THE REIGN OF WILLIAM RUFUS.

a

THE

REIGN OF WILLIAM RUFUS

AND THE

ACCESSION OF HENRY THE FIRST.

BY

EDWARD A. FREEMAN

IN TWO VOLUMES.

VOLUME I.

AMS PRESS
NEW YORK

Reprinted from the edition of 1882, Oxford
First AMS EDITION published 1970
Manufactured in the United States of America

Library of Congress Catalog Card Number: 70-1000518
SBN: complete set: 404-00620-5
volume 1: 404-00621-3

AMS PRESS, INC.
NEW YORK, N. Y. 10003

PREFACE.

I HAVE now been able to carry out the design which I spoke of in the Prefaces to the fifth volume and to the second edition of the fourth volume of my History of the Norman Conquest. I have endeavoured to work out in detail the two sides of the memorable years with which I deal in these volumes, their deep importance for general and specially for constitutional history, and their rich store of personal and local narrative. In the former aspect, I believe I may claim to be the first to have dealt at length with the history of Bishop William of Saint-Calais, a history of deep constitutional importance in itself, and more important still with reference to the career of Anselm. It is no small matter to be able to show that it was not Anselm, but Anselm's enemy, who was the first to appeal from an English court to the see of Rome. In this matter I have, I trust, brought out into its full importance a piece of history which has never, as far as I know, been told at length by any modern writer, though Dr. Stubbs has shown full appreciation of its constitutional bearings. Of less importance, but still more novel, is the mission of Abbot Jeronto to England, to which I have never seen any reference in any modern writer whatever. With regard to the career of Randolf Flambard, I have now worked out more fully many points which have been already spoken of both by myself and by Dr. Stubbs; but I cannot claim to have brought forward anything of great moment that is absolutely new.

In the part which consists of military and other narrative, I have, as usual, given all the attention that I could to the topography. I have visited every place that I could, and I have generally in so doing had the help of friends, often with more observant eyes than my own. I must specially thank Mr. James Parker for his help in Normandy and Maine, the Rev. J. T. Fowler of Durham for his help in Normandy, Maine, and Northumberland, Mr. G. T. Clark in Shropshire, Mr. F. H. Dickinson at Ilchester, the Rev. William Hunt at Bristol, and the Rev. W. R. W. Stephens in Sussex and Kent. I have also to thank His Grace the Duke of Norfolk for free access to Arundel castle, and M. Henri Chardon of Le Mans for much valuable help in that city. And, above all, I must again thank Mr. James Parker for much more than help in preparing the maps and plans which illustrate the book. Without him they could not have been done at all.

In North Wales and in some parts of Normandy and France I was left to my own inquiries. In South Wales I made no particular researches for this volume; but I hope that an old-standing knowledge

of a large part of that country may not have been
useless. Where I feel a real deficiency is in Hampshire. I could not have made any minute inquiries
there without delaying the publication of the book
for many months. But I have in former years been
at Portchester, and I have seen something of the
New Forest. And I feel pretty certain that no
amount of local research can throw any real light
on the death of William Rufus, unless indeed in the
way of showing how local legends grew up. But
something might perhaps be done more minutely to
illustrate the landing and march of Duke Robert
in 1101.

On this last point the place of the conference
between Henry and Robert is satisfactorily fixed in
the new text of Wace published by Dr. Andresen.
I did not come across his volumes till most of the
references to Wace had been copied and printed
from the edition of Pluquet. But in the course of
revision I was able in some cases to refer to Andresen
also. His text is clearly a better one than that of
Pluquet. But I cannot say that I have learned
much from his notes, perhaps from the singularly
repulsive way in which they are printed. Another
German writer, Dr. Liebermann, has done good service to my period by publishing several unpublished
chronicles to which I have often referred. Those of
Saint Edmundsbury are of very considerable local
importance. But there are other things that want
printing. I hear from Mr. E. C. Waters that there
lurks in manuscript a cartulary of Colchester Abbey,

which contains distinct proof that Henry the First spoke English familiarly. I have never doubted the fact, which has always seemed to me as clear as anything that rested on mere inference can be. But it is something to know that there is direct witness to the fact, though it would be more satisfactory if one could refer to that witness for oneself. In the story, as told me by Mr. Waters, a document partly in English is produced in the King's presence; the clerk in whose hands it is put breaks down at the English part; the King takes the parchment, and reads and explains it with ease.

I may mention one point with regard to topography in Normandy and Maine. I have now carefully written the names of all places in Normandy, Maine, and the neighbouring lands, according to the forms now received, as they appear for instance on the French Ordnance map. I am sure that people constantly read names like " Willelmus de Sancto Carilepho," " Robertus de Mellento," without clearly taking in that " Sanctus Carilephus," " Mellentum," &c. are names of real places, as real as any town in England. When one reads, as I have read, of " Bishop Karilef," " the Honour of the Eagle," and so forth, it is plain that those who write in that way have no clear notion of Saint-Calais and Laigle as real places. Yet all these towns are still there; to most of them the railway is open, and there are trains. On the other hand, the confusions of French writers about English places are, if possible, more amazing. A German writer, meanwhile, is pretty

sure to know where any place, either in France or
England, is, though he may be sometimes a little
lifeless in his way of dealing with it.

I have now pretty well done with the history of
the Norman Conquest of England, except so far as
I still hope to put forth my story on a scale intermediate between five — or rather seven — large
volumes and one very small one. But I should be
well pleased to go on with another piece of history
of the same date, the essential importance of which
and its close connexion with that with which I have
been dealing is being always brought more and fully
home to me. The Norman in the great island of
the Ocean and the Norman in the great island of the
Mediterranean naturally form companion pieces. I
have made some acquaintance with the Rogers and
Williams of Sicily in their own home, and I should
be well pleased to make that acquaintance more
intimate. Palermo follows naturally on Winchester
and Rouen. The pleasure-house of William the Bad
is the skeleton of the Conqueror's Tower with a
wholly different life breathed into it by Saracenic
artists. But the points of view from which we may
approach Sicily, the meeting-place of the nations,
and the rich and various sources of interest which
are supplied by the history of that illustrious island,
are simply endless.

In all technical points these volumes follow the
exact pattern of the History of the Norman Conquest. And I take a knowledge of that work for
granted, and I assume all points which I believe

myself to have explained or established in it. But
I have added to these volumes, what I have not
added to any of their predecessors, a Chronological
Summary, distinct from the Table of Contents. It
is, I think, a necessary companion to a narrative in
which I could not strictly follow chronological order,
but had to keep several contemporary lines of story
distinct. Alongside of the History of William Rufus
I set his Annals.

CONTENTS.

CHAPTER I.

INTRODUCTION.

CHAPTER II.

THE EARLY DAYS OF WILLIAM RUFUS. 1087–1090.

§ 1. *The Coronation and Acknowledgement of William Rufus.*
September, 1087.

§ 3. Character of William Rufus.

CHAPTER III.

THE FIRST WARS OF WILLIAM RUFUS.
1090—1092.

§ 1. *Normandy under Robert.* 1087—1090.

                        CHAPTER IV.

            THE PRIMACY OF ANSELM AND THE ACQUISITION
                OF NORMANDY. 1093—1097.

§ 2. *The Vacancy of the Primacy and the Appointment of Anselm.* 1089—1093.

§ 3. *The Assembly at Hastings and the second Norman Campaign.*
1094.

§ 6. *The Crusade and the Mortgage of Normandy.*
November 1095—March 1097.

CHRONOLOGY OF THE YEARS 1087–1102.

1087 September 8 — William Rufus leaves his father's death-bed and hastens to England.

He imprisons Morkere and Wulfnoth.

He is accepted by Lanfranc.

In Normandy Robert of Bellême and others drive out the Duke's garrisons.

September 26 — William is crowned at Westminster.

He makes gifts for his father's soul.

1088 December 25 —January 6 — The Christmas assembly. Odo restored to his earldom.

Death of Abbot Scotland.

Abbot Guy appointed at Saint Augustine's.

March — Conspiracy against the King. Rebellious movements in Kent and Sussex.

Bishop William secures London, Dover, and Hastings for the King.

March—May — The Bishop forsakes the King; his temporalities seized. He is summoned to the King's court, and his lands laid waste.

April 16 — The Easter assembly; the rebel nobles fail to appear.

April—June — Ravaging of Gloucestershire and Somerset. Deliverance of Worcester.

Attempted invasion of Robert. Sieges of Tunbridge, Pevensey, and Rochester.

June — Return of Rhys; Gruffydd and the wikings harry Rhuddlan.

Bishop William at the King's court.

Henry, now Count of the Côtentin, comes to England for his mother's lands.

July 3 — Death of Robert of Rhuddlan.

July — John of Tours consecrated to the bishopric of Somerset void by the death of Gisa.

August— September — Henry and Robert of Bellême go back to Normandy and are imprisoned.

Duke Robert received at Le Mans; sieges of Ballon and Saint Cenery.

Henry is released and restored to his county in the course of the autumn.

	September 6	Agreement between Bishop William and the Counts.
	September 25	Death of Bishop Geoffrey of Chichester.
	November 2	Bishop William before the assembly at Salisbury.
	November 14	Durham castle surrendered to the King.
	after 26	Bishop William crosses to Normandy.
	November ?	Grant of the abbey of Bath to Bishop John; the bishopric of Somerset removed thither.
		The priory of Blyth founded in the course of the year by Roger of Bully.
1089	May 24	Death of Lanfranc.
1090	April 21	Easter assembly at Winchester; war declared against Normandy.
		A large part of eastern Normandy won by William without crossing the sea.
		Maine revolts from Robert; reign of Azo of Este; Howel imprisoned by Helias and visits England.
	June 28	Howel returns to Le Mans.
		Intrigues of Conan at Rouen.
	November 3	Rouen secured to Duke Robert; death of Conan.
		War of Evreux and Conches; peace between them.
		Anselm visits England for the first time as abbot in the course of the year.
1091	December 35 —January 6	Christmas assembly at Winchester.
	January	Siege of Courcy.
	February	Helias buys the county of Maine from Hugh.
		The King crosses to Normandy.
		Treaty of Caen.
	February	William and Robert besiege Henry at Saint Michael's Mount.
	May	Malcolm invades Northumberland and is driven back.
	August	William, Robert, and Henry go back to England. March towards Scotland.
	September 3	Bishop William restored to his bishopric.
	September 29	Loss of ships.
		Treaty with Malcolm.
	October 15	Fall of the tower at Winchcombe.
	October 17	Great wind in London.
		Death of Cedivor; victory of Rhys son of Tewdwr over Gruffydd son of Meredydd in the course of the year.
		In the course of the year come the death of William Bishop of Thetford, the consecration of his successor Herbert Losinga, who also buys the abbey of New Minster for his father, and the consecration of Ralph Luffa Bishop of Chichester.
1092		Fire in London.
	March 28	Consecration of the church of Salisbury.
	April 10	The tower blown down.

May 6	Death of Bishop Remigius; the church of Lincoln remains unconsecrated.
	William's conquest and colonization of Carlisle.
	Marriage of Philip and Bertrada.
September 8	Anselm comes to England; his reception at Canterbury; his first interview with the King.
	Anselm helps Earl Hugh in his changes at Chester.
December 25	Christmas assembly; discussion of the vacancy of the
1093 —January 6	archbishopric.
February	William refuses leave to Anselm to go back to Normandy.
February 3	Death of Bishop Geoffrey of Coutances; Ralph succeeds.
Lent,	Sickness of the King; his repentance and proclamation;
March 2	he grants the see of Lincoln to Robert Bloet.
March 6	The King names Anselm to the archbishopric; his first installation.
April 17	Easter assembly at Winchester; the King recalls his reforms.
	Scottish embassy at Winchester; Malcolm summoned to appear in the King's court.
April 17—24	Defeat and death of Rhys at Brecknock.
April 30	Cadwgan harries Dyfed.
July 1	The Normans enter Ceredigion and Dyfed.
	Advance of the Earls in North Wales; seeming conquest of all Wales.
August 11	Malcolm lays a foundation-stone at Durham.
August 24	Malcolm at Gloucester; William refuses to see him.
	Questions between the King and Anselm; his investiture.
	Intrigues of William of Eu; dealings of William with the Counts of Flanders.
September 25	Enthronement of Anselm.
October 4—13	Death of Robert the Frisian.
October 17	Translation of Saint Julian at Le Mans.
November 13	Death of Malcolm at Alnwick.
November 17	Death of Margaret.
	Donald King of Scots; driving out of Margaret's children.
December 4	Consecration of Anselm.
	Death of Abbot Paul of Saint Alban's.
	Henry received at Domfront and wins back the Côtentin.
December 25	Christmas assembly at Gloucester.
1094 —January 6	
	Challenge received from Robert; Duncan claims the Scottish crown and receives it from William.
	Contributions for the Norman war; Anselm's gift refused.
February 2	Assembly at Hastings.
February 11	Consecration of the church of Battle.
February 12	Robert Bloet consecrated Bishop of Lincoln.
	Bishop Herbert of Thetford deprived of his bishopric.
February 22	Anselm's Lenten sermon; he rebukes the King.

2 c

March 19 William crosses to Normandy.

Campaign of Argentan, Bures, &c.; the French king bought off.

May The foreigners driven out of Scotland.

October 31 Henry and Earl Hugh summoned to Eu; they sail to Southampton.

November Duncan killed; Donald's second reign in Scotland.

December 28 The King goes back to England.

Deaths of Roger of Beaumont, Roger of Montgomery, and Hugh of Grantmesnil, in the course of the year.

In the course of the year the Welsh revolt under Cadwgan and recover the greater part of the country; Pembroke castle holds out.

1095 January 18 Death of Wulfstan.

February 9 Henry goes to Normandy.

February Interview of William and Anselm at Gillingham.

March 1—7 Council of Piacenza.

March 11—14 Assembly at Rockingham.

Gerard and William of Warelwast sent to Pope Urban.

March 25 Assembly at Winchester; Earl Robert of Mowbray summoned, but does not appear.

April 10 Urban at Cremona; Cardinal Walter sent to England.

May 13 Assembly at Windsor; Anselm and William reconciled; Earl Robert fails to appear.

June 10 Anselm receives the pallium at Canterbury.

June 26 Death of Bishop Robert of Hereford.

April 30 Translation of Saint Eadmund.

The King's northern march; Anselm's command in Kent.

July—Sept. Taking of Newcastle and Tynemouth; siege of Bamburgh.

Michaelmas Montgomery taken by the Welsh; the King marches against them.

November 1 The King reaches Snowdon; ill-success of the campaign.

November 18 Council of Clermont.

Pope Urban at Le Mans.

Robert of Mowbray taken at Tynemouth; surrender of Bamburgh.

1096 December 25 —January 6 Christmas assembly at Windsor.

January 1 Death of Bishop William.

January 13 The assembly adjourned to Salisbury; sentences of William of Eu, William of Alderi, and others.

Imprisonment of Robert of Mowbray.

Synod of Rouen; confirmation of the Truce of God.

Mission of Abbot Geronto.

Easter, April 13 He is superseded by the Pope's nephew.

Normandy pledged to William.

June 8 Consecration of Bishop Gerard of Hereford and Samson of Worcester.

August	William takes possession of Normandy.
	Helias takes the cross; mutual defiance between him and William.
September	Duke Robert, Bishop Odo, and others go to the crusade.
	The King spends the winter in Normandy.
	In the course of the year the Welsh take Rhyd-y-gors; Gwent and Brecknock revolt; Pembroke is besieged, but holds out; Gisors is fortified by Pagan Theobald.

1097

February	Odo dies at Palermo.
April 4	William comes back to England.
	Assembly at Windsor.
	The King's campaign in Wales; seeming conquest of the country.
	The King complains of Anselm's knights.
May 14	Whitsun assembly; the charge against Anselm dropped; he asks leave to go to Rome, but is refused.
	Revolt of Cadwgan in Wales.
June— August	The King's last campaign in Wales; its ill-success.
July 24	Death of Howel; Hildebert Bishop of Le Mans.
August	Assembly; an expedition against Donald decreed; Anselm's request again refused.
September	The two Eadgars march to Scotland; exploits of Robert son of Godwine; Donald defeated and blinded; the younger Eadgar King of Scots.
October 14	Assembly at Winchester; Anselm allowed to go, but his temporalities to be seized; his parting with the King.
	Anselm leaves England.
	William demands the French Vexin.
November	He crosses to Normandy for the war with France and Maine. Flambard and Walkelin joint regents.
Nov. 1097— Sept. 1098.	French war; Lewis and William; fortification of Gisors by Robert of Bellême.
December 19	Death of Abbot Baldwin of Saint Eadmund's.
December 25	The King demands money of Walkelin.

1098

January 3	Death of Walkelin.
January	Beginning of the war of Maine; castles occupied by Robert of Bellême.
	Victories of Helias.
April 28	Helias taken prisoner.
May 5	Fulk Rechin at Le Mans.
June	The King invades Maine; he retreats from Le Mans.
July 20	William at Ballon.
August	Convention between Helias and Fulk.
	William enters Le Mans.
	Helias set free; he strengthens himself in his southern castles.
September 27	William's march against France.

	Attacks on Pontoise, Chaumont, and other castles.
	Coming of William of Aquitaine; attacks on the Mont-fort castles; failure of the two Williams.
October 1	Council of Bari; Anselm pleads for William.
	In the course of the year the Welsh withdraw to Anglesey.
	The Earls Hugh in Anglesey.
	Expedition of Magnus of Norway; death of Earl Hugh of Shrewsbury at Aberlleiniog.
	Establishment of Robert of Bellême in England; he buys his brother's earldom.
	His works at Bridgenorth.
	He receives the estates of Roger of Bully.
Christmas	The King spends the winter in Normandy; truce with France.
1099	Mission of William of Warelwast to Rome; he wins over Urban.
April 10	The King in England; Easter assembly.
April 12	Council of Lateran; William's excommunication delayed.
	Anselm leaves Rome for Lyons.
April	Movements of Helias in southern Maine.
May 19	Whitsun assembly in the new hall at Westminster; the bishopric of Durham granted to Randolf Flambard.
June 3	Consecration of Flambard.
June–July	Helias recovers Le Mans; the King's garrisons hold out in the castles; burning of the city.
	The news brought to William; his ride and voyage.
	Helias leaves Le Mans and strengthens himself at Château-du-Loir.
	William passes through Le Mans to southern Maine.
	His failure before Mayet.
	He enters Le Mans.
July 5	Taking of Jerusalem; exploits of Duke Robert.
July 12	Duke Robert refuses the crown of Jerusalem; Geoffrey chosen King.
July 19	Death of Pope Urban the Second.
August 12	Battle of Ascalon.
August 13	Paschal the Second elected Pope.
September	The King returns to England.
November 3	The great tide in the Thames.
December 3	Death of Bishop Osmund of Salisbury.
Dec. 25–Jan. 6, 1100	Christmas assembly at Gloucester.
	In the course of the year Gruffydd and Cadwgan return, and Anglesey and Ceredigion are recovered by the Welsh. Eadgar goes on the crusade. Affairs of Robert son of Godwine in Scotland.
1100 April 1	Easter assembly at Winchester.
May 20	Whitsun assembly at Westminster.

	Great schemes of William Rufus.
May	Death of Richard son of Duke Robert in the New Forest.
June—July	Preparations for war.
July 13	Consecration of Gloucester abbey.
August 1	Abbot Fulchered's sermon at Gloucester.
August 2	Death of William Rufus.
August 3	Burial of William Rufus; Henry elected King; he grants the bishopric of Winchester to William Giffard.
August 5	Coronation of Henry; his charter; he fills the vacant abbeys.
	He imprisons Flambard, and asks Anselm to come back.
	Helias recovers Le Mans; the castle holds out.
September	Duke Robert comes back to Normandy.
	War between Henry and Robert.
September 23	Anselm comes back to England.
	Meeting of Anselm and Henry; question of homage and investiture; truce till Easter; mission to the Pope.
November	Helias recovers the castle.
November 11	Marriage of Henry and Matilda.
November 18	Death of Archbishop Thomas of York.
	Empty legation of Guy of Vienne.
	Plots in England on behalf of Robert.

1101

December 25 —January 6	Christmas assembly at Westminster.
	Escape of Flambard to Normandy; he stirs up Robert to action.
April 21	Easter assembly at Winchester; the question with Anselm again adjourned.
	Growth of the conspiracy.
June 9	Whitsun assembly; mediation of Anselm; renewed promise of good laws.
July	Robert's fleet at Tréport; the English fleet sent against him; some of the crews join him.
	Henry's preparations at Pevensey.
July 20	Robert lands at Portchester; he declines to attack Winchester.
	The armies meet at Alton; conference of Henry and Robert; the treaty of 1101.
Michaelmas	Robert goes back to Normandy.
	Henry's rewards and punishments; banishment of Ivo of Grantmesnil and others.
	Robert of Meulan Earl of Leicester.

1102

December 25 —January 6	Christmas assembly at Westminster.
April 6	Easter assembly at Winchester; Robert of Bellême summoned, but does not appear.
	War against Robert of Bellême in England and Normandy.

		Failure of Duke Robert's troops at Vignats.
		Surrender of Arundel to Henry.
		Surrender of Tickhill.
	Autumn	Henry's Shropshire campaign. Siege of Bridgenorth.
		The King wins over Jorwerth and the Welsh.
		Dealings of Robert of Bellême with Murtagh and Magnus.
		Surrender of Bridgenorth.
		The King's march to Shrewsbury.
		Surrender of Shrewsbury and banishment of Robert of Bellême and his brothers.
1103		Death of Magnus.
		Jorwerth tried at Shrewsbury and imprisoned.
1104		Banishment of William of Mortain.
1106		Battle of Tinchebrai.
1107		Compromise with Anselm.

ADDITIONS AND CORRECTIONS.

VOL. I.

p. 33, l. 17, dele "the father of one of the men who had crossed the sea to trouble England." Robert of Bellême had not come yet; see p. 56.

p. 37, note 3. The comparison of Bristol and Brindisi is a good deal exaggerated; but a certain measure of likeness may be seen.

p. 94, l. 18, dele "of the same kind." See the distinction drawn in p. 604.

p. 96, note 2, for "abjuvare" read "abjurare."

p. 133, note. See vol. ii. p. 330.

p. 180, note. I do not know how "Esparlon"—Épernon—comes to be reckoned among the possessions of Robert of Bellême. We shall find it in vol. ii. p. 251 in the hands of the French house of Montfort.

p. 183, l. 4 from bottom, for "Rotrou" read "Geoffrey."

p. 184, note 1. See vol. ii. p. 396.

p. 214, side-note, for "William of Geroy" read "William son of Geroy."

p. 217, l. 13, for "uncle" read "brother."

p. 238, note 3, for "Aunde" read "Aumale."

p. 243, note 2. I really ought to have mentioned the wonderful forms of torture which the man of Belial inflicted on his lord and his other prisoners (Ord. Vit. 705 A, B); "Per tres menses in castro Brehervallo eos in carcere strinxit, et multotiens, dum nimia hiems sæviret, in solis camisiis aqua largiter humectatis in fenestra sublimis aulæ Boreæ vel Circio exposuit, donec tota vestis circa corpus vinctorum in uno gelu diriguit."

p. 247, l. 3. I suppose that Walter of Rouen, son of Ansgar, who appears high in the King's confidence in vol. ii. pp. 241, 370, is a brother of this William. This is worth noting, as showing how Rufus picked out men likely to serve his purpose from all quarters.

p. 251, l. 5. See below, p. 461, note 3. It would be worth enquiring whether this name *Champ de Mars* is old or new. There is a *Campus Martius* at Autun, whose name is certainly at least mediæval; but, as it is within the Roman walls, it can hardly date from the first days of Augustodunum. It divides the upper and lower city, quite another position from that at Rouen.

p. 298, l. 6. Orderic is hardly fair to Edgar when he says (778 B), "Hic corpore speciosus, lingua disertus, liberalis et generosus, utpote Edwardi regis Hunorum filius [see 701 D and N. C. vol. ii. p. 672], sed dextera segnis erat, ducemque sibi coævum et quasi collectaneum fratrem diligebat."

p. 302, note 1, for "Witan" read "Gemót."

p. 307, l. 6. Something of the kind was actually done somewhat later; see below, p. 435. But that was a challenge through ambassadors.

p. 326, note. In strictness Anselm did not appeal to the Pope at all. See below, p. 598.

p. 335, l. 15, for "unrighteousness" read "unrighteousnesses."

p. 353, l. 6 from bottom. I ought not to have forgotten the character of Ralph Luffa given by William of Malmesbury (Gest. Pont. 205); "Radulfus proceritate corporis insignis, sed et animi efficacia famosus, qui contuitu sacerdotalis officii Willelmo juniori in faciem pro Anselmo archiepiscopo, quem immerito exagitabat, restiterit. Cumque ille, conscientia potestatis elatus, minas ingeminaret, nihil alter reveritus baculum protendit, annulum exuit, ut, si vellet, acciperet. Nec vero vel tunc vel postea austeritatem inflecteret si assertorem haberet. Sed quia discessu suo spem ejus et ceterorum, si qui boni essent, Anselmus enervavit, et tunc causa decidit et postmodum damno succubuit." This seems at first sight to stand in contradiction to Eadmer's picture of all the bishops, except possibly Gundulf (see below, pp. 497, 513, 516), forsaking and renouncing Anselm. We can understand that Eadmer would be inclined to make the worst of the bishops as a body, while William of Malmesbury would be inclined to make the best of the particular bishop of whom he was writing. This is one of the passages in which William of Malmesbury in his second edition watered down the vigorous language of the first. As he first wrote it, the King appeared as "leo ferocissimus Willelmus dico minor." On second thoughts the comparison with the wild beast was left out.

p. 355, l. 15. I have sent Herbert to Rome at this time, in order to bring him back for the meeting at Hastings in 1094. See below, pp. 429, 448. I find that some difficulty has arisen on account of the words of Eadmer (see p. 429), which have been taken as implying that Herbert joined in the consecration of Anselm. Dr. Stubbs puts him on the list in the Registrum. But surely the words might be used if all the bishops came who were in England and able to come.

p. 355, side-note, for "1091–1093" read "1091–1098." See vol. ii. p. 267.

p. 375, note 6, for "perversitatam" read "perversitatem."

p. 385, l. 2, for "undoubtedly" read "by himself."

p. 408, l. 15. There must however have been some exceptions. See the Additions and Corrections to vol. ii. p. 508.

p. 450, l. 3 from bottom. Yet the guarantors, even on William's own side, held him to be in the wrong. See p. 461.

p. 469, note 1. The reference is to the passage of Orderic, quoted in vol. ii. p. 537. But it is hard to understand how Henry can have been at war with William in 1094. Yet there is the passage from Sigebert quoted in p. 471, note 3, where the date must be wrong, but which seems to hang together both with this passage of Orderic and with the suspicions on the King's part implied in the narrative in the Chronicle.

p. 469, l. 10, and note 3, for "son" read "grandson."

p. 485, l. 3, for "of" read "to."

p. 492, l. 2, put semicolon after "within."

p. 506, note 2. This passage is very singular, especially the words "nec ipsum advertere posse putaverunt." On this last point the bishops seem to have been right, as Anselm himself nowhere puts forward any such claim to exemption.

p. 516, note 3. Besides the difficulty about Gundulf, there is the further difficulty about Ralph of Chichester, who, as we have just seen, is said by William of Malmesbury to have taken Anselm's side. He at least stood in no such special position to the Archbishop as the Bishop of Rochester did.

p. 522, side-note, for "May" read "March."

p. 546, l. 12. Worthiest certainly when any actual work was to be done; but the idle sojourn at Laodikeia (see p. 565) makes the general epithet too strong.

p. 551, l. 10, for "Rotrou" read "Geoffrey."

p. 571, l. 3. I believe there is no authority for this English form, "Ever-mouth," though it is not unlikely that "Ebremou" may, like so many other names in Normandy, really be a corruption of some such Teutonic name. The place is in Eastern Normandy, in the present department of Lower Seine.

p. 579, note 1. This is that singular use of the words "Christianitas" and the like which we find in such phrases as "Courts Christian" and "Deanery of Christianity." We must not think of such a "subventio Christianitatis" as the Spanish Bishop sought for at the hands of Anselm. See vol. ii. p. 582.

p. 586, l. 25. For "three" read "four," and add the name of Robert Bloet. He is the Robert referred to in the next page.

p. 604, note 1. The *right* to be tried is confined to the Peers; other persons of course may be so tried, if they are impeached by the Commons.

p. 609, note 1. When I was at Benevento this year (1880), I had hoped to get a sight of the cope, as the treasury of the metropolitan church is rich in vestments. But they are all of much later date, and I could hear nothing of the relic which I sought for.

p. 614, last line. See more in vol. ii. p. 403.

THE REIGN OF WILLIAM RUFUS.

CHAPTER I.

INTRODUCTION.

THE reign of the second Norman king is a period of Character of the reign of William Rufus. English history which may well claim a more special and minute examination than could be given to it when it took its place merely as one of the later stages in the history of the Norman Conquest, after the great work of the Conquest itself was done. There is indeed a point of view in which the first years of the reign of William the Red may be looked on as something more than one of the later stages of the Conquest. They may be looked on, almost at pleasure, either as The Norman Conquest in one sense completed, in another undone. the last stage of the Conquest or as the reversal of the Conquest. We may give either name to a struggle in which a Norman king, the son of the Norman Conqueror, was established on the English throne by warfare which, simply as warfare, was a distinct victory won by Englishmen over Normans on English soil. The truest aspect of that warfare was that the Norman Conquest of England was completed by English hands. But, in so saying, we must understand by the Norman Conquest of England all that is implied in that name to its fullest extent. When Englishmen, by armed support of a Norman king, accepted the fact of the Norman Conquest, they in some measure changed its nature. In the act of completing the Conquest, they in some sort undid it. If we hold that the end of the Conquest came in the days of Rufus, in the days of

CHAP. I.

Feudal development under Rufus and Flambard.

Growth of anti-feudal tendencies.

Extension of the power of England at home.

Wales;

Carlisle.

Rufus also came the beginnings of the later effects of the Conquest. The reign of William the Red, the administration of Randolf Flambard, was, above all others, the time when the feudal side, so to speak, of the Conquest put on a systematic shape. The King and his minister put into regular working, if they did not write down in a regular code, those usages which under the Conqueror were still merely tendencies irregularly at work, but which, at the accession of Henry the First, had already grown into abuses which needed redress. But, on the other hand, it was equally the time when the anti-feudal tendencies of the Conquest, the causes and the effects of the great law of Salisbury,[1] showed how firmly they had taken root. The reign of Rufus laid down the two principles, that, in the kingdom of England, no man should be stronger than the king,[2] but that the king should hold his strength only by making himself the head of the state and of the people. As a stage then in the history of the Conquest and its results, as a stage in the general constitutional history of England, the thirteen years of the reign of Rufus form a period of the highest interest and importance.

But those years are a time of no less interest and importance, if we look at them with regard to the general position of England in the world. Within our own island, the reign of William the Red was marked by a great practical extension of the power of England on the Welsh marches. On another side it was marked yet more distinctly by an enlargement of the kingdom itself, by the settlement of the north-western frontier, by the winning for England of a new land, and by the restoration of a fallen city as the bulwark of the new boundary. What the daughter of Ælfred was at Chester, the son of the Conqueror was at Carlisle. Beyond the

---

[1] See N. C. vol. iv. p. 692.   [2] Will. Malms. iv. 306.

sea, we mark the beginnings of a state of things which
has ceased only within our own memories. The rivalry Beginning
between France and Normandy grows, now that England of rivalry between
is ruled by Norman kings, into a rivalry between France England
and England. In will, if not in deed, the reign of Rufus and France.
forestalls the reigns of Edward the Third and Henry
the Fifth. It sets England before us in a character Wealth of
which she kept through so many ages, the character of England.
the wealthy land which could work with gold as well
as with steel, the land whence subsidies might be looked
for to flow into the less well-filled coffers of the princes
of the mainland. In the reign of Rufus we see England Change
holding an European position wholly different from what in the European
she had held in earlier days. She passes in some sort position of
from the world of the North into the world of the West. England.
That change was the work of the Conqueror; but it is
under his son that we see its full nature and meaning.
The new place which England now holds is seen to be
one which came to her wholly through her connexion
with Normandy; it is no less seen to be one which she
has learned to hold in her own name and by her own
strength.

And, if we pass from the domain of political history
into the domain of personal character and personal incident, we shall find few periods of the same length richer
in both. The character of William Rufus himself, re- Personal
pulsive as from many points it is, is yet a strange and character of William
instructive study of human nature. The mere fact that Rufus.
no prince ever made a deeper personal impression on
the minds of the men of his own age, the crowd of
personal anecdotes and personal sayings which, whether
true or false, bear witness to the depth of that impression, all invite us to a nearer study of the man of
whom those who lived in his own day found so much
to tell, and so much which at first sight seems strange

CHAP. I. and contradictory. William Rufus stands before us as the first representative of a new ideal, a new standard. Our earlier experiences, English and Norman, have hardly prepared us for the special place taken by the king who has some claim to rank as the first distinctly recorded example of the new character of knight and gentleman. In the company of the Red King we are introduced to a new line of thought, a new way of looking at things, of which in an earlier generation we see hardly stronger signs in Normandy than we see in England. For good and for evil, if William Rufus bears the mark of his age, he also leaves his mark on his age. His own marked personality in some sort entitles him to be surrounded, to be withstood, by men whose personality is also clearly marked.

His companions and adversaries. A circle of well-defined portraits, friends and enemies, ministers and rivals, gathers around him. Among them two forms stand out before all. The holy Anselm and Helias. elm at home, the valiant Helias beyond the sea, are the men with whom Rufus has to strive. And the saint of Aosta, the hero of La Flèche, are men who of themselves are enough to draw our thoughts to the times and the lands in which they lived. Each, in his own widely different way, stands forth as the representative of right in the face of a power of evil which we still feel to be not wholly evil. All light is not put out, all better feelings are not trampled out of being, when evil stands in any way abashed before the presence of good.

Rufus and England. Looked at simply as a tale, the tale of Rufus and Anselm, the tale of Rufus and Helias, is worth the telling. But better worth telling still is the tale of Rufus and The last warfare of Normans and English. England. The struggle which kept the crown for Rufus, the last armed struggle between Englishmen and Normans on English ground, the fight of Pevensey and the siege of Rochester, form a stirring portion of our annals, CHAP. I. a portion whose interest yields only to that of a few great days like the days of Senlac and of Lewes. But the really great tale is after all that which is more silent and hidden. This was above all things the time when the Norman Conquest took root, as something which at once established the Norman power in England, and which ruled that the Norman power should step by step change into an English power. The great fact of Rufus' day is that Englishmen won the crown of England for a Norman king in fight against rebellious Normans. On that day the fact of the Conquest was fully acknowledged; it became something which, as to its immediate outward effects, there was no longer any thought of undoing. The house of the Conqueror was to be the royal house; there were to be no more revolts on behalf of the heir of Cerdic, no more messages sent to invite the heir of Cnut. And with the kingship of the Norman all was accepted which was immediately implied in the kingship of the Norman. But on that day it was further ruled that the kingship of the Norman was to change into an English kingship. It became such in some sort even under Rufus himself, when the King of England went forth to subdue Normandy, to threaten France, to dream at least, as a link between Civilis and Buonaparte, of an empire of the Gauls.[1] The success of the attempt, the accomplishment of the dream, would have been the very overthrow of English nationality; the mere attempt, the mere dream, helped, if not to strengthen English nationality, at least to strengthen the national position of England. But these years helped too, in a more silent way, if not to change the Norman rule at home into an English rule, at least to make things

Results of the struggle.

The Conquest accepted and modified.

The Norman kingship becomes English.

Effects of the French War.

---

[1] Tac. Hist. iv. 59.

CHAP. I. ready for the coming of the king who was really to do the work. It was perhaps in the long run not the least gain of the reign of William the Red that it left for Henry the Clerk, not only much to do, but also something directly to undo.

Scheme of the work.

In a former volume we traced the history of the Conqueror in great detail to his death-bed and his burial. In another volume we followed, with a more hasty course, the main features of the reign of William Rufus, looked at specially as bearing on the history of the Conquest and the mutual relations of English and Normans. We will now again take up the thread of our detailed story at the bed-side of the dying Conqueror, and thence trace the history of his successor, from his first nomination by his father's dying voice to his unhallowed burial in the Old Minster of Winchester. And thence, though the tale of Rufus himself is over, it may be well to carry on the tale of England through the struggle which ruled for the second time that England should not be the realm of the Conqueror's eldest son, and, as such, an appendage to his Norman duchy. The accession of Henry is essentially a part of the same tale as the accession of Rufus. The points of likeness in the two stories are striking indeed, reaching in some cases almost to a repetition of the same events. But the points of unlikeness are yet more striking and instructive. And it is from them that we learn how much the reign of Rufus had done alike towards completing the Norman Conquest and towards undoing it.

CHAPTER II.

THE EARLY DAYS OF WILLIAM RUFUS.[1]
1087–1090.

THE way by which the second William became *Character of the accession of Rufus.* fully established on the throne of his father has some peculiarities of its own, which distinguish it from the accessions of most English kings, earlier and later. The only claim of William Rufus to the crown was a nomination by his father which we are told that his father hardly ventured to make. Of election *No formal election.* by any assembly, great or small, we see no trace. Yet the new king is crowned, and he receives the national *His general acceptance.* submission at his crowning, with the fullest outward national consent, with no visible opposition from any quarter, and, as events proved, with the hearty good will of the native English part of his subjects. Yet the King is hardly established in his kingdom before

---

[1] There is not much to say about the authorities for this chapter. The main sources are those with which we have long been familiar, the Peterborough Chronicle, Orderic, Florence, William of Malmesbury. The last three of these increase in value at every step, as they become more and more strictly contemporary. So Henry of Huntingdon, beginning his seventh book in the second year of Rufus, formally puts on the character of a contemporary writer. Hitherto he had written from his reading or from common fame; "nunc autem de his quæ vel ipsi vidimus, vel ab his qui viderant audivimus, pertractandum est." But he still wisely kept the Chronicle before him. He is himself largely followed by Robert of Torigny (or *De Monte*—that is Abbot of Saint Michael's Mount) in his chronicle. From Robert we have also the so-called eighth book of William of Jumièges, which may pass as a History of Henry the First. He is not strictly contemporary for any part of our immediate story. Eadmer, so precious a few years later, gives us as yet only a few touches and general pictures. The French riming chroniclers are of some value later in the reign of Rufus; but we have hardly anything to do with them as yet. A crowd of accessory, occasional, and local writings have to be turned to as usual.

CHAP. II. he has to fight for his crown. William Rufus had, like his father, to win the kingdom of England by war after he was already its crowned king. But, as regards those against whom he fought and those at whose head he fought, his position was the exact reverse of that of his father. Nominated by his father, elected, one might say, by Lanfranc, crowned with no man gainsaying him, William Rufus was at last really established in the royal power by the act of the conquered English. It was they who won the crown for the son of their Conqueror in fight against his father's nearest kinsmen and most cherished comrades.

§ 1. *The Coronation and Acknowledgement of William Rufus. September,* 1087.

One prominent aspect of the reign of William Rufus sets him before us as the enemy, almost the persecutor, of the Church in his realm, as the special adversary of the ecclesiastical power when the ecclesiastical power was represented by one of the truest of saints. And yet there have been few kings whose accession to the throne was in so special a way the act of the ecclesiastical power. William Rufus was made king by Lanfranc in a somewhat fuller sense than that in which every king of those times might be said to be made king by the prelate who poured the consecrating oil upon his head. Nomination by the last king, in the form of recommendation to the electors, had always been taken into account when the people of England came together to set a new king over them. The nomination of Eadward had formed a part, though the smallest part, of the right of Harold to become the chief of his own people.[1] An alleged nomination by Eadward

---

[1] See N. C. vol. iii. p. 583.

formed the only plausible part of the claim by which William asserted his right to thrust himself upon a people of strangers. And now a nomination by William himself was the only right by which his second surviving son claimed to succeed to the crown which he had won. Modern notions of hereditary right would have handed over England as well as Normandy to the eldest son of the last king. English feeling at the time would doubtless, if a formal choice had to be made among the sons of the Conqueror of England, have spoken for his youngest son. Of all the three Henry alone was a true Ætheling; he alone had any right to the name of Englishman; he alone was the son of a crowned king and a man born in the land.[1] But the last wish of William the Great was that his island crown should pass to William the Red. He had not, as our fullest narrative tells us, dared to make any formal nomination to a kingdom which he had in his last days found out to be his only by wrong. He had not dared to name William as his successor; he left the kingdom in the hands of God; he only hoped that the will of God might be that William should reign, and should reign well and happily.[2] And as the best means of finding out whether the will of God were so, he left the actual decision to the highest and wisest of God's ministers in his kingdom. He gave no orders for the

---

[1] See N. C. vol. iv. pp. 228, 795. So Will. Neub. i. 3 ; "Filiorum quidem Willelmi Magni ordine nativitatis novissimus, sed prærogativa primus. Quippe, aliis in ducatu patris natis, solus ipse ex eodem jam rege est ortus." This is noteworthy in a writer in whom (see Appendix A) we see the first sign of a notion of Robert's hereditary right. The author of the Brevis Relatio (9) goes yet further, and seems to assert that a party at least was for Henry's immediate succession; "Sicut postea multi dixerunt, justum fuit ut ipse rex Angliæ post patrem suum esset qui de patre rege et matre regina genitus extitisset."

[2] See N. C. vol. iv. p. 706, note 3.

CHAP. II. coronation of Rufus; he simply prayed Lanfranc to crown him, if the Primate deemed such an act a rightful one.[1] As far as the will of the dying king went, one alone of the Witan of England, the first certainly among them alike in rank and in renown, was bidden to make the choice of the next sovereign on behalf of the whole kingdom.

The special agency of Lanfranc in the promotion of William Rufus is noticed by all the writers who give any detailed account of his accession.[2] Nor was it likely that, when the Archbishop was to be the one elector, the claims of the candidate should be refused. It would seem indeed as if Lanfranc doubted for a moment whether he ought to take upon himself the responsibility of the choice.[3] But everything must have helped to make him ready to carry out the wishes of his late master. That they were the Conqueror's last wishes was no small matter, and Lanfranc had every personal reason to incline him the same way. To make William Rufus king was to promote the man who stood in a special relation to himself, who had been in some sort his pupil, and whom he had himself girded with the belt of knighthood.[4] And it really seems as if there was no other elector besides Lanfranc himself. For once in our history we read of a king succeeding without any formal election, without any meeting of the Witan before the coronation. Within three weeks of the death of the first William, the second William was full king over the land. As soon as he had heard the last wishes of his father, as soon as the dying king had dictated the all-important letter which was to ex-

---

[1] See N. C. vol. iv. p. 706, note 3.   [2] See Appendix A.

[3] See Appendix A.

[4] Will. Malms. iv. 305. "Eum nutrierat et militem fecerat." So Matthew Paris, Hist. Ang. i. 35.

press those wishes to the Primate, William Rufus left
the bedside of his father while the breath was still in
him. He started for the haven of Touques, a spot of
which we shall get a vivid picture later in our story.
With him set forth the bearer of the letter, one of
the great King's chaplains, and, as some say, his Chancellor. This was Robert Bloet, he who was presently
to succeed Remigius of Fécamp in his newly-placed
throne on the hill of Lincoln.[1] Before they had left
Norman ground, the news came that all was over, that
England had no longer a king.[2] William crossed with
all speed, seemingly to Southampton, and found in England no rival, English or Norman. He indeed brought
with him two men, either of whom, if Englishmen had
still heart enough to dream of a king of their own blood,
might have been his rival. Among the captives whom
the Conqueror set free on his death-bed were two men
who represented the mightiest of the fallen houses of
conquered England. These were Morkere the son of
Ælfgar, once the chosen Earl of the Northumbrians,
and Wulfnoth, the youngest son of Godwine and brother[3] of Harold. Two other captives of royal blood, Wulf and
Duncan the son of Malcolm and Ingebiorg, so long a Duncan set
free by
hostage for his father's doubtful faith to his over-lord,[4] Robert.

---

[1] Orderic has two statements as to the port from which William set sail.
In his account of the Conqueror's death (659 D), he makes him sail from
Witsand. But afterwards (763 D), when speaking of Robert Bloet, he
says, "Senioris Guillelmi capellanus fuerat, eoque defuncto de portu
Tolochæ cum juniore Guillelmo mare transfretaverat, et epistolam regis de
coronanda prole Lanfranco archiepiscopo detulerat." This latter is to be
preferred, as the more circumstantial account. Touques moreover is at
once the more likely haven to be chosen by one setting out from Rouen, and
the one less likely to come into the head of a careless narrator. Robert
of Torigny also (Cont. Will. Gem. viii. 2) makes the place Touques.

[2] Ord. Vit. 659 D. "Ibi jam patrem audivit obiisse."

[3] Fl. Wig. 1087. "Willelmus . . . Angliam festinato adiit, ducens secum
Wlnothum et Morkarum." [4] See N.C. vol. iv. p. 517.

CHAP. II. and Wulf the son of Harold and Ealdgyth, the babe who had been taken when Chester fell,[1] were set free at the same time. Duncan and Wulf were in the power of Robert. They in no way threatened his possession of Normandy, and Robert, with all his faults, did not lack generous feeling. They were knighted and set free.[2] Of Wulf we hear no more; Duncan lived to sit for a moment on the throne of his father. The fate of their fellow-sufferers was harsher. Morkere and Wulfnoth had come, by what means we know not, into the power of William. As Morkere had once crossed the sea with the father,[3] he now came back with the son. But their day of freedom was short. The son of Godwine and the grandson of Leofric might either of them be dangerous to the son of William. They therefore tasted the air of freedom only for a few days. William, acting as already king, went to his capital at Winchester, and there thrust the delivered captives once more into the house of bondage.[4] Of Morkere we hear no more; we must suppose that the rest of his days, few or many, were spent in this renewed imprisonment. Wulfnoth seems to have been released at some later time, to enter religion, and to be made the subject of the praises of a Norman poet.[5]

---

[1] See N. C. vol. iv. p. 315.

[2] Fl. Wig. 1087. "Robertus ... Ulfum, Haroldi quondam regis Anglorum filium, Dunechaldumque regis Scottorum Malcolmi filium a custodia laxatos et armis militaribus honoratos, abire permisit."

[3] See N. C. vol. iv. p. 76.

[4] Flor. Wig. 1087. "Mox ut Wintoniam venit, illos, ut prius fuerant, custodiæ mancipavit."

[5] See N. C. vol. iv. p. 855. The Winchester Annals (1087; Ann. Mon. ii. 35) give him, like Prior Godfrey, the title of Earl, and say that he was not released at all. The Conqueror releases all his prisoners in England and Normandy "exceptis duobus comitibus Rogero et Wlnodo." These three captives are joined together in the signatures to an alleged charter of Bishop William of Saint-Calais in the Monasticon, i. 237, and in the Surtees volume,

Such was the first act of authority done by the new CHAP. II.
ruler. Having thus disposed of the men whom he seems
to have dreaded, William found no opposition made
to his succession. But it was important for him to take
possession without delay. The time, September, was
not one of the usual seasons for a general assembly
of the kingdom, and William could not afford to wait
for the next great festival of Christmas. No native
English competitor was likely to appear; but he must
at least make himself safe against any possible attempts
on the part of his brothers beyond the sea. From
Winchester he hastened to the presence of Lanfranc—
seemingly at Canterbury; as the story is told us, it
seems to be taken for granted that it rested with the
Primate to give or to refuse the crown.[1] Whether the
younger William himself brought the news of the death
of the elder is not quite clear; but we are not surprised
to hear from an eye-witness that the first feeling of Lanfranc was one of overwhelming grief at the loss of the
king who was dead, a king who, if he had been to him
a master, had also been in so many things a friend
and a fellow-worker.[2] The formal consecration of his Rufus is
successor was not long delayed; the new king was crowned at
solemnly crowned and anointed by the hands of Lanfranc minster,
in the minster of Saint Peter, on Sunday the feast of the 26, 1087.

Hist. Dun. Scriptt. Tres, v, of which I may have to speak again; "Morkaro
et Rogerio [clearly meant for Roger of Hereford] et Siwardo cognomento
Bran et Wlnoto Haraldi regis germano." They are made to sign, along with
Abbot Æthelwig, who died in 1077, in a Council in London in 1082. The
whole thing is clearly spurious; but what put the signatures of the captives
into anybody's head?

[1] See Appendix A.

[2] Eadmer, Hist. Nov. 13 Selden. "Quantus autem mœror Lanfrancum ex morte ejus perculerit quis dicere possit, quando nos qui circa illum
nuncia morte illius eramus, statim eum præ cordis angustia mori time-
remus?" This seems to imply that the news reached Lanfranc when he
had his monks about him, that is at Canterbury.

CHAP. II. saints Cosmas and Damian. So the day is marked by a
scholar who had specially explored the antiquities of Rome;
Englishmen, who knew less of saints whose holy place
was by the Roman forum, were content to mark it by
its relation to the great festival three days later, or even
by the mere day of the month.[1] On that day, before
the altar of King Eadward's rearing, the second Norman
lord of England took the oaths which bound an English
king to the English people. And, besides the prescribed
oaths to do justice and mercy and to defend the rights
of the Church, Lanfranc is said to have bound the new
king by a special engagement to follow his own counsel
in all things.[2] William Rufus was thus king, and,
if anything had been lacking in the way of regular
election before his crowning, it was fully made up by
the universal and seemingly zealous acceptance of him
at his crowning. "All the men on England to him
bowed and to him oaths swore."[3] The crown which
had passed to Eadward from a long line of kingly
forefathers, the crown which Harold had worn by the
free gift of the English people, the crown which the
first William had won by his sword and had kept by
his wisdom, now passed to the second of his name and
house. And it passed, to all appearance, with the perfect good will of all the dwellers in the land, conquerors
and conquered alike. William the Second, William the
Younger, William the Red, took his place on the seat

---

[1] William of Malmesbury (iv. 305) marks the coronation as being done
"die sanctorum Cosmæ et Damiani." In the Chronicle it is "þreom dagum
ǽr Michaeles mæssedæg;" while Florence simply gives the day of the
month. Wace (14482) says inaccurately "Li jor de feste saint Michiel;"
and the Chronicon de Bello (40) still more inaccurately, "in nativitate
Christi, intrante anno incarnationis ejusdem Verbi Dei mlxxxviii."

[2] See Appendix A.

[3] Chron. Petrib. 1087. "Ealle þa men on Englalande him to abugon,
and him aðas sworon."

of the great Conqueror without a blow being struck or CHAP. II.
a dog moving his tongue against him.

The first act of the uncrowned candidate for the kingly
office had been one of harshness—harshness which was
perhaps politic in the son, but which trod under foot
the last wishes of a repentant father. The first act of
the crowned King was one which might give good
hopes for the reign which was beginning, and which
certainly carried out his father's wishes to the letter.
From Westminster William Rufus went again to Winchester, this time not to make fast the bars of his
father's prison-house, but to throw open the stores of
his father's treasury. Our native Chronicler waxes Wealth
eloquent on the boundless wealth of all kinds, far of the treasury
beyond the powers of any man to tell of, which had at Win-chester.
been gathered together in the Conqueror's hoard during
his one and twenty years of kingship. The Chronicler
had, as we must remember, himself lived in William's
court, and we may believe that his own eyes had
looked on the store of gold and silver, of vessels and
robes and gems and other costly things, which it was
beyond the skill of man to set forth.[1] These were the
spoils of England, and from them were made the gifts
which, in the belief of those days, were to win repose
in the other world for the soul of her despoiler. Every Gifts to
minster in England received, some six marks of gold, churches.
some ten, besides gifts of every kind of ecclesiastical
ornament and utensil, rich with precious metals and
precious stones, among which books for the use of

---

[1] Chron. Petrib. 1087. "Ðisum þus gedone, se cyng ferde to Winceastre, and
sceawode þæt madmehus, and þa gersuman þe his fæder ǽr gegaderode, þa
wæron unasecgendlice ænie man hu mycel þær wæs gegaderod, on golde and
on seolfre and on faton and on pællan and on gimman and on manige oðre
deorwurðe þingon þe earfoðe sindon to ateallene." Yet Henry of Huntingdon (p. 211) knew the exact amount of the silver, sixty thousand pounds, one
doubtless for each knight's fee.

CHAP. II.
Gifts to
Battle
Abbey.

Gifts to the
poor.

divine service was not forgotten.[1] And, above all, the special foundation of his father, the Abbey of the Battle, received choicer gifts than any, the royal mantle of the departed King among them.[2] Every upland church, every one at all events on the royal lordships, received sixty pennies.[3] Moreover a hundred pounds in money was sent into each shire to be given away in alms to the poor for William's soul.[4] Such a gift might be bountiful in a small shire like Bedford, where many Englishmen still kept their own; but it would go but a little way, even after eighteen years, to undo the work of the great harrying of Yorkshire. Meanwhile Robert, already received as Duke of the Normans, was doing the same pious work among the poor and the churches of his duchy.[5] The dutiful son and the rebel were both doing their best for the welfare of their father in the other world.

The Christ-
mas As-
sembly.
1087-1088.

From Winchester the new King went back to Westminster, and there he held the Christmas feast and assembly. It was attended by the two archbishops and by several other bishops, among whom the saint

[1] Florence brings in the books in a list of gifts which is longer than that of the Chronicler; "Cruces, altaria, scrinia, *textos*, candelabra, situlas, fistulas, ac ornamenta varia gemmis, auro, argento, lapidibusque pretiosis, redimita, per ecclesias digniores ac monasteria jussit dividi."

[2] Chron. de Bello, 40. "Regni diadema suscepit. Quod adeptus, paterni mandati non immemor, patris pallium regale et feretrum unde supra meminimus, cum ccc^tis philacteriis, sanctorum pignorum excellentia gloriosis, ecclesiæ beati Martini quantocius delegavit, quæ simul apud Bellum viii Kalendas Novembris suscepta sunt."

[3] The Chronicler says, "to ælcen cyrcean uppe land lx. pæñ." But Florence limits it; "ecclesiis in civitatibus vel villis suis per singulas denarios lx. dari."

[4] Chron. Petrib. 1087. "Into ælcere scire man seonde hundred punda feos, to dælanne earme mannan for his saule."

[5] Flor. Wig. 1087. "Ejus quoque germanus Rotbertus in Normanniam reversus, thesauros quos invenerat monasteriis, ecclesiis, pauperibus, pro anima patris sui largiter divisit."

of Worcester is specially mentioned. At this meeting
too appeared Odo of Bayeux, who received again from
his nephew his earldom of Kent.[1] Released from
his bonds by the pardon which had been so hardly
wrung from the dying Conqueror,[2] he already filled
the first place in the councils of the new Duke of
the Normans,[3] and he hoped to win the like power
over the mind of his other nephew in England. But
before long events came about which showed how
true had been the foresight of William the Great, when
he had said that mighty evils would follow if his brother
should be set free from his prison.

It is certainly something unusual in those times for a
king thus to make his way to his crown by virtue, as
it were, of an agreement between a dead king and a
living bishop, without either the nobles or the nation
at large either actively supporting or actively opposing
his claim. It is clear that men of both races had very
decided views about the matter; but they gave no open
expression to them at the time. The discussion of the
succession came after the coronation, among men who
had already acknowledged the new King. It may be
that all parties were taken by surprise. The accession

[1] Chron Petrib. 1087. "Se cyng wæs on þam midewintre on Lundene."
So Henry of Huntingdon (211); "Rex novus curiam suam ad Natale tenuit
apud Lundoniam." He adds a list of bishops who were present. There were
the two Archbishops, Maurice of London, Walkelin of Winchester, Geoffrey
[it should be Osbern] of Exeter, William of Thetford, Robert of Chester,
William of Durham, as also "Wlnod [sic] episcopus sanctus Wirecestriæ."
On the presence of Odo, see Appendix B. Robert of Torigny (1087) writes
"Vulnof." I cannot see much in his editor's suggestion that the Geoffrey
spoken of is the Bishop of Coutances, because the so-called Bromton, of
all people, has made a blunder about him; X Scriptt. 984.

[2] N. C. vol. iv. p. 708.

[3] Ord. Vit. 664 D. "Totum in Normannia pristinum honorem adeptus est, et consiliarius ducis, videlicet nepotis sui, factus est."

CHAP. II. of William Rufus had not indeed followed the death of
his father with anything like the same speed with which
the accession of Harold had followed the death of his
brother-in-law.   But then the death of Eadward had
long been looked for; the succession of Harold had long
been practically agreed on; above all, the Witan were
actually in session when the vacancy took place.   Everything therefore could be done at a moment's notice
with perfect formal regularity.   Now everything, if
much less sudden, was much more unlooked for.   The
kingdom found itself called on to acknowledge a king
whom no party had chosen, but whom no party had
at the moment the means, perhaps not the will, to
oppose.   The Normans, we may believe, would, if they
had been formally asked, have preferred Robert.   The
English, we may be sure, would, if they had been formally asked, have, at least among Norman candidates,
William preferred Henry.   And practically the choice lay among
the only Norman candidates only, and among them Henry was
available the one who was practically shut out.   All hopes, we
king at the moment. may be sure, had passed away of seeking for a king
either in the house of Cerdic, in the house of Godwine,
or in the house which, if not the house of Cnut, was,
at least by female succession, the house of his father
Swegen.   Of the sons of the Conqueror, Henry, the one
who was at once Norman and Englishman, was young
and beyond the sea.   William was in England, with at
least his father's recommendation to support him.   The
practical question lay between William and Robert.
Was William to be withstood on behalf of Robert?
Comparison Between William and Robert there could at the mo-
between
William ment be little doubt in the minds of Englishmen.   Their
and Robert. father's policy had kept both back from any great opportunity of doing either good or evil to the conquered
kingdom.   But, as far as their personal characters went,

Robert had as yet shown his worst side and William his best. There could be little room for doubt between the man who had fought against his father and the man who had risked his life to save his father. And, besides this, the accession of William would separate England and Normandy. England would again have, if not a king of her own blood, yet at least a king of her own. The island world would again be the island world, no longer dependent on, or mixed up with, the affairs of the world beyond the sea. The harshness which had again thrust back Morkere and Wulfnoth into prison might be passed by, as an act of necessary precaution. Morkere too might by this time be well nigh forgotten, and Wulfnoth had never been known. If a native king was not to be had, William Rufus was at the moment by no means the most unpromising among possible foreign kings.

Political bearing of William's accession.

But in truth neither Normans nor Englishmen were in this case called on to make any real choice. Both were called on, somewhat after the manner of the sham *plebiscita* of modern France, to acknowledge a sovereign who was already in possession. Whatever might have been the abstract preference of the Normans for Robert or of the English for Henry, neither party felt at the moment that degree of zeal which would lead them to brave the dangers of opposition. At any rate, William Rufus was a new king, and a new king is commonly welcome. Men of both races might reasonably expect that the rule of one who had come peacefully to his crown would be less harsh than that of one who had made his entry by the sword. It is further hinted that William partly owed his recognition to his early possession of his father's hoard, perhaps to his careful discharge of his father's will, perhaps, even thus early in his reign, to

No real choice.

Employment of the treasure.

CHAP. II. some other discreet application of his father's treasures.[1] Certain it is that, from whatever cause, all men accepted Rufus with all outward cheerfulness, though perhaps without any very fervent loyalty towards him on any side. It needed the events of the next few months, it needed strong influences and strong opposing influences, to turn the Normans in England into the fierce opponents of the new King, and the native English into his zealous supporters. It needed the further course of his own actions to teach both sides how much they had lost when they passed from the rule of William the Great to that of William the Red.

§ 2. The Rebellion against William Rufus.
March–November, 1088.

The winter of the year which beheld the Conqueror's death passed without any disturbance in the realm of his son.[2] But in the spring of the next year it became plain that the general acceptance which Rufus had met with in England was sincere on the part of his English subjects only. As the native Chronicler puts it, "the land was mightily stirred and was filled with mickle treason, for all the richest Frenchmen that were in this land would betray their lord the King, and would have his brother to King, Robert that was Earl in Normandy."[3] The leaders in this revolt were the bishops

Beginning of the rebellion

---

[1] Will. Malms. iv. 305. "Claves thesaurorum nactus est; quibus fretus totam Angliam animo subjecit suo."

[2] Ib. "Reliquo hiemis quiete et favorabiliter vixit."

[3] Chron. Petrib. 1088. "On þisum geare wæs þis land swiðe astirad, and mid mycele swicdome afylled; swa þæt þa riceste Frencisce men þe weron innan þisan lande wolden swican heore hlaforde þam cynge, and woldon habban his broðer to cynge, Rodbeard, þe wæs eorl on Normandige." The duty of faithfulness to the lord, whoever he may be, is always strongly felt; still William Rufus is only "heora hlaford se cyng," not "heora

whom the Conqueror had clothed with temporal power. CHAP. II.
And foremost among them was his brother, the new Discontent
King's uncle, Odo Bishop of Bayeux, now again Earl of ^{of Odo.}
Kent; and, according to one account, already Justiciar and
chief ruler in England.[1] But whatever might be his formal
position, Odo soon began to be dissatisfied with the
amount of authority which he practically enjoyed. He
seems to have hoped to be able to rule both his nephews
and all their dominions, and, in England at least, to keep
the whole administration in his own hands at least as
fully as he had held it before his imprisonment. In
this hope he was disappointed. The Earl of Kent was
not so great a man under the younger William as he
had been under the elder. The chief place in the confidence of the new King was held by another man of his
own order. This was William of Saint Carilef or Influence
Saint Calais, once Prior of the house from which he took of William of Saint-
his name, and afterwards Abbot of Saint Vincent's with- Calais.
out the walls of Le Mans.[2] He had succeeded the
murdered Walcher in the see of Durham, and he had
reformed his church according to the fashion of the time,
by putting in monks instead of secular canons.[3] His
place in the King's counsel was now high indeed. "So
well did the King to the Bishop that all England went
after his rede and so as he would."[4] Besides this newly

cynehlaford." But the notion that Robert had any special right as the
eldest son seems not to have come into any purely English mind of that
age.

[1] He appears in the list given by Henry of Huntingdon (see above, p. 19)
as "justiciarius et princeps totius Angliæ." Simeon of Durham (1088)
calls him "secundus rex."

[2] See Florence, 1081 ; Sim. Dun. Hist. Eccl. Dun. iv. 1.

[3] See N. C. vol. iv. p. 674.

[4] Chron. Petrib. 1088. "Swa wæll dyde se cyng be þam bisceop þæt
eall Englaland færde æfter his ræde and swa swa he wolde." So Florence;
" Ea tempestate rex prædictus illius, ut veri consiliarii, fruebatur prudentia ;
bene enim sapiebat, ejusque consiliis totius Angliæ tractabatur respublica."

CHAP. II. born jealousy of the King's newly chosen counsellor, Odo had a long standing hatred against the other prelate who had so long watched over the King, and whose advice the King was bound by oath to follow.[1] He bore the bitterest grudge against the Primate Lanfranc, as the inventor of that subtle distinction between the Bishop of Bayeux and the Earl of Kent which had cost the Earl five years of imprisonment.[2]

Action of Odo.

March 1, 1088.

Of the two personages who might thus be joined or separated at pleasure, it is the temporal chief with whom we have now to deal. Lent was now come. Of the spiritual exercises of the Bishop of Bayeux during the holy season we have no record; the Earl of Kent spent the time plotting with the chief Normans in England how the King might be killed or handed over alive to his brother.[3] We have more than one vigorous report of the oratory used in these seditious gatherings. According to some accounts, they went on on both sides of the sea, and we are admitted to hear the arguments which were used both in Normandy and in England.[4] Both agree in maintaining the claims of Robert, as at once the true successor, and the prince best fitted for their purpose. But it is on Norman ground that the necessity for an union between Normandy and England is set forth most clearly. The main

Gatherings of the rebels.

Arguments on behalf of Robert.

Cf. Ann. Wint. 1088. "Episcopus Willelmus Dunelmensis, qui paulo ante quasi cor regis erat."

[1] Will. Malms. iv. 306. "Immortale in eum [Lanfrancum] odium anhelans, quod ejus consilio a fratre se in vincula conjectum asserebat."

[2] See N. C. vol. iv. p. 680.

[3] Chron. Petrib. 1088. "And þæs unræd wearð gewesen innan þam Lengtene." So Florence; "Pars nobiliorum Normannorum favebat regi Willelmo, sed minima; pars vero altera favebat Roberto comiti Normannorum, et maxima; cupiens hunc sibi adsciscere in regnum, fratrem vero aut fratri tradere vivum aut regno privare peremptum." Here is the end of a hexameter.

[4] See Appendix B.

object is to hinder a separation between the two kingdoms, as they are somewhat daringly called.[1] It is clear
that to men who held lands in both countries it would
be a gain to have only one lord instead of two; but, if we
rightly understand the arguments which are put into the
mouths of the speakers, it was held that, if England had
again a king of her own, though it were a king of the
Conqueror's house, the work of the Conquest would be
undone. The men who had won England with their
blood would be brought down from their dominion in
the conquered island.[2] If they have two lords, there
will be no hope of pleasing both; faithfulness to the one
will only lead to vengeance on the part of the other.[3]
William was young and insolent, and they owed him
no duty. Robert was the eldest son; his ways were
more tractable, and they had sworn to him during the
life-time of his father. Let them then make a firm
agreement to stand by one another, to kill or dethrone
William, and to make Robert ruler of both lands.[4]
Robert, we are told, approved of the scheme, and promised that he would give them vigorous help to carry
it out.[5]

---

[1] Ord. Vit. 665 D. "Optimates utriusque *regni* conveniunt, et de duobus
regnis nunc divisis, quæ manus una pridem tenuerat, tractare satagunt."
Cf. the language used at an earlier time about Normandy, N.C. vol. i. p. 221.

[2] Ib. 666 A. "Labor nobis ingens subito crevit, et maxima diminutio
potentiæ nostræ opumque nobis incumbuit. . . . Violenta nobis orta est
mutatio et nostræ sublimitatis repentina dejectio." It is now that he makes
the flourish about "Saxones Angli" (see N. C. vol. i. p. 542); there is also
a good deal about Jeroboam and Polyneikês.

[3] Ib. "Quomodo duobus dominis tam diversis, et tam longe ab invicem
remotis competenter servire poterimus ?"

[4] Ib. B, C. "Inviolabile fœdus firmiter ineamus, et Guillelmo rege
dejecto vel interfecto, qui junior est et protervus, et cui nihil debemus,
Robertum ducem, qui major natu est et tractabilior moribus, et cui jamdudum vivente patre amborum fidelitatem juravimus, principem Angliæ ac
Neustriæ ad servandam unitatem utriusque regni constituamus."

[5] Ib. C. "Decretum suum Roberto duci detexuit. Ille vero, utpote levis

CHAP. II.

Speech of
Odo.

These arguments of Norman speakers are given us
without the names of any ringleaders. We may suspect
that the real speaker, in the idea of the reporter, was
no other than the Bishop of Bayeux.[1] We hear of him
more distinctly on English ground, haranguing his
accomplices somewhat to the same effect; only the
union of the two states is not so distinctly spoken of.
It may be that such a way of putting the case would
not sound well in the ears of men who, if not Englishmen, were at least the chief men of England, and who
might not be specially attracted by the prospect of
another conquest of England, now that England was

Reasons for
preferring
Robert to
William.

theirs. The chief business of the Bishop's speech is to
compare the characters of the two brothers between
whom they had to choose, and further to compare the
new King with the King who was gone. The speaker
seems to start from the assumption that, in the interests
of those to whom he spoke, it was to be wished that
the ruler whom they were formally to acknowledge
should be practically no ruler at all. William the Great
had not been a prince to their minds; William the Red
was not likely to be a prince to their minds either.
Robert was just the man for their purpose. Under
Robert, mild and careless, they would be able to do
as they pleased; under the stern and active William

Comparison
of the
elder and
younger
William.

they would soon find that they had a master. The
argument that follows is really the noblest tribute that
could be paid to the memory of the Conqueror. It sets
him before us, in a portrait drawn by one who, if a
brother, was also an enemy, as a king who did justice
and made peace, and who did his work without shedding

et inconsideratus, valde gavisus est promissis inutilibus, seseque spopondit
eis, si inchoarent, affaturum in omnibus, et collaturum mox efficax auxilium
ad perpetrandum tam clarum fecimus."

[1] See Appendix B.

of blood. It is taken for granted that the death of the
great king, at whose death we are told that peaceable
men wept and that robbers and fiends rejoiced,[1] was
something from which Odo and men like Odo might expect to gain. But nothing would be gained, if the rod of
the elder William were to pass into the hands of the
younger. The little finger of the son would be found
to be thicker than the loins of the father. Their release
from the rule of the King who was gone would profit
them nothing, if they remained subjects of one who
was likely to slay where his father had merely put in
bonds.[2] In this last contrast, though we may doubt
whether there could have been any ground for drawing
it so early in the reign of Rufus, we see that the men of
the time were struck by the difference between the
King whose laws forbade the judicial taking of human
life and the King under whom the hangman began his
work again. To pleadings like these we are told that
the great mass of the Norman nobility in England
hearkened; a small number only remained faithful to
the King to whom they had so lately sworn their oaths.
Thus, as the national Chronicler puts it, "the unrede
was read."[3]

As the chief devisers of the unrede we have the names
of two bishops besides Odo. One name we do not
wonder to find along with his. Geoffrey Bishop of
Coutances was a prelate of Odo's own stamp, one of

Bishop Geoffrey of Coutances joins the rebels.

---

[1] See N. C. vol. iv. p. 710.

[2] Will. Malms. iv. 306. "Multos eodem susurro infecit [Odo];
Roberto regnum competere, qui sit et remissioris animi, et juveniles stulti-
tias multis jam laboribus decoxerit; hunc delicate nutritum, animi ferocia
(quam vultus ipse demonstret), prætumidum, omnia contra fas et jus ausurum; brevi futurum ut honores jamdudum plurimis sudoribus partos amit-
tant; *nihil actum morte patris*, si quos ille vinxerit iste trucidet." (Again
the ending of a hexameter.) A good deal of this seems to come from later
experience of Rufus.

[3] Chron. Petrib. 1088. "Þæs unræd wærð geræd."

CHAP. II. whose doings as a wielder of the temporal sword we have heard in northern, in western, and in eastern England.[1] But we should not have expected to find as partner of their doings the very man whose high promotion had filled the heart of Odo with envy. It was indeed the most unkindest cut of all when the Bishop of Durham, the man in whose counsel the King most trusted, turned against the benefactor who had raised him so that all England went at his rede. What higher greatness he could have hoped to gain by treason it is hard to see. And it is only fair to add that in the records of his own bishopric he appears as a persecuted victim,[2] while all the writers of southern England join in special reprobation of his faithlessness. The one who speaks in our own tongue scruples not to make use of the most emphatic of all comparisons. "He would do by him"—that is, Bishop William would do by King William—"as Judas Iscariot did by our Lord."[3] We should certainly not learn from these writers that, after all, it was the King, and not the Bishop, who struck, or tried to strike, the first blow.

Treason of the Bishop of Durham.

Different statements of his conduct.

It is certainly far from easy to reconcile the different accounts of this affair. At a time a little later the southern account sets Bishop William before us as one who "did all harm that he might all over the North."[4] But at Durham it was believed that at all events a good deal of harm had been already done by the King to the Bishop; and the Bishop claims to have at an earlier time done the best of good service to the King.[5] That service must have been rendered while

---

[1] See N. C. vol. iv. pp. 276, 580, 673.   [2] See Appendix C.

[3] "He þohte to donne be him eall swa Iudas Scarioð dide be ure Drihtene."

[4] "Se bisceop of Dunholme dyde to hearme þæt he mihte ofer eall be norðan."

[5] See Appendix C.

the Lenten conspiracy was still going on; for at no later
time does the Bishop of Durham seem to have been any- His alleged
services to
where in the south of England. Then, according to his the King.
own story, the Bishop secured to the King the possession Lent, 1088.
of Hastings, of Dover, and of London itself. We have
only William of Saint-Calais' own statement for this
display of loyal vigour on his part; but, as it is a statement made in the hearing of the King and of the barons
and prelates of England, though exaggeration is likely
enough, the whole story can hardly be sheer invention.
Bishop William claims to have kept the two southern
havens in their allegiance when the King had almost
lost them. He claims further to have quieted disturb- His action
towards
ances in London, after the city had actually revolted, London.
by taking twelve of the chief citizens to the King's
presence.[1] Our notes of time show that the events of
which the Bishop thus speaks must have happened at
the latest in the very first days of March. It follows Early
movements
that there must have been at the least seditious move- in Kent
ments in south-eastern England, before the time of the and Sussex.
March,
open revolt in the west. In short, the rebellion in Kent 1088.
and Sussex must have begun very early indeed in the
penitential season.

We gather from the Durham narrative that, even at
this early stage, both Bishop Odo and Earl Roger were
already known to the King as traitors. We gather Bishop
William's
further that it was by the advice of the Bishop of advice to
Durham that the King was making ready for military the King.
operations against them, and that, when the Bishop
was himself summoned to the array, he made answer
that he would at once join with the seven knights whom

---

[1] Mon. Angl. i. 248. "Monstrabo quod Dorobernium et Hastingas,
quæ jam pene perdiderat, in sua fidelitate detinui, Londoniam quoque quæ
jam rebellaverat, in ejus fidelitate sedavi, meliores etiam duodecim ejusdem
urbis cives ad eum mecum duxi, ut per illos melius ceteros animaret."

CHAP. II. he had with him — seven chief barons of the bishopric,
as it would seem — and would send to Durham for more.

He forsakes
the King. But, instead of so doing, he left the King's court without his leave; he took with him some of the King's
men, and so forsook the King in his need.[1] Such was
afterwards the statement on the King's side. Certain
it is that, whatever the Bishop's fault was, the royal

His tem-
poralities
seized.
March,
1088. vengeance followed speedily on it. Early in March,
whether with or without the advice of any assembly,[2]
Rufus ordered the temporalities of the bishopric to be
seized, and the Bishop himself to be arrested. The
Bishop escaped to his castle at Durham, whence it
would not be easy to dislodge him without a siege.
Meanwhile the King's men in Yorkshire and Lincolnshire, though they failed to seize the Bishop's own
person, took possession in the King's name of his lands,

He writes
to the
King. his money, and his men. From Durham the Bishop
wrote to the King, setting forth his wrongs, protesting
his innocence, and demanding restitution of all that had
been taken from him. He goes on to use words which
remind us in a strange way at once of Godwine nego-
tiating with his royal son-in-law and of Odo in the
grasp of his royal brother. He offers the services of
himself and his men. He offers to make answer to any
charge in the King's court. But, like Godwine, he asks
for a safe-conduct before he will come;[3] like Odo, he
declares that it is not for every one to judge a bishop,
and that he will make answer only according to his

---

[1] Mon. Angl. i. 247. "Ipse [rex] te summonuit ut cum eo equitares; tu vero
respondisti ei, te cum septem militibus quos ibi habebas libenter iturum, et
pro pluribus ad castellum tuum sub festinatione missurum, et postea fugisti
de curia sua sine ejus licentia, et quosdam de familia sua tecum adduxisti, et
ita in necessitate sua sibi defecisti."

[2] See Appendix C.

[3] Mon. Angl. i. 245. "Præsto sum in curia vestra vobis justitiam facere
convenienti termino, securitate veniendi accepta." Cf. N. C. vol. ii. pp. 149,
150.

order.[1] On the receipt of this letter, the King at once, chap. ii.
in the sight of the Bishop's messenger, made grants of
the episcopal lands to certain of his barons;[2] those
lands were therefore looked on as property which had
undergone at least a temporary forfeiture. He however He is sum-
sent an answer to the Bishop, bidding him come to his moned to
the King's
presence, and adding the condition that, if he would not Court.
stay with the King as the King wished, he should be
allowed to go back safe to Durham. It must however
be supposed that this promise was not accompanied by
any formal safe-conduct ; otherwise, though it is not
uncommon to find the officers of a king or other lord
acting far more harshly than the lord himself, it is hard
to understand the treatment which Bishop William met
with at the hands of the zealous Sheriff of Yorkshire.
That office was now held by Ralph Paganel, a man Action of
who appears in Domesday as holder of lands in various Ralph
Paganel.
parts, from Devonshire to the lands of his present
sheriffdom,[3] and who next year became the founder
of the priory of the Holy Trinity at York.[4] The
Bishop, on receiving the King's answer, sent to York
to ask for peace of the Sheriff. But all peace was re-

---

[1] Mon. Angl. i. 245. " Non est enim omnium hominum episcopos judicare, et ego vobis secundum ordinem meum omnem justitiam offero ; et si
ad præsens vultis habere servitium meum vel hominum meorum, illud idem
secundum placere vestrum vobis offero."

[2] Ib. " Rex acceptis et auditis istis litteris episcopi, dedit baronibus
suis terras episcopi, vidente legato quem sibi miserat episcopus." I suppose
that these barons are no other than the Counts Alan and Odo, of whose share
in the matter we shall hear much more as we go on.

[3] See Ellis, i. 464. It is there remarked that Ralph's lands in Devonshire had largely been Merleswegen's. This is equally true in Yorkshire.
He must have succeeded Hugh the son of Baldric as sheriff. See N. C. vol.
iv. p. 801.

[4] See the foundation charter in the Monasticon, iv. 682; though it is
hard to understand how Pope Alexander could have confirmed anything in
1089. According to the charter, the church had once been held by a body
of canons, which had come to nothing. Ralph now restored it as a Benedictine monastery, a cell to Marmoutiers.

CHAP. II. fused to the Bishop, to his messengers, and to all his
men. A monk who was coming back from the King's
presence to the Bishop was stopped; his horse was
The lands killed, though he was allowed to go on on foot. Lastly,
of the
bishopric the Sheriff ordered all men in the King's name to do
laid waste. all the harm that they could to the Bishop everywhere
March—
May, 1088. and in every way. The Bishop was thus cut off from
telling his grievances; and for seven weeks, we are told,
the lands of the bishopric were laid waste.[1] This date
brings us into the month of May, by which time important
events had happened in other parts of England.

We have seen that, in south-eastern England at least,
the unrede of this year's Lent must have gone beyond
mere words, and must have already taken the form of
General action. But it seems not to have been till after Easter
rebellion. that the general revolt of the disaffected nobles broke
forth throughout the whole land. By this time they
had all thoroughly made up their minds to act. And
we may add that it is quite possible that the King's
treatment of the Bishop of Durham may have had some
share in helping them to make up their minds. They
may have been led to think that open rebellion was
The Easter the safest course. The first general sign was given at
Gemót.
April 16, the Easter Gemót of the year, which, according to rule,
1088. would be held at Winchester. The rebel nobles, instead
The rebels
refuse to of appearing to do their duty when the King wore his
come. crown, kept aloof from his court. They gat them each
man to his castle, and made them ready for war.[2] Soon

---

[1] "Præcepit omnibus regis fidelibus de parte regis ut malum facerent
episcopo ubicumque et quomodo cumque possent. Cumque episcopus per
se vel per legatos suos regem non posset requirere, et terras suas destrui et
vastari absque ulla ultione per vii. septimanas et amplius sustineret," etc.

[2] Their absence from the assembly comes from Florence; "Execrabile hoc
factum clam tractaverunt in quadragesima, quod cito in palam prorumpi
posset post pascha; nam a regali se subtrahentes curia, munierunt castella,
ferrum, flammam, prædas, necem, excitaverunt in patriam." Cf. Orderic,

after the festival the flame burst forth. The great body CHAP. II.
of the Norman lords of England were in open revolt
against the son of the man who had made England theirs.

The list of the rebel nobles reads like a roll of the The rebel
Norman leaders at Senlac or a choice of the names nobles.
which fill the foremost places in Domesday. With a
few marked exceptions, all the great men of the land
are there. Along with Odo, Bishop and Earl, the other Robert of
brother of the Conqueror, Robert of Mortain and of Mortain
Cornwall, the lord of Pevensey and of Montacute, joined
in the revolt against his nephew.[1] So did another kins- and Wil-
man, a member of the ducal house of Normandy and liam of Eu.
gorged with the spoils of England, William son of Robert
Count of Eu, grandson of the elder William and his
famous wife Lescelina.[2] Of greater personal fame, and Earl Roger
of higher formal rank on English soil, was the father and the
border
of one of the men who had crossed the sea to trouble lords.
England, Roger of Montgomery, whose earldom of
Shrewsbury swells, in the statelier language of one of
our authorities, into an earldom of the Mercians.[3] He
brought with him a great following from his own border-
land. Among these was Roger of Lacy, great in the
shires from Berkshire to Shropshire;[4] and with him Osbern.
came the old enemy Osbern of Richard's Castle, whose

---

666 C; " Munitiones suas fossis et hominibus, atque alimentis hominum et
equorum, abundanter instruebant."

[1] On Count Robert, see N. C. vol. ii. p. 296; iv. pp. 78, 168, 170. His name
does not now occur in the Chronicles, nor in Orderic, who does not mention
the siege of his castle of Pevensey. But his action comes out strongly in
Florence, who classes him with Odo as a leader, though in his narrative he
appears merely as his tool. The Hyde writer (297) also dwells fully on his
share in the work, but he has no special facts or legends.

[2] See N. C. vol. iii. pp. 117, 672; iv. pp. 39, 562, 825.

[3] In Orderic, 667 B, he appears as "Rogerius Merciorum comes."

[4] Flor. Wig. 1088. "Rogerius de Laceio, qui jam super regem invaserat
Herefordam." He appears in Domesday in Berkshire, Gloucestershire,
Worcestershire, Shropshire, but most largely in Herefordshire. See Ellis,
i. 442.

CHAP. II. name carries us back to times that now seem far away.[1] With Osbern came his son-in-law Bernard of Neufmarché or Newmarch, sister's son to the noble Gulbert of Hugleville, the man who was soon to stamp his memory on the mountain land of Brecheiniog.[2] From the same border too came the lord of Wigmore, Ralph of Mortemer.[3] But the treason of the great Earl of the central march was not followed by his northern neighbour.

Loyalty of Earl Hugh. Hugh of Chester clave to the King, while the mightiest of his tenants joined the rebels. For the old Hugh of Grantmesnil raised the standard of revolt in Northhamptonshire, and in Leicestershire, the land of his

Rebellion of Robert of Rhuddlan; sheriffdom.[4] And his rebellion seems to have carried with it that of his nephew the Marquess Robert of Rhuddlan, the terror of the northern Cymry.[5] Robert thus found himself in arms, not only against his king, but against his immediate and powerful neighbour and lord Earl Hugh. But the tie which bound a man to his mother's brother was perhaps felt to be stronger than duty towards

of Roger the Bigod; either king or earl. Along with the lords of the British marches stood the guardian of the eastern coast of England against the Dane, Roger the Bigod, father of earls, whose name, fated to be so renowned in later times, appears in the records of these days with a special brand

of Bishop Geoffrey of Coutances; of evil.[6] And with Odo and William of Durham a third prelate joined in the unrede, a prelate the worthy compeer of Odo, the warrior Geoffrey of Coutances, the bishop who knew better how to marshal mailed knights for the battle than to teach surpliced clerks to chant their psalms in the choir.[7] He brought with

---

[1] See N. C. vol. ii. pp. 138, 352.   [2] Ib. vol. iii. p. 132; iv. p. 448.

[3] Ib. vol. iii. p. 737.   [4] Ib. vol. iii. p. 233.

[5] Ord. Vit. 666 D. See N. C. vol. iv. pp. 74, 489.

[6] See below, p. 36.

[7] See his picture in Orderic, 703 B. " Præfatus præsul nobilitate cluebat, magisque peritia militari quam clericali vigebat. Ideoque loricatos milites

him the last of the elder succession of Northumbrian
earls, his nephew Robert of Mowbray, tall of stature,
swarthy of countenance, fierce, bold, and proud, who
looked down on his peers and scorned to obey his
betters, who loved better to think than to speak, and
who, when he opened his lips, seldom let a smile soften
his stern words.[1] With these leaders were joined a
crowd of others, "mickle folk, all Frenchmen," as the
Chronicler significantly marks.[2] The sons of the soil,
we are to believe, had no part in the counsels of that
traitorous Lent, in the deeds of that wasting Easter.

The war now began, a war in which, after the example
of the chief combatants, fathers fought against sons,
brothers against brothers, friends against their former
friends.[3] The rebel leaders, each from the point where
his main strength lay, began to lay waste the land,
specially the lordships of the King and the Archbishop.
And among these evil-doers the loyal monk of Peterborough distinctly sets down William of Saint-Calais,
meek victim as he seems in the records of his own
house. The Bishop may have argued that he was only
returning what the King had done to him; but the
witness is such as cannot be got over; "The Bishop
of Durham did to harm all that he might over all the

---

ad bellandum quam revestitos clericos ad psallendum magis erudire nove-
rat."

[1] See N. C. vol. iv. p. 672. Orderic gives his portrait along with that of
his uncle ; " Robertus Rogerii de Molbraio filius potentia divitiisque admodum pollebat, audacia et militari feritate superbus pares despiciebat, et
superbioribus obtemperare, vana ventositate turgidus, indignum autumabat.
Erat erim corpore magnus, fortis, niger et hispidus, audax et dolosus,
vultu tristis et severus. Plus meditari quam loqui studebat, et vix in con-
fabulatione ridebat."

[2] Chron. Petrib. 1088. " Swiðe mycel folc mid heom, ealle Frencisce
men." He must mean that all the leaders were French. We shall see (see
below, p. 47) that there were both Englishmen and Britons in the rebel
army. [3] Flor. Wig. 1088.

north." Some others of the confederates and their doings are sketched in a few words by the same sarcastic pen ;

" Roger hight one of them that leapt into the castle at Norwich, and did yet the worst of all over all the land." [1] So does the English writer speak of the first Bigod who held the fortress which had arisen on the mound of the East-Anglian kings.[2] Roger had succeeded to the place, though not to the rank, of Ralph of Wader, and, as Ralph had made Norwich a centre of rebellion against the father, so Roger now made it a centre of

rebellion against the son. Then we read how "Hugo eke did nothing better neither within Leicestershire nor within Northampton." [3] This was the way in which the lord of Grantmesnil, so honoured at Saint Evroul, was looked on in the *scriptorium* of the house which had once been the Golden Borough. In some other parts of the country we get fuller accounts than these of the doers and of what was done. Three districts in the west and in the south-east of England became the scene of events which are set down by the writers of the age in considerable detail.

Of Bristol, the great merchant-haven on the West-Saxon and Mercian border, we last heard when the sons of Harold failed to make their way within its walls,[4] and when its greedy slave-traders cast aside, for a while at least, their darling sin at the preaching of Saint Wulfstan.[5] The borough was now beginning to

---

[1] Chron. Petrib. 1088. " Roger hét an of heom se hleop into þam castele æt Norðwic, and dyde git eallra wærst ofer eall þæt land." He is "Rogerius Bigot" in William of Malmesbury. We shall find him behaving better later in our story.

[2] See N. C. vol. iv. pp. 68, 590.

[3] Chron. Petrib. 1088. " Hugo eac an þe hit ne gebette nan þing, ne innan Lægreceastrescire ne innan Norðamtune." He is " Hugo de Grente-mesnil" in William of Malmesbury. See N. C. vol. iv. pp. 74, 232.

[4] See N. C. vol. iv. p. 226.   [5] Ib. p. 382.

put on a new character, one which, in the disturbances CHAP. II. half a century later, won for it the name of the step-mother of all England.[1] A fortress, the forerunner of the great work of Robert Earl of Gloucester,[2] had now arisen, and its presence made Bristol one of the chief military centres of England down to the warfare of the seven-teenth century. The Bristol of those days had not yet Bristol occupied the ground which is now covered by its two in the eleventh chief ecclesiastical ornaments. The abbey of Saint century. Augustine, the creation of Robert Fitz-Harding, had not The chief yet arisen on the lowest slope of the hills to the west, churches not yet nor the priory of Saint James, the creation of Earl built. Robert, on the ground to the north of the borough. These foundations arose in the next age on the Mercian ground without the walls. And any forerunner which may then have been of the church of Saint Mary on the Red cliff, for ages past the stateliest among the parish churches of England, stood beyond the walls, beyond the river, on undisputed West-Saxon ground. The older Peninsular Bristol lay wholly on the Mercian side of the Avon, site of the borough. at the point where the Frome of Gloucestershire still poured its waters into the greater stream in the sight of the sun.[3] But nowhere, unless at Palermo, have the relations of land and water been more strangely turned about than they have been at Bristol. The course of the The two greater river, though not actually turned aside, is dis- rivers. guised by cuts and artificial harbours which puzzle the

---

[1] Gesta Stephani, 41. " Totius Angliæ noverca Bristoa."

[2] Simeon of Durham (1088) speaks of the "castellum fortissimum" at this time.

[3] Gesta Steph. 36. " Est Bristoa civitas . . . ipso situ loci omnium civi-tatum Angliæ munitissima. Sicut enim de Brundusio legimus, quædam provinciæ Glaornensis pars ad formam linguæ restricta, et in longum pro-tensa, duobus fluviis gemina ejus latera proluentibus, inque inferiori parte, ubi ipsa terra defectum patitur, in unam aquarum abundantiam coeuntibus, efficit civitatem."

CHAP. II. visitor till the key is found. The lesser stream of the
Changes in Frome has had its course changed and shortened, and
later times. the remnant is, like the Fleet of London, condemned by
art to the fate which nature has laid on so many of the
rivers of Greece and Dalmatia;[1] it runs, as in a *katabothra*, under modern streets and houses. The marshy
ground lying at the meeting of the streams has been
reclaimed and covered with the modern buildings of the
city. In the twelfth century, still more therefore in the
eleventh, this space was covered at every high tide, when
the waters rushing up the channels of both rivers made
Bristol seem to float on their bosom like Venice or Ra-
The castle. venna.[2] Of the castle again the more part of its site
is covered by modern buildings; a great part of its moat
is filled up; the donjon has vanished; the green is no
longer a green; it is only by searching that we can find
out some parts of the outer walls of the fortress, and
some still smaller parts of the buildings which they
fenced in.[3] But, when the key is once found, it is
not hard to follow the line both of the borough and of
the fortress. Bristol belongs to the same general class
of peninsular towns as Châlons, Shrewsbury, Bern, and
Besançon; but, as at Châlons, the height above the
rivers is not great; and it is at Bristol made quite insig-
nificant by comparison with the hills to the west and
north. Yet on the narrow neck of the isthmus itself,
the actual slope towards the streams on either side is

---

[1] One might quote nearer instances in the streams which flow out of
Mendip; only they have their *katabothra* at the beginning.

[2] Gesta Steph. u. s. "Viva quoque et fortis maris exæstuatio, noctibus
et diebus abundanter exundans, ex ambabus civitatis partibus fluvios ipsos
in latum et profundum pelagus regurgitare in seipsos cogit, portumque mille
carinis habillimum et tutissimum efficiens, ambitum illius adeo prope et con-
juncte constringit ut tota civitas aquis innatare, tota super ripas considere
videatur."

[3] In what was the castle green is a very pretty undercroft of early thirteenth century work, most likely the support of a chapel.

not to be despised. To the west of that isthmus, within
the peninsula, stood the original town, girded to the
north by the original course of the Frome, to the south-
west by the marshy ground at the junction of the rivers.[1]
To the west of the isthmus, outside the peninsula, stood
the castle. Standing on the exposed side, open to an
attack from the east, it was fenced in on three sides by
a moat joining the two rivers at either end. A writer Works of Earl Robert.
of the next age gives us a picture of Bristol Castle as
it then stood, strengthened by all the more advanced
art of that time.[2] But the great keep of Earl Robert,
slighted in the days of the Commonwealth, was not yet.
We can only guess at the state of borough and fortress,
as they had stood when the sons of Harold were driven
back from the walls of Bristol, or as they stood now at
the opening of the civil war which we have now reached.
But there are few towns whose general look must have
been more thoroughly unlike what it is now. The
central and busy streets which occupy the area of the
older Bristol must, allowing for the difference between
the eleventh century and the nineteenth, still keep the
general character of the old merchant-borough. But Growth of the town.
few changes can be greater than those which have
affected Bristol both in earlier and in later times.
One period of change first surrounded the elder town

[1] The course of the stream and the line of the walls have been altered
more than once; but the description in the Gesta Stephani of the peninsula, as long and tongue-shaped, shows that the Frome cannot, when
that was written, have taken the line of the present Baldwin Street. The
town was on the peninsula, but it covered only the north-east part
of it.

[2] Gesta Steph. "Ex una tamen ejus regione ubi ad obsidendum oppor-
tunior magisque pervia habetur, castellum plurimo aggere exaltatum, muro et
propugnaculis, turribus, et diversis machinis firmatum, impugnantium coercet
accessus." This is doubtless equally true in its measure of the state of things
in 1088; but there is not now much sign of the "plurimus agger." The old
prints of Bristol show Earl Robert's keep, a square tower of the best class.

CHAP. II. with a fringe of ecclesiastical buildings, and then took them within a more extended line of wall. Another in later days has swept away well nigh every trace of the fortress which was so famous both in the twelfth century and in the seventeenth, and has covered the whole range of the neighbouring hills with a new and airy city of modern days.

Bristol occupied by Bishop Geoffrey. The castle of Bristol then, though not perched, like so many of its fellows, on any lofty height, was placed on a strong and important site. That site, commanding the lower course of the Avon and the great borough upon it, and guarding the meeting-place, still of two shires, as once of two kingdoms, supplied an admirable centre for the work of those whose object was, not to guard those shires, but to lay them waste.[1] To that end Bristol was occupied and garrisoned by the warrior Bishop of Coutances, Geoffrey of Mowbray. It is not unlikely that he was already in command of the castle. He was not only a land-owner in the two neighbouring shires, a very great land-owner in that of Somerset;[2] His relation to the town. but the meagre notice of Bristol in the Great Survey also shows that he stood in some special relation to the borough as the receiver of the King's dues within it.[3] He doubtless added anything that the castle needed in

[1] The description of the later occupation of Bristol (Gesta Steph. p. 37) will serve equally for this earlier one. "E diversis siquidem provinciis et regionibus emersi, tanto illic abundantius et gratulantius affuerunt, quanto sub divite domino ex munitissimo castello, quicquid libentium animo occurreret, in uberrima committere Anglia fuit eis permissum."

[2] His estates in Somerset are very large. See Domesday, 87 a et seqq. In Gloucestershire (165) he appears as " Episcopus de Sancto Laudo "—the older seat of the bishopric of Coutances.

[3] Domesday, 163. Under " Bertune apud Bristou," now Barton Regis, we read, " Hoc manerium et Bristou reddit regi c. et x. markas argenti. Burgenses dicunt quod episcopus G. habet xxxiii. markas argenti et unam markam auri propter firmam regis." This looks like the Earl's third penny; but Geoffrey certainly had no formal earldom in Gloucestershire.

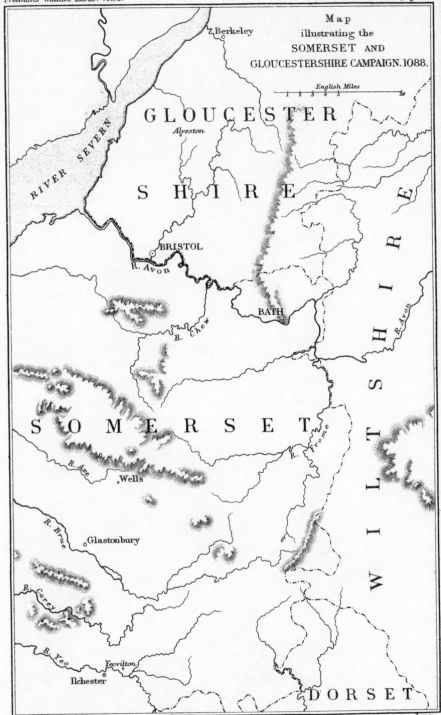

Map
illustrating the
SOMERSET AND
GLOUCESTERSHIRE CAMPAIGN. 1088.

English Miles

Berkeley

GLOUCESTER

RIVER SEVERN

Alveston

SHIRE

BRISTOL

R. Avon

BATH

R. Chew

SOMERSET

WILTSHIRE

R. Frome

R. Axe

R. Avon

Wells

R. Brue

Glastonbury

R. Carey

R. Yeo

Yeovilton

Ilchester

DORSET

Edwᵈ Weller

the way of further defences, and conjecture has attri-
buted to him one of the several lines which the city
walls have taken, that which brought the line of defence most closely to the banks of the Frome.[1] But
whatever were his works, we have no record of them;
we know only that the fierce prelate, at the head of
his partisans, turned Bristol Castle into a den of robbers.
His chief confederates were William of Eu, of whom we
have already spoken[2], and his own nephew Robert of
Mowbray. Among them they harried the land, and
brought in the fruits of their harrying to the castle.[3]
The central position of Bristol made a division of labour
easy. Of Bishop Geoffrey's two younger confederates,
Robert undertook the work in Somerset and William
in Gloucestershire. Robert marched up the valley of the
Avon to the Roman town of Bath, emphatically the "old
borough."[4] At the foot of the hills on either side, lying,
as wicked wits put it, amid sulphureous vapours, at the
gates of hell,[5] the square, small indeed, of the Roman
walls sheltered the abbey of Offa's rearing, now widowed
by the death of its English abbot Ælfsige.[6] The city had
been overthrown by the arms of Ceawlin; it had lain

[1] This is Camden's conjecture; it does not greatly matter for my purpose.

[2] See above, p. 33.

[3] Chron. Petrib. 1088. "Gosfrid bisceop and Rodbeard a Mundbræg
ferdon to Bricgstowe and hergodon, and brohton to þam castele þa hergunge."
So Florence; "Gosfridus episcopus Constantiensis, in castello Brycstowa,
socium conjurationis et perfidiæ habebat secum nepotem suum Rotbertum
de Mulbraio, virum gnarum militiæ."

[4] In the song in the Chronicles, 973, Eadgar is crowned

 "On þære ealdan byrig,   Oþre worde
 Acemannes ceastre,   Beornas Baðan nemnað."
 Eac hie egbuend.

In the prose entries in Worcester and Peterborough this is done "at Hata-
baðum."

[5] See Richard of the Devizes, 62. "Bathonia, in imis vallium, in crasso
nimis aere et vapore sulphureo posita, imo deposita, est ad portas inferi."

[6] See N. C. vol. iv. p. 385.

CHAP. II. waste like the City of the Legions;[1] it had risen again as an English town to share with the City of the Legions in the two chief glories of the days of the peaceful Eadgar. If Chester saw his triumph,[2] Bath had seen his crowning. And now the hand of the Norman, not the Norman Conqueror but the Norman rebel, fell as heavily on the English borough as the hand of the West-Saxon invader had fallen five hundred years before. Bath was a king's town; as such it drew on itself the special wrath of the rebels; the whole town was destroyed by fire, to

He marches through Wiltshire to Ilchester. rise again presently in another character.[3] From Bath, the greatest town of Somerset, but which, as placed in a corner of the land, has never claimed to be one of its administrative centres, the destroyer passed on to another town of Roman origin, which once did aspire to be the head of the Sumorsætan, but from which all traces of greatness have passed away. From Bath Robert first marched into Wiltshire, most likely following the line of the Avon; he there wrought much slaughter and took great spoil. He then turned to the south-west along the high ground of Wiltshire; he made his way into the mid parts of Somerset, and laid siege to the King's town of Givelceaster, Ivelchester, Ilchester,

Position of Ilchester. the Ischalis of a by-gone day.[4] The town lay at the foot of the most central range of the hills of Somerset,

---

[1] Mr. Earle has, I think, made it morally certain that the Old-English poem on a ruined city in the Codex Exoniensis refers to Bath. It is a pity that his account is hidden in the Proceedings of the Bath Natural History and Antiquarian Field Club, vol. ii. no. 3, 1872.

[2] See N. C. vol. iv. p. 310.

[3] Chron. Petrib. 1088. "And syððon foron út of þam castele and hergodon Baðon, and eall þæt land þær abutan." Florence adds the burning; "Rotbertus . . . congregato exercitu invasit Bathoniam, civitatem regiam, eamque igne succendit."

[4] Flor. Wig. 1088. "Illa [Bathonia] deprædata, transivit in Wiltusciram, villasque depopulans, multorumque hominum strage facta, tandem adiit Givelceastram, obsedit, et expugnare disposuit."

on the edge of one of the inlets of the great marshland CHAP. II.
of Sedgemoor. The site was marked by the junction
of the great line of the Fossway with a number of roads
in all directions. The spot was defended by the river,
the Ivel, which gives the town its English name. Here,
at the foot of the high ground, the stream widens to
surround an island, a convenient outpost in the defences of the town which arose on its southern bank.
Ilchester, like Bath, drew on itself the special enmity of The siege.
the rebels as being a king's town, an enmity likely to
be the sharper because Ilchester stands within sight
of Count Robert's castle of Montacute, and is divided
only by the river from lands which were held by
his fellow-rebel William of Eu.[1] The Ilchester of
our day seems a strange place for a siege; but in the
days of the Red King the town was still surrounded
by strong walls, and those walls were defended by
valiant burghers. The walls and gates have perished;
the ditches have been filled up; yet the lasting impress
of the four-sided shape of the Roman *chester* may still
be traced in the direction of the roads and buildings
of the modern town.[2] The importance of Ilchester had
passed away even in the sixteenth century, when of its
five or six churches all but one were in ruins; but, in the
times with which we are dealing, its hundred and seven

[1] Geveltone, now Yeovilton, was held by one Ralph under William of
Eu (Domesday, 96 b). Givele, now Yeovil, was held by Count Robert
(Domesday, 93). All these names come in various corruptions from the
river Givel or Ivel, also called Yeo. Only in *Yeovil* we may trace a bit
of false etymology, which has also set the pattern to Yeovilton.

[2] I took with me to Ilchester a book by the Rev. W. Buckler, "Ilchester
Almshouse Deeds" (Yeovil, 1866), which contains the accounts of Ilchester
from Leland, Camden, and Stukeley, together with Stukeley's map. The
last-named writer may have drawn somewhat on his imagination; but I
could trace the line of the walls, represented in a great part of their course
by modern buildings. Under the circumstances of the site, the usual
carfax is not to be found at Ilchester, any more than at Godmanchester.

CHAP. II. burgesses, with their market held in the old forum at the meeting-place of the roads, held no inconsiderable place Robert of Mowbray driven back from Ilchester. among the smaller boroughs of Western England.[1] What the men of Ilchester had they knew how to defend; the attack and the defence were vigorously carried on on either side. Our one historian of the leaguer—he becomes almost its minstrel—tells us how the besiegers fought for greed of booty and love of victory, while the besieged fought with a good heart for their own safety and that of their friends and kinsfolk. The stronger and worthier motive had the better luck. The dark and gloomy Robert of Mowbray, darker and gloomier than ever, turned away, a defeated man, from the unconquered walls of Ilchester.[2]

This utter failure of a man who stands forth in a marked way as one of the skilful captains of the age was a good omen for success at points which were still William of Eu plunders in Gloucestershire. more important in the struggle. Meanwhile the work of destruction was going steadily on in the lands on the other side of Bristol, among the flock of the holy Wulfstan. Gloucestershire was assigned as the province of William of Eu, and he did his work with a will along the rich valley of the Severn, still the land of pasture, then also the land of vines.[3] The district called Berkeley He harries Berkeley. Harness was laid waste with fire and sword, and the town of Berkeley itself was plundered.[4] Berkeley, once

[1] Domesday, 86 a. "In Givelcestre sunt 107 burgenses, reddentes xx. solidos. Mercatum cum suis appendiciis reddit xi. libras."

[2] Flor. Wig. 1088. "Pugnant exterius spe capti prædæ et amore victoriæ, repugnant intrinsecus acriter pro se suorumque salute. Tandem inter utrumque necessitatis vicit causa; repulsus et tristis recedit Rotbertus privatus victoria." The Chronicle and William of Malmesbury do not speak of Ilchester. William thus sums up the campaign; 'Gaufridus episcopus, cum nepote, Bathoniam et Bercheleiam partemque pagi Wiltensis depopulans, manubias apud Bristou collocabat."

[3] See N. C. vol. ii. p. 144.

[4] Chron. Petrib. 1088. "And eall Beorclea hyrnesse hi awæston."

the abode of Earl Godwine and the scene of the pious CHAP. II.
scruples of Gytha,[1] is now simply marked as a king's
town;[2] the abbey had vanished in a past generation;
the famous castle belongs to a later generation; but the
place was not defenceless. Berkeley is indeed one of Position of
those places which have become strongholds almost by Berkeley.
accident. It looks up at a crowd of points on the bold
outlying promontories of the Cotswolds, points some of
them marked by the earthworks of unrecorded times,
which in Normandy or Maine could hardly fail to have
been seized on for the site of fortresses far sooner than
itself. Nor is it near enough to the wide estuary of the
Severn to have been of any military importance in the
way of commanding the stream. It is rather one of
those places where the English lord fixed his dwelling
on a spot which was chosen more as a convenient
centre for his lands than with any regard to purposes of
warfare. The mound, the church, the town, rose side
by side on ground but slightly higher than the rich
meadows around them. But the mound on which the
great Earl of the West-Saxons had once dwelled had
been, as usual, turned to Norman military uses.
Earl William of Hereford, whose watchful care stretched The castle.
on both sides of the river, had crowned it with
what Domesday marks as "a little castle."[3] One
would be well pleased to know in what such a defence
was an advance on the palisades or other defences which
may have surrounded the hall of Godwine. In after days

Florence more fully; "Willelmus de Owe Glawornensem invadit comitatum,
regiam villam deprædatur Beorchelaum, per totam ferro et flamma grande
perpetrat malum."

[1] See N. C. vol. ii. p. 557.

[2] See Domesday, 164. But it had already given a name to Roger and
Ralph of Berkeley; Domesday, 168. From Roger's descendants it passed
by marriage to Robert the son of Harding. See N. C. vol. iv. p. 758.

[3] Domesday, 163. "In Nesse [Sharpness] sunt v. hidæ pertinentes ad
Berchelai quos W. comes misit extra ad faciendum unum castellulum."

CHAP. II. the "little castle" was to grow into the historic home of that historic house in whom, whether they themselves acknowledge it or not, history must see the lineal offspring, not of a Danish king, but of an English staller.[1] At present however the savage William of Eu had not to assault the stronghold of Robert, son of Harding and grandson of Eadnoth, but merely to overcome whatever resistance could be offered by the *castellulum* of William Fitz-Osbern. Its defences were most likely much less strong than the Roman walls of Ilchester. Berkeley and the coasts thereof were thoroughly ravaged. On the whole, notwithstanding the defeat of Robert of Mowbray, the Bishop of Coutances and his lieutenants had done their work to their own good liking. No small spoil from each of the three nearest shires had been brought in to the robbers' hold at Bristol.

Meanwhile the same work was going on busily to the north and north-west of Bishop Geoffrey's field of action. Of the movements in Herefordshire and Worcester-

Rebel centre at Hereford.

shire we have fuller accounts, accounts which, before we have done, land us from the region of military history into that of hagiography. The centre of mischief in this region was at Hereford. The city which Harold had called back into being, and where William Fitz-Osbern had ruled so sternly, had now no longer an earl; the rebel Roger was paying the penalty of his treason at some point far away alike from Hereford, from Flanders, and from Breteuil.[2] The city had now the King for its immediate lord. It was presently seized by Roger of Lacy,[3] and was turned into a meeting-place

[1] Since I wrote the fourth volume of the Norman Conquest, there has been much controversy about the origin of Robert Fitz-Harding. (See Notes and Queries, Jan. 3rd, 1880.) I am confirmed on the whole in my old belief that he was the son of Harding the son of Eadnoth.

[2] See N. C. vol. iv. pp. 590, 855.　　　　[3] See above, p. 33.

for the disaffected. The host that came together is CHAP. II. marked as made up of "the men that eldest were of Hereford, and the whole shire forthwith, and the men of Shropshire with mickle folk of Bretland."[1] Some of their names, besides that of Roger of Lacy, we have heard already.[2] And we are significantly told that the men of Earl Roger—the men of Shropshire—were with them, Action of Earl Roger. a formula which seems specially meant to shut out the presence of the Earl himself.[3] And though the leaders were "all Frenchmen,"[4] yet among their followers were men of all the races of the land. Not only Normans and Britons, but Englishmen also, were seen in the rebel ranks. So it seemed, if not in the general prospect as it was looked at from distant Peterborough, yet at least in the clearer view which men took from the watch-towers of more nearly threatened Worcester.[5]

For it was the "faithful city" of after days on which The rebels march on Worcester. the full storm of the Western revolt was meant to burst. The Norman lords of the border, with their British allies, now marched on Worcester, as, thirty-three years before, 1055. an English earl of the border, with his British allies, had marched on Hereford.[6] They came of their own will to deal by Worcester, shire and city, as, forty-seven years 1041. before, English earls had been driven against their will to deal with them at the bidding of a Danish king.[7] "They harried and burned on Worcestershire forth, and they came to the port itself, and would then the port burn and the

---

[1] Chron. Petrib. 1088. "þa men þe yldest wæron of Hereforde, and eall þeo scír forþmid, and þa men of Scrobscyre mid mycele folce of Brytlande." [2] See above, p. 33.

[3] Flor. Wig. 1088. "Cum hominibus comitis Rogerii de Scrobbesbyria." Yet the Chronicler says distinctly, "And Rogere eorl wæs eac æt þam unræde." That is, he joined in the conspiracy, but did not take a personal share in the war. [4] See above, p. 35, note 3.

[5] Flor. Wig. 1088. "Congregato magno Anglorum, Normannorum, et Walensium exercitu."

[6] See N. C. vol. ii. p. 395. [7] Ib. vol. i. p. 520.

CHAP. II. minster reave, and the King's castle win to their hands."[1]
But Worcester was not doomed to see in the days of the
second William such a day as Hereford had seen in
the days of Eadward, as Worcester itself had seen in
Deliver- the days of Harthacnut. The port was not burned, the
ance of
Worcester. minster was not reaved, nor was the King's castle won
into the hands of his enemies. And the deliverance of
Worcester is, with one accord, assigned by the writers
of the time to the presence within its walls of its bishop,
the one remaining bishop of English blood, whose un-
shaken loyalty had most likely brought the special wrath
Action of of the rebels upon his city and flock. The holy Wulf-
Wulfstan.
stan was grieved at heart for the woes which seemed
coming upon his people; but he bade them be of good
courage and trust in the Lord who saveth not by sword
or spear.[2] The man who had won the heart of North-
humberland for Harold,[3] who had saved his own city
for the first William,[4] was now to save it again for the
Position of second. At Worcester, castle, minster, and episcopal palace
Worcester.
rose side by side immediately above the Severn. But
Worcester is no hill city like Durham or Le Mans. The
height above the stream is slight; the subordinate buildings of the monastery went down almost to its banks.
The mound, traditionally connected with the name of
Eadgar the Giver-of-peace, has now utterly vanished;

---

[1] Chron. Petrib. 1088. "Þa men ... comon and hergodon and bærndon
on Wiðreceastrescire forð, and hi comon to þam porte sylfan, and woldon
þa þæne port bærnen, and þæt mynster reafian, and þæs cynges castel
gewinnan heom to handa." Florence adds, "grandem de regis incolis
fidelibus sumpturos vindictam." On the deliverance of Worcester, see
Appendix D.

[2] Florence brings in his own Bishop with a panegyric; "Vir magnæ
pietatis et columbinæ simplicitatis, Deo populoque quem regebat in omnibus
amabilis, regi, ut terreno domino, per omnia fidelis, pater reverendus
Wlstanus." In the Chronicle he is simply "se arwurða bisceop Wlfstan."
He goes on to make his exhortation after the manner of Moses.

[3] See N. C. vol. iii. p. 61.   [4] Ib. vol. iv. p. 579.

it then stood to the south of the monastery, and had CHAP. II.
become, as elsewhere, the kernel of the Norman castle.
It will be remembered that it was the sacrilegious extension of its precincts at the hands of Urse of Abetot
which had brought down on him the curse of Ealdred.[1]
But by this time the new minster of Wulfstan's own
building, whose site, we may suppose, was further from the
castle, that is, more to the north, than that of the church
of Oswald,[2] was, if not yet finished, at least in making.
It may be that at this moment the two minsters—the elder
one which has wholly passed away, the newer, where
Wulfstan's crypt and some other portions of his work
still remain among the recastings of later times,—both
stood between the mound of Eadgar and its Norman sur-
roundings, and the bishop's dwelling, whatever may have
been its form in Wulfstan's day. Still along the line of
the river, lay the buildings of the city further to the
north, with the bridge leading to the meadows and low
hills beyond the stream, backed by the varied outline
of the heights of Malvern, the home of the newly-
founded brotherhood of Ealdwine.[3] At the moment when
the rebels drew near to Worcester, all the inhabitants
of the city, of whatever race or order, were of one heart
and of one soul under the inspiration of their holy
Bishop. Like the prophets and judges of old, Wulfstan Wulfstan
suddenly stands forth as first, if not in military action, called to
the com-
at least in military command. We know not whether mand.
the fierce Sheriff or some captain of a milder spirit
formally bore rule in the castle. But we read that the
Norman garrison, by whom the mild virtues of the
English bishop were known and loved, practically put
him at their head. They prayed him to leave his episcopal home beyond the church, and to take up his abode

<hr>

[1] See N. C. vol. iv. p. 174.

[2] See N. C. vol. iv. p. 379.   [3] Ib.

CHAP. II.

Wulfstan
enters the
castle.

Advance of
the rebels.

Sally of
the royal
forces.

with them in the fortress. If danger should be pressing, they would feel themselves all the safer, if such an one as he were among them.[1] Wulfstan agreed to their proposal, and set out on the short journey which he was asked to make, a journey which the encroachments of the Sheriff had made shorter than it should have been.[2] On his way he was surrounded by the inhabitants of Worcester of all classes, all alike ready for battle. He himself had, after the new fashion of Norman prelates, a military following,[3] and the soldiers of the King and of the Bishop, with all the citizens of Worcester, now came together in arms. From the height of the castle mound, Wulfstan and his people looked forth beyond the river. The foes were now advancing; they could be seen marching towards the city, and burning and laying waste the lands of the bishopric.[4] Soldiers and citizens now craved the Bishop's leave to cross the river and meet the enemy. Wulfstan gave them leave, encouraging them by his blessing, and by the assurance that God would allow no harm to befall those who went forth to fight for their King and for the deliverance of their city and people.[5] Grieved further by the sight of the harrying of

---

[1] Flor. Wig. 1088. "Normanni interim, ineuntes consilium, rogant ipsum episcopum ut ab ecclesia transiret in castellam, tutiores se affirmantes de ejus præsentia, si majus incumberet periculum; diligebant enim eum valde. Ipse enim, ut erat miræ mansuetudinis, et pro regis fidelitate, *et pro eorum dilectione*, petitioni eorum adquievit."

[2] See N. C. vol. iv. p. 174.

[3] Flor. Wig. u. s. "Interea audenter in arma se parat episcopalis familia." On the nature of this "familia," see N. C. vol. v. p. 496.

[4] Ib. "Inter quos [hostes] magna belli jam fervebat insania; contumaciter enim episcopi contemnentes mandata, in terram ipsius posuerunt incendia." On the order of events, see Appendix D.

[5] Ib. "Conveniunt castellani et omnis civium turma, occurrere se affirmant hostibus ex altera parte Sabrinæ fluminis, si hoc eis pontificis annueret licentia. Parati igitur et armis instructi, ipsum ad castellum euntem habent obviam, quam optabant requirunt licentiam; quibus libentur annuens, 'Ite,' inquit, 'filii, ite in pace, ite securi, cum Dei et nostra benedictione.

the church-lands, and pressed by the urgent prayer of all CHAP. II.
around him, Wulfstan pronounced a solemn anathema Wulfstan
against the rebellious and sacrilegious invaders.[1] The curses the rebels.
loyal troops, strengthened by the exhortations and
promises of their Bishop, set forth. The bridge was Victory of
made firm; the defenders of Worcester marched across the king's men.
it;[2] and the working of Wulfstan's curse, so the tradition of Worcester ran, smote down their enemies before
them with a more than human power. The invaders,
scattered over the fields for plunder, were at once over-
taken and overthrown. Their limbs became weak and
their eyes dim; they could hardly lift their weapons
or know friend from foe.[3] The footmen were slaugh-
tered; the horsemen, Norman, English, and Welsh, were
taken prisoners; of the whole host only a few escaped
by flight. The men of the King and of the Bishop
marched back to Worcester—so Worcester dutifully
believed—without the loss of a single man from their
ranks. They came back rejoicing in the great salvation
which had been wrought by their hands, and giving
all thanks to God and his servant Wulfstan.[4]

Among the sorrows which rent the breast of the holy
Bishop of Worcester, one may have been to see a man of

Confidens ego in Domino, spondeo vobis, non hodie nocebit vobis gladius, non
quicquam infortunii, non quisquam adversarius.   State in regis fidelitate,
viriliter agentes pro populi urbisque salute."

[1] Ib. "Episcopus ingenti concutitur dolore, videns debilitari res
ecclesiæ, acceptoque inde consilio, gravi eos, ab omnibus qui circumaderant
coactus, percussit anathemate." See Appendix D.

[2] Ib. "Alacres pontem reparatum transeunt, hostes de longinquo
accelerantes conspiciunt."

[3] See Appendix D.

[4] Flor. Wig. u. s. "Cæduntur pedites, capiuntur milites, cum Normannis tam Angli quam Walenses, cæteris vero vix debili elapsis fuga [were
the 'milites' spared for the sake of ransom?] regis fideles cum pontificis
familia, exultantes in gaudio, sine ulla diminutione suorum, redeunt ad
propria; gratias Deo referunt de rerum ecclesiæ incolumitate, gratias
episcopo referunt de consilii ejus salubritate."

CHAP. II. his own order, one whom he had, somewhat strangely perhaps, honoured with his friendship, acting as a temporal leader in the rebellion against which he had to wield his spiritual arms. It was, it may be remembered, Geoffrey of Mowbray, the lord of the robbers' hold at Bristol, who had rebuked the lamb-like simplicity of Wulfstan's garb.[1] The lamb of Severnside had now overthrown alike the wolves of Normandy and the wild cats of the British hills. But, if Wulfstan mourned over the evil deeds of the warlike Bishop of Coutances, he had no such personal cause for grief over either the sins or the sorrows of another bishop who was meanwhile, like himself, besieged in an episcopal city. That bishop however was not, like Wulfstan, defending his own flock with either spiritual or temporal arms ; he was doing all the wrong in his power to the flock of another. The source and leader of the whole mischief,[2] Odo, Bishop and Earl, chose his own earldom of Kent for the scene of his ravages. Our notes of time are very imperfect, and we have seen that there were movements in Kent, movements in which Odo seems to have had a share, much earlier in the year.[3] But it would seem that the great outbreak of rebellion in south-eastern England happened about the same time as the great outbreaks more to the west and north. As the Bishop of Coutances had fixed his head-quarters in the castle of Bristol, so the Bishop of Bayeux now fixed his head-quarters in the castle of Rochester, and thence ravaged the lands of the King and the Archbishop.[4]

Movements of Odo in Kent.

---

[1] See N. C. vol. iv. p. 386.

[2] Chron. Petrib, 1088. "Þe wæs ærur heafod to þam unræde."

[3] See above, p. 29.

[4] Chron. Petrib. 1088. "Ðe bisceop Odo, þe þas cyng of awocan, ferde into Cent to his earldome and fordyde hit swyðe, and þæs cynges land and þæs arcebisceopes mid ealle aweston, and brohte eall þæt gôd into his castele on Hrofeceastre." This follows at once on the accounts of Roger the

Map
illustrating the
KENT AND SUSSEX
CAMPAIGN.
A.D. 1088.
English Miles
1 2 3 4 5

Edw.ᵈ Weller

Another great Kentish fortress, that of Tunbridge, was CHAP. II.
also in rebellion. So in Sussex was Pevensey, the very Tunbridge and
firstfruits of the Conquest, where Odo's brother Count Pevensey.
Robert also held out against the King. These three
fortresses now become the busy scene of our immediate
story; but the centre of all is the post occupied by
the Bishop of Bayeux and Earl of Kent. This part of
the war is emphatically the war of Rochester.

The city by the Medway had been a fortress from the Early history of
earliest times. We have seen that it had already played Rochester.
a part both in foreign and in civil wars. In the days
of Æthelred it still kept the Roman walls parts of which
still remain, walls which were then able to withstand
two sieges, one at the hands of the King himself, and
one at those of the Danish invaders.[1] In truth the Import-ance of its
position of Rochester, lying on the road from London position.
to Canterbury, near to the sea on a navigable river,
made it at all times a great military post.[2] The chief
ornament of the city did not yet exist in the days of
Odo. The noble tower raised in the next age by Arch- The later castle.
bishop Walter of Corbeuil, the tower which in one
struggle held out against John[3] and in the next held
out for his son,[4] and still remains one of the glories of

Bigod and Hugh of Grantmesnil. So William of Malmesbury, who here
brings in the story of Lanfranc's share in Odo's imprisonment in 1082, in
order to account for Odo's special hatred towards the Archbishop.

[1] See N. C. vol. i. pp. 267, 296. On the early history of Rochester
generally, see Mr. Hartshorne's paper in the Archæological Journal,
September, 1863.

[2] This is brought out by Orderic, 667 B; "Oppidum igitur Rovecestræ
sollicita elegerunt provisione, quoniam, si rex eos non obsedisset in urbe,
in medio positi laxis habenis Lundoniam et Cantuariam devastarent, et
per mare, quod proximum est, insulasque vicinas, pro auxiliis conducendis
nuntios cito dirigerent." The islands must be Sheppey and Thanet.

[3] See the siege of Rochester in 1215 and his defence by William of
Albini in Roger of Wendover, iii. 333.

[4] For the siege of 1264 see W. Rishanger, Chron. p. 25 (Camd. Soc.).
On Simon's military engines he remarks that the Earl "exemplum relinquens

CHAP. II.

The cathedral church.

Norman military architecture, had perhaps not even a forerunner of its own class.[1] And the minster of Saint Andrew, which the enlargements of the twelfth and thirteenth centuries have still left one of the least among the episcopal churches of England, had then only the lowly forerunner which had risen, which perhaps was still only rising, under the hands of Gundulf.[2]

The castle site fortified by the Conqueror.

But the steep scarped cliff rising above the broad tidal stream was a stronghold in the Conqueror's days, as it had doubtless been in days long before his. Whether a stone castle had yet been built is uncertain; the fact that such an one was built for William Rufus by Gundulf later in his reign might almost lead us to think that as yet the site, strong in itself, was defended only by earthworks and defences of timber.[3] Below the castle to the south-east lay the city, doubtless fenced

The city.

Anglicis qualiter circa castrorum assultationes agendum sit, qui penitus hujusmodi diebus illis fuerant ignari." A forerunner of Kanarês, he had a fire-ship in the river; he also used mines, as the Conqueror had done at Exeter.

[1] Mr. Hartshorne showed distinctly that the present tower of Rochester was not built by Gundulf, but by William of Corbeuil. See the passages which he quotes from Gervase, X Scriptt. 1664, and the continuator of Florence, 1126. But we have seen (see N. C. vol. iv. p. 366) that Gundulf did build a stone castle at Rochester for William Rufus ("castrum Hrofense lapidum"), and we should most naturally look for it on the site of the later one. On the other hand, there is a tower, seemingly of Gundulf's building and of a military rather than an ecclesiastical look, which is now almost swallowed up between the transepts of the cathedral. But it would be strange if a tower built for the King stood in the middle of the monastic precinct.

[2] The odd position of the cloister at Rochester suggests the notion that Gundulf's church occupied only the site of the present eastern limb, and that the later Norman nave was an enlargement rather than a rebuilding.

[3] Domesday, 2 b. "Episcopus de Rouecestre pro excambio terræ in qua castellum sedet, tantum de hac terra tenet quod xvii.s. et iv.d. valet." This is said of land at Aylesford; but the castle spoken of must surely be that of Rochester. The Domesday phrase "sedet" seems beautifully to describe either the massive square donjon or the shell-keep on the mound; yet it may be doubted whether Rochester had either in the Conqueror's day.

F. Weller.

East Gate

Gundulf's Tower

St. Andrew's

ROCHESTER

Tower of W. of Corbeuil

Bowley Hill

River Medway

100 200 300 400 500 Feet.

For the Delegates of the Clarendon Press.

by the Roman wall; and a large part of its space had CHAP. II.
now begun to form the monastic precinct of Saint
Andrew. The town is said to have been parted from
the castle by a ditch which, as at Le Mans and at
Lincoln, was overleaped by the enlarged church of the
twelfth century;[1] in any case the castle, in all its
stages, formed a sheltering citadel to the town at its
feet. Neither town nor castle by itself occupies a penin- Nature of
sular site; but a great bend of the river to the south the site.
makes the whole ground on which they stand peninsular, with an extent of marshy ground between the
town and the river to the north and east. The stronghold of Rochester, no lofty natural peak, no mound of
ancient English kings, perhaps as yet gathering round
no square keep of the new Norman fashion, but in any
case a well-defended circuit with its scarped sides strengthened by all the art of the time, was the chief fortress
of the ancient kingdom over which the Bishop of Bayeux
now ruled as Earl. It now became, under him, the great The castle
centre of the rebellion. Gundulf, renowned as he was occupied
by Odo.
for his skill in military architecture, must have been sore
let and hindered in the peaceful work of building his
church and settling the discipline of his monks,[2] when
his brother bishop filled the castle with his men of war,
five hundred of his own knights among them.[3] But

---

[1] This ditch is said to have been traced right across the middle of the
cathedral, with the twelfth-century nave to the west of it. I can say
nothing either way from my own observation ; but such an extension of
the church to the west would exactly answer to the extension of the
churches of Le Mans and Lincoln to the east. In both those cases the
Roman wall had to give way.

[2] See N. C. vol. iv. p. 367.

[3] Ord. Vit. 667 A. "Tunc Odo Bajocensis cum quingentis militibus
intra Rofensem urbem se conclusit, ibique Robertum ducem cum suis
auxiliaribus secundum statuta quæ pepigerant præstolari proposuit."
The last clause of course implies the supposed earlier agreement with Duke
Robert, on which see above, p. 25, and Appendix B.

Odo was not satisfied with his garrison. He sent beyond sea to Duke Robert for further help. The prince in whose name Rochester was now held was earnestly prayed to come at once at the head of the full power of his duchy, to take possession of the crown and kingdom which were waiting for his coming.[1]

According to the narrative which we are now following, it would seem that Robert now heard for the first time of the movement which was going on in his behalf in England. His heart is lifted up at the unlooked for news; he tells the tidings to his friends; certain of victory, he sends some of them over to share in the spoil; he promises to come himself with all speed, as soon as he should have gathered a greater force.[2]

At the head of the party which was actually sent were two men whose names are familiar to us.[3] One of them, Count Eustace of Boulogne, united the characters of a land-owner in England and of a sovereign prince in Gaul. This was the younger Eustace, the son of the old enemy of England, the brother of the hero who was within a few years to win back the Holy

---

[1] Flor. Wig. 1088. " Rumore autem percussus insolito, comes exultat, amicis nunciat, quasi jam de victoria securus triumphat, plures ad prædam incitat ; Odoni episcopo, patruo suo, auxiliarios in Angliam legat, se quantocius, congregato majori exercitu, secuturum affirmat."

[2] Ib. " Prædictus episcopus Baiocensis, munita Roveceastra, misit Normanniam, exhortans comitem Rotbertum cito venire in Angliam, nuntians ei rem gestam, affirmans paratum sibi regnum, et si sibi non desisteret paratam et coronam."

[3] Ib. " Missi a comite Rotberto venerunt in Angliam, ab Odone episcopo ad custodiendum receperunt Roveceastram ; et horum ut primates Eustatius junior, comes Bononiæ, et Rotbertus de Beleasmo gerebant curam." Here we have (see Appendix B) the true moment of their coming. From this point we may accept the account in Orderic (667 B) ; " Prædictum oppidum Odo præsul et Eustachius comes atque Robertus Bellesmensis, cum multis nobilibus viris et mediocribus, tenebant, auxiliumque Roberti ducis, qui desidia mollitieque detinebatur, frustra exspectabant." We meet them again in 765 B.

City for Christendom.[1] With him came Robert of Bellême; his share in the rebellion is his first act on
English ground that we have to record. Himself the
eldest son of Earl Roger of Shrewsbury, he had either
brought with him two of his brothers, or else they had
already embraced the cause of Odo in England. Three
sons of Roger and Mabel were now within the walls
of Rochester.[2] The second was Hugh, who was for
a moment to represent the line of Montgomery while
Robert represented the line of Bellême, and who was
to be as fierce a scourge to the Britons of the Northern
border as Robert was to be to the valiant defenders of the
land of Maine.[3] And with them was the third brother,
Roger of Poitou, the lord of the debateable land between
Mersey and Ribble,[4] carrying as it were to the furthest
point of the earldom of Leofric the claim of his father
to the proud title which the elder Roger bears at this
stage of our story. It is as Earl of the Mercians that
one teller of our tale bids us look for a moment on the
lord of Montgomery and Shrewsbury.[5] But the Earl of

---

[1] " Eustatius junior," " Eustatius þe iunga." See N. C. vol. iv. p. 745.

[2] They are mentioned in the Chronicle along with the incidental mention
of Eustace; " Innan þam castele wæron swiðe gode cnihtas, Eustatius þe
iunga, and Rogeres eorles þreo sunan, and ealle þa betstboren men þe
wæron innan þisan lande oððe on Normandige." This is followed by William
of Malmesbury (iv. 306); " Erat tunc apud Roveceastram omnis pene juven-
tutis ex Anglia et Normannia nobilitas; tres filii Rogerii comitis, et Eustachius Bononiæ junior, *multique alii quos infra curam nostram existimo.*"

[3] The three sons of Earl Roger can hardly fail to be his three eldest
sons (see Will. Gem. vii. 16; Ord. Vit. 708 D), Robert, Hugh, and Roger,
all of whom figure in our story. Arnulf does not appear in English history
till later, and Philip the clerk does not appear at all. Geoffrey Gaimar
(Chron. Ang. Norm. i. 35), after setting forth the possessions of Robert of
Bellême, mentions the other three; but one does not exactly see why he
says,

> " Le conte Ernulf ert le quarte frère,
> Par cors valeit un emperère."

Cf. Ord. Vit. 708 D, 808 C.

[4] See N. C. vol. iv. p. 488.   [5] See above, p. 33.

CHAP. II. the Mercians was not with his sons at Rochester any more than he had been with his men before Worcester. He was in another seat of his scattered power. His presence was less needed at Shrewsbury, less needed at the continental or the insular Montgomery, than it was in the South-Saxon land where the lord of Arundel and

He stays at Arundel. Chichester held so high a place. While his men were overthrown before Worcester, while his sons were strengthening themselves at Rochester, Earl Roger himself was watching events in his castle of Arundel.[1] The spot was well fitted for the purpose. Arundel lies in the same general region of England as the three great rebel strongholds of Rochester, Tunbridge, and Pevensey; it lies in the same shire and near the same

Position of Arundel. coast as the last named of the three. But it lies apart from the immediate field of action of a campaign which should gather round those three centres. A gap in the Sussex downs, where the Arun makes its way to the sea through the flat land at its base, had been marked out, most likely from the earliest times, as a

A castle at Arundel T. R. E. fitting spot for a stronghold. The last slope of this part of the downs towards the east was strengthened in days before King William came with a mound and a ditch, and Arundel is marked in the Great Survey as one of the castles few and far between which England

Description of the castle. contained before his coming.[2] The shell-keep which crowns the mound, and the gateway which flanks it, have been recast at various later times from the twelfth century onward, but it would be rash to assert that the mere wall of the keep may not contain portions either of the days of King William or of the days of King Eadward. The traces of a vast hall, more immediately

---

[1] Flor. Wig. 1088. "Rogerus fautor Rotberti erat in castello suo Arundello, comitis prædicti opperiens adventum."

[2] See N. C. iv. 66, v. 808.

overlooking the river, reared as usual on a vaulted sub- CHAP. II.
structure, almost constrain us to see in them the work
of no age earlier or later than that of Roger or his
successor of his own house.[1] The site is a natural watch-
tower, whence the eye ranges far away to various points
of the compass, over the flat land and over the more
distant hills, and over the many windings of the tidal
river which then made Arundel a place of trade as well
as of defence.[2] Less threatening than his vulture's nest
at *Tre Baldwin*,[3] less tempting to an enemy than his
fortresses on the peninsula of Shrewsbury and within the
walls of Chichester,[4] the stronghold of Arundel seems
exactly the place for an experienced observer of men and
things like Earl Roger to look out from and bide his
time. He had to watch the course of things in the three
rebel fortresses; he had further to watch what might
come from a nearer spot, another break in the hill
ground, where, between his doubtful Arundel and re- William of
bellious Pevensey, the twin mounds of loyal Lewes,[5] Warren at
Lewes.
the home of William and Gundrada, looked up to what
was one day to be the battle-ground of English freedom.
Its lord, long familiar to us as William of Warren, stood

[1] See Tierney's History of Arundel, i. 43.

[2] Domesday, 23. "Modo inter burgum et portum aquæ et consuetudinem navium reddit xii. libras et tamen valet xiii. libras. De his habet
S. Nicolaus xxiiii. solidos." "Clerici sancti Nicolai" are mentioned again in
the next column. The church then was secular in 1086; but the clerks
must have soon given way to the priory of Saint Nicolas, founded by Earl
Roger himself as a cell to his abbey at Seez; in 1386 it gave way to the
college of Arundel.

[3] See N. C. iv. p. 501.

[4] Domesday, 23. "Modo est ipsa civitas in manu comitis Rogerii."
Here he had one quarter of a Roman *chester*, while the Bishop had
another; yet there were sixty houses more than there had been T. R. E.

[5] See the customs of Lewes and the rights of William of Warren in
Domesday, 26. The toll on selling a man was threepence. The two mounds
of the castle, the smaller known as Brack Mount, are rare, perhaps unique.
The inner gateway seems to be of Earl William's building.

CHAP. II.

His earl-
dom of
Surrey.

firm in his allegiance, and it was now, according to some accounts, that he received his earldom of Surrey, an earldom to be borne in after times along with that which took its name from Roger's own Arundel.[1] William became the King's chief counsellor, and his position at Lewes must have thrown difficulties in the way of any com-

His loyalty.

munication between Arundel and Pevensey. And in truth, when Earl Roger found it safest to watch and be prudent, we are not surprised to find events presently shaping themselves in such a way as to make it his wisest course to play the part of the Curio of the tale.[2]

Action of
the King.

But meanwhile where was King William? Where was the king who had taken his place on his father's seat with so much ease, but whose place upon it had been so soon and so rudely shaken? We have been called on more than once in earlier studies to mark how the two characters of fox and lion were mingled in the tempers of the Conqueror and his countrymen, and assuredly the Conqueror's second surviving son was fully able to don either garb when need called for it.[3] At this moment we are told in a marked way that William Rufus showed himself in the character of that which is conventionally looked on as the nobler beast. He had no mind to seek for murky holes, like the timid fox, but, like the bold and fearless lion, he gave himself mightily to put down the devices of his enemies.[4] Yet the first time when

---

[1] I suspect that the original title of the Earls of Arundel was Earl of Sussex, and that the name of the castle came to be used, much as the successors of William of Warren, strictly Earls of Surrey, are more commonly called Earls Warren. See more in Tierney's History of Arundel.

[2] Lucan, iv. 819.

[3] See N. C. vol. iii. p. 161.

[4] Ord. Vit. 666 D. "Rex Guillelmus, ut vidit suos in terra sua contra se pessima cogitare, et per singula crebrescentibus malis ad pejora proce-

we distinctly get a personal sight of him, the Red CHAP. II.
King is seen playing the part of the fox with no small He wins over Earl
effect. Earl Roger was assuredly no mean master of Roger.
Norman craft; but King William, in his first essay,
showed himself fully his equal. By a personal appeal
he won the Earl over from at least taking any further
personal share in the rebellion. At some place not mentioned, perhaps at Arundel itself, the Earl, disguising,
we are told, his treason, was riding in the King's company.[1] The King took him aside, and argued the case
with him. He would, he said, give up the kingdom, if
such was really the wish of the old companions of his
father. He knew not wherefore they were so bitter
against him; he was ready, if they wished it, to make
them further grants of lands or money. Only let them
remember one thing; his cause and theirs were really
the same; it was safer not to dispute the will of the
man who had made both him and them what they
were. "You may," wound up Rufus, "despise and
overthrow me; but take care lest such an example
should prove dangerous to yourselves. My father has
made me a king, and it was he alone who made you an
earl."[2] Roger felt or affected conviction, and followed
the King, in his bodily presence at least, during the rest

---

dere; non meditatus est ut timida vulpes ad tenebrosas cavernas fugere,
sed ut leo fortis et audax rebellium conatus terribiliter comprimere."

[1] Will. Malms. iv. 306. "Nec minori astutia Rogerium de Monte
Gomerico, secum dissimulata perfidia equitantem, circumvenit."

[2] Ib. "Seorsum enim ducto magnam ingessit invidiam; dicens,
Libenter se imperio cessurum, si illi et aliis videatur quos pater tutores
reliquerat. Non se intelligere quid ita effrænes sint : si velint, pecunias
accipiant pro libito; si augmentum patrimoniorum, eodem modo; prorsus,
quæ velint, habeant. Tantum videant ne judicium genitoris periclitetur :
quod si de se putaverint aspernandum, de se ipsis caveant exemplum;
idem enim se regem, qui illos duces fecerit. His verbis comes et pollicitationibus incensus, qui primus factionis post Odonem signifer fuit, primus
defecit." Roger of Wendover (ii. 33) adds the words "pœnitentia ductus."

CHAP. II.

Count
Robert at
Pevensey.

of the campaign.[1] But Robert, Count of Mortain and lord of Cornwall, still made Pevensey one of the strongholds of the revolt. Of the third great neighbour of these two lords, Count Robert of Eu, father of the ravager of Berkeley, we hear nothing on this side of the water.

Loyal
Normans.

But, amid the general falling away, the throne of William Rufus was still defended by some men of Norman birth on whom he could better rely than on the doubtful loyalty of the Earl of Shrewsbury. Earl Hugh of Chester remained faithful; so, as we have seen, did Earl Roger's neighbour, now or afterwards Earl William.[2] And to these already famous names we must add one which was now only beginning to be heard of, but which was presently to equal, if not to surpass, the renown of either. This was Robert Fitz-hamon, the son or grandson of Hamon *Dentatus*, the rebel of Val-ès-dunes.[3] But it was not on the swords of the Norman followers of his father that the son of the Conqueror rested his hopes of keeping the crown which the Conqueror had left him. William Rufus had at his side two forces, either of which, when it could put forth its full power, was

Earl Hugh.

William of
Warren.

Robert
Fitz-
hamon.

Forces on
the side of
Rufus,

---

[1] Orderic a little later (667 B) says, "Rogerus Merciorum comes, multique Normannorum, qui cum rege foris obsidebant, clam adminiculari quantum poterant inclusis satagebant."

[2] Orderic (680 C) puts the creation of this earldom somewhat later, at the Gemót held just before the invasion of Normandy in 1090. He adds that the new earl died soon after ("quem paulo post mors nulli parcens e medio rapuit"), and records his burial at Lewes, and adds his epitaph. There is no better authority than that of the Hyde writer (298) for placing the creation at this time or for placing the Earl's death a little later (see below, p. 76). But his narrative is so minute that one would think that he must have had some kind of ground for it. His words are; "Rex Willelmus . . . videns igitur principes regni nutantes et exercitum a se dilabi, sapienti usus consilio, Willelmum de Warennia, virum bellicosum, animo ferum et corpore strenuum famaque præclarum, *in amicitia Asarum* [what this may mean I have no notion, but the editor vouches that such is the reading of the MS.] comitis honore sublimat, multa impendit multaque promittit."

[3] See N. C. vol. ii. p. 251.

stronger by far than the Norman nobles. All that in CHAP. II.
any way represented the higher feelings and instincts
of man was along with him. All that in any shape was
an embodiment of law or right was arrayed against the
men whose one avowed principle was the desire to shake
off the restraints of law in any shape. Against the the Church,
openly proclaimed reign of lawlessness the King could and the
people.
rely on the strength of the Church and the strength of
the people. With the single exception of him of Durham,
the marauding bishops of Bayeux and Coutances found
no followers among the men of their order in England.
Lanfranc stood firmly by the King to whom he had Loyalty
given the crown; and the other bishops, of whatever of the
Bishops.
origin, sought, we are told, with all faithfulness of
purpose, the things which were for peace.[1] Either by The King
their advice or by his own discernment, the King saw appeals
to the
that his only course was to throw himself on the true English.
folk of the land, to declare himself King of the English
in fact as well as in name. A written proclamation went His procla-
forth in the name of King William, addressed, doubtless mation.
in their own ancient tongue, to the sons of the soil, the
men of English kin. The King of the English called
on the people of the English, on the valiant men who
were left of the old stock; he set forth his need to
them and craved for their loyal help.[2] At such a

[1] Ord. Vit. 667 C. "Omnes episcopi Angliæ *cum Anglis* sine dolo
regem juvabant, et pro serena patriæ pace, quæ bonis semper amabiles
est, laborabant."

[2] The appeal to the English is strongly marked in the Chronicle; "Ða
þe cyng undergeat ealle þas þing and hwilcne swicdom hi dydon toweard
his, þa wearð he on his mode swiðe gedrefed. Sende þa æfter Englisce
mannan, and heom fore sæde his neode and gyrnde heora fultumes."
Simeon of Durham gives a free translation quite independent of Florence;
"Hoc audito, rex fecit convocare Anglos, et ostendit eis traditionem
Normannorum, et rogavit ut sibi auxilio essent." But the appeal comes out
no less strongly in Orderic (666 D); "Lanfrancum archiepiscopum cum
suffraganeis præsulibus, et comites, Anglosque naturales convocavit, et
conatus adversariorum, ac velle suum expugnandi eos indicavit." The

CHAP. II. moment he was lavish of promises. All the wrongs of
His pro-   the days of William the Elder were to be put an end
mises.
           to in the days of William the Younger. The English
           folk should have again the best laws that ever before
           were in this land. King William would reign over his
           people like Eadward or Cnut or Ælfred. The two
           great grievances of his father's days were to cease; the
           King's coffers were no longer to be filled by money
           wrung from his people; the King's hunting-grounds
           were no longer to be fenced in by the savage code
           which had guarded the Conqueror's pleasures. All
           unrighteous geld he forbade, and he granted to them
The Eng-   their woods and right of hunting.[1] At the sound of such
lish take promises men's hearts were stirred. At such moments,
up the
King's   men commonly listen to their hopes rather than to their
cause.   reason; the prospects and promises of a new reign are
           always made the best of; and there was no special
           reason as yet why the word of William the Red should
           be distrusted. He had not conquered England; he had
           not as yet had the means of oppressing England; he
           had shown at least one virtue in dutiful attachment

           writ comes from William of Malmesbury, iv. 306; "Ille, videns Normannos
           pene omnes in una rabie conspiratos, Anglos probos et fortes viros, qui
           adhuc residui erant, invitatoriis scriptis accersiit." It is singular that
           Florence mentions the English only in an incidental way a little later;
           "Congregato quantum ad præsens poterat Normannorum, sed tamen
           maxime Anglorum, equestri et pedestri, licet mediocri, exercitu." Does
           the precious document spoken of by William of Malmesbury still lurk in
           any manuscript store?
           [1] Chron. Petrib. "And behet heom þa betsta laga þe æfre ær wæs on
           þisan lande, and ælc unriht geold he forbead, and geatte mannan heora
           wudas and slǽtinge." William of Malmesbury (iv. 306) translates, "Bonas
           leges et tributorum levamen, liberasque venationes pollicens." Florence is
           less literal; "Statuens leges, promittens fautoribus omnia bona." Simeon
           gives another version; "Eo tenore, ut si in hac necessitate sibi fideles exist-
           erent, meliorem legem quam vellent eligere eis concederet, et omnem in-
           justum scottum interdixit, et concessit omnibus silvas suas et venationem.
           Sed quicquid promisit, parvo tempore custodivit. Angli tamen fideliter
           eum juvabant."

to his father; his counsellor was the venerated Primate; chap. ii.
chief in loyalty to him was one yet more venerated, the
one native chief left to the English Church, the holy
Bishop of Worcester. If the English dealt with William
as an English king, he might deal with them as an
English king should deal with his people. In fighting Motives for
for William against the men who had risen up against supporting
William.
him, they would be fighting for one who had not himself
wronged them against the men who had done them the
bitterest of wrongs. If the Bishop of Bayeux and the
Bishop of Coutances, if Robert of Mortain and Robert
of Mowbray, if Eustace of Boulogne and the fierce lord
of Bellême, could all be smitten down by English axes
or driven into banishment from the English shores, if
their estates on English soil could be again parted out
as the reward of English valour, the work of the Norman
Conquest would indeed seem to be undone. And it
would be undone none the less, although the king whose
crown was made sure by English hands was himself the
son of the Conqueror of England.

With such feelings as these the sons of the soil Loyalty
gathered with glee around the standard of King William. of the
English.
Not a name is handed down to us. We know not from
what shires they came or under what leaders they
marched. We see only that, as was natural when the They meet
stress of the war lay in Kent and Sussex, the trysting- in London.
place was London.[1] How did that great city stand at
this moment with regard to the rebellion? It will be
remembered by what vigorous means Bishop William
of Durham claimed to have secured the allegiance of the
citizens some time earlier.[2] At all events, whether by

[1] Flor. Wig. 1088. "Jure regio, militari, ut impiger, fretus audacia,
mittit legatos, vocat quos sibi credit fidos, vadit Lundoniam, belli tracta-
turus negotia, expeditionis provisum, necessaria."
[2] See above, p. 29.

the help of William of Saint-Calais or not, London was
now in the King's hands. There the royal host met,
a motley host, a host of horse and foot, of Normans and
English, but a host in which the English element was
by far the greatest, and in which English feeling gave
its character to the whole movement. Thirty thousand
of the true natives of the land came together of their
own free will to the defence of their lord the King.[1]
The figures are of much the same value as other figures;
it is enough if we take them as marking a general and

zealous movement. The men who were thus brought
together promised the King their most zealous service;
they exhorted him to press on valiantly, to smite the
rebels, and to win for himself the Empire of the whole
island.[2] This last phrase is worth noting, even if it be a

mere flourish of the historian. It marks that the change
of dynasty was fully accepted, that the son of the Conqueror was fully acknowledged as the heir of all the
rights of Æthelstan the Glorious and of Eadmund the
Doer-of-great-deeds. A daughter of their race still sat
on the Scottish throne; but for Malcolm, the savage
devastator of Northern England, Englishmen could not
be expected to feel any love. William was now their
king, their king crowned and anointed, the lord to
whom their duty was owing as his men.[3] Him they
would make fast on the throne of England; for him
they were ready to win the Empire of all Britain. The
English followers of Rufus loudly proclaimed their

[1] Chron. Petrib. 1088. "Ac Englisce men swa þeah fengon to þam
cynge heora hlaforde on fultume." The numbers come from Orderic
(667 A); "Anglorum triginta millia tunc ad servitium regis sponte sua
convenerunt."

[2] Ord. Vit. 667 A. "Passim per totum Albionem *impera*, omnesque
rebelles deice regali justitia."

[3] Ib. "Viriliter age, ut regis filius et legitime ad regnum assumptus;
securus in hoc regno dominare omnibus."

hatred of rebellion. They even, we are told, called on their leader to study the history of past times, where he would see how faithful Englishmen had ever been to their kings.[1]

At the head of this great and zealous host William the Red set forth from London. He set forth at the head of an English host, to fight against Norman enemies in the Kentish and South-Saxon lands. And in that host there may well have been men who had marched forth from London on the like errand only two-and-twenty years before. Great as were the changes which had swept over the land, men must have been still living, still able to bear arms, who had dealt their blows in the *Malfosse* of Senlac amidst the last glimmerings of light on the day of Saint Calixtus. The enemy was nationally and even personally the same. The work before all others at the present moment was to seize the man whose spiritual exhortations had stirred up Norman valour on that unforgotten day, and whose temporal arm had wielded, if not the sword, at least the war-club, in the first rank of the invaders. Odo, the invader of old, the oppressor of later days, the head and front of the evil rede of the present moment, was the foremost object of the loyal and patriotic hatred of every Englishman in the Red King's army. Could he be seized, it would be easier to seize his accomplices.[2] The great object of the campaign was therefore to recover the castle of Rochester, the stronghold where the rebel Bishop, with his allies from

William's march.

The English hatred of Odo.

---

[1] Ord. Vit. 667 A. "Solerter Anglorum rimare historias, inveniesque semper fidos principibus suis Angligenas." Fancy William Rufus sitting down to study the Chronicles, as his brother Henry may likely enough have done.

[2] Chron. Petrib. 1088. "Ferdon þa toweard Hrofeceastre and woldon þone bisceop Odan begytan, þohtan gif hi hæfdon hine, þe wæs ærur heafod to þam unræde, þæt hi mihton þe bet begytan ealla þa oðre."

CHAP. II. Boulogne and from Bellême, bade their defiance to the King and people of England.

It was not however deemed good to march at once upon the immediate centre of the rebellion. A glance at the map will show that it was better policy not to make the attack on Rochester while both the other rebel strongholds, Tunbridge and Pevensey, remained Tunbridge unsubdued. The former of these, a border-post of Kent castle. and Sussex, guarding the upper course of the stream that flows by Rochester, would, if won for the King, put a strong barrier between Rochester and Pevensey. Attack on The march on Rochester therefore took a roundabout the castle. course, and this part of the war opened by an attack on Tunbridge which was the first exploit of the Red Position of King's English army. At a point on the Medway about Tunbridge. four miles within the Kentish border, at the foot of the high ground reaching northward from the actual frontier of the two ancient kingdoms, the winding river receives the waters of several smaller streams, and forms a group of low islands and peninsulas. On the slightly rising ground to the north, commanding the stream and its bridge, a mound had risen, fenced by a ditch on the exposed side to the north. This ancient fortress had grown into the castle of Gilbert the son of Richard, called of Clare and of Tunbridge, the son of the famous Count Gilbert of the early days of the Conqueror.[1] As Tunbridge now stands, the outer defences of the castle stand between the mound and the river, and the

---

[1] It is somewhat singular that, though Richard appears in Domesday as "Ricardus de Tonebrige" as well as "Ricardus filius Gisleberti comitis" (14 et al.), and though his "leva" or "lowy" (see Ellis, i. 212) is often spoken of, yet Tunbridge castle itself is not entered. See on Richard of Bienfaite, Clare, or Tunbridge, N. C. vol. ii. p. 196; iv. 579. A singular story is told in the Continuation of William of Jumièges (viii. 15), how Tunbridge was granted in exchange for Brionne, and measured by the rope. See Appendix S.

mound, bearing the shell-keep, is yoked together in a CHAP. II.
striking way with one of the noblest gateways of
the later form of mediæval military art.[1] The general
arrangements of the latter days of the eleventh century
cannot have been widely different. The mound, doubtless a work of English hands turned to the uses of the
stranger, was the main stronghold to be won. It was
held by a body of Bishop Odo's knights, under the command of its own lord Gilbert; to win it for the King and
his people was an object only second to that of seizing
the traitor prelate himself. The rebel band bade defiance
to the King and his army. The castle held out for
two days; but the zeal of the English was not to be
withstood; no work could be more to their liking
than that of attacking a Norman castle on their own
soil, even with a Norman King as their leader. The The castle
castle was stormed; the native Chronicler, specially stormed.
recording the act of his countrymen, speaks of it, like
the castles of York in the days of Waltheof, as "tobroken."[2] Most likely the buildings on the mound
were thus "tobroken;" but some part of the castle enclosure must have been left habitable and defensible.
For the garrison, with their chief Gilbert, were admitted to terms; and Gilbert, who had been wounded

---

[1] At Tunbridge the mound and the gateway stand side by side, as indeed
they do, though less conspicuously, at Arundel and Lewes. A wall is built
from the gateway to the keep on the mound, losing itself, as it were, in the
side of the mound. The mound thus stands half within and half without
the enclosure formed by the gateway.

[2] Chron. Petrib. 1088. " Þa Englisce men ferdon and tobræcon þone castel,
and þa men þe þærinne wæron griðodon wið þone cyng." So Simeon of
Durham; " Sed viriliter Angli insilientes in illud, destruxerunt totum castrum,
et qui intus erant in manus regi dederunt." Florence gives some further
details; " Tunebrycgiam cui præerat Gilebertus filius Ricardi, contrarium
sibi invenit: obsedit, in biduo expugnavit, vulneratum Gilebertum cum
castello ad deditionem coegit." Is it possible that, according to Orderic's
second account of the rebellion (765 A, B), we are still only in the Easter
week ?

CHAP. II. in the struggle, was left there under the care of a loyal guard.

The first blow had thus gone well to the mark. Such an exploit as this, the capture by English valour of one of the hated strongholds of the stranger, was enough to raise the spirit of William's English followers to the highest pitch. And presently they were summoned to a work which would call forth a yet fiercer glow of national feeling. After Tunbridge had fallen, they set forth on their march towards Rochester, believing that the arch-enemy Odo was there. Their course would be to the north-east, keeping some way from the left side of the Medway; Bishop Gundulf's tower at Malling,[1] if it was already built, would be the most marked point on the road. But they were not to reach Rochester by so easy a path. While they were on their way, news came to the King that his uncle was no longer at Rochester. While the King was before Tunbridge, the Bishop with a few followers had struck to the south-east, and had reached his brother's castle of Pevensey.[2] The Count of Mortain and lord of Cornwall was perhaps wavering, like his neighbour at Arundel. The Bishop exhorted him to hold out. While the King besieged Rochester, they would be safe at Pevensey, and meanwhile Duke Robert and his host would cross the

They march towards Rochester.

Odo at Pevensey.

Odo exhorts Robert of Mortain to hold out.

---

[1] See N. C. vol. iv. p. 366. While I am revising my text, an account of this tower by Mr. Clark has appeared in the Builder, November 27, 1880.

[2] Chron. Petrib. 1088. "Se cyng mid his here ferde toweard Hrofeceastre, and wendon þæt se bisceop wære þærinne, ac hit wearð þam cynge cuð þæt se bisceop wæs afaren to þam castele on Pefenesea." Florence helps us to an hexameter in the middle of his prose; "Relatum erat ei ibi esse episcopum Odonem cum omnibus suis et cohortem ultramarinam ....

Fama volans dicti pervenit Odonis ad aures,

et cum sociis inito consilio, relinquens Roveceastram, cum paucis adiit castrum fratris sui Roberti Moritanensis comitis quod Pevenessa dicitur." Are the "cohors ultramarina" those who had come with Eustace and Robert of Bellême ?

sea. The Duke would then win the crown, and would CHAP. II.
reward all their services.[1]

It is well to be reminded by words like these what Interest
the professed object of the insurgents was. It would of Duke
Robert in
be easy to forget that all the plundering that had been the rebellion.
done from Rochester to Ilchester had been done in
the name of the lawful rights of Duke Robert. The
men who harried Berkeley and who were overthrown at
Worcester were but the forerunners of the Duke of
the Normans, who was to come, as spring went on, with His coming
the full force of his duchy.[2] It was not for nothing looked for.
that King William had gathered his English army,
when a new Norman Conquest was looked for. But He fails to
as yet the blow was put off; Duke Robert came not; help the
rebels.
he seemed to think that the crown of England could
be won with ease at any moment. When the first
news of William's accession came, when those around
him urged him to active measures to support his
rights, he had spoken of the matter with childish scorn.
Were he at the ends of the earth—the city of Alexandria His child-
is taken as the standard of distance—the English would ish boast-
ing.
not dare to make William king, William would not dare
to accept the crown at their hands, without waiting for
the coming of his elder brother.[3] Both the impossible

---

[1] Flor. Wig. 1088. "Fratrem reperiens, cum ut se teneat hortatur, pol-
licens se securos ibi posse esse, et dum rex ad expugnandam Roveceastram
intenderet, comitem Normanniæ cum magno exercitu venturum, seque
suosque liberaturum et magna fautoribus suis dando præmia regnum accepturum."

[2] Ord.Vit. 666 D. "Statuerat præcursores suos vere redeunte sequi cum
multis legionibus militum."

[3] Cont. Will. Gem. viii. 2. "Quum sui fideles eum exhortarentur ut
regnum Angliæ sibi a fratre præreptum velocius armis sibimet restitueret,
simplicitate solita et, ut ita dicam, imprudentiæ proxima, respondisse fertur,
'Per angelos Dei [Gregory's pun in another form], si essem in Alexandria,
exspectarent me Angli, nec ante adventum meum Regem sibi facere aude-
rent. Ipse etiam Willelmus frater meus, quod eum præsumpsisse dicitur,
pro capite suo sine mea permissione minime attentaret."

CHAP. II. things had happened, and Robert and his partisans had now before them the harder task of driving William from a throne which was already his, instead of merely hindering him from mounting it. Up to this time Robert had done

His pro-
mises.

nothing; but now, in answer to the urgent prayers of his uncles, he did get together a force for their help, and promised that he would himself follow it before long.[1]

William
marches on
Pevensey.

The news of Odo's presence at Pevensey at once changed the course of William's march. Wherever the Bishop of Bayeux was, there was the point to be aimed at.[2] Instead of going on to Rochester, the King turned and marched straight upon Pevensey. The exact line of his march is not told us, but it could not fail to cross, perhaps it might for a while even coincide with, the line of march by which Harold had pressed to the South-Saxon coast on the eve of the great battle. Things might seem

The Eng-
lish besiege
Odo in
Pevensey.

to have strangely turned about, when an English army, led by a son of the Conqueror, marched to lay siege to the two brothers and chief fellow-workers of the Conqueror within the stronghold which was the very first-fruits of the Conquest. The Roman walls of Anderida were still there; but their whole circuit was no longer desolate, as it had been when the Conqueror landed, and

The castle
of Pevens-
ey.

as we see it now again. One part of the ancient city had again become a dwelling-place of man. As Pevensey now stands, the south-eastern corner of the Roman en-

---

[1] Chron. Petrib. 1088. "Betwyx þissum se eorl of Normandige Rod-beard, þes cynges broðer, gaderode swiðe mycel folc, and þohte to gewinnane Englelande mid þæra manna fultume þe wæron innan þisan lande ongean þone cyng, and he sende of his mannan to þisum lande, and wolde cuman himsylf æfter."

[2] Florence seems here to translate what the Chronicler had said a little before (see above, p. 67); "Inito itaque salubri consilio, illum eo usque cum exercitu persequitur, sperans se belli citius finem assequuturum, si ante triumphare posset de principibus malorum prædictorum."

closure, now again as forsaken as the rest, is fenced in
by the moat, the walls, the towers, of a castle of the
later type, the type of the Edwards, but whose towers
are built in evident imitation of the solid Roman bastions. Then, or at some earlier time, the Roman wall
itself received a new line of parapet, and one at least of
its bastions was raised to form a tower in the restored
line of defence. When the house of Mortain passed
away in the second generation, the honour of Pevensey
became the possession of the house of Laigle, and from
them, perhaps in popular speech, certainly in the dialect
of local antiquaries, Anderida became the Honour of the
Eagle.[1] Within the circuit of the later castle, close on
the ancient wall, rises, covered with shapeless ruins, a
small mound which doubtless marks the site of the
elder keep of Count Robert. Within that keep the two
sons of Herleva, Bishop and Count, looked down on the
shore close at their feet where they had landed with
their mightier brother two-and-twenty years before.
Within that stern memorial of their victory, they had
now to defend themselves against the sons and brothers
of men who had fallen by their hands, and whose lands
they had parted out among them for a prey.

The siege of Pevensey proved a far harder work than The siege of
the siege of Tunbridge. The Roman wall with its new Pevensey.
Norman defences was less easy to storm than the ancient English mound. William the Red had to wait
longer before Pevensey than William the Great had had
to wait before Exeter. The fortress was strong; the
spirit of its defenders was high; for Odo was among
them. The King beset the castle with a great host;

---

[1] So I find it called in several papers in the Sussex Archæological Collec-
tions. But the local antiquaries seem hardly to have fully grasped the
fact that there is a town in Normandy called *Laigle*, and that the family
with which we are concerned took its name from it.

CHAP. II. he brought the artillery of the time to bear upon its
defences; but for six weeks his rebellious uncles bore
up against the attacks of William and his Englishmen.[1]
Duke Robert at last sends help. And, while the siege went on, another of the chances of
war seemed yet more thoroughly to reverse what had
happened on the same spot not a generation back.
Again a Norman host landed, or strove to land, within
the haven of Pevensey. But they came under other
guidance than that which had led the men who came
before them on the like errand. When William crossed
the sea, his own Mora sailed foremost and swiftest in the
whole fleet, and William himself was the first man in
his army to set foot on English ground. William in
Robert stays behind. short led his fleet; his son only sent his. Robert still
tarried in Normandy; he was coming, but not yet; his
men were to make their way into England how they
could without him. They came, and they found the
South-Saxon coast better guarded than it had been
when Harold had to strive against two invaders at once.
The English hinder the Normans from landing. When Robert's ships drew nigh, they found the ships
of King William watching the coast; they found the
soldiers of King William lining the shore.[2] On such
a spot, in such a cause, no Englishman's heart or hand
was likely to fail him. The attempt at a new Norman
landing at Pevensey was driven back. Those who escaped
the English sailors drew near to the shore, but only
to fall into the hands of the English land-force. It must
not be forgotten that, as the coast-line then stood, when
the sea covered what is now the low ground between the

---

[1] Chron. Petrib. 1088. "And se cyng mid his here ferde æfter, and
besætt þone castel abutan mid swiðe mycele here fulle six wucan." The
artillery comes from Florence; "Accelerat, machinas parat, patruum
utrumque obsidet; locus erat munitissimus; ad expugnationem indies la-
borat." William of Malmesbury cuts the siege of Pevensey short, and
Orderic leaves it out altogether.

[2] See Appendix E.

castle and the beach, the struggle for the landing must have gone on close under the walls of the ancient city and of the new-built castle. The English who beat back the Normans of Duke Robert's fleet as they strove to land must have been themselves exposed to the arrows of the Normans who guarded Count Robert's donjon. But the work was done. Some of the invaders lived to be taken prisoners; but the more part, a greater number than any man could tell, were smitten down by the English axes or thrust back to meet their doom in the waves of the Channel. Some who deemed that they had still the means of escape tried to hoist the sails of their ships and get them back to their own land. But the elements fought against them. The winds which had so long refused to bring the fleet of William from Normandy to England now refused no less to take back the fleet of Robert from England to Normandy. And there were no means now, as there had been by the Dive and at Saint Valery, for waiting patiently by a friendly coast, or for winning the good will of the South-Saxon saints by prayers or offerings.[1] Even Saint Martin of the Place of Battle had no call to help the eldest son of his founder against his founder's namesake and chosen heir. The ships could not be moved; the English were upon them; the Normans, a laughing-stock to their enemies, rather than fall into their enemies' hands, leaped from their benches into the less hostile waters. The attempt of the Conqueror's eldest son to do by deputy what his father had done in person had utterly come to nought. The new invaders of England had been overthrown by English hands on the spot where the work of the former invaders had begun.

After the defeat of this attempt to bring help to the

Utter failure of the invasion.

---

[1] See N. C. vol. iii. p. 395.

CHAP. II.

Alleged death of William of Warren.

besieged at Pevensey, nothing more was heard of Duke Robert's coming in person. If we may believe a single confused and doubtful narrative, the defenders of the castle had at least the satisfaction of slaying one of the chief men in the royal army. We are told that Earl William of Warren was mortally wounded in the leg by an arrow from the walls of Pevensey, and was carried to Lewes only to die there.[1] However this may be, the failure of the Norman expedition carried with it the failure of the hopes of the besieged. Food now began to fail them, and Odo and Robert found that there was nothing left for them but to surrender to their nephew on the best terms that they could get. Of the terms which were granted to the Count of Mortain and lord of Cornwall we hear nothing. The Bishop of Bayeux and Earl of Kent was a more important person, and we have full details of everything that concerned him. The terms granted to the chief stirrer up of the whole rebellion were certainly favourable. He was called on to swear that he would leave England, and would never come back, unless the King sent for him, and that, before he went, he would cause the castle of Rochester to be surrendered.[2] For the better carrying out of the last of his engagements, the Bishop was sent on towards Rochester

The castle surrenders.

Terms granted to Odo.

Rochester to be surrendered.

[1] Liber de Hyda, 299. " Willelmus de Warennia apud obsidionem Peveneselli sagitta in crure valde vulneratus, Leuwias cum omnium mœrore deportatus est." The writer goes on to describe Earl William's last testament and death. It will be remembered (see above, p. 62) that Orderic makes William of Warren die quietly at a later time; but, small as is the authority of the Hyde writer, it is strange if he altogether invented or dreamed this minute account.

[2] Chron. Petrib. 1088. " Syððan heom ateorede mete wiðinnan þam castele, þa gyrndon hi griðas, and agefan hine þam cynge, and se bisceop swór þæt he wolde út of Englelande faran, and ná mare cuman on þisan lande butan se cyng him æfter sende, and þæt he wolde agyfan þone castel on Hrofeceastre." So William of Malmesbury (iv. 306); " Captum ad quod libuit jusjurandum impulit, ut Anglia decederet et Rovecestram traderet."

in the keeping of a small body of the King's troops, CHAP. II.
while the King himself slowly followed.[1] No further
treachery was feared; it was taken for granted that
those who held the castle for Odo would give it up
at once when Odo came in person to bid them do so.
These hopes were vain; the young nobles who were left
in the castle, Count Eustace, Robert of Bellême, and the
rest, were not scrupulous as to the faith of treaties, and
they had no mind to give up their stronghold till they
were made to do so by force of arms. Odo was brought
before the walls of Rochester. The leaders of the party
that brought him called on the defenders of the castle
to surrender; such was the bidding alike of the King
who was absent and of the Bishop who was there in person.
But Odo's friends could see from the wall that the voices
of the King's messengers told one story, while the looks
of the Bishop told another. They threw open the gates; The garri-
they rushed forth on the King's men, who were in no son refuse
to surren-
case to resist them, and carried both them and the der; Odo
taken pri-
Bishop prisoners into the castle.[2] Odo was doubtless soner by
his own
a willing captive; once within the walls of Rochester, friends.
he again became the life and soul of the defence.

[1] Chron. u. s. "Ealswa se bisceop ferde and sceolde agifan þone castel
and se cyng sende his men mid him." So Will. Malms. "Ad quod implen-
dum eum cum fidelibus suis præmisit, lento pede præeuntes subsecutus. . . .
Regii cum episcopo pauci et inermes (quis enim eo præsente insidias time-
ret ?) circa muros desiliunt, clamantes oppidanis ut portas aperiant; hoc episcopum præsentem velle, hoc regem absentem jubere."

[2] Will. Malms. u. s. "At illi, de muro conspicati quod vultus episcopi cum
verbis oratorum non conveniret, raptim apertis portis ruunt, equos involant,
omnesque cum episcopo vinctos abducunt." This explains the shorter
account in the Chronicle; "þa arisan þa men þe wæron innan þam castele,
and namon þone bisceop and þes cynges men, and dydon hi on hæftmenge."
It is now that both the Chronicle and William give the names of the chief
nobles who were in the castle. Henry of Huntingdon (1088, p. 215) strongly
marks Odo's treachery; "Eustachius consul et cæteri proceres qui urbi in-
erant, fallacia ipsius, episcopum regisque ministros ceperunt et in carcerem
retruserunt."

CHAP. II. It perhaps did not tend to the moral improvement of William Rufus to find himself thus shamefully deceived by one so near of kin to himself, so high in ecclesiastical rank. At the moment the treachery of Odo stirred him up to greater efforts. Rochester should be won, though it might need the whole strength of the kingdom to win it. But the King saw that it was only by English hands that it could be won. He gathered around him his English followers, and by their advice put out a proclamation in ancient form bidding all men, French and English, from port and from upland, to come with all speed to the royal muster, if they would not be branded with the shameful name of *Nithing*. That name, the name which had been fixed, as the lowest badge of infamy, on the murderer Swegen,[1] was a name under which no Englishman could live; and it seems to have been held that strangers settled on English ground would have put on enough of English feeling to be stirred in the like sort by the fear of having such a mark set upon them. What the Frenchmen did we are not told; but the *fyrd* of England answered loyally to the call of a King who thus knew how to appeal to the most deep-set feelings and traditions of Englishmen.[2] Men came in crowds to King

William's Niðing Proclamation.

The second English muster.

---

[1] See N. C. vol. ii. p. 104.

[2] Will. Malms. iv. 306. " Ille [rex] .... Anglos suos appellat ; jubet ut compatriotas advocent ad obsidionem venire, nisi si qui velint sub nomine Niðing, quod nequam sonat, remanere. Angli, qui nihil miserius putarent quam hujusce vocabuli dedecore aduri, catervatim ad regem confluunt, et invincibilem exercitum faciunt." This leaves out the fact that the proclamation was addressed both to French and English. The words of the Chronicle are express ; " Ða se cyng undergeat þat þing, þa ferde he æfter mid þam here þe he þær hæfde, and sende ofer eall Englalande, and bead þæt *ælc man þe wære unniðing* sceolde cuman to him, *Frencisce and Englisce,* of porte and of uppelande." We can hardly doubt that we have here the actual words of the proclamation. It must not be forgotten that, by the law of the Conqueror, Frenchmen who had settled in King Eadward's day were counted as English. See N. C. vol. iv. p. 620.

William's muster, and, in the course of May, a vast host CHAP. II.
beset the fortress of Rochester. According to a practice The siege
of which we have often heard already, two temporary of Roches-
forts, no doubt of wood, were raised, so as to hem in the
besieged and to cut off their communications from without.[1] The site of one at least of these may be looked
for on the high ground to the south of the castle, said
to be itself partly artificial, and known as Boley Hill.[2]
The besieged soon found that all resistance was useless.
They were absolutely alone. Pevensey and Tunbridge
were now in the King's hands; since the overthrow of
Duke Robert's fleet, they could look for no help from
Normandy; they could look for none from yet more
distant Bristol or Durham. Till the siege began, they Straits
had lived at the cost of the loyal inhabitants of Kent besieged.
and London. For not only the Archbishop, but most of
the chief land-owners of Kent were on the King's side.[3]
This is a point to be noticed amid the general falling
away of the Normans. For the land-owners of Kent,
a land where no Englishman was a tenant-in-chief, were
a class preeminently Norman. But we can well believe
that the rule of Odo, who spared neither French nor
English who stood in his way,[4] may have been little more
to the liking of his own countrymen than it was to that of

---

[1] Ord. Vit. 667 B. "Animosus rex .... oppidum Maio mense cum
grandi exercitu potenter obsedit, firmatisque duobus castellis omnem exeundi facultatem hostibus abstulit." It must have been late in May, as six
weeks had been spent before Pevensey. Indeed, if the siege did begin in
the Easter week, it must have been June.

[2] See Mr. Clark in the Archæological Journal, vol. xxxii. p. 205.

[3] This appears from the words of Florence; "Hrofenses Cantwarien-
sibus et Lundoniensibus cædes inferunt et incendia. Landfrancus enim
archiepiscopus et pene omnes optimates ejusdem provinciæ erant cum rege."
Orderic too (u. s.) points out the advantageous position of Rochester for
such purposes; "In medio positi laxis habenis Lundoniam et Cantuariam
devastarent."

[4] Seé N. C. vol. v. p. 748.

CHAP. II. the men of the land. But all chance of plunder was now cut off; a crowd of men and horses were packed closely together within the circuit of the fortress, with little heed to health or cleanliness. Sickness was rife among them, and a plague of flies, a plague which is likened to the ancient plague of Egypt, added to their distress.[1] There was no hope within their own defences, and beyond them a host lay spread which there was no chance of overcoming. At last the heart of Odo himself failed him. He and his fiercest comrades, Eustace of Boulogne, even Robert of Bellême, at last brought themselves to crave for peace at the hands of the offended and victorious King.

Plague of flies.

They agree to surrender.

It was a great and a hard lesson which Odo and his accomplices learned at Pevensey and Rochester. It was the great lesson of English history, the great result of the teaching of William the Great on the day of Salisbury, that no one noble, however great his power, however strong the force which he could gather round him, could strive with any hope of success against the King of the whole land. In the royal army itself Odo might see one who had risen as high as himself among the conquerors of England, the father of the fiercest of the warriors who stood beside him, following indeed the King's bidding, but following it against his will. Roger of Montgomery was in the host before Rochester, an unwilling partner in a siege which was waged against his own sons. Both he and other Normans in the King's army are charged with giving more of real help to the besieged than they gave to the King whom

Lesson of the war: the King stronger than any one noble.

Odo and Roger of Montgomery.

---

[1] Ord. Vit. 667 C. "In oppido Rofensi plaga similis Ægyptiorum plagæ apparuit, qua Deus, qui semper res humanas curat et juste disponit, antiqua miracula nostris etiam temporibus recentia ostendit." Nobody could eat, unless his neighbour drove away the flies; so they wielded the flapper by turns.

they no longer dared to withstand openly.[1] But it was
in vain that even so great a lord as Earl Roger sought
to strive or to plot against England and her King. The The unity
policy of the Conqueror, crowning the work of earlier of England.
kings, had made England a land in which no Earl of
Kent or of Shrewsbury could gather a host able to withstand the King of the English at the head of the English
people.[2] When the days came that kings were to be
brought low, it was not by the might of this or that
overgrown noble, but by the people of the land, with
the barons of the land acting only as the first rank of
the people. Those days were yet far away; but an
earlier stage in the chain of progress had been reached.
The Norman nobles had taken one step towards becoming the first rank of the English people, when they
learned that King and people together were stronger
than they.

The defenders of Rochester had brought themselves Rufus re-
to ask for peace; but they still thought that they could fuses terms
to the
make terms with their sovereign. Let the King secure besieged.
to them the lands and honours which they held in his
kingdom, and they would give up the castle of Rochester
to his will; they would hold all that they had as of his
grant, and would serve him faithfully as their natural
lord.[3] The wrath of the Red King burst forth, as well it
might. Odo at least was asking at Rochester for more
favourable terms than those to which he had already sworn

---

[1] See above, p. 62.

[2] Will. Malms. iv. 306. "Nec diutius potuere pati oppidani quin se
traderent, experti quamlibet nobilem, quamlibet consertam manum, nihil
adversus regem Angliæ posse proficere."

[3] Ord. Vit. 667 D. "Guillermum regem nuntiis petierunt ut pacem cum
eis faceret, ac oppidum ab eis reciperet, tali tenore ut terras, fundos, et omnia
quæ hactenus habuerant, ab ipso reciperent, et ipsi eidem ut naturali domino
[cynehlaford] fideliter amodo servirent."

CHAP. II. at Pevensey. William answered that he would grant
no terms; he had strength enough to take the castle,
The King's whether they chose to surrender it or not. And the
threats.
story runs that he added—not altogether in the spirit of
his father—that all the traitors within the walls should
be hanged on gibbets, or put to such other forms of
death as might please him.[1] But those of his followers
who had friends or kinsfolk within the castle came to
Pleadings the King to crave mercy for them. A dialogue follows
for the
besieged. in our most detailed account, in which the scriptural
reference to the history of Saul and David may be set
down as the garnish of the monk of Saint Evroul, but
which contains arguments that are likely enough to
have been used on the two sides of the question. An
appeal is made to William's own greatness and victory,
to his position as the successor of his father. God, who
helps those who trust in him, gives to good fathers a
worthy offspring to come after them. The men in the
castle, the proud youths and the old men blinded by
greediness, had learned that the power of kings had
not died out in the island realm. Those who had come
from Normandy—here we seem to hear an argument
from English mouths — sweeping down upon the land
like kites, they who had deemed that the kingly stock
had died out in England, had learned that the younger
William was in no way weaker than the elder.[2] Mercy

---

[1] Ord. Vit. 667 D. " His auditis rex iratus est, et valde rigidus intumuit, et in nullo flexus legatorum postulationibus non acquievit; sed
perfidos traditores in oppido virtute potenti capiendos juravit, et mox
patibulis suspendendos, et aliis mortium diversis generibus de terra delendos
asseruit."

[2] Ib. "Ecce turgidi juvenes et cupiditate cæcati senes jam satis edocti
sunt quod regiæ vires in hac insula nondum defecerunt. Nam qui de
Normannia, tamquam milvi ad prædam, super nos cum impetu advolarunt,
et in Anglia regiam stirpem defecisse arbitrati sunt, jam Guillelmum juvenem Guillelmo sene non debiliorem, cohibente Deo, experti sunt."

was the noblest attribute of a conqueror; something CHAP. II.
too was due to the men who had helped him to his
victory, and who now pleaded for those who had undergone enough of punishment for their error. Rufus is Answer of
made to answer that he is thankful both to God and the King.
to his faithful followers. But he fears that he should
be lacking in that justice which is a king's first duty,
if he were to spare the men who had risen up against
him without cause, and who had sought the life of a
king who, as he truly said, had done them no harm.[1]
The Red King is made to employ the argument which
we have so often come across on behalf of that severe
discharge of princely duty which made the names of
his father and his younger brother live in men's grateful
remembrance. He fears lest their prayers should lead
him away from the strait path of justice. He who spares
robbers and traitors and perjured persons takes away
the peace and safety of the innocent, and only sows
loss and slaughter for the good and for the unarmed
people.[2] This course is one which the Red King was
very far from following in after years; but it is quite
possible that he may have made such professions at any
stage of his life, and he may have even made them
honestly at this stage. But on behalf of the chiefest Pleadings
of all culprits, the counsellors of mercy had special for Odo.
arguments. Odo is the King's uncle, the companion of
his father in the Conquest of England. He is moreover
a bishop, a priest of the Lord, a sharer in the privileges
to which, in one side of his twofold character, he had

[1] Ord. Vit. 668 B. "Quid sceleratis peccavi? quid illis nocui? quid
mortem meam totis nisibus procuraverunt, et omnes pro posse suo contra
me populos cum detrimento multorum erexerunt?"
[2] Ib. "Quisquis parcit perjuris et latronibus, plagiariis et execratis
proditoribus, aufert pacem et quietem innocentibus, innumerasque cædes et
damna serit bonis et inermibus." We seem to be reading the cover of the
Edinburgh Review.

once appealed in vain. The King is implored not to lay hands on one of Odo's holy calling, not to shed blood which was at once kindred and sacred. Let the Bishop of Bayeux at least be spared, and allowed to go back to his proper place in his Norman diocese.[1] Count Eustace too was the son of his father's old ally and follower—the invasion which Eustace's father had once wrought in that very shire seems to be conveniently forgotten.[2] Robert of Bellême had been loved and promoted by his father; he held no small part of Normandy; lord of many strong castles, he stood out foremost among the nobles of the duchy.[3] It was no more than the bidding of prudence to win over such men by favours, and to have their friendship instead of their enmity.[4] As for the rest, they were valiant knights, whose proffered services the King would do well not to despise.[5] The King had shown how far he surpassed his enemies in power, riches, and valour; let him now show how far he surpassed them in mercy and greatness of soul.[6]

---

[1] Ord. Vit. 668 C. "Baiocensis Odo patruus tuus est et *pontificali sanctificatione* præditus est." "Cum patre tuo Anglos subjugavit"—a merit which would hardly be pleaded in the hearing of the King's army. He is "antistes Domini," and so forth. "Omnes precamur ut illi benevolentiam tuam concedas et illæsum in Normanniam ad diocesim suam abire permittas."

[2] Ib. "Comes Boloniensis patri tuo satis fuit fidelis, et in rebus arduis strenuus adjutor et contubernalis." There must be some confusion between father and son.

[3] Ib. "Magnam Normanniæ partem possidet, fortissimisque castellis corroboratus pene omnibus vicinis suis et Neustriæ proceribus præeminet."

[4] Here (ib. D) a hexameter peeps out;

"Idem qui ⁂lædit, fors post ut amicus obedit."

It is the doctrine of Aias in Sophoklês (659);

ἐγὼ δ' ἐπίσταμαι γὰρ ἀρτίως, ὅτι
ὅ τ' ἐχθρὸς ἡμῖν ἐς τοσόνδ' ἐχθαρτέος,
ὡς καὶ φιλήσων αὖθις.

The balancing clause was not called for.

[5] They were (ib.) "eximii tirones"—"swiðe gode cnihtas"—"quorum servitutem, inclite rex, parvi pendere non debes."

[6] Ib. "Igitur, quos jam superasti potestate, divitiis, et ingenti probi-

To this appeal Rufus yielded. It was not indeed an CHAP. II. appeal to his knightly faith, which was in no way The King yields. pledged to the defenders of Rochester. But it was an appeal to any gentler feelings that might be in him, and still more so to that vein of self-esteem and self-exaltation which was the leading feature in his character. If Rufus had an opportunity of showing himself greater than other men, as neither justice nor mercy stood in the way of his making the most of it, so neither did any mere feeling of wrath or revenge. As his advisers told him, he was so successful that he could afford to be merciful, and merciful he accordingly was. To have hanged or blinded his enemies would not have so distinctly exalted himself, as he must have felt himself exalted, when those who had defied him, those who had tried to make terms with him, were driven to accept such terms as he chose to give them. The Red He grants terms. King then plighted his faith—and his faith when once so plighted was never broken—that the lives and limbs of the garrison should be safe, that they should come forth from the castle with their arms and horses. But they must leave the realm; they must give up all hope of keeping their lands and honours in England, as long at least as King William lived.[1] To these terms they had to yield; but Odo, even in his extremity, craved for one favour. He had to bear utter discomfiture, the Odo asks for the honours of war. failure of his hopes, the loss of his lands and honours; but he prayed to be at least spared the public scorn of the victors. His proud soul was not ready to bear the looks, the gestures, the triumphant shouts and songs, of the people whom he had trodden to the earth, and who

tate, subjuga tibi magnificentia et pietate." On the sense of "magnificentia," cf. N. C. vol. i. p. 261.

[1] Ord. Vit. 668 D. "Omnem spem habendi hæreditates et terras in regno ejus, quamdiu ipse regnaret, funditus abscidit."

CHAP. II. had now risen up to be his conquerors. He asked, it would seem, to be allowed to march out with what in modern phrase are called the honours of war. His particular prayer was that the trumpets might not sound when he and his followers came forth from the castle. This, we are told, was the usual ceremony after the overthrow of an enemy and the taking of a fortress.[1] The King was again wrathful at the request, and said that not for a thousand marks of gold would he grant

Humiliation of Odo. it.[2] Odo had therefore to submit, and to drink the cup of his humiliation to the dregs. With sad and downcast looks he and his companions came forth from the stronghold which could shelter them no longer. The trumpets sounded merrily to greet them.[3] But other sounds more fearful than the voice of the trumpet sounded in the ears of Odo as he came forth. Men saw passing before them, a second time hurled down from his high estate—and this time not by the bidding of a Norman king but by the arms of the English people—the man who stood forth in English eyes as the imbodiment of all that was blackest and basest in the foreign dominion. Odo might keep his eyes fixed on the ground, but the eyes of the

Wrath of the English against him. nation which he had wronged were full upon him. The English followers of Rufus pressed close upon him, crying out with shouts which all could hear, "Halters, bring halters; hang up the traitor Bishop and his accomplices on the gibbet." They turned to the King whose throne they had made fast for him, and hailed him as a national ruler. "Mighty King of the English, let

---

[1] Ord. Vit. 668 D. "Tunc Odo pontifex a rege Rufo impetrare temptavit, ne tubicines in eorum egressu tubis canerent, sicut moris est dum hostes vincuntur et parvum oppidum capitur." Why "parvum"?

[2] Ib. "Nec se concessurum etiam propter mille auri marcos palam asseruit."

[3] Ib. "Oppidanis cum mœrore et verecundia egredientibus, et regalibus tubis cum gratulatione clangentibus."

not the stirrer up of all evil go away unharmed. The
perjured murderer, whose craft and cruelty have taken
away the lives of thousands of men, ought not to live
any longer."[1] Cries like these, mingled with every form
of cursing and reviling, with every threat which could
rise to the lips of an oppressed people in their day of
vengeance, sounded in the ears of Odo and his comrades.[2] But the King's word had been passed, and the
thirst for vengeance of the wrathful English had to be
baulked. Odo and those who had shared with him in *He leaves*
the defence of Rochester went away unhurt; but they *England for ever.*
had to leave England, and to lose all their English lands
and honours, at least for a season. But Odo left England
and all that he had in England for ever.[3] The career
of the Earl of Kent was over; of the later career of the
Bishop of Bayeux we shall hear again.

The rebellion was now at an end in southern Eng- *End of the*
land. Revolt had been crushed at Worcester, at Pe- *rebellion.*
vensey, and at Rochester, and we hear nothing more of
those movements of which Bishop Geoffrey had made
Bristol the centre, and which had met with such a reverse at the hands of the gallant defenders of Ilchester.

[1] Ord. Vit. 669 A. " Multitudo Anglorum quæ regi adhærebat cunctis
audientibus, vociferabatur, et dicebat ; Torques, torques afferte, traditorem
episcopum cum suis complicibus patibulis suspendite. Magne rex Anglorum, cur sospitem pateris abire incentorem malorum ? Non debet vivere
perjurus homicida, qui dolis et crudelitatibus peremit hominum multa
milia."

[2] Ib. " Hæc et alia probra mœstus antistes cum suis audivit."

[3] Chron. Petrib. 1088. " Se bisceop Odo mid þam mannum þe innan
þam castele wæron ofer sæ ferdon, and se bisceop swa forlet þone wurð-
scipe þe he on þis land hæfde." Orderic (669 A) — in his character of
"Angligena" — moralizes ; " Sic irreligiosus præsul de Anglia expulsus
est, et amplissimis possessionibus spoliatus est. Tunc maximos quæstus,
quos cum facinore obtinuit, justo Dei judicio cum ingenti dedecore
perdidit, et confusus Baiocas rediit, nec in Angliam postmodum repe-
davit."

CHAP. II.

Order of events.

The Whitsun Assembly. June 4, 1088.

Confiscations and grants.

Amnesty of the chief rebels.

The chronology of the whole time is very puzzling. We have no exact date for the surrender of Rochester; we are told only that it happened in the beginning of summer.[1] But, as the siege of Pevensey lasted six weeks,[2] it is impossible to crowd all the events which had happened since Easter into the time between Easter and Whitsuntide. Otherwise the pentecostal Gemót would have been the most natural season for some acts of authority which took place at some time during the year. The King was now in a position to reward and to punish ; and some confiscations, some grants, were made by him soon after the rebellion came to an end. "Many Frenchmen forlet their land and went over sea, and the King gave their land to the men that were faithful to him."[3] Of these confiscations and grants we should be glad to have some details. Did any dispossessed Englishmen win back their ancient heritage ? And, if so, did they keep their recovered heritage, notwithstanding the amnesty which at a somewhat later time restored many of the rebels? One thing is clear, that the Frenchmen who are now spoken of were not the men of highest rank and greatest estates among the rebellious Normans. For them there was an amnesty at once. Them, we are told, the King spared, for the love of his father to whom they had been faithful followers, and out of reverence for their age which opened a speedy prospect of their deaths. He was rewarded, it is added, by their repentant loyalty and thankfulness,

---

[1] Ord. Vit. 669 A. "Anno primo Guillelmi Rufi regis, in initio æstatis, Rofensis urbs ei redita est, omniumque qui contra pacem enses acceperant, nequam commotio compressa est." We shall see by the story of Robert of Rhuddlan, to which we shall presently come, that some of the King's followers were at home again by the end of June.

[2] See above, p. 74.

[3] Chron. Petrib. 1088. "Eac manige Frencisce men forleton heora land and ferdon ofer sæ, and se cyng geaf heora land þam mannum þe him holde wæron."

which made them eager to please him by gifts and ser- CHAP. II.
vice of all kinds.[1]

The speed with which some of the greatest among the
rebel leaders were restored to their old rank and their
old places in the King's favour is shown by the way in
which, within a very few months, we find them acting
on the King's side against one who at the worst was
their own accomplice, and who himself professed to have
had no part or lot in their doings. We must now take up Versions of
the story
again the puzzling story of Bishop William of Durham. of the
We left him, according to his own version, hindered Bishop of
Durham.
from coming to the King by the violence of the Sheriff
of Yorkshire, and suffering a seven weeks' harrying of
his lands which carries us into the month of May.[2]
This is exactly the time when the national Chronicler
sets the Bishop himself before us as carrying on a
general harrying of the North country.[3] It is likely
enough that both stories are true; in a civil war above
all it is easy, without the assertion of any direct falsehood, to draw two exactly opposite pictures by simply
leaving out the doings of each side in turn. Anyhow the
King had summoned the Bishop to his presence, and the
Bishop had not come. The King now sends a more The King
special and urgent summons, demanding the Bishop's again sum-
mons the
presence in his court, that is, in all likelihood, at the Bishop.
Whitsun Gemót, or at whatever assembly took its place

---

[1] Ord. Vit. 669 B. "Quorumdam factiones sævissimis legibus puniit,
aliquorum vero reatus ex industria dissimulavit. Antiquis baronibus,
quos ab ipso aliquantum desciverat nequitia, versute pepercit, *pro amore
patris sui* cui diu fideliter inhæserant, et pro senectutis reverentia, sciens
profecto quod non eos diu vigere sinerent morbi et mors propria. Porro
quidam, quanto gravius se errasse in regiam majestatem noverunt, tanto
ferventius omni tempore postmodum ei famulati sunt, et tam muneribus
quam servitiis ac adulationibus multis modis placere studuerunt."

[2] See above, p. 32.   [3] See above, p. 28.

CHAP. II. for that year.[1]   The message was sent by a prelate of
high rank, that Abbot Guy who had just before been
forced by Lanfranc upon the unwilling monks of Saint
Augustine's.[2]   The Bishop was to accompany the Abbot
The to the King's presence.   But, instead of going with Guy,
Bishop's
complaints. Bishop William, fearing the King's wrath and the snares
of his enemies, sent another letter, the bearer of which
went under the Abbot's protection.[3]   The letter curi-
ously illustrates some of the features of the case.   We
Doings of learn more details of the Sheriff's doings.   He had
Counts
Alan and divided certain of the Bishop's lands between two very
Odo. great personages, Count Alan of the Breton and of the
Yorkshire Richmond, and Count Odo, husband of the
King's aunt, and seemingly already lord of Holderness.[4]
The Sheriff had not only refused the King's peace to the
Bishop; he had formally defied him on the part of the
King.[5]   Some of the Bishop's men he had allowed to
redeem themselves; but others he had actually sold.
Were they the Bishop's slaves, dealt with as forfeited
chattels, or did the Sheriff take on himself to degrade
freemen into slavery?[6]   The Bishop protests that he is

[1] See above, p. 88.

[2] See N. C. vol. iv. pp. 409, 825, and below, p. 139.

[3] Mon. Ang. i. 245. "Tandem misi sibi rex abbatem sancti Augustini,
mandans ei ut, sicut prius mandaverat sibi, ad curiam suam cum abbate
veniret.   Episcopus autem, inimicorum suorum insidias cum regis ira
metuens, sine bono conductu se non posse venire respondet et legatos suos
per abbatis conductum cum subscriptis litteris regi misit."

[4] Ib. "Homines meos et terras et pecuniam quam vicecomites vestri
ubicumque poterant, mihi abstulerunt, scilicet Offedene et Welletune quas
diviserunt Odoni et Alano comitibus, cum cæteris terris in Ewerwickschire."
See above, p. 31.   On Count Alan, see N. C. vol. iv. p. 294, and on Odo,
vol. iv. pp. 301, 805.

[5] Ib. "Quod breve cum mississem Radulfo Paganello non solum mihi
pacem negavit sed et de parte vestra me diffidavit." On *diffidatio* see
Ducange *in voce*. In N. C. vol. v. p. 270 we have a case of the man *defying*
his lord. Here the lord *defies* his man. In either case there is the withdrawal
of one side of the mutual duty of lord and man.

[6] Ib. "Hominum vero quosdam vendidit, quosdam redimi permisit."

ready to come with a safe-conduct, and to prove before
all the barons of the realm that he is wholly innocent
of any crime against the King. He adds that he would
willingly come at once with the Abbot. He had full
faith in the King and his barons; but he feared his
personal enemies and the unlearned multitude.[1] Who
were these last? Are we again driven to think of the
old popular character of the Assembly, and did the Bishop
fear that the solemn proceedings of the King's court
would be disturbed by a loyal crowd, ready to deal out
summary justice against any one who should be even
suspected of treason? The King sent the safe-conduct
that was asked for, and the Bishop came to the King's
court.[2]

The Bishop comes with a safe-conduct.

The two Williams, King and Bishop, now met face
to face. William of Saint-Calais pleaded his rights as
a bishop as zealously, and far more fully, than they
had been pleaded by the bishop who was also an earl.
The Bishop of Durham, as Bishop of Durham, held
great temporal rights; but William of Saint-Calais was
not, like his predecessor Walcher, personally earl of any
earldom. Bishop William's assertion of the new ecclesiastical claims reminds us of two more famous assemblies,
in the earlier of which William of Saint-Calais will appear
on the other side. In forming our estimate of the
whole story, we must never forget that the man who
surprised the Red King with claims greater than those
of Anselm is the same man who a few years later became
the counsellor of the Red King against Anselm. In

The Bishop's ecclesias- tical claims.

---

[1] Mon. Ang. i. 245. "Hoc in veritate vobis mando quod libenter cum hoc
abbate venissem, nisi plus inimicos meos et *indoctam populi multitudinem*
timuissem quod de vestro brevi et baronum vestrorum fiducia dubitassem."

[2] Ib. "Rex visis his litteris misit conductum episcopo et bene affidavit
eum per litteras suas quod per eum vel per suos homines nullum ei damnum
eveniret usque quo de rege rediens Dunelmum intraret. Perrexit ergo
episcopus ad regem."

CHAP. II. this first Assembly the Bishop refuses to plead otherwise than according to the privileges of his order. The demand is refused. He craves for the counsel of his Metropolitan Thomas of York and of the other bishops. This also is refused. He offers to make his personal purgation on any charge of treason or perjury. This is refused. The King insists that he shall be tried before He goes the Court after the manner of a layman. This the back to Durham. Bishop refuses;[1] but the King keeps his personal faith, and the Bishop is allowed to go back safely to Durham. We hear much of the ravages done on the Bishop's lands, both while he was away from Durham and after he had gone back thither.[2] Of ravages done by the Bishop we hear nothing in this version. In this version William of Saint-Calais, blackest of traitors in the Peterborough Chronicle, is still the meekest of confessors.

June– September, 1088. We get no further details of the Bishop of Durham's story till the beginning of September. But in the meanwhile the Bishop wrote another letter to the King, again asking leave to make his purgation. The only answer, we are told, on the King's part was to imprison the Bishop's messenger and to lay waste his lands more thoroughly than ever. But, from the beginning of September, the story is told with great detail. By that time southern England at least was at peace, and by that time too men who had taken a leading part in the rebellion were acting as loyal subjects to the King. Agreement On the day of the Nativity of our Lady an agreement was between the Bishop come to between the Bishop and three of the barons of

[1] Mon. Ang. i. 245. "Episcopus . . deprecatus est eum ut rectitudinem sibi consentiret sicut episcopo suo. Rex autem respondit ei, Quod si laicaliter placitare vellet, et extra pacem quam rex ei dederat se mitteret, hoc modo rectitudinem sibi consentiret, et, si hoc modo placitare recusaret, Dunelmum faceret eum reconduci."

[2] Ib. "Dunelmum rediit episcopus, cui rex interim plus quam septingentos homines cum multa præda abstulerat."

the North. Two of these were the Counts Alan and Odo,
who had received grants of the Bishop's lands. They,
it seems clear, had had no share in the rebellion; but
with them was joined a leading rebel, Roger of Poitou,
son of the Earl of Shrewsbury, whom we last heard
of as one of Odo's accomplices at Pevensey. These
three, acting in the King's name, pledged their faith
for the Bishop's personal safety to and from the King's
court. The three barons seem to make themselves in
some sort arbiters between the King and the Bishop.
His personal safety is guaranteed in any case. But the
place to which he is to be safely taken is to differ
according to the result of the trial. The terms seem
to imply that, if the three barons deem justice to be
on the side of the Bishop, he is to be taken back safely
to Durham, while, if they deem justice to be on the
side of the King, he is to be allowed freely to cross
the sea at any haven that he may choose, from Sandwich
to Exeter.[1] In case of the Bishop's return to Durham,
if he should find that during his absence any new
fortifications have been added to the castle, those fortifications are to be destroyed.[2] If, on the other hand,
the Bishop crosses the sea, the castle is to be surrendered
to the King. No agreement contrary to this present one
was to be extorted from the Bishop on any pretext.

---

[1] They were to have (Mon. Ang. i. 246) the "securitas et conductus
regis" till they had crossed—"donec ultra mare ad terram siccam cum
rebus suis essent." The catalogue of the "res suæ" is curious; "Et
liceret eos per conductum regis secum ducere et portare [ἄγειν καὶ φέρειν]
aurum et argentum, equos et pannos et arma et canes et accipitres, et sua
prorsus omnia quæ de terra portari debent." The hawks and hounds
remind us of Harold setting sail from Bosham in the Tapestry. See N. C.
vol. iii. p. 222.

[2] Mon. Ang. i. 246. "Episcopus dedit fidem suam Rogero Pictavensi,
quod si ipse per præscriptam condicionem castellum reduceretur, et major
fortitudo in castello missa vel facta esset in hominibus vel in munitione vel
in castelli fortitudine quam eadem die ibi erat, episcopus totum illud destrui
faceret, ita quod episcopus inde nullum proficuum haberet nec rex damnum."

CHAP. II. The terms were agreed to by the Bishop, and were sworn to, as far as the surrender of the castle was concerned, by seven of the Bishop's men, seemingly the same seven of whom we have heard before and of whom we shall hear again. All matters were to be settled in the King's court one way or the other by the coming feast of Saint Michael; but, as this term was plainly too short, the time of meeting was put off by the consent of both sides to an early day in November.

The Meeting at Salisbury. November 2, 1088.

On the appointed day Bishop William of Durham appeared in the King's court at Salisbury. We have not now, as we had two years before, to deal with a gathering of all the land-owners of England in the great plain. The castle which had been reared within the ditches that fence in the waterless hill became the scene of a meeting of the King and the great men of the realm which may take its place alongside of later meetings of the same kind in the castle by the wood at Rockingham and in the castle by the busy streets of Northampton. We have—from the Bishop's side only, it must be remembered—a minute and lifelike account of a two days' debate in the Assembly, a debate in which not a few men with whose names we have been long familiar in our story, in which others whose names and possessions are written in the Great Survey, meet us face to face as living men and utter characteristic speeches in our ears. We are met at the threshold by

Urse of Abetot.

a well-known form, that of the terrible Sheriff of Worcestershire, Urse of Abetot. Notwithstanding the curse of Ealdred, he flourished and enjoyed court favour, and we now find him the first among the courtiers to meet Bishop William, and to bid him enter the royal presence.[1] That presence the Bishop entered four times

---

[1] Mon. Angl. i. 246. "In quarto nonas Novembris .. venit episcopus Salisbiriam, quem cum Ursus de Habetot unus ex servientibus regis ad regem

in the course of the day, having had three times to CHAP. II.
withdraw while the Court came to a judgement on points
of law touching his case. At every stage the Bishop Conduct
raises some point, renews some protest, interposes some $_{Bishop.}^{of the}$
delay or other. And during the whole earlier part of
the debate, it is Lanfranc who takes the chief part in
answering him; the King says little till a late stage of the
controversy. Before Bishop William comes in to the
King's presence, he prays again, but prays in vain, to have
the counsel of his brother bishops. None of them, not
even his own Metropolitan Thomas, would give him the
kiss of peace or even a word of greeting. When he does
come in, he first raises the question whether he ought not
to be judged, and the other bishops to judge him, in full
episcopal dress. To the practical mind of Lanfranc Lanfranc's
questions about vestments did not seem of first-rate $_{vestments.}^{view of}$
importance. "We can judge very well," he said, "clothed
as we are; for garments do not hinder truth."[1] This point, Case of
it will be remembered, again came up at Northampton, $_{Northamp-}^{Thomas at}$
seventy-six years later. The entrance of Thomas into ton.
the King's hall clad in the full garb of the Primate of $^{1164.}$
all England was one of the most striking features of that
memorable day.[2]

A long legal discussion followed, in which Bishop
William and Lanfranc were the chief speakers. Some
points were merely verbal. Much turned on the con-
struction of the word *bishopric*. The Bishop of Durham

intrare moneret." On Urse of Abetot, see N. C. vol. iv. pp. 173, 383,
579, 820.
[1] Ib. "Episcopus requisivit ab archiepiscopis utrum revestitus ingredi
deberet, dixitque, 'Nihil se prorsus acturum ibi nisi canonice et secundum
ordinem suum et sibi videbatur quod ecclesiastica consuetudo exigebat ut
ipse revestitus ante revestitos causam suam diceret et causantibus canonice
responderet.' Cui Lanfrancus archiepiscopus respondens, 'bene possumus,'
inquit, 'hoc modo vestiti de regalibus tuisque negotiis disceptare, vestes
enim non impediunt veritatem.'"
[2] See William FitzStephen, iii. 56, Robertson.

asked to be restored to his bishopric. Lanfranc answered that he had not been disseized of it.[1] In the course of this dispute one or two facts of interest come out.

It appears from the Bishop's complaint that some of the chief men of the patrimony of Saint Cuthberht had made their way to the meeting at Salisbury, and that not as their bishop's friends. They, his own liegemen, had abjured him; they held the lands of the bishopric in fief of the King; they had made war upon him by the King's orders, and were now sitting as his judges.[2]

But the main point was that the Bishop should, before matters went any further, do right to the King, that is, acknowledge the jurisdiction of the Court.[3] This demand the Bishop tried to evade by every means; but it was firmly pressed both by Lanfranc and by the lay members of the Court. These last seem to act in close concert with the Primate, and the ecclesiastical writer brings out in a lively way the energy of their way of speaking.[4] In answer to them the Bishop spake words which amounted to a casting aside of all the earlier jurisprudence of England, but which were only a natural

---

[1] Mon. Angl. u. s. "Episcopus surgens precatus est regem ut episcopatum suum quem jamdiu sine judicio abstulerat sibi redderet. Lanfrancus vero, rege tacente, dixit, 'Rex de episcopatu tuo nihil tibi abstulit vel aliquis per eum neque breve suum vidisti per quod te de episcopatu tuo dissaisiret vel dissaisiri præciperet.'"

[2] The Bishop now tells his grievances at length. After other wrongs the King "misit comites et barones cum exercitu suo, et per eos totum episcopatum meum vastavit, terras quoque et homines et pecuniam Sancti Cuthberti et meam mihi abstulit. Nostram etiam sedem me ad tempus abjuvare coegit; ipsi etiam casati ecclesiæ qui mei homines ligii fuerant et quidquid habebant de casamento ecclesiæ tenebat ex præcepto regis guerram mihi fecerunt, et terras suas de rege tenentes pacifice hic eos cum rege video adversum me convenisse."

[3] "Rectitudinem facere" is the technical phrase. See Appendix C.

[4] "Tunc laici hujusmodi verbis Lanfranci totius Angliæ primatis animati, adversus episcopum exclamantes dixerunt 'injustum esse quod rex episcopo responderet antequam regi fecisset justitiam.' Laicis vero hæc et alia multa declamantibus et iterantibus, facto silentio, dixit episcopus."

inference from that act of the Conqueror which had CHAP. II.
severed the jurisdictions which ancient English custom
had joined together. He told the barons of the realm He denies
and the other laymen who were present that with them the authority of the
he had nothing to do, that he altogether refused their Court.
jurisdiction; he demanded, that, if the King and the
Bishops allowed them to be present, they should at
least not speak against him.[1] The doctrine of ecclesi- Growth of
astical privilege had indeed grown, since, six and thirty the new doctrines.
years before, the people of England, gathered beneath
the walls of London, had declared a traitorous archbishop to be deprived and outlawed, and had by their
own act set another in his place. Yet the position Position of
of William of Saint-Calais was more consistent than Lanfranc and Bishop
the position of Lanfranc. William of Saint-Calais William.
wholly denied the right of laymen to judge a bishop;
Lanfranc, the assertor of that right, had been placed
in his see on the very ground that the deposition of
Robert and the election of Stigand were both invalid, as
being merely acts of the secular power. Still, however
logical might be the Bishop's argument, his claims
were practically new, either in English or in Norman
ears. If they had ever been heard of before, it had
been only for a moment from the lips of Odo. And
we may mark again that, though the words of William
of Saint-Calais would have won him favour with
Hildebrand, they won him no favour with Lanfranc.
Lanfranc represented the traditions of the Conqueror,
and in the days of the Conqueror, all things, divine and
human, had depended on the Conqueror's nod.[2]

---

[1] "Domini barones et laici, permittite me, quæso, quæ dicturus sum regi
dicere, archiepiscopis et episcopis respondere, quia nihil vobis habeo dicere,
et, sicut huc non veni judicium vestrum recepturus, ita illud omninɔ recuso,
et si domino nostri regi et archiepiscopis et episcopis placuisset vos hic
negotio interesse, nec me taliter obloqui decuisset."

[2] See the complaints from the ecclesiastical side in N. C. vol. iv. p. 436.

At this stage the King speaks for the first time, and, in
this first speech the words of William the Red are mild
enough. He had hoped, he said, that the Bishop would
have first made answer to the charges which had been
brought against him, and he wondered that he had taken
any other course. But the charge had not yet been formally made. Amid the Bishop's protests about the rights
of his order, this somewhat important point was pressed
by one of his fellow-rebels. This was Roger the Bigod,
he who from the castle of Norwich had done such harm
in the eastern lands, but who now appears as an adviser
of the king against whom he had been fighting a few
months before. Let the charge, he said, be brought in
due form, and let the Bishop be tried according to it.[1]
After more protests from the Bishop, the charge was
made by Hugh of Beaumont.[2] It contained a full
statement of the Bishop's treason and desertion, as
already described,[3] and the time is said to have been
when the King's enemies came against him, and when
his own men, Bishop Odo, Earl Roger, and many others,
strove to take away his crown and kingdom.[4] It is
demanded that, on this charge and on any other charges
that the King may afterwards bring, the Bishop shall
abide by the sentence of the King's court. We have

---

[1] Mon. Angl. i. 247. "Tunc Rogerus Bygotus dixit regi, 'Vos debetis
episcopo dicere unde eum appellare vultis, et postea, si ipse nobis voluerit
respondere de responsione sua facite eum judicari ; sin autem, facite inde
quod barones vestri vobis consulerent.'"

[2] I cannot identify this Hugh. "Hugo cognomento pauper" (Ord. Vit.
806 A), son of Count Robert of Meulan, and afterwards Earl of Bedford
(Gest. Steph. 61), was not yet born.

[3] See above, p. 30.

[4] Mon. Angl. u. s. "Rex te appellat quod, cum ipse audivit quod inimici sui
super eum veniebant, et homines sui, episcopus scilicet Baiocensis et Rogerus
comes et alii plures regnum suum pariter sibi et coronam auferre volebant,
et ipse per consilium tuum contra illos equitabat." There is something
odd in this calm mention of Earl Roger as an open rebel.

this statement only in the version of Bishop William CHAP. II.
himself or of a local partisan. Yet there is no reason Its pro-
to doubt that it is a fair representation of the formal bable truth.
charge which was brought in the King's court. That
charge brings out quite enough of overt acts of treason
to justify even the strong words of the Peterborough
Chronicler.[1] With the secret counsels of the rebels during
Lent it does not deal; what share Bishop William had
had in them might be hard to make out by legal proof,
and the charge is quite enough for the King's purpose
without them. But it brings out this special aggra-
vation of the Bishop's guilt, that, after the rebellion had
broken out, after military operations had begun, the
Bishop was still at the King's side, counselling action
while he was himself plotting desertion. The flight of
Bishop William, as we have already told it, really reads
not unlike the flight of Cornbury and Churchill just six
centuries later; and it would be pressing the judgement
of charity a long way to plead in his behalf the doctrine
that in revolutions men live fast.[2] We may notice also Points not
that nothing is said about the Bishop's harryings in dwelled on.
Northern England. They might, according to the custom
of the time, be almost taken as implied in the fact of
his rebellion; or they might be among the other charges
which the King had ready to bring forward if he thought
good.

The formal charge was thus laid before the Court, and The
it was for the Bishop to make his answer. It was the Bishop's
answer.
same as before. Hugh of Beaumont might say what he
chose;[3] only according to his own ideas of canonical rule
would he answer. By this time the wrath of the lay

---

[1] See above, p. 28.

[2] Macaulay, ii. 496–499, 510, 511.

[3] Mon. Angl. u. s. "Episcopus autem Hugoni respondit, ‘Hugo, dicas quidquid volueris, non tibi tamen hodie respondebo.’"

CHAP. II.

Wrath of
the lay
members.

Speech of
Bishop
Geoffrey on
behalf of
William.

Answer of
Lanfranc.

members of the Assembly was waxing hot; they assailed the Bishop, some, we are told, with arguments, some with revilings.[1] At this stage Bishop William found a friend where we should hardly have looked for one. The brigand Bishop of Coutances, already changed from a rebel into a loyal subject, was there among the great men of the realm. England knew him, not as a prelate of the Church, but as one of the greatest of her land-owners; but now, like Odo, he speaks as a bishop. He appeals to the Archbishops at least to give a hearing to Bishop William's objection. They, the bishops and abbots, ought no longer to sit there; they ought to withdraw, taking with them some lay assessors, to dis-cuss the point raised by the Bishop of Durham, whether he ought not to be restored to his bishopric before he is called on to plead[2]. Again the great ecclesiastical statesman is inclined to scorn, almost to mock, the scruples of lesser men. Canonical subtleties might dis-turb the conscience of a bishop who had a few months before headed a band of robbers; but the lawyer of Pavia, the teacher of Avranches, the monk of Bec, the Abbot of Saint Stephen's, the Patriarch of all the nations beyond the sea, had learned, in his long experience, that, as changes of vestments did not greatly matter, so changes of place and procedure did not greatly matter either. As Lanfranc had told Bishop William that they could judge perfectly well in the clothes which they then had on, so now he tells Bishop Geoffrey that they can judge

---

[1] Mon. Angl. u.s. "Tum multum tumultuantes laici, quidam rationibus, quidam vero contumeliis, adversus episcopum deiterarent."

[2] Ib. "Domini archiepiscopi, nos non oporteret diutius hæc ita con-siderare, sed deceret nos surgere et episcopos et abbates convocare, quosdam etiam baronum et comitum istorum nobiscum habere, et cum eis juste decernere si episcopus debeat prius investiri vel ante investituram de querelis regis intrare in placitum." The text has "S. Constantiensis episcopus," but Bishop Geoffrey must be meant.

perfectly well in the place and company in which they CHAP. II.
were now sitting. There was no need to rise ; let the The Bishop
Bishop of Durham and his men go out, and the rest of goes out.
the Court, clergy and laity alike, would judge what
was right to be done.[1] The Bishop warned the Court
to act according to the canons, and to let no one judge
who might not canonically judge a bishop. Lanfranc
calmly, but vaguely, assured him that justice would be
done.[2] Hugh of Beaumont told him more plainly, " If Defiance of
I may not to-day judge you and your order, you and Hugh of Beaumont.
your order shall never afterwards judge me." [3] With one
more protest, one more declaration that he would disown any judgement which was not strictly canonical,[4]
Bishop William and his followers left the hall of
meeting.

Our only narrative of these debates, the narrative of Debate
Bishop William himself or of some one writing under in the Bishop's
his inspiration, complains of the long delay before the absence.
Bishop was allowed to come back, and gives a description, one which reads like satire, of the assembly which
stayed to debate the preliminary point of law. There was Constitu-
the King, with the bishops and earls, the sheriffs and the tion of the Court.
lesser reeves, with the King's huntsmen and other offi-
cials.[5] The great officers of state, Justiciar, Chancellor,

---

[1] Mon. Angl. u. s. " Ad hæc Lanfrancus archiepiscopus, 'Non est necesse,'
inquit, 'nos surgere, sed episcopus et homines sui egrediantur, et nos
remanentes, tam clerici quam laici, consideremus equaliter quid inde juste
facere debeamus."

[2] Ib. " Vade, nos enim juste faciemus quidquid fecerimus."

[3] Ib. " Si ego hodie te et tuum ordinem judicare non potero, tu vel
tuus ordo nunquam me amplius judicabitis."

[4] Ib. " Vide autem qui in domo ista remanent et me judicare disponunt
ut et canonicos judices habeant et canonice me judicent ; si enim aliter
agerent, eorum judicia penitus recusarem."

[5] Ib. " Rege, cum suis episcopis et consulibus et vicecomitibus et
præpositis et venatoribus aliisque quorumlibet officiorum, in judicio re-
manente.

CHAP. II. Treasurer, had not yet risen to their full importance; still it is odd to find them, as they would seem to be, thrust in, after the manner of an *et cetera*, after, it may be, Osgeat the reeve and Croc the huntsman.[1] But anyhow, in this purely official assembly, we may surely see the *Theningmannagemót* gradually changing into the *Curia Regis*.[2] The Court, however constituted, debated in the Bishop's absence on the point of the law which he had raised. On his return, his own Metropolitan, Thomas of York, announced to him the decision of the Assembly. Till he acknowledged the jurisdiction of the Court, the King was not bound to restore anything that had been taken from him. We seem to hear the voice of Flambard, when, in announcing this decision, Thomas makes use of the word *fief*, which had not hitherto been heard in the discussion.[3] Bishop William catches in vain at the novelty; Archbishop Thomas declines all verbal discussion; whether it is called bishopric or fief, nothing is to be restored till the jurisdiction of the court is acknowledged.[4] Thus baffled, Bishop William has only to fall back on his old protests, his old demand for the counsel of his brother bishops. Lanfranc meets him as a lawyer; the bishops

The Bishop comes back.

Debate on the word fief.

---

[1] We have met with Osgeat the Reeve in Domesday. See N. C. vol. v. p. 812. Croc the hunter, like others of his craft, appears in 49, 74 b. See Ellis, i. 403. This odd mixture of great and small officials is not unusual. In the "Constitutio Domus Regis" in Hearne's Liber Niger, i. 341, the descent from the Chancellor to the bakers and cooks—the huntsmen come at the end—is more sudden than one would have looked for, though certain chaplains and seneschals break the fall.

[2] See N. C. vol. v. pp. 423, 878.

[3] Mon. Angl. u. s. "Dominus noster archiepiscopus et regis curia vobis judicat quod rectitudinem regi facere debetis antequam de *vestro feodo* revestiat."

[4] Ib. "Nullus mihi hodie vel ego alicui de feodo feci verbum," says Bishop William. To which Archbishop Thomas answers, "Vobis judicat curia ista, quia de nulla re debet vos rex resaissire antequam sibi rectitudinem faciatis."

are his judges, and therefore cannot be his counsel.[1] CHAP. II.
The King now steps in; the Bishop may take counsel
with his own men, but he shall have no counsel from
any man of his.[2] The Bishop answers that, in the seven The
men whom he has with him—clearly the same seven Bishop's
of whom we have twice heard already—he will find but seven men.
little help against the power and learning of the whole
realm which he sees arrayed against him.[3] But he He goes
gets no further help; he withdraws the second time for out the
consultation, but it is only with the seven men of his time.
own following.

The result of their secret debate suggests that Bishop
William in truth took counsel with no one but himself.
Surely no seven men of English or Norman birth could
have been found to suggest the course which William
of Saint-Calais now took. For he came back to utter
words which must have sounded strange indeed either in
English or in Norman ears. "The judgement which has He comes
here been given I reject, because it is made against the back and
canons and against our law; nor was I canonically Rome.
summoned; but I stand here compelled by the force of
the King's army, and despoiled of my bishopric, beyond
the bounds of my province, in the absence of all my
comprovincial bishops. I am compelled to plead my
cause in a lay assembly; and my enemies, who refuse
me their counsel and speech and the kiss of peace, laying aside the things which I have said, judge me of
things which I have not said; and they are at once
accusers and judges; and I find it forbidden in our
law to admit such a judgement as I in my folly was

---

[1] Mon. Ang. u. s. "Episcopi sunt judices, et eos ad consilium tuum
habere non debes."

[2] Ib. "Cum tuis ibi consule, quia de nostris in consilio tuo nullum
prorsus habebis."

[3] Ib. "Parum consilii in his septem hominibus habeo contra virtutem et
scientiam totius hujus regni quod hic adversum me video congregatum."

CHAP. II. willing to admit.[1] The Archbishop of Canterbury and my own Primate ought, out of regard for God and our order, to save me of their good will from this encroachment. Because then, through the King's enmity, I see you all against me, I appeal to the Apostolic See of Rome, to the Holy Church, and to the Blessed Peter and his Vicar, that he may take order for a just sentence in my affair; for to his disposition the ancient authority of the Apostles and their successors and of the canons reserves the greater ecclesiastical causes and the judgement of bishops." [2]

Character of the appeal.

Such an appeal as this was indeed going to the root of the matter. It was laying down the rule against which Englishmen had yet to strive for more than four hundred years. William of Saint-Calais not only declared that there were causes with which no English tribunal was competent to deal, but he laid down that among such causes were to be reckoned all judgements where any bishop—if not every priest—was an accused party. Bishop William could not even claim that, as one charged with an ecclesiastical offence, he had a right to appeal to the highest ecclesiastical judge. Even such a claim as this was a novelty either in Normandy or in England; but William of Saint-Calais was not charged with any ecclesiastical offence. Except so far as the indictment involved the charge of perjury, that debateable ground of the two jurisdictions, the offence

---

[1] Mon. Angl. u. s. "In *lege nostra* prohibitum invenio, ne tale judicium suspiciam." This strange phrase, twice repeated, most likely refers to the False Decretals, of which he seems to have had a copy with him. See below, p. 109.

[2] Ib. "Apostolicam sedem Romanam, sanctam ecclesiam et beatum Petrum ejusque vicarium appello, ut ipsius ordinatione negotii mei justam sententiam suscipere merear, cujus dispositioni majores causas ecclesiasticas et episcoporum judicia antiqua apostolorum eorumque successorum atque canonum auctoritas reservavit." Yet, according to the doctrine held long after by Thomas Stubbs (see N. C. vol. iv. p. 260), the Bishop of Durham need not have gone very far to find a Vicar of Saint Peter.

laid to the Bishop's charge was a purely temporal one,
that of treason against his lord the King. So arraigned,
he refuses the judgement of the King of the English and
his Witan, and appeals from them to the Bishop of
Rome. He justifies his appeal by referring to some
law other than the law of England, some special law
of his own order, by which, he alleges, he is forbidden to submit to any such judgements as that of the
national assembly of the realm of which he is a subject.
We again instinctively ask, how would William the
Great have dealt with such an appeal, if any man had
been so hardy as to make it in his hearing? But we
again see how the ecclesiastical system which William
the Great had brought in was one which needed his
own mighty hand to guide.[1] He was indeed, in all
causes and over all persons, ecclesiastical and temporal,
within his dominions supreme. But the moment he
himself was gone, that great supremacy seems to have
fallen in pieces. Lanfranc himself, steadily as he main- Arguments
tains the royal authority throughout the dispute, seems franc.
to shrink from boldly grappling with the Bishop's claim.
Some lesser fallacies we are not surprised to find passed
over. The daring statement that the sole right of the
Bishop of Rome to judge other bishops was established by
the Apostles may perhaps have seemed less strange even
to Lanfranc than it does to us. But Lanfranc must have William's
smiled, and Thomas of York must have smiled yet more, vincials.
at the Bishop of Durham's grotesque complaint that he
was deprived of the help of his comprovincial bishops.[2]
It was a vain hope indeed, if he thought that King Malcolm would allow him the comfort of any brotherly
counsel from Glasgow or Saint Andrews. But the real

[1] See N. C. vol. iv. p. 338.
[2] Mon. Angl. u. s. "Dispoliatus episcopio extra provinciam meam, ab-
sentibus omnibus comprovincialibus meis, in laicali conventu causam meam
dicere compellor."

CHAP. II. point is that Lanfranc seems to avoid giving any direct answer to Bishop William's claim to appeal to a court beyond the sea. Instead of stoutly denying the right of any English subject to appeal to any foreign power from the judgement of the highest court in England, he falls back into Bishop William's own subtleties about "fief" and "bishopric;" and he appeals to the case of Odo, where it was only the Earl and not the Bishop who was dealt with.[1] The verbal question goes on, till the Bishop declares that he has no skill to dispute against the wisdom of Lanfranc; he has been driven to appeal to the apostolic see, and he wishes to have the leave of the King and the Archbishop to go to the see to

The Bishop goes out the third time. which he has appealed.[2] A third time does he, at Lanfranc's bidding, leave the hall while this question is debated by the King and his council. On his return the

He comes back, and sentence is pronounced. final sentence is pronounced by the mouth of Hugh of Beaumont. As the Bishop has refused to answer the charges brought against him by the King, as he invites the King to a tribunal at Rome, the Bishop's fief is declared forfeited by the judgement of the King's court and the barons. It really says a good deal for the long-suffering of the prelates and barons, and of the Red

He renews his appeal. King himself, that Bishop William again ventured to make his appeal in more offensive terms than before. He is ready, in any place where justice reigns and not violence, to purge himself of all charges of crime and perjury. He will prove in the Roman Church that the

---

[1] Mon. Ang. u. s. "Nos non de episcopio sed de tuo te feodo judicamus, et hoc modo judicavimus Baiocensem episcopum ante patrem hujus regis de feodo suo, nec rex vocabat eum episcopum in placito illo, sed fratrem et comitem."

[2] Ib. "Quia Dei gratia sapientissimus et nominatissimus estis, in hoc sapere vestrum tam sublime intelligo, quod parvitas mea illud comprehendere non potest; sed apostolicam sedem quam ex necessitate appellavi per licentiam regis et vestram adire volo."

judgement which has just been pronounced is false and CHAP. II.
unjust.[1] Hugh of Beaumont is driven to a retort; "I
and my companions are ready to confirm our judgement
in this court." The Bishop again declares that he will
enter into no pleadings in that court. Let him speak
never so well, his words are perverted by the King's partisans. They have no respect for the apostolic authority,
and, even after he has made his appeal, they load him
with an unjust judgement. He will go to Rome to seek
the help of God and of Saint Peter.[2]

Up to this time the King has taken only a secondary
part in the lively dispute which has been going on in his
presence. We have listened chiefly to the pithy sayings
of Lanfranc and to the official utterances of Hugh of
Beaumont. But now Rufus himself steps in as a chief Speeches of
the King.
speaker, and that certainly in a characteristic strain.
His patience had borne a good deal, but it was now
beginning to give way. The King's short and pointed
sentences, uttered, we must remember, with a fierce look
and a stammering tongue, are a marked contrast to the
long-turned periods and legal subtleties of the Bishop.
He now steps into the dispute from a very practical side;
"My will is that you give me up your castle, as you will
not abide by the sentence of my court."[3] More distinctions, more protests, more appeals to Rome, only
stir up the Red King to the use of his familiar oath;

[1] Mon. Ang. u. s. "In omni loco in quo non violentia sed justitia
dominetur, de scelere et perjurio me purgare paratus sum, et hoc quod hic
pro judicio recitasti in Romana ecclesia falsum et injuste dictum esse
monstrabo."

[2] Ib. "In curia ista nullum ad præsens placitum subintrabo, quia nihil
ibi tam bene dicerem quin fautores regis depravando perverterent, qui ipsam et non reverentes apostolicam auctoritatem post ejus appellationem me
judicio non legali gravant, sed Dei et Sancti Petri postulans auxilium Romam
vadam."

[3] Ib. "Tunc rex ait, 'Modo volo ut castellum tuum mihi reddas, quoniam
judicium meæ curiæ non sequeris.'"

"By the face of Lucca, you shall never go out of my hands till I have your castle." [1] The Bishop was now fairly in the mouth of the lion; yet he again goes through the whole story of his wrongs and his innocence, with some particulars which we have not hitherto heard. When his possessions were seized by the King's officers, though a hundred of his own knights looked on, no resistance had been offered to the King's will.[2] He had now nothing left but his episcopal city; if the King wished to take that, he would offer no resistance, save by the power of God. He would only warn him, on behalf of God and Saint Peter and his Vicar the Pope, not to take it. He would give hostages and sureties that, while he went to Rome, his own men should keep the castle, and that, if the King wished, they should keep it for his service.[3] The King again spoke; "Be sure, Bishop, that you shall never go to Durham, nor shall your men hold Durham, nor shall you escape my hands, unless you freely give up the castle to me." [4]

The Bishop appeals to Counts Odo and Alan. The Bishop now for once says not a word about canonical rights; he appeals, more shortly and more prudently, to the plighted faith of the two Counts who had promised that he should go back to Durham. But Lanfranc argues that the Bishop has forfeited his safe-conduct, and that, if he refuses to give up the castle, the

---

[1] Mon. Ang. i. 248. "Per vultum de Luca nunquam exibis de manibus meis donec castellum habeam."

[2] Ib. "Ego passus sum per tres servientes vestros aufferri mihi terras et pecuniam ecclesiæ, præsentibus centum meis militibus, et in nullo prorsus vobis restiti."

[3] Durham is described as "Urbs ipsa in qua sedes est ecclesiæ." The Bishop adds; "Paratus sum bonos obsides et fiducias dare vobis, quod homines mei quos ibi dum Romam vado volo dimittere in fidelitate vestra eam custodient, et, si volueritis, libenter vobis servient."

[4] "Tunc rex ait, 'In veritate credas, episcope, quod nullo modo Dunelmum reverteris et quod homines tui Dunelmi nullatenus remane-bunt, nec tu manus meas evades donec castellum tuum liberum mihi reddas.'"

King may rightly arrest him.[1]   At this hint the lay CHAP. II.
members of the Assembly joined in with one voice, the Cries of the lay members.
foremost among them being that Randolf Peverel of
whose possessions and supposed kindred we have had
elsewhere to speak.[2]   "Take him," was the cry, "take
him; for that old gaoler speaks well."[3]   But at this
stage the Bishop finds friends in the Counts whose faith
had been pledged to his safe-conduct.   Count Alan Intervention of Count Alan.
formally states the terms of the agreement, and prays
the King — Odo and Roger joining with him in the
prayer — that he may not be forced to belie his faith,
as otherwise the King should have no further service
from him.[4]   But in Lanfranc's view the second of the
two cases which were contemplated in the agreement
had taken place.   The King was not bound to let the
Bishop go back to Durham; all that he was now bound
to do was to give him ships and a safe-conduct out of
the realm.[5]   The dispute goes on in the usual style.
The Bishop continues his appeal to Rome; he again in- The Bishop appeals yet again.
vokes what he calls specially the Christian law, point-
ing, it would seem, to a volume in his own hand;[6] while

---

[1] Mon. Ang. u. s.   "Si episcopus amplius castellum suum vobis contra-
dixerit, bene eum capere potestis, quia conductum quem hactenus habuit
nunc dimittit, cum prior conventionem frangit, et barones vestros probare
appetit quod fidem suam servarent non bene."

[2] On Randolf Peverel and his alleged connexion with William, see N. C.
vol. iii. p. 662; iv. 200; v. 26.

[3] Mon. Angl. i. 248.   "Tunc Radulfus Piperellus et omnes laici unanimiter conclamantes dixerunt; 'Capite eum, capite eum, bene enim loquitur
iste vetustus ligaminarius.'"   One would like to have the original French of
this somewhat irreverent description of the Archbishop, but gaoler seems
to be the most likely meaning of the unusual word ligaminarius.

[4] Ib.   "Multum precor dominum meum regem ne fidem meam inde
faciat me mentiri, nullum enim proficuum in me haberet ulterius."

[5] Ib.   "Rex bene vos adquietavit; plenam namque rectitudinem episcopo obtulit. et ipse eam vobis audientibus recusavit, regem quoque Romam
injuste invitavit; recognoscat igitur episcopus hoc justum fecisse judicium,
et si illud sequi nollet, et rex sibi naves inveniet et conductum."

[6] "Christianam legem quam hic scriptam habeo, testem invoco."   See
above, p. 104.

CHAP. II. Lanfranc asserts the authority of the King's court.[1] The King then steps in with one of his short speeches; "You may say what you will, but you shall not escape my hands, unless you first give up the castle to me."[2] The Bishop then makes a shorter protest than usual, the drift of which seems to be that he is ready to suffer

The final sentence. any loss rather than be personally arrested.[3] The sentence of the Court is now finally passed. A day is fixed by which the Bishop's men should leave the city of Durham and the King's men take possession of it instead.[4]

The judgement of the Assembly had thus formally gone against the claims of the Bishop of Durham; but his resources were not at an end. Defeated on all points of law, he makes an appeal to the King's generosity.

The Bishop asks for an allowance. Will his lord the King, he now prays, leave him something from his bishopric on which he may at least be

Answer of Lanfranc. able to live? Lanfranc again answers; "Shall you go to Rome, to the King's hurt and to the dishonour of all of us, and shall the King leave lands to you? Stay in his land, and he will give back to you all your bishopric, except the city, on the one condition that you do right to him in his court by the judgement of his barons."[5]

---

[1] Mon. Ang. u. s. "Non est justum ut placitum vel judicium regis pro aliqua contradictione longius procedat, sed quotiens in curia sua judicium agitur, ibidem necesse est ut concedatur vel contradicatur, tu ergo judicium nostrum vel hic concede, vel hic evidenti ratione contradicito."

[2] Ib. "Rex ait, ʻDicas licet quidquid velis, non tamen effugies manus meas nisi castellum prius mihi reddas.'" The Bishop has just before spoken of "Roma, ubi debeo et ubi justitia magis quam violentia."

[3] Ib. "Cum vos non solum episcopatum, verum et omnia mea, injuste abstuleritis, et ipsam modo sedem violenter auferre velitis, pro nulla re quam facere possim capi me patiar."

[4] Ib. "Constituta est ergo dies qua episcopus urbem suis hominibus vacuaret et rex ibi suos poneret."

[5] Ib. "Tu pro regis damno et omnium nostrorum dedecore vadis Romam, et ipse tibi terram dimitteret? Remane in terra sua, et ipse episcopatum tuum præter urbem tibi reddet, ea conditione quod in curia sua judicio baronum suorum rectitudinem sibi facias."

Bishop William, almost parodying the words of a much earlier appeal to Rome, says that he has appealed to the Apostolic See, and to the Apostolic See he will go.[1] Lanfranc retorts; "If you go to Rome without the King's leave, we will tell him what he ought to do with your bishopric." Bishop William answers in a long speech, renewing his protests of innocence and his offers of purgation, and setting forth the services which he claimed to have done for the King at Dover, Hastings, and London. The Bishop many times makes his prayer, and the King as often refuses. Then Lanfranc counsels him to throw himself wholly on the King's mercy; if he will do so, he himself will plead for him at the King's feet. But the Bishop still goes on about the authority of the canons and the honour of the Church; he will earnestly pray for the King's mercy, but he will accept no uncanonical judgement. The King then makes a new proposal; "Let the Bishop give me sureties that he will do nought to my hurt on this side the sea, and that neither my brother nor any of my brother's men shall keep the ships which I shall provide to my damage or against the will of their crews."[2] It certainly was demanding a good deal to expect Bishop William to go surety for either the will or the power of Duke Robert to do or to hinder anything. The Bishop pleads that the Counts pledged their faith that he should not be obliged to enter into any agreement except the one which had been made at Durham. And the Sheriff of Yorkshire, Ralph Paganel, the same who had been the

CHAP. II.

The King's offers.

The King and Ralph Paganel.

---

[1] Mon. Ang. u. s. "Ego apostolicam sedem appellavi, quia in curia ejus nullum justum judicio audio et nullo modo dimittam quin illuc vadam."

[2] Ib. "Tunc rex ait, 'Faciat mihi episcopus fiduciam quod damnum meum citra mare non quærat vel recipiat, et quod naves meas quas sibi inveniam non detinebit frater meus vel aliquis suorum ad damnum meum contra nautarum voluntatem.'"

CHAP. II. spoiler of the Bishop's goods, bears witness that his claim was a just one.[1] By this time the wrath of the Red King was gradually kindling; he turns on the Sheriff with some sharpness; "Hold your peace; for no surety will I endure to lose my ships; but if the Bishop will give this surety which I ask, I will ask for no other."[2] The Bishop falls back on his old plea; he will enter into no agreement save that into which he entered with the Counts. The King again swears by the face of Lucca that the Bishop shall not cross the sea that year, unless he gives the required surety for the ships.[3] The Bishop then protests that, rather than be arrested, he will give the surety and more than the surety which is demanded; but he calls all men to witness that he does this unwillingly and through fear of arrest.[4] He gives the surety, and another stage in the long debate ends.

Question of the safe-conduct.

A new point, happily the last, was raised when the Bishop, having given the required surety, asked for ships and a safe-conduct. The King says that he shall have them as soon as the castle of Durham is in the King's power; till then, he shall have no safe-conduct, but shall stay at Wilton.[5] He again meekly protests; he will endure the wrong against which he has no means of

[1] Mon. Ang. u. s. "Reginaldus Paganellus ait, 'Certe comites vestri promiserunt hoc quod dicit episcopus et convenienter inde eos custodite.'" "Reginaldus" must surely be a slip for "Radulfus."

[2] Ib. "'Tace,' inquit rex, 'quia pro nullius fiducia naves meas perdere patiar, sed, si episcopus inde se fiduciam fecisse cognoverit, super illam aliam non requiram.'"

[3] Ib. "Tunc rex iratus ait, 'Per vultum de Luca, in hoc anno mare non transibis, nisi fiduciam quam de navibus requiro prius modo feceris.'"

[4] Ib. "Faciam hanc et multo majorem, si necesse fuerit, fiduciam antequam hic in captione detinear; sed bene omnes audiant quod ea invitus faciam et captionis timore coactus."

[5] Ib. "Rex ait, 'Nullum conductum habebis, sed Wiltone moraberis donec ego vere sciam quod castellum habeam in mea potestate, et tunc demum naves recipies et conductum.'" Wilton seems an odd place for the purpose; should it be "Wintonie?"

striking.[1] Then a man of Bishop Geoffrey of Coutances
steps in with a new count. The men who held the
Bishop of Durham's castle had—before the Bishop came
to the King's court; therefore, it might be inferred, with
his knowledge—taken two hundred beasts belonging to
the Bishop of Coutances which were under the King's safe-
conduct. Bishop Geoffrey had surely seen more than two
hundred beasts brought into Bristol as the spoil of loyal
men in Somerset, Gloucestershire, and Wiltshire; but he
is careful to exact the redress of his own loss from his
brother bishop and rebel. The men of the Bishop of
Durham had refused to pay the price of the beasts; they
refused even when Walter of Eyncourt—we have met him
in Lincolnshire[2]—bade them do so in the King's name;
he William, the man of Bishop Geoffrey, demands that
the price be paid to his lord.[3] The King puts it to the
barons whether he can implead the Bishop on this
charge also.[4] Lanfranc, for the first time helping his
brother prelate, rules that this cannot be done. Bishop
William cannot be impleaded any further, because he
now holds nothing of the King—the surrender of the
castle of Durham is thus held to be already made—and
is entitled to the King's safe-conduct.[5] The Assembly
now breaks up for the day; the Bishop is to choose the
haven from which he will sail, and to make known his
choice on the morrow.

The next day the Court again comes together. The

---

[1] Mon. Ang. u. s. "Cum quod vellem et deberem facere non valeam, hoc ipsum quod dicitis injuste patiar et coactus."

[2] See N. C. vol. iv. p. 215. "Walterus de Haiencora," or "Haiencorn," must be a corruption of his name.

[3] Mon. Angl. i. 249. "Precamur vos ut faciatis domino meo reddi pecuniam." The name of the speaker is given as "Willelmus de Merlao."

[4] Ib. "Rex ait, 'Videant barones isti si ego juste possum implacitare episcopum.'"

[5] Ib. "Injustum esset si amplius implacitaretis eum, cum de vobis mihi teneat et securum conductum habere debeat."

Bishop of Durham asks Count Alan to find him a haven
and ships at Southampton. The King steps in; "Know
well, Bishop, that you shall never cross the channel till
I have your castle"—adding, with a remembrance of the
doings of another prelate at Rochester—"for the Bishop
of Bayeux made me smart with that kind of thing."[1] If
the castle of Durham was in the King's hands by the
fixed day, the fourteenth day of November, the Bishop
should have the ships and the safe-conduct without further

delay. The King then bids Count Alan and the Sheriff
Gilbert[2] to give the Bishop at Southampton such ships
as might be needful for his voyage seven days after the
day fixed for the surrender of the castle. Meanwhile, on

the appointed day, the castle of Durham was received
into the King's hands by Ivo Taillebois and Erneis of
Burun—names with which we have long been familiar.[3]
They disseized the Bishop of his church and castle and
all his land; but they gave to the Bishop's men a writ
under the King's seal, promising the most perfect safety
to the Bishop and his men through all England and in
their voyage.[4] And, according to the most obvious
meaning of the narrative, Heppo, the King's *balistarius*
—a man of whom, like Ivo Taillebois, we have heard in
Lincolnshire—was put into their hands as surety for the
observance of the safe-conduct.

It might have seemed that the Bishop's troubles were
now ended, so far as they could be ended by leaving the
land which he professed to look on as a land of perse-

---

[1] Mon. Ang. u.s. "Bene scias, episcope, quod nunquam transfretabis donec
castellum tuum habeam ; episcopus enim Baiocensis inde me castigavit."

[2] Gilbert of Bretevile appears as a considerable landowner in Hampshire
(Domesday, 48) and Wiltshire (71). He may have been Sheriff of either shire.

[3] See N. C. vol. iv. pp. 215, 800. Besides Erneis himself, we have heard
of a Ralph Fitz-Erneis at Senlac, vol. iii. p. 494.

[4] Mon. Ang. u. s. "Dissaisiverunt episcopum de ecclesia et de castello
et de omni terra sua xviii. Kal. Dec., et liberaverunt hominibus episcopi
Helponem balistarium regis." The King's writ follows. *Helpo* must be
Heppo. See N. C. vol. iv. p. 216. See Appendix C.

cution. But a crowd of hindrances were put in the way of his voyage. Notwithstanding the safe-conduct given to the Bishop's men, a number of wrongs were done to them by Ivo Taillebois, whose conduct may be thought to bear out his character as drawn in the legendary history of Crowland. The great grievance was that in defiance—so men thought at Durham—of Lanfranc's judgement that Bishop William was not bound to plead in the matter of the beasts taken from the Bishop of Coutances, two of his knights were forced to plead on that charge.[1] Meanwhile the day came which had been appointed for the Bishop's voyage. He had been waiting at Wilton, under the care of a certain Robert of Conteville, who had been assigned, at his own request, to keep him from all harm.[2] The castle had been duly given up; all seemed ready for his crossing. Bishop William asked the Sheriff Gilbert and his guardian Robert for ships, to cross in the company of Robert of Mowbray.[3] Under orders from the King,[4] they kept him for five days longer, when Robert of Conteville took him to Southampton. The wind was favourable, and the Bishop craved for leave to set sail at once. The King's officers forbade him to sail that day; the next day, when the wind had become contrary, they, seemingly in mockery, gave him

[1] Mon. Ang. u.s. "Accepit Ivo Taillesbosci duos milites episcopi, et coegit eos placitare de animalibus Constantiensis episcopi de quibus judicatum fuerat ante regem Dunelmensi episcopo non debere respondere." It is of course possible that there might be some ground for impleading the knights, though not for impleading the Bishop.

[2] He had before asked; "dum in Anglia fuero, habetote mecum unum bonum hominem, qui et hospitia mihi inveniat et ab impedimento me defendat." The "good man" assigned is "Robertus de Comitisvilla." One would think that he was a kinsman of the husband of Herleva, the King's step-grandfather.

[3] *Roger* in the text; but Robert must surely be meant.

[4] Mon. Ang. u. s. "Illi responderunt se nullam sibi navem liberaturos, et dixerunt regem sibi præcepisse ut bene servarent episcopum, ne de potestate regis exiret usque quo quid de eo fieri præciperet, illis per suas sigillatas literas remandaret."

CHAP. II.

Charge against the monk Geoffrey.

leave to sail. While he waited for a favourable wind, a new charge was brought against him, founded on the alleged doings of one of his monks, Geoffrey by name, of whom we shall afterwards hear as being in his special confidence. By the sentence of forfeiture pronounced by the Court, all the Bishop's goods had become the property of the Crown. It was therefore deemed an invasion of the King's rights when, after the Bishop had gone to the King's court, Geoffrey took a large number of beasts from the Bishop's demesne. He had also taken away part of the garrison of the castle, who had killed

New summons against the Bishop.

a man of the King's. On this charge Bishop William was summoned to appear in the King's court at the Christmas Gemót to be held in London. One of the bearers of the summons was no less famous a man than Bishop Osmund of Salisbury, a man of a local reputa-

His argument with Osmund.

tion almost saintly.[1] Bishop William again appeals to the old agreement; he protests his innocence of any share in the acts of Geoffrey, though he adds that he might lawfully have done what he would with his own up to the moment when he was formally disseized.[2] These words might seem to imply that the act of Geoffrey, though done after the Bishop had left Durham, was done before the sentence was finally pronounced. But he cannot go to the King's court; he has nothing left; he has eaten his horses; that is seemingly their price.[3] He is

[1] Mon. Ang. u. s. "Venerunt ad eum Salesberiensis episcopus et Robertus de Insula et Ricardus de Cultura, et summonuerunt eum de parte regis, Kal. Decembr., ut in nativitate Domini esset Londoniæ ad curiam regis, et faceret ei rectitudinem de Gaufrido monacho suo, qui, postquam episcopus ad curiam venerat, de dominicatu episcopi quingenta et triginta novem animalia acceperat, et munitionem castelli abstulerat de quibusdam suis aliis hominibus, qui unum hominem regis occiderant." The Gemót was therefore to be at We. tminster, not in its regular place at Gloucester.

[2] Ib. "Quamvis juste facere potuissem, potui enim de meis facere quidquid volui, usquequo de mea sede me dissaisivit."

[3] Ib. "Ad curiam ejus amplius ire non possum, ipse enim omnia mea mihi abstulit, et equos meos jam venditos manducavi."

still repeatedly forbidden to cross, even alone.[1] In chap. ii.
answer to an earnest message that he might be allowed
to go to Rome, the King sent Walkelin Bishop of Win- The Bishop
chester with two companions, one of them Hugh of Port, again summoned by
a well-known Domesday name, to summon him to send Walkelin.
Geoffrey for trial to Durham and to appear himself in
London at the Christmas Gemót to answer for the deeds
of his men.[2] In defiance of all prayers and protests, the
King's officers kept the Bishop in ward night and day; in
his sadness he sent a message to the Counts who had given
him the safe-conduct, praying them by the faith of their
baptism to have him released from his imprisonment and
allowed to cross the sea.[3] They answered his appeal. Interposition of the
At their urgent prayer, the King at last let him cross. Counts.
He sailed to Normandy, where he was honourably re- He at last
ceived by Duke Robert, and—so the Durham writer crosses to
Normandy.
believed—entrusted with the care of his whole duchy.[4]
Perhaps it was owing to these new worldly cares that,
though we often hear of him again, we do not hear of
him as a suppliant at the court of Rome.

The tale of Bishop William of Durham is long, perhaps Importance of the
in some of its stages it is wearisome; but it is too story of
important a contribution to our story to be left out William of
Saint-
or cut short. It sets before us the earliest of those Calais.
debates in the King's court of which we shall come

[1] He offers, "Solus, si liceat, transfretabo."

[2] Mon. Angl. u. s. "Rex misit ei Wintoniensem episcopum et Hugonem
de Portu et Gaufridum de Traileio, et per illos sibi mandavit ut Gaufridum
monachum ad placitandum de prædictis forisfactis Dunelmum mitteret, et
ipse Londoniam iret, ut in nativitate Domini de hominibus suis ibi rectitudinem regi faceret."

[3] Ib. "Episcopus tristis misit ad comites Alanum et Rogerum et
Odonem, mandans eis impedimenta sua, et conjuravit eos per eam fidem
quam in baptismo susceperant et quam sibi promiserant."

[4] Ib. "A Roberto fratre regis comite Normannorum honorifice susceptus, totius Normanniæ curam suscepit."

CHAP. II.

Illustrations of jurisprudence.

across other memorable examples before the reign of Rufus is over. We see the forms and the spirit of the jurisprudence of England in the days immediately following the Norman Conquest, a jurisprudence which, both in its forms and its spirit, has become strongly technical, but which still has not yet become the exclusive possession of a professional class. Bishops, earls, sheriffs, are still, as of old, learned in the law, and are fully able to carry on a legal discussion in their own persons. And we see that a legal discussion in those days could be carried out with a good deal of freedom

Legal trickery of the Bishop.

of speech on all sides. As to the matter of the debate, all that we know of Bishop William, both afterwards and at this time from other sources, can leave hardly any doubt that he was simply availing himself of every legal subtlety, of every pretended ecclesiastical privilege, in order to escape a real trial in which he knew that he would have no safe ground on the merits of the case.

Reasons for proceeding against him.

And, if it be asked why the Bishop of Durham should have been picked out for legal prosecution, while his accomplices were forgiven and were actually sitting as his judges, the answer is to be found in the circumstances of the case. As we read the tale in all other accounts, as we read of it in the formal charge brought by Hugh of Beaumont, we see that there was a special treachery in Bishop William's rebellion which distinguished his case from that of all other rebels. Why he should have joined the revolt at all, how he could expect that any change could make him greater than he already was, is certainly a difficulty; but the fact seems certain, and, if it be true, it quite accounts for the special enmity with which he was now pursued. The idea of the Bishop which the story conveys to us is that of a subtle man, full of resources, well able to counterfeit innocence, and to employ the highest ecclesiastical claims as a

means to escape punishment for a civil crime. It was CHAP. II.
from the mouth of William of Saint-Calais that, for the The first appeal to
first time as far as we can see, men who were English Rome made
by birth or settlement heard the doctrine that the King by William of Saint-
of the English had a superior on earth, that the ·decrees Calais.
of the Witan of England could be rightly appealed
from to a foreign power. The later career of the
Bishop makes him a strange champion of any such
teaching. The largest charity will not allow us to give
him credit for the pure single-mindedness of Anselm, or
even for the conscious self-devotion of Thomas. We
feel throughout that he is simply using every verbal
technicality in order to avoid any discussion of the
real facts. A trial and conviction would hardly have
brought with them any harsher punishment than the
forfeiture and banishment which he actually underwent.
But it made a fairer show in men's eyes to undergo
forfeiture and banishment in the character of a persecuted confessor than to undergo the same amount of
loss in the character of a convicted traitor.

The part played by Lanfranc is eminently character- Behaviour
istic. Practically he maintains the royal supremacy on of Lan-franc ;
every point; but he makes no formal declaration which
could commit him to anti-papal theories. As for William of the King.
Rufus, one is really inclined for a long while to admire
his patience through a discussion which must have been
both wearisome and provoking, rather than to feel any
wonder that, towards the end of the day, he begins to
break out into somewhat stronger language. But in the
latter part of the story, like Henry the Second but unlike
Henry the First, he stoops from his own thoroughly good
position. He shows a purpose to take every advantage
however mean, and to crush the Bishop in any way,
fair or foul. So at least it seems in our story; but one
would like to hear the other side, as one is unwilling

CHAP. II. to fancy either Bishop Walkelin or Bishop Osmund
directly lending himself to sheer palpable wrong. But,
The lesser after all, not the least attractive part of the story is
actors.
the glimpse which it gives us of the lesser actors, some
of them men of whom we know from other sources the
mere names and nothing more. We feel brought nearer
to the real life of the eleventh century every time that
we are admitted to see a Domesday name becoming
something more than a name, to see Ralph Paganel, Hugh
of Port, and Heppo the *Balistarius* playing their parts
in an actual story. The short sharp speeches put into
the mouths of some of the smaller actors, as well as those
which are put into the mouth of the King, both add to
the liveliness of the story and increase our faith in
Conduct of its trustworthiness. As in some other pictures of the
the laity,
kind, the laity, both the great men and the general
body, stand out on the whole in favourable colours. It
not favour is perfectly plain, from Bishop William's own words,[1]
able to the
Bishop. that he had not, like Anselm and Thomas, the mass
of the people on his side. It is equally plain that
the majority of the assembly, though they certainly
gave him a fair hearing, were neither inclined to his
cause nor convinced by his arguments. And the conduct
of the Counts Alan and Odo and their companion
Roger of Poitou is throughout that of strictly honourable men, anxious to carry out to the letter every
point to which they have pledged their faith. The Red
King, having merely pledged his faith as a king, and
not in that more fantastic character in which he always
held his plighted word as sacred, is less scrupulous
on this head.

The affair of Bishop William brings us almost to
the last days of the year of the rebellion. But, much

---

[1] See above, p. 91, where he is afraid of the "indocta multitudo."

earlier in the year, events of some importance had been CHAP. II.
happening in other parts of the island. We are almost No re-
corded
tempted to take for granted that so great a stir in movement
northern England as that which accompanied the banish- in Scot-
land.
ment of the Bishop of Durham must have been accom-
panied or followed by some action on the part of King
Malcolm of Scotland. None such however is spoken
of. But the stirs on the Western border had been taken Move-
ments in
advantage of by the enemies of England on that side. Wales.
We have seen that British allies played a part on the
side of the rebels in the attack on Worcester. Further
north, independent Britons deemed that the time was
come for a renewal of the old border strife. When Earl
Hugh of Chester and the Marquess Robert of Rhuddlan
took opposite sides in a civil war, it was indeed an inviting
moment for any of the neighbouring Welsh princes. The
time seems to have been one of even more confusion than
usual among the Britons. The year after the death of State of
Wales.
the Conqueror is marked in their annals as a special time
of civil warfare, in which allies were brought by sea
from Scotland and Ireland. Rhys the son of Tewdwr, Rhys
restored by
of whom we have already heard,[1] was driven from his a fleet from
kingdom by the sons of Bleddyn, and won it again by Ireland.
the help of a fleet from Ireland.[2] Men were struck by
the vast rewards in money and captives with which he
repaid his naval allies, who are spoken of as if
some of them were still heathens.[3] These movements

---

[1] See N. C. vol. iv. pp. 502, 675.

[2] Ann. Camb. 1087. "Resus filius Teudur a regno suo expulsus est
a filiis Bledint, scilicet Madauc, Cadugan, et Ririt. Resus vero ex
Hibernia classem duxit et revertitur in Britanniam." The Brut is to
the same effect.

[3] Ib. "Ingentem censum captivorum gentilibus et Scotis filius Teudur
tradidit." The Brut for "gentiles et Scoti" has "Yscotteit ar Gúydyl,"
marking the Gwyddyl as heathen Ostmen. This is the most common use
of the word in the British writers; but we can hardly think that the Scots
here spoken of are Scots in the elder sense.

CHAP. II. are not recorded by any English or Norman writer, nor do the Welsh annals record the event with which Norman and English feeling was more deeply concerned. But there was clearly a connexion between the two. Gruffydd the son of Cynan appears in the British annals Gruffydd's as an ally of the restored Rhys,[1] and we now find a
Irish allies. King Gruffydd, not only carrying slaughter by land into the English territory, but appearing in the more unusual character of the head of a seafaring expedition. We may feel pretty sure that it was the presence of the allies from Ireland—both native Irish, it would seem, and Scandinavian settlers—which combined with the disturbed state of England to lead Gruffydd to a frightful inroad on the lands of the most cruel enemy of the
He attacks Britons, the Marquess Robert. The Welsh King and his
Rhuddlan. allies marched as far as the new stronghold of Rhuddlan; they burned much and slew many men, and carried off many prisoners, doubtless for the Irish slave-market.[2] It was clearly through this doubtless far more profitable raid on the English territory that Rhys and Gruffydd found the means of rewarding their Irish and Scandinavian allies.

Robert of　　This inroad took place while the civil war in England
Rhuddlan. was going on,[3] a war in which it must be remembered that other British warriors had borne their part.[4] While

[1] In Ann. Camb. 1082, Trahaern (see N. C. iv. 675), with others, "a Reso filio Teudur et a Grifino filio Conani occidisus est." This Gruffydd must be distinguished from Gruffydd son of Meredydd. He may be the "Grifin puer" of Domesday, 180 b. "Griffin rex" in p. 269 is surely Gruffydd son of Llywelyn.

[2] Ord. Vit. 669 B. "Grithfridus rex Guallorum cum exercitu suo fines Angliæ invasit, et circa Rodelentum magnam stragem hominum et incendia fecit, ingentem quoque prædam cepit, hominesque in captivitatem duxit."

[3] Orderic (u. s.) specially marks Gruffydd's invasion as happening "cum supradicta tempestate vehementer Anglia undique concuteretur et mutuis vulneribus incolæ regni quotidie mactarentur."

[4] See above, pp. 34, 47. Now is the time for the exploits of the grandsons of Jestyn ap Gwrgan. See N. C. vol. v. p. 822, and Appendix DD.

the lands of Rhuddlan were wasted, the Marquess Robert CHAP. II.
was busy far away at the siege of Rochester.   This would His
make us think that, like Earl Roger, he changed sides change of
early,[1] and that he was now in the royal camp, helping party.
to besiege Odo and his accomplices.   After the surrender He returns
of Rochester, the news of the grievous blow which had Wales.
been dealt to himself and his lands brought Robert back
to North Wales, wrathful and full of threats.[2]   The
enemy must by this time have withdrawn from the
neighbourhood of Rhuddlan; for we now hear of the
Marquess in the north-western corner of the land which
he had brought under his rule.   He was now in the The penin-
peninsula which ends to the north in that vast headland Dwyganwy.
which, like the other headland which ends the peninsula of Gower to the west, bears the name of the Orm's
Head.[3]   The mountain itself, thick set with remains
which were most likely ancient when Suetonius passed
by to Mona, forms a strong contrast to the flat ground
at its foot which stretches southward towards the tidal
mouth of the Conwy.   But that flat ground is broken
by several isolated hills, once doubtless, like the Head
itself, islands.   Of these the two most conspicuous, two
peaks of no great height but of marked steepness and
ruggedness, rise close together, one almost immediately
above the Conwy shore, the other landwards behind it.
They are in fact two peaks of a single hill, with a dip
between the two, as on the Capitoline hill of Rome.

[1] We have seen him among the rebels. See above, p. 34.

[2] Ord. Vit. u. s.   "Robertus Rodelenti princeps de obsidione Rofensi
rediens, et tam atroces damnososque sibi rumores comperiens, vehementer
dolens ingemuit, et terribilibus minis iram suam evidenter aperuit."

[3] Ib. 670 B.   "Tertio die Julii Grithfridus rex Guallorum cum tribus
navibus sub montem qui dicitur Hormaheva littori appulsus est."   It
needs a moment's thought to see that *Hormaheva* is *Ormesheafod*, the
Orm's Head.   Here the name bears the Scandinavian form given to it
doubtless by Northern rovers.   The *Worm's Head* in Gower, in its English
form, marks the presence of Low-Dutch settlers, whether Flemish or Saxon.

CHAP. II.

The castle
of Dwy-
ganwy. Here was the old British stronghold of Dwyganwy,
famous in early times as the royal seat of Maelgwyn,
him who is apostrophized in the lament of Gildas by the
name of the dragon—the *worm*—of the island.[1] That
stronghold had now passed into the hands of the Marquess Robert, and had been by him strengthened with
all the newly imported skill of Normandy. The castle
of Dwyganwy plays a part in every Welsh war during
the next two centuries, and we can hardly fancy that
much of Robert's work survives in the remains of buildings which are to be traced on both peaks and in the
dip between them. But it is likely that at all times
the habitable part of the castle lay between the two
peaks, while the peaks themselves formed merely mili-

Robert
at Dwy-
ganwy. tary defences. Here then Robert was keeping his head-
quarters in the opening days of July. At noon on one
of the summer days the Marquess was sleeping—between
the peaks, we may fancy, whether in any building or in
the open air. He was roused from his slumber by

Approach
of Gruf-
fydd.
July 3,
1088. stirring tidings. King Gruffydd, at the head of three
ships, had entered the mouth of the Conwy; he had
brought his ships to anchor; his pirate crews had
landed and were laying waste the country. The tide
ebbed; the ships stood on the dry land; the followers
of Gruffydd spread themselves far and wide over the
flat country, and carried prisoners and cattle to their
ships.[2] The Marquess rose; he climbed the height im-

---

[1] Ord. Vit. 670 B. "Incolis Britonibus sævo Marte repulsis, fines suos
dilatavit, et in monte Dagaunoth, qui mari contiguus est, fortissimum
castellum condidit." Orderic has clearly got hold of the right names
and the right incidents; but he has misconceived the topography.

Dwyganwy passes as the stronghold of that Maglocunus or Maelgwyn,
whom Gildas (Ep. 33) addresses as "insularis draco, multorum tyrannorum
depulsor, tam regno quam etiam vita" (cf. Nennius, c. 62, and Ann. Camb.
547, the year of his death). See Giraldus, It. Kamb. ii. 10; Descrip. Kamb.
i. 5 (where he calls it "nobile castellum "), vol. vi. pp. 136, 176.

[2] Ord. Vit. 670 C. "Interim mare fluctus suos retraxit, et in sicco litore

mediately above him, a height which looks on the flat
land, the open sea, the estuary now crowned on the
other side by Conwy with its diadem of towers, over the
inland hills, and on the Orm's Head itself rising in the
full view to the northward. He saw beneath him a
sight which might have stirred a more sluggish soul.
As King Henry had looked down on the slaughter of
his troops at Varaville,[1] so Robert, from his fortified
post of Dwyganwy, saw his men carried off in bonds
and thrown into the ships along with the sheep.[2] He
sent forth orders for a general gathering, and made ready
for an attack on the plunderers at the head of such men
as were with him at the moment. They were few; they
were unarmed; but he called on them to make their
way down the steep hillside and to fall on the plunderers on the shore before the returning tide enabled
them to carry off their booty.[3] The appeal met with
no hearty answer; the followers of the valiant Marquess pleaded their small numbers and the hard task

Eagerness of Robert.

classis piratarum stetit. Grithfridus autem cum suis per maritima discurrit,
homines et armenta rapuit, et ad naves exsiccatas festine remeavit."

[1] See N. C. vol. iii. p. 176.

[2] Ord. Vit. u. s. "Clamor vulgi Robertum meridie dormitantem ex-
citavit, eique hostilem discursum per terram suam nuntiavit. Ille vero,
ut jacebat, impiger surrexit, et mox præcones ad congregandum agmen
armatorum per totam regionem direxit. Porro ipse cum paucis bellatoribus
imparatus Guallos prosecutus est, et de vertice montis Hormohevæ, qui
nimis arduus est, captivos a piratis ligari, et in naves cum pecoribus
præcipitari speculatus est."

Orderic must surely have confounded the Orm's Head itself with the
lower hill of Dwyganwy. It is there, in or near his own castle, that
we must conceive Robert sleeping, not on the Orm's Head itself, or on any
casual point of the flat ground between the two. To climb the higher
of the two peaks of Dwyganwy would be perfectly natural, and would
give him a wide enough view over the whole country. But to conceive
him first crossing the flat, and then climbing a huge mountain for no
particular object, seems quite out of the question.

[3] Ib. "Marchisus audax, ut leo nobilis, vehementer infremuit, hominesque paucos qui secum inermes erant, ut, antequam æstus maris rediret,
super Guallos in sicco litore irruerent, admonuit."

of making their way down the steep and rocky height.[1] But Robert was not to be kept back; he still saw what was doing through the whole of the peninsular lowlands. He could not bear to let the favourable moment pass by. Without his cuirass, attended only by a single knight, Osbern of Orgères, he went down to attack the enemy on the shores of the estuary.[2] When the Britons saw him alone, with only a single companion and no defence but his shield, they gathered round him to overwhelm him with darts and arrows, none daring to attack him with the sword.[3] He still stood, wounded, with his shield bristling with missiles, but still defying his enemies. At last his wounds bore him down. The weight of the encumbered shield was too much for him; he sank on his knees[4], and commended his soul to God and His Mother. Then the enemy rushed on him with one accord; they smote off his head in sight of his followers, and fixed it as a trophy on the mast of one of the ships.[5] Men saw all this from the hilltop with grief and rage; but they could give no help.

Death of Robert.

[1] Ord. Vit. 670 C. "Prætendunt suorum paucitatem, et per ardui montis præcipitium descendendi difficultatem."

[2] Ib. "Nimis doluit, impatiensque moræ per difficilem descensum sine lorica cum uno milite nomine Osberno de Orgeriis, ad hostes descendit." I cannot identify this Osbern, unless he be "Osbernus filius Tezonis," who in Domesday (267 b, 268 b) holds a good deal of land in Cheshire under Earl Hugh, but none seemingly under Robert himself. For Orgères see Stapleton, ii. lxxxv.

[3] Ib. 670 D. "Quem cum viderent solo clypeo protectum et uno tantum milite stipatum, omnes pariter in illum missilia destinant, et scutum ejus jaculis intolerabiliter onerant, et egregium militem letaliter vulnerant. Nullus tamen, quamdiu stetit et parmam tenuit, ad eum comminus accedere, vel eum ense impetere ausus fuit." Cf. the account of the death of Siccius in Dion. Hal. xi. 26. He has an ὑπασπιστής to play the part of Osbern of Orgères.

[4] Ib. "Bellicosus heros spiculis confossus genua flexit, et scutum missilibus nimis onustum viribus effœtus dimisit."

[5] Ib. "In conspectu suorum caput ejus abscindunt ac super malum navis pro signo victoriæ suspendunt."

A crowd came together on the shore; but it was too late; the lord of Rhuddlan was already slain. By this time the invaders were able to put to sea, and the followers of Robert were also able to get their ships together and follow them. They followed in wrath and sorrow, as they saw the head of their chief on the mast.[1] Gruffydd must have felt himself the weaker. He ordered the head to be taken down and cast into the sea. On this the pursuers gave up the chase; they took up the body of the slain Marquess, and, amidst much grief of Normans and English,[2] buried him in Saint Werburh's minster at Chester.[3]

His burial at Chester.

We are well pleased to have preserved to us this living piece of personal anecdote, which reminds us for a moment of the deaths of Harold and of Hereward. Its preservation we doubtless owe to the connexion of Robert of Rhuddlan with the house of Saint Evroul. Otherwise we might have known no more of the conqueror of North Wales than we can learn from the entries in Domesday which record his possessions.[4] But Robert, nephew of Hugh of Grantmesnil, had enriched his uncle's foundation with estates in England, and in the city of Chester itself.[5] He was therefore

Connexion of Robert with Saint Evroul.

---

[1] Ord. Vit. 670 D. "Classe parata piratas per mare fugientes persequebantur nimis tristes, dum caput principis sui super malum puppis intuebantur."

[2] Ib. 671 A. "Cum nimio luctu Anglorum et Normannorum." This may be well believed. Normans and English soon forgot their own differences in warfare with the Welsh.

[3] But Orderic has forgotten his dates when he says, "Nuper illud coenobium Hugo Cestrensis consul construxerat, eique Ricardus Beccensis monachus abbas praeerat." We shall see as we go on that the monks were not planted at Saint Werburh's till 1092 (see N. C. vol. iv. pp. 312, 491). It is now that Orderic speaks of the "belluini coetus"—we are not told whether they were Norman, English, or Welsh—among whom Abbot Richard had to labour.

[4] See N. C. vol. iv. p. 489.

[5] His gifts in lands, tithes, and villains, in Normandy and in England, are reckoned up by Orderic, 669 C, D. Among them was "in civitate Cestra ecclesiam sancti Petri de mercato et tres hospites."

CHAP. II. not allowed to sleep for ever in the foreign soil of Chester. He had a brother Arnold, a monk of Saint Evroul, zealous in all things for his house, who had begged endless gifts for it from his kinsfolk in Eng-

His translation to Saint Evroul.

land, Sicily, and elsewhere. Some years after Robert's death, Arnold came to England, and, by the leave of Bishop Robert of Chester or Coventry—Bishop of the Mercians in the phrase of the monk who was born in his diocese—translated the body of Robert to the minster of Saint Evroul. There a skilful painter, Reginald surnamed Bartholomew—most likely a monk who had taken the apostolic name on entering religion—was employed to adorn the tomb of Robert and the arch which sheltered it with all the devices of his art.[1]

Orderic writes his epitaph.

And the English monk Vital—we know him better by his English and worldly name—was set to compose the epitaph of one who had in some sort, like himself, passed from Mercia to Saint Evroul.[2] In his history Orderic deemed it his duty to brand Robert's dealings with the Welsh as breaches of the natural law which

Its character.

binds man to man.[3] And it may be that something of the same feeling peeps out in the words of the epitaph itself, which prays with unusual fervour for the forgiveness of Robert's sins.[4] Yet in the verses which record his acts, his campaigns against the Briton appear as worthy exploits alongside of his zeal for holy things and his special love for the house of Ouche. It is not

---

[1] Ord. Vit. 671 B. "Rainaldus pictor, cognomento Bartolomæus, variis coloribus arcum tumulumque depinxit."

[2] Ib. "Vitalis Angligena satis ab Ernaldo rogatus epitaphium elegiacis versibus hoc modo edidit."

[3] See N. C. vol. iv. p. 490.

[4] Ord. Vit. 672 A ;

"Eripe tartareis Robertum, Christe, camœnis [caminis] ;
Est nimis ipse reus; terge, precor, facinus ; "

with four more lines to the same effect.

easy to track out all these exploits, even in the narrative of Orderic himself, much less in the annals of
Robert's British enemies. But all the mightiest names
of the Cymry are set forth in order, as having felt the
might of the daring Marquess. He had built Rhuddlan
and had guarded it against the fierce people of the land.
He had ofttimes crossed beyond Conwy and Snowdon
in arms. He had put King Bleddyn to flight and had
won great spoil from him. He had carried off King Howel
as a prisoner in bonds. He had taken King Gruffydd
and had overthrown Trahaern. That Howel, his former
captive, should rejoice at his fall is in no way wonderful; but the epitaph speaks further of the treachery
of a certain Owen, of which there is no mention in the
prose narrative.[1] In any case Robert of Rhuddlan
stands out as one of the mightiest enemies of the
Northern Cymry, and the tale of his end is one of the
most picturesque in this reign of picturesque incidents.

The rebellion was now over, and the new King was
firm upon his throne. And with the rebellion, the last
scene, as we have already said, of the Norman Conquest

End of the
Norman
Conquest.

---

[1] Ord. Vit. 671 C, D.

> " Montem Snaudunum fluviumque citum Colvenum,
>   Pluribus armatis transiliit vicibus.
> Præcipuam pulcro Blideno rege fugato
>   Prædam cum paucis cepit in insidiis.
> Duxit captivum lorisque ligavit Hoëllum
>   Qui tunc Wallensi rex præerat manui.
> Cepit Grithfridum regem vicitque Trehellum ;
>   Sic micuit crebris militiæ titulis.
> Attamen incaute Wallenses ausus adire,
>   Occidit æstivi principio Julii.
> Prodidit Owenius, rex est gavisus Hovellus ;
>   Facta vindicta monte sub Hormaheva.
> Ense caput secuit Grithfridus, et in mare jecit,
>   Soma quidem reliquum possidet hunc loculum."

The exploits of Robert fully entitled him to Orderic's pet Greek word.
"Colvenus" must be some corrupt form of *Conwy*.

CHAP. II. was over also. Englishmen and Normans had, for the last time under those names, met in open fight on English soil. Whether of the two had won the victory? Such a question might admit of different answers when the Norman King vanquished the Norman nobility at the head of the English people. In one sense the Conquest was confirmed; in another sense it was undone. Men must have felt that the Conquest was undone, that the *wergeld* of those who fell two-and-twenty years back was indeed paid, when the second Norman host that strove to land on the beach of Pevensey, instead of marching on to Hastings, to Senlac, to London, and to York, was beaten back from the English coast by the arms of Englishmen. They must have felt that it was undone, when the castles on which Englishmen looked as the darkest badges of bondage were stormed by an English host, gathered together at the same bidding which had gathered men together to fight at Sherstone and at Stamfordbridge. He must have been *Nithing* indeed who did not feel that the wrongs of many days were paid for, when the arch-oppressor, the most loathed of all his race, came forth with downcast looks to meet the jeers and curses of the nation on which he had trampled. Days like the day of Tunbridge, the day of Pevensey, and the day of Rochester, are among the days which make the heart of a nation swell higher for their memory. They were days on which the Englishman overcame the Norman, days which ruled that he who would reign over England must reign with the good will of the English people. The fusion of Normans and English was as yet far from being brought to perfection; indeed nothing could show more clearly than those days that the gap between the two nations still yawned in all its fulness. But nothing did more than the work of those days at once to fill up the gap and to rule in what

The Conquest confirmed and undone.

How far undone.

Tendencies to union.

way it should be filled up. Those days showed that the CHAP. II. land was still an English land, that the choice of its ruler rested in the last resort with the true folk of the land. Those days ruled that Normans and English should become one people; but they further ruled, if there could be any doubt about the matter, that they were to become one people by the Normans becoming Englishmen, not by the English becoming Normans. It is significant that, in recording the next general rebellion, the Chronicler no longer marks the traitors as "the richest Frenchmen that were on this land;" they are simply "the head men here on land who took rede together against the King." [1]

But, if in this way the Conquest was undone, if it was How far confirmed. ruled that England was still to be England, in another way the Conquest was confirmed. The English people showed that the English crown was still theirs to bestow; but at the same time they showed that they had no longer a thought of bestowing it out of the house of their Conqueror. When the English people came to-The Norman dynasty accepted. gether at the bidding of the Conqueror's son, when they willingly plighted their faith to him and called on him, as King of the English, to trust himself to English loyalty, they formally accepted the Conquest, so far as it took the form of a change of dynasty. Men pressed to fight for King William against the pretender Robert; not a voice was raised for Eadgar or Wulf or Olaf of Denmark. The stock of the Bastard of Falaise was received as the *cynecyn* of England, instead of the stock of Cerdic and Woden; for there must have

---

[1] We have seen that, in describing the rebellion of 1088, the words of the Chronicler are, "þa riceste Frencisce men þe weron innan þisan lande wolden swican heora hlaforde þam cynge." In 1101 we read simply, "þa sona þæræfter wurdon þa heafod men her on lande wiðerræden togeanes þam cynge."

CHAP. II. been few indeed who remembered that William the Red, unlike his father, unlike Harold, unlike Cnut, did come of the stock of Cerdic and Woden by the spindle-side.[1] And, in admitting the change of dynasty, all was admitted which the change of dynasty immediately implied. Men who accepted the son could not ask for the wiping out of the acts of the father. They could not ask for a new confiscation and a new Domesday the other way. In accepting the son of the Conqueror, they also accepted

Acceptance of the Norman nobility in an English character.
the settlement of the Conqueror. His earls, his bishops, his knights, his grantees of land from Wight to Cheviot, were accepted as lawful owners of English lands and offices. But the very acceptance implied that they could hold English lands and offices only in the character of Englishmen, and that that character they must now put on.

In this way the reign of William Rufus marks a stage in the developement or recovery of English nationality and freedom. And yet at the time the days of Rufus

Rufus' breach of his promises.
must have seemed the darkest of all days. No reign ever began with brighter promises than the real reign of William the Red; for we can hardly count his reign as really beginning till the rebellion was put down. No reign ever became blacker. No king was ever more distinctly placed on his throne by the good will of his people. No other king was ever hated as William Rufus lived to be hated. No other king more utterly and shamefully broke the promises of good government by

Englishmen not oppressed as such;
which he had gained his crown. And yet we may doubt whether William Rufus can be fairly set down as an oppressor of Englishmen, in the sense which those words would bear in the mouths of a certain school of writers. His reign is rather a reign of general wrong-doing, a reign of oppression which regarded no distinctions of

[1] See N. C. vol. ii. p. 308.

race, rank, or order, a time when the mercenary soldier,
of whatever race, did what he thought good, and when
all other men had to put up with what he thought good.
In such a state of things the burthen of oppression would but the
undoubtedly fall by far the most heavily upon the native general
English ; they would be the class most open to suffering touches
and least able to obtain redress. The broken promises them most.
of the King had been specially made to them, and they
would feel specially aggrieved and disheartened at his
breach of them. Still the good government which Rufus
promised, but which he did not give, was a good government which would have profited all the King's men, French
and English, and the lack of it pressed, in its measure, on
all the King's men, French and English. There is at least
nothing to show that, during the reign of Rufus, Englishmen, as Englishmen, were formally and purposely picked
out as victims. We must further remember that no legal
barrier parted the two races, and that the legal innovations of the reign of Rufus, as mainly affecting the King's
military tenants, bore most hardly on a class which was
more largely Norman than English. On the other hand, Rufus
it is certain that native Englishmen did sometimes, if and the
rarely, rise to high places, both ecclesiastical and tem- English.
poral, in the days of Rufus. Of the many stories current
about this king, not above one or two throw any light
on his relations to the native English class of his subjects.
The one saying of his that bears on the subject savours
of good-humoured banter rather than of dislike or even
contempt.[1] On the whole, dark as is the picture given
us of the reign of Rufus, we cannot look on it as having

---

[1] I refer to the passage which I have already quoted in N. C. vol. v. p.
830, where William Rufus, just before his death (Ord. Vit. 782 B), mocks
at the English regard for omens ; "Num prosequi me ritum autumat
Anglorum, qui pro sternutatione et somnio vetularum dimittunt iter suum
seu negotium?"

CHAP. II.

The merce-
naries.

at all turned back or checked the course of national advance. When mercenary soldiers have the upper hand, they are sure to be chosen rather from strangers of any race than from natives of the land of any race. There is indeed no reason to think that either a native Englishman or a man of Norman descent born in England would, if he were strong, brave, and faithful, be shut out from the Red King's military family. The eye of Rufus must have been keen enough to mark many an act of good service done on the shore of Pevensey or beneath the stronghold of Rochester. But all experience shows that the tendency of such military families is to recruit themselves anywhere rather than among the sons of the soil. And nothing draws the sons of the soil more closely together than the presence of strangers on

Their
favour
helps the
fusion of
races.

the soil. In their presence they learn to forget any mutual grievances against one another. In after times Normans and English drew together against Brabançons and Poitevins. We may feel sure that they did so from the beginning, and that the reign of Rufus really had its share in making ready the way for the fusion of the two races, by making both races feel themselves fellow-sufferers in a time of common wrong-doing.

The rebellion and its suppression, the affairs of the Bishop of Durham, and the striking episode by the Orm's Head, fill up the first stirring year of the Red King. But the year of the rebellion is also marked by one or two ecclesiastical events, which throw some light on the state of things in the early days of Rufus, while he still had

Sale of ec-
clesiastical
offices.

Lanfranc to his guide. The great ecclesiastical crimes of the Red King in his after days were the bestowal of bishoprics and abbeys for money, and the practice of keeping them vacant for his own profit. Of these two abuses, the former seems to have been the earlier in date. The keeping prelacies vacant was one of the chap. ii. devices of Randolf Flambard, and it could hardly Prolonging of vacan- have been brought into play during the very first cies. year of Rufus. The influence of Lanfranc too would be powerful to hinder so public an act as the keeping vacant of a bishopric or abbey; it would be less powerful to hinder a private transaction on the King's part which might be done without the Primate's know-ledge. Add to this, that, while the filling a church or keeping it vacant was a matter of fact about which there could be no doubt, the question whether the King had or had not received a bribe was a matter of surmise and suspicion, even when the surmise and suspicion hap-pened to be just. It is then not wonderful that we find Rufus charged with corrupt dealings of this last kind at a very early stage of his reign. We have seen Case of Thurstan of Glaston- bury. that Thurstan, the fierce Abbot of Glastonbury, was, by one of the first acts of Rufus, restored to the office which he had so unworthily filled, and from which the Conqueror had so worthily put him aside. And we have seen that it was at least the general belief that his restoration was brought about by a lavish gift to the King's hoard.[1] But three prelacies, two bishoprics and a great abbey, which either were vacant at the moment of the Conqueror's death or which fell vacant very soon after, were filled without any unreasonable delay. Stigand, Bishop of Chichester, died about the Geoffrey Bishop of Chichester; time of the Conqeror's death, whether before or after, and his see was filled by his successor before the end of the year.[2] Geoffrey's own tenure was short; he dies Sep- tember 25, 1088. died in the year of the rebellion, and, as his see did

---

[1] See N. C. vol. iv. p. 393.

[2] Stigand appears in the list of deaths which accompanied that of William in the Chronicle, where one would think that the persons spoken of died after him; but in the less rhetorical account of the same year

CHAP. II.

Death of
Scotland
of Saint
Augus-
tine's
and Ælf-
sige of
Bath.

Death of
Bishop
Gisa.
1088.

The bishop-
ric of
Somerset
granted to
John of
Tours.

He removes
the see to
Bath.

then remain vacant three years, we may set that down as the beginning of the evil practice.[1] About the same time died Scotland Abbot of Saint Augustine's, and the English Ælfsige, who still kept the abbey of Bath.   Not long after died Ælfsige's diocesan, the Lotharingian Gisa, who had striven so hard to bring in the Lotharingian discipline among his canons of Wells.[2] The bishopric of the Sumorsætan was thus among the first sees which fell to the disposal of William the Red, and his disposal of it led to one of the most marked changes in its history. The bishopric was given to John, called *de Villula*, a physician of Tours, one of the men of eminence whom the discerning patronage of William the Great had brought from lands alike beyond his island realm and beyond his continental duchy.   John was a trusty counsellor of the Red King, employed by him in many affairs, and withal a zealous encourager of learning.[3] But he had little regard to the traditions and feelings of Englishmen, least of all to those of the canons of Wells.   Like Hermann, Remigius, and other bishops of his time, he carried out the policy of transferring episcopal sees to the chief towns of their dioceses.   But the way in which he carried out his scheme, if not

in Florence they seem to have died before him. The Life of Lanfranc at the end of the Chronicles records the consecrations and benediction of all the three prelates with whom we are concerned, Geoffrey, Guy, and John, in 1088 ; "Cantuariæ, in sede metropoli, examinavit atque sacravit." Cf. Gervase, X Scriptt. 1654.

[1] See Stephens' Memorials of Chichester, p. 47.

[2] See N. C. vol. ii. p. 459.

[3] Will. Malms. Gest. Pont. 195 draws a curious picture of him ; "Erat medicus probatissimus, non scientia sed usu, ut fama, nescio an vera, dispersit. Litteratorum contubernio gaudens, ut eorum societate aliquid sibi laudis asciaceret ; salsioris tamen in obloquentes dicacitatis quam gradus ejus interesse deberet." He had just before described him as "natione Turonicus, professione medicus, qui non minimum quæstum illo conflaverat artificio." The local writer in the Historiola (21) calls him " vir prudens et providus."

exactly like the violent inroad of Robert of Limesey
on the church of Coventry,[1] was at least like the first
designs of Hermann on the church of Malmesbury,
which had been thwarted by the interposition of Earl
Harold.[2] The change was made in a perfectly orderly
manner, but by the secular power only. The abbey of
Bath was now vacant by the death of its abbot Ælfsige.
Bishop John procured that the vacant post should be
granted to himself and his successors for the increase of
the bishopric of Somerset. This was done by a royal
grant made at Winchester soon after the suppression
of the rebellion, and confirmed somewhat later in a
meeting of the Witan at Dover.[3] John then transferred
his *bishopsettle* from its older seat at Wells to the church
which had now become his. He next procured a grant Grant of
of the temporal lordship of the "old borough," which the tempo-
was perhaps of less value after its late burning by ship. ral lord-
Robert of Mowbray.[4] Thus, in the language of the time,
Andrew had to yield to Simon, the younger brother to
the elder.[5] That is, the church of Saint Peter at Bath,
with its Benedictine monks, displaced the church of
Saint Andrew at Wells, with its secular canons freshly
instructed in the rule of Chrodegang, as the head church
of the bishopric of Somerset. The line of the independent abbots of Bath came to an end; their office was
merged in the bishopric, by the new style of Bishop
of Bath. Thus the old Roman city in a corner of the
land of the Sumorsætan, which has never claimed the
temporal headship of that land, became for a while
the seat of its chief pastor.

[1] See N. C. vol. iv. p. 417.   [2] See N. C. vol. ii. p. 411.
[3] See Appendix F.   [4] See above, p. 41.
[5] Will. Malms. Gest. Pont. 196. "Cessit Andreas Simoni, frater fratri,
minor majori." Yet before the west front of the church of Wells there can
be no doubt who was there looked on as the very chiefest apostle.

CHAP. II.
The change
made
wholly by
the civil
authority.
That so great an ecclesiastical change should be wrought by the authority of the King and his Witan—perhaps in the first instance by the King's authority only—shows clearly how strong an ecclesiastical supremacy the new king had inherited from his father and his father's English predecessors. By the authority of the Great Council of the realm, but without any licence from Pope or synod, an ancient ecclesiastical office was abolished, the constitution of one church was altered, and another was degraded from its rank as an episcopal see. The change was made, so says the Red King's charter, for the good of the Red King's soul, and for the profit of his kingdom and people. It is more certain that it was eminently distasteful to both the ecclesiastical bodies which were immediately concerned. The treatment which they met with illustrates the absolute power which the bishops of the eleventh century exercised over their monks and canons, but which so largely passed away from them in the course of the twelfth. To the canons of Wells Bishop John was as stern a master or conqueror as Bishop Robert was to the monks of Coventry. They were deprived of their revenues, deprived of the common buildings which had been built for them by Gisa, and left to live how they might in the little town which had sprung up at the bishop's gate.[1] To the English monks of Offa's house at Bath the new bishop was hardly gentler; he deemed them dolts and barbarians, and cut short their revenues and allowances. It was not till he was surrounded by a more enlightened company of monks of his own choosing that he began to restore something for the relief of their poor estate.[2] But in his architectural works he was magnificent. His long reign of thirty-four years

Dislike to
the change
on the part
of the
canons of
Wells

---

[1] See Appendix F.　　　　　　　　　　[2] See Appendix F.

allowed him, not only to begin, but seemingly to finish, CHAP. II.
the great church of Saint Peter of Bath, of which a few
traces only remain, and the nave only of which is represented by the present building.[1] And though, since the The church
days of Ælfsige, there has never been an Abbot of Bath called
distinct from the Bishop, yet *abbey*, and not *minster* or *abbey*.
cathedral, is the name by which the church of Bath is
always known to this day.[2]

The disturbances at Saint Augustine's which followed Disturb-
the death of Abbot Scotland, and the chief features of the ap-
which have been described elsewhere, must have taken pointment
place earlier in the year. For the appointment or in- Saint Au-
trusion of Guy took place while Odo was still acting as gustine's.
Earl of Kent.[3] But the great outbreak, in which the
citizens of Canterbury took part with the monks against
the Abbot, did not happen till after the death of Lanfranc. Then monks and citizens alike made an armed
attack on Guy, and hard fighting, accompanied by many
wounds and some deaths, was waged between them and
the Abbot's military following.[4] The Abbot himself Flight of
escaped only by fleeing to the rival house of Christ Guy.
Church. Then came two Bishops, Walkelin of Win-

---

[1] Will. Malms. 195. "Sepultus est in ecclesia sancti Petri, quam a
fundamentis erexerat, magno et elaborato parietum ambitu."

[2] The like usage is still more remarkable at Durham and Carlisle,
churches which never had an abbot distinct from the bishop. At Carlisle
the "abbey" seems to mean the monastic precinct rather than the church
itself.

[3] See N. C. vol. iv. p. 409. The story is told in the Winchester Appendix to the Chronicles.

[4] Chron. Wint. App. 1089. " Post ejus [Lanfranci] obitum, monachi sancti
Augustini, præfato abbati suo Widoni palam resistentes, cives Cantuariæ
contra eum concitaverunt, qui illum armata manu in sua domo interimere
temptaverunt. Cujus familia cum resisteret, pluribus utrimque vulneratis
et quibusdam interfectis, vix abbas inter manus illorum illæsus evasit,
et ad matrem ecclesiam, quærendo auxilium, *Cantuariam, fugit*." This
last odd expression must be owing to the fact that Saint Augustine's stood
outside the walls.

CHAP. II. chester and Gundulf of Rochester, accompanied by some lay nobles, with the King's orders to punish the of-

Punishment of the rebellious monks.

fenders. The monks were scourged; but, by the intercession of the Prior and monks of Christ Church, the discipline was inflicted privately with no lay eyes to behold.[1] They were then scattered through different monasteries, and twenty-four monks of Christ Church, with their sub-prior Anthony as Prior, were sent to

Punishment of the citizens.

colonize the empty cloister of Saint Augustine's.[2] The doom of the citizens was harder; those who were found guilty of a share in the attack on the Abbot lost their eyes.[3] The justice of the Red King, stern as it was, thus drew the distinction for which Thomas of London strove in after days. The lives and limbs of monastic offenders were sacred.

§ 3. *The Character of William Rufus.*

Death of Lanfranc. May 24, 1089.

The one great event recorded in the year after the rebellion was the death of Archbishop Lanfranc, an

[1] Chron. Wint. App. "Coram populo subire disciplinam, quia palam peccaverant, ii qui advenerant, decreverunt; sed prior et monachi ecclesiæ Christi, pietate moti, restiterunt; ne, si palam punirentur, infames deinceps fierent, sicque eorum vita ac servitus contemneretur. Igitur concessum est ut in ecclesia fieret, ubi non populus, sed soli ad hoc electi admitterentur."

Thierry, who of course colours the whole story after his fashion, becomes (ii. 140) not a little amusing at this point. The flogging was done by two monks of Christ Church, "Wido et Normannus." If one stopped to think of matters of nationality at such a moment, we might admire the impartiality of the Norman bishops in entrusting the painful duty to a monk of each nation, somewhat on the principle of a mixed jury. For no one can doubt that Normannus, *Northman*, was as good an Englishman as Northman the son of Earl Leofwine and other English bearers of that name. Thierry, on the other hand, tells us that the whipping was done by "deux religieux étrangers, appelés Guy et Le Normand." He seemingly mistook the Christian name "Normannus" for the modern surname "Lenormand," and he forgot that this last could be borne only by one whose forefathers had moved from Normandy to some other French-speaking land.

[2] Chron. Wint. App.   [3] Ib. See N. C. vol. iv. p. 410.

event at once important in itself, and still more important in the effect which it had on the character of
William Rufus, and in its consequent effect on the general
march of events. The removal of a man who had played
so great a part in all affairs since the earliest days
of the Conquest, who had been for so many years, both
before and after the Conquest, the right hand man of
the Conqueror, was in itself no small change. For
good or for evil, the Lombard Primate had left his
mark for ever on the Church and realm of England.
One of the abetters of the Conquest, the chief instrument of the Conqueror, he had found the way to the
good will of the conquered people, with whom and with
whose land either his feelings or his policy led him
freely to identify himself.[1] It must never be forgotten
that, if Lanfranc was a stranger in England, he was no
less a stranger in Normandy. As such, he was doubtless better able to act as a kind of mediator between
the Norman King and the English people ; he could do
somewhat, if not to lighten the yoke, at least to make
it less galling. In the last events of his life we have
seen him act as one of the leaders in a cause which was
at once that of the English people and of the Norman
King. We have seen too some specimens of his worldly
wisdom, of his skill in fence and debate. An ecclesiastical statesman rather than either a saint or strictly
a churchman, it seems rather a narrow view of him
when the national Chronicler sends him out of the
world with the hope that he was gone to the heavenly
kingdom, but with the special character of the venerable father and patron of monks.[2] His primacy of

[1] See Lanfranc, Ep. 67 (i. 80, ed. Giles) ; N. C. vol. iv. p. 439.

[2] Chron. Petrib. 1089. "On þisum geare se arwurða muneca feder and
frouer Landfranc arcebisceop gewat of þissum life, ac we hopiað þæt he ferde
to þæt heofanlice rice."

CHAP. II.

His burial at Christ Church.

nearly nineteen years ended in the May of the year following the rebellion.[1] He was buried in the metropolitan church of his own rebuilding, and, when his shorter choir gave way to the grander conceptions of the days of his successor, the sweet savour that came from his tomb made all men sure that the pious hope of the Chronicler had been fulfilled.[2]

Lanfranc was borne to his grave amid general sorrow.[3] But the sorrow might have been yet deeper, if men had known the effect which his death would have

Change for the worse in the King's character.

on the character of the King and his reign. Up to this time the worst features of the character of William Rufus had not shown themselves in their fulness. As long as his father lived, as long as Lanfranc lived, he had in some measure kept them in check. We need not suppose any sudden or violent change. It is the manifest exaggeration of a writer who had his own reasons for drawing as favourable a picture as he could of the Red King, when we are told that, as long as Lanfranc lived, he showed himself, under that wholesome influence, the perfect model of a ruler.[4] There

[1] The exact date comes from his Life, 52 (i. 312, ed. Giles); "anno archiepiscopatus xix, v. calendas Junii diem clausit extremum." The Latin Chronicler gives us the exact measure of his primacy; "In sede pontificali sedit annis decem et octo, mensibus ix. duobus diebus." The Life gives us his epitaph, which begins;

"Hic tumulus claudit quem nulla sub orbe Latino
　　　Gens ignoravit."

See N. C. vol. ii. p. 636.

[2] Vita Lanfranci, 52 (i. 312, ed. Giles). "Cum immineret dies ipsius dedicationis, sicut mos est, omnia corpora de ecclesia elata fuerunt. Tunc quidam frater, sive curiositate, seu quod magis credibile est, pro reliquiis habendam de casula gloriosi Lanfranci abscidit particulam; de qua miri odoris suavitas efflagrabat. Ostendit aliis, qui et ipsi senserunt odoris fragrantiam. Qua de re intellegi datur, quod anima illius in magna suavitate requiescit; cujus corporis indumenta tanto odore redolent."

[3] Vita Lanf. ib. "Dolor omnibus incomparabilis, et luctus inconsolabilis suis."

[4] See the passages from William of Malmesbury quoted in Appendix G.

can be no doubt that, while Lanfranc yet lived, William
Rufus began to cast aside his fetters, and to look on his
monitor with some degree of ill will.   The Primate had
already had to rebuke him for breach of the solemn promises of his coronation, and it was then that he received the
characteristic and memorable answer that no man could
keep all his promises.   But there is no reason to doubt
that the death of Lanfranc set Rufus free from the last
traces of moral restraint.[1] His dutiful submission to
his father had been the best feature in his character;
and it is clear that some measure of the same feeling
extended itself to the guardian to whose care his father,
both in life and in death, had entrusted him.   But now
he was no longer under tutors and governors; there was
no longer any man to whom he could in any sense look
up.   He was left to his own devices, or to the counsels of men whose counsels were not likely to improve
him.   It was not a wholesome exchange when the
authority of Lanfranc and William the Great was exchanged for the cunning service of Randolf Flambard and
the military companionship of Robert of Bellême.

As soon then as Lanfranc was dead, William Rufus
burst all bounds, and the man stood forth as he was, or
as his unhappy circumstances had made him.   We may
now look at him, physically and morally, as he is drawn
in very elaborate pictures by contemporary hands.   William, the third son of the Conqueror, was born before
his father came into England ; but I do not know that
there is any evidence to fix the exact year of his birth.

---

[1] Eadmer, Hist. Nov. 14. "Cum posthac in regno fuisset confirmatus,
postposita pollicitatione sua, in contraria dilapsus est. Super quo cum a
Lanfranco modeste redargueretur, et ei sponsio fidei non servatæ oppone-
retur, furore succensus, 'Quis,' ait, 'est qui cuncta quæ promittit implere
possit?' Ex hoc igitur non rectis oculis super pontificem intendere valebat, licet a nonnullis ad quæ illum voluntas sua trahebat, ipsius respectu,
eo superstite, temperaverit."

He is spoken of as young[1] at the time of his accession,
and from the date of the marriage of the Conqueror and
Matilda, it would seem likely that their third son would
then be about twenty-seven years of age. He would
therefore be hardly thirty at the time of the death of
Lanfranc. The description of his personal appearance

is not specially inviting. In his bodily form he seems,
like his brother Robert,[2] a kind of caricature of his
father, as Rufus, though certainly not Robert, was also
in some of his moral and mental qualities. He was a
man of no great stature, of a thick square frame, with
a projecting stomach. His bodily strength was great;
his eye was restless; his speech was stammering, especially when he was stirred to anger. He lacked the power
of speech which had belonged to his father and had even
descended to his elder brother; his pent-up wrath or
merriment, or whatever the momentary passion might be,
broke out in short sharp sentences, often showing some

readiness of wit, but no continued flow of speech. He
had the yellow hair of his race, and the ruddiness of
his countenance gave him the surname which has stuck
to him so closely. The second William is yet more emphatically the Red King than his father is either the
Bastard or the Conqueror. Unlike most other names
of the kind, his surname is not only used by contemporary writers, but it is used by them almost as a proper
name.[3] Up to the time of his accession, he had played no
part in public affairs; in truth he had no opportunity of

---

[1] See above, p. 25.

[2] Will. Malms. iv. 321. "Si quis desiderat scire corporis ejus qualitatem,
noverit eum fuisse corpore quadrato, colore rufo, crine subflavo, fronte
fenestrata, oculo vario, quibusdam intermicantibus guttis distincto; præ-
cipuo robore, quamquam non magnæ staturæ, et ventre paullo projectiore.
Eloquentiæ nullæ, sed titubantia linguæ notabilis, maxime cum ira succres-
ceret." Cf. the description of Robert, N. C. vol. iv. p. 633.

[3] So for instance Orderic (667 B); "Rex ergo Rufus indigenarum hortatu

playing any. The policy of the Conqueror had kept CHAP. II.
his sons dependent on himself, without governments or
estates.[1] We have a picture of Rufus in his youthful Rufus in
days, as the young soldier foremost in every strife, who youth.
deemed himself disgraced, if any other took to his arms
before himself, if he was not the first to challenge an
enemy or to overthrow any enemy that challenged his
side.[2] Above all things, he had shown himself a dutiful His filial
son, cleaving steadfastly to his father, both in peace and duty.
war. His filial zeal had been increased after the rebellion of his brother, when the hope of the succession had
begun to be opened to himself.[3] By his father's side,
in defence of his father, he had himself received a wound
at Gerberoi.[4] Such was his character beyond the sea;

promptior surrexit," and William of Malmesbury (iv. 306), "Quomodo
adversarios rex Rufus vicerit." So again Wace (14496);

   "Por devise del nom k'il out,   Kar chescun Willame aveit nom,
   Ki à son pere ressemblout,   Out li filz poiz Ros à sornom."

Presently (14513) he is "li reis Ros." The use of the nickname in this
way was the more easy, because Rufus was a real name which had been
borne by other men, while nobody had ever been called *Curthose*. See on
the name Martel, N. C. vol. ii. p. 280; vol. v. p. 569.

I do not know that any one except Matthew Paris has turned the Red King
into a Red Dragon. He does so twice. Hist. Angl. i. 97, "Rex Willelmus,
qui a multis rubeus draco cognominabatur;" and again, i. 167, "Rex Willelmus, draco rubeus—sic enim eum appellabant propter tyrannidem."

[1] M. Gaston le Hardy, the apologist of Duke Robert (Le Dernier des
Ducs Normands, Caen, 1880, p. 41), refers to the Monasticon and Orderic
for the statement that William Rufus was called "comes" in his father's
life-time. But I cannot find the places. Has he got hold of any signature
of Earl William Fitz-Osbern?

[2] Will. Malms. iv. 305. "Emensa pueritia, in militari exercitio adoles-
centiam egit; equitari, jaculari, certare cum primævis obsequio, cum æquævis
officio. Jacturam virtutis putare si forte in militari tumultu alter eo prior
arma corriperet, et nisi primus ex adverso provocaret, vel provocantem
dejiceret."

[3] Ib. "Genitori in omnibus obsequelam gerens, ejus se oculis in bello
ostentans, ejus lateri in pace obambulans. Spe sensim scaturiente, jam
successioni inhians, maximum post abdicationem fratris majoris, cum et
tirocinium minoris nonnihil suspiceret."

[4] See N. C. vol. iv. p. 644.

CHAP. II. but the one. fact known of him in England before his father's death is that he had, like most men of his time who had the chance, possessed himself in some illegal way of a small amount of ecclesiastical land.[1]

It is quite possible that both his father and Lanfranc **His na-** may have been deceived as to his real character. In **tural gifts.** the stormy times which followed his accession, he had shown the qualities of an able captain and something more. He had shown great readiness of spirit, great power of adapting himself to circumstances, great skill in keeping friends and in winning over enemies. No man could doubt that the new King of the English had in him the power, if he chose to use it, of becoming a **His** great and a good ruler. And assuredly he could not **conduct** **during the** be charged with anything like either cruelty or breach **rebellion.** of faith at any stage of the warfare by which his crown was made fast to him. If he anywhere showed the cloven foot, it was in the matter of the Bishop of **Case of the** Durham. Even there we can have no doubt that he **Bishop of** **Durham.** spared a traitor; but he may have been hasty in the earliest stage of the quarrel; he certainly, in its latter stages, showed signs of that small personal spite, that disposition to take mean personal advantages of an enemy, which was so common in the kings of those days. Still, whatever Lanfranc may have found to rebuke, whatever may have been the beginnings of evil while the Primate yet lived, no public act of the new king is as yet recorded which would lead us to pass any severe sentence upon him, if he is judged according to the measure of his own times.

It is indeed remarkable that the pictures of evil-doing which mark the reign of Rufus from the Chronicle onwards are, except when they take the form of personal

---

[1] See N. C. vol. iv. p. 629.

anecdote, mainly of a general kind. Those pictures, CHAP. II.
those anecdotes, leave no room to doubt that the reign General
of Rufus was a reign of fearful oppression; but his op- against
pression seems to have consisted more in the unrestrained Little
licence which he allowed to his followers than in any personal
special deeds of personal cruelty done by his own hands
or by his immediate orders. Rufus certainly did not compa-
share his father's life-long shrinking from taking human his father
life anywhere but in battle; but his brother Henry, the and
model ruler of his time, the king who made peace for man
and deer, is really chargeable with uglier deeds in his
own person than any that can be distinctly proved
against the Red King. We are driven back to our
old distinction. The excesses of the followers of Rufus,
the reign of unright and unlaw which they brought
with them, did or threatened harm to every man in his
dominions; the occasional cruelties of Henry hurt only
a few people, while the general strictness of his rule
profited every one. What makes William Rufus stand out His profli-
personally in so specially hateful a light is not so much irreligion.
deeds of personal cruelty, as indulgence in the foulest forms
of vice, combined with a form of irreligion which startled
not only saints but ordinary sinners. And the point Redeeming
is that, hateful as these features in his character were, in his
they did not hinder the presence of other features which character.
were not hateful in the view of his own age, of some
indeed which are not hateful in the view of any age.

The marked personality of William Rufus, the way His
in which that personality stamped itself on the memory person-
of his age, is shown by the elaborate pictures which ality.
we have of his character, and by the crowd of personal
anecdotes by which those pictures are illustrated. Allowing
for the sure tendency of such a character to get worse,
we may take our survey of the Red King as he seemed
in men's eyes when the restraints of his earlier life were

CHAP. II. taken away. As long as his father lived, he had little
power to do evil; as long as Lanfranc lived, he was kept
within some kind of bounds by respect for the man to
whom he owed so much. When Lanfranc was gone, he
either was corrupted by prosperity, or else, like Tiberius,[1]
his natural character was now for the first time able to
Comparison show itself in the absence of restraint. His character
with his
father. then stood out boldly, and men might compare him with
his father. William the Red may pass for William the
Great with all his nobler qualities, intellectual and moral,
left out.[2] He could be, when he chose, either a great
captain or a great ruler; but it was only by fits and
His alleged starts that he chose to be either. His memory was
firmness of
purpose. strong; he at least never forgot an injury; he had also
a kind of firmness of purpose; that is, he was earnest
in whatever he undertook for good or for evil, and could
His not easily be turned from his will.[3] But he lacked that
caprice. true steadiness of purpose, that power of waiting for
the right time, that unfailing adaptation of means to
ends, which lends somewhat of moral dignity even to

[1] A great part of the description of Tiberius given by Tacitus (Ann vi.
51) applies to William Rufus; only we cannot make out quite so many
stages in the moral downfall of the Red King. "Egregium vita famaque
quoad privatus vel in imperiis sub Augusto fuit; occultum et subdolum fin-
gendis virtutibus donec Germanicus ac Drusus superfuere: idem inter bona
malaque mixtus, incolumi matre." These are words of almost the same
meaning as some of the expressions of Eadmer and William of Malmesbury.
See specially Eadmer, Hist. Nov. 14; "Confestim [after Lanfranc's death]
rex foras expressit quod in suo pectore, illo vivente, confotum habuit." In
any case we may say, "postremo in scelera simul ac dedecora prorupit, postquam, remoto pudore et metu, suo tantum ingenio utebatur." The change in
William after Lanfranc's death is most strongly brought out by Matthew
Paris, Hist. Angl. i. 38.

[2] This is well drawn out by Dean Church, Anselm, 156, 157.

[3] Ord. Vit. 680 A. "Tenacis memoriæ, et ardentis ad bonum seu malum
voluntatis erat." Nearly to the same effect are the words of the Hyde
writer (299); "Erat quidem operibus levis, sed verbis, ut aiunt, in tantum
stabilis ut, si cui bonum vel malum promisisset, certus inde satis exsistere
posset."

the worst deeds of his father. The elder William, we chap. ii.
may be sure, loved power and loved success; he loved
them as the objects and the rewards of a well-studied
and abiding policy. The younger William rather loved
the excitement of winning them, and the ostentatious
display of them when they were won. Hard as it was
for others to turn him from his purpose, no man was
more easily turned from it by his own caprice. No
man began so many things and finished so few of them.
His military undertakings are always ably planned and His un-
set on foot with great vigour. But his campaigns come campaigns.
to an end without any visible cause. After elaborate
preparations and energetic beginnings, the Red King turns
away to something else, often without either any marked
success to satisfy him or any marked defeat to discourage
him. If he could not carry his point at the first rush,
he seems to have lacked steadiness to go on. We have
seen what he could do when fighting for his crown at
the head of a loyal nation. He does not show in so
favourable a light, even as a captain, much less as a
man, when he was fighting to gratify a restless ambition
at the head of hirelings gathered from every land.

The two qualities for which he is chiefly praised by His " mag-
the writer who strives to make the best of him are his nanimity."
magnanimity and his liberality. The former word must
not be taken in its modern English use. It is reckoned
as a virtue; it therefore does not exactly answer to
the older English use of the word "high-minded;" but
it perhaps comes nearer to it than to anything that
would be spoken of as magnanimity now. It was at
all events a virtue which easily degenerated into a
vice; the magnanimity of William Rufus changed, it is
allowed, by degrees into needless harshness.[1] The
leading feature of the Red King's character was a

[1] See Appendix G.

CHAP. II. boundless pride and self-confidence, tempered by occasional fits of that kind of generosity which is really
His bound-less pride. the offspring of pride. We see little in him either of
real justice or of real mercy; but he held himself too
high to hurt those whom he deemed it beneath him to
hurt. His overweening notion of his own greatness,
personal and official, his belief in the dignity of kings
and specially in the dignity of King William of England,
led him, perhaps not to a belief in his star like
Buonaparte, certainly not to a belief in any favouring
power, like Sulla,[1] but to a kind of conviction that neither
human strength nor the powers of nature could or ought
to withstand his will. This high opinion of himself
he asserted after his own fashion. The stern and
dignified aspect of his father degenerated in him into
the mere affectation of a lofty bearing, a fierce and
His private demeanour. threatening look.[2] This was for the outside world;
in the lighter moments of more familiar intercourse,
the grim pleasantry into which the stately courtesy
of his father sometimes relaxed degenerated in him into
a habit of reckless jesting, which took the specially
shameless form of mocking excuses for his own evil
deeds.[3] Indeed his boasted loftiness of spirit sometimes
laid him open to be mocked and cheated by those around
Trick of his chamberlain. him. One of the endless stories about him, stories which,
true or false, mark the character of the man, told how,
when his chamberlain brought him a pair of new boots,
he asked the price. Hearing that they cost three
shillings only—a good price, one would have thought,

---

[1] See Historical Essays, Second Series, p. 343.

[2] Will. Malms. iv. 312. "Erat in foris et in conventu hominum tumido vultu erectus, minaci oculo adstantem defigens, et affectato rigore feroci voce colloquentem reverberans."

[3] Ib. "Intus et in triclinio cum privatis, omni lenitate accommodus, multa joco transigebat; facetissimus quoque de aliquo suo perperam facto cavillator, ut invidiam facti dilueret et ad sales transferret."

in the coinage of those times—he bade his officer take
them away as unworthy of a king and bring him a
pair worth a mark of silver. The cunning chamberlain
brought a worse pair, which he professed to have bought
at the higher price, and which Rufus accordingly pronounced to be worthy of a King's majesty.[1] Such a
tale could not have been believed or invented except
of a man in whose nature true dignity, true greatness
of soul, found no place, but who was puffed up with a
feeling of his own importance, which, if it could sometimes be shaped into the likeness of something nobler,
could also sometimes sink into vanity of the silliest
and most childish kind.

But the quality for which the Red King was most His "liber-
famous in his own day, a quality which was, we are
told, blazed abroad through all lands, East and West,
was what his own age called his boundless liberality.
The wealth of England was a standing subject of wonder
in other lands, and in the days of Rufus men wondered
no less at the lavish way in which it was scattered
abroad by the open hand of her King.[2] But the liberality
of Rufus had no claim to that name in its higher sense.[3]
It was not that kind of liberality which spends un-

---

[1] This tale is told by William of Malmesbury (iv. 313) in illustration of
the general character of Rufus, as "homo qui nesciret cujuscumque rei
effringere pretium vel æstimare commercium." He adds, " vestium suarum
pretium in immensum extolli volebat, dedignans si quis alleviasset." In the
story which follows, the King's speech to the chamberlain is character-
istically vigorous ; "Indignabundus et fremens, 'Fili,' ait, 'meretricis, ex
quo habet rex caligas tam exilis pretii ?'" We are not surprised to hear that
the officer got rich in the service of such a master ; "Ita cubicularius ex
eo pretium vestimentorum ejus pro voluntate numerabat, multa perinde suis
utilitatibus nundinatus." So there is a story told of a rich patient who
despised the cheapness of Galen's prescriptions, and asked him to order
something dearer. See Friedländer, Sittengeschichte Roms, i. 339.

[2] Take for instance Suger (Duchèsne, iv. 283) ; "Ille opulentus et An
glorum thesaurorum profusor, mirabilisque militum mercator et solidator."

[3] See Appendix G.

grudgingly for good purposes out of stores which have been honestly come by; it was a liberality which gave for purposes of wrong out of stores which were brought together by wrong. It was a liberality which consisted in the most reckless personal waste in matters of daily life, and which in public affairs took the form of lavish bribes paid to seduce the subjects of other princes from their allegiance, of lavish payments to troops of mercenary soldiers, hired for the oppression of his own dominions and the disquieting of the dominions of others. It was said of him that the merchant could draw from him any price for his wares, and that the soldier could draw from him any pay for his services.[1] The sources which supplied William with his wealth were of a piece with the objects to which his wealth was applied; under him the two ideas of liberality and oppression can never be separated. What was called liberality by the foreign mercenary was called extortion by the plundered English- man. The hoard at Winchester, full as the Conqueror had left it, could not stay full for ever; it is implied that it was greatly drawn upon by gifts to those who saved William's crown and kingdom at Pevensey and Rochester.[2] This was of a truth the best spent money of the Red King's reign; for it rewarded true and honest service, and service done by the hands of Englishmen. But to fill the hoard again, to keep it filled amid the constant drain, to keep up with the lavishness of one to whom prodigality had become part of his nature,[3] needed

---

[1] Will. Malms. iv. 313. "Cui pro libito venditor distraheret mercimonium et miles pacisceretur stipendium." This comes in the passage quoted in the last page.

[2] Ib. "Cum primis initiis regni metu turbarum milites congregasset, nihil illis denegandum putabat, majora in futurum pollicitus. Itaque quia paternos thesauros evacuaret impigre, et modicæ ei pensiones numerabantur, jam substantia defecerat."

[3] Ib. "Sed animus largiendi non deerat, quod usu donandi pene in naturam verterat."

every kind of unrighteous extortion. The land was bowed CHAP. II.
down by what, in the living speech of our forefathers, His extortions.
was called *ungeld;* money, that is, wrung from the
people by unrede, unright, and unlaw.[1] Like his father, His generally
Rufus was, as a rule, strict in preserving the peace of the strict
land; his hand was heavy on the murderer and the government.
robber. The law of his father which forbade the punishment of death[2] was either formally repealed or allowed
to fall into disuse. The robber was now sent to the
gallows; but, when he had got thither, he might still
save his neck by a timely payment to the King's
coffers.[3] And the sternness of the law which smote
offenders who had no such prevailing plea was relaxed
also in favour of all who were in the immediate
service of the King.[4] The chief objects of William's His lavish-
boasted liberality were his mercenary soldiers, picked ness to his mercena-
men from all lands. A strong hand and a ready ries.
wit, by whomsoever shown and howsoever proved,
were a passport to the Red King's service and to his
personal favour.[5] And those who thus won his personal
favour were more likely to be altogether strangers than
natives of the land, whether of the conquering or of the
conquered race. We may suspect that the settled inhabit- Chiefly foreigners.
ants of England, whether English or Norman, knew the
King's mercenaries mainly as a body of aliens who had
licence to do any kind of wrong among them without
fear of punishment. The native Englishman and his
Norman neighbour had alike to complain of the chartered

[1] See the extract from the Chronicle, below, p. 155.

[2] See N. C. vol. iv. p. 621.

[3] Will. Malms. iv. 314. "Cujuscumque conditionis homunculus, cujuscumque criminis reus, statim ut de lucro regis appellasset, audiebatur; ab
ipsis latronis faucibus resolvebatur laqueus si promisisset regale com-
modum."

[4] See Appendix G.

[5] We shall see some instances as we go on, specially the story told by
William of Malmesbury, iv. 309.

CHAP. II.　brigands who went through the land, wasting the sub-
stance of those who tilled it, and snatching the food out
of the very mouths of the wretched.[1]　A more detailed
picture sets before us how, when the King drew near
to any place, men fled from their houses into the woods,
or anywhere else where they could hide themselves.
For the King's followers, when they were quartered in
any house, carried off, sold, or burned, whatever was
in it.　They took the householder's store of drink to
wash the feet of their horses, and everywhere offered the
cruellest of insults to men's wives and daughters.[2]　And
for all this no redress was to be had; the law of the
land and the discipline of the camp had alike become a
dead letter in the case of offenders of this class.　The
oppressions of the King's immediate company were often
complained of in better times and under better kings;
but they seem to have reached a greater height under
William Rufus than at any time before or after.　We
hear of no such doings under the settled rule of the
Conqueror; under Henry they were checked by a statute
of fearful severity.[3]　As usual, the picture of the time
cannot be so well drawn in any words as those in which
the native Chronicler draws it in our own tongue.　King
William "was very strong and stern over his land and
his men and his neighbours, and very much to be feared,
and, through evil men's rede that to him ever welcome
were, and through his own greediness, he harassed his
land with his army and with *ungeld*.　For in his days

Their
wrong-
doings.

Statute of
Henry
against
them.
1108.

---

[1] William of Malmesbury, iv. 314. "A buccis miserorum cibos abstra-
hentes."

[2] See Appendix G.

[3] See N. C. vol. v. p. 159.　The evil went on under Henry until the
passing of this statute, as we see by the terrible complaint of the
Chronicler in the year 1104; "æfre ealswa se cyng for, full hergung þurh
his hired uppon his wreccea folc wæs, and þær onmang for oft bærneta
and manslihtas."

ilk right fell away, and ilk unright for God and for world CHAP. II.
uprose." [1]

Thus were the promises with which William Rufus
had bought the help of the English people in his day
of danger utterly trampled under foot. He had promised
them good laws and freedom from unrighteous taxes;
he had promised them that they should have again, as
in the days of Cnut,[2] the right of every man to slay
the beasts of the field for his lawful needs. Instead
of all this, the reign of the younger William became,
above all other reigns, a reign of *unlaw* and of *ungeld*.
The savage pleasures of the father, for the sake of which Stricter
he had laid waste the homes and fields of Hampshire, forest laws.
were sought after by the son with a yet keener zest,
and were fenced in by a yet sterner code. In the days
of William the Red the man who slew a hart had, what
he had not in the days of William the Great, to pay
for his crime with his life.[3] The working of this stern
law is shown in one of the many stories of William
Rufus, a story of which we should like to hear the end
a little more clearly.[4] Fifty men were charged with Story of
having taken, killed, and eaten the King's deer. We the fifty
are so generally left to guess at the nationality of the English-
lesser actors in our story that our attention is specially men.
called to the marked way in which we are told that

---

[1] Chron. Petrib. 1100. "He wæs swiðe strang and reðe ofer his land
and his mænn and wið ealle his neahheburas, and swiðe ondrædendlic, and
þurh yfelra manna rædas þe him æfre gecweme wæran and þurh his agene
gitsunga, he æfre þas leode mid here and mid ungylde tyrwigende wæs,
forþan þe on his dagan ælc riht afeoll and ælc unriht for Gode and for
worulde úp aras."

[2] See N. C. vol. i. pp. 436, 754.

[3] Will. Malms. iv. 319. "Venationes, quas rex primo indulserat, adeo
prohibuit ut capitale esset supplicium prendisse cervum." Contrast this
with his father's law in N. C. vol. iv. p. 621.

[4] The story is told by Eadmer, Hist. Nov. 48. It is brought in as an
illustration of the impiety of Rufus rather than of his cruelty.

they were men of Old-English birth, once of high rank in the land, and who had contrived still to keep some remnants of their ancient wealth.[1] They belonged doubtless to the class of King's thegns; if we were told in what shire the tale was laid, Domesday might help us to their names. This is one of the very few passages which might suggest the notion that Englishmen, as Englishmen, were specially picked out for oppression. And it may well be true that the forest laws pressed with special harshness on native Englishmen; no man would have so great temptation to offend against them as a dispossessed Englishman. What is not shown is that a man of Norman birth who offended in the same way would have fared any better. The mention of the accused men as Englishmen comes from the teller of the story only; and he most likely points out the fact in order to explain what next follows. On their denying the charge, they were sent to the ordeal of hot iron. Granting that killing a deer was a crime at all, this was simply the ancient English way of dealing with the alleged criminal. We are therefore a little surprised when our informant seems to speak of the appeal to the ordeal as a piece of special cruelty.[2] The fiery test was gone through; but God, we are told, took care to save the innocent, and on the third day, when their hands were

---

[1] Eadmer, Hist. Nov. 48. "Quinquaginta circiter viri quibus adhuc illis diebus ex antiqua Anglorum ingenuitate divitiarum quædam vestigia arridere videbantur."

[2] Ib. "Negant illi; unde statim ad judicium rapti, judicantur injectam calumniam examine igniti ferri a se propulsare debere. Statuto itaque die præfixi pœnæ judicii pariter subacti sunt, remota pietate et misericordia." Yet, unless there was some special circumstance of hardship which is not recorded, this was only the old law of England kept on by the Conqueror. (See N. C. vol. iv. p. 624; v. pp. 400, 874.) That is, if the accuser was English, and the King's reeves and huntsmen were largely English. If the accuser was French, the accused were entitled to a choice between the ordeal and the wager of battle. Can Eadmer mean that this choice was not allowed them?

formally examined, they were found to be unhurt. The CHAP. II.
King in his wrath uttered words of blasphemy. Men said The King's
blasphe-
that God was a just judge; he would believe it no mous com-
longer. God was no judge of these matters; he would ment.
for the future take them into his own hands.[1] To
understand the full force of such words, we must remember that the ordeal was, in its own nature, an
appeal to the judgement of God in cases when there
was no evidence on which man could found a judgement.[2] What happened further we are not told; it can
hardly be meant that the men in whose favour the
judgement of God was held to have been given were
sent to the gallows all the same.

In this last story the most distinctive feature of the Special
vices of
character of William Rufus comes out. In many of his Rufus.
recorded deeds we see the picture of an evil man and an
evil king, but still of a man and a king whose deeds
might find many parallels in other times and places.
But the story in which he mocks at the ordeal leads us
to those other points in him which give him a place of
his own, a place which perhaps none other in the long
roll-call of evil kings can dispute with him. Other
kings have been cruel; others have been lustful; others
have broken their faith with their people, and have said
in their hearts that there was no God. But the Red King
stands well nigh alone in bringing back the foulest vices
of heathendom into a Christian land, and at the same

---

[1] Eadmer, Hist. Nov. 48. "Cum principi esset relatum condemnatos
illos tertio judicii die simul omnes inustis manibus apparuisse, stomach-
atus taliter fertur respondisse, 'Quid est hoc? Deus est justus judex?
Pereat qui deinceps hoc crediderit. Quare per hoc et hoc meo judicio
amodo respondebitur. Non Dei quod pro voto cujusque hinc inde
plicatur.'"

[2] "Judicium" is the usual Domesday name. See N. C. vol. v. p.
875.

CHAP. II. time openly proclaiming himself the personal enemy
of his Maker.

Contrast
between
Rufus and
his father.

It is with regard to his daily life and to the beliefs
and objects which his age looked on as sacred that
William Rufus stands out in the most glaring contrast
to his father.   William the Great, I need hardly repeat,
was austere in his personal morals and a strict observer
of every outward religious duty.   His court was decent;
the men who stood before him kept, we are told, to the

Old and
new
fashions
of dress.

modesty of the elder days.   Their clothes were fitted
to the form of their bodies, leaving them ready to run or
ride or do anything that was to be done.[1]   They shaved
their beards—all save penitents, captives, and pilgrims—
and cut their hair close.[2]   But with the death of William, of Pope Gregory, and of other religious princes,
the good old times passed away, and their decorous
fashions were forgotten through all the Western lands.[3]
Then vain and foppish forms of attire came in.   The
gilded youth of Normandy and of Norman England
began to wear long garments like women, which hindered walking or acting of any kind; they let their
hair grow long like women; they copied the walk and

The
pointed
shoes.

mien of women.[4]   Above all, their feet were shod with
shoes with long curved points, like the horns of rams
or the tails of scorpions.   These long and puffed shoes

[1] Ord. Vit. 682 C. "Illi modestis vestiebantur indumentis optimeque
coaptatis ad sui mensuram corporis.   Et erant habiles ad equitandum et
currendum et ad omne opus quod ratio suggerebat agendum."

[2] Ib. "Olim pœnitentes et capti et peregrini usualiter intonsi erant,
longasque barbas gestabant, judicioque tali pœnitentiam, seu captionem,
vel peregrinationem spectantibus prætendebant."

[3] Ib. "Post obitum Gregorii papæ et Guillelmi Nothi aliorumque
principum religiosorum, in occiduis partibus pene totus abolitus est honestus
patrum mos antiquorum."   Yet, unless we go as far north as the sainted
Cnut of Denmark, it is not easy to find any specially devout princes who
died about the same time as Gregory and William.

[4] See Appendix G.

were the device of a courtier of Rufus, Robert henceforth CHAP. II. surnamed the *Cornard*, and they were further improved by Count Fulk of Anjou, when he wished to hide the swellings on his gouty feet.[1] The long hair and the long-pointed shoes serve as special subjects for declamation among the moral writers of the time.[2] But these unseemly fashions were only the outward signs of the deeper corruption within. The courtiers, the minions, of Rufus, forerunners of the minions of the last Henry of Valois, altogether forsook the law of God and the customs of their fathers. The day they passed in sleep ; the night in revellings, dicing, and vain talk.[3] Vices before unknown, the vices of the East, the special sin, as Englishmen then deemed, of the Norman, were rife among them. And deepest of all in guilt was the Red King himself. Into the details of the private life of Rufus it is well not to grope too narrowly. In him England might see on her own soil the habits of the ancient Greek and the modern Turk. His sins were of a kind from which his brother Henry, no model of moral perfection, was deemed to be wholly free, and which he was believed to look upon with loathing.[4]

Fashionable vices of the time.

Personal crimes of the King.

Sinners, even of the special type of the Red King, have before now been zealous supporters of orthodoxy. If William persecuted Anselm, Constans defended Athanasius. But the foulness of William's life was of a piece with his open mockery of everything which other men in his day held sacred. Whatever else divided Englishman and Norman, they were at least one in religious doctrine

His irreligion.

---

[1] See Appendix G.

[2] Take, above all, the story of Bishop Serlo's most practical sermon in Orderic, 815, 816. See N. C. vol. v. p. 844, and Appendix G.

[3] Ord. Vit. 682 B. "Nocte comessationibus et potationibus vanisque confabulationibus, aleis et tesseris aliisque ludicris vacabant; die vero dormiebant."

[4] See Appendix G.

CHAP. II. and religious worship. In matters of dogma Stigand was as orthodox as Lanfranc. But now, among the endless classes of adventurers whom the Conquest brought to try their luck in the conquered land, came men of a race whom Normans and Englishmen alike looked on as cut off from all national and religious

Coming of the Jews. fellowship. In the wake of the Conqueror the Jews of Rouen found their way to London,[1] and before long we find settlements of the Hebrew race in the chief cities and boroughs of England, at York, Winchester, Lincoln, Bristol, Oxford, and even at the gates of the Abbots of Saint Edmund's and Saint Alban's.[2] They came as the

Their position in England. King's special men, or more truly his special chattels, strangers alike to the Church and to the commonwealth of England, but strong in the protection of a master who commonly found it to his interest to defend them against all others. Hated, feared, and loathed, but far too deeply feared to be scorned or oppressed, they stalked defiantly among the people of the land, on whose wants they throve. They lived safe from harm or insult, save now and then, when popular wrath burst all bounds, and when their proud mansions and fortified quarters could shelter them no longer from raging crowds eager to wash out their debts in the blood of their creditors.[3] The romantic picture of the de-

---

[1] See N. C. vol. v. p. 818. In some manuscripts of William of Malmesbury (iv. 317) he says distinctly, "Judæi qui Lundoniæ habitabant, quos pater a Rothomago illuc traduxerat."

[2] The Jews meet us at every turn in the twelfth and thirteenth centuries. At Lincoln and Saint Eadmundsbury they have left their works. Those of Winchester — their Jerusalem — shared in the perfection which marked all classes of men in that city (see Ric. Div. c. 82). In the genuine "Annals of an English Abbey" (Gest. Abb. i. 193) we may see something of the "superbia magna et jactantia" which the Jew Aaron (of Lincoln) displayed at Saint Alban's.

[3] As in the great massacre at York in 1189. Or the King himself might, like John, do as he would with his own chattels.

spised, trembling, Jew, cringing before every Christian CHAP. II.
that he meets, is, in any age of English history, simply
a romantic picture. In the days of Rufus at all events, Favour
the Jews of Rouen and London stood erect before the shown to
prince of the land, and they seem to have enjoyed no Rufus.
small share of his favour and personal familiarity. The
presence of the unbelieving Hebrew supplied the Red
King with many opportunities for mocking at Christianity and its ministers. He is even said to have shown
himself more than once, when it was to his interest so to
show himself, as a kind of missionary of the Hebrew faith.
He was not the only prince of his age who discouraged
conversions to Christianity on the part of distinct races
who could be made more useful, if they remained distinct,
and who could in no way be kept so distinct as if they
remained in the position of infidels. Count Roger of Comparison
Sicily found that the unbelieving Saracens,[1] and William Sicilian
Rufus found that the unbelieving Hebrews, were, each in Saracens.
their own way, more profitable to their several masters
than if they had been allowed to lose their distinct being
among their Christian neighbours. But in the whole William's
dealings of Rufus with the Jews there is a vein of vein of
mockery in which, if Roger shared, it is not recorded.
It is true that we do not find Rufus taking the part of
the Jew, except when the Jew made it worth his while
to do so. But when he did take the Jew's part, he clearly
found a malicious pleasure in taking it. He enjoyed
showing favour to the Jew, because so to do gave annoyance to the Christian.

Whether Rufus was in any strict sense an intellectual Question of
sceptic may be doubted. That he was such cannot be sceptic.
inferred from his bidding in bitter mockery the Jewish
rabbis and the bishops of England to dispute before
him on the tenets of their several creeds, promising to

[1] See Eadmer, Vit. Ans. iii. 5. We shall come across them again.

CHAP. II.

The dispute between Jews and Christians.

embrace the faith of the strangers, if they should have the better in the discussion. The discussion took place in London, most likely when the prelates were gathered for some Whitsun Gemót. The Christian cause was supported by several bishops and clerks—one would like to have their names—who argued, we are told, in great fear on behalf of the faith which was thus jeoparded.[1] As is usual in such cases, each side claimed the victory;[2] but in any case the arguments on the Hebrew side were not so overwhelming as to make the King become an avowed votary of Moses. Still he did what he could to hinder the ranks of the Church from being swelled at the cost of the synagogue. In a story which must belong to the latter part of his reign, we read how the Jews of Rouen began to be frightened at the great numbers of their body

Jews turn back again.

who fell away from the law of their fathers. They came to the King, and, by a large bribe, obtained from him a promise that the converts should be constrained to go back to the faith which they had forsaken. They were brought before Rufus, and most of them were by his terrible threats forced again to apostatize.[3] The tale

---

[1] Will. Malms. iv. 317. "Apud Londoniam contra episcopos nostros in certamen animati [Judæi], quia ille ludibundus, credo, dixisset quod, si vicissent Christianos apertis argumentationibus confutatos, in eorum sectam transiret. Magno igitur timore episcoporum et clericorum res acta est, pia sollicitudine fidei Christianæ timentium."

[2] Ib. "De hoc quidem certamine nihil Judæi præter confusionem retulerunt, quamvis multotiens jactarint se non oratione sed factione superatos."

[3] Eadmer, Hist. Nov. p. 47. "Ferebant ... ad eum convenire, conquerentes nonnullos ex suis, spreto Judaismo, Christianos tunc noviter factos fuisse, atque rogantes ut, sumpto pretio, illos, rejecto Christianismo, ad Judaismum redire compelleret. Adquiescit ille, et, suscepto pretio apostasiæ, jubet ex Judæis ipsis adduci ad se. Quid plura? Plures ex illis minis et terroribus fractos, abnegato Christo, pristinum errorem suscipere fecit." Eadmer brings in this story, without pledging himself to its truth, as one which he, when in Italy, heard from those who came from Rouen. "Sicut illa accepimus, simpliciter ponam, non adstruens vera an secus exstiterint, an non. Ferebant igitur hi qui veniebant," &c. It is the

of the Red King's success in this crooked kind of missionary enterprise reached the ears of a Jew father—where
we are not told—whose only and well-beloved son was lost
to him by conversion to the Christian faith. The young
man had been favoured with a vision of the protomartyr
Stephen, who had bidden him ask for baptism and take
his own name at the font.[1] He went to a priest, told
his tale, and was admitted to baptism by the name
which was appointed to him. His father, mourning for
his loss, went to King William and made his complaint;
praying that at his command his son might be restored
to his old faith.[2] Rufus held his peace; the argument
which alone persuaded him to meddle in such matters
had not yet been urged.[3] A promise of sixty marks
of silver, payable on the second conversion of the youth,
brought the King to another mind,[4] and Stephen was
called into the royal presence. A dialogue took place

same story as that which William of Malmesbury tells, iv. 317; "Insolentiæ
in Deum Judæi suo tempore dedere indicium; semel apud Rothomagum,
ut quosdam ab errore suo refugas ad Judaismum revocarent, muneribus
inflectere conati."

[1] Eadmer, Hist. Nov. p. 47. The protomartyr pleads his own example;
"Uno dierum per viam forte eunti apparuit alter juvenis, vultu et veste
decorus, qui interrogatus unde vel quis esset, dixit se jam olim ex Judæo
Christianum effectum, Stephanum protomartyrem esse."

[2] Ib. "Æstuans quonam modo suis sacris filium posset restituere, didicit
quemadmodum Willielmus rex Anglorum nonnullos hujusmodi, pecuniæ
gratis, nuper Judaismo reddiderit." This way of speaking might almost
make us think that the Jew was not living in William's dominions; yet
the whole tenor of the story, which seems to be laid at Rouen, looks
otherwise. One phrase is odd; "paternis rogat legibus *imperiali sanctione*
restitui." William Rufus, as we shall see, did not forget his imperial as
well as his royal dignity, but Rouen was an odd place in which to show
himself in the imperial character.

[3] Ib. "Tacet ille ad rogata, nondum audiens quamobrem tali negotio
sese deberet medium facere."

[4] Ib. "Advertit Judæus mysterium cur suis precibus non responderet,
et e vestigio sexaginta marcas argenti se illi daturum, si Judaismo restitueret filium suum, pollicetur." This almost looks as if the Jew thought
at first that the King, out of zeal for the Hebrew cause, would do the job
for him for nothing.

CHAP. II.

Dispute
between
Stephen
and the
King.

between the King and the neophyte, in which Rufus, remembering perhaps the one redeeming feature in his own
life, pressed Stephen's return to Judaism as a matter of
filial duty. The youth humbly suggests that the King is
joking. Rufus waxes wroth, and takes to words of abuse
and to his usual oath. Stephen's eyes shall be torn out,
if he does not presently obey his bidding.[1] The youth
stands firm, and even rebukes the King. He can be no
good Christian who, instead of trying to win to Christ
those who are estranged from him, strives to drive back
those who have already embraced his faith. Rufus, put
to shame by the answer, has nothing to say, but drives
Stephen from his presence with scorn.[2] The Jew father
is waiting without. His son overwhelms him with words
of abuse which even zeal for his new faith would hardly
justify. He would no longer acknowledge a father in
one whose own father was the Devil, and who, not
satisfied with his own damnation, sought the damnation
of his son.[3] With ·this somewhat harsh way of putting
matters, the zealous youth vanishes from the story; the

The King's
compro-
mise with
Stephen's
father.

Jew father has yet another turn with the Red King. He
is called in, and Rufus says that he has done what he had
been asked to do, and demands the promised payment for
his pains.[4] The Jew expostulates. His son, he says, is
firmer than ever in his Christian faith and in his hatred
towards himself. Yet the King says that he has done what

---

[1] Eadmer, u. s. "Tecum jocarer, stercoris fili ? Recede potius et præceptum meum velocius imple, alioquin per vultum de Luca faciam tibi oculos
erui." On the oath, see Appendix G.

[2] Ib. "Confusus princeps in istis, contumeliis affectum juvenem cum
dedecore jussit suis conspectibus eliminari."

[3] Ib. "Fili mortis et pabulum externæ perditionis, non sufficit tibi
damnatio tua, nisi et me tecum præcipites in eam ? Ego vero cui jam
Christus patefactus est absit ut te unquam pro patre agnoscam, quia pater
tuus diabolus est." The reference must be to St. John viii. 44 ; but the
pedigree was a dangerous one for a presumptive grandson to meddle with.

[4] Ib. "Ecce feci quod rogasti, redde quod promisisti."

he had been asked, and demands payment. "Finish," he goes on, with a boldness which challenges some sympathy, "what you have begun, and then we will settle about my promise; such was our agreement."[1] It is characteristic of Rufus not to be angry at a really bold word. Evidently entering into the grotesque side of the dispute, he rejects the doctrine of payment by results; he answers that he has done his best, and that, though he had not succeeded, he cannot go away with nothing for his trouble.[2] At last, after some further haggling, the parties in this strange dispute come to a compromise. The Jew pays, and the King receives, half the sum which had been promised in the beginning.

A king of whom such stories as these could be told, whether every detail is literally true or not, must have utterly cast aside all the decencies of his own or of any other age. But Rufus, according to the tales told of him, went even further than this. He is charged with a kind William's of personal defiance of the Almighty, quite distinct alike defiance from mere carelessness and from speculative unbelief. of God. When he recovered from the sickness which forms such 1093. an epoch in his life, "God," he said, "shall never see me a good man; I have suffered too much at his hands."[3] He mocked at God's judgement and doubted his justice—his disbelief in the ordeal is quoted as an

---

[1] Eadmer, u.s. "Filius meus jam nunc et in Christi confessione constantior et mihi est solito factus infestior ; et dicis"—mark the scriptural turn— "'Feci quod petisti, redde quod promisisti?' Immo quod cœpisti primo perfice, et tunc demum de pollicitis age. Sic enim convenit inter nos."

[2] Ib. "Feci quantum potui; verum, quamvis non proficerim, minime tamen feram me sine fructu laborasse."

[3] Ib. 54. "Quod Deus nunquam eum bonum habiturus esset pro malo quod sibi inferret." The words are spoken to Bishop Gundulf. Eadmer comments; "In cunctis erat fortunatus, ac si verbis ejus hoc modo respondit Deus, 'Si te pro malo, ut dicis, numquam bonum habebo, probabo an saltem pro bono possim te bonum habere, et ideo in omni quod tu bonum æstimas velle tuum adimplebo."

CHAP. II.   instance.   Either God did not know the deeds of men,
or else he weighed them in an unfair balance.[1]   He was
wroth if any one ventured to add the usual reserve of
God's will to anything which he, King William, undertook or ordered to be undertaken.   He had that belief
in himself that he would have everything referred to his
own wisdom and power only.[2]   Modern ideas might be
His con-   less shocked at another alleged sign of his impiety.   He
tempt for
the saints.   was said to have declared publicly that neither Saint
Peter nor any other saint had any influence with God,
and that he would ask none of them for help.[3]   In all
this we are again left in doubt whether we are dealing
with a speculative unbeliever, or only with one who was
so puffed up with pride that he liked not to be reminded
of any power greater than his own, least of all of a
power which might some day call him to account for
Frequency   his evil deeds.   And though William Rufus clearly went
of blas-
phemy.   lengths in his defiance of God to which even bad men
were unaccustomed, we must remember that something
of the same kind in a less degree was not uncommon
in his time.   Blasphemy strictly so called, that is, neither

[1] Eadmer, 48.   "Ad hoc quoque lapsus est ut Dei judicio incredulus fieret,
injustitiæque illud arguens, Deum aut facta hominum ignorare, aut
æquitatis ea lance nolle pensare adstrueret."   Then follows the story
of the deer-stealers which I have told in p. 155.   Mark Eadmer's firm belief
in the ordeal, which had not yet been condemned by the Church.

[2] Ib. 47.   "Ferebatur eum in tantam mentis elationem corruisse ut
nequaquam patienter audire valeret, si quivis ullum negotium quod vel a se
vel ex suo præcepto foret agendum, poneret sub conditione voluntatis Dei
fieri.   Sed quæque acta simul et agenda suæ soli industriæ ac fortitudini
volebat adscribi."   We have his like in Kapaneus, Æsch. Sept. c. Theb.
409;

θεοῦ τε γὰρ θέλοντος ἐκπέρσειν πόλιν
καὶ μὴ θέλοντος φησὶν, οὐδὲ τὴν Διὸς
ἔριν πέδῳ σκήψασαν ἐκποδὼν σχέθειν.

[3] Ib.   "Quæ mentis elatio ita excrevit in eo ut, quemadmodum dicebatur,
crederet et publica voce assereret nullum sanctorum cuiquam apud Deum
posse prodesse, et ideo nec se velle, nec aliquem sapientem debere, beatum
Petrum seu quemlibet alium quo se juvaret interpellare."

simple irreverence nor intellectual unbelief, but direct re- CHAP. II.
viling and defiance of a power which, by the very terms
of the defiance, is believed in, is a vice of which Englishmen of our own day have hardly any notion. But, as it
has many parallels in heathen creeds, as it has not yet
died out in all parts of Christendom, so it was by no
means unknown in the days with which we are dealing.
Its frequency at a somewhat later time is shown when Contrast
the biographer of Saint Lewis sets it down as one of his of Saint Lewis.
special virtues, that he never, under any circumstance,
allowed any reviling of God or the saints.[1] On the Case of
other hand, we find Henry the Second, whom there is no Henry the Second.
reason whatever to look on as a speculative unbeliever,
indulging, as in lesser forms of irreverence, so also in
direct reviling of God.[2] But the vice, to us so revolt-
ing and unintelligible, seems to have reached its highest
point in the King of whom men said in proverbs that
he every morning got up a worse man than he lay down,
and every evening lay down a worse man than he
got up.[3]

Thus far we are inclined to see in our second William
a character of unmixed blackness, alike as a man and
as a King. There seems no room left for even pagan
virtues in the oppressor, the blasphemer, the man given

[1] Joinville, p. 217 ed. Michel; "Le roy ama tant Dieu et sa douce mère
que touz ceulz que il pooit atteindre qui disoient de Dieu ne de sa mère
chose déshoneste ne vilein serement, que il les feṣoit punir griefment." He
goes on to tell how, like Saint Wulfstan (see N. C. vol. iv. p. 386) but' unlike Saint Eadward (ib. ii. p. 26), he never swore nor mentioned the devil.

[2] Giraldus (de Inst. Prin. c. iii. 11) gives a specimen of his blasphemies,
and adds, " quibus ne memoriæ refricatio facinus atque blasphemiam
posteris ad mentem revocet, supersedere potius quam paginam nostram
commaculare dignum duximus."

[3] Eadmer, Hist. Nov. 54. "In tantum ex successibus suis profecit ut, sicut
hi qui factis ejus die noctuque præsentes exstiterunt attestantur, nụmquam
vel de lecto surgeret vel in lecto se collocaret, quin seipsum aut collocante
aut surgente semper deterior esset."

up to vices at whose foulness ordinary sinners stood
aghast. Yet nothing is plainer than that there was something in the character of William Rufus which made
him not wholly hateful in the eyes of his own age.
There was a side to him which, if we may not strictly
call it virtuous, has yet in it something akin to virtue,
as compared with other sides of him. There is, as I have
already hinted, amidst all the general oppressions of his
reign, amidst all the special outrages which he at least
allowed to go unpunished, no sign in him of that
direct delight in human suffering which marks some
of his contemporaries. I have spoken of his dutiful
obedience to his father while he lived; and the sentiment
of filial duty lived on after his father's death, and showed
itself in some singular forms of respect for his memory.
Elsewhere the enemy and spoiler of the Church, towards
his father's ecclesiastical foundations Rufus appears as a
benefactor. Saint Stephen's, the monument of his father's
penance, Battle, the monument of his father's victory,
were both the objects of his bounty.[1]   But it is singularly characteristic that the means for bounty towards
Saint Stephen at Caen were found in the plunder of
the Holy Cross at Waltham.[2] At York, strangely out
of the common range of his actions, we find him counted
as a second founder of the hospital of Saint Peter;
we find him changing its site, enlarging its buildings and
revenues, but specially setting forth that he was confirming the gifts of his father.[3] We shall see that, in all his
wars, it was his special ambition to keep whatever had
been his father's; whatever he lost or won, it was a point
of honour to hold the great trophy of his father's continental victories. In other warfare the Red King might
halt or dally or put up with an imperfect conquest.
But when Le Mans, castle and city, was to be kept or

[1] See Appendix G.   [2] See Appendix G.   [3] See Appendix G.

won, when the royal tower of his father was in jeopardy CHAP. II.
or in hostile hands, then the heart of Rufus never
waxed weak in counsel, his arm never faltered in the
fight.

But one form of words which I have just used opens His
to us one special side of the character of the Red King chivalrous
spirit.
which is apt to be overlooked. I have spoken of the
point of honour. I am not sure that, in the generation
before Rufus, those words could have applied in all their
fulness either to Harold of England or to William of
Normandy, either to Gyrth of East-Anglia or to Roger
of Beaumont. But to no man that ever lived was the Chivalry a
whole train of thoughts and feelings suggested by new thing.
those words more abidingly present than they were to
the Red King. It might be going too far to say that
William Rufus was the first gentleman, as his claim to
that title might be disputed by his forefather Duke
Richard the Good.[1] But he was certainly the first
man in any very prominent place by whom the whole
set of words, thoughts, and feelings, which belong to
the titles of knight and gentleman were habitually and
ostentatiously thrust forward.

We have now in short reached the days of chivalry, True character of
the days of that spirit on which two of the masters of chivalry.
history have spoken in words so strong that I should
hardly venture to follow them.[2] Of that spirit, the
spirit which, instead of striving to obey the whole law
of right, picks out a few of its precepts to be observed
under certain circumstances and towards certain classes
of people, William the Red was one of the foremost
models. The knight, like the monk, arbitrarily picks The knight
and the
out certain virtues, to be observed in such an exclusive monk.
and one-sided way as almost to turn them into vices.

---

[1] See N. C. vol. i. p. 255.   [2] See Appendix H.

He has his arbitrary code of honour to supplant alike the law of God and the law of the land. That code teaches the duties of good faith, courtesy, mercy—under *His word when kept and when broken.* certain circumstances and towards certain people. Was William Rufus a man of his word? His subjects as a body had no reason to think so; the princes of other lands had no reason to think so. His promises to his people went for nothing; his treaties with other princes went for nothing.[1] To observe both of these was the dull every-day duty of a Christian man whom it had pleased God to call to a particular state of life, that namely of a king. Holding, as Rufus did, that no man could keep all his promises,[2] these were the class of promises that he thought it needless to try to keep. But when William plighted his word in the character of the *probus miles*, the *preux chevalier*, in modern phrase, as "an officer and a gentleman," no man kept it more strictly. No man cared less for the justice of his wars; no man cared less for the wrong and suffering which *His knightly courtesy.* his warfare caused. But no man ever more scrupulously observed all the mere courtesies of warfare. He was not like Robert of Bellême. The life and limb of the prisoner of knightly rank were safe in his hands. Indeed any man of any rank who appealed to his personal generosity was always safe. Under the influence of the law of honour, the tyrant, the blasphemer, the extortioner, the oppressor who neither feared God nor regarded man, puts on an air of unselfishness, of *His trust in the knightly word of others.* unworldliness. Strict in the observance of his own knightly word, he places unbounded confidence in the knightly word of others. He thrusts indignantly aside the suggestion of colder spirits that a captive knight

---

[1] Twice under the same year 1091 the Chronicler adds to the record of a treaty concluded by Rufus that it " litle hwile stode."

See above, p. 143.

may possibly break his *parole*.[1] We shall see all this CHAP. II.
as we follow the tale of his strife with Helias of Maine, Contrast
one who was as scrupulous an observer of the law of with Helias.
honour as himself, but one who did not let the law of
honour stand in the place of higher and older laws. And Import-
this is a side of the character of Rufus on which it is im- ance of this side of his
portant to dwell, as it is one which the popular conception character.
of him, a conception perfectly true as far as it goes, is apt
to leave out. We have not grasped the likeness of the
real man, unless we remember that the man whose
crimes and vices the popular picture has not exaggerated,
carried with him through life a sentimental standard
of filial duty and reverence, and a knightly conscience,
if the phrase may pass, as quick to speak and as sure
to be obeyed as the higher conscience of Anselm or
Helias. Without fully taking this in, we shall not easily
understand the twofold light in which Rufus looked to
the men of his own age, in whose eyes he clearly was
not wholly hateful. And without fully taking it in, we
shall fail to give him his place in the general history
of England, Normandy, and mankind in general. In He marks
William Rufus we have not only to study a very varied the begin-ning of a
and remarkable phase of human nature; we have also new æra.
to look on a man who marks the beginning of a new
age and a new state of feeling.

The Red King has indeed this advantage, that the
other parts of his character are so bad that the chivalrous side of him stands out as a relief, as at least com-
parative light amid surrounding darkness. There are Chivalry
other princes in whom the chivalrous side is the dark the bad side of
side, because there are other parts of their character some princes;
better than chivalry. The essence of chivalry is that
the fantastic and capricious law of honour displaces all

---

[1] I refer to the story of the Angevin knights at Ballon, told by Orderic
(772 C, D). We shall come to it in a later chapter.

the forms of the law of right. The standard of the good knight, the rule of good faith, respect, and courtesy, as due from one knight to another, displaces the higher standard of the man, the citizen, and the Christian. There are perhaps whole ages, there certainly are particular men, in which this lower standard has its use. Any check, any law, is better than no check and no law.

He who cannot rise to the higher rank of an honest man had better be a knight and gentleman than a mere knave and ruffian. If a man cannot be kept back from all crimes by the law of right, it is a gain that he should be kept back from some crimes by the law of honour. It was better that William Rufus should show mercy and keep his word in some particular kind of cases than that he should never show mercy or keep his word at all. But the very fact that such an one as Rufus could feel bound by the law of honour shows how feeble a check the law of honour is. And we must remember that the very feeling of courtesy and deference towards men of a certain rank led only to more reckless and contemptuous oppression of all who lay without the favoured pale. And, at least as regards particular men, the beginning of the days of chivalry

was the falling back from a higher standard. We have come across men in our own story who showed that they obeyed a better law than that of honour. It was not at the bidding of chivalry or honour, it was not in the character of knight or gentleman, that Herlwin made light of his own wrongs by the side of those of his poor peasants,[1] or that Harold refused to harry the lands

of the men who had chosen him to be their king.[2] But the law of honour and chivalry was most fully obeyed, the character of knight and gentleman was shown in its full perfection, when the Knight without Fear and with-

---

[1] See N. C. vol. ii. p. 220.   [2] See N. C. vol. iii. p. 438.

out Reproach refused to expose himself to toils of war CHAP. II.
which were too dangerous for any but the base churl.[1] Bayard.
It was fully carried out when the mirror of chivalry, the The Black
Black Prince himself, gave their lives to the French Prince.
knights who fought against him, and murdered the unarmed men, women, and children, who craved for mercy.[2]
It was no less worthily carried out by the king who Francis
ever had the faith of a gentleman on his lips, who the First of France.
boasted that he had never broken his word except to
women, and who betrayed, not only the women, but the
allied princes and commonwealths who trusted in him.
William the Red at least need not shrink from a comparison with Francis of Valois.[3] But it must not be for- Twofold
gotten that one of the chivalrous heroes on our list had character of the
a side to him better than his chivalry. William the Black Prince.
Great assuredly, and I believe William the Red also,
would have shrunk from such a deed as the slaughter of
Limoges. But he who wrought the slaughter of Limoges

[1] This was at the siege of Padua in 1509. " Maximilien fit proposer à La Palisse de faire mettre pied à terre à sa gendarmerie pour monter à l'assaut avec les landsknechts. Mais d'après le conseil de Bayard, La Palisse répondit que la gendarmerie française était toute composée de gentilshommes, et qu'il ne serait pas convenable de la faire combattre pêle-mêle avec les fantassins allemands, qui étaient roturiers." Sismondi, Rép. Ital. xiv. 26.

[2] The story of the massacre of Limoges, the most truly chivalrous deed ever done, is well known. It will be found in Froissart, i. 289 (vol. i. p. 401, ed. Sauvage).

[3] Hallam, who thoroughly understood Henry the Eighth, adds in a note (Const. Hist. i. 36) ; "After all, Henry was every whit as good a king and man as Francis I, whom there are still some, on the other side of the channel, servile enough to extol; not in the least more tyrannical and sanguinary, and of better faith towards his neighbours." The famous letter of Francis about all being lost except honour is now disbelieved, but it is characteristic all the same. I have said something about this in the Fortnightly Review, December, 1876.

It is singular enough that in 1546 some reader of the "Normanniæ Nova Chronica," after the entries about the misdeeds of William Rufus in 1098, bursts out (p. 9) into a fierce invective against the vices and oppressions of Francis the First, as far surpassing those of Rufus. If men murmured in 1098, how much more reason had they to murmur in 1546.

CHAP. II. was also the patriotic statesman of the Good Parliament.
The knight, courteous and bloody as became his knighthood, could turn about and act as something better than
a knight.   In such a man we must measure the balance
of good and evil as we can, and the chivalrous side of
him is the evil side.   In William Rufus the chivalrous
side is the better side; it is the comparatively bright
spot in a picture otherwise of utter blackness.

Grouping
of events
in the reign
of Rufus.
The chief events of the reign of William Rufus fall
into two classes.   There is the military side; there is
the ecclesiastical and constitutional side.   There is the
side which shows us the noblest and the basest type
of the warrior in Helias of La Flèche and in Robert
of Bellême.   There is the side which shows us the noblest
and the basest type of the priest in Anselm of Canterbury
and in Randolf of Durham.   The two sides go on together.
The most striking features in both belong to a somewhat
later time than that which we have now reached.   But
it is the military side in its earlier stages which most
directly connects itself with the tale which we have gone
through in the present chapter.   The first Norman
campaign of the Red King comes in date before the
archiepiscopate of Anselm; it comes in idea before the
administration of Randolf Flambard.   On the other
hand, it is directly connected with the war of Pevensey
and Rochester, with the banishment of Bishop Odo and
Bishop William.   We will therefore pass to it as the
chief subject of our next chapter.

CHAPTER III.

THE FIRST WARS OF WILLIAM RUFUS.

1090–1092.[1]

Character of the year 1089.

THE rest of the year in which Lanfranc died was unmarked by any striking public event, political or military. The causes of evil which had begun to play their part before the Primate's death, which were

---

[1] There is nothing special to note as to the authorities for this chapter, except that we now begin to make some little use of the Lives of the Bishops of Le Mans in Mabillon's Vetera Analecta, of which we shall have to make much larger use in a later chapter.

Since this chapter was written and partly printed, I have come across a book called "Le Dernier des Ducs Normands. Étude de Critique Historique sur Robert Courte-Heuse; par Gaston le Hardy (Caen, 1880)." It is a gallant apology for Duke Robert, who however, it seems, cannot be set up without a cruel setting down both of Orderic and of King Henry. M. le Hardy believes in the false Ingulf and seems to be an enemy to Italian freedom. He has worked with care at his authorities, and I have to thank him for a few references; but his style of criticism is odd. In p. 47 he argues against the last speech of the Conqueror in Orderic—a speech very open to argument against it on other grounds—because William is there made to confess that he had no right to the English crown. This at least cannot be. "Comment croire que le Conquérant, dont les droits légitimes à la couronne d'Angleterre étaient au moins fondés sur des apparences très-respectables, *puisqu'elles décidèrent le Pape à se prononcer en sa faveur*, se soit appliqué à les désavouer, et à démentir ainsi toute sa vie." I think more highly both of the intellect and of the conscience of William the Great. I can conceive his being led to repent of his sins, even though the Pope told him that they were no sins. M. le Hardy, like so many of his countrymen, seems unable to understand any English matter, and he seems never to have looked at any English or German book.

I let my estimate of Robert stay where it was. His character is best summed up in the portrait drawn by William of Malmesbury at the end of his fourth book;

"Patria lingua facundus ut sit jocundior nullus; in aliis consiliosus ut nihil excellentius; militiæ peritus ut si quis unquam; pro mollitie tamen animi nunquam regendæ reipublicæ idoneus judicatus."

I think I have throughout done justice to Robert's military skill—it was more than mere daring—and to his gifts as a counsellor of others.

CHAP. III.

Natural
phæno-
mena.

The great
earth-
quake.
Aug. 11,
1089.

enabled to play it so much more powerfully after his death, were no doubt already at work; but they had as yet not wrought any open change, or done anything specially to impress men's minds. The writers of the time have nothing to record, except natural phænomena, and it must be remembered that natural phænomena, and those mostly of a baleful kind, form a marked feature of the reign of William Rufus. Even he could hardly be charged with directly causing earthquakes, storms, and bad harvests; but, in the ideas of his day, it was natural to look on earthquakes, storms, and bad harvests, either as scourges sent to punish his evil deeds, or else as signs that some more direct vengeance was presently coming upon himself. The ever-living belief of those times in the near connexion between the moral and the physical world must always be borne in mind in reading their history. And in the days of William Rufus there was plenty in both worlds to set men's minds a-thinking. Lanfranc had not been dead three months before the land was visited with a mighty earthquake. The strongest buildings—the massive keeps and minsters lately built or still building—seemed to spring from the ground and sink back again into their places.[1] Then came a lack of the fruits of the earth of all kinds; the harvest was slow in ripening and scanty when it came; men reaped their corn at Martinmas and yet later.[2]

---

[1] Chron. Petrib. 1089. "Swilc eac gewarð ofer eall Engleland mycel eorðstyrunge, on þone dæg iii. Id. Aug." Will. Malms. iv. 322. "Secundo anno regni ejus terræ motus ingens totam Angliam exterruit tertio idus Augusti, horrendo miraculo, ut ædificia omnia eminus resilirent, et mox pristino more residerent." Some annals, as those of Plympton (Liebermann, 26), directly connect the events. "Obiit Lanfrancus archiepiscopus, et terra mota est."

[2] Chron. u. s. "And wæs swiðe lætsum gear on corne and on ælces cynnes wæstmum, swa þæt manig man ræpon heora corn onbuton Martines mæssan and gyt lator." "Vix ad festum sancti Andreæ," says William of Malmesbury.

The next year we find no entries of this kind. There CHAP. III.
was a mighty stir in England and in Normandy; but Character
it was not a mere stirring of the elements. We now enter 1090.
on the record of the foreign pólicy and the foreign wars of Beginnings
the Red King, and we hear the first wail going up from the adventure.
oppressed folk within his kingdom. Throughout his reign
the growth of the prince's power and the grievances of his
people go together. In the former year there was nothing
to chronicle but the earthquake and the late harvest. This First men-
year we hear of the first successes of the King beyond the domestic
sea, and we hear, as their natural consequence, that the opposition.
"land was fordone with unlawful gelds." [1]

The two years which followed the death of Lanfranc saw The years
the attempt of the first year of Rufus reversed. Instead 1090–1091.
of the lord of Normandy striving to win England, the lord Successes
of England not only strives, but succeeds, in making him- mandy.
self master of a large part of the Norman duchy. Having Supremacy
thus become a continental potentate, the King comes land.
back to his island kingdom, to establish his Imperial 1091.
supremacy over the greatest vassal of his crown, and tion of
to do what his father had not done, to enlarge the borders Cumber-
of his immediate realm by a new land and a new city.   1092.

Through a large part then of the present chapter the
scene of our story will be removed from England to Normandy. Yet it is only the scene which is changed, not the Close con-
actors. One main result of the coming of the first William English
into England was that for a while the history of Nor- and Normandy and that of England cannot be kept asunder. tory.
The chief men on the one side of the water are the chief The same
men on the other side. And the fact that they were so is in both.
the main key to the politics of the time. We have in the
last chapter seen the working of this fact from one side;

[1] Chron. Petrib. 1090. "And betwyx þisum þingum þis land wæs swiðe
fordón on unlaga gelde and on oðre manige ungelimpe."

CHAP. III. we shall now see its working from the other side. The same men flit backwards and forwards from Normandy to England and from England to Normandy. But of warfare, public and private, during the reign of William Rufus and still more during the reign of Henry the First, Normandy rather than England is the chosen field. Without warfare of some kind a Norman noble could hardly live. And for that beloved employment Normandy gave many more opportunities than England. The Duke of the Normans, himself after all the man of a higher lord, could not be—at least no duke but William the Great could be—in his continental duchy all that the King of the English, Emperor in his own island, could be within his island realm. Private war was lawful in Normandy—the Truce of God itself implied its lawfulness; it never was lawful in England. And wars with France, wars with Anjou, the endless struggle in and for the borderland of Maine, went much further towards taxing the strength and disturbing the peace of the Norman duchy, than the endless strife on the Welsh and Scottish marches could go towards taxing the strength and disturbing the peace of the English kingdom. Normandy then will be our fighting-ground far more than England; but the fighting men will be the same in both lands.

The old companions of the Conqueror were by this time beginning to make way for a new generation. The rebellion of 1088 saw the last exploits of some of them. Yet others among them will still be actors for a while. Bishop Odo, cut off from playing any part in England, still plays a part in Normandy. The great border earls, Hugh of Chester and of Avranches, Roger of Shrewsbury and of Montgomery, die in the course of our tale, but not till we have something more to tell about both of them, and a good deal to tell about the longer-lived of the two. Their younger fellow, Robert of Mowbray, after becoming the

Marginal notes:

Normandy the chief seat of warfare.

Contrast between Normandy and England as to private war.

The old and the new generation.

Bishop Odo.

Hugh. d. 1101. Roger. d. 1094.

Robert of Mowbray.

chief centre of one part of our story, leaves the world chap. iii.
by a living death. The new Earl of Surrey, if not William of
already dead, passes away without anything further to Warren.
record of him; Walter Giffard, old as a man, but young Walter
as an earl, still lives on. But younger men are coming d. 1102.
into sight. William of Eu, the son of the still living William
Count Robert, has already come before us as a chief of Eu.
actor in our story, and we shall see him as the chiefest
sufferer. But above all, two men, whom we have
hitherto seen only by fits and starts, now come to the
front as chief actors on both sides of the sea. Before
we enter on the details of Norman affairs, it will be well
to try clearly to take in the character and position of
two famous bearers of the same name, great alike in England, in Normandy, and in France, Robert of Bellême, Robert of
afterwards of Shrewsbury, of Bridgenorth, and of both Bellême.
Montgomeries, and Robert, Count of the French county of Robert of
Meulan, heir of the great Norman house of Beaumont, Meulan.
and forefather of the great English house of Leicester.

The two Rogers, fathers of the two Roberts, are still
living; but for the rest of their days they play a part
quite secondary to that played by their sons. Robert History
of Bellême, the eldest son of Roger of Montgomery, has racter of
already come before us several times, most prominently Robert of
as a sharer in the rebellion raised by the present Duke
against his father in Normandy[1] and in the rebellion
raised on his behalf against his brother. As son of Succeeds
the slain Countess Mabel,[2] he was heir of the house Mabel.
of Talvas, heir alike of their possessions and of their 1082.
reputed wickedness. Lord through his mother of the Her in-
castle from which he took his name, lord of a crowd
of other castles on the border-lands of Normandy,
Perche, and Maine, Robert of Bellême, Robert Talvas,
stands forth for the present as the son of Mabel rather

---

[1] See N. C. vol. iv. pp. 558, 638.   [2] Ib. p. 493.

CHAP. III.

Succeeds
his father
at Mont-
gomery,
1094;

and his
brother at
Shrews-
bury,
1098.

His wife
Agnes of
Ponthieu.

Guy Count
of Ponthieu.
1053-1100.

Greatness
of Robert's
possessions.

than as the son of Roger. In after times counties and
lordships flowed in upon him from various sources and
in various quarters. The death of his father gave him
the old Norman possessions of the house of Montgomery;
the death of his brother gave him the new English
possessions of that house, the great earldom of Shrewsbury and all that went with it. We seem to be carried
back to past times when we find that Robert of Bellême
was married to the daughter of Guy of Ponthieu, the
gaoler of Harold, and that, at the accession of William
Rufus, Guy had still as many years to reign as the Red
King himself. Guy's death at last added Ponthieu to
the possessions of the house of Bellême, nominally in
the person of Robert's son William Talvas, practically
in that of Robert himself. The lord of such lands,
master of four and thirty castles,[1] ranked rather with
princes than with ordinary nobles; and even now, when
Robert held only the inheritance of his mother, the
extent and nature of his fiefs gave him a position almost
princely. The man alike of Normandy and of France,
he could make use of the profitable as well as the
dangerous side of a divided allegiance, and it is not

---

[1] Ord. Vit. 708 B. He does not say distinctly at what stage he means.
Geoffrey Gaimar (Chron. Angl. Norm. i. 35) has an elaborate picture of
Robert at his greatest;

"Li quens Robert, cil de Belesme,   Roche-Mabilie estait en sa pœs.
  Mil chevalers out en son esme ;   En Rom out rues assez.
  En Engleterre out treis contez,   Il esteit quen de sis contez ;
  Quens de Pontif estait clamez,   Ço ert le meillur chevaler
  Si ert conte de Leneimeis,   Ke l'em séust pur querreier.
  D'Esparlon e de Sessuneis ;   Cil vint à son seignur le rei,
  Sue estait Argenton, Seis,   Mil chevalers menat od sei."

He then goes on to mention his brothers. (See above, p. 37.) Many of
the places on this list will come in our story. "Rom," it is hardly needful
to say, is only the capital of Normandy, not of the world. But what are the
three counties in England? There is Shropshire, and most likely Sussex.
What is the third? Yorkshire, on the strength of Tickhill? But Robert
had no earldom there.

without reason that we find the lord of the border-land CHAP. III.
spoken of by the fitting title of Marquess[1]. From the Great part played by him.
death of the Conqueror onwards, through the reigns
of Robert and William, till the day when Henry sent
him to a life-long prison, Robert of Bellême fills in
the history of Normandy and England a place alongside of their sovereigns.

With the inheritance of Mabel and William Talvas, His cha- racter.
their son and grandson was believed to have succeeded
in full measure to the hereditary wickedness of their
house. That house is spoken of as one at whose deeds
dæmons themselves might shudder,[2] and Robert himself His sur- name.
bears in the traditions of his Cenomannian enemies the
frightful surname which has been so unfairly transferred to
the father of the Conqueror. His name lives in proverbs.
In the land of Maine his abiding works are pointed
to as the works of Robert the Devil. Elsewhere the
"wonders of Robert of Bellême" became a familiar
saying.[3] That Robert was a man of no small natural
gifts is plain; to the ordinary accomplishments of the
Norman warrior he added a mastery of the more in-
tellectual branches of the art of warfare. As the His skill in engineer- ing.
Cenomannian legend shows, he stood at the head of
his age in the skill of the military engineer.[4] Firm
and daring, ready of wit and ready of speech, he had
in him most of the qualities which might have made
him great in that or in any other age. But, even in His special and wanton cruelty.
that age, he held a place by himself as a kind of in-

---

[1] Ord. Vit. 675 D

[2] Hen. Hunt. De Cont. Mund. 11. " Gens ipsis dæmonibus horrenda."

[3] See N. C. vol. i. p. 468. The Archdeacon of Huntingdon himself, with a slight contempt of sex and species, calls him " Pluto, Megæra, Cerberus, vel si aliquid horrendi scribi potest." He speaks of the proverb, " Mirabilia Roberti de Belesme."

[4] See his two pictures in Orderic, 675 C, D, and 707 C, D. In his character of engineer we shall meet him at Gisors. See 766 B.

CHAP. III. carnation of evil. Restless ambition, reckless contempt of the rights of others, were common to him with many of his neighbours and contemporaries. But he stands almost alone in his habitual delight in the infliction of human suffering. The recklessness which lays waste houses and fields, the cruelty of passion or of policy which slays or mutilates an enemy, were common in his day. But even then we find only a few men of whom it was believed that the pangs of other men were to them a direct source of enjoyment. In Robert sheer love of cruelty displaced even greediness ; he refused ransom for his prisoners that he might have the pleasure of putting them to lingering deaths.[1] The received forms of cruelty blinding and mutilation, were not enough for him; he brought the horrors of the East into Western Europe ; men, and women too, were left at his bidding to writhe on the sharp stake.[2] Distrustful of all men, artful, flattering, courteous of speech, his profession of friendship was the sure path to destruction.[3] The special vices of William Rufus are not laid to his charge; it is at least to the credit of Latin Christendom in the eleventh century that it needs the union of its two worst sinners

---

[1] Ord. Vit. 707 D. "Magis affectabat supplicia miseris inferre quam per redemptionem captivorum pecunias augere." So Hen. Hunt. u. s. Yet, as some of his captives escaped, he lost the ransom for nothing.

[2] Ib. "Homines privatione oculorum et amputatione pedum manuumve deformare parvipendebat, sed inauditorum commeditatione suppliciorum in torquendis miseris more Siculi Phalaris tripudiabat. Quos in carcere pro reatu aliquo stringebat, Nerone seu Decio vel Diocletiano sævior, indicibiliter cruciabat, et inde jocos cum parasitis suis et cachinnos jactabundus exercebat. Tormentorum quæ vinctis inferebat delectatione gloriabatur, hominumque detractione pro pœnarum nimietate crudelis lætabatur." The special detail of the impaling comes from Henry of Huntingdon, who says also, "Erat ei cædes horribilis hominum cibus jucundus animæ."

[3] Will. Malms. v. 398. "Simulationis et argutiarum plenus, frontis sereno et sermonum affabilitate credulos decipiens, gnaros autem malitiæ exterritans, ut nullum esset majus futuræ calamitatis indicium quam prætensæ affabilitatis eloquium." Something of the same kind was said of King Henry himself. See N. C. vol. v. p. 841.

to form the likeness of an Ottoman Majesty, Excellency, chap. iii.
or Highness in the nineteenth. But his domestic life
was hardly happy. His wife Agnes, the heiress of His treatment of
Ponthieu, the mother of his one child William Talvas, his wife
was long kept by him in bonds in the dungeons of
Bellême.[1] And, more piteous than all, we read how and his godson.
a little boy, his own godchild, drew near to him in all
loving trust. Some say, in the sheer wantonness of
cruelty, some say, to avenge some slight fault of the
child's father, the monster drew the boy under his cloak
and tore out his eyes with his own hands.[2]

The list of the men, great and small, who were simply
wronged and dispossessed by Robert of Bellême, is
long indeed.[3] Some of them, it is true, were now
and then able to revenge their wrongs with their own
arms. He seems, as might have been expected, to His enmity
have been the special enemy of all that was specially
good in individuals or in communities. He was the to the
bitter foe of the valiant and faithful men of Domfront.[4] men of Domfront;
He was before all things the enemy of Helias of La to Helias;
Flèche. He was the enemy of his neighbour Count to Rotrou
Rotrou of Perche, who also bears a good character among of Perche;
the princes of his day.[5] As temporal lord of Seez, he to the
was the enemy of its churches, episcopal and abbatial; prelates of Seez.
he had not that reverence for the foundation of his

[1] Ord. Vit. 708 B. She at last escaped to Countess Adela at Chartres,
and got to her own land of Ponthieu.

[2] The story is told with the difference spoken of in the text by Henry of
Huntingdon (de Cont. Mundi, 11) and by William of Malmesbury (v. 398).
Henry says only, "Filioli sui oculos sub chlamide positi quasi ludens
pollicibus extraxit." William supplies a kind of motive; "Puerulum ex
baptismo filiolum, quem in obsidatum acceperat, pro modico delicto patris
excæcarit, lumina miselli unguibus nefandis abrumpens." That is, the
Archdeacon makes the ugly story still uglier, just as in the case of the
children of Juliana. See N. C. vol. v. pp. 157, 841.

[3] Ord. Vit. 708 A. "Ob insolentiam et cupiditatem plurima contra collimi-
taneos prælia cœpit; sed sæpe victus cum damno et dedecore aufugit."

[4] See further on in this chapter.   [5] Ord. Vit. 675 D.

CHAP. III.

Abbot Ralph, afterwards Archbishop of Canterbury.

father which is one of the redeeming features in the character of the Red King. He underwent excommunication from the zeal of Bishop Serlo, and by the wrongs done by him to Abbot Ralph of Seez, which drove that prelate to seek shelter in England, he unwittingly gave England a worthy primate and Anselm a worthy successor.[1] One is inclined to wonder how such a man gained the special favour of the Conqueror, whose politic sternness had nothing in common with the fiendish brutality of Robert.[2] Perhaps, as in William Rufus, the worst features of his character may for a while have been hidden. It is less surprising that, in the days of William's sons, we find him in honour at the courts of England, Normandy, and France.

His imprisonment by Henry. 1110.

But at last vengeance came upon him. When King Henry sent him to spend his days in prison, it was in a prison so strait and darksome that the outer world knew not whether he were dead or alive, nor was the time of his death set down in any record.[3]

Robert Count of Meulan and Earl of Leicester.

His father Roger of Beaumont.

The other Robert, the son of the other Roger, was a man of a different mould, a man who would perhaps seem more in place in some other age than in that in which he lived. He was the son of the old and worthy Roger of Beaumont, the faithful counsellor of princes, who, like Gulbert of Hugleville, refused to share in

---

[1] See Ord. Vit. 707 D for the Bishop; ib. 678 A and Will. Malms. Gest. Pont. 127 for the Abbot. With the bishopric there was a question of the right of advowson; "Episcopium contra jus et fas comprimebat, et Guillelmo Belesmensi avo ejus a Ricardo duce datum asserebat." Cf. on the bishopric of Le Mans, N. C. vol. iii. p. 194. From the Abbot too he demanded an oath of allegiance, "de sacramento et homagio abbatem exagitare." This was in Henry's time.

[2] Ord. Vit. 668 C. "Robertus Belesmensis qui patri tuo fuit valde dilectus, et multis honoribus olim ab ipso promotus." See above, p 84.

[3] Hen. Hunt. u. s. "Quem tantopere fama coluerat dum viveret, in carcere utrum viveret vel obisset, nescivit, diemque mortis ejus obmutescens ignoravit."

the spoils of England.[1]   Great, like his namesake, in CHAP. III.
France, Normandy, and England, Robert passed through
a long life unstained by any remarkable crime, though
it was hinted that, of his vast possessions on both sides
of the sea, some were not fairly come by.[2]   He is known He inherits
in history by the name of his French county of Meulan, Meulan from his
which he inherited from his mother's brother, Count uncle,
Hugh, son of Count Waleran, who withdrew to become
a monk of Bec.[3]   From his father, when he too had and Beau-
gone to end his days in his father's monastery of Preaux, his father.
Robert inherited the lordship of Beaumont, called, from
his father's name, Beaumont-le-Roger.[4]   He shared in His earl-
the Conqueror's distribution of lands in England, and in Leicester.
after days he received the earldom of Leicester from
King Henry, as his less stirring brother Henry had
already received that of Warwick from the Red King.
That he was a brave and skilful soldier we cannot His ex-
doubt; his establishment in England was the reward of Senlac.
good service done at one of the most critical moments of
the most terrible of battles.[5]   But the warrior of Senlac
hardly appears again in the character of a warrior; he
lives on for many years as a cold and crafty states- His fame
man, the counsellor of successive kings, whose wisdom, for wisdom
surpassing that of all men between Huntingdon and

---

[1] Will. Malms. v. 407. "Homo antiquæ simplicitatis et fidei, qui
crebro a Willelmo primo invitatus ut Angliam veniret, largis ad voluntatem
possessionibus munerandus, supersedit, pronuncians patrum suorum hæredi-
tatem se velle fovere, non transmarinas et indebitas possessiones vel
appetere vel invadere." (Cf. N. C. vol. iv. p. 448.) We have heard of
him already; N. C. vol. ii. p. 201; iii. 288, 380, 386; iv. 82, 192, 475,
645.

[2] See the story in p. 186.

[3] Will. Malms. u. s.; Will. Pict. 134; Will. Gem. vii. 4; Ord Vit.
709 A.

[4] This Norman Beaumont must be distinguished from the French and
Cenomannian Beaumonts which we shall meet with, just as there is a
Norman, a French, and a Cenomannian Montfort.

[5] See N. C. vol. iii. p. 487.

CHAP. III. Jerusalem, was deemed, like that of Ahithophel, to be like
the oracle of God.[1] His counsels were not always of an
Character amiable kind. Under Rufus, without, as far as we can
of his
influence see, sharing in his crimes, he checked those chivalrous in-
with Rufus
and Henry. stincts which were the King's nearest approach to virtue.[2]
Under Henry his influence was used to hinder the promotion of Englishmen in their own land.[3] Yet on the
whole his character stands fair. He discouraged fop-
pery and extravagance by precept and example ; he was
the right-hand man of King Henry in maintaining the
peace of the land, and he seems to have shared the
higher tastes of the clerkly monarch.[4] Of Anselm he was
His sons. sometimes the enemy, sometimes the friend.[5] His sons
were well taught, and they could win the admiration of
Pope and cardinals by their skill in disputation.[6] The
eldest, Waleran, his Norman heir, plays an unlucky part
in the reign of Henry ;[7] his English heir Robert con-

---

[1] Will. Malms. v. 407. " Cum superiorum regum tempore, spe sensim
pullulante, in gloriam procederet, hujus [Henrici] ætate summo provectu
effloruit, habebaturque ejus consilium quasi quis divinum consuluisset sacra-
rium." So Hen. Hunt. de Cont. Mund. 7. " Fuit Robertus consul de Mel-
lend in rebus secularibus sapientissimus omnium hinc usque in Jerusalem
degentium."

[2] We shall see this presently in the story of Helias. See Ord. Vit. 773 B.

[3] See N. C. vol. v. p. 828.

[4] Hen. Hunt. u. s. " Fuit scientia clarus, eloquio blandus, astutia per-
spicax, providentia sagax, ingenio versipellis, prudentia insuperabilis, consilio profundus, sapientia magnus." A goodly string of synonyms. William
of Malmesbury (u. s.) gives more details. He was " suasor concordiæ, dis-
suasor discordiæ," " in placitis propugnator justitiæ, in guerris provisor
victoriæ, dominum regem ad severitatem legum custodiendam exacuens,
ipse non eas sequens sed proponens, expers in regem perfidiæ, in ceteros
ejus persecutor." He was " ingentis in Anglia momenti, ut inveteratum
vestiendi vel comedendi exemplo suo inverteret morem." He brought in
the " consuetudo semel prandendi," contrary to the custom of Harthacnut.

[5] We shall see him in both characters as we go on. See Appendix Y.
He stood firmly by the King in the matter of investiture. See Will.
Malms. v. 417.

[6] Will. Malms. v. 406. This was when Pope Calixtus came into Normandy
in 1110. See N. C. vol. v. p. 191.　　　[7] See N. C. vol. v. pp. 197, 207, 288.

tinued the line of the Earls of Leicester.[1] His last days CHAP. III.
were clouded by domestic troubles;[2] and he is said to His last days.
have formally perilled his own soul in his zeal for the
temporal welfare of his sons. On his death-bed, so the His death.
story runs, Archbishop Ralph and other clergy bade him, 1118.
for his soul's health, to restore whatever lands he had Story of his death-bed.
gained unjustly.[3] What then, he asked, should he leave
to his sons? "Your old inheritance," answered Ralph,
"and whatever you have acquired justly. Give up the
rest, or you devote your soul to hell." The fond father
answered that he would leave all to them, and would trust
to their filial piety to make atonement for his sins.[4]
But we are told that Waleran and Robert were too busy
increasing by wrong what had been won by wrong to do
anything for the soul of their father.[5]

These are the two men who, of secondary importance
in the tale of the Conquest and of the reign of the first

---

[1] See N. C. vol. iv. p. 192.

[2] I do not quite understand the story in Henry of Huntingdon (8) about
another earl depriving Robert of his wife or bride; "Contigit quemdam
alium consulem sponsam ei tam factione quam dolosis viribus arripuisse.
Unde in senectute sua mente turbatus et angaria obnubilatus, in tenebras
mœroris incidit, nec usque ad mortem se lætum vel hilarem sensit." Earl
Robert's widow, Elizabeth or Isabel of Crépy or Vermandois, was presently
married again to the younger Earl William of Warren. (See Ord. Vit. 686 B,
723 D, 805 D; Will. Gem. viii. 40, 41.) Was there anything irregular or
scandalous about the marriage? Count Robert married her in 1096, so
that, as he was distinctly old at his death in 1118, she must have been far
from young. His children therefore were children of his advanced life,
which lessens the difficulty about the child whom his daughter Isabel
is said to have borne to King Henry late in his reign. (Will. Gem. viii.
29; cf. 37; and see N. C. vol. v. p. 844.)

[3] Hen. Hunt. u. s. "Ut terras quas vi vel arte multis abstulerat, pœnitens redderet, et erratum lacrimis lavaret." Would this extend to English
grants from the Conqueror? One might almost suspect that his father
thought so.

[4] Ib. "Filiis omnia tradam; ipsi pro salute defuncti misericorditer agant."

[5] Ib. "Filii ejus magis injuste congregata injuste studuerunt augere
quam aliquid pro salute paterna distribuere."

William, become the most prominent laymen of the reign of the second.   The churchmen of the time who stand forth conspicuously for good and for evil will have

Prominence of the two Roberts.

their place in another chapter.   But the two Roberts will, next to the King and the Ætheling, hold the first place in the tale which we have immediately to tell, as they held it still in days of which we shall not have the telling, long after the Ætheling had changed into the King.   The force of him of Bellême, the wit of him of Meulan, had their full place in the affairs both of Normandy and of England, and both were brought to bear against the prince and people of Maine.

§ 1. *Normandy under Robert.*   1087–1090.

Temptations to the invasion of Normandy.

That the thought of an invasion of his elder brother's duchy should present itself to the mind of William Rufus was not very wonderful.   The fact that it was his elder brother's duchy might perhaps be of itself enough to suggest the thought.   The dutiful son of his father, whom alone his father had called to rule of his own free will, might feel himself in some sort defrauded, if any part of his father's dominions was held by a brother whose only claim was the accident of his elder birth, and whose personal unfitness for the rule of men his father had emphatically set forth.   Indeed, without seeking for any special motive at all, mere ambition, mere love of enterprise, might be motive enough to lead a prince like Rufus to a campaign beyond the sea, a campaign which might make him master of the native dominion of his

Interest of those who held land in both countries.

father, the land of his own birth.   And such schemes would be supported on grounds of reasonable policy by a large part of the Norman possessors of the soil of England.   Holding, many of them, lands on both sides of the sea, it was their interest that the same prince should reign on both sides of the sea, and that they themselves should not be left open to the dangers of a divided allegiance. They had failed to carry out this purpose by putting Robert in possession of England; they might now carry it out by putting William in possession of Normandy. And the attempt might even Provoca- be made with some show of justice. The help which given by Robert had given to the rebellion against Rufus might, Robert. in the eyes of Rufus, or of a much more scrupulous prince than Rufus, have been held to justify reprisals. And to a prince seeking occasions or excuses for an State of invasion of Normandy the actual condition of that Normandy. duchy might seem directly to invite the coming of an invader. The invader might almost comfort himself with the belief that his invasion was a charitable work. Any kind of rule, almost any kind of tyranny, might seem an improvement on the state of things which was now rife through the whole length and breadth of the Norman land. William Rufus might reasonably think His inva- that no small part of the inhabitants of Normandy to be would welcome invasion from an invader of their own largely welcome. blood, the son of their greatest ruler. And the event showed that he was by no means mistaken in so thinking.

No words of man were ever more truly spoken than The Con- the words in which William the Great, constrained, as foretells he deemed himself, to leave Normandy in the hands of the cha- racter of Robert, was believed to have foretold the fate of the Robert's land which should be under his rule. Robert was, so his father is made to call him, proud and foolish, doomed to misfortune; the land would be wretched where he was master.[1] The Conqueror was a true pro-

---

[1] Ord. Vit. 659 B. "Indubitanter scio quod vere misera erit regio quæ subjecta fuerit ejus dominio. Superbus enim est et insipiens nebulo, trucique diu plectendus infortunio." See N. C. vol. iv. pp. 705, 854. The words

CHAP. III. phet; when Robert stepped into his father's place, the

Utter
anarchy of
the duchy.
work of the fifty years' rule of his father was undone
in a moment. Normandy at once fell back into the
state of anarchy from which William had saved it, the
state into which it fell when the elder Robert set forth
for Jerusalem.[1] Once more every man did what was
right in his own eyes. And the Duke did nothing to
hinder them. Again we are brought to that standard
of the duties of a sovereign of which we have heard so
often, that standard which was reached by the Conqueror and by his younger son, but which neither Robert in this generation nor Stephen in the next strove

Character
of Robert.
to reach. Robert, it must always be noticed, is never
charged with cruelty or oppression of any kind in his

His weak
good-na-
ture.
own person. His fault was exactly of the opposite kind.
He was so mild and good-natured, so ready to listen to
every suppliant, to give to every petitioner, to show
mercy to every offender, that he utterly neglected the
discharge of the first duty of his office, that which the
men of his time called doing justice.[2] William the Great

must of course take their share of the doubts which can hardly fail to attach
to the long speech of which they form a part; but they are more likely than
most parts of it to have been preserved by a trustworthy tradition. On
the speech see Church, Anselm, 147.

[1] See N. C. vol. ii. p. 191.

[2] There is more than one passage in Orderic setting forth the wretched
state of things in Normandy under Robert. See 664 B; 672 B, C; 675
A, B; 677 B. In the first passage he gives a personal description, not
unlike that quoted in N. C. vol. iv. p. 633; "Omnes ducem Robertum
mollem esse desidemque cognoscebant, et idcirco facinorosi eum despicie-
bant et pro libitu suo dolosas factiones agitabant. Erat quippe idem dux
audax et validus, multaque laude dignus, eloquio facundus, sed in regimine
sui suorumque inconsideratus, in erogando prodigus, in promittendo diffusus,
ad mentiendum levis et incautus, misericors supplicibus, ad justitiam super
iniquo faciendam mollis et mansuetus, in definitione mutabilis, in conversatione omnibus nimis blandus et tractabilis, ideoque perversis et insipientibus
despicabilis. Corpore autem brevis et grossus, ideoque *Brevis-ocrea* a
patre est cognominatus." Cf. Roman de Rou, 14470.

The words about Robert's tendency to falsehood would seem to imply,

had done justice and made peace. The smaller brood CHAP. III.
of thieves and murderers had been brought to feel the Revival of
avenging arm of the law. Thieves and murderers on a brigandage and private
greater scale, the unruly nobles of the duchy, had been war.
forced to keep back their hands from that form of
brigandage which they dignified with the name of private
war. Under Robert both classes of offenders found full
scope for their energies. He did nothing to restrain
either. He neither made peace nor did justice. Brave, Lack of
liberal, ready of speech, ready of wit and keen of sight "justice."
in supporting the cause of another, Robert undoubtedly
could be. But stronger qualities were needed, and those
qualities Robert had not. Sunk in sloth and dissipation, no
man heeded him; the land was without a ruler. Forgetful
alike of injuries and of benefits, Robert, from the first
moment of his reign, tamely endured the most flagrant
outrages to the ducal authority, without doing anything
to hinder or to avenge.[1]

not so much deliberate lying as that kind of carelessness of truth which is
quite of a piece with the rest of his character.

On the technical use of the word *justice*, see N. C. vol. v. pp. 157, 253,
320, 520; cf. ii. 33, 40, 173.

[1] Ord. Vit. 672 B. " Provincia tota erat dissoluta, et prædones catervatim discurrebant per vicos et per rura, nimiumque super inermes debaccha-
batur latrunculorum caterva. Robertus dux nullam super malefactores
exercebat disciplinam, et grassatores per octo annos sub molli principe
super imbecillem populum suam agitabant furiam." Perhaps the most
striking character of Robert is that which is given of him by one who had
studied him in two parts of the world, Ralph of Caen in his Gesta Tancredi,
c. xv. (Muratori, v. 291). The virtues of Robert were "pietas"—in the
sense of *pity*—and "largitas." But he carried both virtues so far that they
became vices. "Pietas largitasque valde fuissent mirabiles ; sed quia
in neutra modum tenuit, in utraque erravit." He goes on to describe
Robert at greater length ; "Siquidem misericordiam ejus immisericordem
sensit Normannia, dum eo consule per impunitatem rapinarum nec homini
parceret nec Deo licentia raptorum. Nam sicariis manibus, latronum gutturi,
mœchorum caudæ salaci, eamdem quam suis se reverentiam debere consul
arbitrabatur. Quapropter nullus ad eum vinctus in lacrimis trahebatur,
quin solutus mutuas ab eo lacrimas continuo impetraret. Ideo, ut dixi,

CHAP. III.

Spread
of vice
and evil
fashions.

In other respects also Normandy suddenly changed from what it had been under the great King-duke. William the Great, strict to austerity in his private life, careful in the observance of all religious duties, a zealous supporter of ecclesiastical discipline, had made his duchy into a kind of paradise in ecclesiastical eyes. All this was now swept away. The same flood of foolish and vicious fashions which overspread England overspread Normandy also. There is nothing to convict Robert personally of the special vices of Rufus; but the life of the unmarried Duke was very unlike the life of his father. And vice of the grossest kind, the vices of Rufus himself, stalked forth into broad daylight, unabashed and unpunished.[1] The ecclesiastical power, no longer supported by the secular arm, was too weak to restrain or to chastise.[2] As every form of violence, so every form of licentiousness, had its full swing in the Normandy of Robert Curthose.

Weakness
of the
spiritual
power.

Building
of castles.

The Conqueror
keeps garrisons in
the castles
of the
nobles.
Instances
at Evreux,

But, above all, this time stood out, like all times of anarchy, as a time of building and strengthening of castles. One of the means by which the Conqueror had maintained the peace of the land had been by keeping garrisons of his own in the castles of such of his nobles as were likely to be dangerous. He had followed this wise policy with the castle of Evreux, the stronghold of his kinsman Count William. He had followed it with the crowd of castles which, as the inheritance of his

---

nullis sceleribus fraenum, immo omnibus additum calcar ea tempestate Normannia querebatur." Of Robert's bounty he goes on to say that he would give any sum for a hawk or a dog; "Hujus autem pietatis sororculam eam fuisse patet largitatem, quae accipitrem, sive canem argenti summa quantalibet comparabat."

[1] Orderic is plain-spoken enough on this head in 672 B.

[2] Ib. "Episcopi ex auctoritate Dei exleges anathematizabant. Theologi *prolatis sermonibus* Dei reos admonebant. Sed his omnibus tumor et cupiditas cum satellitibus suis immoderate resistebant."

mother, had passed to Robert of Bellême, the man who CHAP. III.
is to be the leading villain of our present drama. But and in the Bellême
the precautions of the Conqueror lasted no longer than castles.
his life; his successor might be defied without danger.
At the moment of the King's death, Robert of Bellême
was on his way to the court to "speak with the King,"
in the ordinary phrase,[1] on some affairs of his own.   He
had reached Brionne when he heard of the Conqueror's
death.   Instead of going on to offer his homage or sup- Robert of
port to the new Duke, he turned back, gathered his Bellême drives out
own followers, marched on Alençon, and by a sudden the ducal forces.
attack drove the ducal garrison out of the fortress by
the Sarthe, the southern bulwark of Normandy.   He did
the same with better right on his own hill of Bellême,
which was not strictly Norman soil.   He did so with all
his other castles, and with as many of the castles of his
neighbours as he could.[2]   The lord of Bellême in short
established himself as a prince who might well bear himself as independent of the lord of Rouen.   Count William The like
of Evreux followed his example; the late King's garrison done by the Count of
was driven out of the fortress which had arisen within Evreux and others.
the walls of the Roman Mediolanum.   William of Breteuil,
Ralph of Toesny or of Conches, the nobles of Normandy
in general wherever they had the power, all did the
like.[3]   They drove out the garrisons; they strengthened
the old fortresses; they raised new ones, adulterine

---

[1] See N. C. vol. v. p. 46.   Cf. vol. iv. p. 688.

[2] Orderic (664 B) records Robert's doings at Alençon and Bellême, and
adds, " Hoc quoque fecit Bellismæ, et omnibus aliis castellis suis, et non
solum suis, sed et in vicinorum suorum, quos sibi pares dedignabatur habere,
municipiis, quæ aut intromissis clientibus sibi subjugavit, aut penitus, ne
sibi aliquando resistere possent, destruxit."

[3] Ib.   He adds a reflexion in his character of "Angligena."   " Sic
proceres Neustriæ de munitionibus suis omnes regis custodes expulerunt,
patriamque divitiis opulentam propriis viribus vicissim exspoliaverunt.
Opes itaque quas Anglis aliisque gentibus violenter rapuerunt, merito
latrociniis et rapinis perdiderunt."

castles in the phrase of the day, built without the Duke's
licence and placed beyond his control. Those who
were strong enough seized on the castles of weaker
neighbours. The land was again filled with these robbers' nests, within whose walls and circuit law was
powerless, lairs, as men said, of grievous wolves, who
entered in and spared not the flock.[1] Some nobles indeed had the decency to go through the form of asking
the Duke for gifts which they knew that he would not
have strength of mind to refuse them. One of them was
William of Breteuil, the son of the famous Earl William
of Hereford, the brother of the rebel Roger,[2] and once a
sharer in Robert's rebellion against his father. He asked
and received the famous tower of Ivry, the tower of
Albereda, the now vanished stronghold which once looked
down on the plain where Henry of Navarre was in after
ages to smite down the forces of the League. This gift
involved a wrong to the old Roger of Beaumont, who had
held that great fortress by the Conqueror's commission.
Roger was accordingly recompensed by a grant of
Brionne, the island stronghold in the heart of Normandy,
which had played such a part in the early wars of the
Conqueror.[3] Thus places specially connected with the
memory of the great William, places like Alençon and

Robert's
lavish
grants.

Ivry.

Brionne.

[1] Ord. Vit. 672 C. "Adulterina passim municipia condebantur, et ibidem
filii latronum ceu catuli luporum ad dilacerandas bidentes nutriebantur."
Our Chronicler was yet more vigorous when he peopled the castles with
devils and evil men, A.D. 1135. The "adulterina municipia" are the castles
built without the Duke's licence. See N. C. vol. ii. p. 193. For the German
laws on the same subject, see Maurer, Einleitung, p. 24. M. le Hardy (60)
amusingly mistakes the "municipia" for "quelques communes."

[2] See N. C. vol. iv. pp. 537, 638.

[3] Ord. Vit. 664 C. "Guillelmo de Britolio dedit Ibericum, ubi arx quam
Albereda proavia ejus fecit fortissima est. Et Rogerio de Bellomonte, qui
solebat Ibericum jussu Guillelmi regis custodire, concessit Brioniam, quod
oppidum munitissimum et in corde terræ situm est." On Ivry, see N. C.
vol. i. p. 258. See Will. Gem. viii. 15, where the same story is told as by
Orderic. On Brionne, see N. C. vol. ii. pp. 196, 268, 624.

Brionne, which had cost him no small pains to win or to
recover, passed away from his son without a thought.
Robert gave to every man everything that he asked for,
to the impoverishment of himself and to the strengthening of every other man against him.[1]

In one corner only of the duchy was there a better
state of things to be seen. The Ætheling Henry had
received from his dying father a bequest in money, but
no share in his territorial dominions.[2] He claimed however the English lands which had been held by his
mother Matilda, but which the late King had kept in his
own hands after her death.[3] This claim had not as yet
been made good, and Henry's possessions still consisted
only of his five thousand pounds in money. With part
of this he was presently to make a splendid invest-
ment. While Henry had money but no lands, Robert
had wide domains, but his extravagance soon left him
without money. The Norman portion of the Conqueror's hoard was presently scattered broadcast among
his mercenary soldiers and other followers. Of these
he kept a vast number; men flocked eagerly to a prince
who was so ready to give; but before long he was

The Æthel-
ing Henry.

He claims
his mo-
ther's
lands.

Lavish
waste of
Robert.

[1] Ord. Vit. 664 C. "Cunctis placere studebat, cunctisque quod petebant
aut dabat aut promittebat vel concedebat. Prodigus dominium patrum
suorum quotidie imminuebat, insipienter tribuens unicuique quod petebat,
et ipse pauperescebat, unde alios contra se roborabat."

[2] See N. C. vol. iv. p. 709.

[3] The passages from Orderic which set forth Henry as the heir of his
mother have been discussed in N. C. vol. iv. p. 854 (cf. pp. 320, 629), as also
the expression of William of Malmesbury (v. 392) which implies that the
Conqueror bequeathed Matilda's lands to Henry, or directed that Matilda's
earlier bequest should take effect. The same writer also just before speaks
(v. 391) of Henry, after his father's death, as "paterna benedictione et
materna hæreditate simul et multiplicibus thesauris ["gersuman unateal-
lendlice" in the Chronicle] nixus." Wace also says (14484),

" E Henris out des déniers asez   Partie out del tresor son pere
   Ke sis peres li out donez,   E grant partie out de sa mere."

CHAP. III.

He asks
a loan of
Henry.

Henry
buys the
Côtentin
and Av-
ranchin.

without the means of giving or paying any more. He asked Henry for a gift or a loan. The scholar-prince was wary, and refused to throw his money away into the bottomless pit of Robert's extravagance.[1] The Duke then proposed to sell him some part of his dominions. At this proposal Henry caught gladly, and a bargain was struck. For a payment of three thousand pounds, Henry became master of a noble principality in the western part of the Norman duchy. The conquest of William Longsword,[2] the colony of Harold Blaatand,[3] the whole land from the fortress of Saint James to the haven of Cherbourg, the land of Coutances and Avranches, the castle and abbey of Saint Saviour,[4] and the house that was castle and abbey in one, the house of Saint Michael in Peril of the Sea—all this became the dominion of Henry, now known as Count of the Côtentin. With these territories he received the superiority over a formidable vassal; he became lord over the Norman possessions of Earl Hugh of Chester.[5] Thus the English-born son of the Norman Conqueror held for his first dominion no contemptible portion of his father's duchy, as ruler of the Danish land which in earlier days had beaten back an English invasion.[6] In that land, under

---

[1] Ord. Vit. 665 C. "Opes quas habebat militibus ubertim distribuit, et ·tironum multitudinem pro spe et cupidine munerum sibi connexuit. Deficiente ærario Henricum fratrem suum, ut de thesauro sibi daret, requisivit. Quod ille omnino facere noluit."

[2] N. C. vol. i. p. 170.

[3] Ib. vol. i. p. 191.   [4] Ib. vol. ii. p. 249.

[5] The purchase is thus described by Orderic (ib.); "Henricus duci tria millia librarum argenti erogavit, et ab eo totum Constantinum pagum, quæ tertia Normanniæ pars est, recepit. Sic Henricus Abrincas et Constantiam, Montemque sancti Michaëlis in periculo maris, totumque fundum Hugonis Cestrensis consulis, quod in Neustria possidebat, primitus obtinuit." This of course does not mean any disseisin of Earl Hugh, but only the transfer of his homage from Robert to Henry. For other versions of the transaction, see Appendix I.

[6] See N. C. vol. i. p. 302.

the rule of him who was one day to be called the Lion CHAP. III.
of Justice, there was a nearer approach to peace and Henry's
order than could be found in other parts of Normandy. firm rule.
The young Count governed his county well and firmly;
no such doings went on in the lands of Coutances and
Avranches as went on in the rest of the duchy under
the no-rule of Duke Robert.[1]

Henry, Ætheling on one side of the sea and now Henry
Count on the other side,[2] next thought of crossing the goes to
England.
channel to seek for those estates in his native land Summer,
which he claimed in right of his mother.[3] These lands, 1088.
in Cornwall, Buckinghamshire, and specially in Gloucestershire, had mostly formed a part of the forfeited possessions of Brihtric, the man whose name legend has so
strangely connected with that of Matilda.[4] Henry
must have reached England about the time when the
rebellion had been put down, and when the new King
might be expected to be in a mood inclined either to
justice or to generosity. William received his brother William
graciously, and granted, promised, or pretended to grant, promises
him the
the restitution of the lands of their mother.[5] Henry, lands of
already a ruler on one side of the sea, a sharer in his Matilda.
father's inheritance, went back to his peninsula in a

---

[1] Ord. Vit. 665 C. "Constantiniensem provinciam bene gubernavit,
suamque juventutem laudabiliter exercuit." He was hardly twenty years
old. So 689 C; "Constantinienses Henricus clito strenue regebat."

[2] He is " Henricus clito [Ætheling], Constantiniensis comes " in Orderic,
672 D; "comes Henricus" in Will. Gem. viii. 3.

[3] Ord. Vit. 672 D. " In Angliam transfretavit et a fratre suo terram
matris suæ requisivit." The date is fixed by the words "postquam
certus rumor de Rofensis [oppidi] deditione citra mare personuit."

[4] See N. C. vol. iv. pp. 164, 759.

[5] Ord. Vit. 672 D. " Rex Guillelmus benigniter eum, ut decuit fratrem,
suscepit, et quod poterat fraterne concessit. Deinde, peractis pro quibus
ierat, in autumno regi valefecit." An actual possession of something
seems implied in the words of Orderic, 689 C, " Regi Angliæ hostis erat
pro terra matris suæ, qua rex eumdem in Anglia dissaisiverat, et Roberto
Haimonis filio dederat."

CHAP. III. character which was yet newer to him, that of a sharer in his father's conquest, a great land-owner on the other side of the sea. But his luck, which was to shine forth so brightly in after times, forsook him for the present. If Henry ever came into actual possession of his English

He seizes them again. estates, his tenure of them was short. At some time which is not distinctly marked, the lands which had

They are granted to Robert Fitz- hamon. been Matilda's were again seized by William. They were granted to one of the rising men of the time, one of the few who had been faithful to the King in the late times of trouble, to Robert Fitz-hamon, perhaps already the terror of the southern Cymry. Thus the old posses- sions of Brihtric passed into the hands of the lord of the castle of Cardiff, the founder of the minster of Tewkes- bury.[1] In the next generation the policy of Henry was to win them back, if not for himself, yet for his son.[2]

Influence of Odo with Robert. If the Count of Coutances failed of his objects in Eng- land, a worse fate awaited him for a season on his return to Normandy. He had enemies at the court of Duke Robert; first of all, it would seem, his uncle Odo, lately Earl of Kent and still Bishop of Bayeux. He was now driven from his earldom to his bishopric, like a dragon, we are told, with fiery wings cast down to the earth.[3]

Autumn, 1088. The tyrant of Bayeux, the worst of prelates—such are the names under which Odo now appears in the pages of our chief guide[4]—had again become Robert's chief counsellor. His counsel seems to have taken the

---

[1] See Appendix GG.

[2] See N. C. vol. v. p. 853; Ord. Vit. 681 A.

[3] This flight is Orderic's own. In 673 A we have, "Baiocensis Odo, velut ignivolus draco projectus in terram."

[4] Ib. 672 D, "Baiocensis tyrannus;" 673 A, "pessimus præsul Odo." This last phrase comes at the beginning of Odo's speech in the Duke's council; at the end of it our historian has waxed milder, and tells us (674 A) how "exhortatoriam antistitis allocutionem omnes qui aderant laudaverunt."

form of stirring up the Duke's mind to abiding wrath CHAP. III. against his brother of England, and against all who were, or were held to be, his partisans.[1] When Henry left England to come back to Normandy, he brought with him a dangerous companion in the person of Robert of Bellême. That rebel of a few months back was now thoroughly reconciled to Rufus. Duke Robert was even made to believe that his namesake of Bellême, so lately his zealous supporter, was joined with Henry by a mutual oath to support the interests of the King of the English at the expense of the Duke of the Normans.[2] The measures of Robert or of Odo were speedily taken; the coasts were watched; the voyagers were seized before they could disembark from their ships.[3] They were put in fetters, and presently consigned to prisons in the keeping of the Bishop. They had not even the comfort of companionship in bonds. While the Ætheling, Count of the Côtentin, was kept in Odo's episcopal city, the place of imprisonment for the son of the Earl of Shrewsbury was the fortress of Neuilly, in the most distant part of Odo's diocese, near the frontier stream of Vire which parts the Bessin from Henry's own peninsula. The less illustrious captive was the first to find a champion. Earl Roger, by the licence of the King, left England, crossed into Normandy, entered into open war with the Duke on behalf of his son, and garrisoned all his own castles and those of his son against him. Vassal of three lords, the lord

Henry brings back Robert of Bellême.

They are seized and imprisoned.

Earl Roger makes war on the Duke.

---

[1] Ord. Vit. 673 A. "Variis seditionibus commovebat Normanniam, ut sic de aliquo modo nepoti suo, a quo turpiter expulsus fuerat, machinaretur injuriam."

[2] Orderic here (672 D) speaks only of "quidam malevoli discordiæ satores ... falsa veris immiscentes." But surely the Bishop was at their head.

[3] I think we may accept this circumstantial account of Orderic. For other versions, see Appendix I.

of Montgomery and Shrewsbury, the father of the lord of Bellême, might almost rank as their peer. As a prince rather than as a mere baron, Earl Roger took to arms.

His fortresses.

The border-fortresses on the frontier ground of Normandy, Maine, and Perche were all put into a state of defence.[1] Alencon, by the border stream, was again, as in the days when its burghers mocked the Tanner's grandson,[2] garrisoned against his son and successor. Bellême itself, the cradle of the house of Talvas—the Rock of Mabel, bearing the name of her who had united the houses of Talvas and Montgomery, and whose blood had been the price of its possession—Saint-Cenery on its peninsula by the Sarthe, another of the spoils of Mabel's bloody policy—all these border strongholds, together with a crowd of others lying more distinctly within the Norman dominions, had again become hostile spots where the Duke of the Normans was defied.

The episcopal gaoler of Bayeux, in his character of chief counsellor of Duke Robert, is described as keeping his feeble nephew somewhat in awe. But his counsels, it is added, were sometimes followed, sometimes despised.[3] Now that all Normandy was in a blaze of civil war, Odo came to Rouen, and had an audience of the Duke, seemingly in an assembly of his nobles.[4] If our guide is to be trusted, Robert, who had no love for hearing sermons even from the lips of his father, was now condemned to hear a sermon of no small length from the perhaps even readier lips of his uncle. Odo

Odo's exhortation to Robert.

---

[1] Ord. Vit. 672 D. "Rogerius comes Scrobesburiæ, ut Robertum filium suum captum audivit, accepta a rege licentia, festinus in Neustriam venit, et omnia castella sua militari manu contra ducem munivit."

[2] See N. C. vol. ii. p. 297.

[3] Ord. Vit. 673 A. "Ipsum nempe dux multum metuebat, et quibusdam consiliis ejus adquiescebat, quædam vero flocci pendebat."

[4] At least there were others besides the Duke to hear and to cheer. See p. 198, note 4.

gave Robert a lecture on the good government of his CHAP. III.
duchy, on the duty of defending the oppressed and
putting down their oppressors. A long list of princes
are held up as his examples, the familiar heroes of
Persia, Macedonia, Carthage, and Rome, among whom,
one hardly sees why, Septimius Severus takes his place
along with the first Cæsar. On the same list too Rivalry of
Normandy
come the princes of his own house, the princes whom and
the warlike French had ever feared, winding up France.
with the name of his own father, greatest of them all.[1]
In all this we hear the monk of Saint Evroul rather
than the Bishop of Bayeux; but any voice is worth
hearing which impresses on us a clearer understanding
of the abiding jealousy between Normandy and France.
But we may surely hear Odo himself in the practical
advice that follows. Now is the time to root out the The line of
Talvas to
whole accursed stock of Talvas from the Norman duchy. be rooted
They were an evil generation from the beginning, not out.
one of whom ever died the death of other men.[2] It is
as the son of Mabel, not as the son of Roger, that Robert
of Bellême comes in for this frightful inheritance, and
Odo could not foresee how pious an end the Earl of
Shrewsbury was to make in a few years.[3] He reminded the Duke that a crowd of castles, which had
been ducal possessions as long as his father lived, had
been seized on his father's death by Robert of Bellême,
and their ducal garrisons driven out.[4] It was the

---

[1] Ord. Vit. 673 B. "Reminiscere patrum et proavorum, quorum mag-
nanimitatem et virtutem pertimuit bellicosa gens Francorum." It is curious
to see how often Norman patriotism falls back on the memory of the wars
with France rather than on the conquest of England. So it is in the speech
of Walter of Espec before the battle of the Standard. See N. C. vol. v.
p. 832.

[2] Ib. 673 D. "Hoc nimirum horrenda mors eorum attestatur, quorum
nullus communi et usitato fine, ut cæteri homines, defecisse invenitur."

[3] See Ord. Vit. 708 B.   [4] See above, p. 193.

Duke's duty, as the ruler of the land, as a faithful son
of Holy Church, to put an end to the tyranny of this
usurper, and to give to all his dominions the blessing of
lawful government at the hand of their lawful prince.

But the overthrow of the house of Talvas was not
the only work to which Odo stirred up his nephew.
Affairs of There was another enterprise to be undertaken before
Maine.
the great lord of the Cenomannian border could be
safely attacked. These early days of Robert lead us
on at once to that side of the continental wars and
continental policy of Rufus which seems to have drawn
to itself the smallest amount of English interest at the
time,[1] but which is that on which we are now led to
look with a deeper interest than any other. Before
Robert could safely attack Bellême, he must make sure
of Le Mans and of all Maine. Every mention of that
noble city, of its counts and its bishops, its renowned
church, and its stout-hearted citizens, has a charm which
is shared by no other spot between the Loire and the
Helias and Channel. And at no stage of its history did the Ceno-
Hildebert.
mannian state stand forth with greater brilliancy than in
the last days of its independent being, when Le Mans
had Helias to its count and Hildebert to its bishop.
Those days are still parted from us by a few years; but
the advice given by Odo to Robert brings us to the beginning of the chain of events which leads straight to
them. The historian of William Rufus must now begin
to look forward to the days when Rufus, like his
father, tried his strength against the valiant men of
the Cenomannian land and city, and tried it at a time

---

[1] The only entry which the Chronicler has on Rufus' wars in Maine
is the short one in 1099 (more was said about the expedition of the
elder William in 1063), but some parts of the Norman war are given in
great detail.

when land and city could put forth their full strength
back again under a leader worthy of them. But as
yet the land of Maine has neither to deal with so
mighty a foe nor to rejoice in the guardianship of so
worthy a champion. In the stage of the tale which
we have now reached, Rufus plays no part at all, and
Helias plays only a secondary part. The general story of History
Le Mans and Maine has been elsewhere carried down of Maine under the
to the last mention of them in the days of the Con- Conqueror.
queror.[1] It has been told how the land passed under
William's power in the days before he crossed the sea 1063.
to win England[2]—how the city and land had revolted
against the Norman—how, after trying the rule of a
foreign branch of their own princely house, its people had
risen as the first free commonwealth north of the Loire 1073.
—how they had been again brought into William's
hand, and that largely by the help of his English warriors[3]—and how, after the final submission of the city,
isolated spots of the Cenomannian land had again risen
against the Norman power. The last act of this earlier
drama was when a single Cenomannian fortress success- 1083.
fully withstood the whole strength of Normandy and
England.[4] We have seen how Hubert of Beaumont beheld the Conqueror baffled before his hill fortress of
Sainte-Susanne, the shattered keep which still stands,
sharing with Dol in the Breton land the honour of being
the two spots from which William had to turn away,
conqueror no longer.[5] But, if Hubert had beaten back 1086.
William from his castle, he had found it expedient to
return to his allegiance; and, at the death of the Conqueror, Maine seems to have been as thoroughly under
William's power as Normandy and England. Things

---

[1] See N. C. vol. v. pp. 543–563, 652–655.
[2] Ib. vol. iii. pp. 182–215. [3] Ib. vol. iv. pp. 483, 557, 827.
[4] Ib. vol. iv. p. 652. [5] Ib. vol. iv. pp. 635, 657.

CHAP. III.

Dissatisfaction in Maine.

Relations with Fulk of Anjou.

changed as soon as the great King had passed away. The land and city which had striven so often against the Conqueror himself were not likely to sit down quietly under the feeble rule of Robert. And, besides the standing dislike of the people of Maine to Norman rule, there was a neighbour who was likely to be stirred up by his own ambition to meddle in the affairs of Maine, and to whom the actual provisions of treaties gave at least a colourable claim to do so. By the terms of the peace of Blanchelande, the new Duke of the Normans had become the man of Count Fulk of Anjou for the county of Maine.[1] It is true that the homage had been of the most formal kind. There had been no reservation of authority on the part of the superior lord, nor, as far as we can see, was any service of any kind imposed on the

Robert's homage to Fulk.

fief, if fief it is to be called. The homage might almost seem to have been a purely personal act, a homage expressing thankfulness for the surrender of all Angevin rights over Maine, rather than an acknowledgement of Angevin superiority over the land and city. Still Robert, as Count of Maine, had, in some way or other, become Count Fulk's man, and Count Fulk had, in some way or other, become Robert's lord. A relation was thus established between them of which the *Rechin* was sure to take advantage, whenever the time came.

Robert Count of Maine.

State of things in Maine.

Robert, on his father's death, had taken his title of Prince of the Cenomannians as well as that of Duke of the Normans,[2] and his authority seems to have been acknowledged at Le Mans no less than at Rouen. We may suspect that there was no very deep felt loyalty in the minds of a people whose rebellious tendencies had deeply impressed the mind of William the Great. He is

---

[1] N. C. vol. iv. p. 563.

[2] Ord. Vit. 673 C. "Normannorum dux et Cœnomannorum princeps nomine tenus multis annis factus est."

said—though we may guess that the etymology comes CHAP. III.
rather from the reporter than from the speaker—to have
derived the name of their land and city from their currish
madness.[1] But there was as yet no open resistance. Of
the three chief men in Church and State, Bishop Howel Howel.
was an active supporter of the Norman connexion, while
Geoffrey of Mayenne and Helias of La Flèche were at
least not ready openly to throw it off. Geoffrey, who Geoffrey of
had fought against the Conqueror twenty-five years Mayenne.
before,[2] who had betrayed the young commonwealth of
Le Mans fifteen years before,[3] must have been now advanced in life; but we shall still hear of him for some years
to come. Helias, the chief hero of later wars, was of a Helias.
younger generation, and now appears for the first time.
He was, it will be remembered, the son of John of La His descent
Flèche and of Paula the youngest sister of the last Count position.
Herbert.[4] He was therefore, before any other man in
the land, the representative of Cenomannian independence, as distinguished both from Norman rule and from
Angevin superiority. But his father had, in the Conqueror's second Cenomannian war, remained faithful to
the Norman, alike against commonwealth, Lombard, and
Angevin.[5] His son for the present followed the same
course. Bishop Howel was in any case a zealous Norman Story of
partisan; according to one story he was a special nominee Howel's
of the Conqueror, appointed for the express purpose of appoint-
helping to keep the people of Maine in order. According ment.
to the local historian, he had been appointed Dean of
Saint Julian's by his predecessor Arnold, and was, on

---

[1] Ord. Vit. 531 A. "Cœnomanis, *a canina rabie dicta*, urbs est antiqua,
et plebs ejus finitimis procax et sanguinolenta, dominisque suis semper
contumax et rebellionis avida." Following the diphthongal spelling of the
text, one might rather be tempted to derive the name from the *commune*
or κοινόν set up by its *men*.

[2] N. C. vol. iii. pp. 167, 203, 209-212.   [3] Ib. iv. 546-555.

[4] Ib. vol. iii. p. 197.   [5] Ib. vol. iv. pp. 545, 560, 563.

Arnold's death, freely and unanimously chosen to the
bishopric.[1] In Normandy it was believed that King
William, on Arnold's death, offered the bishopric to one
of his own clerks, Samson of Bayeux, who declined the
offer on the ground that a bishop, according to apostolic
rule, ought to be blameless, while he himself was a
grievous sinner in many ways. The King said that
Samson must either take the bishopric himself or find
some fit person in his stead. Samson made his nomination at once. There was in the King's chapel a clerk,
poor, but of noble birth and of virtuous life, Howel by
name, and, as his name implied, of Breton birth or
descent.[2] He was the man to be bishop of Le Mans.
Howel was at once sent for. He came, not knowing to
what end he was called. Young in years, slight and mean
in figure, he had not the stately presence with which
Walcher of Durham had once impressed the mind of
Eadgyth, perhaps of William himself.[3] But Howel was
not called upon, like Walcher, to be a goodly martyr,
but only a confessor on a small scale. William was at
first tempted to despise the unconscious candidate for
the chair of Saint Julian. But Samson, who, sinner as
he may have been, seems not to have been a bad preacher
or reasoner, warned the King that God looked not at the

*Samson re-
commends
him for
the see.*

---

[1] Mabillon, Vet. An. 288. "Favore totius cleri ejusdem ecclesiæ
decanum statuerat; in quo gradu tanto amore totius populi erga se illexit
affectum, ut eo jam tempore non minorem quam episcopo omnes illi reverentiam exhiberent. . . . Unde factum est, ut post decessum memorati antistitis
in electionem ipsius omnes unanimiter convenirent, ipsumque episcopatu
dignissimum voce consona proclamarent."

[2] Ord. Vit. 531 B. "'Ecce in capella tua est quidam pauper clericus,
sed nobilis et bene morigeratus. Huic præsulatum commenda in Dei
timore, quia dignus est (ut æstimo) tali honore.' Regi autem percunctanti
quis esset, Samson respondit : 'Hoëlus dicitur, et est genere Brito ; sed
humilis est, et revera bonus homo.'" On Samson himself, see N. C. vol.
iv. p. 641.

[3] N. C. vol. iv. p. 478.

outward appearance, but at the heart. William examined
further into Howel's life and conversation, and presently
gave him the temporal investiture of the bishopric.[1] At
the same time a *congé d'élire* went to Le Mans, which
led to Howel's "pure and simple" election by the Chapter.[2] A point both of canon and of feudal law turned
up. The old dispute between the Norman Duke and the Temporal
relations
of the
Angevin Count about the advowson of the bishopric had
never been settled; the Peace of Blanchelande was silent bishopric
of Le
on that point. Legally there can be no doubt that the Mans.
true temporal superior of the Bishop of Le Mans was
neither Fulk nor William, but their common, if forgotten,
lord King Philip.[3] But, whoever might be his temporal
lord, no one doubted that the Bishop of Le Mans was a
suffragan, and the suffragan highest in rank, of the Archbishop of Tours.[4] Yet, as things stood, as Tours was in
the dominions of Fulk, a subject of William who went
to that metropolis for consecration might have been called
on to enter into some engagement inconsistent with his
Norman loyalty. By a commission therefore from Arch- Howel consecrated at
bishop Ralph of Tours, Howel received consecration at Rouen.
April 21,
1085.

[1] Ord. Vit. 531 C. "Ei curam et seculare jus Cœnomanensis episcopa-
tus commisit." I have elsewhere spoken of this kind of document in
England (N. C. vol. ii. p. 588). Only it would seem that in England the
King either acted wholly of himself or else confirmed an election already
made by the Chapter. Here the Chapter, as in later times, elects on the
King's recommendation.

[2] Ib. "Decretum regis clero insinuatum est, et præfati clerici bonæ
vitæ testimonium ab his qui noverunt ventilatum est. Pro tam pura et
simplici electione devota laus a fidelibus Deo reddita est, et electus pastor ad
caulas ovium suarum ab episcopis et reliquis fidelibus, quibus hoc a rege
jussum fuerat, honorifice perductus est." The *regale*, or rather *ducale*,
comes out strongly in these matters, as it always does in Normandy.

[3] See N. C. vol. iii. p. 194.

[4] Vet. An. 290. "Celeberrimum est enim Cenomannensis ecclesiæ
præsulem post Turonensem archiepiscopum totius Turonensis diœceseos
obtinere primatum." *Diœcesis* here stands for province, as *parochia* constantly stands for diocese.

CHAP. III. Rouen from the Primate of the Normans, William the Good Soul.[1]

This story is worth telling, as it is thoroughly characteristic of the Conqueror; but there is this difficulty about it, that we can hardly understand either how the historian of the Bishops of Le Mans could fail to know the succession of the deans of his own church, or else how the head of the chapter of Saint Julian's could be lurking as a poor clerk in King William's chapel. Be this as it may, there is thorough agreement as to the episcopal virtues of Howel, as to his zeal in continuing

Howel's Norman loyalty.

the works in the church of Saint Julian,[2] and as to his unwavering loyalty to the Norman house. And, builder and adorner of the sanctuary as he was, he did not scruple to rob the altars of the saints of their gold and silver to feed the poor in the day of hunger.[3] His loyalty to Robert seems to have carried with it, for a time at

Robert before Le Mans.

least, the submission of the city. The Duke drew near at the head of his army. Bishop Odo was again in harness as one of his nephew's chief captains. With him came not a few of the lords who had seized castles in the Duke's despite, but who were nevertheless ready to follow his

[1] Vet. An. 288. "Quia propter contentionem quæ inter Vvillum regem Anglorum, et Fulconem Andegavorum comitem de eodem episcopatu exorta erat, Radulfus Turonorum archiepiscopus Turonis eum ordinare non potuit, ipsius assensu atque præcepto omniumque suffraganeorum ejus, cum magno honore ordinatus est in Rotomago civitate, a domno Willelmo ejusdem urbis archiepiscopo xi. Kalend. Maii, anno ab Incarnatione Domini millesimo lxxxv." [2] See Appendix MM.

[3] Vet. An. 290. "Cum fames populum oppressisset, essetque impossibile unius copiis generalem afflictorum indigentiam sustentari, *ex communi cleri plebisque consilio*, aurum et argentum quod erat in tabula altaris sanctorum martyrum Gervasii et Protasii pius temerator accepit; illudque fideli dispensatione pauperibus erogavit." Compare the action of Abbot Leofric of Saint Alban's, and the "prædictæ rationes" which led him so to act, together with the argument of Matthew Paris with regard to its lawfulness; Gest. Abb. i. 29, 30.

banner. There was the elder Ralph of Toesny, he who had taken the strange message to King Henry after the day of Mortemer, and who had refused to bear the banner of Normandy on the day of Senlac.[1] With him was his nephew, William of Breteuil, the elder and more lucky of the two sons of William Fitz-Osbern. He had been one of Robert's companions in his day of rebellion, along with the younger Ralph of Toesny and with Robert of Bellême, now their enemy.[2] The host entered Le Mans without resistance, and was received, we are told, with joy by clergy and citizens alike.[3] Messages were sent forth to summon the chief men of the county to come and do their duty to their new lord. Helias came; so did Geoffrey of Mayenne. When two such leaders submitted, others naturally followed their example. All the chief men of Maine, it would seem, became the liegemen of Duke Robert. One obstinate rebel alone, Pagan or Payne of Montdoubleau, defended with his followers the castle of Ballon against the new prince.[4]

General submission of the county.

Ballon holds out.

The fortress which still held out, one whose name we shall again meet with more than once in the immediate story of the Red King, was a stronghold indeed. About twelve miles north of Le Mans a line of high ground ends to the north in a steep bluff rising above the Cenomannian Orne, the lesser stream of that name which mingles its waters with the Sarthe. The river is not the same prominent feature in the land- scape which the Sarthe itself is at Le Mans and at some of the other towns and castles which it washes; it does not in the same way flow directly at the foot of the hill. But it comes fully near enough to place

The castle of Ballon.

---

[1] See N. C. vol. iii. pp. 159, 465.
[2] Ib. vol. iv. p. 659.   [3] See Appendix KK.
[4] Ord. Vit. 674 B. "Paganus de Monte Dublabelis, cum aliis con- tumacibus castrum Balaonem tenebat et venienti duci cum turmis suis acriter resistebat."

Ballon in the long list of peninsular strongholds. The
hill forms a prominent feature in the surrounding landscape; and the view from the height itself, over the
wooded plains and gentle hills of Maine, is wide indeed.
He who held Ballon against the lord of Normandy, the
new lord of Le Mans, might feel how isolated his hill-
fort stood in the midst of his enemies. To the south
Le Mans is seen on its promontory; and, if the mighty
pile of Saint Julian's had not yet reached its present
height, yet the twin towers of Howel, the royal tower
by their side, the abbey of Saint Vincent then rising
above all, may well have caught the eye even more
readily than it is caught by the somewhat shapeless mass
of the cathedral church in its present state. To the north
and north-west the eye stretches over lands which in any
normal state of things would have been the lands of
enemies, the lands of the houses of Montgomery and
Bellême. But at the moment of Robert's siege the
defenders of Ballon must have looked to them as
friendly spots, joined in common warfare against the
Norman Duke. To the north the eye can reach beyond
the Norman border at now rebellious Alençon, to the
butte of Chaumont, the isolated hill which looks down
upon the Rock of Mabel. To the north-east the horizon
skirts the land, at other times the most dangerous of all,
but which might now be deemed the most helpful, the
native home of the fierce house of Talvas. But, even if
Ballon had been begirt on all sides by foes, its defenders
might well venture to hope that they could defy them
all. The hill had clearly been a stronghold even from
præhistoric times. The neck of the promontory is cut
off by a vast ditch, which may have fenced in a Cenomannian fortress in days before Cæsar came. This
ditch takes in the little town of Ballon with its church.
A second ditch surrounds the castle itself, and is carried

fully round it on every side. The castle of Ballon there- CHAP. III.
fore does not, like so many of its fellows, strictly over-
hang the stream or the low ground at its foot. At no
point does it, like many other fortresses in the same land,
mingle its masonry with the native rock. Ballon is more
like Arques[1] on a smaller scale than like any of the
strictly river fortresses. Within the ditch, the wall of the
castle remains, a gateway, a tower, a house of delicate
detail; but every architectural feature at Ballon is later
than the days of Rufus; the greater part of the present
castle belongs to the latest days of mediæval art. This Siege of Ballon.
stronghold, to be fought for over and over again in the
course of our story, now underwent the earliest of its
sieges which concerns us. It held out stoutly for some August—September, 1088.
time during the months of August and September. The
loss on both sides was great. At last the besieged The castle surrenders.
surrendered, and were admitted to the Duke's grace.[2]
Robert was for a moment the undisputed lord of all
Maine.

The first part of Bishop Odo's counsel was thus suc- Further schemes of Odo.
cessfully carried out. But the submission of Maine was
in Odo's scheme only a means to the thorough rooting
out of the house of Bellême. And Robert found himself
in such sure possession of Le Mans and Maine that he
could call on the warriors of city and county to follow him
in carrying out the second part of the Bishop's scheme.
The first point for attack among the fortresses held on Robert attacks Saint Cenery.
behalf of Earl Roger or his captive son was the castle of
Saint Cenery. This was a border fortress of Normandy Description and history of the fortress.
and Maine, one which could boast of a long and stirring
history, and its small remains still occupy a site worthy

---

[1] N. C. vol. iii. p. 122.

[2] Ord. Vit. 674 B. "Post plurima damna utriusque partis, Balaonenses
pacem cum duce fecerunt."

CHAP. III. of the tale which they have to tell. Just within the Norman border, some miles west of the town and castle of Alençon, not far from the junction of the lesser stream of Sarthon with the boundary river, a long narrow peninsula is formed by the windings of the Sarthe. It forms an advanced post of Normandy thrust forward with the Cenomannian land on three sides of it. The greater part of the peninsula consists of a steep and rocky hill,[1] which, as it draws near to its point, is washed by the stream on either side, though nearer to the isthmus the height rises immediately above alluvial meadows between its base and the river. The site was a tempting one for the foundation of a castle, in days when, though there might be hostile ground on three sides, yet no bow-shot or catapult from any hostile point could reach the highest part of the hill. Yet, as the name of the place is ecclesiastical, so its earliest memories are ecclesiastical, and its occupation as a fortress was, in the days of our story, a thing of yesterday. Cenericus or Cenery, a saint of the seventh

Monastery of Saint Cenery. century, gave the place its name. A monastery arose, where a hundred and forty monks prayed around the tomb of their patron. His memory is still cherished on his own ground. A church contemporary with our story, a church of the eleventh century crowned by a tower of the twelfth, rises boldly above the swift stream which flows below the three apses of its eastern end. Within, the art of a later but still early age has adorned its walls with the forms of a series of holy persons, among whom the sainted hero of the spot holds a chief place.[2] But if

---

[1] Ord. Vit. 674 D. "Habitatoribus hujus municipii quies et pax pene semper defuit, finitimique Cenomannenses, seu Normanni insistunt. Scopulosum montem anfractus Sartæ fluminis ex tribus partibus ambit, in quo sanctus Cerenicus venerandus confessor tempore Milehardi Sagiorum pontificis habitavit."

[2] In local belief, Saint Cenery on his own ground seems to have supplanted the Archangel himself as the weigher of souls.

the name of Saint Cenery first suggests the ecclesiastical history of the place, its surname[1] marks a chief feature in its secular history. The place is still Saint Cenery-*le-Gerey*. That is, it keeps the name of the famous house of Geroy, the name so dear to the heart of the monk of Saint Evroul.[2] For the monastery of Saint Cenery was but short-lived. When the wiking Hasting was laying The monks waste the land, the monks of Saint Cenery fled away flee to Château-with the body of their patron, like that of Saint Cuth-Thierry. berht in our own land, to the safer resting-place of Château-Thierry in the land of Soissons.[3] As things now stand, the peninsula of Saint Cenery, with its church and the site of its castle, might suggest, as a lesser object suggests, a greater, the grouping of abbey and castle on that more renowned peninsula where the relics of Saint Cuthberht at last found shelter. The forsaken monastery was never restored. The holy place lost its holiness; over the tombs of the ancient monks arose a den of thieves, a special fortress of crime.[4] In other words, after a century and a half of desolation, a castle arose on the tempting site which was supplied by the neck of the peninsula.[5] Fragments of its masonry may still be

---

[1] On surnames of places, see N. C. vol. v. p. 573.

[2] Ib. vol. ii. p. 233.

[3] Ord. Vit. 674 D. "Carolo Simplice regnante, dum Hastingus Danus cum gentilium phalange Neustriam depopulatus est, sanctum corpus a fidelibus in castrum Theodorici translatum est et dispersis monachis monasterium destructum." Yet at a later time (see Ord. Vit. 706 D) Saint Cenery still possessed an arm of the eponymous saint, though monks of Seez, not of Saint Cenery, were its keepers; and there is still a bone or fragment of a bone under the high altar of the parish church which claims to be a relic of him.

[4] Ib. "Sanguinarii prædones ibi speluncam latronum condiderunt," "scelesti habitatores," &c.

[5] Unless Orderic's words just quoted are mere rhetoric, we must infer that the site of the castle, and not the site of the present church, had been the site of the forsaken monastery. Well suited as the whole peninsula was for the purposes of a castle, the actual isthmus, where three small knolls

seen, and its precinct seems to have taken in the church and the whole peninsula, though in the greater part of its circuit no defence was needed beyond the steep and scarped sides of the rocky hill itself. The castle was the work of a man whose name has been familiar to us for thirty years, a man who was still living, and who was actually in the host before the fortress of his own rearing. Geoffrey of Mayenne was closely connected, as kinsman and as lord, with William the son of Geroy. When Geoffrey fell into the hands of William Talvas, the faithful vassal ransomed his lord by the sacrifice of his own castle of Montacute, which stood just beyond the Sarthon within the borders of Maine. To repair this loss of his friend, no doubt also to repay the invasion of Cenomannian soil by a like invasion of Norman soil, and to put some check in the teeth of the house of Bellême, Geoffrey built the castle of Saint Cenery on the left bank of the Sarthe, and gave it as a gift of thankfulness to the son of Geroy.[1] But the inhabitants of the new stronghold, in their dangerous border position, never knew peace or good luck, but were visited with every kind of evil.[2] The sons of the pious and virtuous Geroy yielded to the influence of the spot; they fell into crime and rebellion, and were punished by banishments and strange deaths. The second lord of Saint Cenery, Robert the brother of William, had rebelled against the Conqueror; he had held his fortress against him, and he had died in a mysterious way of a poisoned apple.[3] His son and successor Arnold found how

The castle founded by Geoffrey of Mayenne for William of Geroy.

History of the descendants of Geroy.

rise above the general level of the hill, must have been the most tempting spot of all. On two of the knolls remains of its masonry are still to be seen, and the outworks reach far down the hill on its western side. The place seems to have been a simple fortress, with no town or village, beyond such houses as may have grown up around the castle.

[1] Orderic tells the story, 674 C.

[2] See the extract in the last page.

[3] N. C. vol. iv. p. 184.

dangerous was the greed and hate of a powerful and un- CHAP. III.
scrupulous neighbour. Nearly north from Saint Cenery, Roche-
at much the same distance as Alençon is to the east, not Mabille.
far from the foot of the hill of Chaumont which makes
so marked a feature in the whole surrounding landscape,
on a peninsula formed by a bend of the Sarthon, just
within the borders of Maine as Saint Cenery is just
within the borders of Normandy, rises the solitary rock
which once had been known as Jaugy. There we still
trace the ruins of the castle which bore the name of the
cruel Countess, the despoiler of the house of Jaugy, the
castle of the Rock of Mabel.[1] To the possessor of the
Rock of Mabel the mightier rock of Saint Cenery, forming part of the same natural line of defence, could not
fail to be an object of covetousness. Arnold died of
poison, by the practice of the ruthless wife of Roger
of Montgomery. Saint Cenery became part of the pos- Saint
sessions of the fierce line of Bellême; and, under its Cenery
seized by
present master, it doubtless deserved the strongest Mabel.
of the names bestowed on it by the monk of Saint
Evroul.

At this moment Saint Cenery was held on behalf of Saint
Cenery
Robert of Bellême by a specially valiant captain named held by
Robert Carrel.[2] We have no details of the siege. We are Robert
Carrel.
told nothing of the positions occupied by the besiegers, or The siege.
how they became masters of the seemingly impregnable
height. We are told that the resistance was long and
fierce; but at last the castle was taken; and, as failure of Surrender
of Saint
provisions is spoken of as the cause, we may guess that Cenery.

[1] N. C. vol. iii. p. 169.
[2] Ord. Vit. 674 D. "Ibi familia Roberti Belesmensis erat, cui Robertus
Quadrellus, acerrimus miles et multo vigore conspicuus, præerat, qui hortatu
Rogerii comitis obsidentibus fortiter obstabat." The modern form of
"Quadrellus" would be "Carrel." "Fulcherius Quarel" appears among
the knights of Perche bearing harness under Philip Augustus; Duchèsne,
p. 1032.

CHAP. III.   the garrison was driven to surrender.   If so, the surrender

must have been to the Duke's mercy, and the mercy of

Robert   Duke Robert or of his counsellors was cruel.   The Duke,
Carrel
blinded.   we are told, in his wrath, ordered the eyes of Robert

Other mu-   Carrel to be put out.   The personal act of the Duke in
tilations.
the case of the rebel leader seems to be contrasted with

the sentence of a more regular tribunal of some kind, by

which mutilations of various kinds were dealt out to

others of the garrison.[1]   Yet personal cruelty is so in-

consistent with the ordinary character of Robert that

we are driven to suppose either that some strong personal

influence was brought to bear on the Duke's mind, or

else that Robert Carrel had given some unpardonable

offence during the course of the siege.   But it is worth

while to notice the words which seem to imply that the

punishment of the other defenders of Saint Cenery was the

work of some body which at least claimed to act in a judi-

Question   cial character.   We can hardly look as yet for the subtlety
of the
military   of a separate military jurisdiction, for what we should
tribunal.
now call a court-martial.   That can hardly be thought

of, except in the case of a standing body of soldiers, like

Cnut's housecarls, with a constitution and rules of their

own.[2]   But as in free England we have seen the army—

that is, the nation in arms—act on occasion the part of

a national assembly, so in more aristocratic Normandy

the same principle would apply in another shape.   The

chief men of Normandy were there, each in command of

his own followers.   If Robert or his immediate counsellors

wished that the cruel punishments to be dealt out to the

revolted garrison should not be merely their own work,

[1] Ord. Vit. 674 D. "Præfatus municeps jussu irati ducis protinus oculis
privatus est. Aliis quoque pluribus qui contumaciter ibidem restiterant
principi Normanniæ [this almost sounds like the wording of an indictment]
debilitatio membrorum inflicta est ex sententia curiæ."

[2] N. C. vol. i. pp. 445, 476.

if they wished the responsibility of them to be shared by
a larger body, the means were easy.   There was a court
of peers ready at hand, before whom they might arraign
the traitors.

But if there were those within Saint Cenery who Claims of
were marked for punishment, there was one without its Robert, grandson of
walls who claimed restitution.   A son of Geroy's son Geroy.
Robert, bearing his father's name, had, like others of
his family, served with credit in the wars of Apulia
and Sicily.   He was now in the Duke's army, seemingly
among the warriors of Maine, ready to play his part in
winning back the castle of his father from the son of the
murderess of his uncle.   Geoffrey of Mayenne and the
rest of the Cenomannian leaders asked of the Duke that
the son of the former owner of the castle, Geoffrey's own
kinsman and vassal, should be restored to the inheritance
of his father, the inheritance which his father held in the
first instance by Geoffrey's own gift.   The warfare which
was now waging was waged against the son of the
woman by whom one lord of Saint Cenery had been
treacherously slain.   The triumph of right would be
complete, if the banished man were restored to his own,
at the prayer of the first giver.   The Duke consented; The castle
Saint Cenery was granted afresh to the representative of granted to him.
the house of Geroy; Geoffrey saw the castle of his own
rearing once more in friendly hands.   The new lord
strengthened the defences of his fortress, and held it as a
post to be guarded with all care against the common
enemy, the son of Mabel.[1]

Two fortresses were thus won from the revolters; and
the success of the Duke at both places, his severity at

---

[1] This is told by Orderic, 674 D.   He adds, "Ille fere xxxvi annis
postmodum tenuit, muris et vallis zetisque munivit, et moriens Guillermo et
Roberto filiis suis dereliquit."   Yet he lost it for a season to the old
enemy.   See 706 D.

CHAP. III.

Surrender of Alencon,

of Bellême.

The other castles ready to surrender.

one of them, had their effect on those who still defended other castles for Robert of Bellême.[1] Alençon, where the great William had wrought so stern a vengeance for the mockeries of its citizens, stood ready to re- ceive his son without resistance. So did Bellême itself, the fortress which gave its name to the descendants of the line of Talvas, the centre of their power, where their ancient chapel of Mabel's day still crowns the elder castle hill, standing isolated below the town and fortress of later date.[2] Its defenders made up their minds to submit to the summons of the Duke, if only the Duke would come near to summon them. So did the gar- risons of all the other castles which still remained in rebellion. Frightened at the doom of Robert Carrel and his companions, they stood ready to surrender as soon as the Duke should come. But it is not clear whether the Duke ever did draw near to receive the fortresses which were ready to open their gates to him. Robert had had enough of success, or of the exertions which were needful for success. It would almost seem as if the siege of Saint Cenery had been as much as he could go through, and as if he turned back at once on its surrender. At all events he stopped just when complete victory was within his grasp. He longed for the idle

[1] Ord. Vit. 675 A. "Municipes Alencionis et Bellesmi aliarumque munitionum, ut audierunt quam male contigerit Roberto Quadrello et com- plicibus qui cum eo fuerant, valde territi sunt, et ut debitas venienti duci munitiones redderent, consilium inierunt." But the words which imme- diately follow are ; "Verum Robertus ab incœpta virtute cito defecit, et mollitie suadente ad tectum et quietem avide recurrit, exercitumque suum, ut quisque ad sua repedaret, dimisit." This leaves it not quite clear, whether he stayed to receive in person the surrenders which were ready for him.

[2] The site of the true castle of Bellême may easily be distinguished from the later fortress. The native home of Mabel stands quite apart from the hill on which the town and the later castle stand, being cut off from it by art. The chapel is but little altered, and has a crypt, the way down to which reminds one of Saint Zeno and other Italian churches.

repose of his palace. His army was disbanded; every CHAP. III.
man who followed the Duke's banner had the Duke's Robert disbands
licence to go to his own home.[1] his army.

All this while, it will be remembered, Robert of Bellême Robert of
himself was actually in bonds in the keeping of Bishop Bellême still in
Odo. The war had been waged rather against his father prison.
Earl Roger than against himself. But it was wholly on
Robert's account that it had been waged. Whatever we
may think of the right or wrong of his imprisonment
at the moment when it took place, there can be no
doubt that it was for the general good of the Norman
duchy that Robert of Bellême should be hindered from
doing mischief. He was the arch-rebel against his sovereign, the arch-plunderer of his neighbours, the man who,
in that fierce age, was branded by common consent as the
cruellest of the cruel. It was to break his power, to win
back the castles which he had seized, that the hosts of
Normandy and Maine had been brought together; it was
for the crime of maintaining his cause that Robert Carrel
and his comrades had undergone their cruel punishment.
But the fates of the chief and of his subaltern were
widely different. Duke Robert, weary of warfare, was
even more than ever disposed to mercy, that is more
than ever disposed to gratify the biddings of a weak
good-nature. Earl Roger marked the favourable moment, Earl Roger
when the host was disbanded, and when the Duke had prays for his son's
gone back to the idle pleasures of Rouen. He sent elo- release.
quent messengers, charged with many promises in his
name—promises doubtless of good behaviour on the part
of his son—and prayed for the release of the prisoner.[2]

[1] See note 1, last page.

[2] Ord. Vit. 675 A. "Per dicaces legatos a duce pacem filiique sui abso-
lutionem postulans, multa falso pollicitus est." Robert, he adds, "qui
improvidus erat et instabilis, ad lapsum facilis, ad tenendum justitiæ rigorem
mollis, ex insperato frivolis pactionibus infidorum adquievit." It is now that
Orderic gives us his full picture of Robert of Bellême and his doings.

CHAP. III. With Duke Robert an appeal of this kind from a man
like Earl Roger went for more than all reasonable fore-
thought for himself and his duchy. The welfare of
thousands was sacrificed to a weak pity for one man.

Robert of
Bellême set
free.
Robert of Bellême was set free. His promises were of
course forgotten; gratitude and loyalty were forgotten.

His career. Till a wiser sovereign sent him in after days to a prison
from which there was no escape, he went on with his
career of plunder and torture, of utter contempt and
defiance of the ducal authority.[1] But, under such a
prince as Robert, contempt and defiance of the ducal
authority was no disqualification for appearing from time
to time as a ducal counsellor.[2]

Robert of Bellême was thus set free, because his father
had asked for his freedom. A prince who sought to keep
any kind of consistency in his acts could hardly have
kept his own brother Henry in ward one moment after
the prison doors were opened to his fellow-captive. But
it would seem that the gaol-delivery at Bayeux did not

Henry set
free.
follow at once on that at Neuilly. Henry was still kept
in his prison, till, at the general request of all the chief
lords of Normandy, he was set free.[3] He went back to
his county of the Côtentin with no good will to either
of his brothers.[4] Here he strove to strengthen himself

[1] Ord. Vit. 675 B. "Liberatus intumuit, jussa ducis atque minas minus
appretiavit, præsentisque memor injuriæ diutinam multiplicemque vindictam
exercuit."

[2] Ib. 681 D. "Tunc Edgarus Adelinus, et Robertus Bellesmensis, atque
Guillelmus de Archis monachus Molismensis præcipui ducis consiliarii
erant "—an oddly assorted company. This is in 1090.

[3] Ib. 677 A. "Optimatum suorum supplicationibus adquiescens. Henricum fratrem suum concessit, et a vinculis in quibus cum Roberto Belesmensi
constrictus fuerat absolvit."

[4] Ib. 689 C. "Constantienses Henricus clito strenue regebat, rigidus-
que contra fratres suos persistebat. Nam contra ducem inimicitias agitabat
pro injusta captione quam nudiustertius, ut prædictum est, ab illo per-
pessus fuerat. Regi nihilominus Angliæ hostis erat pro terra matris
suæ."

in every way, by holding the castles of his principality, CHAP. III.
by winning friends and hiring mercenaries. He strength- Henry
ened the castles of Coutances and Avranches, those of strengthens
his castles.
Cherbourg by the northern rocks and of Gavray in the
southern part of the Côtentin. Among his counsellors His
and supporters were some men of note, as Richard of partisans.
Redvers, and the greater name of the native lord of
Avranches, Earl Hugh of Chester.[1] Indeed all the lords
of the Côtentin stood by their Count, save only the
gloomy, and perhaps banished, Robert of Mowbray, Earl
of Northumberland. That we find the lords of two
English earldoms thus close together in a corner of Normandy shows how thoroughly the history of the kingdom
and that of the duchy form at this moment one tale.
While the Count and Ætheling was strengthened by such His good
support, the land of Coutances and Avranches enjoyed government.
another moment of peace and order, while the rest of
Normandy was torn in pieces by the quarrels of Robert
of Bellême and his like.

§ 2. The first Successes of William Rufus.

1090.

While the duchy of Normandy had thus become Schemes
of William
one scene of anarchy under the no-government of Rufus.
its nominal prince, the King of the English had been
carefully watching the revolutions of his brother's
dominions. He now deemed that the time had come
to avenge the wrongs which he deemed that he had
suffered at his brother's hands. He must have seen that
he had not much to fear from a prince who had let slip

---

[1] Ord. Vit. 689 C. " Oppida sua constanter firmabat, et fautores sibi de proceribus patris sui plurimos callide conciliabat. Abrincas et Cæsarisburgum et
Constantiam atque Guabreium, aliasque munitiones possidebat, et Hugonem
comitem et Ricardum de Radveriis, aliosque Constantinienses, præter
Robertum de Molbraio, secum habuit, et collectis undique viribus prece
pretioque quotidie crescebat."

CHAP. III. such advantages as Robert had held in his hands after
the taking of Saint Cenery. He watched his time; he
made his preparations, and was now ready to take the
decisive step of crossing the sea himself or sending
others to cross it. But even William Rufus in all his pride
and self-confidence knew that it did not depend wholly
on himself to send either native or adopted Englishmen
on such an errand. He had learned enough of English
constitutional law not to think of venturing on a foreign
war without the constitutional sanction of his kingdom.

He con-
sults the
Assembly
at Win-
chester.
Easter,
1090.
His speech.

In a Gemót at Winchester, seemingly the Easter Gemót
of the third year of his reign,[1] he laid his schemes
before the assembled Witan, and obtained their consent
to a war with the Duke of the Normans. If we may
trust the one report which we have of his speech, William
the Red had as good reasons to give for an invasion of
Normandy as his father had once had to give for an invasion of England. He went forth to avenge the wrongs
which his brother had done to him, the rebellion which
he had stirred up in his kingdom. But he went also
from the purest motives of piety and humanity. The
prince who had tried to deprive him of his dominions had
shown himself utterly unable to rule his own. A cry
had come into the ears of him, the Red King, to which

---

[1] Ord. Vit. 680 B. " Turmas optimatum adscivit, et Guentoniæ congregatis
quæ intrinsecus ruminabat sic ore deprompsit." The Chronicler tells us,
under 1090, how " se cyng wæs smægende hu he mihte wrecon his broðer
Rodbeard swiðost swencean, and Normandige of him gewinnan." The
custom of holding the Easter Gemót at Winchester seems to fix this
assembly to Easter, 1090.

The continuance of the three yearly assemblies is well marked by William
of Malmesbury in the Life of Wulfstan (Ang. Sac. iii. 257); " Rex Wille!-
mus consuetudinem induxerat [that is, he went on with what had been done
T. R. E.], quam successores aliquamdiu tritam consenescere permisere. Ea
erat, ut ter in anno cuncti optimates ad curiam convenirent, de necessariis
regni tractaturi, simulque visuri regis insigne, quomodo iret gemmato fasti-
giatus diademate."

he could not refuse to hearken. It was the cry of the
holy Church, the cry of the widow and the orphan.
All were alike oppressed by the thieves and murderers
whom the weakness of Robert allowed to do their will
throughout the Norman land. That land looked back
with a sigh to the days of William the Great, who had
saved Normandy alike from foreign and from domestic
foes. It became his son, the inheritor of his name and
crown, to follow in his steps, and to do the same
work again. He called on all who had been his father's
men, on all who held fiefs of his granting in Normandy
or in England, to come forward and show their prowess
for the deliverance of the suffering duchy.[1] But it
was for them to take counsel and to decide. Let the His consti-
Assembly declare its judgement on his proposal. His language.
purpose was, with their consent, to send over an army
to Normandy, at once to take vengeance for his own
wrongs, and to carry out the charitable work of de-
livering the Church and the oppressed, and of chastising
evil-doers with the sword of justice.[2]

This constitutional language in the mouth of William
Rufus sounds somewhat strange in our ears; the profession of high and holy purposes sounds stranger still.
There is of course no likelihood that we are reading a
genuine report of an actual speech; still the words of
our historian are not without their value. No one would
have been likely to invent those words, unless they
had fairly represented the relations which still existed

---

[1] Ord. Vit. 680 C. "Commoneo vos omnes qui patris mei homines fuistis
et feudos vestros in Normannia et Anglia de illo tenuistis, ut sine dolo ad
probitatis opus mihi viriliter unanimiter faveatis."

[2] Ib. "Colligite, quæso, concilium, prudenter inite consilium, sententiam
proferte, quid in hoc agendum sit discrimine. Mittam, si laudatis, exercitum
in Normanniam, et injuriis quas mihi frater meus sine causa machinatus est
talionem rependam. Ecclesiæ Dei subveniam, viduas et orphanos inermes
protegam, fures et sicarios gladio justitiæ puniam."

CHAP. III. between a King of the English and the Assembly of
his kingdom. The piety may all come from the brain
Its witness of the monk of Saint Evroul; but the constitutional
to consti-
tutional doctrines which he has worked into the speech cannot
usage. fail to set forth the ordinary constitutional usage of
the time. Even in the darkest hour in which England
had any settled government at all, in the reign of the
worst of all our kings, it was not the will of the King
alone, not the will of any private cabal or cabinet, but
the will of the Great Council of the nation, which, just
as in the days of King Eadward,[1] decided questions of
peace and war.

The Witan unanimously agreed to the King's proposal,
and applauded, so we are told, the lofty spirit—the
War voted technical name is used—of the King himself.[2] War was
by the
Witan. at once voted, and it might have been expected that
a brilliant campaign would at once have followed on
the warlike vote. We might have looked to see the
Red King, the mirror of chivalry, cross the sea, as his
father had done on the opposite errand, at the head
of the whole force of his realm. We might have looked
to see a series of gallant feats of arms take place between the two hostile brothers. The real story is
The King widely different. William Rufus did not cross the sea
stays in
England. till a year after war had been declared, and remark-
ably little fighting happened, both while he stayed in
His policy. England and after he set forth for Normandy. But we
have seen that William Rufus, as a true Norman, was,
with all his chivalry, at least as much fox as lion.[3]
And a ruler of England, above all, a son of William the

---

[1] See N. C. vol. ii. pp. 93, 95.

[2] Ord. Vit. 680 C. "His dictis omnes assensum dederunt et *magna-
nimitatem* regis collaudaverunt."

[3] See above, p. 60.

Great, had many weapons at his command, one only CHAP. III.
of which could the Duke of the Normans hope to
withstand with weapons of the like kind. Robert was His advan-
in his own person as stout a man-at-arms as Rufus, tages in a
and, if the chivalry of Normandy could only be per- with
suaded to rally round his banner, he might, as the Robert.
valiant leader of a valiant host, withstand on equal
terms any force that the island monarch could bring
against him. But courage, and, we may add, whenever he chose to use it, real military skill, were the
only weapons which Robert had at his bidding. The
armoury of the Red King contained a choice of many
others, any one of which alone might make courage
and military skill wholly useless. William, headstrong
as he often showed himself, could on occasion bide
his time as well as his father, and, well as he
loved fighting, he knew that a land in such a state
as Normandy was under Robert could be won by
easier means. Besides daring and generalship equal
to that of Robert, Rufus had statecraft; and he was
not minded to use even his generalship as long as his
statecraft could serve his turn. He knew, or his ready
wit divined, that there were men of all classes in
Normandy who would be willing to do his main work
for him without his striking a blow, without his crossing
the sea in person, almost without a blow being struck
in his behalf. He had only to declare himself his
brother's rival, and it was the interest of most of the
chief men in Normandy to support his claims against
his brother. The very same motives which had led Interest of
the Normans in England to revolt against William on Normans.
behalf of Robert would now lead the Normans in
Normandy to revolt against Robert on behalf of William.
Norman nobles and land-owners who held lands on
both sides of the sea had deemed it for their interest

Q

CHAP. III that one lord should rule on both sides of the sea.
They had then deemed it for their interest that that
lord should be Robert rather than William. The former
doctrine still kept all its force; on the second point they
had learned something by experience. If England and
Normandy were to have one sovereign, that sovereign
must needs be William and not Robert. There was not
the faintest chance of placing Robert on the royal throne
of England; there was a very fair chance of placing
William in the ducal chair of Normandy. Simply as
a ruler, as one who commanded the powers of the state
and the army, William had shown that he had it in
his power to reward and to punish. Robert had shown
that it was quite beyond his power to reward or to
punish anybody. He who drew on himself the wrath
of the King was likely enough to lose his estates in
England; he who drew on himself the wrath of the
Duke had no need to be fearful of losing his estates
in Normandy. And William had the means of making
a yet more direct appeal to the interests of not a few
of his brother's subjects, in a way in which it was still
more certain that his brother would not appeal to any
of his subjects. The hoard at Winchester was still well
filled. If it had been largely drawn upon, it was again
filled to the brim with treasures brought in by every
kind of unrighteous exactions. Already was the land
"fordone with unlawful gelds;"[1] but the King had the
profit of them. But there was no longer any hoard
at Rouen out of which Robert could hire the choicest
troops of all lands to defend his duchy, as William
could hire them to attack it. And the wealth at William's
command might do much even without hiring a single
mercenary. The castles of Normandy were strong; but

Position of William and Robert.

Power of William's wealth.

Hiring of mercenaries.

---

[1] See above, p. 177.

few of them were so strong that, in the words of King CHAP. III.
Philip—Philip of Macedon, not Philip of France—an Bribes.
ass laden with gold could not find its way into them.[1]
Armed at all points, master alike of gold and steel, able
to work himself and to command the services of others
alike with the head and with the hand, William Rufus
could, at least in contending with Robert, conquer when He con-
he chose and how he chose. And for a while he chose, quers without leaving
like the Persian king of old, to win towns and castles England.
without stirring from his hearth.[2]

The first point of the mainland which the Red King Submission
of Saint
won was one which lay beyond the strict bounds of Valery.
the Norman duchy; but no spot, either in Normandy
or in England, was more closely connected with the
fortunes of his house. And it was one which had a
certain fitness as the beginning of such a campaign.
The first spot of continental ground which was added to
the dominion of one who called himself King of the
English, and who at least was truly King of England,
was the spot from which his father had set forth for the
conquest of England. He won it by the means which
were specially his own. "By his cunning or by his
treasures he gat him the castle at Saint Valery and the
havens."[3] Englishmen had fought for the elder William

[1] Plutarch, Reg. et Imp. Apoph. Philip. 15.

[2] Æsch. Pers. 861 ;

ὅσσας δ᾽ εἷλε πόλεις, πόρον οὐ διαβὰς Ἅλυος ποταμοῖο,
οὐδ᾽ ἀφ᾽ ἑστίας συθείς.

[3] Chron. Petrib. 1090. "Ðeah þurh his geapscipe, oððe þurh gærsuma
he begeat þone castel aet Sée Waleri and þa hæfenan, and swa he begeat
þone æt Albemare." This is followed by William of Malmesbury, iv. 307,
who translates the passage, "Castrum Sancti Walerici, et portum vicinum,
et oppidum quod Albamarla vocatur, sollertia sua acquisivit, pecunia custodes corrumpens." Florence however calls it "castellum Walteri de
Sancto Walarico." This might be understood of any castle belonging to
Walter of Saint Valery ; and the change might be taken either as having

CHAP. III. in Maine and before Gerberoi;[1] but that was merely to win back the lost possessions of the Norman Duke. Now the wealth and the arms of England were used to win castles beyond the sea for a prince whose possessions and whose titles up to that moment were purely English.

Beginning of English action on the continent.

In the history of England as a power—and the history of England as a power had no small effect on the history of the English as a people—the taking of Saint Valery is the beginning of a chain of events which leads on, not only to the fight of Tinchebray and the first loss of Rouen, but to the fight of Crecy and the fight of Chastillon, to the taking of Boulogne and the loss of Calais.

Saint Valery had, by the forced commendation of the still reigning Count Guy, passed under Norman superiority;[2] but it was no part of the true Norman land. The

Submission of Stephen of Aumale.

first fortress within the Norman duchy which passed into the hands of Rufus was the castle of Aumale, standing just within the Norman border, on the upper course of the river of Eu. Its lord, the first of the great Norman nobles to submit to William and to receive his garrison into his castle, was Stephen, son of Count Odo of Champagne and of Adelaide, whole sister of the Conqueror, cousin-german therefore of the two contending princes.[3] Aumale was won, as Saint Valery had been won, by cunning or by treasure. Stephen may simply have learned to see that it was better for him to have the same lord at Aumale and in Holderness, or his eyes may have been yet further enlightened by the brightness of

the force of a correction or as showing that Florence did not understand what he found in the Chronicles. I do not find any mention of the taking of Saint Valery, or of any possession of Walter of Saint Valery, anywhere except in the English writers. Walter, who is more than once mentioned by Orderic (724 B, 729 D) as a crusader, was of the house of the Advocates of Saint Valery of whom I have spoken elsewhere (N. C. vol. iii. pp. 131, 393).

[1] N. C. vol. iv. pp. 557, 643.

[2] Ib. vol. iii. p. 157.

[3] Ib. vol. ii. p. 632.

English gold. But the Red King had other means at his chap. iii.
disposal, and it seems that other means were needed, if
not to win, at least to keep Aumale.   The defences of Aumale
the castle were greatly strengthened at the King's cost,[1] strength-
and it became a centre for further operations.   "Therein the King's
he set his knights, and they did harms upon the land, in quarters.
harrying and in burning."[2]   Other castles were soon
added to the Red King's dominion. Count Robert of Submission
Eu, whom we have heard of alike at Mortemer and in Robert of
Lindesey,[3] the father of the man whom we have more Eu and his
lately heard of at Berkeley, still held the house where liam;
William the Great had received Harold as his guest,[4]
hard by the church where he had received Matilda as
his bride.[5] The Count had been enriched with lands in
southern England; he is not recorded as having joined
in his son's rebellion; and the lord of Eu now transferred
the allegiance of his Norman county to the prince of
whom he held his command on the rocks of Hastings.[6]
Aumale and Eu, two of the most important points on
the eastern border of Normandy, are thus the first
places which we hear of as receiving Rufus on the mainland. We shall hear of both names again, but in quite
another kind of tale, before the reign of Rufus is over.

The next Norman noble to join the cause of William of Gerard of
was another lord of the same frontier, who held a point Gournay.
of hardly less importance to the south of Eu and Aumale.

---

[1] Ord. Vit. 681 A. "Primus Normannorum Stephanus de Albamarla
filius Odonis Campaniæ comitis regi adhæsit, et regiis sumptibus castellum
suum super Aucium flumen vehementer munivit, in quo validissimam regis
familiam contra ducem suscepit." Florence calls it "castellum Odonis de
Albamarno."

[2] Chron. Petrib. 1090. "And þarinne he sette his cnihtas, and hi dydon
hearmes uppon þam lande on hergunge and on bærnete."

[3] N. C. vol. iii. p. 153 ; vol. iv. p. 280.

[4] Ib. vol. iii. p. 226.   [5] Ib. vol. iii. p. 93.

[6] Domesday, 18. "Rex W. dedit comiti [de Ow] castellariam de
Hastinges."

CHAP. III. This was Gerard of Gournay, son of the warrior of Mortemer who had gone to end his days as a monk of Bec,[1]
son-in-law of the new Earl of Surrey,[2] husband of perhaps
the only woman on Norman ground who bore the name
of English Eadgyth.[3] His castle of Gournay, from
which many men and more than one place[4] in England
have drawn their name, stood on the upper course of the
Epte, close to the French border. The fortress itself has
vanished; but the minster of Saint Hildebert, where the
massive work of Gerard's day has been partly recast in
the lighter style of the next century, still remains, with
its mighty pillars, its varied and fantastic carvings, to
make Gournay a place of artistic pilgrimage. Nor is it
hard to trace the line of the ancient walls of the town,
showing how the border stream of Epte was pressed into
the service of the Norman engineers. The adhesion of
the lord of Gournay seems to have been of the highest
importance to the cause of Rufus. The influence of
Gerard reached over a wide district north of his main
dwelling. Along with Gournay, he placed at the King's
disposal his fortress of La Ferté Saint Samson, crowning
a height looking over the vale of Bray, and his other
fortress of Gaillefontaine to the north-east, on another
height by the wood of its own name, overlooking the
early course of the Bethune or Dieppe, the stream
which joins the eastern Varenne by the hill of Arques.[5]
Gerard too was not only ready in receiving the King's
forces into his own castles, but zealous also in bringing
over his neighbours to follow his example.[6] Among

The
church of
Gournay.

Other
castles of
Gerard.

---

[1] See N. C. vol. iii. p. 152.
[2] See above, p. 59.   [3] N. C. vol. iv. p. 733; vol. v. p. 560.
[4] As Barrow *Gurney* in Somerset.
[5] See N. C. vol. iii. p. 121.
[6] Ord. Vit. 681 A. "Gornacum et Firmitatem et Goisleni fontem,
aliasque munitiones suas regi tradidit, finitimosque suos regiæ parti subjicere studuit."

these was the lord of Wigmore, late the rebel of
Worcester, Ralph of Mortemer.[1]   Old Walter Giffard
too, now Earl of Buckingham in England, had English
interests far too precious to allow him to oppose his
island sovereign.   He held the stronghold of Longueville—the north-eastern Longueville by the Scie, the
stream which, small as it is, pours its waters inde-
pendently into the Channel between Dieppe and Saint
Valery-in-Caux.   There, from a bottom fenced in by
hills on every side, the village, the church where the
hand of the modern destroyer has spared only a few
fragments of the days of Norman greatness, the priory
which has been utterly swept away, all looked up to a
hill on the right bank of the stream which art had
changed into a stronghold worthy to rank alongside of
Arques and Gisors.   Girt about with a deep ditch, on the
more exposed southern side with a double ditch, the hill
was crowned by a shell-keep which still remains, though
patched and shattered, and a donjon which has been
wholly swept away.   In this fortress the aged warrior
of Arques and Senlac received, like so many of his neighbours, the troops which William of England had sent to
bring the Norman duchy under his power.

The domains of all these lords lay in the lands on
the right bank of the Seine, the oldest, but, as I have
often remarked, not the truest Normandy.   But the Red
King also won a valuable ally in quite another part of
the duchy.   This was Ralph of Conches or of Toesny,
with whom we are now most concerned as the husband
of the warlike Isabel of Montfort, and, in that character
rather than in any other, the enemy of the Countess
Heloise and of her husband Count William of Evreux.
The rival lords were in fact half-brothers.   The old

---

[1] N. C. vol. iv. pp. 39, 737.

CHAP. III. Roger of Toesny, the warlike pilgrim of Spain,[1] was succeeded by Ralph, who has so often played his part in our story, and whom we last met in Duke Robert's army before Le Mans.[2] The widow of Roger, the mother of Ralph, had married Richard Count of Evreux, and was

Enmity of their wives.

by him the mother of the present Count William.[3] But this near kindred by birth had less strength to bind the brothers together than the fierce rivalry of their wives had to set them at feud with one another. The jealousy of these two warlike ladies kept a large part of Normandy in a constant uproar. Our historian bitterly laments the amount of bloodshed and havoc which was

Countess Heloise of Evreux.

the result of their rivalry.[4] Heloise was of the house of the Counts of Nevers, the Burgundian city by the Loire, a descent which carries us a little out of our usual geographical range.[5] Tall, handsome, and ready of speech, she ruled her husband and the whole land of Evreux with an absolute sway. Her will was everything; the counsels of the barons of the county went for nothing.[6] Violent and greedy, she quarrelled with many

[1] See N. C. vol. ii. p. 201.   [2] See above, p. 209.

[3] Will. Gem. vii. 4. See N. C. vol. i. p. 465. The kindred is also implied in the fact that William of Breteuil was the nephew of both Ralph and William. See Ord. Vit. 688 B, D, and below, p. 266.

[4] Ord. Vit. 687 D. "Perstrepentibus undique præliis in Neustria, securitate pacis perfrui non poterat Ebroicensis provincia. Illic nempe plus quam civile bellum inter opulentos fratres exortum est, et maligna superbarum æmulatione mulierum malitia nimis augmentata est. Heluisa namque comitissa contra Isabelem de Conchis pro quibusdam contumeliosis verbis irata est, comitemque Guillelmum cum baronibus suis in arma per iram commovere totis viribus conata est. Sic per suspiciones et litigia feminarum in furore succensa sunt fortium corda virorum, quorum manibus paulo post multus mutuo cruor effusus est mortalium, et per villas et vicos multarum incensa sunt tecta domorum."

[5] She was the daughter of William the First, Count of Auxerre and Nevers, by his first wife Ermengarde, daughter of Reginald Count of Tonnerre. See Art de Vérifier les Dates, ii. 559.

[6] Orderic has two pictures of her. In the second (834 B), drawn a few years later than our present time, when Count William "natura senioque

of the nobles of Normandy, with Count Robert of Meu- CHAP. III.
lan among them, and stirred up her husband to many
disputes and wars to gratify her fierce passions.[1] At
this time some slight which she had received from the
lady of Conches had led her to entangle her husband in
a bitter feud with his half-brother. Isabel or Elizabeth Isabel of
Montfort.
—the two names are, as usual, given to her indifferently—
the wife of Ralph of Toesny, was a daughter of the French
house of Montfort,[2] the house of our own Simon. Like
her rival, she must now have been long past her youth;
but, while Heloise was childless,[3] Isabel was the mother
of several children, among them of a son who has
already played a part in Norman history. This was
that younger Ralph of Toesny who married the
daughter of Waltheof and who had taken a part in
the present Duke's rebellion against his father.[4] Handsome, eloquent, self-willed, and overbearing, like her
rival, Isabel had qualities which gained her somewhat more of personal regard than the Countess of
Evreux. She was liberal and pleasant and merry of

---

aliquantum hebescebat," we read, ' Uxor ejus totum consulatum regebat,
quæ in sua sagacitate plus quam oporteret confidebat. Pulcra quidem et
facunda erat, et magnitudine corporis pene omnes feminas in comitatu Ebro-
arum consistentes excellebat, et eximia nobilitate, utpote illustris Guillelmi Nivernensis comitis filia, satis pollebat. Hæc nimirum consilio
baronum mariti sui relicto, æstimationem suam præferebat, et ardua nimis
secularibus in rebus plerumque arripiebat atque immoderata temptare properabat." Elsewhere (688 A), he says, " Ambæ mulieres quæ talia bella
ciebant, loquaces et animosæ, ac forma elegantes erant, suisque maritis im-
perabant, subditos homines premebant, variisque modis terrebant." When
Orderic (576 C), recording Isabel's widowhood and religious profession,
speaks of her as " letalis lasciviæ cui nimis in juventute servierat pœnitens,"
the word need not be taken in the worst sense. He uses (864 A) the same
kind of language of Juliana daughter of Henry the First, who, whatever she
was as a daughter, seems to have been a very good wife and mother.

[1] Ord. Vit. 834 B. "Pro feminea procacitate Rodberto comiti de Mellento aliisque Normannis invidiosa erat."

[2] Ord. Vit. 576 B, C. [3] Ib. 834 C.

[4] See N. C. vol. iv. pp. 605, 643.

CHAP. III. speech, and made herself agreeable to those immediately
about her.   Moreover, while of Heloise we read indeed
that she stirred up wars, but not that she waged them in
her own person, Isabel, like the ancient Queens of the
Amazons, went forth to the fight, mounted and armed,
War   and attended by a knightly following.[1] The struggle be-
between
Conches   tween the ladies of Evreux and Conches was at its height
and
Evreux.   at the moment when the castles of eastern Normandy
were falling one by one into the hands of Rufus.   Isabel
Ralph in   and Ralph were just now sore pressed.   The lord of
vain asks
help of the Conches therefore went to Duke Robert and craved his
Duke.   help;[2] but from Duke Robert no help was to be had
He sub-   for any man.   Ralph then bethought him of a stronger
mits to
William.   protector, in the sovereign of his English possessions.
King William gladly received such a petition, and bade
Count Stephen and Gerard of Gournay, and all who had
joined him in Normandy, to give all the help that they
Advance of   could to the new proselyte.[3]   The cause of the Red
William's
party.   King prospered everywhere; well nigh all Normandy to
the right of Seine was in the obedience of Rufus.   All
its chief men had, in a phrase which startles us in that

[1] Ord. Vit. 688 A.   " Magna in eisdem morum diversitas erat. Heluisa
quidem solers erat et facunda, sed atrox et avara. Isabel vero dapsilis et
audax atque jocosa, ideoque coessentibus amabilis et grata. In expedi-
tione inter milites, ut miles, equitabat armata, et loricatis equitibus ac spicu-
latis satellitibus non minori præstabat audacia quam decus Italiæ Turni
manipularibus virgo Camilla."   He goes on to liken her to Penthesileia
and all the other Amazons.

[2] Ib. " Radulfus Robertum ducem adivit, querelas damnorum quæ
a contribulibus suis pertulerat intimavit, et herile adjutorium ab eo
poposcit ; sed frustra, qui nihil obtinuit."

[3] Ib. B. " Hinc alias conversus est, et utile sibi patrocinium quærere
compulsus est. Regem Angliæ per legatos suos interpellatur, eique sua
infortunia mandavit, et si sibi suffragaretur, se et omnia sua permisit. His
auditis rex gavisus est, et efficax adminiculum indigenti pollicitus est.
Deinde Stephano comiti et Gerardo de Gornaco, aliisque tribunis et centu-
rionibus qui præerant in Normannia familiis ejus, mandavit ut Radulfum
totis adjuvarent nisibus et oppida ejus munirent necessariis omnibus."

generation, "joined the English."[1] And for them the
King of the English was open-handed. Into the hoard
at Winchester the wealth of England flowed in the shape
of every kind of unlawful exaction. Out of it it flowed
as freely to enable the new subjects of King William to
strengthen the defences of their castles and to hire mercenaries to defend them.[2]

During all this time Duke Robert himself does not seem Helias of
to have thought of striking a blow. But there was one Saint-Saens.
man at least between Seine and Somme who was ready
both to give and to take blows on his behalf. Robert He marries
had given one of his natural children, a daughter born Robert's
daughter.
to him in his wandering days,[3] in marriage to Helias,
lord of Saint-Saens.[4] Helias, like so many of the Nor- His
man nobles, came of a house which had risen to im- descent.
portance through the loves of Gunnor and Richard the
Fearless.[5] A daughter of one of Gunnor's sisters married Richard Viscount of Rouen, and became the mother
of Lambert of Saint-Saens, the father of Helias.[6] Helias
and the daughter of Robert had thus a common, though
distant, forefather in the father of Gunnor. With his He has
wife Helias received a goodly dowry, nothing less, we Caux as
his wife's
are told, than the whole land of Caux.[7] Helias' own dowry.
lordship of Saint-Saens lies on the upper course of the Position of
Saint-Saens.

---

[1] Ord. Vit. 681 A. "Robertus Aucensium comes, et Gauterius Gifardus
et Radulfus de Mortuomari, et pene omnes qui trans Sequanam usque ad
mare habitabant, *Anglicis conjuncti sunt.*"

[2] Ib. " De regiis opibus ad muniendas domos suas armis et satellitibus
copiosam pecuniam receperunt."

[3] See N. C. vol. iv. p. 644.

[4] Ord. Vit. 681 A. "Robertus dux contra tot hostes repagulum paravit,
filiamque suam quam de pellice habuerat, Heliæ filio Lamberti de Sancto
Sidonio conjugem dedit."

[5] N. C. vol. i. p. 253.   [6] Will. Gem. viii. 37.

[7] Ord. Vit. 681 B. "Archas cum Buris et adjacente provincia in ma-
ritagio tribuit, ut adversariis resisteret Calegiique comitatum defenderet.
Ille vero jussa viriliter complere cœpit."

CHAP. III. Varenne, in a deep bottom girt on all sides by wooded hills, one of which, known as the *Câtelier*, overhanging the town to the north, seems to have been the site of the castle of Helias. His stronghold has vanished; but the church on which the height looks down, if no rival to Saint Hildebert of Gournay, still keeps considerable remains of an age but little later than that with which we have to do. The possessions of Helias, both those which he inherited and those which he received with his wife, made his resistance to the invader of no small help to the cause of his father-in-law. They barred the nearest way to Rouen, not indeed from Gournay, but from Eu and Aumale. They came right between these last fortresses and the domain of Walter Giffard at Longueville. Of the three streams which meet by Arques, while Helias himself held the upper Varenne at Saint-Saens, his wife's fortress of Bures held the middle course of the Bethune or Dieppe below Gerard's Gaillefontaine, and below Drincourt, not yet the New Castle of King Henry.[1] The massive church, with parts dating from the days of Norman independence, rises on the left slope of the valley above an island in the stream. But the site of the castle which formed part of the marriage portion of Duke Robert's daughter is hard to trace. But lower down, nearer the point where the streams meet, the bride of Helias had brought him a noble gift indeed. Through her he was lord of Arques, with its donjon and its ditches, the mighty castle whose tale has been told in recording the history of an earlier generation.[2] A glance at the map will show how strong a position in eastern Normandy was held by the man who commanded at once Saint-Saens, Bures, and Arques. But the son-in-law of Duke Robert deserves our notice

Importance of his position.

Bures.

Helias holds Arques.

---

[1] Neufchâtel-en-Bray, famous for cheeses.

[2] See N. C. vol. iii. p. 121.

for something better than his birth, his marriage, or his CHAP. III.
domains. Helias of Saint-Saens was, in his personal Faithful-
character, a worthy namesake of Helias of La Flêche. ness of
Helias
Among the crimes and treasons of that age, we dwell towards
Robert.
with delight on the unswerving faithfulness with which,
through many years and amidst all the ups and downs
of fortune, he clave to the reigning Duke and to his son
after him.[1]   But this his later history lies beyond the
bounds of our immediate tale.   What directly concerns
us now is that Helias was the one noble of Normandy
whom the gold of England could not tempt.   It would
be almost ungenerous to put on record the fact that,
unlike most of his neighbours, he had no English estates
to lose.   The later life of Helias puts him above all
suspicion of meaner motives.   Saint-Saens, Arques,
Bures, and all Caux, remained faithful to Duke Robert.

With this honourable exception, an exception which
greatly lessened the value of his new conquests, William
Rufus had won, without hand-strokes, without his personal presence, a good half of the original grant to Rolf,
the greater part of the diocese of Rouen.   He was soon William's
dealings
to win yet another triumph by his peculiar policy.   By with
those arms which were specially his own, he was to win France.
over an ally, or at least to secure the neutrality of an
enemy, of far higher rank, though perhaps of hardly
greater practical power, than the Count of Aumale and
the aged lord of Longueville.   Robert in his helplessness Robert
asks help
cried to his over-lord at Paris.   Had not his father done of Philip.
the same to Philip's father?   Had not King Henry
played a part at least equal to that of Duke William
among the lifted lances of Val-ès-dunes?[2]   Philip had

---

[1] Ord. Vit. 681 B.   " Roberto duci et Guillelmo filio ejus semper fidelis
fuit, et sub duobus regibus Guillelmo et Henrico multa pertulit, labores
videlicet ac exhæreditationem, damna, exsilium, ac multa pericula."   See
N. C. vol. v. pp. 84, 182.

[2] N. C. vol. ii. p. 254.

CHAP. III. had his jest on the bulky frame of the Conqueror, and his jest had been avenged among the candles of the bloody churching at Mantes.[1] By this time at least, so some of our authorities imply, Philip had brought himself to a case in which the same jest might have been

Philip comes to help.

made upon himself with a good deal more of point. At the prayer of his vassal the bulky King of the French left his table and his dainties, and set forth, sighing and groaning at the unusual exertion, to come to the help of the aggrieved Duke.[2] It was a strange beginning of the

Meeting of the Norman and French armies.

direct rivalry between England and France. King Philip came with a great host into Normandy. And Robert must somewhere or other have found forces to join those of his royal ally. And now was shown the value of the position which was held by the faithful Helias in the land

They march on Eu.

of Caux. It must have been by his help that the combined armies of Robert and Philip were able to march to the furthest point of the Red King's new acquisitions, to the furthest point of the Norman duchy itself, to the castle of Eu, which was held, we are told, by a vast host, Norman and English.[3] Let an honest voice from Peter-

---

[1] N. C. vol. iv. p. 700.

[2] Will. Malms. iv. 307. "Domino suo regi Franciæ per nuntios violentiam fratris exposuit, suppetias orans. Et ille quidem iners, et quotidianam crapulam ructans, ad bellum singultiens ingluvie veniebat."

[3] The place is not mentioned in the Chronicles nor in any other of our accounts, except by Robert of Torigny in the Continuation of William of Jumièges, viii. 3. He tells his story backwards in a very confused way, and mixes up the events of this year and the next; "Facta est itaque tandem inter eos [Robertum et Willelmum] apud Cadomum, ut diximus, adminiculante Philippo rege Francorum, qui in auxilium ducis contra Willelmum regem apud oppidum Auci ingenti Anglorum et Normannorum exercitu tunc morantem venerat, qualiscumque concordia." This means the peace of 1092, when William was in Normandy, and when Philip certainly did not come to Eu. On the other hand, William was certainly not at Eu in 1091. But as Philip did in 1091 come to some castle which must have been either Eu, Aunde, or Gournay, we may perhaps accept this as evidence in favour of Eu.

borough tell what followed. "And the King and the
Earl with a huge *fyrd* beset the castle about where the
King's men of England in it were. The King William
of England sent to Philip the Franks' King, and he for
his love or for his mickle treasure forlet so his man the
Earl Robert and his land, and went again to France and
let them so be."[1] A Latin writer does not think it
needful to allow Philip the perhaps ironical alternative
of the English writer. Love between Philip and
William Rufus is not thought of. We are simply told
that, while Philip was promising great things, the money
of the King of England met him—the wealth of Rufus
seems to be personified. Before its presence his courage
was broken; he loosed his girdle and went back to
his banquet.[2]

Thus the special weapons of Rufus could overcome
even kings at a distance. But, ludicrous as the tale
sounds in the way in which it is told, this negotiation
between Philip and William is really, in an European,
and even in an English point of view, the most important event in the whole story. We should hardly
be wrong in calling this payment to Philip the first
instance of the employment of English money in the
shape of subsidies to foreign princes. For such it in
strictness was. It was not, like a Danegeld, money paid
to buy off a foreign invader. Nor was it like the simple
hiring of mercenaries at home or abroad. It is, like
later subsidies, money paid to a foreign sovereign, on

[1] Chron. Petrib. 1090. "Se cyng Willelm of Englalande sende to
Philippe Francena cynge, and he *for his lufan* oðð*e for his* mycele
gersuma, forlet swa his man þone eorl Rodbeard and his land, and ferde
ongean to France, and let heom swa weorðan." The spirit is lost in the
Latin of Florence; "Quod cum regi Willelmo nuntiatum esset, non modica pecuniæ quantitati regi Philippo occulte transmissa, ut obsidione
dimissa, domum rediret, flagitavit et imperavit."

[2] Will. Malms. iv. 307. "Occurrerunt magna pollicenti nummi regis
Angliæ, quibus infractus cingulum solvit et convivium repetiit."

CHAP. III. condition of his promoting, or at least not thwarting, the policy of a sovereign of England. The appetite [1] which was now first awakened in Philip of Paris soon came to be shared by other princes, and it lasted in full force for

First direct dealings between England and France.

many ages. Again, we have now for the first time direct political dealings between a purely insular King of England—we may forestall the territorial style when speaking of England as a state rather than of Englishmen as a nation—and a French King at Paris. The embassies which passed between Eadward and Henry, even when Henry made his appeal on behalf of Godwine,[2] hardly

Different position of the two Williams.

make an exception. William the Great had dealt with France as a Norman duke; if, in the latter part of his reign, he had wielded the strength of England as well as the strength of Normandy, he had wielded it, as far as France was concerned, wholly for Norman purposes. But William the Red, though his position arose wholly out of the new relations between England and Normandy, was still for the present a purely English king.

Relation of England, Normandy, and France.

The first years of Rufus and the first years of Henry the First are alike breaks in the hundred and forty years of union between England and Normandy.[3] Had not a Norman duke conquered England, an English king would not have been seeking to conquer Normandy; but, as a matter of fact, an English king, who had no dominions on the mainland, was seeking to conquer Normandy. And he was seeking to win it with

[1] Macaulay, Hist. Eng. iv. 265. "The Elector of Saxony . . . had, together with a strong appetite for subsidies, a great desire to be a member of the most select and illustrious orders of knighthood." For this last passion there was as yet no room, but William Rufus did a good deal towards bringing about the state of things in which it arose.

[2] N. C. vol. ii. p. 318.

[3] So are the Norman reigns of Geoffrey Plantagenet and his son Henry. But their position in Normandy was quite different from Robert's, while they claimed England in quite a different sense from the claims of Robert, and had—the son at least had—partisans there.

the good will, or at least the neutrality, of the French
King. This was a state of things which could have
happened only during the few years when different sons
of the Conqueror ruled in England and in Normandy.
Whenever England and Normandy were united, whether
by conquest or by inheritance, the old strife between
France and Normandy led England into the struggle.
But at the present moment an alliance between England
and France against Normandy was as possible as any
other political combination. And the arts of Rufus Results of
secured, if not French alliance, at least French neu- Rufus'
trality. But either alliance or neutrality was in its with
own nature destructive of itself. Let either Normandy Philip.
win England or England win Normandy, and the old
state of things again began. The union of England and
Normandy meant enmity between England and France,
an enmity which survived their separation.[1] Friendly
dealings between William and Philip were a step towards the union of England and Normandy, and thereby
a step towards that open enmity between England and
France which began under Rufus himself and which lasted
down to our fathers' times. The bribe which Philip took
at Eu has its place in the chain of events which led to
Bouvines, to Crécy, and to Waterloo.

But while things were thus, unknown to the actors in State of
them, taking a turn which was permanently to affect the Normandy.
history of mankind, the immediate business of the time
went on as before in the lands of Northern Gaul. In
Normandy that immediate business was mutual destruction—civil war is too lofty a name; in Maine it was
deliverance from the Norman yoke. I am not called on
to tell in detail the whole story of every local strife between one Norman baron and another, not even in those

[1] N. C. vol. v. pp. 85, 95, 96.

CHAP. III.

Private wars not interrupted by the invasion.

Action of Robert of Bellême.

rare cases when the Duke himself stepped in as a judge or as a party in the strife. Those who loved nothing so well as slaughter, plunder, and burning, had now to make up for the many years during which the strong hand of William the Great had kept them back from those enjoyments. They had no thought of stopping, though the kings of England and France, or all the kings of the earth, should appear in arms on Norman soil. Many a brilliant feat of arms, as it was deemed in those days, must be left to local remembrance; even at events which closely touched many of the chief names of our story we can do no more than glance. The revolt of Maine will have to be spoken of at length in another chapter; among strictly Norman affairs we naturally find Robert of Bellême playing his usual part towards his sovereign and his neighbours, and we find the tower of Ivry and the fortified hall of Brionne ever supplying subjects of strife to the turbulent nobles. We see Robert of Bellême at war with his immediate neighbour Geoffrey Count of Perche,[1] and driving Abbot Ralph of Seez to seek shelter in England.[2] We also find him beaten back from the walls of Exmes by Gilbert of Laigle and the other warriors of his house, the house of which we have heard in the Malfosse of Senlac

---

[1] The character of this Count Geoffrey (son of the Rotrou who figures in the war of the Conqueror and his son, N. C. vol. iv. pp. 637, 639) as drawn by Orderic (675 D; see above, p. 183) is worth studying; "Erat idem consul magnanimus, corpore pulcher, et callidus, timens Deum et ecclesiæ cultor devotus, clericorum pauperumque Dei defensor strenuus, in pace quietus et amabilis, bonisque pollebat moribus." Yet he was also "in bello gravis et fortunatus, finitimisque intolerabilis regibus et inimicus [cis?] omnibus." Moreover "multas villas combussit multasque prædas hominesque adduxit." The truth is that the curse of private warfare drew the best men, no less than the worst, into the common whirlpool; and, once in arms, they could not keep back their followers from the usual excesses, even if any such thought occurred to themselves. Cf. Ord. Vit. 890 B for another mention of Geoffrey.

[2] See above, p. 184.

and beneath the rocks of Sainte-Susanne.[1] William of CHAP. III.
Breteuil loses, wins, and loses again, his late grant of
the tower of Ivry, and the second time he is driven to
give both the tower and the hand of his natural daughter
as his own ransom from a specially cruel imprisonment
at the hands of a rebellious vassal.[2] Brionne forms the
centre of a tale in which its new lord and his son, the
other Roger and the other Robert of our story, play
over again the part of the Earl of Shrewsbury and
his son of Bellême. Robert of Meulan comes from Robert of
England to assert his claim among others to the much- Meulan
claims the
contested tower of Ivry. The Duke reminds him that tower of
Ivry.
he had given Brionne to his father in exchange for
Ivry. The Count of Meulan gives a threatening
answer.[3] The Duke, with unusual spirit, puts him in He is imprisoned,
prison, seizes Brionne, and puts it into a state of de- but set free
fence. Then the old Roger of Beaumont, old a genera- at the intercession
tion earlier,[4] obtains, by the recital of his own exploits, of his
father.

[1] Ord. Vit. 685 A, B. This Gilbert is son of Eginulf, who died at Senlac
(N. C. vol. iii. p. 503, note), and brother of Richer, who died before Sainte-
Susanne (N. C. vol. iv. p. 659). His sister Matilda married Robert of
Mowbray.

[2] Ib. 684 D, 685 C, D; Will. Gem. viii. 15. The offender, a man of
Belial, was Ascelin surnamed Goel. The marriage was blessed or cursed
with the birth of seven sons, all, according to both our authorities, of evil
report.

[3] See above, p. 194. The bandying of words, as given by Orderic
(686 A), is worth notice; "Robertus comes Mellenti muneribus et pro·
missis Guillelmi regis turgidus de Anglia venit, Rothomagum ad ducem
accessit, et ab eo arcem Ibreii procaciter repetiit. Cui dux respondit,
Æquipotens mutuum patri tuo dedi Brioniam nobile castrum pro arce
Ibreii. Comes Mellenti dixit, Istud mutuum non concedo, sed quod pater
tuus patri meo dedit habere volo. Alioqui per sanctum Nigasium faciam
quod tibi displicebit. Iratus igitur dux illico eum comprehendi et in
carcere vinciri præcepit, et Brioniam Roberto Balduini filio custodiendam
commisit." This Robert in 686 D sets forth his pedigree, as grandson
of Count Gilbert the guardian of the Conqueror (see N. C. vol. ii. pp. 195,
196). He was nephew of Richard of Bienfaite (see above, p. 68), the
founder of the house of Clare.

[4] He is now brought in as "callidus senex."

CHAP. III.   the deliverance of his son.[1]   He then prays, not without

Robert   golden arguments, for the restitution of Brionne.[2]   The
takes
Brionne.   officer in command, Robert son of Baldwin, asserts his
own hereditary claim, and, at the head of six knights
only, stands a siege, though not a long one, against the
combined forces of the Duke and of the Count of Meulan
and his father.[3] This siege is remarkable. The summer
days were hot; all things were dry; the besiegers shot
red-hot arrows against the roof of the fortified hall, and
set fire to it.[4]   So Duke Robert boasted that he had
taken in a day the river-fortress which had held out for
three years against his father.[5]

These events concern us only because we know the
actors, and because they helped to keep up that state of
confusion in the Norman duchy which supplied the Red
King at once with an excuse for his invasion, and with

Advance of the means for carrying out his schemes. It must be
Rufus.   remembered that the two stories are actually contemporary; while Robert was besieging Brionne, the fortresses of eastern Normandy were already falling one by
one into the hands of Rufus. It is even quite possible that

[1] Ord. Vit. 686 C. The Duke speaks of the old Roger's " magna *lega-litas*," "*loyalty*," according to its etymology. Is it characteristic of the " callidus senex " that he addresses the Duke as " vestra sublimitas," " vestra serenitas," and thanks him for imprisoning his son, " temerarium juvenem "? Yet it was twenty-four years since the exploits of Robert of Meulan at Senlac.

[2] Ib. D. " Ob hoc ingens pecuniæ pondus promisit."

[3] Ib. 687 A.

[4] Ib. A, B. "Tunc calor ingens incipientis æstatis, et maxima siccitas erant, quæ forinsecus expugnantes admodum juvabant. Callidi enim obsessores in fabrili fornace quæ in promptu structa fuerat, ferrum missilium calefaciebant, subitoque *super tectum principalis aulæ* in munimento jacie-bant, et sic ferrum candens sagittarum atque pilorum in arida veterum lanugine imbricum totis nisibus figebant."

[5] Ib. "Sic Robertus dux ab hora nona Brioniam ante solis occasum obtinuit, quam Guillelmus pater ejus cum auxilio Henrici Francorum regis sibi vix in tribus annis subigere potuit." See N. C. vol. ii. p. 268.

Robert of Meulan's voyage from England to Normandy, CHAP. III.
and the demands made by him and his father on the
Duke, were actually planned between the cunning Count
and the Red King as a means of increasing the confusion
which reigned in the duchy. But there are tales of local
strife which concern us more nearly. The war of the The war of
half-brothers, the war of the Amazons, the strife between Conches and
Conches and Evreux, between Isabel and Heloise, is an Evreux.
immediate part of the tale of William Rufus. The lord
of Conches was strengthened in his struggle with his
brother by forces directly sent to his help by the King's
order.[1] The war went on; and, while it was still going Movement
on, a far more important movement began in the greatest at Rouen.
city of Normandy, a movement in which the King of the
English was yet more directly concerned. Up to this
time his plans had been everywhere crowned with success.
His campaign, if campaign we can call it, had begun soon
after Easter. Half a year had passed, and nearly the
whole of the oldest, though not the truest, Normandy
had fallen into his hands without his stirring out of his
island realm. It now became doubtful whether Robert
could keep even the capital of his duchy.

The month of November of this year saw stirring November,
scenes alike in the streets of Rouen and beneath 1090.
the walls of Conches. But, while Conches was openly
aided by the King's troops, no force from England
or from the parts of Normandy which William had
already won had as yet drawn near to Rouen.
Rufus knew other means to gain over the burghers
of a great city as well as the lords of castles and
smaller towns. The glimpse which we now get of the State of
internal state of the Norman metropolis tells us, like things in
so many other glimpses which are given us in the his-Rouen.
tory of these times, just enough to make us wish to be

[1] See above, p. 234.

CHAP. III. told more. A state of things is revealed to us which we are not used to in the history of Normandy. Rouen appears for a moment as something like an independent commonwealth, though an enemy might call it a commonwealth which seemed to be singularly bent on its own destruction. The same municipal spirit which we have seen so strong at Exeter and at Le Mans[1] shows itself now for a moment at Rouen. We may be sure that under the rule of William the Great no man had dreamed of a *commune* in the capital of Normandy. His arm, we may be sure, had protected the men of Rouen, like all his other subjects, in the enjoyment of all rights and privileges which were not inconsistent with his own dominion. But in his day Rouen could have seen no demagogues, no tyrants, no armies in civic pay, no dealings of its citizens with any prince other than their own sovereign. But the rule of William the Great was over; in Robert's days it may well have seemed that the citizens of so great a city were better able to rule themselves, or at all events that they were entitled to choose their own ruler. When the arts of Rufus, his gifts and his promises, began to work at Rouen in the same way in which they had worked on the castles of the eastern border, his agents had to deal, not with a prince or a lord, but with a body of citizens under the leadership of one of whom one doubts whether he should be called a demagogue or a tyrant. We seem to be carried over two hundred and forty years to the dealings of Edward the Third with the mighty brewer of Ghent. The Artevelde of Rouen was Conan — the name suggests a Breton origin — the son of Gilbert surnamed Pilatus. He was the richest man in the city; his craft is not told us; but we must always remember that a citizen was not necessarily a trader.[2] His wealth

The municipal spirit.

Conan demagogue or tyrant.

---

[1] See N. C. vol. iv. pp. 145, 451.   [2] Ib. vol. v. pp. 466, 474.

was such that it enabled him to feed troops of mercenaries and to take armed knights into his pay.[1] Another
leading citizen, next in wealth to Conan, was William
the son of Ansgar,[2] whose name seems to imply the
purest Norman blood. Conan had entered into a treaty Conan's
with William, the object of which, we are told, was to William.
betray the metropolis of Normandy and the Duke of the
Normans—the sleepy Duke, as our guide calls him—into
the power of the island King.[3] Nor was this merely The citi-
the scheme of Conan and William; public feeling in the William.
city went heartily with them. A party still clave to the
Duke; but the mass of the men of Rouen threw in their
lot with Conan, and were, like him, ready to receive
William as their sovereign instead of Robert.[4] They
may well have thought that, in the present state of
things, any change would be for the better; the utter
lawlessness of the time, which might have its charms
for turbulent nobles, would have no charms for the
burghers of a great city. Or the men of Rouen may have
argued then, much as the men of Bourdeaux argued ages
later, that they were likely to enjoy a greater measure
of municipal freedom, under a King of the English,
dwelling apart from them in his own island, than they
would ever win from a Duke of the Normans, holding

[1] Ord. Vit. 689 D. "Hujus nimirum factionis incentor Conanus
Gisleberti Pilati filius erat, qui inter cives, utpote ditissimus eorum, præ-
cellebat. Is cum rege de tradenda civitate pactum fecerat, et immensis
opibus ditatus in urbe vigebat, ingentemque militum et satellitum familiam
contra ducem turgidus jugiter pascebat."

[2] Ib. 691 A. "Guillelmus Ansgerii filius, Rodomensium ditissimus."
This is after Conan's death.

[3] Ib. 689 D. "Cives Rothomagi regiis muneribus et promissis illecti
de mutando principe tractaverunt, ac ut Normanniæ metropolim *cum somno-
lento duce* regi proderent consiliati sunt."

[4] Ib. "Maxima pars urbanorum eidem adquiescebant. Nonnulli tamen
pro fide duci servanda resistebant, et opportunis tergiversationibus de-
testabile facinus impediebant."

CHAP. III.

A party for
Robert.

A day fixed
for the sur-
render to
William.

Robert
sends for
help.

Henry and
Robert of
Bellême
come to
the Duke's
help.

his court and castle in Rouen itself. Yet the friends of Robert might have their arguments too. The party of mere conservatism, the party of order, would naturally cleave to him. But other motives might well come in. True friends of the *commune* might doubt whether William the Red was likely to be a very safe protector of civic freedom. They might argue that, if they must needs have a master, their liberties were less likely to be meddled with under such a master as Robert. But the party of the Duke's friends, on whatever grounds it stood by him, was the weaker party. A majority of the citizens was zealous for William. A day was fixed by Conan with the general consent, on which the city was to be given up,[1] and the King's forces were invited to come from Gournay and other points in his obedience. Robert seems to have stayed in the capital which was passing from him; but he felt that, if he was to have supporters, he must seek for them beyond its walls. He sent to tell his plight to those of the nobles of Normandy in whom he still put any trust.[2] And he also hastened to seek help in a reconciliation with some neighbours and subjects with whom he was at variance.

It is certainly a little startling, after the history of the past year, to find at the head of the list of Duke Robert's new allies the names of the Ætheling Henry and of Robert of Bellême. We may well fancy that they took up arms, not so much to support the rights of the Duke against the King as to check the dangerous example of a great city taking upon itself to choose among the

[1] Ord. Vit. 689 D. "Conanus de suorum consensu *contribulium* securus, terminum constituit." Orderic most likely means nothing in particular by this odd word "contribules." But the later history of free cities supplies a certain temptation to begin thinking of gilds, *Zünfte, Geschlechter, abbayes,* and *alberghi.*

[2] Ib. "Dux, ubi tantam contra se machinationem comperiit, amicos in quibus confidebat ad se convocavit."

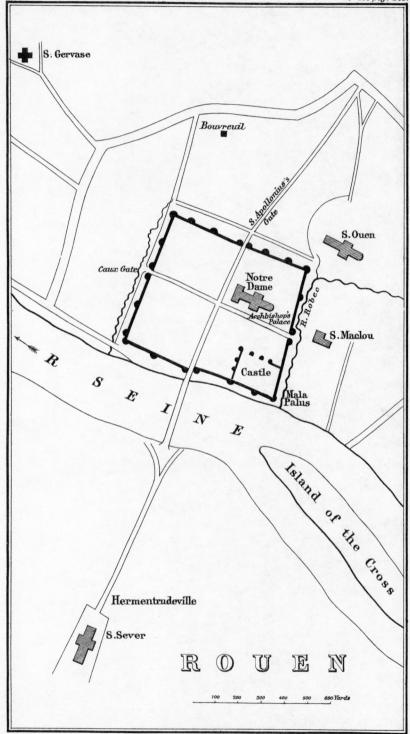

S. Gervase

Bouvreuil

S. Apollonius's Gate

S. Ouen

Caux Gate

Notre Dame

R. Robec

Archbishop's Palace

S. Maclou

Castle

Mala Palus

R. SEINE

Island of the Cross

Hermentrudeville

S. Sever

ROUEN

100   200   300   400   500   600 Yards

claims of kings, dukes, and counts. Robert of Bel- CHAP. III.
lême may indeed have simply hastened to any quarter Danger of the ex-
from which the scent of coming slaughter greeted him. ample of Rouen.
But Henry the Clerk could always have given a reason
for anything that he did. Popular movements at Rouen
might supply dangerous precedents at Coutances. The
Count of Coutances too might have better hopes of becoming Duke of Rouen, if Rouen were still held for a
while by such a prince as Robert, than he could have if
the city became either the seat of a powerful commonwealth or the stronghold of a powerful king. But, from
whatever motive, Henry came, and he was the first to
come.[1] Others to whom the Duke's messengers set forth Others who help Robert.
his desolate state [2] came also. Robert of Bellême, so lately
his prisoner, Count William of Evreux and his nephew
William of Breteuil, all hastened, if not to the deliverance of Duke Robert, at least to the overthrow of
Conan. And with them came Reginald of Warren,
the younger son of William and Gundrada,[3] and Gilbert of Laigle, fresh from his victory over his mightiest
comrade.[4] At the beginning of November Duke Robert November 3, 1090.
was still in the castle of Rouen; but his brother Henry Henry at Rouen.
was now with him within its walls, and the captains
who had come to his help were thundering at the gates
of the rebellious city.

The Rouen of those days, like the Le Mans, the York, Rouen in the eleventh century.
and the Lincoln, of those days, was still the Roman city,
the old Rothomagus. As in those and in countless other
cases, large and populous suburbs had spread themselves
over the neighbouring country; at Rouen, as at York,

---

[1] Ord. Vit. 690 A. "Henricus igitur primus ei suppetias venit, et primo
subsidium fratri contulit, deinde vindictam viriliter in proditorem exercuit."

[2] Ib. "Fidelibus suis desolationem sui cita legatione intimavit."

[3] Ib. See above, p. 76, and N. C. vol. iv. p. 654.

[4] See above, p. 242. He was killed next year. See Ord. Vit. 685 B.

CHAP. III. those suburbs had passed the river; but the city itself, the walled space to be attacked and defended in war-time, was still of the same extent as it had been in the days before Rolf and before Chlodwig. The rectangular space marking the Roman camp stretched on its southern side nearly to the Seine, whose stream, not yet fenced in by quays, reached further inland on that side Position of than it now does. Rouen is essentially a river city, not the city. a hill city. The metropolitan church does indeed stand on sensibly higher ground than the buildings close to the river; but to one fresh from Le Mans or Chartres the rise which has to be mastered seems trifling indeed. For a hill city the obvious site would have been on the natural akropolis supplied by the height of Saint Katharine to the south-east. Yet Rouen is a city of the mainland; the islands which divide the waters of the Seine must have been tempting points for Rolf in his Wiking days; but even the largest of them, the Isle of the Cross, was hardly large enough for a town to grow upon it. Of the walls of Rothomagus not a fragment is left; yet the impress of a Roman *chester* is hard to wipe out; it is still easy to trace its lines among the streets and build-ings of the greatly enlarged mediæval and modern city. Frightful as has been the havoc which the metropolis of Normandy has undergone in our own time, merci-lessly as the besom of destruction has swept over its ancient streets, churches, and houses, the dæmon of modern improvement has spared enough to enable us, if not to tell the towers, yet in idea to mark well the bulwarks, of the city where the Conqueror reigned. The ducal Near the south-west corner of the parallelogram, not castles. far from the river-side, had stood the earlier castle of the Dukes. Its site in after times became the friary of the Cordeliers, a small fragment of whose church, as well as another desecrated church within the castle

precinct, does in some faint way preserve the memory CHAP. III.
of the dwelling-place of Rolf.[1] But by the days of
Robert, the dukes had moved their dwelling to the
south-eastern corner, also near the river, where the site
of the castle is marked by the vast *halles,* and by the
graceful Renaissance porch, where the chapter of our
Lady of Rouen yearly, on the feast of the Ascension,
exercised the prerogative of mercy by saving one prisoner condemned to die. Here the memory of the castle,
though only its memory, lives in the names of the *Haute*
and the *Basse Vieille Tour,* one of which is soon to be
famous in our story. On the eastern side the wall was The eastern
side of the
washed by a small tributary of the Seine, the Rebecq, city.
a stream whose course has withdrawn from sight almost
as thoroughly as the Fleet of London or the Frome of
Bristol.[2] On this side of the city lay a large swampy
tract, whose name of *Mala palus* still lives in a
Rue Malpalu[3], though a more distant part of it has
taken the more ambitious name of the Field of Mars.
Within the wall lay the metropolitan church of our The archbishopric.
Lady and the palace of the Primate of Normandy. If
this last reached to anything like its present extent to
the east, the Archbishops of Rouen, like the Counts of

[1] This earlier castle of the dukes must be carefully distinguished from
the *Vieux Palais,* which, though it is no longer standing, still lives in street
nomenclature. This last was the work of our Henry the Fifth, and lay to
the west, between the Roman wall and the wall of Saint Lewis.

On this side of the city the modern street lately called *Rue de l'Impératrice,*
and now promoted to the name of *Rue Jeanne Darc,* is not a bad guide.
It runs a little outside of the Roman wall and may fairly represent its
fosse. So the other great modern street called *Rue de l'Hôtel de Ville,* and
now *Rue Thiers,* runs a little further outside the northern wall of the ancient
city, which is marked by the *Rue de la Ganterie.*

[2] On this side again a modern street helps us. The *Rue de la République,*
lately *Rue Impériale,* marks, though less accurately than the others, the
eastern side of the city. The Rebecq may be traced for a little way, but
it presently loses itself, or at least is lost to the inquirer.

[3] Ord. Vit. 690 B. See below, p. 255.

CHAP. III.

Abbey of Saint Ouen.

Maine,[1] must have been reckoned among the men who sat on the wall. Outside the city, but close under the wall, near its north-eastern corner, stood the great abbey of Saint Ouen, the arch-monastery,[2] still ruled by its Abbot Nicolas, though his long reign was now drawing to an end.[3] At the opposite north-western angle, but much further from the walls, where the higher ground begins to rise above the city, stood the priory of Saint Gervase, the scene of the Conqueror's death.[4]

Priory of Saint Gervase.

Castle of Bouvreil.

Walls of Saint Lewis.

Saint Gervase indeed stood, not only far beyond the Roman walls, but beyond those fortifications of later times which took Saint Ouen's within the city. For Rouen grew as Le Mans grew. On the higher ground like Saint Gervase, but more to the east, rose the castle of Bouvreil, which Philip of Paris, after the loss of Norman independence, reared to hold down the conquered city. Between his grandfather's castle and the ancient wall Saint Lewis traced out the newer line of fortification which is marked by the modern *boulevards*. His walls are gone, as well as the walls of Rothomagus; but of the house of bondage of Philip Augustus one tower still stands, while of the dwelling-place of her own princes even mediæval Rouen had preserved nothing.

The gates.

The four sides of the Roman enclosure were of course pierced by the four chief gates of the city, of three of which we hear in our story. Of these the western, the gate of Caux, is in some sort represented by the Renaissance gate of the Great Clock [5] with its adjoining

[1] See N. C. vol. iii. p. 203.

[2] "Archimonasterium" is a title of Saint Ouen's. See Neustria Pia, 1.

[3] See N. C. vol. ii. pp. 183, 468.

[4] See N. C. vol. iv. p. 704.

[5] The "Tour de la Grosse Horloge" and the gate close by are conspicuous features in that quarter of Rouen. The noble Palace of Justice was not even represented in the times with which we have to do.

tower. The northern gate bore the name of Saint CHAP. III.
Apollonius. The river was spanned by at least one
bridge, which crossed it by way of the island of the
Cross, near the second ducal castle. Beyond the Suburbs
stream lay the suburb of Hermentrudeville, now Saint beyond the Seine.
Sever, where Anselm had waited during the sickness
of the Conqueror.[1] There too the Duchess Matilda,
soon to be Queen, had begun the monastery of the
meadow, the monastery of our Lady of Good News, the
house of *Pratum* or *Pré*, whose church still stood unfinished, awaiting the perfecting hand of her youngest
son.[2]

Meanwhile the elder and best-beloved son of Matilda Fright of Duke Robert.
was trembling within the city on the right bank of the
broad river. Luckily he had the presence of his youngest
brother, the English Ætheling, the Count of the Côtentin,
to strengthen him. Personal courage Duke Robert never
lacked at any time; but something more than personal
courage was now needed. Robert was perhaps not
frightened, but he was puzzled; at such a moment he
seemed to the calm judgement of Henry to be simply
in the way; it was for wiser heads to take counsel
without him. But deliverance was at hand. Both sides Approach of Gilbert and Reginald.
of the Seine sent their helpers. Gilbert of Laigle crossed
the bridge by the island close under the ducal tower, and
turned to the left to the attack of the southern gate.
Reginald of Warren at the head of three hundred
knights drew near to the gate of Caux.[3] Against Efforts of Conan.
this twofold attack Conan strove hard to keep up the
hearts of his partisans. He made speeches exhorting
to a valiant defence. Many obeyed; but the city was Division among the citizens.
already divided; while one party hastened to the
southern gate to withstand the assault of Gilbert,

---

[1] See N. C. vol. iv. p. 706.   [2] Neustria Pia, 611.
[3] Ord. Vit. 690 A. " Ad Calcegiensem portam properavit."

another party sped to open the western gate and to
let in the forces of Reginald. Soldiers of the King of
the English, the advanced guard doubtless of a greater
host to come, were already in the city, stirring up the
party of Conan to swifter and fiercer action.[1] Soldiers
and citizens were huddled together in wild confusion;
shouts passed to and fro for King and Duke; men at
either gate smote down neighbours and kinsmen to the
sound of either war-cry.[2] The strength of the city was
turned against itself. The hopes of the commonwealth
of Rouen, either as a free city or as a favoured ally
of the island King, were quenched in the blood of its
citizens. Le Mans and Exeter had fallen; but they had
fallen more worthily than this.

Meanwhile Henry and those who were with him in
the castle deemed that the time had come for the defenders of the ducal stronghold to join their friends
within and without the city. But there was one inha-
bitant of the castle whose presence was deemed an
encumbrance at such a moment. Men were shouting
for the Duke of the Normans; but the wiser heads of
his friends deemed that the Duke of the Normans was
just then best out of the way. Robert came down
from the tower, eager to join in the fray and to give
help to the citizens of his own party.[3] But all was

---

[1] Ord. Vit. 690 A. "Jampridem quidam de regiis satellitibus in urbem
introierant, et parati, rebellionem tacite præstolantes, seditionis moram
ægre ferebant."

[2] Ib. B. "Dum militaris et civilis tumultus exoritur, nimius hinc et
inde clamor attollitur, et tota civitas pessime confunditur, et in sua viscera
crudeliter debacchatur. Plures enim civium contra cognatos vicinosque
suos ad utramque portam dimicabant, dum quædam pars duci, et altera
regi favebant. . . . Dum perturbationis ingens tumultus cuncta confunderet,
et nesciretur quam quisque civium sibi partem eligeret."

[3] Ib. B. "Dux ubi furentes, ut dictum est, in civitate advertit, cum
Henrico fratre suo et commanipularibus suis de arce prodiit, suisque velo-
citer suffragari appetiit."

wild tumult; it needed a cooler head than Robert's to CHAP. III.
distinguish friend from foe. He might easily rush on
destruction in some ignoble form, and bring dishonour
on the Norman name itself.[1] He was persuaded by
his friends to forego his warlike purposes, and to
suffer himself to be led out of harm's way. While
every other man in the metropolis of Normandy was
giving and taking blows, the lord of Normandy, in
mere personal prowess one of the foremost soldiers in his
duchy, was smuggled out of his capital as one who could
not be trusted to let his blows fall in the right place.
With a few comrades he passed through the eastern gate
into the suburb of the Evil Swamp, just below the
castle walls. It is to be noticed that no fighting on this No attacks from the east.
side of the city is mentioned. The King's troops were
specially looked for to approach from Gournay, and the
east gate was the natural path by which an army from
Gournay would seek to enter Rouen. One would have
expected that one at least of the relieving parties would
have hastened to make sure of this most important point.
Yet one division takes its post by the southern gate,
another by the western, none by the eastern. Were
operations on that side made needless, either by the
neighbourhood of the castle, by any difficulties of the
marshy ground, or by the disposition of the inhabitants
of the suburb? Certain it is that Duke Robert's nearest
neighbours outside his capital were loyal to him. The
men of the Evil Swamp received the Duke gladly as
their special lord.[2] He allowed himself to be put into
a boat, and ferried across to the suburb on the left bank.

---

[1] Ord. Vit. 690 B. "Ne perniciem inhonestam stolido incurreret,
cunctisque Normannis perenne opprobrium fieret."

[2] Ib. "Fugiens cum paucis per orientalem portam egressus est, et mox
a suburbanis vici, qui Mala-palus dicitur, fideliter ut specialis herus susceptus est."

CHAP. III. There he was received by one of his special counsellors, William of Arques, a monk of Molesme, and was kept safely in his mother's monastery till all danger was over.[1]

It was clearly not wholly for the sake of such a prince as this that so many Norman leaders, Henry of Coutances among them, had made up their minds that the republican movement at Rouen was to be put down. The moment for putting it down had come. Gilbert of Laigle had by this time, by the strength of his own forces and by the help of the citizens of his party, entered Rouen through the southern gate. His forces now joined the company of Henry; they thus became far more than a match for the citizens of Conan's party, even strengthened as they were by those of the King's men who were in the city. A great slaughter of the citizens followed; the soldiers of Rufus contrived to flee out of the city, and to find shelter in the neighbouring woods;[2] the city was full of death, flight, and weeping; innocent and guilty fell together; Conan and others of the ringleaders were taken prisoners. Conan himself was led into the castle, and

Gilbert enters Rouen.

Slaughter of the citizens.

Conan taken prisoner.

---

[1] Ord. Vit. 690 B. "Cimba parata Sequanam intravit, et relicto post terga conflictu trepidus ad Ermentrudis-villam navigavit. Tunc ibidem a Guillelmo de Archis Molismensi monacho susceptus est, ibique in basilica sanctæ Mariæ de Prato finem commotæ seditionis præstolatus est." On this William of Arques, see above, p. 220.

William of Malmesbury (v. 392) has quite another account, in which the Duke's flight is not spoken of, and in which Henry at least urges him to action; "Regios eo interdiu venientes, qui dolo civium totam jampridem occupaverant urbem, probe expulit [Henricus], admonito per nuntios comite ut ille a fronte propelleret quos ipse a tergo urgeret." This account does not come in its chronological place, but in William's account of the early life of Henry. And he misconceives the date, placing the revolt of Rouen after the coming of William into Normandy; "Willelmo veniente in Normanniam uti se de fratre Roberto ulcisceretur, comiti obsequelam suam exhibuit [Henricus], Rotomagi positus."

[2] Ord. Vit. 690 C. "Regia cohors territa fugit, latebrasque silvarum quæ in vicinio erant, avide poscens, delituit; et subsidio noctis discrimen mortis seu captionis difficulter evasit."

there Henry took him for his own share of the spoil, chap. iii. not indeed for ransom, but to be dealt with in a strange and dreadful fashion. It is one of the contrasts of human nature that Henry, the great and wise ruler, the king who made peace for man and deer, the good man of whom there was mickle awe and in whose day none durst hurt other, should have been more than once guilty in his own person of acts of calm and deliberate cruelty which have no parallel in the acts of his father, nor in those of either of his brothers. So now Conan was doomed to a fate which was made the sterner by the bitter personal mockery which he had to endure from Henry's own mouth. The Ætheling led his victim up through the several stages of the loftiest tower of the castle, till a wide view was opened to his eyes through the uppermost windows.[1] Henry bade Conan look out on the fair prospect which lay before him. He bade him think how goodly a land it was which he had striven to bring under his dominion.[2] These words well express the light in which Conan's schemes would look in princely eyes; the question was not whether Robert or William should reign in Rouen; it was whether Conan should reign there as demagogue or tyrant in the teeth of all princely rights. Henry went on to point out the beauties of the landscape in detail; the eyes of the scholar-prince could perhaps better enjoy them than the eyes of Rufus or of Robert of Bellême. Beyond the river lay the pleasant park, the woody land rich in beasts of chase. There was the Seine washing the walls of the city, the river rich in fish, bearing on its waters the ships which enriched Rouen with the wares of many

Fate of Conan.

Henry and Conan in the tower.

---

[1] On the different versions of the death of Conan in Orderic and in William of Malmesbury. see Appendix K.

[2] Ord. Vit. 690 C. "Considera, Conane, quam pulcram tibi patriam conatus es subjicere."

CHAP. III. lands.[1] On the other side he bade him look on the city itself thronged with people, its noble churches, its goodly houses. The modern reader stops for a moment to think that, of the buildings which then met the eye of Conan, churches, castles, halls of wealthy burghers like himself, clustering within and without the ancient walls, all doubtless goodly works according to the sterner standard of that day, hardly a stone is left to meet his own eye as he looks down from hill or tower on the great buildings of modern Rouen. It was another Saint Romanus, another Saint Ouen, of far different outline and style from those on which we now gaze, which Henry called on Conan to admire at that awful moment. He bade him mark the splendour of the city; he bade him think of its dignity as the spot which had been from of old the head of Normandy.[2] The trembling wretch felt the mockery; all that was left to him was to groan and cry for mercy. He confessed his guilt; he simply craved for grace in the name of their common Maker. He would give to his lord all the gold and silver of his hoard and the hoards of his kinsfolk; he would wipe out the stain of his past disloyalty by faithful service for the rest of his days.[3] The Conqueror would have granted such a prayer in sheer greatness of soul; the Red King might well have deemed it beneath him to harm so lowly a suppliant. But the stern purpose of Henry was fixed, and his wrath, when it was

[1] Ord. Vit. 690 C. "En, ad meridiem delectabile parcum patet oculis tuis. En saltuosa regio silvestribus abundans feris. Ecce Sequana piscosum flumen Rotomagensem murum allambit, navesque pluribus mercimoniis refertas huc quotidie devehit."

[2] Ib. D. "En ex alia parte civitas populosa, mœnibus sacrisque templis et urbanis ædibus speciosa, cui jure a priscis temporibus subjacet Normannia tota."

[3] Ib. "Pro redemptione mei domino meo aurum dabo et argentum, quantum reperire potero in thesauris meis meorumque parentum, et pro culpa infidelitatis fidele usque ad mortem rependam servitium."

once kindled, was as fierce as that of his father or his CHAP. III.
brother. "By the soul of my mother"—that seems to
have been the most sacred of oaths with Matilda's defrauded heir, as he looked out towards the church of her
building—"there shall be no ransom for the traitor, but
rather a hastening of the death which he deserves."[1]
Conan no longer pleaded for life; he thought only of the
welfare of his soul. "For the love of God, at least grant
me a confessor."[2] Had the Lion of Justice reached that
height of malice which seeks to kill the soul as well as
the body? At Conan's last prayer his wrath reached its
height;[3] Conan should have no time for shrift any more
than for ransom. If the clergy of Saint Romanus
already enjoyed their privilege of mercy, they were to
have no chance of exercising it on behalf of this arch-
criminal. With all the strength of both his hands, Henry Death of Conan.
thrust Conan, like Eadric,[4] through the window of the
tower. He fell from the giddy height, and died, so it
was said, before he reached the ground. His body was
tied to the tail of a pack-horse and dragged through
the streets of Rouen to strike terror into his followers.
The spot from which he was hurled took the name of
the Leap of Conan.[5] The tower, as I have said, has
perished; the site of the Leap of Conan must be

[1] Ord. Vit. 690 C. "Per animam matris meæ, traditori nulla erit re-
demptio, sed debitæ mortis acceleratio."

[2] Ib. "Conanus gemens clamavit alta voce; Pro amore, inquit, Dei,
confessionem mihi permitte."

[3] Ib. "Henricus acer fraternæ ultor injuriæ præ ira infremuit." Simple
wrath is an attribute which we are more used to assign to Henry the Second,
with his hereditary touch of the Angevin devil, than to the calm, deliberate,
Henry the First. Yet we can understand how, through the stages of the
"ironica insultatio," as Orderic calls Henry's discourse to Conan, a determination taken in cold blood might grow into the fierce delight of
destruction at the actual moment of carrying it out.

[4] See Appendix K.

[5] Ord. Vit. 691 A. "Locus ipse, ubi vindicta hujusmodi perpetrata
est, saltus Conani usque in hodiernam diem vocitatus est."

CHAP. III. sought for in imagination, at some point, perhaps the
south-eastern corner, of the vast *halles* of ancient Rouen.

Policy of
Henry.
The rule of Robert was now restored in Rouen, so far
as Robert could be said to rule at any time in Rouen
or elsewhere. It is remarkable that after the death of
Conan we lose sight of Henry; that is, as far as Rouen is
concerned, for we shall before long hear of him again in
quite different relations towards his two brothers. He may
well have thought that one fearful example was needed,
but that one fearful example was enough. He would
secure the punishment of the ringleader, even by doing
the hangman's duty with his own hands; but mere havoc
and massacre had no charms for him at any time. His
policy might well have forestalled the later English rule,
"Smite the leaders and spare the commons." If Robert
or anybody else was to reign in Rouen, nothing would
be gained by killing, driving out, or recklessly spoiling,
the people over whom he was to reign. But there were
men at his side to whom the utmost licence of warfare
was the most cherished of enjoyments. The Duke, never

Robert
brought
back.
personally cruel,[1] was in a merciful mood. When all
danger was over, he was brought across the river from
his monastery to the castle. He saw how much the city
had already suffered; his heart was touched, and he was

Treatment
of the
citizens.
not minded to inflict any further punishment. But he
had to yield to the sterner counsels of those about
him, and to allow a heavy vengeance to be meted out.[2]
He seems however to have prevailed so far as to
hinder the shedding of blood. At least we hear nothing
of any general slaughter. The fierce men who had
brought him back seem to have contented themselves
with plunder and leading into captivity. The citizens

---

[1] See above, p. 190.

[2] Ord. Vit. 691 A. " Robertus dux, ut de prato ad arcem rediit et quæ
gesta fuerant comperit, pietate motus infortunio civium condoluit, sed,
fortiori magnatorum censura prævalente, reis parcere nequivit."

of Rouen were dealt with by their countrymen as men CHAP. III.
deal with barbarian robbers. They were spoiled of all
their goods and led away into bondage. Robert of
Bellême and William of Breteuil, if they spared life,
spared it only to deal out on their captives all the
horrors of the prison-house.[1] The richest man in Imprison-
Rouen after the dead Conan, William the son of ment and
ransom of
Ansgar, became the spoil of William of Breteuil. After William
son of
a long and painful imprisonment, he regained his liberty Ansgar.
on paying a mighty ransom of three thousand pounds.[2]

Before his captive was set free, the lord of Breteuil
himself learned what it was to endure imprisonment,
this time doubtless of a milder kind than that which he
inflicted on William the son of Ansgar or that which
himself endured at the hands of Ascelin.[3] The Count of Count
Evreux and his nephew of Breteuil must have marched William
marches
almost at once from their successful enterprise at Rouen against
Conches.
to a less successful enterprise at Conches. For it was November,
still November when Count William or his Countess 1090.
resolved on a great attack on the stronghold of their
rival.[4] Evreux was doubtless the starting-point for
an undertaking which followed naturally on the work
which had been done at Rouen. The Count of Evreux
might keep on the garb of Norman patriotism which
he had worn in the assault on the rebellious capital, and

[1] Ord. Vit. 691 A. " Robertus Belesmensis et Guillelmus Bretoliensis
affuerunt, et Rodomanos incolas velut exteros prædones captivos abduxe-
runt, et squaloribus carceris graviter afflixerunt. . . . . Sic Belesmici et
Aquilini ceterique ducis auxiliarii contra se truculenter sæviunt, civesque
metropolis Neustriæ vinculatos attrahunt, cunctisque rebus spoliatos, ut
barbaros hostes male affligunt."

[2] Ib. " A Guillelmo Bretoliensi ducitur captivus, et post longos carceris
squalores redimit se librarum tribus millibus."

[3] See above, p. 243.

[4] Ib. 688 B. " Mense Novembri Guillelmus comes ingentem exercitum aggregavit, et Conchas expugnare cœpit." One would like to know
what number passed for " ingens exercitus " in this kind of warfare.

CHAP. III. his Countess might add to the other crimes with which she charged Ralph and Isabel a share in the crime of Conan, that of traitorous dealing with the invading enemy. The forces of Evreux and Breteuil were therefore arrayed to march together against the stronghold of the common kinsman and enemy at Conches.

No contrast could well be greater than the contrast between the spot from which Count William set forth and the spot which he led his troops to attack.

Position of Evreux and Conches. Near as Conches and Evreux are, they are more thoroughly cut off from one another than many spots which are far more distant on the map. The forest of Evreux parts the hills of Conches from the capital of Count William's county. The small stream of the Iton flows by the homes of both the rival heroines. But at Conches it flows below the hill crowned by castle, church, and abbey; at Evreux its swift stream had ages before been taught to act as a fosse to the four walls of

Position of Medio-lanum or Evreux. a Roman *chester*. Low down in the valley, like our own Bath, with the hills standing round about his city, the Count of Evreux lived among the memorials of elder days. The walls of Mediolanum, which can still be traced through a large part of their circuit, fenced in to the south the minster of Our Lady and the palace of the Bishop, then still tenanted by the eloquent Gilbert.[1] His home, like that of his metropolitan at Rouen,[2] might seem to stand upon the Roman wall itself. At the north-west corner, the wall fenced in the castle from which Count William had driven out the Conqueror's garrison, and where he, either then or at some later time,

History of Evreux. overthrew the Conqueror's donjon.[3] The wall of Mediolanum, like the wall of the Athenian akropolis, had

---

[1] See N. C. vol. iv. p. 713.   [2] Ib. p. 713.

[3] Ord. Vit. 834 C. " Prædictus comes et Heluisa comitissa dangionem regis apud Ebroas funditus dejecerunt."

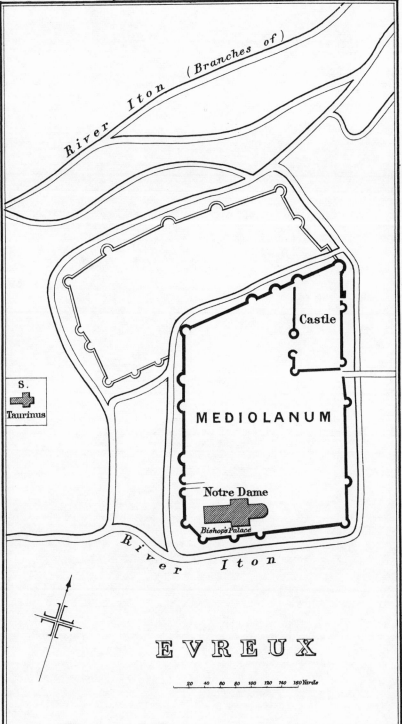

River Iton (Branches of)

Castle

S.
Taurinus

MEDIOLANUM

Notre Dame

Bishop's Palace

River Iton

EVREUX

20 40 60 80 100 120 140 160 Yards

E. Weller.

fragments of ornamental work, shattered columns, capi-
tals, cornices, built in among its materials. It would
thus seem to belong to a late stage of Roman rule, when
the Frank was dreaded as a dangerous neighbour, perhaps when he had already once laid Mediolanum waste.
To the north, much as at Le Mans and at Rouen, the city
in later times enlarged its borders, as, in later times still,
it has enlarged them far to the south. The "Little City"
—a name still borne by a street within the Roman circuit—is a poor representative of the Old Rome on the
Cenomannian height;[1] but both alike bear witness to
the small size of the original Roman encampments, and
to the gradual process by which they were enlarged into
the cities of modern times. But in the days of William The
and Heloise the circuit of Roman Mediolanum was still Roman
walls.
the circuit of Norman Evreux. And, as in so many
other places, the oldest monuments have outlived many
that were newer. Neither church, castle, nor episcopal Small
palace, keeps any fragments of the days of the warlike traces
of the
Countess; it is only in the minster of Saint Taurinus eleventh
century at
without the walls that some small witnesses of those times Evreux.
are to be found. Even the Romanesque portions of the
church of Our Lady must be later than Count William's
day, and the greater part of the building of the twelfth
century has given way to some of the most graceful conceptions of the architects of the fourteenth. The home of
the Bishop has taken the shape of a stately dwelling in
the latest style of mediæval art; the home of the Count
has vanished like the donjon which Count William overthrew. But the old defences within which bishops and
counts had fixed themselves in successive ages still live
on, to no small extent in their actual masonry, and in
the greater part of their circuit in their still easily
marked lines. And, high upon the hills, the eye rests

[1] See N. C. vol. iii. p. 204.

on the stronghold of yet earlier days, bearing the local
name of the *Câtelier*, the earth-works which rise above
Evreux as the earth-works of Sinodun rise above the
northern Dorchester. Here we may perhaps see the
point where the Gaul still held out on the hill, when
the Roman had already entrenched himself by the river-
side. At Evreux the works of the earliest times, the
works of the latest times, the works of several intermediate times, are there in their fulness. But there is
nothing whatever left in the city directly to remind us
of the times with which we are now dealing. A man
might pass through Evreux, he might make a diligent
search into the monuments of Evreux, and, unless he
had learned the fact from other sources, he might fail to
find out that Evreux had ever had counts or temporal
lords of any kind.

It is otherwise with the fortress of the warlike lady
of the hills, against which the warlike lady of the
river-city now bade the forces of her husband's county
to march. The home of Isabel has no more of her actual
work or date to show than the home of Heloise; but the
impress of the state of things which she represents is
stamped for ever on the stronghold of the house of
Toesny. At Evreux the Count and his followers lived
in the midst of works which, even in their day, were
ancient; at Conches, on the other hand, all was in that
day new. Conches had already its minster, its castle,
most likely its growing town; but all were the works
of its present lord or of his father. The hill of Conches
is another of those peninsular hills which, as the chosen
sites of castles, play so large a part in our story. But
the castle of Conches does not itself crown a promontory,
like the castle of Ballon. The cause doubtless was that
at Conches the abode of peace came first, and the abode
of warfare came only second. Either Ralph himself, the

first of his house who bears the surname of Conches as CHAP. III.
well as that of Toesny, or else his fierce father in some Foundation of the
milder moment, had planted on the hill a colony of monastery.
monks, the house of Saint Peter of Conches or Castellion.[1] The monastery arose on that point of the high
ground which is most nearly peninsular, that stretching
towards the north. To the south of the abbey presently
grew up the town with its church, a town which, in after
times at least, was girded by a wall, and which was sheltered or threatened by the castle of its lords at the end The castle.
furthest from the monastery. To the east, the height
on which town and castle stand side by side rises sheer
from a low and swampy plain, girt in by hills on every
side, lying like the arena of a natural amphitheatre. On
the hill-side art has helped nature by escarpments; the
mound of the castle, girt by its deep and winding ditch,
rises as it rose in the days of Ralph and Isabel; but the
round donjon on the mound and the other remaining
buildings of the fortress cannot claim an earlier date
than the thirteenth century. The donjon and the apse
of the parish church, a gem of the latest days of French
art, now stand nobly side by side; in Isabel's day they
had other and ruder forerunners. But of the abbey, The abbey.
which must have balanced the castle itself in the general
view, small traces only now remain; it has become quite

[1] On the foundation of the abbey of Conches or Castellion, see Neustria
Pia, 567, and the passages from Orderic and William of Jumièges there
cited. William (vii. 22) puts it among the monasteries founded in the
reign of William the Great, and calls its founder Ralph. But Orderic (460
A) attributes the foundation to a Roger, seemingly the old Roger who
came back from Spain. I can hardly accept the suggestion in Neustria
Pia that the Roger spoken of is the young Roger of whom we shall presently hear, the son of Ralph and Isabel, and that he was joint-founder
with his father Ralph.

Orderic twice (493 B, 576 A) distinguishes Ralph of *Conches*, the husband
of Isabel, from his father Roger of *Toesny*; " Rodulphus de Conchis, Rogerii
Toenitis filius," " Radulfus de *Conchis*, filius Rogerii de Toënia."

CHAP. III. secondary in the general aspect of the place, which gathers wholly round the parish church and the donjon. The western side of the hill, towards the forest which takes its name from Conches, shows nearly the same features as the eastern side on a smaller scale. It looks down on another plain girt in by hills; but on this side the slope of the hill of Conches itself is gentler, and the town is here defended by a wall. Altogether it was a formidable undertaking when the lord of the ancient city in the vale carried his arms against the fortress, the work of his brother, which had arisen within his own memory on the height overlooking his own river.

Siege of
Conches.

Count William thus began his winter siege of Conches; but, as usual, we get no intelligible account of the siege as a military operation. We are told nothing of the Count's line of march, or by what means he sought to bring the castle to submission. But, as usual too, we have no lack of personal anecdotes, anecdotes some of which remind us how near were the family ties between the fierce nobles who tore one another in pieces. We have already mentioned one nephew of the Count of Evreux who came with him to the attack of Conches. But William of Breteuil was nephew alike of both the contending brothers. His mother Adeliza, daughter of Roger of Toesny, wife of Earl William of Hereford before he went to seek a loftier bride in Flanders,[1] was the whole sister of Ralph of Conches and the half-sister of Count William of Evreux.[2] Another nephew and follower of Count William, Richard of Montfort, son of his whole sister, was moreover a brother of the Penthesileia of Conches.[3] The fate of these two kinsmen was different. Richard, in warring against his sister's castle, with some chance of meeting his sister personally in the

Near
kindred of
the com-
batants.

Death of
Richard of
Montfort.

---

[1] See N. C. vol. iv. p. 534.   [2] Will. Gem. vii. 22.

[3] Ord. Vit. 688 B.

field, did not respect the sanctity of the neighbouring CHAP. III. abbey of her husband's foundation. He heeded not the tears of the monks who prayed him to spare the holy place. A chance shot of which he presently died was looked on as the reward of his sacrilege. Both sides mourned for one so nearly allied to both leaders.[1] William of Breteuil, the ally of his uncle of Evreux, William of became the captive of his uncle of Conches. That wary Breteuil taken captain, when the host of Evreux came a-plundering, was prisoner. at the head of a large force of his own followers and of the King of England's soldiers.[2] But he bade his men keep back till the foe was laden with booty; they were then to set upon them in their retreat. His orders were successfully carried out. Many of the party became the prisoners of the lord of Conches, among them the lord of Breteuil, the gaoler of William the son of Ansgar.[3] Of this incident came a peace which ended the three years' warfare of the half-brothers.[4] The captive William of Breteuil procured his freedom by a ransom of three thousand pounds paid to his uncle of Conches, which

[1] Ord. Vit. 688 B. "Dum cœnobialem curiam beati Petri Castellionis invaderet, nec pro reverentia monachorum, qui cum fletibus vociferantes Dominum interpellabant, ab incœptis desisteret, hostili telo repente percussus est, ipsoque die cum maximo luctu utriusque partis mortuus est." He is described as "formidabilis marchisius."

[2] Ib. C. "Radulfus pervalidum agmen de suis, et de familia regis habuit."

[3] Ib. "Cupidis tironibus foras erumpere dixit, Armamini et estote parati, sed de munitione non exeatis donec ego jubeam vobis. Sinite hostes præda onerari, et discedentes mecum viriliter insectamini. Illi autem principi suo, qui probissimus et militiæ gnarus erat, obsecundarunt, et abeuntes cum præda pedetentim persecuti sunt." Cf. the same kind of policy on the part of the Conqueror, N. C. vol iii. p. 152.

[4] Ib. "Ebroicenses erubescentes quod guerram superbe cœperant et inde maximi pondus detrimenti cum dedecore pertulerant, conditioni pacis post triennalem guerram adquieverunt." The peace was clearly made about the end of 1090 or the very beginning of 1091. The three years of war must therefore be reckoned from the death of the Conqueror, or from some time not long after.

CHAP. III. was presently made good to him by the ransom of his
Settlement own victim from Rouen.   Moreover, as he had no lawful
of the
county of   issue,[1] he settled his estates on his young cousin
Evreux on   Roger, the younger son of Ralph and Isabel.   The same
young
Roger of   youthful heir was also chosen by his childless uncle
Conches.   of Evreux to succeed him in his county.[2]   Perhaps Duke
Robert confirmed all these arrangements as a matter of
course; perhaps the consent of such an over-lord was
not deemed worth the asking.

The young Roger of Toesny thus seemed to have a brilliant destiny opened to him, but he was not doomed to be
lord either of Evreux or of Breteuil. He was, it is implied,
too good for this world, at all events for such a world
Character as that of Normandy in the reign of Robert.   Pious,
of Roger.
gentle, kind to men of all classes, despising the pomp
of apparel which was the fashion of his day,[3] the young
Roger attracts us as one of a class of whom there may
have been more among the chivalry of Normandy than
we are apt to think at first sight.   An order could not
be wholly corrupt which numbered among its members
such men as Herlwin of Bec, as Gulbert of Hugleville,[4]

[1] Ord. Vit. 688 D.   He had at least two natural children, a daughter
Isabel, of whom we have already heard (see above, p. 243), and a son
Eustace, who succeeded his father in the teeth of all collateral claimants.
Eustace is best known as the husband of Henry the First's natural
daughter Juliana (see N. C. vol. v. p. 157, *note*), in whose story we come
again to the ever-disputed tower of Ivry. See Will. Gem. viii. 15 ; Ord. Vit.
577 B; 810 C ; 848 B, C.

[2] Ib.   "Ebroicensis quoque comes eundem Rogerium, utpote nepotem
suum, consulatus sui heredem constituit." This was to the prejudice of his
nephew Amalric of Montfort, son of his whole sister Agnes, and half-brother
of Isabel.   After Count William's death in 1108, the strivings after his
county were great and long, till Amalric recovered full possession in 1119.
Ord. Vit. 863 C.

[3] Ib.   "Pretiosis vestibus quibus superbi nimis insolescunt, uti dedignabatur, et in omni esse suo sese modeste regere nitebatur." This must be
taken in connexion with Orderic's various protests against the vain fashions
of the day, especially the great one in p. 682.

[4] See N. C. vol. ii. p. 219; iv. p. 448.

and the younger son of Ralph of Conches. A tale is CHAP. III.
told of him, a tale touching in itself and one which gives
us our only glimpse of the inner and milder life of the
castle of Conches under the rule of its Amazonian mis-
tress. A number of knights sat idle in the hall, sporting
and amusing themselves with talk in the presence of
the lady Isabel.[1] At last they told their dreams. One, The three
dreams.
whose name is not given, said that he had seen the form
of the Saviour on the cross, writhing in agony and
looking on him with a terrible countenance. All who
heard the dream said that some fearful judgement was
hanging over the head of the dreamer. Then spoke Baldwin of
Boulogne.
Baldwin the son of Count Eustace of Boulogne, one of
the mightier sons of an ignoble father.[2] He too had
seen his Lord hanging on the cross; but the divine
form was bright and glorious; the divine face smiled
kindly on the dreamer; the divine hand blessed him
and traced the sign of the cross over his head.[3] All
said that rich gifts of divine favour were in store for
him. Then the young Roger crept near to his mother, Roger's
dream.
and told her that he too knew one not far off who had
beheld his vision also. Isabel asked of her son of whom
he spoke and what the seer had beheld. The youth
blushed and hesitated, but, pressed by his mother and
his comrades, he told how there was one who had lately
seen his vision of the Lord, how the Saviour had placed
his hand on his head, and had bidden him, as his beloved, to come quickly that he might receive the joys of
life. And he added that he knew that he who was thus
called of his Lord would not long abide in this world.

---

[1] Ord. Vit. 688 D. "Quondam milites otiosi simul in Aula Conchis
ludebant et colloquebantur, et coram domina Elisabeth de diversis thema-
tibus, ut mos est hujusmodi, confabulabantur." Then follows this beautiful
story of the three dreams. 　　　　[2] See N. C. vol. iv. p. 130.

[3] Ord. Vit. 689 A. "Dextera sua me benedicentem, signumque crucis
super caput meum benigniter facientem."

CHAP. III.   Such talk as this in the hall of Conches, in the presence of its warlike lady, whether we deem it the record
of real dreams or a mere pious imagining after the fact,
seems like a fresh oasis in the dreary wilderness of un-
Fulfilment   natural war.   Each vision was of course fulfilled.   The
of the
dreams.   nameless knight, wounded ere long in one of the combats
of the time, died without the sacraments.   Baldwin of
Boulogne, afterwards son-in-law of Ralph and Isabel,[1]
was indeed called to bear the cross, but in a way which
men perhaps had not thought of six years before Pope
Urban preached at Clermont.   Count of Edessa, King of
Jerusalem, the name of Baldwin lives in the annals of
crusading Europe; to Englishmen it perhaps comes home
most nearly as the name of a comrade of our own Robert
Death of   son of Godwine.[2]   But a brighter crown than that of Bald-
young
Roger.   win's kingdom was, long before Baldwin reigned, the reward of the young Roger.   A few months after the date
of the tale, he died peacefully in his bed, full of faith and
hope, and, amid the grief of many, his body was laid in
the minster of Saint Peter of his father's rearing.[3]

Later   There was thus peace between Conches and Evreux, a
treaty
between   peace which does not seem to have been again broken.
the two
brothers.   Ten years later, in a time of renewed licence, we find
1100.   the two brothers joining in a private war against Count
Banish-   Robert of Meulan.[4]   Eight years later again, when
ment and
death of   Count William and his Countess were busy building a
Count
William.   monastery at Noyon, they fell under the displeasure of
April 18,   King Henry, and died in banishment in the land of
1108.   Anjou.[5]   Ralph of Toesny was succeeded by his son

---

[1] He married their daughter Godehild, the former wife of Robert, son of
Henry Earl of Warwick. See Ord. Vit. 576 C; Will. Gem. viii. 41. The
strange story of his two later marriages does not concern us, and the way
in which he became Count of Edessa was hardly becoming in a holy warrior.

[2] See N. C. vol. v. pp. 94, 819, and Appendix HH.

[3] Ord. Vit. 689 C.   [4] Ib. 784 B.

[5] Ib. 834 C. There is a singular contrast in the words with which

the younger Ralph, and Isabel, after a long widowhood, CHAP. III. withdrew as a penitent to atone for the errors of her youth, one would think of her later days also, in a life of religion.[1]

It is after recording the war of Conches and the sack of Rouen that the monk of Saint Evroul takes up his parable to set forth the general wretchedness of Normandy in the blackest colours with which the pictures of Hebrew prophets and Latin poets could furnish him. And it is Orderic the Englishman[2] that speaks. In his Norman cell he never forgot that he first drew breath by the banks of the Severn. In his eyes the woes of Normandy were the righteous punishment for the wrongs of England. The proud people who had gloried in their conquest, who had slain or driven out the native sons of the land, who had taken to themselves their possessions and commands, were now themselves bowed down with sorrows. The wealth which they had stolen from others served now not to their delight but to their torment.[3] Normandy, like Babylon, had now to drink of the same cup of tribulation, of which she had given others to drink even to drunkenness. A Fury without a curb raged through the land, and smote down its inhabitants.

Orderic's picture of Normandy.

His English feelings.

Orderic disposes of the dead bodies of the Count and the Countess; "*Comitissa* nempe defuncta prius apud Nogionem *quiescit;* comes vero, postmodum apoplexia percussus, sine viatico decessit, et *cadaver ejus* cum patre suo Fontinellæ *computrescit.*"

[1] See above, p. 233. [2] See N. C. vol. iv. p. 496.

[3] Ord. Vit. 691 A, B. "Ecce quibus ærumnis superba profligatur Normannia, quæ nimis olim victa gloriabatur Anglia, et naturalibus regni filiis trucidatis sive fugatis usurpabat eorum possessiones et imperia. Ecce massam divitiarum quas aliis rapuit eisque pollens ad suam perniciem insolentur tumuit, nunc non ad delectamentum sui sed potius ad tormentum miserabiliter distrahit." He has an earlier reflexion to the same effect (664 B); "Sic proceres Neustriæ . . . . patriam divitiis opulentam propriis viribus vicissim exspoliaverunt, opesque quas Anglis aliisque gentibus violenter rapuerunt merito latrociniis et rapinis perdiderunt."

CHAP. III. The clergy, the monks, the unarmed people, everywhere wept and groaned. None were glad save thieves and robbers, and they were not long to be glad.[1] And so he follows out the same strain through a crowd of prophetic images, the locust, the mildew, and every other instrument of divine wrath. We admit the aptness of his parallel when he tells us that in those days there was no king nor duke in the Norman Jerusalem; we are less able to follow the analogy when he adds that the rebellious folk sacrificed at Dan and Bethel to the golden calves of Jeroboam.[2] At last, when his stock of metaphors is worn out, he goes back to his story to tell the same tale of crime and sorrow in other parts of the Norman duchy.[3]

§ 2. *Personal Coming of William Rufus.*

1091.

In a general view of the state of affairs, William Rufus had lost much more by the check of his plans at Rouen

[1] Ord. Vit. 691 A, B. "Soli gaudent, sed non diu nec feliciter, qui furari seu prædari possunt pertinaciter."

[2] Ib. "In diebus illis non erat rex neque dux Hierusalem, aureisque vitulis Jeroboam rebellis plebs immolabat in Dan et Bethel." We are used to this kind of analogy whenever any one goes after a wrong Pope; but Normandy, with all its crimes, seems to have been perfectly orthodox.

[3] Ib. C. "Multa intueor in divina pagina quæ subtiliter coaptata nostri temporis eventui videntur similia. [Every age, except perhaps the eighteenth, has made the same remark.] Ceterum allegoricas allegationes et idoneas humanis moribus interpretationes studiosis rimandas relinquam, simplicemque Normannicarum historiam rerum adhuc aliquantulum protelare satagam." This praiseworthy resolve reminds us of an earlier passage (683 B) where he laments the failure of the princes and prelates of his day to work miracles, and his own inability to force them to the needful pitch of holiness; "Ast ego vim illis ut sanctificentur inferre nequeo. Unde his omissis super rebus quæ fiunt veracem *dictatum* facio."

It would seem from this that Orderic dictated his book. (See also his complaint in 718 C, when at the age of sixty he felt too old to write and had no one to write for him.) We need not therefore infer in some other cases that, because an author dictated, therefore he could not write.

than he could gain by any successes of his Norman CHAP. III.
allies at Conches. The attempt of the Count of Evreux
on the castle of his new vassal had been baffled; but
his own far greater scheme, the scheme by which he
had hoped to win the capital of Normandy, had been
baffled also. It may have been this failure which led
the King to see that his own presence was needed
beyond the sea. The Christmas Gemót of the year was Christmas
held, not, as usual, at Gloucester, but at Westminster. Gemót at West-
At Candlemas the King crossed to Normandy with a great minster.
fleet.[1] The two things are mentioned together, as if to 1090.
The King
imply that a further sanction of the assembled Witan was crosses to Normandy.
given to this new stage of the war. War indeed between February,
William and Robert there was none. It does not seem 1091.
that a single blow was struck to withstand the invader. But blows were given and taken in Normandy
throughout the winter with as much zeal as ever. And
this time Duke Robert himself was helping to give and
take them. Stranger than all, he was giving and taking Duke
them in the character of an ally of Robert of Bellême Robert helps
against men who seem to have done nothing but defend Robert of Bellême.
themselves against the attacks of the last-named common
enemy of mankind. Old Hugh of Grantmesnil, once the Hugh of
Conqueror's lieutenant at Winchester and afterwards his Grantmesnil and
Sheriff of Leicestershire,[2] was connected by family ties Richard of
with Richard of Courcy,[3] and the spots from which they Courcy.

---

[1] The Chronicle (1091) says expressly, "On þisum geare se cyng Willelm
heold his hired to Xpes messan on Wæstmynstre, and þæræfter to Candelmæssan he ferde for his broðær unþearfe ut of Englalande into Normandige."
So Florence; "Mense Februario rex Willelmus junior Normanniam petiit."
Orderic (696 D) seems to place his voyage a little earlier; "Mense
Januario Guillelmus Rufus rex Anglorum cum magna classe in Normanniam
transfretavit." But he places it late in the month; for in 693 B, having
recorded the death of Bishop Gerard on January 23, he adds that the King's
voyage happened " eadem septimana." [2] See N. C. vol. iv. pp. 72, 234.
[3] Richard of Courcy's son Robert married Rohesia, one of the many
daughters of Hugh of Grantmesnil. Ord. Vit. 692 A.

took their names, in the diocese of Seez, between the Dive
and the Oudon, lay at no great distance from one another.
They thus lay between Earl Roger's own Montgomery[1]
and a series of new fortresses on the Orne and the neighbouring streams, by which Earl Roger's son hoped to extend his power over the whole land of Hiesmes.[2] Hugh
and Richard strengthened themselves against the tyrant
—such is the name which Robert bears—gathering their
allies and putting their castles in a state of defence.
Their united forces were too much for the lord of Bellême. He sought help from his sovereign, and the Duke,
who was not allowed to strike a blow for his own
Rouen, appeared as the besieger of Courcy, no less than
of Brionne. He who had fought to turn the tyrant out
of Ballon and Saint Cenery now fought to put Courcy
into the tyrant's power.

Siege of
Courcy.
January,
1091.
News of
William's
coming.
February.

The siege
raised.

The siege of Courcy began in January.[3] At the end
of the month or the beginning of the next, a piece of
news came which caused the Duke and the other besiegers to cease from their work. Robert himself could
see that there was something else to be done besides
making war on Hugh of Grantmesnil on behalf of
Robert of Bellême, when the King of the English was
in his own person on Norman ground. The host before
Courcy broke up; some doubtless went to their own
homes;[4] but we may suspect that some found their
way to Eu. For there it was that King William had
fixed his quarters; there the great men of Normandy
were gathering around him. They did not come empty-
handed. They welcomed the King with royal gifts; but it

---

[1] See N. C. vol. ii. p. 197.   [2] Ord. Vit. 691 C.
[3] See Appendix L.
[4] Ord. Vit. 693 B. "Cujus [Guillelmi] adventu audito, territus dux
cum Roberto aliisque obsidentibus actutum recessit, et unusquisque propria
repetiit." He is more emphatic in 697 A; "Robertus de Belesmo cum
suis complicibus aufugit."

was to receive far greater gifts in return. Thither too CHAP. III.
men were flocking to him, not only from Normandy, but Men flock
to William
from France, Flanders, Britanny, and all the neighbour- from all
parts.
ing lands. And all who came went away saying that the
King of the English was a far richer and more bountiful
lord than any of their own princes.[1] In such a state of
things it was useless for Robert to think of meeting his
brother in arms. His only hope was to save some part
of his dominions by negotiation before the whole Norman land had passed into the hands of the island king.
A treaty of peace was concluded, by which Robert kept Treaty of
his capital and the greater part of his duchy, but by Caen.
1091.
which William was established as a powerful and dangerous continental neighbour, hemming in what was left
of Normandy on every side.

The treaty was agreed to, seemingly under the mediation of the King of the French, in a meeting of the rival
brothers at Caen.[2] The territorial cession made by Ro- Cession of
bert mainly took the form of recognizing the commenda- Norman
territory
tions which so many Norman nobles had made to the to William.
Red King. They had sought him to lord, and their lord
he was to be. The fiefs held by the lords of Eu, Aumale,
Gournay, and Conches, and all others who had submitted
to William, passed away from Robert. They were to be
held of the King of the English, under what title, if any,
does not appear. To hold a fief of William Rufus meant
something quite different from holding a fief of Robert.
The over-lordship of Robert meant nothing at all; it did

---

[1] Ord. Vit. 693 B. "Mox omnes pene Normannorum optimates certatim
regem adierunt, eique munera, recepturi majora, cum summo favore contule-
runt. Galli quoque et Britones et Flandritæ, ut regem apud Aucum
in Neustria commorari audierunt, aliique plures de collimitaneis provinciis,
ad eum convenerunt. Tunc magnificentiam ejus alacriter experti sunt,
domumque petentes cunctis cum principibus suis divitiis et liberalitate
præposuerunt."

[2] On the Treaty of 1091, see Appendix M.

CHAP. III. not hinder his vassal from making war at pleasure either on his lord or on any fellow-vassal. But the over-lord-ship of William Rufus, like that of his father, meant real sovereignty; the lords who submitted to him had given themselves a master. If any of them had a mind to live in peace, their chance certainly became greater; in any case the dread of William's power, combined with the attractions of the rich hoard which was so freely opened, might account for the sacrifice of a wild independence.

Their geographical aspect. The territory thus ceded to the east, the lands of Eu, Aumale, and Gournay, involved a complete surrender of the eastern frontier of the duchy. The addition of the lands of Conches formed an outpost to the south. Rouen was thus hemmed in on two sides. But this was not enough, in the ideas of the Red King, to secure a scientific frontier. The lord of the island realm must hold some points to strengthen his approach to the main-land, something better than the single port of Eu in one corner of the duchy. Robert had therefore to surrender two points of coast which had not, as far as we have heard, been occupied by William or by his Norman allies.

Cession of Fécamp and Cherbourg. Rouen was to be further hemmed in to the north-west, by the cession of Fécamp, abbey and palace. The occupation of this point had the further advantage for William that it put a check on the districts which had been kept for Robert by Helias of Saint-Saen. These were now threatened by Fécamp on one side and by Eu and Aumale on the other. And William's de-mands on the Duke of the Normans contained one clause which could be carried out only at the cost of the Count of the Côtentin. Henry's fortress of Cherbourg, not so long before strengthened by him,[1] was also to pass to William. So early was the art known by which a more powerful prince, with no ground to show except his own

[1] See above, p. 221.

will, claims the right to shut out a weaker prince or
people from the seaboard which nature has designed for
them.

Besides Cherbourg, the Red King demanded the island William demands Saint Michael's Mount.
fortress of Saint Michael's Mount, the abbey in peril of
the sea. Otherwise he seems to have claimed nothing
in the west of Normandy. Robert might reign, if he
could, over the lands which his father had brought into
submission on the day of Val-ès-Dunes. Nor were
the great cessions which Robert made to be wholly
without recompence. It might be taken for granted
that the Duke whose territories were thus cut off was
to have some compensation in another shape out of the
wealth of England. So it was; vast gifts were given Money paid to Robert.
by the lord of the hoard at Winchester to the pauper
prince at Rouen.[1] But he was not to be left without
territorial compensation also. William not only under- The lost dominions of the Conqueror to be restored to Robert.
took to bring under Robert's obedience all those who
were in arms against him throughout Normandy; he
further undertook to win back for him all the dominions which their father had ever held, except those
lands which, by the terms of the treaty, were to fall to
William himself. This involved a very considerable
enlargement of Robert's dominions, besides turning his
nominal rule into a reality in the lands where he was
already sovereign in name. It was aimed at lands both
within and without the bounds of the Norman duchy.
Maine, city and county, was again in revolt against its Projected recovery of Maine.
Norman lords.[2] By this clause of the treaty William
bound himself to recover Maine for Robert. This obligation he certainly never even attempted to fulfil. He
did not meddle with Maine till the Norman lord and the
English King were again one. Then the recovery of

[1] Ord. Vit. 693 B. "Tunc ingentia Robertus dux a rege dona recepit."
[2] See Appendix M; and for the affairs of Maine, see below, Chapter VI.

CHAP. III. Maine, or at least of its capital, became one of the chief objects of his policy.

But this clause had also a more remarkable application. Its terms were to be brought to bear on one nearer by blood and neighbourhood to both the contending princes than either Cenomannian counts

Henry to be despoiled of the Côtentin. or Cenomannian citizens. The terms of the treaty amounted to a partition of the dominions of the Count of the Côtentin between his two brothers. Cherbourg and Saint Michael's Mount were, as we have seen, formally assigned to William, and the remainder of Henry's principality certainly came under the head of lands which had been held by William the Great and which the treaty did not assign to William the Red. As such they were to be won back for Robert by the help of William. That is to say, William and Robert agreed to divide between themselves the territory which Henry had fairly bought with money from Robert. No

Character of the agreement. agreement could be more unprincipled. As between prince and prince, no title could be better than Henry's title to his county; while, if the welfare of the people of Coutances and Avranches was to be thought of, the proposed change meant their transfer from a prince who knew the art of ruling to a prince whose nominal rule was everywhere simple anarchy. Neither Robert nor William was likely to be troubled with moral scruples; neither was likely to think much of the terms of a bargain and sale; but one might have expected that Robert would have felt some thankfulness to his youngest brother for his ready help in putting down the rebellious movement at Rouen.[1] William

---

[1] William of Malmesbury (v. 392) is becomingly strong on this head; "Parum hic labor apud Robertum valuit, virum animi mobilis, qui statim ad ingratitudinem flexus, bene meritum urbe cedere coegit." This comes just after the death of Conan. His whole account is very confused.

might indeed on that same account look on Henry as an enemy; but such enmity could hardly be decently professed in a treaty of alliance between Robert and William. We may perhaps believe that the chief feeling which the affair of Rouen had awakened in Robert's mind was rather mortification than gratitude. A brother who had acted so vigorously when he himself was not allowed to act at all was dangerous as a neighbour or as a vassal. The memory of his services was humiliating; it was not well to have a brother so near at hand, and in command of so powerful a force, a brother who, if he had at one moment hastened to his elder brother's defence, might at some other moment come with equal speed on an opposite errand. But whatever were their motives, King and Duke agreed to rob their youngest brother of his dominions. And the importance Henry attacked at once. which was attached to this part of the treaty is shown by the speed and energy with which it was carried out. While the recovery of Maine was delayed or forgotten, the recovery of the Côtentin was the first act of the contracting princes after the conclusion of the treaty.

But, when we look to some other terms of the treaty, Probable objects of William. it is possible that, in the mind of William at least, the spoliation of Henry had a deeper object. One purpose of the treaty was to settle the succession both to Settlement of the English and Norman succession. the kingdom of England and to the duchy of Normandy. Neither the imperial crown nor the ducal coronet had at this moment any direct and undoubted heir, according to any doctrine of succession. Both William and Robert were at this time unmarried; Robert had more than one illegitimate child; no children of William Rufus are recorded at any time. The treaty provided that, William and Robert to succeed one another. if either King or Duke died without lawful issue during the lifetime of his brother, the survivor should succeed

Constitutional aspect of the agreement.

Growth of the hereditary principle,

and of the doctrine of legitimacy.

The two Æthelings.

to his dominions. I have spoken elsewhere of the constitutional aspect of this agreement.[1] It was an attempt to barter away beforehand the right of the Witan of England to bestow the crown of a deceased king on whatever successor they thought good. And, like all such attempts, before and after, till the great act of settlement which put an end to the nineteen years' anarchy,[2] it came to nothing. But that such an agreement should have been made shows what fresh strength had been given by the Norman Conquest to the whole class of ideas of which the doctrine of hereditary succession to kingdoms forms a part.[3] But, putting this view of the matter aside, the objects of the provision, as a family compact, were obvious. It was William's manifest interest to shut out Robert's sons from any share in the inheritance of their father. This was easily done. The stricter doctrine of legitimacy of birth was fast growing.[4] It was but unwillingly that Normandy had, sixty years earlier, acknowledged the bastard of an earlier Robert; it was most unlikely that Normandy would submit to a bastard of the present Robert, while there yet lived lawful sons of him who had made the name of Bastard glorious. Robert, on the other hand, might not be unwilling to give up so faint a chance on the part of his own children, in order to be himself declared presumptive heir to the crown of England. But there were others to be shut out, one of whom at least was far more dangerous than the natural sons of Robert. There were then in Normandy two men who bore the English title of Ætheling, one of the old race, one of the new; one whom Englishmen had once chosen as the last of the old race, another to whom Englishmen looked

---

[1] See N. C. vol. v. pp. 87-90.   [2] Ib. vol. v. p. 328.
[3] Ib. vol. v. p. 388.   [4] Ib. vol. v. p. 89.

as the first of the new race who had any claim to the CHAP. III.
privileges of kingly birth. We must always remember Henry;
that, in English eyes, Henry, the son of a crowned
King of the English, born of his crowned Lady on
English ground, had a claim which was not shared by
his brothers, foreign-born sons of a mere Norman
Duke and Duchess.[1] The kingly and native birth of Eadgar.
Henry might put his claims at least on a level
with those of Eadgar, who, male heir of Ecgberht and
Cerdic as he was, was born of uncrowned parents
in a foreign land.[2] Indeed it might seem that by
this time all thoughts of a restoration of the West-
Saxon house had passed out of the range of practical
politics, and that the claims of Eadgar were no longer
entitled to a thought. The Red King however seems
to have deemed otherwise. He was clearly determined
to secure himself against the remotest chances of danger.
Henry was to be despoiled; Eadgar was to be banished. Eadgar
Eadgar had come back from Apulia;[3] he was now banished from
living in Normandy on terms of the closest friendship Normandy.
with the Duke, who had enriched him with grants of
land, and, as we have seen, admitted him to his inmost
counsels.[4] We know not whether Eadgar had given
the Red King any personal offence, or whether William
was simply jealous of him as a possible rival for the
crown. At any rate, whether by a formal clause of the
treaty or not, he called on Robert to confiscate Eadgar's
Norman estates and to make him leave his dominions.[5]
Neither towards Henry nor towards Eadgar would the William's
policy of William Rufus seem to have been wise; but policy towards

[1] See N. C. vol. iv. pp. 288, 796.
[2] Ib. vol. iii. p. 7 ; see vol. ii. p. 376.   [3] Ib. vol. iv. p. 694.
[4] We have seen him already as a counsellor ; see above, p. 220. Orderic,
giving a picture of him some years later (778 B), adds that " ducem sibi
coævum et quasi collectaneum fratrem diligebat."
[5] See Appendix M.

CHAP. III.

Henry and
Eadgar.

sound policy, in any high sense, was not one of the attributes of William Rufus. Whatever may be said of Henry's relations towards Normandy, he was more likely to plot against his brother of England if he became a landless wanderer than if he remained Count of Coutances and Avranches. As for Eadgar, it might possibly have been a gain if he could have been sent back to Apulia or provided for in his native Hungary. As it was, he straightway betook himself to a land where he was likely to be far more dangerous than he could ever be in Normandy. As in the days of William the Great,[1] he went at once to the court of his brother-in-law of Scotland.[2] It may be that William presently saw that he had taken a false step in the treatment of both the Æthelings. At a later time we shall see both Henry and Eadgar enjoying his full favour and confidence.

Eadgar
goes to
Scotland.

The man before whose eyes the crown of England had twice been dangled in mockery, and the man who was hereafter to grasp that crown with a grasp like that of the Conqueror himself, were thus both doomed to be for the moment despoiled of lands and honours. To men of less exalted degree the treaty was more favourable. King and Duke alike, so far to the credit of both of them, stipulated for the safety and restoration of their several partisans in the dominions of the other. All supporters of William in any of those parts of Normandy which were not to be ceded to him were to suffer no harm at the hands of Robert. And, what was much more important, all those who had lost their lands in England three years before on account of their share in the rebellion on behalf of Robert were to have their

The fol-
lowers of
each side
to be
restored.

The rebels
of 1088
to be
restored.

[1] See N. C. vol. iv. pp. 194, 508, 567.
[2] Chron. Petrib. 1091. "And ut of Normandig for to þam cynge his aðume to Scotlande and to his swustor."

lands back again. An exception, formal or practical, CHAP. III.
must have been made in the case of Bishop Odo. He
certainly was not restored to his earldom of Kent.

The treaty was sworn to by twelve chief men on each *The treaty*
side.[1] The English Chronicler remarks, with perfect *sworn to.*
It stands
truth, that it stood but a little while.[2] But one part *but a little*
while.
at least was carried out at once and with great vigour.
Within less than a month after William had landed in *William*
and Robert
Normandy to dispossess Robert, he and Robert marched *march*
together to dispossess Henry. They spent their Lent in *against*
Henry.
besieging him in his last stronghold. When the Count *Lent, 1091.*
of Coutances heard of the coalition against him, he made
ready for a vigorous resistance. He put his two cities *Henry's*
position.
of Coutances and Avranches and his other fortresses
into a state of defence, and gathered a force, Norman
and Breton, to garrison them.[3] Britanny indeed was
the only quarter from which he received any help in his
struggle.[4] Those who seemed to be his firmest friends *Earl Hugh*
of Chester
turned against him. Even Earl Hugh of Chester, the fore- *and others*
most man in the land from which his father had taken *betray*
their
his name,[5] had no mind to jeopard his great English *castles to*
William.
palatinate for the sake of keeping his paternal Avranches
in the obedience of the Ætheling. Henry's other supporters, Richard of Redvers, it is to be supposed, among
them, were of the same mind. They saw no hope that
Henry could withstand the might, above all the wealth,
of Rufus; they accordingly surrendered their fortresses

---

[1] Chron. Petrib. 1091. "Ðas forewarde gesworan xii. þa betste of þes
cynges healfe, and xii. of þes eorles." In Florence the "betste" become
"barones."

[2] "þeah hit syððan litle hwile stode."

[3] Ord. Vit. 697 A. "Aggregatis Britonibus et Normannis, Constantiam
et Abrincas aliaque oppida munivit, et ad resistendum totis nisibus insur-
rexit."

[4] Ib. 697 B. "Britones, qui sibi solummodo adminiculum contulerant."

[5] See N. C. vol. ii. p. 209.

CHAP. III. into the King's hands.[1] One stronghold only was
Henry now left to Henry, one of the two which had been
takes up
his quarters specially marked out to be taken from him, the moat Saint
Michael's nastic fortress of Saint Michael. The sacred mount
Mount. was then famous and venerable through all Normandy,
The build- and far beyond the bounds of Normandy. Of that vast
ings on the
Mount. and wondrous pile of buildings, halls, cloister, church,
buildings which elsewhere stand side by side, but which
here are heaped one upon another, little could then have
been standing. The minster itself, which crowns all,
had begun to be rebuilt seventy years before by the
Abbot Hildebert,[2] and it may be that some parts of his
work have lived through the natural accidents of the
next age[3] and the destruction and disfigurement of
later times. But the series of pillared halls, knightly
and monastic, which give its special character to the
abbey of the Mount, are all of far later date than the
war of the three brothers. Yet the house of the
warrior archangel was already at once knightly and
Abbot monastic. The reigning abbot Roger was, in strict
Roger.
1085. ecclesiastical eyes, a prelate of doubtful title. He
had come in—as countless other bishops and abbots
of Normandy and England had come in—less by free
election of the monks than by the will of the great

[1] Ord. Vit. 697 A. "Hugo Cestrensis comes aliique fautores, ejus pau-
pertatem perpendentes, et amplas opes terribilemque potentiam Guillelmi
regis metuentes, egregium clitonem in bellico angore deseruerunt, et municipia sua regi tradiderunt." Wace tells quite another tale, more favourable
to Earl Hugh, but much less likely. See Appendix N.

[2] Ann. S. Mich. 1023. "Hoc anno inchoatum est novum monasterium
a Richardo secundo comite et Hildeberto abbate, qui abbas ipso anno
obiit." This is Hildebert the Second, appointed in 1017.

[3] Ib. 1100. "Hoc anno pars non modica ecclesiæ montis sancti Michaelis corruit . . . . in cujus ruina portio quædam dormitorii monachorum destructa atque eversa est." Ib. 1112. "Hoc anno combusta est
hæc ecclesia sancti Michaelis igne fulmineo, cum omnibus officinis monachorum."

Duke and King.[1] What personal share Roger took in the CHAP. III.
struggle is not recorded; but some at least of his monks,
like the monks of Ely in the days of Hereward,[2] wel-   The monks
welcome
comed the small body of followers who still clave to   Henry.
Henry, and at whose head he now took up his last
position of defence in the island sanctuary.[3]

Here Henry was besieged by his two brothers, Duke   Siege of
the Mount.
and King. Yet we hear of nothing which can in strict-   Lent, 1091.
ness be called a siege. The Mount stands in the mouth
of a bay within a bay. At high water it is strictly an   Its
island; at low water it is surrounded by a vast wilder-   position.
ness of sand—those treacherous sands from which thirty
years before Harold had rescued the soldiers of the elder
William[4], and which stretch back as far as the rocks of
Cancale on the Breton shore. In this sense the bay of   The inner
bay.
Saint Michael may be counted to stretch from Cancale
to the opposite point on the Norman coast, where the
land begins to bend inwards to form the narrower bay.
This last may be counted to stretch from the mouth of
the border stream of Coesnon below Pontorson to Genetz
lying on the coast nearly due west from Avranches.
The Mount itself and its satellite the smaller rock of
Tombelaine lie nearly in a straight line between these
two points. Alternately inaccessible by land and by
water, accessible by land at any time only by certain
known routes at different points, the Mount would seem
to be incapable of direct attack by any weapons known
in the eleventh century. On the other hand, it would
be easy to cut it off from all communication with the
outer world by the occupation of the needful points on

---

[1] Ann. S. Mich. 1085. "Huic [Rannulfo] successit Rogerius Cado-
mensis, non electione monachorum, sed vi terrenæ potestatis."

[2] See N. C. vol. iv. p. 468.

[3] See Florence's account in Appendix N.

[4] See N. C. vol. iii. p. 235.

CHAP. III.
Later
sieges.
1417-1424.

No men-
tion of
ships.

Positions
of the
besiegers.

Character
of the
siege.

the shore and by the help of a blockading fleet. And in
the great siege three hundred and thirty years later —
when Normandy had again a kingly duke of the blood
of Rolf and Henry, but when the Mount clave to the
King of Paris or of Bourges—we hear both of the blockading fleet of England and of the series of posts with
which the shore was lined. Without a fleet the Mount
could hardly be said to be besieged; but, on the other
hand, its insular position would be of no use to its
defenders, unless they had either ships at command
or friends beyond sea. In the present case we hear
nothing of ships on either side, nor of any help coming
to the besieged. Nor do we hear of any systematic
occupation of the whole coast. We hear only that the
besiegers occupied two points which commanded the
two sides of the inner bay, On the north the Duke
took up his quarters at Genetz; to the south the besiegers occupied Arderon, not far from the mouth of
the Coesnon, while King William of England established himself in the central position of Avranches.[1]
The siege thus became an affair of endless small
attacks and skirmishes. We hear of the plundering
expeditions which Henry was able to make into the
lands of Avranches and even of Coutances, lands which
had once been his own, but which had now become
hostile ground.[2] We hear too how, before each of the

---

[1] I take this from Wace, 14660 ;

    "Li Munt asistrent environ,   N'issent del mont se par els non.
    De Genez de si à Coisnon   A Avrenches li reis séeit
    E la rivière d'Ardenon ;   Et a Genez li dus esteit."

On the value of Wace's general story, see Appendix N ; but we may trust
the topography of the Jerseyman.

[2] See Florence's account in Appendix N.   So Will. Malms. iv. 308 ;
"Crebris excursibus obsidentem militiam germanorum contristavit." Wace
(14652) says,

    "Sovent coreit par Costentin,   Li vilains prist, si fist raendre,
    E tensout tot Avrencin ;   Ne leissout rien k'il péust prendra."

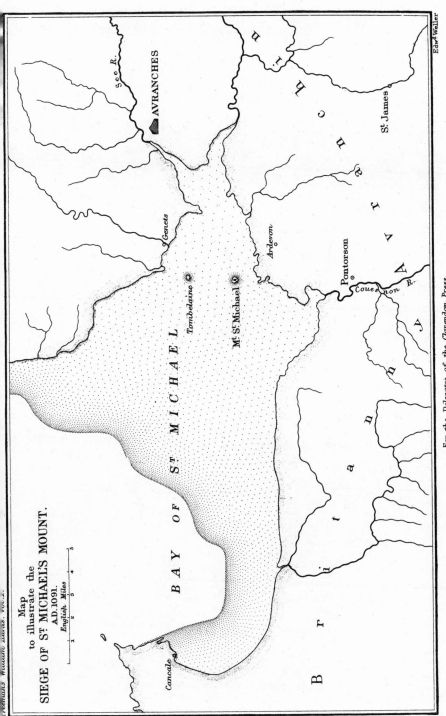

Freeman's William Rufus. Vol. I.

Map
to illustrate the
SIEGE OF St MICHAEL'S MOUNT.
A.D. 1091.

English Miles

1 2 3 4 5

B A Y   O F   St M I C H A E L

Cancale

Tombelaine

Mt St Michael

Genets

See R.

AVRANCHES

St. James

Ardevon

Pontorson

Couesnon R.

B r i t t a n n y

N o r m a n d y

Edwᵈ Weller

For the Delegates of the Clarendon Press.

extreme points occupied by the besiegers, before Genetz CHAP. III. and before Arderon, the knights on both sides met every Combats. day in various feats of arms, feats, it would seem, savouring rather of the bravado of the tourney than of any rational military purpose.[1]

We now get, in the shape of those personal anecdotes Personal anecdotes. in which this reign is so rich, pictures of more than one side of the strangely mixed character of the Red King. At the other end of Normandy William had won lands and castles without dealing a single blow with his own sword, and with a singularly small outlay of blows from the swords of others. At Eu, at Aumale, and at Gournay, the work had been done with gold far more than with steel. Beneath Saint Michael's Mount steel was to have its turn; and, when steel was the metal to be used, William Rufus was sure to be in his own person the foremost among those who used it. The change of scene seemed to have turned the wary trafficker into the most reckless of knights errant. Amidst such scenes he became, in the eyes of his own age, the peer of the most renowned of those Nine Worthies the tale of whom was made up only in his own day. We shall see at a later William compared to Alexander. stage how the question was raised whether the soul of the Dictator Cæsar had not passed into the body of the Red King; by the sands of Saint Michael's bay he was held to have placed himself on a level with the Macedonian Alexander. The likeness could hardly be carried on through the general military character of the two princes; for Alexander, when he began an enterprise, commonly carried it on to the end. And it may be doubted whether Alexander ever jeoparded his own life

---

[1] Wace, 14666;

"Mult véissiez joster sovent,   E la rivière de Coisnon.
  E tornéier espessement   Chescun jor al flo retraiant
  Entre li Munt et Ardenon   Vint chevaliers jostes menant."

CHAP. III. in the senseless way in which Rufus in the tale is made
to jeopard his.   We must picture to ourselves the royal
head-quarters between the height of Avranches and
the sands of Saint Michael's bay.   The King goes
Knight-   forth from his tent, and mounts the horse which he had
errantry of
William.   that morning bought for fifteen marks of silver.[1]   He
sees the enemy at a distance riding proudly towards
him.   Alone, waiting for no comrade, borne on both
by eagerness for the fray and by the belief that no one
would dare to withstand a king face to face, he gallops
forward and charges the advancing party.[2]   The newly
The King   bought horse is killed; the King falls under him; he
upset.   is ignominiously dragged along by the foot, but the
strength of his chain-armour saves him from any actual
wound.[3]   By this time the knight who had unhorsed
him has his hand on the hilt of his sword, ready to deal
a deadly blow.   William, frightened by the extremity of
his danger, cries out, "Hold, rascal, I am the King of
England."[4]   The words had that kind of magic effect
which is so often wrought by the personal presence of
royalty.   From any rational view of the business in
hand, to slay, or better still to capture, the hostile
king should have been the first object of every man in
Henry's garrison.   To no case better applied the wise
order of the Syrian monarch, "Fight neither with small
nor great, save only with the King of Israel."[5]   But as
soon as a voice which some at least of them knew proclaimed that it was a king who lay helpless among
them, every arm was stayed.   The soldiers of Henry
tremble at the thought of what they were so near

---

[1] On the two versions of this story, if they are meant to be the same
story, in William of Malmesbury and in Wace, see Appendix N.

[2] Will. Malms. iv. 309.   "Solus in multos irruit, alacritate virtutis
impatiens, simulque confidens nullum sibi ausurum obsistere."

[3] Ib. "Fides loricæ obstitit ne læderetur."

[4] Ib. "Tolle, nebulo, Rex Angliæ sum."   [5] 1 Kings xii. 31.

doing; with all worship they raise the King from the CHAP. III.
ground and bring him another horse.[1] William springs His treatment of the
unaided on his back; he casts a keen glance on the knight
band around him,[2] and asks, "Who unhorsed me?" As who unhorsed him.
they were muttering one to another, the daring man who
had done the deed came forward and said, "I, who took
you, not for a king but for a knight." A bold answer
was never displeasing to Rufus; he looked approval,
and said, "By the face of Lucca,[3] you shall be mine;
your name shall be written in my book,[4] and you shall
receive the reward of good service." Here the story
ends; we are to suppose that William, instead of being
carried a prisoner to the Mount, rode back free to
Avranches, having lessened the small force of Henry by
a stout knight and two horses.

The tale is told as an example of the magnanimity of Character of the
the Red King. And there is something which moves a story.
kind of admiration in the picture of a man, helpless
among a crowd of enemies, yet bearing himself as if they
were his prisoners, instead of his being theirs. The point
of the story is that Rufus did no harm, that he felt
no ill will, towards the man who had unhorsed, and all
but killed him; that he honoured his bold deed and bold
bearing, and promised him favour and promotion. But
had the soldiers of Henry done their duty, William would
have had no opportunity, at least no immediate opportunity, of doing either good or harm to his antagonist.

---

[1] Will. Malms. iv. 309. "Tremuit, nota voce jacentis, vulgus militum,
statimque reverenter de terra levato equum alterum adducunt."

[2] Ib. "Non expectato ascensorio, sonipedem insiliens, omnesque circumstantes vivido perstringens oculo, Quis, inquit, me dejecit?"

[3] See Appendix G. We have had this favourite oath already.

[4] Will. Malms. u. s. "Meus amodo eris, et meo albo insertus laudabilis
militiæ præmia reportabis." Of William's "album" or muster-roll we
hear elsewhere. Wace, 14492;

"N'oïst de chevalier parler   Ki en son brief escrit ne fust,
  Ke de proesce oïst loer,   E ki par an del suen n'éust."

William assumes that the enemy will not dare to withstand him, and his assumption is so far justified that
he is withstood only by one who knows not who he
is, and whose words imply that, if he had known, he
would not have ventured to withstand him.   Trusting
to this kind of superstitious dread, William is able to
speak and act as he might have spoken if the man who
unhorsed him had been brought before him in his own
Comparison tent.   Richard of the Lion-heart, when the archer who
with
Richard   had given him his death-wound was brought before him,
the First.   first designed him for a death of torture, and then, on
hearing a bold answer, granted him life and freedom.[1]
In this, as in some other cases, the Red King, the earliest
model of chivalry, certainly does not lose by comparison
with the successor who is more commonly looked on as
its ideal.[2]

Another and perhaps better known story which is told
of this siege puts the character of William Rufus in
another light, while it brings out the character of Robert
Contrast   in a lively form.   The Duke, heedless of the consequences
between
William   of his acts but not cruel in his own person, was, above
and
Robert.   all men, open to those passing bursts of generosity which
are quite consistent with utter weakness and want of
principle.   William Rufus was always open to an appeal
to his knightly generosity, to that higher form of self-
assertion which forbade him to harm one who was beneath him, and which taught him to admire a bold deed
or word even when directed against himself.   But the ties

[1] See Roger of Howden, iv. 83.   The King is wounded before Chaluz ;
the castle is taken, " quo capto, præcepit rex omnes suspendi, excepto illo
solo qui eum vulneraverat, quem, ut fas est credere, turpissima morte
damnaret, si convaluisset."

[2] See N. C. vol. v. p. 73.   Where did William of Malmesbury find his
story of Alexander, " qui Persam militem se a tergo ferire conatum, sed pro
perfidia ensis spe sua frustratum, incolumem pro admiratione fortitudinis
conservavit"?   The story in Arrian, i. 15, is quite different.

of kindred, still more the ties of common humanity, sat CHAP. III.
very lightly on him. The gentler soul of Robert was by
no means dead to them. He did not shrink from
waging an unjust war against his brother and deliverer;
he did not shrink from despoiling that brother and deliverer of dominions which he had sold to him by his own
act for a fair price; but he did shrink from the thought
of letting the brother against whom he warred suffer
actual bodily hardships when he could hinder them.
The defenders of the Mount had, according to one account, plenty of meat; but all our narratives agree as to
the difficulty of providing fresh water for the fortress
which twice in the day was surrounded by the waves.[1]
Henry sent a message to the Duke, praying that he
might be allowed access to fresh water; his brothers
might, if they thought good, make war on him by the
valour of their soldiers; they should not press the
powers of nature into their service, or deprive him of
those gifts of Providence which were open to all human
beings.[2] Robert was moved; he gave orders to the
sentinels at Genetz not to hinder the besieged from
coming to the mainland for water.[3] One version even
adds that he added the further gift of a tun of the best
wine.[4] This kind of generosity, where no appeal was
made to his own personal pride, was by no means to

Lack of
water on
the Mount.

Henry asks
to be
allowed to
take water.

Answer of
Robert and
William.

---

[1] The stock of meat comes from Wace, 14700;

"De viande aveient plenté,   Asez aveient a mengier,

Maiz de bevre aveient grant chierté; Maiz molt trovoent li vin chier."
The lack of water is secondary in his version. See Appendix N.

[2] Will. Malms. iv. 310. "Impium esse ut eum aqua arceant, quæ esset
communis mortalibus ; aliter, si velit, virtutem experiatur ; nec pugnet
violentia elementorum sed virtute militum." If this represents a real message from Henry, it must surely have been meant as an *argumentum ad
hominem* for Robert.

[3] Ib. "Genuina mentis mollitie flexus, suos *qua prætendebant* laxius
habere se jussit." This must mean the quarters of Robert at Genetz, as
distinguished from those of William.

[4] See Appendix N.

U 2

CHAP. III. the taste of Rufus; as a commander carrying on war, he was ready to press the rights of warfare to the uttermost. When he heard what Robert had done, he mocked at his brother's weakness; it was a fine way of making war to give the enemy meat and drink.[1] Robert answered, in words which do him honour, but which would have done him more honour if they had been spoken at the beginning as a reason for forbearing an unjust attack on his brother—"Shall we let our brother die of thirst? Where shall we find another, if we lose him?"[2]

Such are these two famous stories of the war waged beneath the mount of the Archangel. Both are eminently characteristic; there is no reason why both may not be true. But we must withhold our belief when one of our tale-tellers adds that William turned away from the siege in contempt for Robert's weakness.[3] A more sober guide tells us that when, for fifteen days, Henry and his followers had held up against lack of water and
Henry surrenders. threatening lack of food,[4] the wary youth saw the hopelessness of further resistance, and offered to surrender the Mount on honourable terms. He demanded a free

---

[1] Will. Malms. iv. 310. "Belle scis actitare guerram, qui hostibus præbes aquæ copiam; et quomodo eos domabimus si eis in pastu et in potu indulserimus?"

[2] Ib. "Ille renidens illud come et merito famosum verbum emisit, Papæ, dimitterem fratrem nostrum mori siti? et quem alium habebimus si eum amiserimus?" For the other version, see Appendix N. M. le Hardy (80), who is a knight of the order of Pius the Ninth, translates "Papæ," "par le Pape."

[3] See Appendix N.

[4] Ord. Vit. 697 A. "Fere xv. diebus cum suis aquæ penuria maxime coarcuerunt. Porro callidus juvenis, dum sic a fratribus suis coarctaretur, et a cognatis atque amicis et confœderatis affinibus undique destitueretur, et multimoda pene omnium quibus homines indigent inedia angeretur," &c. The siege began "in medio quadragesimæ," and lasted fifteen days. Florence is therefore wrong in saying "per totam quadragesimam montem obsederunt."

passage for himself and his garrison. William, already CHAP. III.
tired of a siege in which he had made little progress and
which had cost him many men and horses,[1] gladly accepted the terms. Henry, still Ætheling, though no
longer Count, marched forth from his island stronghold
with all the honours of war.[2] We are to suppose that,
according to the terms of the treaty, the King took
possession of the Mount itself, and the Duke of the rest
of Henry's former county. William stayed on the main- William
land, in the parts of Normandy which had been ceded to at Eu.
him, for full six months, having his head-quarters at
Eu.[3] In August the affairs of his island kingdom called He goes
him back again; and, strange to say, both his brothers back to
England.
went with him as his guests and allies.[4] August,
1091.

At this moment the past and the future alike lead us Fortunes of
to look with more interest on the fates of the dispos- Henry.
sessed Ætheling than on those of any other of the actors
in our story. But there is at first sight some little difficulty in finding out what those fates were. From our His pre-
English authorities we could only gather that Henry sence in
England in
was in England before the end of the year in which the 1091.
siege took place, and that three years later he was again
beyond sea, in favour with William and at enmity with
Robert. From other writers we get a version, which

[1] Flor. Wig. 1091. "Frequenter cum eo prœlium commiserunt, et homines
et equos nonnullos perdiderunt. At rex, cum obsidionis diutinæ pertæsus
fuisset, impacatus recessit."

[2] Ord. Vit. 697 A. "Liberum sibi sociisque suis exitum de monte ab
obsidentibus poposcit. Illi admodum gavisi sunt, ipsumque cum omni
apparatu suo egredi *honorifice* permiserunt." On the honours of war, see
above, p. 86. See Appendix N.

[3] Ib. "Rex in Neustria usque ad Augustum permansit, et dissidentes
qui eidem adquiescere voluerunt regali auctoritate pacavit." So in 693 C he
mentions the lands of Eu, Gournay, and Conches, and adds, " ubi præfatus
rex a Januario usque ad kal. Augusti regali more cum suis habitavit."
I assume Eu as his actual head-quarters, as it was before and after.

[4] Ib. D. See the next chapter.

CHAP. III.

Story of
Henry's
adventures. takes no notice of any visit to England, but which gives
us a moving tale of Henry's experiences in Normandy
and the neighbouring lands. It is one of those cases
where a writer, telling his own part of the story, altogether forgets, perhaps without formally contradicting,
other parts. In such a case he is likely to stumble in
some of his dates and details; but this need not lead us
altogether to cast aside the main features of his story.
It is plain that, for some time after the surrender of the
Mount, Henry was, to say the least, landless. In the
pictures of his actual distress and adversity there may
well be somewhat of exaggeration; but they draw from
one who is not a flatterer the important remark that,
having known adversity himself, he learned to be gracious in after years to the sufferings of others.[1] We are
perhaps startled by such a saying when we think of
some particular acts of Henry; but this witness does
not stand alone; and, among the contradictions of
human nature, there is nothing impossible in the belief
that such a spirit may have existed alongside of many
particular acts of cruelty.[2] But it is certain that
Henry's season of adversity must have been shorter
than it appears in the picture of it which is given to

His alleged
wander-
ings. us. We are told that, soon after he left the Mount,
he found himself very nearly a solitary wanderer.
He first went into Britanny, the only land from
which he had received any help, and thanked his
friends there for their services. Thence he betook himself to France, and spent, we are told, nearly two years
in the borderland of the Vexin, the land which had been
the scene of his father's last and fatal warfare, and which

---

[1] Ord. Vit. 697 B. "Sic regia proles in exsilio didicit pauperiem perpeti,
ut futurus rex optime sciret miseris et indigentibus compati, eorumque
dejectioni vel indigentiæ regali potentia seu dapsilitate suffragari, et ritus
infirmorum expertus eis pie misereri."

[2] See N. C. vol. v. pp. 156, 843.

was again to be the scene of warfare before his brother's reign was ended. There, with a train cut down to one knight, one clerk, and three esquires, Henry wandered to and fro, seeking shelter where he could.[1] Whatever truth there may be in these details, the time of Henry's probation could not have been spread over anything like a period of two years. He may have been a wanderer during the few months which immediately followed the surrender of the Mount; but, if so, he was reconciled to both his brothers long before the end of the year. Or he may, from some unexplained reason, have again become a wanderer during some months of the following year. There is nothing in any way impossible or unlikely in either story. What is certain is that, before the end of the next year, Henry had again an establishment on Gaulish ground, and one gained in the most honourable way. And it is equally certain that when King William went back to England in the month of August in the present year he took both of his brothers with him.[2]

Robert and Henry accompany William to England.

§ 4. The Scottish Expedition of William Rufus. *August—October*, 1091.

The business which called William back to his king-dom was a serious one; it was no other than to drive back or to avenge a Scottish invasion. King Malcolm, who seems to have stayed quiet during the rebellion three years before, now took up arms. We cannot help connecting this step with the visit of his brother-in-law, and the words of the Chronicler seem directly to imply that Malcolm's invasion was the consequence of

Affairs of Scotland.

---

[1] See Appendix O.

[2] Will. Malms. iv. 310. " In regnum se cum ambobus fratribus recepit." I should hardly have accepted this evidence, if it had not been confirmed by the signatures to a charter of which I shall presently speak. See below, p. 305.

CHAP. III. Eadgar's coming.[1] From one version we might almost
think that Malcolm had been called on to do homage
and had refused.[2] This is perfectly possible in itself;
but the time of William's special occupation with Norman affairs seems oddly chosen for such a summons.
An earlier time, some point in the blank period between
the rebellion and the Norman campaign, would have
seemed more natural for such a purpose. However this
may be, now, in the month of May, Malcolm took advantage of William's absence in Normandy to invade
Northumberland for the fourth time. He designed, we
are told, to go much further and do much more, words
which might almost suggest a purpose of asserting the
claims of Eadgar to the English crown. Whatever were
his objects, they were not carried out, save one which
was doubtless not the least among them, that of carrying
off great spoil from Northumberland.[3] The furthest point
that Malcolm reached was Chester-le-Street, a point un-
pleasantly near to the bishopless monks of Durham.[4]
There the men in local command went against him and
drove him back. In the national Chronicle they appear
as "the good men who guarded this land."[5] In this way

*Malcolm's
invasion of
Northum-
berland.
May, 1091.*

*He is
driven
back.*

---

[1] Immediately after the words quoted in p. 282, follows the entry about
Malcolm; "Onmang þam þe se cyng W. ut of Englelande wæs ferde se
cyng Melcolm of Scotlande hider into Englum, and his mycelne dæl ofer
hergode."

[2] Ord. Vit. 701 A. "In illo tempore Melcoma rex Scotorum contra
regem Anglorum rebellavit, debitumque servitium ei denegavit." See
Appendix P.

[3] Flor. Wig. 1091. "Mense Maio rex Scottorum Malcolmus cum magno
exercitu Northymbriam invasit; si proventus successisset, ulterius proces-
surus, et vim Angliæ incolis illaturus. Noluit Deus: ideo ab incepto est
impeditus: attamen antequam rediisset, ejus exercitus de Northymbria
secum non modicam prædam abduxit."

[4] Sim. Dun. 1093 (where he reckons up Malcolm's invasions); "Quarto,
regnante Willelmo juniore, cum suis copiis infinitis usque Ceastram, non
longe a Dunelmo sitam, pervenit, animo intendens ulterius progredi."

[5] Chron. Petrib. 1091. "Oð þæt þa gode men þe þis land bewiston, him

of speaking, as in many other phrases in our own and other tongues, the word "good" means rank and office rather than moral goodness. Yet the latter idea is not wholly absent; the name would hardly be given to men who were engaged in a cause which the writer wholly condemned. The "good men" here spoken of must have been mainly Normans, with Earl Robert of Mowbray at their head. Earl Robert was not likely to have won much love from the English people. Yet he passed for a "good man," when he did his duty for England, when he guarded the land and drove back the Scottish invader. Of any wish to put Malcolm in the place of either the elder or the younger William we see no trace at any stage of our story. Beyond this emphatic sentence, we get no details. As in so many other cases, if conquest was the object of Malcolm's expedition, plunder was the only result.

CHAP. III.

The "good men."

The news of this harrying of the northern part of his kingdom brought King William back from Normandy in the course of August. With him, as we have said, came Robert and Henry. Why was the Duke's presence needed? One account hints that his coming had some reference to the actors in the late rebellion, some of whom at least were now restored to their estates.[1] Another version speaks of an old friendship between Robert and Malcolm;[2] and there was a tie of spiritual affinity between

William and Robert in England. August, 1091.

Relations between Robert and Malcolm.

fyrde ongean sændon and hine gecyrdon." Did they not go in their own persons?

[1] See above, p. 282. The words of Orderic (701 A) are odd; "Guillelmus rex . . . cum Roberto fratre suo pacem fecerat, ipsumque contra infidos proditores qui contra regem conspiraverant secum duxerat." This surely cannot mean the Scots; it must mean the rebels of three years before. Robert cannot have been brought to act in any way against them; yet the words of Orderic must have a confused reference to some real object of his coming.

[2] Will. Malms. iv. 311. "Satagente Roberto comite, qui familiarem jamdudum apud Scottum locaverat gratiam, inter Malcolmum et Willelmum concordia inita." See Appendix P.

CHAP. III. them arising out of Robert's relation as godfather to a child of Malcolm.[1] It was perhaps in this character that Robert came to act, if need should be, as a welcome Stronger side of Robert and Eadgar. negotiator with his Scottish gossip. One strange thing is that, on more than one occasion in our story, both Robert and Eadgar, two men who seem so incapable of vigorous or rational action on behalf of themselves, play a distinctly creditable part when acting on behalf of others. But this is really no uncommon inconsistency of human nature; men are often found who are good advisers in the affairs of others, while they are by no means wise managers of their own. Robert in truth appears to most advantage anywhere out of his own duchy. Neither the warrior of the crusade nor the negotiator with the Scot seems to be the same man as the Duke who could not be trusted to defend his own palace.

William sets forth. In the present case there was more of negotiation than of warfare. Of actual fighting there seems to have been none. William got together, as his father had done in the like case,[2] a great force by land and sea for the invasion of Scotland. With the land force the King and the Duke set forth; but seemingly with no haste, as time was found for a great ecclesiastical ceremony on Durham in the absence of Bishop William. the way. For three years the church of Durham had been without a shepherd, and the castle of Durham had been in the hands of the King. The monks of Saint Cuthberht's abbey had feared that this irregular time would be an evil time for them. But they put their trust in God and their patron saint, and went to the King The King's favourable treatment of the monks. to ask his favour. Rufus was specially gracious and merciful; he rose up to greet Prior Turgot, the head of the embassy, and he gave orders that the monks of Durham should be in no way disturbed, but should keep full

[1] See Appendix BB.   [2] See N. C. vol. iv. p. 513.

possession of their rights and property, exactly as if the CHAP. III.
Bishop had remained in occupation of his see.[1]   We
may even venture to guess that they had a somewhat
fuller possession of them during the Bishop's absence.
We are expressly told by the local historian that the Red
King did not deal with Durham as he dealt with other
churches; he took nothing from the monks, and even
gave them something of his own.[2]   The new society — Works at
Durham.
for it must be remembered that the monks of Durham
were a body of Bishop William's own bringing in[3]—
flourished so greatly during this irregular state of things
that it was now that they built their refectory.[4]   But a
time of more settled order was now to come.   Bishop Reconcilia-
tion of
Bishop
William of Saint-Calais, whatever had been his crimes Bishop
three years back, was among those whom King William William
with the
had engaged by his treaty with his brother to restore to King.
their lands and honours.   Besides this general claim, it
was believed, at Durham at least, that the banished
prelate had earned his restoration by a signal service
done to the King.   In the third year of his banishment
an unnamed Norman fortress was holding out for the
King; but its garrison was sore pressed, and its capture
by the enemy seemed imminent.   The Bishop, by what
means of persuasion we are not told, but it does not
seem to have been by force, caused the besiegers to raise
the siege.[5]   This service won the King's thorough good

[1] Sim. Dun. Hist. Eccl. Dun. iv. 8.   "Priori ad se venienti humiliter
assurgens, benigne illum suscepit, et ita per omnia sub se, quemadmodum
sub episcopo, curam ecclesiæ cum omni libertate agere præcepit."

[2] Ib.   "Licet in alia monasteria et ecclesias ferocius ageret, ipsis tamen
non solum nihil auferebat, sed etiam de suo dabat, et ab injuriis malignorum
sicut pater defendebat."

[3] See N. C. vol. iv. p. 674.

[4] Sim. Dun. u. s.   "Hoc tempore refectorium, quale hodie cernitur,
monachi ædificaverunt."

[5] Ib.   "Tertio anno expulsionis episcopi, cum homines regis quoddam in
Normannia castellum tenentes obsiderentur, et jamjamque capiendi essent,

CHAP. III. will, and William, on his march to Scotland, personally
He is re-   put the Bishop once more in possession of his see and of
stored to his
bishopric. all its rights and belongings, temporal and spiritual.[1]
September
3, 1091.   Bishop William did not come back empty-handed; he
brought with him costly gifts for his church, ornaments,
gold and silver vessels, and, above all, many books.[2]
And, at some time before the year was out, we find him
confirming with great solemnity, with the witness of
the great men of the realm, certain grants of the Conqueror to the monks of his church.[3] The return of the
Bishop was an event not only of local but of national
His   importance. He was restored by the King, not only to
renewed
influence   his formal favour, but to a high place in his innermost
with the
King.   counsels. Bishop William was not one of those who
come back from banishment having learned nothing and
forgotten nothing. He had, in his sojourn beyond the
sea, learned an altogether new doctrine as to the relations between bishops and kings.

The march which had been interrupted by the ceremony at Durham was clearly a slow one. William was
at Durham in the first days of September; much later
in the month a heavy blow fell on one part of the ex-
Loss of   pedition. The greater part of the ships were lost a few
the ships.
Michael-   days before the feast of Michaelmas, and we are told that
mas, 1091. this happened before the King could reach Scotland.
The King was therefore several weeks in journeying

eos episcopus a periculo liberavit, et consilio suo ut obsidio solveretur
effecit."

[1] Sim. Dun. Hist. Eccl. Dun. iv. 8. "Unde rex placatus, universa quæ
in Anglia prius habuerat, ei restituit." More formally in the Gesta Regum,
1091; "Veniens Dunelmum, episcopum Willelmum restituit in sedem suam,
ipso post annos tres die quo eam reliquit, scilicet tertio idus Septembris."
The time of three years is not quite exact; see above, p. 94.

[2] Hist. Eccl. Dun. u. s. "Ille nequaquam vacuus rediit, sed non
pauca ex auro et argento sacra altaris vasa et diversa ornamenta, sed
et libros plurimos ad ecclesiam præmittere curavit."

[3] See above, p. 295, and below, p. 305.

from Durham to the border of the true Scotland, the CHAP. III.
Firth of Forth; and we are told that many of the land
force also perished of cold and hunger.[1] The army
however which remained was strong enough to make
Malcolm feel less eager for deeds of arms than he had
most likely felt in May. At last, near the shore of the *Scots' Water*, the estuary which parted English Lothian
from Scottish Fife, the two kings met face to face,
seemingly in battle array, but without coming to any
exchange of blows. It is marked in a pointed way that
Malcolm had crossed from his kingdom to his earldom.
He "went out of Scotland into Lothian in England, and
there abode." [2] There a negotiation took place. The
ambassadors or mediators were Duke Robert and the
Ætheling Eadgar.[3] According to the most picturesque
version, Malcolm, who is conceived as still keeping on
the northern side of the firth, sends a message to

William and Malcolm by the Scots' Water.

Mediation of Robert and Eadgar.

[1] Chron. Petrib. 1091. "Se cyng W. . . . . sona fyrde hét ut abeodan ægðer scipfyrde and landfyrde; and seo scipferde, ær he to Scotlande cuman mihte, ælmæst earmlice forfór, feowan dagon toforan Sĉe Michæles mæssan." Florence calls the host "classis non modica et equestris exercitus," and adds that "multi de equestri exercitu ejus fame et frigore perierunt."

[2] Chron. Petrib. 1091. "Ac þa þa se cyng Melcolm gehyrde þæt hine man mid fyrde secean wolde, he for mid his fyrde ut of Scotlande into Loðene on Englaland, and þær abad." Florence, followed by Simeon, oddly enough translates this; "Rex Malcolmus cum exercitu in provincia Loidis occurrit." Hence some modern writers have carried Malcolm as far south as *Leeds*, I presume only to Leeds in Yorkshire. Orderic (701 A), though, as we shall see, he somewhat misconceives the story, marks the geography very well; "Exercitum totius Angliæ conglobavit, ut usque ad magnum flumen, quod Scotte Watra dicitur, perduxit." The "Scots' Water" is of course the Firth of Forth. So Turgot in the Life of Margaret (Surtees Simeon, p. 247) speaks of "utraque litora maris quod Lodoneium dividit et Scotiam." See Appendix P.

[3] Chron. Petrib. ib. "Ða ða se cyng William mid his fyrde genealehte þa ferdon betwux Rodbeard eorl and Eadgar æþeling, and þæra cinga sehte swa gemacedon." So Florence; "Quod videns comes Rotbertus, clitonem Eadgarum, quem rex de Normannia expulerat, et tunc cum rege Scottorum degebat, ad se accersivit : cujus auxilio fretus, pacem inter reges fecit." On the details in Orderic, see Appendix P.

CHAP. III. William to the effect that he owes no homage to him, but that, if he can have an interview with Robert, he Conference will do to him whatever is right. By the advice of his of Robert and Wise Men,[1] William sends his brother, who is cour-Malcolm. teously received by the Scottish King for three days. Somewhat like the Moabite king of old, though with quite another purpose, Malcolm takes his visitor to the tops of various hills, and shows him the hosts of Scotland encamped in the plains and dales below. With so mighty a force he is ready to withstand any one who should try to cross the firth; he would be well pleased Malcolm's if any enemy would make the attempt. He then sud-homage to Robert. denly turns to the question of homage. He had received the earldom of Lothian from King Eadward, when his great-niece Margaret was betrothed to him. The late King William had confirmed the gifts of his predecessor, and, at his bidding, he, Malcolm, had become the man of his eldest son, his present visitor Duke Robert. To him he would discharge his duty; to the present King William he owed no duty at all. He appealed to the Gospel for the doctrine that no man could serve two lords, the doctrine which had been so practically pressed on Robert's behalf three years before.[2] Robert admitted the truth of Malcolm's statement; but he argued that times were changed, and that the decrees of his father had lost their old force. It would be wise to accept the reigning King as his lord, a lord nearer, richer, and more powerful, than he could pretend to be himself. Malcolm might be sure of a gracious reception from William, if he came on such an He submits errand. Malcolm was convinced; he went to the King to William. of the English; he was favourably received, and a peace

---

[1] "Ex consultu sapientum," says Orderic. These ancient formulæ cleave to us wherever we go, even in the camp. On the action of the military Witan, see above, p. 216.   [2] See above, p. 25.

was agreed on. It is added that the two kings then CHAP. III. disbanded their armies, and went together into England.[1]

This last statement throws some doubt upon the whole of this version; for Malcolm's alleged journey to England at this moment is clearly a confusion with events which happened two years later. The references Question as to the betrothal of Margaret. too to the earldom of Lothian and to an earlier betrothal of Margaret are a little startling; yet it is perhaps not quite hopeless to reconcile them with better ascertained facts. As I have elsewhere suggested, this earlier betrothal of Margaret to Malcolm is not necessarily inconsistent with his later marriage with her after the intermediate stage of Ingebiorg.[2] Malcolm may at one time have been in no hurry to carry out a marriage dictated by political reasons; yet he may have afterwards become eager for the same marriage after he had seen her whose hand was designed for him. As for the Lothian earldom, Question of Lothian. we here see the beginning of the later Scottish argument, that homage was due from the Scottish to the English king only for lands held within the kingdom of England. At this stage Lothian was the land held within the kingdom of England; it was what Northumberland, Huntingdon, or any other confessedly English land held by the Scottish king, was in later times. When Malcolm was restored to his crown by the arms of Siward,[3] no doubt Lothian was granted to him among other things. Only Malcolm takes up the line, or our historian thinks it in character to make him take up the line, of implying, though not directly asserting, that Lothian was the only possession for which homage was due. And, on the strictest view of English claims, Malcolm would be right in at least drawing a marked

---

[1] See Appendix P.   [2] See N. C. vol. iv. p. 175.
[3] Ib. vol. ii. p. 272.

CHAP. III.   distinction between Scotland and Lothian. He owed both
kingdom and earldom to the intervention of Eadward
and Siward; but Lothian was a grant from Eadward in
a sense in which Scotland was not. Over Scotland
neither Eadward nor William could claim more than an
external superiority. Lothian was still English ground,
as much as the land which is now beginning to be distinguished as Northumberland.

Treaty
between
William
and
Malcolm.

The version of Malcolm's submission which I have
just gone through is certainly worth examining, and
I do not see that it contradicts the simpler and more
certain version. According to this account, the negotiation was carried on between Robert and Eadgar. The
agreement to which the mediators came was that Malcolm should renew to the younger William the homage
which he had paid to the elder.[1] On the other hand, he
was to receive all lands and everything else that he had
before held in England, specially, it would seem, twelve
vills or mansions for his reception on his way to the

Malcolm
does
homage.

English court.[2] On these terms Malcolm became the
man of William; Eadgar also was reconciled to William.
The two kings parted on good terms, but the Chronicler
notices, in a phrase of which he is rather fond, that it
" little while stood." [3]

William, Robert, and Eadgar now took their journey

[1] It is specially marked that the homage now done was the renewal of
the old homage. So the Chronicle, 1091; "Se cyng Melcolm to uran cynge
com, and his man wearð to ealle swilcre gehyrsumnisse swa he ǽr his fæder
dyde, and þæt mid aðe gefestnode." So Florence; "Ea conditione, ut
Willelmo, sicut patri suo obedivit, Malcolmus obediret."

[2] The Chronicle says only; "Se cyng William him behét on lande and
on ealle þinge þæs þe he under his fæder ǽr hæfde." Florence is fuller;
"Et Malcolmo xii. villas, quas in Anglia sub patre illius habuerat, Willelmus redderet, et xii. marcas auri singulis annis daret." See Appendix P.

[3] Chron. Petrib. u. s. "On þisum sehte wearð eac Eadgar eþeling wið
þone cyng gesæhtlad, and þa cyngas þa mid mycclum sehte tohwurfon, ac
þæt litle hwile stod." Florence is to the same effect. See Appendix P.

back again, as it is specially marked, from Northum- CHAP. III.
berland into Wessex.[1] The realm of Ælfred is still looked Return of
on as the special dwelling-place of his successors from William.
beyond the sea. But it would seem that, at some stage
of their southward journey, at some time before the
year was out, they joined with other men of royal and
princely descent in setting their crosses to a document,
in itself of merely local importance, but which is clothed
with a higher interest by the names of those who sign
it. A grant of certain churches to the convent of Dur- Evidence
ham becomes a piece of national history when, besides the of the
Durham
signatures for which we might naturally look, it bears the charters.
names of King William the Second, of Robert his brother,
of Henry his brother, of Duncan son of King Malcolm, of
Eadgar the Ætheling, and of Siward Barn.[2] This is the
only time when all these persons could have met. There is
no sign of any later visit of Robert to England during
the reign of William. But the signatures of Henry and
Duncan teach us more. Duncan, it will be remembered, Duncan.
had been given as a hostage at Abernethy;[3] he had been
set free by the Conqueror on his death-bed; he had been
knighted by Robert, and allowed to go whither he would.[4]
Had he already made his way back to his own land, or
did he come in the train of his latest benefactor? In
the former case, had he been again given as a hostage?
Or had William found out that the son of Ingebiorg
might possibly be useful to him? It is certain that, two
years later, Duncan was at William's court and in William's favour; and it looks very much as if he had, in
whatever character, gone back to England with the

---

[1] Flor. Wig. 1091. "Post hæc rex de Northymbria per Merciam in
West-Saxoniam rediit." [2] See Appendix P.

[3] See N. C. vol. v. p. 121. The Chronicle in 1093 brings him in as
"Dunecan ... se on þæs cynges hyrede W. wæs, swa swa his fæder hine
ures cynges fæder ær to gisle geseald hæfde."

[4] See above, p. 14.

King. The signature of Eadgar shows that the document must be later than the treaty with Malcolm by which he was reconciled to William, that is, that it was signed on the journey southward, not on the journey northward. The signature of Henry is our only hint that he had any share at all in the Scottish business, and it throws a perfectly new light on this part of his history. He was plainly in England, seemingly in favour with both his brothers, and things look as if he too, though he is nowhere mentioned, must have gone on the march to Scotland. Siward Barn, like Duncan, was one of those who were set free by William the Great on his death-bed. We now learn that he shared the good luck of Duncan and Wulf, not the bad luck of Morkere and Wulfnoth. He signs as one of the great men of the north, with Arnold of Percy, with the Sheriff Morel, and with Earl Robert himself.

One thing is plain, namely, that this document was not signed in the regular Christmas Assembly of the year. By that time Robert and Eadgar were no longer in England. By that time Robert and William had again quarrelled. We may guess that some of Robert's old partisans had been less lucky than the Bishop of Durham. At all events, some points in the treaty of Caen remained unfulfilled. Then, as in later times, a diplomatic engagement was not found strong enough to carry itself out by its own force, like a physical law of nature. We are not told what was the special point complained of; but something which the Red King should have done for Robert or for his partisans was left undone.[1] It was simply as a man and a king that Rufus had entered into any engagements with his brother. His knightly honour was not pledged; the treaty therefore came under the head of those promises which no man can

_____
[1] Could there be any reference to the non-restoration of Odo? See above, p. 283.

CHAP. III.
Eadgar.

Henry.

Siward
Barn.

Fresh
dispute
between
William
and
Robert.

fulfil.[1] We are told in a pointed way that Robert stayed CHAP. III. with his brother till nearly the time of Christmas. The matter in dispute, whatever it was, might have been fittingly discussed in the Christmas Assembly; only it might have been hard to find the formula by which the Duke of the Normans was to appeal the King of the English of bad faith before his own Witan. Two days Robert and Eadgar leave England. December 23, 1091. before the feast Robert took ship in Wight, and sailed to Normandy, taking the Ætheling Eadgar with him.[2]

Either the reign of Rufus was really richer than other Natural phænomena. times in striking natural phænomena, or else they were specially noticed as signs of the times. About the time Fall of the tower at Winchcombe. October 15, 1091. of the King's Scottish expedition, the tower of the minster at Winchcombe was smitten by a mighty thunderbolt, and fell in ruins on the body of the church, crushing the most hallowed images in its fall. The Chthonian Zeus had no place in the mythology of the times; but this destruction, which left behind it a thick smoke and an evil smell, was deemed to be the work of the evil one, the signs of whose presence were got rid of only by the most solemn chants and processions.[3] Two days later,

---

[1] See above, p. 143.

[2] Chron. Petrib. 1091. "And se eorl Rodbeard her oð Xpes mæsse forneah mid þam cynge wunode, and litel soðes þær onmang of heora forewarde onfand; and twam dagon ær þære tide on Wiht scipode and into Normandig fôr, and Eadgar æþeling mid him." So Florence; "Rex . . . secum fere usque ad nativitatem Domini comitem retinuit, sed conventionem inter eos factam persolvere noluit. Quod comes graviter ferens, xo. kal. Januarii die cum clitone Eadgaro Normanniam repetiit."

[3] Florence (1091) tells this tale; "Magnus fumus cum nimio fœtore subsecutus, totam ecclesiam replevit, et tamdiu duravit, quoad loci illius monachi cum aqua benedicta et incensu et reliquiis sanctorum, officinas monasterii psalmos decantando circumirent." William of Malmesbury (iv. 323) gives more details, and is better certified as to the cause; "Secutus est odor teterrimus, hominum importabilis naribus. Tandem monachi, felici ausu irrumpentes, benedictæ aquæ aspergine prœstigias inimici effugarunt." A modern diplomatist might have said that the prestige of the evil one was lowered.

CHAP. III. London was visited by a fearful wind, which blew down

Great wind seven churches and houses to the number of six hundred.
in London.
October 17, Above all, the wooden roof of the church of Saint Mary-
1091.
le-bow was carried off, and its beams were hurled to the
ground with such force that they were driven into the
hard earth, and had to be sawn off as they stood.[1] Two
men who were in the church were crushed. The citizens
could have hardly repaired their houses before another

Fire in blow came upon them. Early in the next year the greater
London.
March 28, part of London was destroyed by fire.[2] By Eastertide
1092.
the cathedral churches of two of the dioceses whose
seats had been moved in the late reign stood ready for

Consecra- consecration. On the waterless hill which then was
tion of the
church of Salisbury, within the everlasting ditches of the elder
Salisbury. time, looking down on the field of battle which had
April 5,
1092. decreed that Britain should be English[3] and on the
field of council which had decreed that England should
be one,[4] Norman Osmund, the doctor of the ritual lore
of England, had finished the work which Lotharingian
Hermann had began. The new mother church of the
lands of Berkshire, Wiltshire, and Dorset, the elder
minster of Saint Mary, whose stones were borne away
to build the soaring steeple of its successor but whose
foundations may still be traced on the turf of the forsaken city, now awaited its hallowing. There was then

---

[1] Florence again tells the tale; but William of Malmesbury (iv.324) again is
far more emphatic, and seems to look on the winds as moral agents; "Quid
illud omnibus incognitum sæculis? Discordia ventorum inter se dissiden-
tium, ab Euro-austro veniens decimo sexto kal. Novembris Londoniæ plusquam secentas domos effregit ... Majus quoque scelus furor ventorum ausus,
tectum ecclesiæ sanctæ Mariæ quæ 'ad Arcus' dicitur pariter sublevavit."
But Florence is simply setting down events under their years, while William
is making a collection of " casualties," to illustrate the position that " plura
sub eo [Willelmo Rufo] subita et tristia acciderunt," and notes this year as
specially marked by " tumultus fulgurum, motus turbinum."

[2] Flor. Wig. 1092. " Civitas Lundonia maxima ex parte incendio con-
flagravit."

[3] See N. C. vol. i. p. 321.   [4] See N. C. vol. iv. p. 691.

no archbishop in southern England; the rite was done CHAP. III.
by Osmund himself with the help of his two nearest
episcopal neighbours, Walkelin of Winchester and
John of Bath.[1] The ceremony had thus a specially
West-Saxon character. The three bishops who came
together at Salisbury represented the three—once four—
churches, among which the old West-Saxon diocese, the
diocese of Winchester, had been parted asunder.[2] But
at Salisbury too, the elements, if somewhat less hostile
than at Winchcombe and London, were by no means
friendly. Five days only after the hallowing, the light- The tower
ning fell, as at Winchcombe; the peaked roof or low thrown
spire which sheltered the tower—doubtless of wood down.
covered with lead—was thrown down, and its fall did April 10.
much damage to the walls of the new minster.[3]

A day later by a month had been fixed for another
ceremony of the same kind, the crowning of the work of
a prelate who seems to have wished for a more stately
ceremony and a greater gathering than the almost domestic rite which had satisfied Bishop Osmund. Remigius,
Almoner of Fécamp, Bishop of Dorchester, Bishop of

[1] Flor. Wig. 1092. "Osmundus Searesbyriensis episcopus, ecclesiam
quam Searesbyriæ in castello construxerat, cum adjutorio episcoporum
Walcelini Wintoniensis et Johannis Bathoniensis, nonis Aprilis feria ii.
dedicavit." Cf. Will. Malms. Gest. Pont. 183. The foundation charter
(Mon. Ang. vi. 1299) was signed in 1091, "Willelmo rege monarchiam
totius Angliæ strenue gubernante anno quarto regni ejus, apud Hastinges "
—most likely on his return from Normandy in August. The signatures
come in a strange order. Between the earls and the Archbishop of York
come "Signum Wlnoti. Signum Croc venatoris." Wulfnoth here turns up
in the same strange way in which he so often does. Croc the huntsman
we have heard of already. See above, p. 102. We get also the signatures
of Howel Bishop of Le Mans, and of Robert the *dispenser*, who invented the
surname Flambard (see below, p. 331). On the signature of Herbert Losinga,
see Appendix X.   [2] See N. C. vol. ii. p. 606.
[3] Will. Malms. iv. 325. "Eadem violentia fulminis apud Salesbiriam
tectum turris ecclesiæ omnino disjecit, multamque maceriam labefactavit,
quinta sane die postquam eam dedicaverat Osmundus, præclaræ memoriæ
episcopus."

CHAP. III.   Lincoln, was drawing near the end of his famous epi-
Remigius   scopate. He had reformed the constitution of his chapter
of Lincoln.
and diocese; and we hear that he was no less zealous
in reforming the manners of his flock.[1] The darling
sin of Bristol—most likely the darling sin of every great
trading-town—was rife at Lincoln also; and Remigius,
like Wulfstan, preached against the wicked custom by
which men sold their country-folk, sometimes their kinsfolk, to a life of shame or of bondage in foreign lands.[2]
Completion   But beyond all this, he had finished his great work on
of the
minster.   the hill of Lincoln; the elder church of Saint Mary had
grown into the great minster of which later rebuildings
and enlargements have still left us some small remnants.[3]
The eastern limb had as yet no need to overleap the
Roman wall of Lindum; but Remigius had reared, and
sought to consecrate, no fragment, but a perfect church.
His doorways are there in the western front to show that
the building has received no enlargement on that side
from Remigius' day to our own. The work was done,
and its founder felt his last end coming. He was eager
to see the house which he had builded dedicated to
its holy use before he himself passed away. But an
unlooked-for hindrance came. The only archbishop in
the land, Thomas of York, claimed the district in which

[1] See N. C. vol. iv. p. 419, and Giraldus, Vita Rem. c. 3, 4, 5 (vol. vii.
p. 17 et seqq. Dimock). Giraldus is, I believe, the only writer who makes a
saint of Remigius. He enlarges on the effects of Remigius' preaching, and
consequently on the wickedness of those to whom he had to preach.

[2] Giraldus, Vit. Rem. ch. v. "Prolem propriam quam genuerat, nepotes
etiam et neptes, alienigenis in servitutem detestanda avaritia venalem ex
consuetudine prostituebant." Cf. N. C. vol. iv. p. 381, and the stories
in Will. Malms. ii. 200, about Godwine's supposed first wife. See N. C.
vol. i. p. 737.

[3] I mentioned in N. C. vol. iv. p. 212, that Lincoln minster grew out of
an earlier church of Saint Mary. The history of John of Schalby printed
by Mr. Dimock shows that this elder parish church went on within the
minster. This is a very important case of a double church. See Giraldus,
vii. xxx. 194, 209.

Remigius had built his church as belonging to his own CHAP III.
diocese.[1] This does not seem to have been by virtue of Thomas of York
the claim that the whole diocese of Dorchester came claims the jurisdic-
within his metropolitan jurisdiction.[2] The argument tion of Lindesey.
was that Lindesey, won for the Christian faith by
Paullinus, won for the Northumbrian realm by Ecgfrith,
was part of the diocesan jurisdiction of the Bishop of
York. And, whatever the truth of the case might be,
the warmest of all admirers of Remigius goes some way
to strengthen the doctrine of Thomas, when he speaks
of Lindesey almost as a conquered land won by the
prowess of Remigius from the Northumbrian enemy.[3]
The time was not one for doubtful disputations. Re- Remigius
migius, saint as he is pictured to us, knew how to use wins over the King.
those baser arguments which were convincing above all
others in the days of the Red King. His original
appointment in the days of the Conqueror had not been
altogether beyond suspicion;[4] and it was now whispered that it was by the help of a bribe that he won
the zealous adhesion of William Rufus to his cause.
Rufus was at least impartial; he was clearly ready to
give a fair day's work for a fair day's wages, and what he
would do for a Jew he would also do for a bishop. All

---

[1] See N. C. vol. iv. p. 369.   [2] See N. C. vol. iv. p. 355.

[3] Giraldus, Vit. Rem. ch. iv. "Operam erga regem et archiepiscopum,
excambium Eboracensi pro Lindeseia donantes, prudenter effectui, Deo
cooperante mancipavit. Et sic Lindeseiam terramque totam inter Widhemam
scilicet Lincolniæ fluvium et Humbriam diocesi suæ provinciæque Cantuariensi viriliter adjecit." This is Giraldus' improvement on the local record
copied by John of Schalby (Giraldus, vii. 194); "Datis per regem prædictum
Eboracensi archiepiscopo in excambium possessionibus, totam Lyndesyam
suæ diocesi et provinciæ Cantuariensi conjunxit." It must be remembered
that a bishopric of Lindesey had once been set up by the Northumbrian
Ecgfrith. See Bæda, iv. 12.

[4] See N. C. vol. iv. pp. 90, 354. This seems to be delicately referred to
in the record copied by John of Schalby (Giraldus, vii. 193); "Remigius
natione Normannus ac monachus Fiscanensis, qui ob certam causam venerat
cum eodem [Willielmo rege] in episcopum Dorkecestrensem."

CHAP. III.

Gathering
for the
consecra-
tion at
Lincoln.
May 9,
1092.

Death of
Remigius.
May 6,
1092.

the bishops of England were bidden by royal order to come together at the appointed day for the dedication of the church of Lincoln.[1] A vast crowd of men of all ranks came to Lincoln; the course of the story suggests that the King himself was there; all the bishops came, save one only. Robert of Hereford, the friend of Wulfstan, the Lotharingian skilled in the lore of the stars, knew by his science that the rite would not take place in the lifetime of Remigius. He therefore deemed it needless to travel to Lincoln for nothing.[2] His skill was not deceived; three days before the appointed time Remigius died.[3] The dedication of the church was delayed; it was done in the days of his successor, some years later.[4] Meanwhile Remigius himself won the honours of a saint in local esteem, and wonders of healing were wrought at his tomb for the benefit of not a few of divers tongues and even of divers creeds.[5]

---

[1] So says Florence. Remigius is eager to dedicate his church, "quia sibi diem mortis imminere sentiebat." Thomas objects, "affirmans eam in sua parochia esse constructam." "At rex Willelmus junior, *pro pecunia quam ei Remigius dederat,* totius fere Angliæ episcopis mandavit ut, in unum convenientes, septennis idibus Maii ecclesiam dedicarent." Of course there is nothing about the bribe in Giraldus, nor yet in William of Malmesbury, Gest. Pont. 313, where the King's order to the bishops is issued "magnanimi viri"—Remigius has got the King's own epithet— "hortatu." Matthew Paris, in the Historia Anglorum, i. 42, credits the Red King with an unlooked-for degree of zeal; "Postea rex Willelmus, cujus consilio et auxilio ecclesia illa fuit a primo loco suo remota, et quam *pro anima patris sui* [this at least is characteristic] multis ditaverat possessionibus, procuravit ut ea magnifice consummaretur."

[2] Will. Malms. Gest. Pont. 313. "Solus Rotbertus Herefordensis venire abnuerat, et certa inspectione siderum dedicationem tempore Remigii non processuram viderat, nec tacuerat."

[3] On the exact date, see Mr. Dimock's note to Giraldus, vii. 20. Ascension Day came on the feast of Saint John *ante Portam Latinam.*

[4] "Ecclesiæ per hoc remansit dedicatio." William of Malmesbury (u. s.) says, "Rem dilatam successor ejus non graviter explevit, utpote qui in labores alterius delicatus intrasset." There seems to be no mention of this in the Lincoln writers.

[5] Giraldus (vii. 22–31) has fifteen chapters, very short ones certainly, of the miracles of Remigius. One takes most to the healings of the crippled

§ 5. *The Conquest and Colonization of Carlisle.* CHAP. III.
1092.

It was seemingly from this fruitless gathering at Lin- William's conquest of Carlisle.
coln that William the Red went forth to what was in
truth the greatest exploit of his reign. He went on a
strange errand, to enlarge the bounds of England by
overthrowing the last shadow of independent English
rule. Hitherto the northern border of England had shown
a tendency to fall back rather than to advance, and a
generation later the same tendency showed itself again.
But Rufus did what neither his father nor his brother
did ; he enlarged the actual kingdom of England by the
addition of a new shire, a new earldom—in process of
time a new bishopric—and he raised as its capital a renewed city whose calling it was to be the foremost bulwark
of England in her northern wars. Whatever any other
spot on either side of the sea may be bound to do, Carlisle,
city and earldom, is bound to pay to the Red King the
honours of a founder. And the Saxon branch of the
English people must see in him one who planted a strong
colony of their blood on the lands of men of other races,
kindred and alien. There is a certain amusement in see- Mistakes as to the position of Cumberland and Westmoreland.
ing the endless discussions in which men have entangled
themselves in order to explain the simple fact that
Cumberland and Westmoreland are not entered in Domesday, forgetful that it was just as reasonable to look
for them there as it would have been to look there for

women Leofgifu and Ælfgifu ; Remigius " huic præcipue languori se pro-
pitium dedit." A Norman, Richard by name, who tried to pull a hair
from the beard of the saint's uncorrupted body (cf. N. C. vol. iii. p. 32),
became crippled himself. But a certain deaf and dumb Jewess, who came
to blaspheme—doubtless mentally—was smitten to the earth and suddenly
endowed with hearing and speech, beginning by uttering the name of
Remigius in French. " Ex quo patet, quia non propter merita semper aut
devotionem, sed ut manifestetur gloria Dei, miracula fiunt." She was bap-
tized by Bishop Alexander, and was carried about by him hither and
thither to declare the praises of his predecessor.

CHAP. III. Caithness or the Côtentin. Cumberland and Westmoreland, by those names, formed no part of the English kingdom when the Conqueror drew up his Survey. Parts of the lands so called, those parts which till recent changes formed part, first of the diocese of York, afterwards of that of Chester, are entered in Domesday in their natural place, as parts of Yorkshire.[1] The other parts are not entered, for the simple reason that they were then no part of the kingdom of England. It was now, in the third or fourth year of William Rufus, that they became so.

History of Carlisle.

603-685.

Lugubalia or *Caerluel* was reckoned among the Roman cities of Britain. It was reckoned too among the cities of the Northumbrian realm, in the great days of that realm, from the victory of Æthelfrith at Dægsanstan to the fall of Ecgfrith at Nectansmere.[2] Then the Northumbrian power fell back from the whole land between Clyde and Solway, and all trace of Lugubalia is lost in the confused history of the land of the Northern Britons. Its site, to say the least, must have formed part of that northern British land whose king and people sought Eadward the Unconquered to father and lord.[3] It must have formed part of that well nigh first of territorial fiefs which Eadmund the Doer-of-great-deeds granted to his Scottish fellow-worker.[4] It must have formed part of the under-kingdom which so long served as an appanage for the heirs of Scottish kingship. But, amidst all these changes, though the land passed under the over-lordship of the Basileus of Britain, yet it never, from Ecgfrith to Rufus, passed under the immediate dominion of any English king. And, as far as the city itself was concerned, for the last two centuries before Rufus the site was all

---

[1] See Appendix R.

[2] See Bæda, Hist. Eccl. iv. 29. But we have a more distinct notice in the Life of Saint Cuthberht, c. 27 (ii. 101 Stevenson), of "Lugubalia civitas, quæ a populis Anglorum corrupte Luel vocatur." In Ecgfrith's day there might be seen "mœnia civitatis, fonsque in ea miro quondam Romanorum opere extractus." [3] See N. C. vol. i. pp. 58, 576. [4] Ib. vol. i. pp. 63, 580.

that was left to pass to any one. The history of Scandinavian influence in Cumberland is one of the great
puzzles of our early history. The Northman is there to
speak for himself; but it is not easy to say how and
when he came there.[1] But one result of Scandinavian
occupation or Scandinavian inroad was the overthrow
of Lugubalia. We gather that it fell, as Anderida fell
before Ælle and Cissa, as Aquæ Solis fell before Ceawlin,
as the City of the Legions fell before Æthelfrith.[2] But
now the son of the Conqueror was to be to Lugubalia
what the daughter of Ælfred had been to the City of
the Legions. The king who made the land of Carlisle
English bade the walls of Carlisle again rise, to fence in
a city of men, a colony of the Saxon land.

At this moment the land of Carlisle, defined, as we
can hardly doubt, by the limits of the ancient diocese,
was the only spot of Britain where any man of
English race ruled. Its prince, lord, earl—no definite
title is given him—was Dolfin the son of Gospatric, a
scion of the old Northumbrian princely house and sprung
by female descent from the Imperial stock of Wessex.[3]
When or how Dolfin had got possession of his lordship
we know not; but it can hardly fail to have been a
grant from Malcolm, and it must have been held by
him in the character of a man of the Scottish king.

We are not told whether either Dolfin or Malcolm had
given any new offence to William, or whether there
was any other motive for the King's action at this
moment. We can record only the event. Rufus went
northward with a great force to Carlisle. He drove out
Dolfin; he restored the forsaken city; he built the castle;
he left a garrison in it, and went southward again.[4]

---

[1] See N. C. vol. i. p. 647.

[2] Flor. Wig. 1092. "Hæc civitas, ut illis in partibus aliæ nonnullæ,
a Danis paganis ante cc. annos diruta, et usque ad id tempus mansit
deserta."   [3] See N. C. vol. iv. p. 134.

[4] Chron. Petrib. 1092. "On þisum geare se cyng W. mid mycelre fyrde

But this was not all. Not only was the restored city to be a bulwark of England, but the conquered land was to become a colony of Englishmen. Many churlish folk were sent thither with wives and cattle, to dwell in the land and to till it.[1] We thus see, what seems always to be forgotten in discussions of Cumbrian ethnology, that, at least in the immediate district of Carlisle, the last ele

Supposed
connexion
with the
making of
the New
Forest. ment in its mixed population was distinctly Saxon.[2] Ingenious writers have guessed that the men who were now settled at Carlisle were the very men who had been deprived of their homes and lands at the making of the New Forest. There is no evidence for this guess, and every likelihood is against it. Though I hold that the dispossessed land-owners and occupiers of Hampshire are not an imaginary class,[3] yet I cannot think that they can have formed so large a class as to have gone any way towards colonizing even so small a district as the old diocese of Carlisle. But it is plain that the land needed inhabitants, and that the new inhabitants were sought for in the south of England. In the Carlisle district then the order of settlement among the races of Britain is different from what it is anywhere else. Elsewhere it is Briton, Angle or Saxon, Dane or Northman. Here, as far as one can see, the order must be Briton, Angle, Pict, Northman, Saxon.

ferde horð to Cardeol, and þa burh geæðstaþelede, and þone castel arerde, and Dolfin ūt adraf, þe æror þær þæs landes weold, and þone castel mid his mannum gesette." Florence seems to connect this with the unwrought ceremony at Lincoln; "His actis, rex in Northymbriam profectus, civitatem quæ Brytannice Cairleu, Latine Lugubalia vocatur, restauravit et in ea castellum ædificavit." Orderic brings together the old and the new when he speaks (917 B) in David's time of "Carduilum validissimum oppidum, quod Julius Cæsar, ut dicunt, condidit."

[1] The Chronicler goes on; "And syððan hider suð gewænde, and mycele mænige cyrlisces folces mid wifan and mid orfe þyder sænde þær to wunigenne þæt land to tilianne." So Henry of Huntingdon, vii. 2; "Rex reædificavit civitatem Carleol, et ex australibus Angliæ partibus illuc habitatores transmisit." Florence leaves out both the colonization and the driving out of Dolfin.   [2] See Appendix R.   [3] See N. C. vol. iv. p. 858.

The land now added to England is strictly the land of
Carlisle. We do not hear the names of Cumberland or
Westmoreland till after the times with which we are
dealing. The restored city gave its name to the land, to its
earls, when it had earls, to its bishops when it had bishops.[1]
And truly of all the cities of England none is more
memorable in its own special way than that which now
for the first time became a city of united England. The
local history of Carlisle stands out beyond that of almost
any other English city on the surface of English history.
It has not, as local history so often has, to be dug out of
special records by special research. Called into fresh
being to be the bulwark of England against Scotland,
Carlisle remained the bulwark of England against Scotland
as long as England needed any bulwark on that
side. In every Scottish war, from Stephen to George
the Second, Carlisle plays its part. Nor is it perhaps
unfit that a city whose special work was to act as a
check upon the Scot should itself have in its general
look somewhat of a Scottish character. The site of the
city and castle instinctively reminds us of the sites of
Edinburgh and Stirling. It is a likeness in miniature;
but it is a likeness none the less. The hill which is
crowned by Carlisle castle is lower than the hills which
are crowned by the two famous Scottish fortresses; but
in all three cases the original city climbs the hill whose
highest point is crowned by the castle. At Carlisle the
castle stands at the northern end of the city, and its
look-out over the Eden, towards the Scottish march, is
emphatically the look-out of a sentinel. It looks out
towards the land which so long was hostile; but it
looks out also on one spot which suggests the memories
of times when Scots, Picts, and Britons may have been
there, but when they found no English or Danish adversaries
to meet them. The Roman wall avoids Lugubalia

[1] See Appendix R.

itself, though the inner line of foss, which runs some way south of the wall itself, is said to be traced along the line which divides the castle from the city. But among the most prominent points of view from the castle is Stanwix, the site of the nearest Roman station, which seems to bear about it the memory of the stones of the ancient builders. Here, on the brow of the hill, cut off by a ditch like so many headlands of the same kind, on a site which had doubtless been a place of strength for ages before the Roman came, the Red King reared the new bulwark of his realm. Of the works of his age there are still large remains; how much is the work of Rufus himself, how much of his successor, it might be hard to say. The square keep is there, though sadly disfigured by the unhappy use of the castle as a barrack; a large part of the wall, both of city and castle, is still, after many patchings and rebuildings, of Norman date; it is still in many places plainly built out of Roman stones. Here and there one is even tempted to think that some of those stones in the lower part of the wall may have stood there since Carlisle was Lugubalia. Castle and city bear about them the memories of many later times and many stirring scenes in history. But on that spot we are most called on to trace out, in church and city and castle, every scrap that reminds us of the two founders of Carlisle, the two royal sons of the Conqueror. The names which before all others live on that site are those of William who raised up city and fortress from the sleep of ages, and of Henry who completed the work by adding Carlisle to the tale of English episcopal sees.[1]

The wall and the castle.

Work of Rufus and Henry at Carlisle.

Fortunes of Henry. In the same year in which King William of England thus advanced and strengthened the borders of his

---

[1] On the bishopric, see N. C. vol. v. p. 230.

kingdom by strength of arms, his youngest brother again CHAP. III.
became a ruler of men by a nobler title.   Whatever was
the date or the length of Henry's day of distress, it came
to an end about the time of the restoration of Carlisle.
No call could be more honourable than that which again
set him in a place of power.   Among the many victims Domfront
of Robert of Bellême were the people of Domfront, the Robert of
old conquest of William the Great.   The castle had Bellême.
passed into the hands of the tyrant, and grievous was
the oppression which Domfront and the coasts thereof
suffered at his hands.   The inhabitants, under the lead The men of
of a chief man of the place, Harecher or Archard by choose
name, rose in revolt, and chose the banished Count of Henry to
the Côtentin as their lord and defender against the com- 1093.
mon enemy of mankind.   In company with this local
patriot, Henry came to Domfront; he accepted the
offered lordship, and entered into the closest relations
with those who had chosen him.   He bound himself to
respect all their local customs, and never to give them
over to any other master.   Henry kept his word; amidst
all changes, he clave to Domfront for the rest of his days
as a specially cherished possession.[1]

It was indeed, both in its position and in its asso- Position of
ciations, a noble starting-point for one who had to Domfront.
carve out a dominion for himself by his wits or by his
sword.   It was a place of happy omen for a son of
William the Conqueror, as the place where his father
first began to deserve that title, his first possession beyond the elder bounds of his own duchy.[2]   Henry was
now lord of the rocky peninsula, which, impregnable as
it had once been deemed, had yielded to the terror of his
father's name, and where the donjon of his father's
rearing opened its doors to receive his greatest son as a
prince and a deliverer.   On one side, the Varenne flowed

---

[1] On Henry's election at Domfront, see Appendix P.
[2] See N. C. vol. ii. p. 287 ; vol. iii. p. 165.

CHAP. III. far beneath the rock, parting it from the wilder rocks beyond the stream. On the other side, on the same level as the castle, but with a slight dip between the two, just like the dip which parts town and castle at Notting-ham,[1] was the walled town, in after days itself a mighty fortress, girded with double walls and towers in thick array, and entered by a grim and frowning gateway with two massive flanking towers grounded on the solid rock. But, of all spots in the world, Domfront is one whose lord could never bear to be lord of Domfront only. From few spots not fixed on actual Alps or Pyrenees can the eye range over a wider prospect than it ranges over from the castle steep of Henry's new lordship. To the north the view is by comparison shut in; but on this side lies the way into the true heart of Normandy, to Caen and Bayeux and all that lies be-tween. To the west the eye catches the hills of the Avranchin; to the south the land of Maine stretches far away, the land of his father's victories at Ambrières and at Mayenne, the land whose sight suggests that the land of Anjou lies yet beyond it. To the south Henry might look on lands which were to be the inheritance of his children; to the north he looked on lands which were one day to be his own; but to the south-west, towards Mortain and Avranches and the Archangel's Mount, his eye might light on a region some of the most famous spots of which he was presently to win with his own right hand.

Change in Henry's affairs.

His old friends join him.

Earl Hugh.

For the tide in Henry's affairs turned fast, as soon as the wanderer of the Vexin became the chosen lord of Domfront. His old friends in his former principality began to flock around him once more. Earl Hugh was again on his side, with Richard of Redvers and the rest.[2]

And he had now a mightier friend than all. King

[1] See N. C. vol. iv. p. 198.   [2] See Appendix P.

William of England soon found out that he had not ^{CHAP. III.}
played a wise part for his own interests, or at least for ^{Henry re-}
his own plans, in strengthening his elder brother at the ^{stored to William's}
expense of the younger. He was now again scheming ^{favour.}
against Robert; he therefore favoured the growth of the ^{Henry at}
new power on the Cenomannian border. It was with the ^{war with Robert.}
Red King's full sanction that Domfront became the
head-quarters of a warfare which Henry waged against
both Roberts, the Duke and the tyrant of Bellême.[1] He
made many expeditions, which were largely rewarded
with plunder and captives, and in the course of which
some picturesque incidents happened which may call for
some notice later in our story.[2] For the present we are
concerned rather with the re-establishment of Henry's
power, of which his possession of Domfront was at once
the earnest and the beginning. Favoured by William, ^{He gets}
helped by his former friends, Henry was soon again a ^{back his county.}
powerful prince, lord of the greater part of his old
county of Coutances and Avranches. And this dominion
was secured on his southern border by the occupation of
another fortress almost as important as Domfront itself,
and no less closely connected with the memory of
Henry's father.

This was the castle of Saint James, the stronghold ^{Castle of}
which the Conqueror reared to guard the Breton march,[3] ^{Saint James oc-}
which stands close on that dangerous frontier, in the ^{cupied by Henry.}
southernmost part of the land of Avranches. That hilly
and wooded land puts on at this point a somewhat
bolder character. A peninsular hill with steep sides, ^{Its}
and with a rushing beck, the Beuvron, between itself ^{position.}
and the opposite heights, was a point which the eye of
William the Great had marked out as a fitting site for a
border-castle. Yet the castle did not occupy the exact
spot where one would have looked for it. We should have

---

[1] See Appendix P.   [2] See Appendix P.   [3] See N.C. vol. iii. p. 253.

thought to find it at the very head of the promontory, commanding the valley on all sides. It is so at Ballon; it is not so at Saint Cenery or at Conches. But in a more marked way than either of these, the castle of Saint James stood on one side of the hill, the south side certainly, the side looking towards the dangerous land, but still not occupying the most commanding position of all. In this choice of a site we may perhaps see a mark of the Conqueror's respect for religion. The ecclesiastical name of the place shows that, in William's day, the church of Saint James already occupied the lofty site which its successor still keeps. Castle-builders less scrupulous than the great William might perhaps have ventured, like Geoffrey of Mayenne at Saint Cenery,[1] to build their fortress on the holy ground. The Conqueror had been content with the less favourable part of the hill, and at Saint James, as at Conches, church and castle stood side by side. The natural beauty of the site cannot pass away; the look-out over the valley on either side is fairer and more peaceful now than it was in William's day; but every care has been taken to destroy or to mutilate all that could directly remind us of the days when Saint

Slight re-
mains of
the castle.

James was a stronghold of dukes and kings. The elder church has given way to a structure strangely made up of modern buildings and ancient fragments. The tower of the Conqueror still gives its name to the Place of the Fort; but there are no such remains as we see in the shattered keep of Domfront, hardly such remains as may be traced out at Saint Cenery and on the Rock of Mabel. A line of wall to the south, strengthening the scarped hill-side like the oldest walls of Rome, is all that is left to speak to us of the castle which was William's most famous work on that border of his dominions. Nothing beyond these small scraps is left of the fortress whose

---

[1] See above, p. 213.

building led to that memorable march against the Breton chap. iii.
in which William and Harold fought as fellow-soldiers.[1]

We are not told what were Henry's relations with The castle
Britanny at the time when this great border fortress granted to Earl Hugh.
passed into his hands. Bretons had been his only
friends at the time of the siege of the Mount; but their
friendship for the Count of the Côtentin was perhaps
felt for him, not so much in that character as in that of
the enemy of the Norman Duke and the English King.
It may possibly mark a feeling that the Celtic peninsula
might again become a dangerous land, when the guardianship of the chief bulwark against the *Bretwealas* of the
mainland was given to one who had full experience of
warfare with the *Bretwealas* of the great island. The
Earl of Chester had a hereditary call to be the keeper
of the castle of Saint James. The fortress had, on its
first building, been entrusted by the Conqueror to the
guardianship of Earl Hugh's father, the Viscount Richard
of Avranches. Hugh's treason when King and Duke
came against him was now forgotten; his earlier and
later services were remembered; and the restored prince,
now once more Count as well as Ætheling, granted the
border castle, not as a mere castellanship, but as his own
proper fief, to the lord of the distant City of the Legions.[2]

We have thus seen the power of William the Red
firmly established on both sides of the sea. He had
received the homage of Scotland; he had enlarged the

---

[1] See N. C. vol. iii. p. 228.

[2] Will. Gem. viii. 4. "Quia in hoc negotio et in aliisque plerisque suis
necessitatibus Hugo comes Cestrensis ei fidelis exstiterat, concessit ei ex
integro castellum quod sancti Jacobi appellatum est, in quo idem comes
tunc temporis nihil aliud habebat, præter custodiam munitionis istius
oppidi." He goes on to describe the building of the castle, in words partly
borrowed from William of Poitiers, and the grant to Richard of Avranches.
On Richard, see N. C. vol. ii. pp. 209, 296.

CHAP. III. bounds of England; he had won for himself a Norman
dominion hemming in the dominions which are left to
the nominal sovereign of the Norman land. And it is
wonderful with how little fighting all this had been done.
It was only before the island rock of Saint Michael that
the chivalrous King had any opportunity of winning
renown by feats of chivalry. A year follows, crowded
with events, but all of them events which happened within
the four seas of our own island. Our next chapter will
therefore deal mainly with English affairs, and with some
aspects of English affairs which yield in importance to
none in the whole history of England. One of the chief
personages of our story now comes before us in the form
of the holy Anselm. Few more striking personal contrasts are to be found in the whole range of history than
those parts of our tale where Anselm and William meet
face to face. But more memorable still, in a general
aspect of English history, is the work which has been
silently going on ever since William Rufus was made
fast on his throne, the work which stands broadly forth
as a finished thing when the controversy between King
and Primate begins. Assuredly no "feudal system" was
ever introduced into England by any law of William
the Great; but it is only a slight stretch of language
to say that something which, if any one chooses, may
be called a "feudal system" was, during these years,
devised in and for England by the craft and subtlety
of Randolf Flambard.

CHAPTER IV.

THE PRIMACY OF ANSELM AND THE ACQUISITION
OF NORMANDY.[1]

1093–1097.

THE story of the first five years of the Red King's reign may be written with little, if any, forsaking of strict chronological order. The accession, the rebellion, the affairs of Normandy, the affairs of Scotland, Character of the early years of William Rufus. 1087-1092.

[1] During this chapter, the authorities for the life of Anselm become of primary importance. We have the invaluable help of the two works of Anselm's friend and faithful companion, the English monk Eadmer, afterwards Bishop-elect of Saint Andrews. Both Orderic and William of Malmesbury speak of Eadmer with the deepest reverence, and cut short their own accounts of Anselm, referring to his. He first wrote the *Historia Novorum*, and then the *Vita Anselmi* as a kind of supplement, to bring in certain points more purely personal to his hero. The subject of the *Historia Novorum* we might call "Anselm and his Times." The subject of the *Vita* is naturally Anselm himself. Eadmer's history is of course most minute and most trustworthy for all that concerns Anselm; other matters he cuts short. In most cases one can see his reasons; but it is not easy to see why he should have left out the mission of Geronto recorded by Hugh of Flavigny (see Appendix AA). Along with the works of Eadmer, we have also a precious store in the Letters of Anselm himself (see Appendix Y), which, besides the picture which they give of the man, throw a flood of light on the history. All these materials, with the other writings of Anselm, will be found in two volumes of Migne's Patrologia, 158 and 159. I have used this edition for the Letters and for the Life; the *Historia Novorum* I have gone on quoting in the edition of Selden.

I need hardly say that Anselm's English career, with which alone I am concerned, is only one part of his many-sided character. I have kept mainly to the history of Anselm in England; I have cut short both his early life and even the time of his first banishment. With his theology and philosophy I have not ventured to meddle at all. Anselm has had no lack of biographers from the more general point of view; Hasse (Anselm von Canterbury, Leipzig, 1852), Charles de Rémusat (Saint Anselme de Cantorbéry, Paris, 1853), Charma (Saint-Anselme, Paris, 1853), Croset-Mouchet (S. Anselme

follow one another in successive or nearly successive
years, as the main subjects which challenge our atten-
Chronolo- tion.   One set of events leads to another.   The rebellion
gical se-
quence of followed naturally on the accession ; the interference of
the history. Rufus in Normandy followed naturally on the rebellion ;
the Scottish invasion seems to have been the immediate
occasion of the banishment of Eadgar from Normandy.
But during the whole of the five years there is no great
interlacing of different parts of the main story; at no
stage are two distinct sets of events of equal moment
going on at the same time; the historian is hardly called
on to forsake the arrangement of the annalist.   While
the events recorded by the annalist were in doing, some
of the greatest changes in English history were silently
going on; but they were not changes of a kind which
More com- could be set down in the shape of annals.   From the
plicated
character end of the year which saw the restoration of Carlisle the
of the next
period. nature of the story changes.   Different scenes of the
1093-1098. drama of equal importance are now acting at once.
For the next five years we have three several lines of
contemporary story, which are now and then inter-

d'Aoste, Archevêque de Cantorbéry, Paris, 1859).   I have made some use
of all these ; but the value even of Hasse and De Rémusat for my strictly
English purpose is not great.   M. Croset-Mouchet writes with a pleasant
breeze of local feeling from the Prætorian Augusta, but he is utterly at sea
as to everything in our island.

In our own tongue the life of Anselm has been treated by a living and a
dead friend of my own, holding the same rank in the English Church.   Dean
Hook, I must say with regret, utterly failed to do justice to Anselm.
This is the more striking, as he did thorough justice to Thomas.   From Dr.
Hook's point of view it needed an effort to do justice to either, a smaller
effort in the case of Anselm, a greater in the case of Thomas.   As sometimes
happens, he made the greater effort, but not the smaller.   I am however able
to say that he came to know Anselm better before he died.   Dean Church,
on the other hand, has given us an almost perfect example of a short sketch
of such a subject.   The accuracy of the tale is as remarkable as the beauty
of the telling.   It lacks only the light which is thrown on the story of Anselm
by the earlier story of William of Saint-Calais.   It is most important to
remember that Anselm was not the first to appeal to the Pope.

twined, but which on the whole did not seriously affect one another. Each is best told by itself, with as little reference to either of the others as may be. And each begins in the year of which we have now reached the threshold. The sixth year of William Rufus saw the beginning of the primacy of Anselm, the beginning of the main dealings of the reign with Wales and Scotland, the beginning of renewed interference in the Norman duchy. It will be well to keep these three lines of narrative as distinct as may be. They show the Red King in three different characters. In the first story he appears as the representative of the new form which the kingship of England has taken with reference both to temporal and to spiritual matters within the kingdom. In the second story we see him asserting the powers of the English crown beyond the kingdom of England, but within the island of Britain. And here, alongside of the affairs of Scotland, perhaps not very closely connected with them by any chain of cause and effect, but forming one general subject with them as distinguished alike from purely domestic and from continental affairs, will come the relations between England and Wales during the reign of William Rufus. In the third story we see the beginning of the events which led to those wider schemes of continental policy which almost wholly occupy the last three years of the reign. One event only of much moment stands apart from the general thread of any of the three stories. It stands by itself, as one of those events which might easily have led to great changes, but which, as a matter of fact, passed away without much result. This is the conspiracy and revolt of Robert of Mowbray and William of Eu, which may, dramatically at least, be connected with either the Scottish or the Norman story, but which, as a matter of actual English history, stands apart from all.

CHAP. IV.

Three distinct sets of contemporary events.

Aspects of Rufus with regard to each.

Primacy of Anselm.

Affairs of Scotland and Wales.

Continental schemes.

Revolt of Robert of Mowbray. 1095.

CHAP. IV.

Relations between Rufus and Anselm. Working of the new ideas.

Of these three the first on the list must claim the precedence. The relations between Rufus and Anselm involve the whole civil and ecclesiastical policy of the reign. The dispute between King and Primate was the outcome of all that had been working in silence while the Red King was winning castles in Normandy, receiving the homage of Scotland, and enlarging the bounds of England. During those years one side of the results of the Norman Conquest was put into formal shape. Between the fall of Rochester and the restoration of Carlisle, new ideas, new claims, had come to their full

New position of the King.

growth. Those ideas, those claims, had made the kingship of William the Red something marked by not a few points of difference from the kingship either of the Con-

Ecclesiastical position of the Conqueror.

fessor or of the Conqueror. Nowhere does the difference between the elder and the younger William stand forth more clearly than in their dealings with the spiritual power. No king, as I have often shown, was more truly Supreme Governor of the Church within his realm than was the Conqueror of England, her defender against the

William and Lanfranc.

claims of Rome. But William the Great sought and found his fellow-worker in all things in an archbishop likeminded with himself. We can hardly conceive the reign of the Conqueror without the primacy of Lan-

Opposite conduct of Rufus.

franc. But the great object of William the Red was to avoid the restraints which could not fail to be placed upon his self-will, if he had one standing at his side whose place it was to be at once the chief shepherd of the English Church and the tribune of the English

Vacancy of the see of Canterbury. 1089-1093.

people. For three years and more from the death of Lanfranc the see of Canterbury remained vacant. Such a vacancy was without precedent; but it was designed itself to become a precedent. It was by no accident, from no momentary cause, that William delayed the appointment of any successor to his old guardian and coun-

sellor. It was part of a deliberate policy affecting the CHAP. IV.
whole ecclesiastical and civil institutions of the realm. Its policy.
And that policy, there can be little doubt, was the device Influence
of a single subtle and malignant genius by whom the of Randolf
Flambard.
whole internal administration of the Red King's reign
was guided.

§ 1. *The Administration of Randolf Flambard.*
1089–1099.

The chief minister, if we may so call him, of William
Rufus, during these years, and indeed to the end of his
reign, was that Randolf Flambard or Passeflambard of
whom we have already heard.[1] His early history is Early history of
not easy to trace, beyond the general fact that he rose Flambard.
to power by the same path by which so many others
rose in his day, by service in the King's chapel and
chancery.[2] It has been generally thought that he was Said to
settled in England as early as the days of Eadward; have been
settled in
but it may be doubted whether the evidence bears out England
T. R. E.
this belief. And the course of his life is certainly easier to
understand, if we do not bring him into England so soon,
or attribute to him so great a length of life, as we must
do if we look on him as having been already a land-
owner in England before the Conquest.[3] On the other Said to
have been
hand, if we accept the story which makes him pass to in the
the King's service from the service of Maurice Bishop of service of
Bishop
London, he must have been the King's clerk for so short Maurice
a time before the death of the Conqueror as hardly to [Bishop of
London
give room for the usual stages of official promotion. 1086–
1107].
Another version places him in the King's service from his
earliest years.[4] Perhaps we may guess that the name of

---

[1] See N. C. vol. v. p. 131.   [2] Ib. p. 135.
[3] Ib. vol. iv. p. 521, and see Appendix S.
[4] See the extract from Orderic (678 C) in Appendix S.

CHAP. IV. the Bishop of London is wrongly given, and that Flambard had really been in the service of one of Maurice's predecessors, of Hugh of Orival or of the more famous William. His reason for leaving his episcopal patron is said to have been that a deanery which he held was taken from him, a story which oddly connects itself with another, according to which he was at one time dean or other head of the canons of Twinham—better known as Christchurch—in Hampshire.[1] The story, true or false, like the earlier life of Thomas of London, illustrates the way in which the highest ecclesiastical preferments short of bishoprics and abbeys were held by these clerical servants of kings and bishops. Clerical they often were only in the widest sense; they were sometimes merely tonsured, and they seldom took priest's orders till they were themselves promoted to bishoprics.[2] Randolf Flambard however was a priest;[3] he could therefore discharge the duties of his deanery in person, if he ever troubled himself to go near it. Otherwise there was very little of the churchman, or indeed of the Christian, about the future Bishop of Durham and builder of Saint Cuthberht's nave. At all events it was wholly by his personal qualities, such as they were, that Randolf Flambard made his way to the highest places in Church and State. In his day the Church supplied the readiest opening for the service of the State, and service to the State was again rewarded by all but the highest honours of the Church.

The man who was practically to rule England had at least little advantage on the score of birth. He is set

Marginal notes:

Said to have held the deanery of Twinham.

Preferments held by the clerks of kings and bishops.

Flambard a priest.

Character of Flambard.

His parents.

---

[1] See Appendix S.

[2] So Liebermann truly remarks (Einleitung in den Dialogus de Scaccario, 40). He adds; " Diese pflegten die Priesterweihe möglichst spät zu empfangen; desto eifriger erjagten sie fette Pfründen."

[3] Florence (1100) notices emphatically that the doings of Flambard were done " contra jus ecclesiasticum, et sui gradus ordinem, presbyter enim erat." So he is marked by Anselm (Epp. iv. 2) as " sacerdos."

before us as the son of a low-born priest in the diocese CHAP. IV.
of Bayeux and of a mother who bore the character of a
witch, and who was reported to have lost an eye through
the agency of the powers with which she was too
familiar.[1] Handsome in person, ready of wit, free of
speech and of hand, unlearned, loose of life, clever and
unscrupulous in business of every kind, he made friends
and he made enemies; but he rose. The surname which The name
cleaves to him in various shapes and spellings is said to *Flambard.*
have been given to him in the court of the Conqueror by
the *dispenser* Robert, because he pushed himself on at the
expense of his betters, like a burning flame.[2] But his His finan-
genius lay most of all in the direction of finance, in cial skill.
days when finance meant to transfer, by whatever means,
the greatest amount of the subject's money into the
coffers of the King. One story describes him as sent Mention of
on such an errand by the Conqueror into the lands of the Con-
his future bishopric, and as smitten for his crime by queror's
the wonder-working hand of Saint Cuthberht himself.[3] His share
There is every reason to believe that he had a hand in in Domes-
drawing up the Great Survey.[4] But, while William the day.
Great lived, he seems not to have risen to any high
place. Towards the end of his reign the Conqueror did
begin to give away bishoprics to his own clerks,[5] but
still hardly to such clerks as Randolf Flambard. Nor

---

[1] See Appendix S. The story about Flambard's mother, which Sir
Francis Palgrave suggests may have come from a ballad, is told by Orderic
in another place (787 A); " Mater, quæ sortilega erat et cum dæmone
crebro locuta, ex cujus nefaria familiaritate unum oculum amiserat." One
thinks of a later dabbler in mischief; " Our minnie's sair mis-set, after her
ordinar, sir—she'll hae had some quarrel wi' her auld gudeman—that's
Satan, ye ken, sirs." William of Malmesbury (Gesta Regum, iv. 314)
calls him " fomes cupiditatum, Ranulfus clericus, ex infimo genere hominum
lingua et calliditate provectus ad summum." In the Gesta Pontificum, 274,
he is more guarded, and says only " ex quo ambiguum genere."

[2] See Appendix S. [3] See N. C. vol. iv. p. 522.
[4] See Stubbs, Const. Hist. i. 348. [5] See N. C. vol. iv. p. 687.

CHAP. IV. did the Conqueror need a minister, in the sense of needing one who should in some sort fill his place and exercise his powers. The elder William could rule his kingdom himself, or at most with the advice of the special counsellor whom ancient custom gave him in the person of Lanfranc. But the younger William, sultan-like in his mood, needed, like other sultans, the help of a vizier. And he found the fittest of all viziers for his purpose in the supple clerk from the Bessin.

His rise under Rufus.

The reign of Flambard seems to have begun as soon as Lanfranc was gone. He thoroughly suited the Red King's views. He was ready to gather in wealth for his master from every quarter; he knew how to squeeze the most out of rich and poor; when a tax of a certain amount was decreed, he knew how to make it bring in double its nominal value.[1] He alone thoroughly knew his art; no one else, said the laughing King, cared so little whose hatred he brought on himself, so that he only pleased his master.[2] He stands charged in one account of his deeds with declaring the Great Survey to be drawn up on principles not favourable enough to the royal hoard, and with causing it to be supplanted by a new inquisition which made the Red King richer than his father.[3] This story is very doubtful; but it is thoroughly in character. In any case Flambard rose to the highest measure both of power and of official dignity that was open to him. His office and its duties are described in various ways; in that age official titles and functions

His alleged new Domesday.

His official position.

---

[1] Will. Malms. iv. 314. "Is, si quando edictum regium processisset ut nominatum tributum Anglia penderet, duplum adjiciebat."

[2] Ib. "Subinde, cachinnantibus quibusdam ac dicentibus, solum esse hominem qui sciret sic agitare ingenium nec aliorum curaret odium dummodo complacaret dominum." This is one of the passages where William of Malmesbury thought it wise to soften what he first wrote. For "cachinnantibus quibusdam ac dicentibus" some manuscripts read "cachinnante rege ac dicente."   [3] See Appendix U.

were less accurately distinguished than they were a little chap. iv.
later.[1] But there seems no doubt that Flambard, the He holds
lawyer whom none could withstand,[2] held the formal the Justi-ciarship.
office of Justiciar. Till his time that post had not, as
a distinct office, reached the full measure of its greatness.
It was Flambard himself who raised it to the height of Growth of
power and dignity which accompanied it when it was the office under him.
held by Roger of Salisbury and Randolf of Glanville.
He was to the post of Justiciar what Thomas of London
two generations later was to the post of Chancellor; he
was the man who knew how to magnify his office.[3] In His
that office "he drave all the King's gemóts over all Eng- "driving" of the
land."[4] The King's thegns who had come to the local Gemóts.
assembly on the King's errand in the days of Æthelred
and Cnut[5] had now grown into a mighty and terrible
power. How Flambard drave the gemóts we learn elsewhere. He was fierce alike to the suppliant and to the
rebel.[6] Suppliant and rebel alike were in his eyes useful
only as means for further filling the mighty chest at Winchester. Strangely enough, he himself, clerk and Norman He loses
as he was, had found neither birth nor order protect him his land for the New
when the Conqueror had needed a part of his land for the Forest.
creation of the New Forest.[7] On the principle that man His zeal
is ever most ready to inflict on others the wrongs which for the King's
he has borne himself, Flambard, who himself in some interests.

---

[1] See N. C. vol. v. p. 430.

[2] Will. Malms. iv. 314. "Invictus causidicus, et tam verbis tam rebus immodicus." One thinks of Lanfranc's successes in the law-courts of Pavia (see N. C. vol. ii. p. 226); but knowledge of the Imperial law was a matter of professional learning; with the simpler law of England age and experience were enough.

[3] See Stubbs, Const. Hist. i. 384, and Appendix T.

[4] Chron. Petrib. 1099. "Rannulfe his capellane ... þe æror ealle his gemot ofer eall Engleland draf and bewiste."

[5] See N. C. vol. v. p. 445.

[6] Will. Malms. iv. 314. "Juxta in supplices ut in rebelles furens."

[7] See Appendix T.

sort ranked among the disinherited, was of all ministers of the royal will the most eager to draw the heritage of every man, without respect to birth or order, into the hands of the master whom he served too faithfully.

But we shall altogether misunderstand both Flambard and his master, if we take either of them for vulgar spoilers, living as it were from hand to mouth, and casually grasping any sources of gain which chanced to be thrown in their way. Whatever Flambard did he did according to rule and system; nay more, he did it according to the severest rules of logic. Amidst the vague declamations which set him before us as the general robber of all men, we light on particular facts and phrases which give us the clue to the real nature of his doings. It is worth notice that, in more than one picture, the rich are enlarged on as the special victims of his extortions; in one the Ætheling Henry himself is spoken of as having suffered deeply at his hands.[1] We may guess that this has some special reference to the way in which Henry was defrauded of the lands of his mother, a business in which Flambard is likely enough to have had a share.[2] These references to the wrongs done to the rich have their significance; they point to a cunningly devised system of Flambard's, by which, the greater a man's estate was, the more surely was he marked for extortion. The legislation of Flambard, if we can call that legislation which seems never to have been set down in any formal statute,[3] was not at all of the kind which catches the small flies and lets the large ones get through. As we have seen in some other cases,[4] a seemingly casual expression of our native

His changes and exactions systematic.

His alleged spoliation of the rich.

His dealings with the Ætheling Henry.

Witness of the Chronicle.

---

[1] See the extract from Orderic, 786 C, in Appendix T.

[2] See above, p. 198.　　　　　　　[3] See N. C. vol. v. p. 398.

[4] As in the case of the general redemption of lands (see N. C. vol. iv. p. 25) and the great confiscation and distribution in the midwinter Gemót of 1067 (ib. p. 127).

Chronicler is the best record of a matter of no small CHAP. IV.
constitutional importance. The Red King "would be The King
ilk man's heir, ordered and lewd."[1] In those words lay everyman's
the whole root of the matter. The great work of the heir.
administration of Flambard, the great work of the reign lasting
of Rufus, was to put in order a system of rules by burthens
which the King might be the heir of every man. Those exactions.
few words, which might seem to have dropped from
the Chronicler in a moment of embittered sarcasm, do
indeed set forth the formal beginning of a series of
burthens and exactions under which Englishmen, and
preeminently the rich and noble among Englishmen,
groaned for not much less than six hundred years after
Flambard's days.

In short the "unrighteousness" ordained by William The Feudal
Rufus and Randolf Flambard[2] are no other than those Tenures.
feudal tenures and feudal burthens which even the Par- Abolished
liament which elected Charles the Second, in the midst of 1660.
its self-abasement and betrayal of its own ancient rights,
declared to have been "much more burthensome, grievous, and prejudicial to the kingdom than they have
been beneficial to the king."[3] Assuredly they were as
burthensome, grievous, and prejudicial to the kingdom
in the eleventh century as they were in the seventeenth;
but assuredly they were found in the eleventh century
to be highly beneficial to the King, or they would not
have been ordained by Rufus and Flambard. We have Tenure in
reached the age of chivalry; and tenure in chivalry, chivalry.

[1] Chron. Petrib. 1100. "Forðan þe he ælces mannes gehadodes and
læwedes yrfenuma beon wolde."

[2] William of Malmesbury (v. 393) seems to sum up the reforms of
Henry in the words "injustitias a fratre et Rannulfo institutas prohibuit."
"Justitiæ" is a technical phrase (see N. C. vol. iv. pp. 559, 560). "Injus-
titiæ," as here used, is something like our "unlaw" and "ungeld."

[3] Revised Statutes, i. 725. By some chance this statute is printed in
this collection, which commonly leaves out the statutes which are of most
historical importance.

CHAP. IV. with all its mean and pettifogging incidents, was put into a systematic form for the special benefit of the coffers of the king who was before all things the good knight, the *preux chevalier,* the *probus miles.* The King "would be the heir of ilk man, ordered and lewd." To

Wardship. that end the estate of the minor heir was to be made a prey; he was himself to be begged and granted and sold

Marriage. like an ox or an ass;[1] the heiress, maid or widow, was in the like sort to be begged and granted, sold into unwilling wedlock, or else forced to pay the price which a chivalrous tenure demanded for the right either to remain unmarried or to marry according to her own will.

Dealings with bishoprics and abbeys. The bishopric or the abbey was to be left without a pastor, and its lands were to be let to farm for the King's profit, because the King would be the heir of the priest as well as of the layman. That all this, in its fully developed

Agency of Flambard in systematizing the feudal tenures. and systematic form, was the work of Randolf Flambard, I hope I may now assume. I have argued the point at some length elsewhere,[2] and I need not now do more

The evidence. than pass lightly over some of the main points. Certain tendencies, certain customs, of which, under the Con-

Henry's charters. queror and even before the Conqueror, we see the germs, but only the germs, appear at the accession of Henry the First as firmly established rules, which Henry does not promise wholly to abolish, while he does promise to redress their abuses. It follows that they had put on their systematic shape in the intermediate time, that is, during the reign of Rufus. One of these abuses, that which for obvious reasons was most largely dwelled on by our authorities, namely the new way of dealing with ecclesiastical property, is distinctly spoken of as a

---

[1] I borrow this phrase from the story of Count William of Evreux in Orderic, 814 C (see Appendix K), though he was not to be given in quite the same sense.

[2] See N.C. vol. v. pp. 373-381.

novelty, and a novelty of Flambard's devising. The CHAP IV.
obvious inference is that the whole system, a system
which logically hangs together in the most perfect way,
was the device of the same subtle and malignant brain.
And having got thus far, we are now enabled to see the Import-
full force of those seemingly casual expressions in the ance of
writers of the time of which I have already spoken. It casual
phrases.
was the royal claims of relief, of wardship, and marriage, systematically and mercilessly enforced, no less
than the royal claim to enjoy the fruits of vacant
ecclesiastical benefices, which are branded in Latin as
the *injustitiæ* of Rufus and Flambard, and which in
our own tongue take the shape of the King's claim to be
the heir of every man.

This last pithy phrase takes in all the new claims
which were now set up over all lands, whether held
by spiritual or temporal owners, and, in some cases at
least, over personal property also. All the "unrighteousnesses," all "the evil customs," which the charter of
Henry promises to reform[1] come under this one head.
In Flambard's system of tenure there could be no such Flambard's
thing as an ancient *eðel* or *allod*, held of no lord, and theory of
land-hold-
burthened only with such payments or duties as the ing.
law might lay upon its owner. With him all land was in
the strictest sense *loanland*.[2] The owner had at most
a life-interest in it; at his death it fell back to the king,
for the king was to be the heir of every man. The king Relief and
might grant it to the son of the last owner; but, if so, it redemption.
was by a fresh grant,[3] for which the new grantee had
to pay. And the terms of Henry's charter imply that

See the charter of Henry, Select Charters, 97; "Et omnes malas consuetudines quibus regnum Angliae injuste opprimebatur inde aufero, quas
malas consuetudines ex parte hic pono." He then goes through the grievances
in order, relief, marriage, wardship, and the rest.

[2] I borrow our ancient word *lœnland*, which survives in the German
lehn.   [3] See N. C. vol. v. pp. 379, 867.

CHAP. IV. the payment was arbitrary and extortionate. Henry promises that the heir of a tenant-in-chief shall not be constrained to *redeem*—to buy back—his father's lands as had been done in his brother's time; he shall *relieve* them by a just and lawful relief.[1] Under Rufus then it was held that the land had, by the former holder's death, actually passed to the king, as the common heir of all men, and that, if the son or other representative of the former holder wished to possess it, he must, in the strictest sense, buy it back from the king. Henry acknowledges the rights of the heir, while still maintaining the theory of the fresh grant. The heir is not to *redeem*—to buy back—his father's land; he is merely to *relieve* it—to take it up again, and he is to pay only the sum prescribed by legal custom, the equivalent of the ancient heriot or the modern succession-duty. So it is

Dealings with men's wills.

with personal property. The Red King, it is plain, claimed to be the heir of men's money, as well as of their land. For one of Henry's promised reforms is that the wills of his barons and others his men shall stand good, that their money shall go to the purposes to which they may have bequeathed it, and that, if they die without wills, their wives, children, kinsfolk, or lawful men, shall dispose of it as they may think best for the dead man's soul.[2] Such a reform could not have been needed unless William Rufus had been in the habit of interfering with

Older theory of wills.

men's free right of bequest. And it might have been plausibly argued that the right of bequest was no natural

---

[1] Select Charters, 97. "Si quis baronum, comitum meorum sive aliorum qui de me tenent, mortuus fuerit, hæres suus non *redimet* terram suam sicut faciebat tempore fratris mei, sed justa et legitima relevatione *relevabit* eam."

[2] Ib. "Et si quis baronum vel hominum meorum infirmabitur, sicut ipse dabit vel dare disponet pecuniam suam, ita datam esse concedo. Quod si ipse præventus armis vel infirmitate, pecuniam suam non dederit vel dare disposuerit, uxor sua sive liberi aut parentes, et legitimi homines ejus, eam pro anima ejus dividant, sicut eis melius visum fuerit."

right of man, that the most ancient legal doctrine both CHAP. IV.
of Rome and of England was that a will was an exceptional act, which needed the confirmation of the sovereign power. If such a doctrine had anyhow come to the
knowledge of Flambard, it would assuredly seem to him
a natural inference that no such confirmation should be
granted save at such a price as the king might see fit to
demand.

But of all the devices of Flambard, there was one which, Wardship.
it would seem, was specially his own, one which was at
once the most oppressive of all and that which followed
most logically from the nature of feudal tenure. This
was the lord's right of wardship. This claim starts from
the undoubted doctrine that the fief is after all only a
conditional possession of its holder, that he holds it only
on the terms of discharging the military service which is
due from it. Nothing was easier than to argue that, when
the fief passed to an heir who was from his youth incapable
of discharging that service, the fief should go back into
the lord's hands till the heir had reached the time of life
when he could discharge it. The abuses and oppressions
which such a right led to need hardly be dwelled on; they
are written in every page of our legal history from the
days of Rufus to the days of Charles the First. Nothing
now enriches an estate like a long minority; in those
times the heir, when at last he came into possession,
found his estate impoverished in every way by the temporary occupation of the king or of the king's favourite
to whom the wardship had been granted or sold. Yet it Its logical
cannot be denied that the argument by which the right character.
of wardship was established was, as a piece of legal
argument, quite unanswerable. And of all the feudal
exactions certainly none was more profitable. The Its
tenant-in-chief who died, perhaps fighting in the king's oppressive
working.
cause, and who left an infant son behind him, had the

CHAP. IV. comfort of thinking that his estate would, perhaps for the next twenty years, go to enrich the coffers of his sovereign.   On this head Henry speaks less clearly than he speaks on some other points; but his words certainly seem to imply that the wardship of the tenant-in-chief was to go, not to the king, but to the mother or to some kinsman.[1] If so, either Henry himself or his successors thought better of the matter.   The right of wardship, as a privilege of the king or other lord, appears in full force in the law-book of Randolf of Glanville.[2]

Extent of Flambard's changes.

When we attribute all these exactions and "unrighteousnesses" to the device of Flambard, it is of course not meant that they were altogether unheard of either before his day or beyond the lands over which his influence reached.   Traces of these claims, or of some of them, are to be found wherever and whenever feudal notions about the tenure of land had crept in.   All that is meant is that claims which were vaguely growing up were put by Flambard into a distinct and systematic shape.   What William the Great did on occasion, for reasons of state, William the Red did as a matter of course, as an ordinary means of making money.[3]   And it is significant that two of the most oppressive of these claims, that of wardship and the kindred claim of marriage, were, in their fully developed shape, peculiar or nearly so to the lands where Rufus reigned and Flambard governed, to the English kingdom and the Norman duchy[4]   I have said elsewhere that, of the two sides of feudalism, our Norman kings carefully shut out the side which tended to

Wardship and marriage special to England and Normandy.

The two sides of feudalism.

[1] Select Charters, 97. "Et terræ et liberorum custos erit sive uxor sive alius propinquorum qui justius esse debeat."

[2] See Tractatus de Legibus, vii. 9. 10; and Phillips, Englische Reichs- und Rechtsgeschichte, ii. 204.

[3] See N. C. vol. v. p. 374.

[4] This was pointed out by Hallam, Middle Ages, i. 128, ed. 1846.

weaken the royal power, and carefully fostered the side chap. iv. which tended to strengthen it.[1] Both sides of this process were busily at work during the reign of Rufus. The great law of the Conqueror, the law of Salisbury, which decreed that duty to the king should come before all other duties, was practically tried and practically confirmed in the struggle which showed that no man in England was strong enough to stand against the king.[2] England was not to become feudal in the sense in which Germany and France became feudal. But in all those points where the doctrines of feudal tenure could be turned to the king's enrichment, England became of all lands the most feudal. Enactor of no statute, author of no code or law-book, Randolf Flambard was in effect the lawgiver of feudalism, so far as that misleading word has any meaning at all on English soil.

England in what sense feudal.

Flambard the lawgiver of English feudalism.

All this exactly falls in with those phrases in our authorities which speak of Flambard as the spoiler of the rich, the plunderer of the inheritances of other men. It also bears out what I have said already,[3] that there is no evidence to show that Rufus was a direct oppressor of the native English as such. The subtle devices of tyranny of which we have just spoken directly concerned those only who were the King's tenants-in-chief. That is to say, they touched a class of estates which were far more largely in Norman than in English hands. Most likely, even in that reign, a numerical majority of the King's tenants-in-chief would have been found to be of English blood. But such a majority would have been chiefly made up of the very smallest members of the class; the greater landowners, those whose wrongs, under such a system, would be, if not heavier, at least more conspicuous, were mainly the

Flambard's oppression falls most directly on the greatest estates.

No special oppression of the native English.

[1] See N. C. vol. v. p. 381.
[2] See above, p. 81.   [3] See above, p. 133.

conquerors of Senlac or their sons. It was a form of oppression which would strike men as specially falling upon the rich. A special meaning is thus given to phrases which might otherwise be thought to be merely those common formulæ which, in speaking of any evil which affects all classes, join rich and poor together. The devices of Flambard were specially aimed at the

Indirect oppression of other classes.

rich. The great mass of the English people, and that large class of Normans who held their lands, not straight of the king but of some intermediate lord, were touched by them only when the lords who suffered by Flambard's exactions tried to make good their own losses by exactions of the same kind on their own tenants.

Dealings of the tenants-in-chief with their under-tenants.

That they did so is shown by the reforming charter of Henry. When he promises to deal fairly and lawfully by his barons and his other men in the matters of relief and marriage, he demands that his barons shall deal fairly and lawfully by their men in the like cases.[1] But in the first instance it was mainly the rich, mainly the Normans, whom the feudal devices of Flambard touched.

Strange submission of the nobles.

And it is not the least strange thing in these times to see a race of warlike and high-spirited nobles, conquerors or sons of conquerors, submit to so galling a yoke, a yoke which must have been all the more galling when we think of the origin and position of the man by whom it

Position of the king's clerks.

was devised. We cannot think that the king's clerks were ever a popular body with any class, high or low, native or foreign. Their position appealed to no sentiment of any kind, military, religious, or national; their rule rather implied the treading under foot of all such sentiments. The military tenants must have looked on them with the dislike which men of the sword, specially in such

---

[1] Select Charters, 97. "Similiter et homines baronum meorum justa et legitima relevatione relevabunt terras suas de dominis suis. . . . Et præcipio quod barones mei similiter se contineant erga filios et filias vel uxores hominum suorum."

an age, are apt to look on the rule of men of the pen.
In the eyes of strict churchmen they must have passed
for ungodly scorners of the decencies of their order.
To the mass of the people they must have seemed
foreign extortioners, and nothing more. They represented the power of the king, and nothing else. In
some states of things the power of the king, even of a
despotic king, may be welcomed as the representative of
law against force. But under Rufus the power of the *The reign of unlaw.*
king was before all things the representative of unlaw.
Yet though all murmured, all submitted. The son of *General submission.*
the poor priest of the Bessin, clothed with a power
purely official, lorded it over all classes and orders.
Earls, prelates, and people, were alike held down by
the guide and minister of the royal will.

One cause of this general submission is doubtless to be *Position of Rufus favourable for his schemes.*
found in the immediate circumstances of the time. The
alliance of the King and the English people had for the
moment broken the power of the Norman nobles. The
ecclesiastical estate was left without a head by the death
of Lanfranc. The popular estate was left without a head,
as soon as the King turned away from the people who
had given him his crown, and broke all the promises that
he had made to them. There was no power of combination; the great days when nobles, clergy, and commons,
could join together against the king, as three orders in
one nation, were yet far distant. Each class had to bear
its own grievances as it could; no class could get any help
from any other class; and the King's picked mercenaries,
kept at the expense of all classes, were stronger than any
one class by itself. Yet we cannot doubt that even the *Effect on national unity.*
rule of Rufus and Flambard did something towards the
great work of founding national unity. All the inhabitants of the land, if they had nothing else in common, had common grievances and a common oppressor.

CHAP. IV. For a moment we can believe that the English people would feel a certain pleasure in seeing the men who had once conquered them and whom they had more lately conquered, brought under the yoke, and under such a yoke as that of Flambard. But such a feeling would be short-lived compared with the far deeper feeling of common grievances and common enmities.

Other forms of exaction.

For the yoke of Flambard was one which, in different ways, pressed on all classes. If the native English, and the less wealthy men generally, were less directly touched by his feudal legislation than those who ranked above them, Flambard had no mind to let poor men, or native Englishmen, or any other class of men, go scot free. If his new devices pressed mainly on the great, he knew how to use the old forms of law so as to press on great and small alike. No one was too high, no one was too low, for the ministers of the King's Exchequer to keep their eyes on him. No source of profit was deemed too small or too mean, if the coffers of a chivalrous king could be filled by it. If Flambard sought to seize upon every man's heritage, he also *drave* all the King's gemóts over all England. We have no details; but it is easy to see how the ancient assemblies, and the judicial and administrative business which was done in them, might be turned into instruments of extortion. We have seen that the worst criminals could win their pardon by a bribe,[1] and means might easily be found, by false charges and by various tricks of the law, for wringing money out of the innocent as well as the guilty. We may again turn to Henry's charter. It is a very speaking clause which forgives all "pleas" and debts due to his brother, except certain classes of them which were held to be due of lawful right.[2] In the days of

Working of the old laws.

"Driving" of the Gemóts.

Witness of Henry's charter.

[1] See above, p. 153.

[2] Select Charters, 97. "Omnia placita et omnia debita quæ fratri meo

Rufus and Flambard the presumption was that a demand made on behalf of the crown was unlawful.

But there is one form of the exactions of the Red King which, for obvious reasons, stands forth before all others in the pages of the writers of the time. When the King would be the heir of every man, he was fully minded to be the heir of the clerk or the monk as well as of the layman. And Flambard, priest and chaplain as he was, had no mind to sacrifice the interests of his master to the interests of his order. By his suggestion William began early in his reign, as soon as the influence of Lanfranc was withdrawn, to make himself in a special way the heir of deceased bishops and abbots. These great spiritual lords were among the chief land-owners of the kingdom. The kings therefore naturally claimed to have a voice in their appointment. They invested the new prelate with his ring and staff; and this right, so fiercely denied to the successor of Augustus, was exercised without dispute by the successor of Cerdic and Rolf.[1] The

debebantur condono, exceptis rectis firmis meis et exceptis illis quæ pacta erant pro aliorum hæreditatibus vel pro eis rebus quæ justius aliis contingebant."

[1] See N. C. vol. iv. pp. 429, 821. Eadmer says emphatically in the Preface to the Historia Novorum; "Ex eo quippe quo Willelmus Normanniæ comes terram illam [Angliam] debellando sibi subegit, nemo in ea episcopus vel abbas ante Anselmum factus est qui non primo fuerit homo regis, ac de manu illius episcopatus vel abbatiæ investituram per dationem virgæ pastoralis suscepit." He excepts the bishops of Rochester, who received investiture from the Archbishop of Canterbury, their lord as well as their metropolitan.

A distinct witness to the antiquity of the royal rights in England is borne by William of Malmesbury (v. 417), where he is speaking of the controversy in Henry the First's time. The King refused to yield to the new claims of the Pope, "non elationis ambitu, sed procerum et maxime comitis de Mellento instinctu, qui, in hoc negotio magis *antiqua consuetudine* quam recti tenore rationem reverberans allegabat multum regiæ majestati diminui, si *omittens morem antecessorum*, non investiret electum per baculum et annulum."

Another remarkable witness is given by one of the continuators of Sigebert (Sigeberti Auctarium Ursicampinum, Pertz, vi. 471). He records the

CHAP. IV. new prelate received, by the king's writ, as a grant from the king, the temporal possessions which were attached to the spiritual office.[1] We have seen that this action on the part of the king by no means wholly shut out action either on the part of the local ecclesiastical body or on

Grant of the temporalities by the king.

the part of the great council of the kingdom.[2] But it was from the king personally that the newly chosen or newly nominated prelate received the actual investiture of his office and its temporalities. The temporalities with which he was invested might have their special

Church lands become fiefs.

rights and privileges; but at least they were not exempt from the three burthens which no land could escape, among which was the duty of providing men for military service in case of need.[3] As feudal ideas grew, the inference was easy that lands granted by the king and charged with military service were a fief held of the king by a military tenure. We have seen signs of change in that direction in the days of the Conqueror;[4] in the days of Rufus the doctrine was fully established, and it was pushed to its logical results by the lawyer-like

Flambard's inferences.

ingenuity of Flambard. If the lands held by a bishop or abbot were a fief held by military tenure, they must be liable to the same accidents as other fiefs of the same

Analogy between lay and ecclesiastical fiefs.

kind. When a bishop or abbot died, or otherwise vacated his office, the result was the same as when the lay holder of a fief died without leaving an heir of full age.

death of Lanfranc under a wrong year, 1097, and adds; "Anselmus abbas Beccensis, pro sua sanctitate et doctrina non solum in Normannia, sed etiam in Anglia jam celeberrimus, successit in præsulatu. Qui licet a rege Willelmo et principibus terre totiusque ecclesiæ conventu susceptus honorifice fuisset, multas tamen molestias et tribulationes postmodum sub ipso rege passus est pro statu ecclesiæ corrigendo. Nam reges Angliæ hanc injustam legem *jam diu tenuerant*, ut electos ecclesiæ præsules ipsi per virgam pastoralem ecclesiis investirent."

This is of course written by the lights of Henry the First's reign, as Anselm never objected to the royal investiture in the time of Rufus.

[1] See N. C. vol. ii. p. 588.   [2] Ib. p. 590.
[3] See N. C. vol. i. pp. 93, 601.   [4] See N. C. vol. iv. p. 372.

There was the fief; but there was no one ready to perform the duties with which it was charged. The fief must
therefore fall back to the lord till it should be granted
afresh to some one who could discharge those duties.
The king thus, in the words of the Chronicler, became
the heir of the deceased bishop or abbot, even more
thoroughly than he became the heir of the deceased baron
or other lay tenant-in-chief. For in the latter case,
except when the late holder's family became extinct by
his death, there was always some one person who had
by all law and custom a right above all other men
to succeed him. The son or other natural successor
might be constrained to buy back the lands of the
ancestor,[1] or, if a minor, he might be kept out of them
till his time of wardship was over. Still even Flambard
would have allowed that such a natural successor had,
if he could pay the price demanded, a claim upon the
land which was not shared by any one else. But on the
lands of a deceased bishop or abbot no man, even of his
own order, had any better claim than another till such a
claim was created by election or nomination. The king Vacant
prelacies
was the only heir; the lands and all the other property of held by the
the vacant office passed into his hands; and, as no election King.
or nomination could hold good without his consent, it
was in his power to prolong his possession as heir as long
as he thought good. That is to say, by the new device of
Flambard, when a bishop or abbot died, the king at once
entered on his lands, and kept them as long as the see or
abbey remained vacant. And, as it rested with the king Power of
prolonging
when the see or abbey should be filled, he could prolong the va-
the vacancy for any time that he thought good. And cancy.
William Rufus commonly thought good to prolong the Sale of
bishoprics
vacancy till some one offered him such a price in ready and abbeys.
money as made it worth his while to put an end to it.[2]

[1] See N. C. vol. iv. p. 37.   [2] See Appendix W.

CHAP. IV. The result was that, in the words of the Chronicler, "God's Church was brought low."[1] The great ecclesiastical offices, as they fell vacant, were either kept vacant for the King's profit, or else were sold for his profit to men who, by the very act of buying them, were

Innovations of Rufus. shown to be unworthy to hold them.[2] We are distinctly told that this practice was an innovation of the days of Rufus, and that it was an innovation of which Flambard was the author.[3] The charge of simony, like all other charges of bribery and corruption, is often much easier to bring than to disprove; but it is not likely to be spoken of as a systematic practice, unless it

Earlier cases of simony. undoubtedly happened in a good many cases. We have come across cases in our earlier history where it was at least suspected that ecclesiastical offices had been sold, or, what proves even more, that they were looked on as likely to be sold.[4] And that the practice was common among continental princes there can be little doubt.

Not systematic before Rufus. But there is nothing to make us believe that it was at all systematic in England at any earlier time, and the Conqueror at all events was clear from all scandal of the kind. But the chain of reasoning devised by Flambard would make it as fair a source of profit for the king to take money on the grant of a bishopric as to take it on the grant of a lay fief. And there is no reason to doubt that Rufus systematically acted on this principle, and that, save at the moment of his temporary repentance, he seldom or never gave away a bishopric or abbey for nothing. The other point of the

---

[1] This comes in the great passage under 1100; "Godes cyrcean he nyðerade, and þa bisceoprices and abbotrices þe þa ealdras on his dagan feollan, ealle he hi oððe wið feo gesealde, oððe on his agenre hand heold and to gafle gesette."

[2] See the passage quoted from Eadmer in Appendix W.

[3] See Appendix W.

[4] See N. C. vol. i. pp. 505. 527; vol. ii. p. 69.

charge, that bishoprics and abbeys were kept vacant CHAP. IV.
while the king received the profits, was not a matter of Treatment of vacant
surmise or suspicion, but a matter of fact open to all churches.
men. When a prelate died, one of the king's clerks
was sent to take down in writing a full account of all
his possessions. All was taken into the king's hands.
Sometimes the king granted out the lands for money or
on military tenure, in which case the new prelate, when
one was appointed, might have some difficulty in getting
them back.[1] In other cases the king kept the property in
his own hands, letting it out at the highest rent that he
could get, and, as his father did with the royal demesnes,
at once making void his bargains if a higher price
was offered.[2] In the case of the abbeys and of those
churches of secular canons where the episcopal and
capitular estates were not yet separated, the king
took the whole property of the church, and allowed the
monks or canons only a wretched pittance.[3] We have
seen that, in one case where local gratitude has recorded
that he did otherwise, it is marked as an exception to his
usual practice.[4] And, in all these doings, Flambard, as Flambard the chief agent.
he was the deviser of the system, was its chief adminis-
trator. The vacant prelacies were put under his
management; he extorted, for his own profit and for
the king's, such sums both from the monks or clergy
and from the tenants of the church lands that they all
said that it was better to die than to live.[5]

---

[1] See Stubbs, Const. Hist. i. 299. We have come across a good many
cases which illustrate the difficulty of getting back church lands, even
when they had been granted away only for a season. See N. C. vol. ii.
p. 565; vol. iv. p. 803.

[2] See N. C. vol. iv. p. 617.

[3] See Appendix W.   [4] See above, p. 298.

[5] Ann. Wint. 1097. "Radulfus xvi. ecclesias carentes pastoribus sub
tutela sua habebat, episcopatus, et abbatias, quas ad extremam pauper-
tatem perduxit. Ecclesiæ quibus pastores præerant, dabant singulis annis
regi ccc. vel cccc. marcas, aliæ plus, aliæ vero minus. In tanta erant tam

CHAP. IV.
The prac-
tice a new
one.

These doings on the part of Rufus are by the writers of the time put in marked contrast with the practice of earlier kings, and especially with the practice of his own father. As the old and inborn kings had done nothing of the kind, so neither had the Conqueror from beyond sea. In their days, when an abbot or bishop died, his spiritual superior, the bishop of the diocese or the archbishop of the province, administered the estates of his church during the vacancy, bestowing the income to pious and charitable uses, and handing the estates over to the new prelate on his appointment.[1] In later legal language, the guardian of the spiritualties was also the guardian of the temporalities. Bishoprics and abbeys were dealt with as smaller preferments have always been dealt with, as holdings in *frank-almoign*. The novelty lay, not in receiving the bishopric or abbey from the king, but in receiving it on the terms of a lay fief. One prelate, Odo Abbot of Chertsey, the Norman successor of the English Wulfwold,[2] resigned his post rather than hold it on such terms.[3] For the rest of the reign of Rufus the estates of the abbey were left in the hands of Flambard. One of the earliest among the reforms of Henry and Anselm was the restoration of Odo.[4]

If we look more minutely into the chronology of this reign, it will appear that these long vacancies were more usual in the case of the abbeys than in that of the

The olden
practice.

Tenure in
*frank-
almoign.*

Odo Abbot
of Chertsey
resigns,
1092.

Restored
by Henry,
1100.

Vacancies
longer in
abbeys
than in
bishoprics.

---

ordinati miseria quam laici, quod tædebat eos vitæ eorum." The annalist had said a little earlier (1092), in nearly the same words, "Prædictus Radulphus, vir quo in malo nemo subtilior, ecclesias sibi commissas exspoliavit bonis omnibus, et divites simul et pauperes [see p. 341] ad tantam deduxit inopiam, ut mallent mori quam sub ejus vivere dominatu."

[1] See Appendix W.

[2] See N. C. vol. iv. pp. 383, 385, 481.

[3] Ann. Wint. 1092. "Odo abbas abbatiam dimisit, nolens eam de rege more sæcularium tenere." Here is a distinct protest against the new tenure.

[4] Ib. 1100. "Odoni reddidit [Henricus] abbatiam Certesiæ."

bishoprics. At the time of William's death he had in his
hands, besides the archbishopric of the absent Anselm,
the two bishoprics of Winchester and Salisbury and
eleven abbeys.[1] Of these Winchester had been vacant
rather more than two years and a half, Salisbury had
been vacant only eight months. And the bishoprics
which were filled in his reign had mostly been
vacant one, two, or at most three years, shorter times
than bishoprics were often kept vacant in much later
times.[2] The reason for the difference seems clear. The
bishoprics, when they were filled, commonly went to
the king's clerks, to Flambard himself and his fellows.
The great temporal position of a bishopric was ac-
ceptable to men of this class, and they found in the
king's service the means of making up a purse such as
would tempt the king to end the vacancy in their
favour[3]. A bishopric was therefore likely to be filled,
unworthily filled doubtless, but still filled, before any
very long time had passed. The abbeys, on the other
hand, would have small attractions for the king's servants, who in fact, as secular clerks, could not hold
them. And the men for whom such a post would have
attractions, the monks of the vacant abbey or the abbots
or priors of lesser houses, would not have the same
means as the king's servants of making up a purse.

Vacant bishoprics. Walkelin dies. Jan. 3, 1098. Osmund dies. Dec. 3, 1099.

Differences between bishoprics and abbeys.

[1] Chron. Petrib. 1100.

[2] Take two cases at random with a great interval between them, the
vacancy of the see of Lincoln under Henry the Second, and that of Oxford,
which one might have thought hardly worth keeping vacant, under
Elizabeth. Hugh Curwin (see Godwin, 405) died in 1568, and his successor
John Underhill was not appointed till 1589.

[3] Orderic (764 A) gives a picture of the kind of men who became
bishops under this system; " Sic utique capellani regis et amici præsulatus
Angliæ adepti sunt, et nonnulli ex ipsis *præposituras ad opprimendos inopes,*
sibique augendas opes nihilominus tenuerunt. . . . Plerumque leves et
indocti eliguntur ad regimen ecclesiæ tenendum, non pro sanctitate vitæ
vel ecclesiasticorum eruditione dogmatum liberaliumve peritia litterarum,
sed nobilium pro gratia parentum et potentum favore amicorum."

CHAP. IV. The abbeys therefore were likely to remain vacant longer than the bishoprics. When they were filled, it was not without simony, or at least not without a pay-
Case of
Peter-
borough.
1098.
ment of some kind to the King. For it is rather harsh to apply the word simony to the payment by which the monks of Peterborough bought of the King the right to choose an abbot freely—a free *congé d'élire* in short, without any letter missive.[1] Another thing may be noticed. The bishops appointed at this time all bear Norman names ; Normans were the most likely men to
English
abbots.
find their way into the King's chapel and chancery. But the abbots are still not uncommonly English.[2] Rufus, who welcomed brave mercenaries from any quarter, also welcomed bribes from any quarter, with little of narrow prejudice for or against particular nations. An English monk was as likely as his Norman fellow to have, by some means quite inconsistent with his rule, scraped together money enough to purchase preferment. And when a body of monks bought the right of free election, they were likely to choose an Englishman rather than a stranger. At all times the kings interfered less with the elections to abbeys than they did with the elections to bishoprics.[3] And, if there is any truth, even as a legendary illustration, in a tale which is told both of Rufus and of other kings, there were moments when the
Story of
the ap-
pointment
to an
unnamed
abbey.
Red King could prefer a practical joke to a bribe. An abbey—the name is not given—is vacant; two of its monks come to the King, trying to outbid one another in offers of money for the vacant office. A third brother

---

[1] See N. C. vol. v. p. 224.   [2] Ib.

[3] See Stubbs, Const. Hist. vol. iii. pp. 318, 319. He gives amongst the reasons for the difference ; " The abbots were not so influential as the bishops in public affairs, nor was the post equally desirable as the reward for public service ; with a very few exceptions the abbacies were much poorer than the bishoprics, and involved a much more steady attention to local duties, which would prevent attendance at court."

has come with them, and the King asks what he will give. He answers that he will not give anything; he has simply come to receive the new abbot, whoever he may be, and to take him home with all honour. Rufus at once bestows the abbey on him, as the only one of the party worthy of it.[1] The tale is not impossible; had it been placed in Normandy and not in England, we might have even said that it was not unlikely. For we shall see, as we go on, that, from whatever cause, Rufus dealt with ecclesiastical matters in Normandy in a different spirit from that in which he dealt with them in England.

At the point which we have reached in our general story, the time of the restoration of Carlisle, two English sees only were vacant. Two had been filled during the year of the Norman campaign, and both of them by prelates of some personal mark. Ralph Luffa, Bishop of Chichester, holds a high place in the history of his own church, as the founder alike of the existing fabric and of the existing constitution of its chapter.[2] He bears altogether so good a character that he is not likely to have come to a bishopric in the way which was usual in the days of Rufus. Did the King give him his staff in some passing better moment, like that in which he gave the staff to the worthy abbot at the nameless monastery? But the other episcopal appointment of the same

[1] This story has no better authority than that of the Hyde writer (299); still it is, to say the least, remarkable that it should be told of William Rufus. But there is an element of fun in the tale, and the Red King may for once have preferred a joke to a bribe. The description of the three monks at all events is good; "Cum coram rege astarent pariter, et uno plura promittente, alius pluriora promitteret, rex sagaciter cuncta perscrutans, tacentem monachum tertium quid quæsivit, ille se nil omnino promittere aut dare respondit, sed ad hoc tantum venisse ut abbatem suum cum honore suscipiendo domum deduceret."

[2] See Stephens, Memorials of Chichester, p. 47.

CHAP. IV. year was one of the usual kind, as far as the motive of the appointment went, though the person to whom the bishopric was given or sold was not one of the class who in this reign commonly profited by such transactions.

Death of William Bishop of Thetford. 1091.

Bishop William of Thetford, the successor of the unlearned Herfast,[1] died in the year of negotiations, the year of the peace with Robert and the peace with Malcolm.[2] His bishopric was not long kept vacant; before the end of the year the church of Thetford had a new pastor, and one who plays no small part in local history.

Herbert Losinga.

This was the famous Herbert Losinga,[3] who, if we may trust such accounts of him as we have, made so bad a beginning and so good an ending. Norman by birth, an immediate countryman of the Conqueror, as sprung from the land of Hiesmes, a man of learning and

Prior of Fécamp.

evident energy, he became a monk of Fécamp and prior of that great house.[4] Early in the reign of

Abbot of Ramsey. 1087.

Rufus or in the last days of the Conqueror, he was raised to the abbey of Ramsey, when the long and varied life of Æthelsige came to an end.[5] He now,

He buys the see of Thetford.

on Bishop William's death, at once bought for himself the see of Thetford for one thousand pounds.[6] Before the end of the year he was consecrated by Archbishop Thomas of York, making his profession to a future Archbishop of Canterbury.[7] At the same

---

[1] See N. C. vol. ii. p. 666.

[2] On the chronology, see Appendix X.

[3] I have already sketched his career, N. C. vol. iv. p. 420.

[4] So says Bartholomew Cotton, in his History of the Norwich Bishops; Hist. Angl., ed. Luard, p. 389; "Hic prius fuit prior Fiscanni, postea abbas Ramesseye, et pater suus Robertus abbas Wintoniæ. Hic Herbertus in pago Oxymensi natus, Fiscanni monachus, post ejusdem loci prioratum strenue administratum, translatus in Angliam a rege Willelmo, qui secundus ex Normannis obtinuit imperium, Ramesseye abbatis jure prælatus est."

[5] See N. C. vol. iv. pp. 36, 747.

[6] See Appendix X.

[7] See Appendix X.

time he also bought preferment for his father Robert, CHAP. IV.
who, it must be supposed, had embraced the monastic
life. The New Minster of Winchester had now been for Three
three years, since the death of its last Abbot Ralph, in years' vacancy
the hands of Flambard.[1] Herbert now bought the abbacy of New Minster.
for his father.[2] This twofold simony naturally gave great 1088-1091.
offence, and formed a fertile subject for the eloquence Robert Losinga
of the time, both in prose and verse.[3] The reign of the Abbot.
father was short; two years later Flambard again held 1091-1093.
the wardship of New Minster.[4] The career of the son in
his East-Anglian bishopric was longer and more varied,
and we shall come across him again in the course of our
story. At present it is only needful to say that Herbert Herbert repents and
very soon repented of the shameful way by which he receives
had climbed into the sheepfold, that he went to Rome, his bishopric again
that he gave up his ill-gotten bishopric into the hands from the Pope.
of Pope Urban, and received his staff from him again in c. 1093.
what was deemed to be a more regular way.[5] Herbert's
repentance was to his credit; and, as things stood at the
moment, there was perhaps no better way of making
amends. But the course which he took was not only
one which was sure to bring on him the displeasure of
the Red King; it was in the teeth of all the customs of
William the Great and of the kings before him. A
journey to Rome, without the royal licence, and seemingly taken by stealth,[6] the submission to a Pope whom
the King had not acknowledged,[7] the surrender to any

---

[1] Ann. Wint. 1088. "Radulfo abbate Wintoniæ defuncto, commisit rex
abbatiam Radulfo Passeflabere capellano suo."

[2] See Appendix X.

[3] See Appendix X.

[4] Mon. Angl. ii. 431.

[5] See Appendix X.

[6] "Latenter," says the extract from Florence quoted in Appendix X.

[7] See N. C. vol. iv. p. 437. So in Eadmer, Vit. Ans. ii. 3. 23. William
Rufus says, "Se illum [Urbanum] pro papa non tenere, nec suæ consue-

CHAP. IV.

Novelty of Herbert's act.

Pope of the staff which he had received from the King of the English, were all of them offences, and the last act was distinctly a novelty. Ulf, Ealdred, Thomas, Remigius, had all been deprived of their staves and had received them again;[1] but no English prelate of those times had of his own act made the Pope his judge in such a matter. When the holy Wulfstan was threatened with deposition, he had, even in the legend, given back his staff, not to the Pope who ruled at Rome, but to the King who slept at Westminster.[2] No wonder then that the Red King was moved to anger by a slight to his authority which his father could not have overlooked, and which might have stirred the Confessor himself to one of his passing fits of wrath. The return of Herbert from Rome forms part of a striking group of events to which we shall presently come.

Vacancy of Lincoln. 1092-1094.

The two bishoprics of Chichester and Thetford were thus filled soon after they became vacant. In the year after the consecration of Ralph and Herbert, a third see, as we have seen, fell vacant by the death of Remigius of Lincoln.[3] That see was not filled so speedily as Chichester and Thetford had been; still it did not remain vacant so long as some of the abbeys. But a longer vacancy befell, a lasting vacancy seemed designed to befall, the mother church of all of them. All this while the metropolitan throne of Canterbury remained empty. No successor to Lanfranc was chosen or nominated; it was the fixed purpose of the Red King to make no nomination himself, to allow no choice on the part of the ecclesiastical electors. Here at least the doctrines of Randolf Flam-

Vacancy of Canterbury. 1089-1093.

tudinis esse, ut absque sua electione alicui liceret in regno suo papam nominare."

[1] See N. C. vol. ii. pp. 118, 464; vol. iv. p. 354.

[2] See N. C. vol. iv. pp. 376, 820.

[3] See above, p. 312.

bard were to be carried out in their fulness. It is the CHAP. IV.
state of ecclesiastical matters during this memorable
vacancy, and the memorable nomination which at last
ended it, which call for our main attention at this stage
of our story.

§ 2. *The Vacancy of the Primacy and the Appointment of Anselm.* 1089–1093.

It needs some little effort of the imagination fully to Effects
take in all that is implied in a four years' vacancy of the of the vacancy of
see of Canterbury in the eleventh century. For the the see of Canter-
King to keep any bishopric vacant in order to fill his bury.
coffers with its revenues was a new and an unrighteous
thing, against which men cried out as at once new and
unrighteous.   But to deal in this way with the see of Special
Canterbury was something which differed in kind from position of the metro-
the like treatment of any other see. That the bishopric politan see.
of Lincoln was vacant, that the Bishop of Durham was
in banishment, was mainly a local grievance. The
churches of Lincoln and Durham suffered; they were
condemned to what, in the language of the times, was
called a state of widowhood. The tenants of those
churches suffered all that was implied in being handed
over from a milder lord to a harsher one. The dioceses
were defrauded of whatever advantages might have
flowed from the episcopal superintendence of Robert
Bloet or of William of Saint-Calais. But the general
affairs of the Church and realm might go on much the
same; there was one councillor less in the gemót or the
synod, and that was all. It was another thing when the
patriarchal throne was left vacant, when Church and
realm were deprived of him who in a certain sense
might be called the head of both. An Archbishop of
Canterbury was something more than merely the first

CHAP. IV.

Its antiquity and dignity.

Place of the Archbishop in the assembly.

His leadership of the nation.

of English bishops. Setting aside his loftier ecclesiastical claims as the second Pontiff of a second world, he held within the realm of England itself a position which was wholly his own.[1] He held an office older and more venerable than the crown itself. There were indeed kings in England before there were bishops; but there were Archbishops of Canterbury before there were Kings of the English. The successor of Augustine, the "head of Angle-kin,"[2] had been the embodiment of united English national life, in days when the land was still torn in pieces by the rivalry of the kings of this or that corner of it.[3] This lofty position survived the union of the kingdoms; it survived the transfer of the united kingdom to a foreign Conqueror. Lanfranc stood by the side of William, as Dunstan had stood by the side of Eadgar. In every gathering of the Church and of the people, in every synod, in every gemót, the Archbishop of Canterbury held a place which had no equal or second, a place which was shared by no other bishop or earl or ætheling. If we reckon the King as the head of the assembly, the Archbishop is its first member. If we reckon the King as a power outside the assembly, the Archbishop is himself its head. He is the personal counsellor of the King, the personal leader of the nation, in a way in which no other man in the realm could be said to be. As of old, under the Empire of Rome, each town had its *defensor civitatis*, so now, under the kingship of England, the successor of Augustine might be said to hold the place of *defensor regni*. The position which

---

[1] See N. C. vol. v. pp. 661, 662.

[2] In the poem on the captivity of Ælfheah in the Chronicles, 1011, he is

"Se þe ær wæs heafod
Angelcynnes
And Cristendomes."

[3] Cf. Stubbs, Const. Hist. i. 211 et seqq. with 245.

Lanfranc had held, and in which during these dreary CHAP. IV. years he had no successor, was a position wholly unlike that of the class of bishops to which we are now getting accustomed, royal officials who received bishoprics as the payment of their temporal services. It was equally unlike that of the statesman-bishops of later times, who might or might not forget the bishop in the statesman, but whose two characters, ecclesiastical and temporal, were quite distinct and in no way implied one another. An archbishop of those times was a statesman by virtue of his spiritual office; he was the moral guardian and moral mouth-piece of the nation. The ideal archbishop was at once saint, scholar, and statesman; of the long series from Augustine to Lanfranc, some had really united all those characters; none perhaps had been altogether lacking in all three. Hence the special care Appointments to the archbishopric. with which men were chosen for so great a place both before and for some time after the time with which we are dealing. The king's clerks, his chancellor, his treasurer, even his larderer,[1] might beg or buy some bishopric of less account; but, seventy years after this time, the world was amazed when King Henry bethought him of placing Chancellor Thomas, not in the Thomas of London. 1162. seat of Randolf of Durham or Roger of Salisbury, but in the seat of Ælfheah, Anselm, and Theobald.[2] The surprise which was then called forth by what was looked The King's fixed purpose to keep the see vacant. on as a new-fangled and wrongful nomination to the archbishopric of Canterbury may help us to judge of the surprise and horror and despair which came over the minds of men, as it became plain that the wish, perhaps

[1] So we read of Henry the First in Florence, 1102; "Duos de clericis duobus episcopatibus investivit, Rogerium videlicet cancellarium episcopatu Saresbyriensi, et Rogerium larderarium suum pontificatu Herefordensi."

[2] See N. C. vol. v. p. 662, and Contemporary Review, 1878, pp. 493, 496.

the fixed purpose, of the Red King was to get rid of archbishops of Canterbury altogether.

The King's motives. The motives of the King are plain. He sought something more than merely to get possession of the rich revenues of the archbishopric, though that was doubtless not a small matter in the policy of either Rufus or Flambard. The estates of the see. The estates of the see of Canterbury furnished a very perceptible addition to the royal income, and they gave the King a convenient means of rewarding some of his favourites, to whom he granted archiepiscopal lands on military tenure.[1] Lanfranc himself had already done something like this;[2] but the usual tendency of lands so granted to pass away from the Church would be greatly strengthened when it was not the Archbishop, but the King, at whose hands they had been received, and to whom the first homage had been paid. But all Further motives. this was doubtless very secondary. In the case of other sees it was a mere reckoning of profit; Rufus had no objection to fill them at once, if any one would make it worth his while to do so. But it is plain that he had a fixed determination to keep the archbishopric vacant, if possible, for ever, at all events as long as the patience of his kingdom would endure such a state of things. To Rufus, whether as man or as king, the appointment of an archbishop was the thing of all others which was least to be wished. To fill the see of Canterbury would be at once to set up a disagreeable monitor by his side, and to put some check on the reign of unright and unlaw, public and private. William doubtless remembered how, as long as Lanfranc lived, he had had to play an unwilling part, and to put a bridle on his worst and most cherished instincts. An archbishop of his own naming could not indeed have the personal authority of his ancient guardian; but any archbishop would have

---

[1] See below, p. 418. [2] See N. C. vol. iv. p. 372.

a charge to speak in the name of the Church and the CHAP. IV.
nation in a way which could hardly be pleasing in his
ears. The metropolitan see therefore remained unfilled
till the day when William Rufus became for a short
season another man.

It is worth remarking that what might have seemed a No fear of
very obvious way out of the difficulty clearly did not a bad appointment.
come into the head of the King or of any one else. The
long vacancy of the archbishopric made men uneasy;
they were grieved and amazed as to what might happen
in so unusual a case; but they felt sure that the present
distress must end some time, and they seem to have
taken for granted that, when it did end, it would end by
the appointment of some one worthy of the place. Men
were troubled at the King's failure to appoint any archbishop; they do not seem to have been at all troubled
by fear that he might appoint a bad archbishop.[1] Rufus
himself seems never to have thought of granting or
selling the metropolitan see to any of his own creatures,
to Flambard for instance or to Robert Bloet. He might
so deal with Lincoln or Durham; something within
or without him kept him from so dealing with Canterbury. It is throughout taken for granted that the choice
lay between a good archbishop or none at all. A good
archbishop was the yoke-fellow of a good king, the
reprover of an evil king. William Rufus wanted neither
of those. But even William Rufus had not gone so far,
his subjects did not suspect him of going so far, as to
think of appointing an evil archbishop in order to be
the tool of an evil king. The precedent of making the Primates
patriarchal throne of Britain the reward of merely tem- between
Anselm
poral services[2] did not come till it had been filled by and
Thomas.

---

[1] We shall come to this again. This state of feeling is implied in Eadmer's
whole description of the time immediately before Anselm's appointment.

[2] We have seen even under the reign of the Confessor (see N. C. vol. ii.

CHAP. IV. four more primates, all taken from the regular orders, numbering among them at least one saint and one statesman, but no mere royal official. The first degradation of the archbishopric led to its greatest exaltation, in the person of Thomas of London. But Thomas of London, even in his most worldly days, was a very different person from Randolf Flambard.

Seemingly no thought of election.

Another point to be remarked is how utterly the notion either of ecclesiastical election or of election in the Great Council of the realm seems to have passed away.

No action of the monks.

There is nothing like an attempt at the choice of an archbishop, either by the monks of Christ Church, the usual electors, or by the suffragan bishops, who afterwards claimed the right. It might have been too daring a step if the monks had done as they once had done in the days of King Eadward,[1] if they had chosen an archbishop freely, and then asked for the King's approval of their choice. Eadward had rejected the prelate so chosen; William Rufus might have done something more than reject him. But we do not hear of their even venturing to petition for leave to elect; they do not, like the monks of Peterborough,[2] make such a petition, and enforce it

No action of the Witan.

by the strongest of arguments. Nor do bishops, earls, thegns, the nation at large, venture to act, any more than the monks. They murmur, and that is all. No action on the subject is recorded to have been taken in any of the gemóts till the vacancy had lasted nearly four years; and we shall see that the action which was at last taken

p. 69, and above, p. 348) a notion afloat that the archbishopric of Canterbury was to be had by bribery; but it was to be bribery carried on in some very underhand way, not in the form of open gifts either to King Eadward or to Earl Godwine. The appointment of Stigand (see N. C. vol. ii. p. 347) might be said to be the reward of temporal services; but they were services done to the whole nation, and the reward was bestowed by the nation itself.

[1] See N. C. vol. ii. p. 69. Cf. Appendix I.

[2] See above, p. 352.

showed more strongly than anything else that, as far chap. iv.
as this world was concerned, it rested wholly with the _{Silent en-} _{durance of}
King whether England should ever again have another _{the action.}
primate or not. Through the whole time, the nation
suffers, but it suffers in silence. We have already had
to deal with a king on whose nod all things human
and divine were held to hang;[1] we are now dealing
with a king who would have no petition made, no act
ascribed, within his realm, to any God or man except
himself.[2]

The state of things during the time when William _{Results,}
Rufus held firm to his purpose that no man should be _{of the} _{vacancy.}
archbishop but himself,[3] and when the revenues of the
archbishopric were paid into the hands of Randolf Flam-
bard,[4] was one of general corruption. It is immediately _{Corruption}
after recording the King's way of dealing with bishoprics _{of the} _{clergy.}
and abbeys that one of our chief guides breaks forth into
his most vehement protest against the vices of the time,
and specially against the corruption and degradation of
the clergy.[5] That they took to secular callings, that
they became pleaders of causes and farmers of revenues,
was not wonderful. Under the rule of Flambard there

---

[1] See N. C. vol. iv. p. 436.

[2] Eadmer, Vit. Ans. ii. 3. 23. The King and his courtiers, " quid dicerent
non habentes, eum in regem blasphemare uno strepitu conclamavere, quandoquidem ausus erat in regno ejus, nisi eo concedente, quidquam vel Deo
ascribere."

[3] Eadmer, Hist. Nov. 16. "Et adjecit, Sed per sanctum vultum de
Luca (sic enim jurare consueverat) [see Appendix G] nec ipse hoc tempore
nec alius quis archiepiscopus erit, me excepto."

[4] The action of Flambard in the matter comes out most strongly in the
Winchester Annals, 1089, where a motive is assigned for Flambard's zeal ;
"Hoc anno commisit rex Radulfo Passeflabere archiepiscopatum Cantuariæ,
defuncto Lanfranco. Ipse autem regi quicquid inde aliquo modo lucrari
poterat, ut de ejus cogitaret promotione, donavit." But he had to wait
eight years for his reward.

[5] I refer to the well-known outburst of William of Malmesbury, iv. 314,
some passages of which I have quoted in Appendix G.

were endless openings for employments of this kind, employments for which, as in the case of Flambard himself, the clerk was commonly better fitted than the layman.

And the general fiscal spirit of the time, the endless seeking after gold and silver of which the King set the example, naturally spread through all classes; every rich man, we are told, turned money-changer.[1] The constant demands for actual coin, the large outlay of actual coin in the payment of the King's mercenaries, must have led to an increased activity in the circulation of the precious metals. The newly-come Jews, strong in royal favour, doubtless found their account in this turn of things; but some classes of Christians seem to have

found their account in it also. But, besides all this, the writers of the time seem clearly to connect the frightful profligacy of the time, specially rife among the King's immediate following, with the vacancy of the archbishopric. It is true that things were not much better in Normandy, where the good soul of Archbishop William must have been daily grieved at the unlawful deeds of almost every one around him. But an Archbishop of Rouen had never been held to have the same authority over either prince or people as an Archbishop of Canterbury. Whatever power, moral or formal, was at any time wielded by the ecclesiastical state for the reformation of manners was altogether in abeyance, now that there was no Primate either to call together a synod of the national Church or to speak with that personal authority which belonged to none of the chiefs of the national Church but himself. Even darker times were in store, when there was a Primate in the land, but when his authority was defied and his person insulted.

---

[1] Will. Malms. iv. 314. "Nullus dives nisi nummularius, nullus clericus nisi causidicus, nullus presbyter nisi (ut verbo parum Latino utar) firmarius."

But as yet the darkest times that men had known were CHAP. IV.
the four years during which the sons of the English
Church were left as sheep without a shepherd.

The shepherd was at last to come, like his immediate
predecessor, in one sense from a distant land, in another
sense from a land which was only too near. The house
of Bec, the house of Herlwin, was for the second time to
give a patriarch to the isle of Britain. It had given us Anselm.
Lanfranc the statesman; it was now to give us Anselm
the saint. We may reckon it, not as the shame, but as Debt of
the glory of our nation that we have so often won foreigners.
strangers, and even conquerors, to become our national
leaders, and to take their place among the noblest
worthies of the soil. Alongside of the lawgiver from
Denmark, of the deliverer from France, we rank, as
holding the same place among bishops which they hold
among kings and earls, the holy man from the Prætorian
Augusta.[1] The annals of the eleventh and twelfth centuries are thick set with the names of foreign prelates
holding English sees; and among them both Normandy
and Lorraine, to say nothing of Pavia, had sent us some
whom we might well be glad to welcome. But the two The Bur-
whose names shine out above them all, the two from gundian
saints.
whose names all thought of their foreign birth passes
away, the two whom we hail as our own by adoption
and love, came from a more distant realm, and a realm
which is well nigh forgotten. Hugh of Avalon and of Hugh of
Lincoln came from the more favoured and famous district Avalon.
where the Imperial Burgundy rises to the Alps and sinks

---

[1] Of the birthplace of Anselm and its buildings, some of which must
have been fresh in his childhood, I attempted a little picture in my
Historical and Architectural Sketches. The nature of the country is
brought out with all clearness by Dean Church, Anselm, p. 8. Before him
it had stirred up the local patriotism of M. Croset-Mouchet to the best
things in his book.

again to the Rhone.[1]   Anselm of Aosta and of Canterbury came from that deep valley which, after all changes, is still Cisalpine Gaul. He came from that small outlying fragment of the Middle Kingdom which has not risen to the destiny of Unterwalden and Bern, of Lausanne and Geneva, but which has escaped the destiny of Bresse and Bugey, of Chablais and Nizza, of royal Arles and princely Orange, and of Hugh's own home by the city of Gratian.[2] The vale of Aosta, still Burgundian in its speech and buildings, the last remnant of the great Burgundian dominion of its lords, still gives a title to princes of the house of its earliest and of its latest

Humbert. The father of Anselm, no less than the father of Lanfranc, was of Lombard birth. But Gundulf had been fully adopted at Aosta, and his son, born on Burgundian soil, son of a Burgundian mother of lofty, perhaps of princely stock,[3] must be reckoned as belonging to the

---

[1] I must venture to admire, though the poet has forsaken the natural Saturnian of Nævius and Walter Map for the foreign metre of Homer, the lines in which one of the biographers of Saint Hugh (Metrical Life, Dimock, p. 2) describes the country of his hero;

"Imperialis ubi Burgundia surgit in Alpes,
    Et condescendit Rhodano, convallia vernant,
    Duplicibus vestitur humus; sunt gramina vestis
    Publica, sunt flores vestis sollennis, et uno
    Illa colore nitent, sed mille coloribus illi."

[2] Eadmer (Vit. Ans. i. 1. 1) carefully marks the geography of Aosta. It is "Augusta civitas, confinis Burgundiæ et Langobardiæ." I have collected some passages on this head in Historical Geography, p. 278. The French writers De Rémusat (Saint Anselme, 21), Charma (4), and specially M. Croset-Mouchet (55), as a neighbour, seem to have caught the Burgundian birth of Anselm better than the English. Yet Charma, who knows that Aosta was Burgundian, calls Anselm an Italian, perhaps on account of the Lombard birth of his father.

[3] M. Croset-Mouchet (57) is very anxious to connect Anselm's mother with the house of the Counts of Savoy. He gives a genealogical table at the end of his book, where the pedigree of Ermenberga is traced up to Ardoin the Third, Count of Turin and Marquess in Italy. He seems however to be not very certain about the matter, and it does not greatly affect Anselm's career either at Bec or at Canterbury.

Burgundy in which he was born and bred rather than to the Italy which in after days he visited as a stranger.[1] There, in the last home of old Gaulish freedom, in an Augusta named after the first Augustus—an Augusta which we doubt whether to call Prætorian from the conquerors or Salassian from the conquered—in the long valley fenced in by the giant Alps on either side—at the foot of the pass where local belief holds that Hannibal had crossed of old and where Buonaparte was to cross in days to come—there where the square walls of the Roman town rise almost untouched above the rushing Dora—where the street still bearing the name of Anselm leads from the Roman gate to the Roman arch of triumph, where the towers of Saint Gratus and Saint Urse, fellows of kindred towers at Verona and at Lincoln, at Schaffhausen and at Cambridge, rose fresh in all their squareness and sternness when Anselm lay as a babe beneath their shadow—there, among the sublimest works of nature and among some of the most striking works of man, was born the teacher of Normandy, the shepherd of England, the man who dived deeper than any man before him into the most awful mysteries of the faith, but whom we have rather to deal with as one who ranks by adoption among the truest worthies of England, the man

---

[1] Pope Urban (Hist. Nov. 45) counsels Anselm to avoid the unhealthy season at Rome, "quia urbis istius aër multis et maxime peregrinæ regionis hominibus nimis est insalubris." Later in the story (Hist. Nov. 72), Ivo of Chartres gives him a like piece of advice about Italy generally; "Accepit ab Ivone et a multis non spernendi consilii viris, satius fore cœptum iter in aliud tempus differendum, quam *Italicis ardoribus* ea se tempestate cum suis tradere cruciandum. Nimis etenim fervor æstatis ita ubique, sed maxime, ut ferebatur, in Italia, tunc temporis quæque torrebat, ut incolis vix tolerabilis, peregrinis vero gravis et importabilis." The difference of air between Aosta and Rome or Italy generally does not depend upon the boundaries of kingdoms; but here Anselm is distinctly reckoned as a "peregrinus homo" in Italy no less than Eadmer or Ivo or Pope Urban himself.

who stood forth as the champion of right against both political and moral wrong in the days when both political and moral wrong were at their darkest.

Comparison of Lanfranc and Anselm.

I have already pointed out the contrast between the characters of Lanfranc and Anselm, in recording one memorable discourse between them, in which Anselm won Lanfranc over to a better mind in the matter of our English Ælfheah.[1] The calling and the work of the two men were different; and the work of Anselm implied the earlier work of Lanfranc. Lanfranc was, after all, in some sort a conqueror of the English Church, and the character of a conqueror was one in which Anselm could never have shown himself. Lanfranc was a statesman, one whose policy could spread itself far beyond the bounds of this or that kingdom or nation, but whose very policy compelled him not to let the distinctions of kingdoms and nations slip out of his sight. To Anselm we could almost fancy that such distinctions were of small account. He was the servant of God and the friend of all God's creatures; he perhaps hardly stopped to think whether those whose souls and bodies he was ever ready to help were Burgundian, Norman, or English. With such a spirit as this, he could not have done Lanfranc's work; and it is worthy of remark that the Conqueror, who so greatly valued him, seems never to have thought of him for any preferment in England. Lanfranc had to carry out a policy, in some measure harsh and worldly, but which, granting his own position and that of his master, could not be avoided. Anselm fittingly came after him, at a time when national distinctions and national wrongs were almost forgotten in the universal reign of evil, to protest in the name of universal right, and in so doing to protest against particular and national wrongs. He would have been out of place

Anselm not preferred in England by the Conqueror.

[1] See N. C. vol. iv. p. 441.

in the first days of the Conquest; as a stranger, though CHAP. IV. only as a stranger, he would have been out of place in the days of our earlier freedom. When he did come, he Various was thoroughly in place, as one who was before all sides of Anselm's things a preacher of righteousness, but who could, when character. need called for it, put on the mantle of the statesman and even that of the warrior. Like our own Wulfstan, in many things his fellow, we find him the friend and counsellor of men of a character most opposite to his own. And, as we have seen Wulfstan, if not commanding, at least directing, armies,[1] so we shall see Anselm, if not waging war in his own person, at least hallowing more than one camp by his presence. And we can hardly blame him if, at some later stages of his career, he allowed himself to be swayed by scruples which he had never thought of at its beginning, if, in his zeal for eternal right, he allowed himself to sin against the ancient laws and customs of England. When England, Normandy, France, and the Empire, were as they all were in his day, we can forgive him for looking on the Roman Bishop as the one surviving embodiment of law and right, and for deeming that, when he spake, it was as when a man listened to the oracles of God.

The tale of the early life of Anselm has been handed Anselm down to us by a loving companion, a man of our own and Eadmer. nation, who was won in his youth by the kind words of the foreign saint when he came to England as a momentary visitor, and who in after times became the most faithful of disciples through all the changes of his fortunes. It is one of the marked features of the story that we know so little of Anselm, except from his own writings and from the narrative of Eadmer. Our own historians of the time

_____
[1] See above, p. 49, and N. C. vol. iv. p. 579.

CHAP. IV.

References to Eadmer in other writers.

Church's Life of Anselm.

speak of Anselm with the deepest reverence; but they say little of him beside the broad facts which lie on the surface of English history. Some of them directly refer to his special biographer for fuller accounts.[1] In telling his story I find myself in the like case. I am tempted to refer once for all for the acts of Anselm to his Life as written in our own day by a master both of description and of comment.[2] I could be well pleased to send my readers elsewhere to study Anselm the monk and abbot, and to concern myself only with his career as archbishop in our own land. But the earlier and the later career of Anselm hang together, and he has already made his appearance at more than one earlier stage of our own story. I must therefore attempt some general notice, though at less length than if the ground had not been thus forestalled, of the primate who came to us from Aosta, as his predecessor did from Pavia, and who, like his predecessor, made Bec a halting-place on the way to Canterbury.

Childhood of Anselm.

In the life of Anselm a childhood and a manhood of eminent holiness are parted by a short time of youthful licence. The little child in his dream climbed his native mountains to seek for the palace of God on a Christian Olympos. He reported the idleness of the handmaids of his Lord; he sat at the feet of his Lord; he was refreshed by the steward of the divine household with a meal of the purest bread.[3] The scholarly boy was so eager for the monastic life that he prayed for some

[1] Will. Malms. iv. 315. "Simul et supersedendum est in historia, quam reverendissimi Edmeri præoccupavit facundia."

[2] I feel towards Dean Church almost as William of Malmesbury felt towards Eadmer. But he of course looks at Anselm from a point of view somewhat different from mine. And he had not been led to notice that earlier action of William of Saint-Calais which from my point of view is all-important for the story of Anselm.

[3] This beautiful story is told by Eadmer at the very beginning of the Life, i. 1. 2.

sickness that might drive him into the cloister.[1] But CHAP. IV.
the youth for a while cast aside his piety; he cast aside His youthful licence.
his learning; he gave himself to the thoughts and sports
of the world; he even yielded to those temptations of
the flesh which Wulfstan had withstood in the midst of
his military exercises,[2] and which Thomas withstood
in the midst of his worldly business.[3] But the love of
his tender and pious mother kept him from wholly
falling away. The yearning for a monastic life came
upon him again, though his wishes were greatly opposed
by his father. At last, in his twenty-fourth year, Anselm He leaves
Aosta.
left his own land. After three years' sojourn in Bur- 1057.
gundy and France, he reached Normandy, and, in the His sojourn at
steps of Lanfranc, first took up his abode at Avran- Avranches.
ches.[4] But Lanfranc was now at Bec. Thither Anselm, He becomes a
fully bent on the monastic calling, followed the great monk at
scholar. He had doubted for a while between Bec and Bec.
1060.
Clugny. We shall hardly think the worse of him for
his frank confession of human feelings. He doubted,
because at Clugny his human learning would be of no
use, while at Bec it would be overshadowed by that of
Lanfranc.[5] In the end, by the advice of Lanfranc him-

---

[1] Eadmer, Vit. Ans. i. 1. 3. "Ille in suo proposito perstans oravit
Deum, quatenus infirmari mereretur, ut vel sic ad monachicum quem desi-
derabat ordinem susciperetur."

[2] Will. Malms. Vita Wlst. 245. See N. C. vol. ii. p. 470. The confession of Anselm in this matter comes out in his sixteenth Meditation, p. 793
of Migne's edition. The passage seems to imply more serious offences
than would have been guessed from the more general words of Eadmer,
i. 1. 4. The meditation is addressed to a sister. If this means his own
sister Richeza or Richera, it must have been before her marriage with Bur-
gundius. See his Epistles, iii. 43.

[3] See William Fitz-Stephen, iii. 21, Robertson, and the remarkable
story in William of Canterbury, i. 5, Robertson.

[4] Vit. Ans. i. 1. 45. See N. C. vol. ii. p. 228.

[5] Vit. Ans. i. 1. 6. He is made to say; "Ecce, inquit, monachus fiam.
Sed ubi? Si Cluniaci vel Becci, totum tempus quod in discendis litteris
posui, perdidi. Nam et Cluniaci districtio ordinis, et Becci supereminens
prudentia Lanfranci, qui illic monachus est, me [al. mihi] aut nulli prodesse,

self and of Archbishop Maurilius, he became a monk of
Bec, and, when Lanfranc became Abbot of Saint Stephen's,
Anselm succeeded him in the office of prior.[1]

This first preferment Anselm seems to have taken willingly. A crowd of beautiful stories, setting forth his faith
towards God and his kindliness towards all men, belong
to this part of his career, the time when he was specially
employed in writing his theological works. We admire
the mixture of wisdom and kindness with which he re-
proved the abbot of another house who complained that
the boys who were entrusted to his teaching got more
and more unruly, even though they were whipped day
and night.[2] We are tempted to feel a slight grudge when
he counsels a knight who seems to have been leading a
good and devout life in the world to embrace the monastic
calling.[3] Much as that age needed men like Anselm,
it still more needed men like Gulbert of Hugleville and
Helias of La Flèche. But we note with some interest
the comment of Eadmer, so curiously illustrating the
common rivalry between one monastery and another.
In such cases Anselm did not counsel profession at
Bec rather than in any other house, and this par-

ticular convert took the cowl at Marmoutiers. At last,
on the death of Herlwin, the unanimous choice of the
convent called him to the place of abbot. His deep
reluctance to accept so great a charge was overcome
only by the express command of Archbishop Maurilius,

aut nihil valere comprobabit. Itaque in tali loco perficiam quod dispono,
in quo et scire meum possim ostendere, et multis prodesse."

[1] See N. C. vol. ii. p. 110. His election to the priorship is recorded in the
Life, i. 2. 9. There is no mention of any such dislike to the promotion
on Anselm's part as is recorded at his later election as abbot. The whole
account of Anselm's monastic life, as given by Eadmer and followed by his
modern biographers, is of the deepest interest. I have noticed only a few
special points here and there.

[2] See the story in the Life, i. 4. 30.

[3] Ib. i. 4. 35. His name is given as Cadulus.

who, on his election to the priorship, had bidden him
by virtue of holy obedience to accept both that and any
higher preferment which might come in his way.[1] The
election of Anselm to the abbacy marks a stage in our
story. It was in his character of abbot that he was first
brought into relations with England; in that character
he paid his first visit to the land which was presently
to make him her own.

The fame of the new Abbot of Bec and of his house,
great already, now grew still greater. Learning had
shone at Bec ever since Lanfranc came thither; but
hitherto it had shone only in the second rank. It now
took the chief seat in the person of Abbot Anselm. He
was sought by men from all parts as a friend, a teacher,
a spiritual adviser. Of the open-handed hospitality of
Bec it was not, we are told, for Norman neighbours to
speak; those might speak who had found their way
thither from the distant lands of Burgundy and Spain.[2]
The whole Latin world drank in with eagerness the
teaching of Anselm.[3] Scholars of all lands came to sit
at his feet. Noble ladies in their widowhood sought his
neighbourhood and spiritual direction, and received the

---

[1] Eadmer, Vit. Ans. i. 36. The scene between the monks and the abbot-elect,
the mutual prayers and prostrations, are very like to the later scene when he
is named archbishop at Gloucester. The command of the Archbishop of
Rouen comes out emphatically; "Vicit quoque et multo maxime vicit
præceptum, quod, ut supra retulimus, ei fuerat ab archiepiscopo Maurilio
per obedientiam injunctum, videlicet, ut, si major prælatio quam illius
prioratus exstiterat ipsi aliquando injungeretur, nullatenus eam suscipere
recusaret."

[2] Ord. Vit. 530 B. "De hospitalitate Beccensium sufficienter eloqui
nequeo. Interrogati Burgundiones et Hispani, aliique de longe seu de
prope adventantes respondeant: et quanta benignitate ab eis suscepti fuerint,
sine fraude proferant, eosque in similibus imitari sine fictione satagant.
Janua Beccensium patet omni viatori, eorumque panis nulli denegatur
charitative petenti."

[3] Ib. A. "Fama sapientiæ hujus didascoli per totam Latinitatem divul-
gata est, et nectare bonæ opinionis ejus occidentalis Ecclesia nobiliter
debriata est."

CHAP. IV.

His corre-
spondence.

Intercourse
between
Bec and
England.

honourable title of mothers of the house.[1] Like all the saints and scholars of his day, he had a crowd of correspondents of all classes ; amongst them we see Countess Ida of Boulogne and the Conqueror's renowned daughter Adela.[2] And throughout his life and letters we see constant signs of the daily intercourse which, as naturally followed on the circumstances of the time, was ever going on between Normandy and England. The endless going to and fro between the two countries strikes us at every step.[3] There was an interchange of men; if many Normans found their way to England, some Englishmen found their way to Normandy. Bec had already begun to give bishops to England. Lanfranc had placed two monks of his old house in the episcopal chair of Rochester.[4] The second of them, the famous Gundulf, had been, when at Bec, the familiar friend of Anselm, who spoke little himself, but who listened to the great teacher, and wept at his touching words.[5] On the other hand, in the house of Bec itself there were monks who were English of the Old-English stock, monks whom Lanfranc thought fit to call back to their own land and to the monastery of which he was the spiritual father.[6]

---

[1] See Appendix Y.　　　　　　　[2] See Appendix Y.

[3] See Appendix Y.　　　　　　　[4] See N. C. vol. iv. p. 366.

[5] There is something amusing in the picture of the two in the Life of Gundulf, Anglia Sacra, ii. 275. "Anselmus, quia in scripturis eruditior erat, frequentior loquebatur. Gundulfus vero, quia in lacrimis profusior erat, magis fletibus rigabatur. Loquebatur ille; plorabat iste. Ille plantabat; iste rigabat. Divina ille proferebat eloquia; profunda iste trahebat suspiria. Christi vices ille, iste gerebat Mariæ." There are not a few letters of Anselm addressed to Gundulf. See Appendix Y.

[6] Among these was one of the men named Osbern—there would seem to be more than one—who play a part in the life of Anselm. There is the Osbern mentioned in the Life, i. 2. 13, 14, as first the bitter enemy and then the chosen friend of Anselm. He seems to live and die at Bec, and after his death he appears to Anselm and tells him how the old serpent thrice rose up against him, but the Lord's bearward, "ursarius Domini Dei" (comp. N.C. vol. ii. p. 26), saves him. Then there is the Osbern

Anselm had thus many ties of friendship and CHAP. IV. kindly association with England, even before he had any official connexion with the land or its inhabitants. And a strictly official connexion began long before he became archbishop. The Abbot of Bec had both tem- Lands of poral possessions and spiritual duties within our island. Bec in
England. He was the lord of English estates and the spiritual father of brethren settled on English soil. The house of Bec appears in four places in Domesday as holder of lands in England; but one manor only was held in chief of the king. The church of Saint Mary of Bec held the lordship of Deverel in Wiltshire, once the possession of Brihtric, whether the son of Ælfgar or any less famous bearer of the name. This had been the gift of Queen Matilda, and it is worth noting that the value of the land had lessened in the few years between her death and the taking of the Survey.[1] A smaller estate at Swinecombe in Oxfordshire, held of Miles Crispin, was more lucky; it had grown in value by one third.[2] In Surrey the house held lands at Tooting

mentioned in the Letters, i. 57, 58. This last Osbern is demanded by Lanfranc for his monastery at Canterbury ("domnus Osbernus quem ad se reduci auctoritas vestra jubet"), and he is sent to Prior Henry at Christ Church with a letter of recommendation from Anselm. In this are the words, "domnus Osbernus vester, qui ad vos redit, pristinæ vitæ perversitatam sponte accusat et execratur." This and a good deal more would exactly suit the Osbern of the Life, yet it is hardly possible that they can be the same. But this second Osbern may be the same as the one who writes the most remarkable letter to Anselm (iii. 2), on which see Appendix Y. Osbern, Osbiorn, is one of those names which are both English—or at least Danish—and Norman. That the second Osbern at least was English seems clear from Epp. i. 60, 65, where we hear of "domnus Hulwardus [Wulfward] Anglus, consobrinus domni Osberni." Did Lanfranc claim all English monks anywhere?

[1] Domesday, 69 b. "Totum manerium valet xii. libras; valebat xv. libras vivente Mathilde regina, quæ dedit eidem ecclesiæ." There were six hides and a half in demesne, and one hide held by the church of the place.

[2] Domesday, 159 b. "Valuit xl. solidos; modo lx. solidos. Hæc terra nunquam geldum reddidit." This exceptional privilege, designed or casual, might become a ground of disputes.

and Streatham, the gift of Richard of Clare or of Tunbridge, him of whom we have so often heard. The possessions of Bec at Tooting, which had sunk to one fifth of their ancient value at the time of their grant to the abbey, had risen again to the value at which they were rated in the days of King Eadward.[1] The business arising out of these lands, all seemingly held in demesne, with a mill, churls, slaves, and other dependents, must have called for some care on the part of the abbot or of those whom he employed for the purpose. And it would seem that, on the whole, the monastic body had been a careful husband of its English estates. In after times also Bec became the head of several alien priories in England; but one only of these can be carried back with certainty to Anselm's day. This was the priory of Clare in Suffolk, afterwards moved to Stoke, which was founded as a cell to Bec while Anselm was abbot.[2] It was the gift of Gilbert of Clare, brother of Richard the other benefactor of the house, a house which seems to have had special attractions for the whole family of Count Gilbert.

The dependent priory of Clare. 1090.

Law-suits. Anselm was thus a land-owner on both sides of the sea, and, little as he loved temporal business, he could

---

[1] Domesday, 34 b. "Sancta Maria de Bech tenet de dono Ricardi Totinges . . . . T. R. E. et modo val. c. solidos; cum recepit xx. solidos." On these possessions of Bec in England during the reign of the Conqueror, see N. C. vol. iv. p. 440.

[2] See Mon. Angl. vii. 1052. An earlier church of secular canons was changed by Gilbert of Clare into a cell of Bec. It was removed to Stoke in 1124, made denizen in 1395, and restored to seculars in 1415. See Mon. Angl. vi. 1415. Weedon Beck in Northamptonshire is also said to have had a cell of Bec, founded shortly after the Conquest. Weedon appears three times in Domesday, 223, 224 b, 227; but there is no mention of Bec. Ernulf of Hesdin is also said to have founded a cell to Bec at Ruislip in Middlesex, Mon. Angl. vii. 1050. Ruislip appears in Domesday, 129 b, as a possession of Ernulf, but there is no mention of Bec. The chief dependency of Bec in England, Oakburn in Wiltshire, does not claim an earlier date or founder than Matilda of Wallingford, daughter of Robert of Oily, in 1149.

not wholly escape it. No man, no society of men, in CHAP. IV.
either the Normandy or the England of those days,
could hope to keep clear of law-suits. The house of
Herlwin, new as it was and holy as it was, seems to
have been entangled in not a few. Anselm's chief wish Anselm's
desire to
was that in these disputes justice should be done to all do justice.
concerned. There were among the monks of Bec, as
among the monks of other houses, men who knew the
law and who were skilful in legal pleadings. The Abbot
had sometimes to charge them to make no unfair use
of their skill, and not to strive to win any advantage for
the house but such as was strictly just.[1] Otherwise, as
far as he could, he entrusted mere worldly affairs—the
serving of tables—to others.[2] Yet he could not avoid
journeys beyond sea on behalf of the house. He was
thus more than once compelled to visit England. He His first
visit to
crossed the sea in the first year of his appointment as England.
abbot. He came to Canterbury; he was received with 1078.
mickle worship by Lanfranc and the monks of Christ
Church.[3] The first touch of English soil seems to have
changed the Burgundian saint, the Norman abbot, into an
Englishman and an English patriot. It was now that he
made the memorable discourse in which he showed that
English Ælfheah was a true martyr.[4] The Abbot of His friendship with
Bec did not scorn to be admitted into the brotherhood the monks

[1] Eadmer, Vit. Ans. i. 5. 37. "Abominabile quippe judicabat, si
quidvis lucri assequeretur ex eo quod alius contra moderamina juris quavis
astutia perdere posset. Unde neminem in placitis patiebatur a suis aliqua
fraude circumveniri, observans ne cui faceret quod sibi fieri nollet." Compare the cunning lawyers whom Abbot Adelelm found among the monks of
Abingdon, N. C. vol. iv. p. 476.

[2] Ib. "Delegatis monasterii causis curæ ac sollicitudini fratrum, de quorum vita et strenuitate certus erat."

[3] Ib. 41. "Cum igitur Anselmus, transito mari, Cantuariam veniret, pro
sua reverentia et omnibus nota sanctitate, honorifice a conventu ecclesiæ
Christi in ipsa civitate sitæ susceptus est." His discourse to the monks is
given at great length. [4] See N. C. vol. iv. p. 441.

of the monks of Christ Church, and to dwell with them as one of themselves.[1] It was the time when Lanfranc was doing his work of reform among them,[2] a work which was doubtless helped by the sojourn and counsel of Anselm. With the more learned among them he lived familiarly, putting and answering questions, both in profane and sacred lore.[3] And among them he made one friend, English by blood and name, whose memory is for ever entwined with his own. It was now that Eadmer, then a young monk of the house, won his deep regard, and attached himself for ever to the master whose acts he was in after times to record.[4]

But it was not only in the church which was one day to be his own, or among men of his own order only, that Anselm made friends in England. He made a kind of progress through the land, being welcomed everywhere, as well in the courts of nobles as in the houses of monks, nuns, and canons.[5] Everywhere he scattered the good seed of his teaching, speaking to all according to their several callings, to men and women, married and unmarried, monks, clerks, laymen, making himself, as far as was lawful, all things to all men.[6] Scholar and

---

[1] Vit. Ans. i. 5. 41. "Accepta fraternitate monachorum, factus est inter eos unus ex eis. Degens per dies aliquot inter eos et quotidie, aut in capitulo, aut in claustro, mira quædam et illis adhuc temporibus insolita de vita et moribus monachorum coram eis rationabili facundia disserens."

[2] See N. C. vol. iv. p. 361.

[3] Vit. Ans. u. s. "Privatim quoque aliis horis agebat, cum his qui profundioris ingenii erant, profundas eis de divinis nec non sæcularibus libris quæstiones proponens, propositasque exponens."

[4] Ib. "Quo tempore et ego ad sanctitatis ejus notitiam pervenire merui, ac, pro modulo parvitatis meæ, beata illius familiaritate utpote adolescens, qui tunc eram, non parum potiri."

[5] Ib. 6. 45. "Vadens et ad diversa monasteria monachorum, canonicorum, sanctimonialium, nec non ad curias quorumque nobilium, prout eum ratio ducebat, perveniens, lætissime suscipiebatur, et suscepto quæque charitatis obsequia gratissime ministrabantur."

[6] Ib. "Solito more cunctis se jucundum et affabilem exhibebat, moresque singulorum in quantum sine peccato poterat, in se suscipiebat."

theologian as Anselm was, his teaching was specially CHAP. IV.
popular; he did not affect the grand style, but dealt His preaching.
largely in parables and instances which were easy to
be understood.[1] The laity therefore flocked eagerly
to hear him, and every man rejoiced who could win the
privilege of personal speech with the new apostle.[2]
The men of that age, stained as many of them were
with great crimes—perhaps all the more because their
crimes were of a kind which they could not help feeling
to be crimes—commonly kept enough of conscience and
good feeling to admire in others the virtues which they
failed to practise themselves. William Rufus himself
had moments when goodness awed him. It was only
a few exceptional monsters like the fiend of Bellême
whom no such feelings ever touched. Anselm became His love for England.
the idol of all the inhabitants of England, without distinction of age or sex, of rank or race. The land became
to him yet another home, a home which he loved to
visit, and where he was ever welcome.[3] Men sought to His alleged miracles.
him for the cure of bodily as well as spiritual diseases;
and we read of not a few cases of healing in which he
was deemed to be the agent, cases in which modern times
will most likely see the strong exercise of that power
which, from one point of view, is called imagination,

Eadmer draws out the apostolic rule at some length, and gives specimens
of Anselm's discourses to these different classes.

[1] Vit. Ans. i. 6. 47. "Non eo, ut aliis mos est, docendi modo exercebat, sed longe aliter singula quæque sub vulgaribus et notis exemplis
proponens, solidæque rationis testimonio fulciens, ac remota omni am-
biguitate, in mentibus auditorum deponens."

[2] Ib. "Lætabatur ergo quisquis illius colloquio uti poterat, quoniam in
eò quodcumque petebatur divinum consilium in promptu erat." He had
said yet more strongly, "Corda omnium miro modo in amorem ejus verte-
bantur, et ad eum audiendum famelica aviditate replebantur."

[3] Ib. 48. He became "pro sua excellenti fama totius Angliæ partibus
notus, ac pro reverenda sanctitate charus cunctis effectus." And directly
after, "Familiaris ergo ei dehinc Anglia facta est, et prout diversitas
causarum ferebat, ab eo frequentata."

CHAP. IV.

His friendship with the Conqueror;

with Earl Hugh.

Hugh's changes at Chester.

and from another faith.[1] The highest in estate and power were the most eager of all to humble themselves before him. We have seen how the elder William, ever mild to good men, was specially mild to Anselm, how he craved his presence on his death-bed, and how Anselm, unable to help his master in life, was among those who did the last honours to him in death.[2] We are told that there was not an earl or countess or great person of any kind in England, who did not seek the friendship of Anselm, who did not deem that his or her spiritual state was the worse if any opportunity had been lost of doing honour or service to the Abbot of Bec.[3] Like some other saints of his own and of other times, he drew to himself the special regard of some whose characters were most unlike his own. Earl Hugh of Chester, debauched, greedy, reckless, and cruel, beyond the average of the time, is recorded as being a special friend of the holy man.[4] He who rebuked kings doubtless rebuked earls also; but it would have been a better sign of reformation, if Hugh, under the teaching of Anselm, had learned to spare the eyes either of brother nobles or of British

[1] No strictly physical miracle is alleged to have been wrought by Anselm's own hands; but several stories are told by Eadmer in the sixth chapter of the first book of the Life, in which cures were believed to be done by water in which he had washed, and the like. In another class of stories in the third chapter, the bodily wants of Anselm or his friends are supplied in an unexpected way, but without any physical miracle. Thus the well-known Walter Tirel, entertaining Anselm, makes excuses for the lack of fish. The saint announces that a fine sturgeon is on the road, and it presently comes.

Eadmer's book of the Miracles of Anselm, which forms No. xvi. in Dr. Liebermann's collection, consists of wonders of the usual kind at or after Anselm's death.

[2] See N. C. vol. iv. pp. 704, 713.

[3] Eadmer, Vit. Ans. i. 6. 47. "Non fuit comes in Anglia seu comitissa, vel ulla persona potens, quæ non judicaret se sua coram Deo merita perdidisse, si contingeret se Anselmo abbati Beccensi gratiam cujusvis officii tunc temporis non exhibuisse."

[4] See N. C. vol. iv. p. 491. So Hist. Nov. 15, "Certe amicus meus familiaris ab antiquo comes Cestrensis Hugo fuit."

captives, than if he was merely led to place monks chap. iv. instead of canons at Saint Werburh's, and in the end to take the cowl among them himself.

But the planting of monks at Saint Werburh's had no small effect on the destiny of Anselm and of England. In the course of the year which saw the annexation of Cumberland men began to be thoroughly wearied of the long vacancy of the archbishopric. It may be that the great gathering at Lincoln had brought home to every mind the great wrong under which the Church was suffering. The bishops of the land had come together to a great ecclesiastical rite; but they had come together as a body without a head. And they had parted under circumstances which made the state of things even worse than it had been when they met. The death of Remigius had handed over another bishopric to the wardship of Flambard. The land from the Thames to the Humber, the great diocese which took in nine shires, was to be left without a shepherd as long as Rufus and Flambard should think good. That is, it was to be left till some one among the King's servants should be ready to do by Lincoln as Herbert Losinga had done by Thetford. Men began to say among themselves that such unlaw as this could not go on for ever; the land could not abide without a chief pastor; an archbishop must soon come somehow, whether the King and Flambard willed it or not. The feeling was universal; and with it another feeling was almost equally universal; when the archbishop should come, he could come only in the shape of the man who was of all men most worthy of the office, the man whom all England knew and loved as if his whole life had been spent within her seas, the holy Abbot of Bec.[1] That such was

Feeling as to the vacancy of the archbishopric.

1092.

Vacancy of Lincoln.

Anselm looked to as the coming archbishop.

---

[1] Eadmer, Hist. Nov. 14. "Jam enim, quodam quasi præsagio mentes quorundam tangebantur, et licet clanculo, nonnulli adinvicem loquebantur, eum, si Angliam iret, archiepiscopum Cantuariensem fore." William of Malmesbury (Gest. Pont. 78), "Erat tamen spes nonnulla his malis posse

the general feeling in England soon became known out of England; it became known at Bec as at other places; it was not hidden from the Abbot of Bec himself.

Earl Hugh seeks help from Anselm in his reforms. 1092.

At the time which we have now reached Earl Hugh was planning his supposed reforms at Saint Werburh's. Designing to fill the minster with monks, he would have his monks from the place where the monastic life was most perfectly practised; the men who were to kindle a new light at Chester must come from Bec.[1] It was in the end from Bec that the first abbot Richard and his brethren came to wage that strife which we are told was so specially hard-fought in that region.[2] But the founder further wished the work to be done under the eye of the Abbot of Bec himself; so, trusting in his old friendship, Earl Hugh prayed Anselm to come to him. His prayer was backed by that of other nobles of England;[3] the monks of Bec too deemed that either the affairs of Saint Werburh's or some other business of the monastery called for their abbot's presence in England.[4] But Anselm at

imponi finem, si quando Cantuariensem archiepiscopum viderent, qui esset os omnium, vexillifer prævius, umbo publicus. Spargebaturque in vulgus rumor, haud equidem sine mente et numine Dei, ut arbitror, Anselmum fore archiepiscopum, virum penitus sanctum, anxie doctum, felicem futuram hujus hominis benedictionibus Angliam."

[1] See N. C. vol. iv. pp. 312, 491. We might have guessed from Eadmer (Hist. Nov. 14) that it is Saint Werburh's of which he is speaking, when he says, "Hugo comes Cestrensis volens in sua quadam ecclesia monachorum abbatiam instituere, missis Beccum nuntiis, rogavit abbatem Anselmum Angliam venire, locum inspicere, eumque per monachos suos regulari conversatione informare." But it is William of Malmesbury (Gest. Pont. 78) who distinctly mentions Chester. Anselm comes to England, "ut abbatiam apud Cestrum firmaret, quam ejusdem civitatis comes Hugo monachis potissimum Beccensibus implere volebat."

[2] He had to dwell among "belluini cœtus." See N. C. vol. iv. p. 491, and above, p. 127.

[3] Vit. Ans. ii. 1. 1. "Invitatus, imo districta interpellatione adjuratus, ab Hugone Cestrensi comite, multisque aliis Anglorum regni principibus, qui eum animarum suarum medicum et advocatum elegerant."

[4] Ib. "Insuper ecclesiæ suæ prece atque præcepto pro communi utilitate coactus."

first steadily refused to go; the general rumour had
reached his own ears; he had been told that, if he went
to England, he would certainly become Archbishop of
Canterbury. He shrank from the acceptance of such
an office; he shrank yet more from doing anything
which might even have the look of seeking for such
an office. It might be a question of casuistry whether
the command of Maurilius to accept any preferment
that might be offered could have any force beyond
the life and the province of Maurilius; yet that command may have made Anselm yet more determined to
keep out of the way of all danger of having the see of
Canterbury offered to him. He refused to go to England,
when it was possible that his object in going might
be cruelly misconstrued.[1] Another message came, announcing that Earl Hugh was smitten with grievous
sickness, and needed the spiritual help of his friend.
Moreover Anselm need not be afraid; there was nothing
in the rumours which he had heard; he stood in no
danger of the archbishopric.[2] In this Hugh most likely
spoke the truth. Others had brought themselves to believe that there must soon be an archbishop, and that
that archbishop must be Anselm. But they had no
ground for thinking that anything of the kind would
happen, except that it was the best thing that could
happen. The Earl of Chester was as likely as any man
except Flambard to know the King's real mind; and
what followed makes it plain that as yet Rufus had no
thought of filling the archbishopric at all. Still Anselm
would not go till a third message from the Earl appealed

[1] Hist. Nov. 14. "Quia hoc [his purpose not to accept the archbishopric]
non omnes intelligebant (providendo bona, non tantum coram Deo, sed etiam
coram omnibus hominibus), Angliam intrare noluit, ne se hujus rei gratia
intrasse quisquam suspicaretur."

[2] Ib. 15. "Si timor suscipiendi archiepiscopatus ne veniat eum detinet,
fateor, inquit, in fide mea, quoniam id, quod rumor inde jactet, nihil est."

to another motive. It would not be for the soul's health of Anselm himself if he stayed away when his friend so deeply needed his help.[1] To this argument Anselm yielded; for the sake of friendship and of his friend's spiritual welfare, he would go, let men say what they would about his motives for going.[2]

He is bidden to go by his monks.

But the invitation of Earl Hugh was not Anselm's only motive for his journey. Another cause was added which a little startles us. The business of the abbey in England, business to be done with the King, still called for the abbot's presence there. The monks sought to have the royal exactions on their English lands made less heavy.[3] At this moment Anselm was not at Bec; he was spending some days at Boulogne with his friend and correspondent Countess Ida.[4] While there, he received a message from Bec, bidding him, by virtue of the law of obedience, not to come back to the abbey till he had gone into England and looked after the matters about which he was needed there.[5] Such a message as this from monks to their abbot sounds to

[1] Hist. Nov. 15. "Tertio mandat illi hæc, si non veneris, revera noveris, quia nunquam in vita æterna in tanta requie eris quin perpetuo doleas te ad me non venisse." There is something very striking in the frequent mixture of strong faith with evil practice in men of Earl Hugh's stamp. But his cleaving to such a man as Anselm is at least more enlightened than the fetish-worship of Lewis the Eleventh. Cf. Church, Anselm, 173.

[2] Eadmer (Hist. Nov. 15) gives his reflexions at some length. They are summed up in the words of William of Malmesbury, Gest. Pont. 78; "Cæterum quid homines loquerentur ipsi viderent, cum quantum sua interesset, eorum obloquia, honesta diu conversatione vitasset." He adds, "Simul et jam rumor de ejus archiepiscopatu, minas olim intentans, longinquitate temporis detepuerat."

[3] Will. Malms. Gest. Pont. 79. "Ut prædiorum suorum vectigalia lenito intercessionibus suis rege levigaret."

[4] Eadmer, Hist. Nov. 15. Several letters of Anselm are addressed to her. See Appendix Y.

[5] Hist. Nov. 15. "Mandatum est illi a Beccensibus ne, si peccato inobedientiæ notari nollet, ultra monasterium repeteret, donec transito mari, suis in Anglia rebus subveniret."

us like a reversal of all monastic order ; but it seems to CHAP. IV. have been held that, while each monk undoubtedly owed obedience to the abbot, the abbot himself owed obedience to the general vote of the convent. To these two influences, the law of obedience and care for Earl Hugh's soul, Anselm at last yielded. He set sail from Boulogne Anselm or Whitsand, and landed at Dover. He was now within goes to England. what was presently to be his own province, his own diocese; and that province he was not again to leave till he sought shelter on the mainland in the character of archbishop and confessor.

The immediate business of Anselm led him to Chester, and to the place, wherever it was, where the King was to be found. We are told that he made the best of his way to his sick friend,[1] who was so eager for Anselm's coming that he despised all other spiritual help.[2] But it is plain that he tarried on the road to see the King. From Dover his first stage was Canterbury. There he was Anselm alarmed by the welcome given him by a crowd of monks at Canterbury. and laymen who hailed him as their future archbishop. September 8, 1092. It was a high festival, the Nativity of our Lady; but Anselm, wishing to give no encouragement to such greetings as he had just received, declined to officiate at the celebration of the feast. He tarried but one night in the city, and left it early the next morning.[3] He then went to His first the King. The reception which he met with showed that interview with Rufus. Rufus must have been for the moment in one of his better moods. Anselm indeed was a chosen friend of his father,

[1] "Citato gressu, ad comitem venit," says Eadmer (Hist. Nov. 15), where he leaves out the interview with the King which he describes in the Life.

[2] Will. Malms. Gest. Pont. 79. "Hugo .... quanquam in supremis positus, omnium in confessione supercilium recusans, Anselmum expetebat; veteris amicitiae pignus apud eum depositurus si moreretur."

[3] Vit. Ans. ii. 1. 1. "Cum quasi ex præsagio futurorum multi et monachi et laici conclamarent illum archiepiscopum fore, summo mane a loco decessit, nec ullo pacto acquiescere petentibus, ut ibi festum celebraret, voluit."

CHAP. IV. and he had given him no personal offence. As soon as the approach of the Abbot of Bec was announced, the King arose, met him at the door, exchanged the kiss of peace, and led him by the hand to his seat.[1] A friendly discourse followed. Perhaps the very friendliness of William's greeting brought it more fully home to Anselm's mind that it would be a failure of duty on his own part if he spoke only of the worldly affairs of his abbey. He must seize the moment to give a word of warning to a sinner whose evil deeds were so black, and who disgraced at the same time so lofty an office and such high natural gifts. Anselm asked that all others might withdraw; he wished for a private interview with the King. The affairs of the house of Bec were, for the moment at least, passed by; the welfare of the kingdom of England, and the soul's health of its king, were objects which came first. Anselm told Rufus in plain words that the men of his kingdom, both secretly and openly, daily said things of him which in no way became his kingly office.[2] From later appeals of Anselm to the conscience of Rufus, we may conceive that this general description took in at once the special wrongs done to the Church, the general abuses of William's government, and the personal excesses of William's own life. Anselm was not the man to hold his peace on any one of those three subjects ; but we have no details of Anselm's discourse from his own biographer, nor does he give us any notice of the way in which William received his rebuke.[3] Yet it would seem

Anselm's rebuke of the King.

---

[1] Vit. Ans. ii. 1. 1. "Rex ipse solio exsilit, et ad ostium domus viro gaudens occurrit, ac in oscula ruens per dexteram eum ad sedem suam perducit."

[2] Ib. "Regem de his quæ fama de eo ferebat Anselmus arguere cœpit, nec quidquam eorum quæ illi dicenda esse sciebat, silentio pressit. Pene etenim totius regni homines omnes talia quotidie nunc clam nunc palam de eo dicebant, qualia regiam dignitatem nequaquam decebant."

[3] The language of Eadmer quoted in the last note is quite vague. In William of Malmesbury (Gest. Pont. 79) we get one of those remarkable cases in which he first wrote something strong, and then altered it. He seems

that the milder mood of the Red King had not wholly CHAP. IV. passed away. If Anselm had been thrust aside with any violent or sarcastic answer, it would surely have passed into one of the stock anecdotes of the reign. Our only other description of the scene paints Rufus as held back from any disrespectful treatment of Anselm by a lingering reverence for the friend of his parents. He turned the matter off with a laugh. He could not hinder what men chose to say of him; but so holy a man as Anselm ought not to believe such stories.[1] It is not even clear whether Anselm brought himself to speak at all on the particular business which had brought him to the King's presence. King and Abbot parted; it Settlement would seem that nothing was done about the affairs of of the affairs of Bec for the present; but we may gather that, at some Bec. later time, the lands of the monastery were relieved from the burthens of which they complained.[2]

Anselm now went on to Chester, where he found his Anselm at friend Earl Hugh restored to health. But the change in Chester. the foundation at Saint Werburh's still needed his presence, and the special affairs of his own house had also

(see his editor's note) to have first written, "Data secreti copia, *flagitiorum obscœnitatem* quibus regem accusabat fama incunctanter aperuit." He then struck out the strong words in Italics and changed them to the vague "cuncta."

[1] Will. Malms. Gest. Pont. 79. "Famæ licentiæ non se posse obviare dictitans; ceterum sanctum virum non debere illa credere. Neque enim procaciore responso exsufflare hominem tunc volebat, sciens quanti eum pater et mater pendere soliti essent dum adviverent."

[2] Eadmer, in the passage quoted above, distinctly implies that nothing was said about the affairs of Bec, and adds, "Finito colloquio divisi ab invicem sunt, et de ecclesiæ suæ negotiis ea vice ab Anselmo nihil actum est." William of Malmesbury, on the other hand, describes Anselm as speaking of them at this interview ("necessitates quoque suas modeste allegans"), and William as settling them as Anselm wished ("ille omnia negotia Beccensis ecclesiæ ad arbitrium rectoris componens"). I should infer from this, and from the words "ea vice" in Eadmer, that things were settled in the end as the monks of Bec wished, but not at this interview. William of Malmesbury is never very strict as to chronological order.

CHAP. IV. to be looked to. Between these two sets of affairs,

The King Anselm was kept in England for five months. He then
refuses him
leave to go wished to go back to Normandy; but the King's leave,
back.
February, it seems, was needed, and the King's leave was refused.[1]
1093.
This refusal is worth notice. It does not seem to have
been done in enmity; at least it was not followed by any
kind of further wrong-doing on the King's part towards

William's Anselm. It really looks as if William had, not indeed
feeling
towards   any fixed purpose of appointing Anselm to the arch-
Anselm.
bishopric, but a kind of feeling that he might be driven to
appoint him, a feeling that things might come to a stage
in which he could not help naming some archbishop, and
that, if it came to that stage, he could not help naming
Anselm. It is plain from what follows that the thought
of Anselm as a possible archbishop was in the King's
mind as well as in the minds of others. But certainly
no offer or hint was at this stage made by William, nor
was anything said to Anselm about the matter by any
one else.[2] Men no doubt knew Anselm's feelings, and
avoided the subject. But at one point during these
five months the vacancy of the archbishopric was
brought very strongly before Anselm's mind, though
not in a way which suggested his own appointment

Christmas rather than that of anybody else. When the Midwinter
Assembly,
1092–1093. Gemót of this year was held, the long vacancy, and

The   the evils which flowed from it, became a matter of
vacancy
discussed   discussion among the assembled Witan. But they did
by the
Witan.   not venture to attempt any election, or even to make any
suggestion of their own; they did not even make any

---

[1] Eadmer, Hist. Nov. 15. "Post hæc in Normanniam regredi volens,
negata a rege licentia, copiam id agendi habere non potuit." It is not easy,
as Dean Church remarks (Anselm, 175), to see why the King's leave was
needed for the subject of another prince to go back to his own country.

[2] Ib. "Sic hujus temporis spatium transiit, ut de pontificatu Cantuariensi nihil ad eum vel de eo dictum actumve sit; ipseque sui periculi et
antiqui timoris securus effectus fuerit."

direct petition to the King to put an end to the vacancy.
A resolution was passed — our contemporary guide
doubted whether future ages would believe the fact—
that the King should be humbly petitioned to allow
prayers to be put up throughout the churches of England craving that God would by his inspiration move
the King's heart to put an end to the wrongs of his
head church and of all his other churches by the appointment of a worthy chief pastor.[1] We thus see that
the power of ending or prolonging the vacancy is
acknowledged to rest only with the King; it is not for
the Witan to constrain, but only for God to guide, the
royal will. But we further see that the right of or-
daining religious ceremonies is held to rest with the
King and his Witan, just as it had rested in the days of
Cnut.[2] The unanimous petition of the Assembly was
laid before the King. He was somewhat angry, but he
took no violent step. He agreed to the matter of the
address, but in a scornful shape. "Pray as you will; I
shall do as I think good; no man's prayers will do anything to shake my will."[3] To draw up a proper form
of prayer was the natural business of the bishops; and
they had among them one specially skilled in such
matters in the person of Osmund of Salisbury. But they
all agreed to consult the Abbot of Bec, and to ask him to

[1] Eadmer tells the story, with the comment, "quod posteris mirum
dictu fortasse videbitur."

[2] See N. C. vol. i. p. 435.

[3] Eadmer, u. s. "Ipse, licet nonnihil exinde indignatus, tamen fieri
quod petebatur permisit, dicens quod quidquid ecclesia peteret, ipse sine
dubio pro nullo dimitteret quin faceret omne quod vellet." Will. Malms.
Gest. Pont. 79. "Respondit ludibundus, risu iram dissimulans; 'Orate quod
vultis; ego faciam quod placebit, quia nullius unquam oratio voluntatem
meam labefactabit.'" The *oratio directa* of William sounds as if it came
nearer to the King's actual words than the *oratio obliqua* of Eadmer. But
we lose much in many of these stories from not having the Red King's own
vigorous French.

CHAP. IV.

Anselm
draws up
a form of
prayer.

draw up a prayer fitted for the purpose. Anselm, after much pressing, agreed; he drew up the prayer; it was laid before the Assembly, and his work was approved by all.[1] The Gemót broke up, and prayers were offered throughout England, according to Anselm's model, for the appointment of an archbishop, a prayer which on most lips doubtless meant the appointment of Anselm himself.[2]

The year
1093.

Before the Assembly broke up, a memorable year had begun. It is a year crowded with events, with the deaths of memorable men, with one death above all which led to most important results on the relations between the two great parts of the isle of Britain. With these events I shall deal in another chapter; we have now mainly to trace the ecclesiastical character of the year as the greatest of all stages in the career of Anselm. The Assembly had doubtless been held at Gloucester, and, after the session was over, the King tarried in the neighbourhood, at the royal house of Alvestone, once a

William's
sickness at
Alvestone.

lordship of Earl Harold.[3] There he was smitten with a heavy sickness. The tale has a legendary sound; yet there is nothing really incredible in the story that he fell sick directly after he had been guilty of a mocking speech

Discourse
about
Anselm
before the
King.

about Anselm. Some nobles were with the King at Alvestone, and one of them spoke of the virtues of the Abbot of Bec. He was a man who loved God only, and sought for none of the things of this world. The King says in mockery, "Not for the archbishopric of Canterbury?" The remark at least shows that Anselm and the

---

[1] Eadmer, Hist. Nov. 13. Anselm's chief objection was that the making of prayers was a specially episcopal business; " Episcopi, ad quos ista maxime pertinebant, Anselmum super reipsa consuluerunt. Et quod ipse orationis agendæ modum et summam ordinaret, vix optinere suis precibus ab eo potuerant. Episcopis enim præferri in tali statuto ipse abbas fugiebat."

[2] Ib. "Institutæ igitur preces sunt per Anglorum ecclesias omnes."

[3] See Domesday, 163. The entry of Alvestone comes immediately before the entry of Berkeley.

archbishopric went together in the King's thoughts as
well as in the thoughts of other men.[1] The lord who
had spoken answered that, in his belief and in that of
many others, the archbishopric was the very thing which
Anselm least wished for.[2] The King laughed again, and
said that, if Anselm had any hope of the archbishopric,
he would clap his hands and stamp with his feet, and
run into the King's arms. But he added, "By the face of
Lucca, he and every other man who seeks the archbishopric
may this time give way to me; for I will be archbishop
myself."[3] He repeated the jest several times. Presently
sickness came upon him, and, in a few hours, he took to
his bed. He was carried in haste from Alvestone to
the neighbouring city, where he could doubtless find
better quarters and attendance.[4] He lay sick during the
whole of Lent; but, unless his sickness began somewhat
earlier, the whole of the events with which we have to
deal must have been crowded into the first few days of
the penitential season. At all events, during the first
week of Lent, William Rufus was lying at Gloucester,

[1] This story is told by Eadmer (Hist. Nov. 15, 16) and William of
Malmesbury (Gest. Pont. 80). One would like to know the name of this
"unus de principibus terræ, cum rege familiariter agens," who held Anselm
in such high esteem. If it had been Earl Hugh, one might expect that
Eadmer would have said so.

[2] Ib. "Nec illum quidem maxime, sicut mea multorumque fert
opinio."

[3] Ib. "Obtestatus est rex quod manibus ac pedibus plaudens, in am-
plexum ejus accurreret, si ullam fiduciam haberet se ad illum posse ullatenus
aspirare, et adjecit, Sed per sanctum vultum de Luca (sic enim jurare consueverat), nec ipse hoc tempore nec alius quis archiepiscopus erit, me
excepto."

[4] Ib. "Hæc illum dicentem e vestigio valida infirmitas corripuit,
et lecto deposuit, atque indies crescendo ferme usque ad exhalationem
spiritus egit." He mentions Gloucester directly after, but the minute
geography comes from Florence (1093); "Rex Willelmus junior, in regia
villa quæ vocatur Alwestan vehementi percussus infirmitate, civitatem
Glawornam festinanter adiit, ibique per totam quadragesimam languosus
jacuit."

CHAP. IV. sick of a sickness which both himself and others deemed
to be unto death.[1]

Repentance of Rufus. The heart of the Red King was not yet wholly
hardened; with sickness came repentance. Believing
himself to be at the gates of the next world, his conscience awoke, and he saw in their true light the deeds
which he had been so long doing in this world. He no
longer jested at his own crimes and vices; he bemoaned
them and began to think of amendment. The great
men of the realm, bishops, abbots, and lay nobles,
pressed around his sick bed, looking for his speedy
death, and urging him to make what atonement he
Advice of the prelates and nobles. could for his misdeeds, while he yet lived. Let him
throw open his prisons; let him set free his captives;
let him loose those who were in chains; let him forgive
his debtors—it is again assumed that a debt to the Crown
must be a wrongful debt—let him provide pastors for
the churches which he holds in his hands; above all, let
him set free the head church of all, the church of Canterbury, whose bondage was the most crying wrong of
his kingdom.[2] All this they pressed, each to the best
of his power, on the no longer unwilling mind of the
King. It bethought them moreover that there was one
not far off, who was more skilled than any of them in
healing the diseases of the soul, and whose words would

---

[1] Here we have the pithy words of the Chronicle; "On þisum geare to
þam længtene warð se cyng W. on Gleaweceastre to þam swiðe geseclod,
þæt he wæs ofer eall dead gekyd." So says Eadmer (Hist. Nov. 16); "Omnes totius regni principes coeunt; episcopi, abbates, et quique nobiles, nihil
præter mortem ejus præstolantes."

[2] The good resolutions of the King come out with all force in the
Chronicle; "And on his broke he Gode fela behæsa behét, his agen lif on
riht to lædene, and Godes cyrcean griðian and friðian, and næfre má eft wið
feo gesyllan, and ealle rihte lage on his þeode to habbene." The exhortations come out most clearly in Eadmer; Florence seems to attribute them
to the King's lay counsellors; "Cum se putaret cito moriturum, ut ei sui
barones suggesserint," &c.

strike deeper into the heart of the penitent than the words
of any other. The Abbot of Bec was still in England;
he was even, knowing nothing of what was going on,
tarrying at no great distance from Gloucester.[1] A messenger was sent, bidding him come with all speed; the
King was dying, and needed his spiritual help before all
was over. Anselm came at once; he asked what had
passed between the sick man and his directors, and he
fully approved of all the counsel that they had given to
the repentant sinner.[2] The duties of confession, of amendment, of reparation, the full and speedy carrying out of
all that his advisers had pressed upon him, was the
only means, the only hope. By the general voice of all,
Anselm was bidden to undertake the duty of making
yet another exhortation to the royal penitent. Anselm
spoke, and William hearkened. He more than hearkened; he answered, and for the moment he acted. He
accepted all that Anselm told him; he promised to
amend his ways, to rule his kingdom in mildness and
righteousness. To this he pledged his faith; he made
the bishops his sureties, and bade them renew the promise in his name to God before the altar.[3] More practical still, a proclamation was put forth under the royal
seal, promising to the people, in the old form, good

---

[1] Eadmer, Hist. Nov. 16. "Hac tempestate Anselmus inscius horum morabatur in quadam villa non longe a Glocestria ubi rex infirmabatur."

[2] Ib. "Ingreditur ad regem, rogatur quid consilii salubrius morientis animæ judicet. Exponi sibi primo postulat, quid se absente ab assistenti- bus ægro consultum sit. Audit, probat, et addit, scriptum est, Incipite Domino in confessione." He goes on at somewhat further length on the duty of confession. There is something striking in the kind of profes- sional air with which the duty is undertaken. The spiritual physician, called in from a distance, approves the treatment of the local practitioners, just as a physician of the body might do.

[3] Ib. "Spondet in hoc fidem suam, et vades inter se et Deum facit episcopos suos, mittens, qui hoc votum suum Deo super altare sua vice promittant."

CHAP. IV. laws, strict heed to right, strict examination into wrong. The vacant churches should be filled, and their revenues should be restored to them. The King would no longer sell them or set them to farm. All prisoners should be set free; all debts to the crown should be forgiven; all offences against the King should be pardoned, and all

General satisfaction.

suits begun in the King's name stopped.[1] Great was the joy through the land; a burst of loyal thankfulness was in every heart and on every mouth. The rule of King William was henceforth to be as the rule of the best of the kings who had gone before him. Thanksgivings went up to God through the whole land, and earnest prayers for the welfare of so great and so good a king.[2]

This was the second time that the people of England had greedily swallowed the promises of the Red King. He had already deceived them once; but kings are easily trusted, and the awful circumstances under which reform was now promised might well lead men to believe that

Beginnings of reform.

the promise was sincere. Sincere for the moment it doubtless was; nor did the proclamation remain altogether a dead letter. The reforms were actually begun; some at least of the prisoners were set free. William

[1] Eadmer, Hist. Nov. 16. "Scribitur edictum, regioque sigillo firmatur, quatenus captivi quicunque sunt in omni dominatione sua relaxentur, omnia debita irrevocabiliter remittantur, omnes offensiones antehac perpetratæ, indulta remissione, perpetuæ oblivioni tradantur." More general provisions followed; "Promittuntur insuper omni populo bonæ et sanctæ leges, inviolabilis observatio juris, injuriarum gravis, et quæ terreat cæteros, examinatio." We may specially regret that we have not the English text of this momentary Great Charter. Its language seems to assume, like the charter of Henry (see above, pp. 344, 392), that suits brought in the King's name would be unjust, and that his claims for debts would be unjust also.

[2] Ib. "Gaudetur a cunctis, benedicitur Deus in istis, obnixe oratur pro salute talis ac tanti regis." This is the real language of the moment, which is weakened by William of Malmesbury, Gest. Pont. 80; "Plausu exceptum est verbum, ibatque clamor cælo bona et salutem regi optantium."

also now made grants to some monasteries,[1] and, what CHAP. IV.
was more important than all, he filled the vacant
bishoprics. The fame of one of the two appointments He grants the bishop-ric of Lincoln to Robert Bloet.
so fills the pages of our guides that we might easily forget
that it was now that the staff of Remigius was given
to Robert Bloet.[2] We have heard of him already as an
old servant of William the Great, and as trusted by him
with the weighty letter which ruled the succession of the
crown on behalf of William the Red.[3] He was now the
King's Chancellor. He bears a doubtful character; he
was not a scholar, but he was a man skilful in all worldly
business; he was not a saint, but he was perhaps not the
extreme sinner which some have painted him.[4] His consecration was put off for nearly a year; and we shall
meet him again in the midst of a striking and busy scene
when the next year has begun. For the present we need
only remember that two bishops, and not one only, were
invested, according to the ancient use of England, by the
royal hand at the bedside of William Rufus.

We may take for granted that it took no such struggle
to change the King's Chancellor into the Bishop-elect
of Lincoln as it took to change the man on whom all
eyes were now fixed into an Archbishop-elect of Canterbury. It was now a Sunday, the first Sunday in Lent; March 6, 1093.
a gathering of bishops and other chief men stood around
the King who was believed to be dying. He had
solemnly repented; he must now make restitution. The

---

[1] So says the Chronicle; "to manegan mynstren land geuðe."

[2] There is something odd in the way in which the Chronicler and
Florence couple the two prelates now appointed; "And þæt arcebiscoprice
on Cantwarbyrig, þe ær on his agenre hand stód. Anselme betæhte, se wæs
ær abbot on Bæc, and Rodbeard his cancelere þæt biscoprice on Lincolne."
That is to say, they cut the whole story short; or more truly they tell it
on the same scale on which they tell other things, while we are used to
Eadmer's minute narrative of all that concerns Anselm.

[3] See above, p. 13.   [4] See Appendix Z.

CHAP. IV. best men among those who stood around him pressed yet more strongly on his mind the duty of at once filling the metropolitan see. The sick man answered that such was his purpose. They asked whom he deemed worthy of such a post; none dared suggest any name; the choice rested wholly with the royal will.[1] The King made an effort; he sat up in his bed; he pointed out the Abbot of Bec among those who filled the room, and spake the words; "I choose this holy man Anselm."[2] The feeling which now bids men to listen in silence to the official utterances of royal lips was then unheard of; even the fear of danger to the sick man yielded to the universal joy; a loud shout of applause rang through the chamber which was soon, as men deemed, to be the chamber of death. One man alone joined not in the shout; one man grew pale and trembled in every limb. The moment so long dreaded had at last come; the burthen from which he shrank was at last to be forced on the shoulders of the struggling abbot. For in the case of Anselm the struggle was no metaphor. He was dragged to the King's bedside to receive the investiture[3]—no thought of the elective rights of the monks of distant Christ Church seems to have come into the head of any man. Pouring out reasons against his own appointment, Anselm withstood by main force all efforts to

Rufus names Anselm to the archbishopric.

General delight.

Unwillingness of Anselm.

---

[1] Eadmer, Hist. Nov. 16. They exhort the King to appoint. He consents willingly; "Sed cunctis ad nutum regis pendentibus, prænunciavit ipse et concordi voce subsequitur acclamatio omnium, abbatem Anselmum tali honore dignissimum."

[2] I think we may for a moment turn from the *oratio obliqua* of Eadmer to the vivid little picture in William of Malmesbury; "Ille cubito sese attollens, 'Hunc,' ait, 'sanctum virum Anselmum eligo,' ingenti subsecuto fragore faventium." One is reminded of the death-bed of Eadward, as drawn in the Tapestry. See N. C. vol. iii. p. 13, note.

[3] Eadmer, u. s. "Cum raperetur ad regem, ut per virgam pastoralem investituram archiepiscopatus de manu ejus susciperet, toto conamine restitit, idque multis obsistentibus causis nullatenus fieri posse asseruit."

drag him nearer to the King. The bishops at last succeeded in drawing him apart from the crowd, and began
to argue with him more quietly.[1] They warned him not
to withstand the will of God, or to refuse the work to
which he was called. He saw that Christianity had
almost died out in England; everything had fallen into
confusion; every abomination was rife. One bolder
voice—was it the voice of English Wulfstan or of Norman Gundulf?—added words such as are not often
uttered in the chamber of a king, and which even then
perhaps were not meant to reach kingly ears. "By the
tyranny of that man"[2]—pointing to the sick king on his
bed—"we and the churches which we ought to rule have
fallen into danger of eternal death; wilt thou, when
thou canst help us, scorn our petition?" The appeal
went on; Anselm was told how the church of Canterbury, in whose oppression all were oppressed, called to
him to raise up her and them; could he, casting aside all
thought for her freedom, all thought for the help of his
brethren, refuse to share their work, and seek only his
own ease? Anselm pleaded at length; he was old; he was
unused to worldly affairs. He prayed to be allowed
to abide in the peaceful calling which he loved. The
bishops all the more called on him to take the rule over
them which was offered to him; let him guide them in
the way of God; let him pray to God for them, and they
would manage all worldly affairs for him.[3] He then
pleaded that he was the subject of another realm;[4] he
owed obedience to his own prince, to his own archbishop; he could not cast off his duty to them without

---

[1] "Accipiunt eum episcopi, et ducunt seorsum de multitudine."

[2] "Per tyrannidem istius hominis."

[3] "In Deo pro nobis intende, et nos secularia tua disponemus pro te."

[4] "Abbas sum monasterii regni alterius." "Regnum" of course means
Normandy, an inaccurate phrase, but one that we have had already (see
above, p. 25).

their leave; nay, he could not, without the consent of his own monks, cast off the duties which he owed to them. The bishops told him that the consent of all concerned would be easily gained. He protested that all that they did, all that they purposed, was nought.[1]

Anselm dragged to the King's bedside.

The bishops had certainly the better in the argument; they had also the better in the physical struggle; for they now dragged Anselm close to the King's bedside. They set forth to Rufus what they called the obstinacy of the Abbot;[2] it was for the King to try what his personal authority could do. The sick man, lately so proud and scornful, was stirred even to tears; he made a speech far longer than his wont, but which seems to carry with it the stamp of genuineness. He had raised himself to speak his formal choice with a voice of authority; he now spoke, in plaintive and beseeching words, in the ear of the holy man beside him. In the mind of Rufus at that moment it was his own personal salvation that was at stake. "O Anselm," he whispered, "why do you condemn me to eternal torments? Remember, I pray you, the faithful friendship which my father and my mother had to you and which you had to them; by that friendship I adjure you not to let their son perish both in body and soul. For I am sure that I shall perish if I die while I still have the archbishopric in my hands.[3] Help me then, help me, lord and father; take the bishopric for the holding of which I am already greatly confounded, and fear that I shall be confounded for ever." Still Anselm drew back and excused himself. Then the

Pleadings of the King.

---

[1] "Nihil est omnino, non erit quod intenditis."

[2] "Rapiunt hominem ad regem aegrotum, et pervicaciam ejus exponunt."

[3] "Contristatus est rex, pene ad suffusionem oculorum, et dixit ad eum, 'O Anselme quid agis? Cur me poenis aeternis cruciandum tradis?'" He adds presently, "Certus sum enim quod peribo, si archiepiscopatum in meo dominio tenens, vitam finiero."

bishops again took up their parable in a stronger tone. CHAP. IV.
What madness had possessed him? He was harassing Further pleadings
the King, almost killing him; his last moments were of the bishops
embittered by Anselm's obstinacy.[1] They gave him to
know that whatever disturbances, oppressions, and
crimes, might hereafter disturb England would all lie at
his door, if he did not stop them that day by taking on
him the pastoral care. Still—so he himself witnessed
afterwards—wishing rather, if it were God's will, to die
than to take on him the archbishopric, he turned to two
of his own monks who had come with him, Eustace
and Baldwin of Tournay, and asked them to help
him.[2] Baldwin answered, "If it be the will of God and of his own monks.
that it shall be so, who are we that we should with-
stand the will of God?" His words were followed
by a flood of tears, his tears by a gush of blood from
his nostrils. Anselm, surely half-smiling, said, "Alas,
how soon is your staff broken." The King then, seeing
that nothing was gained, bade the bishops fall at Anselm's
feet and implore him to take the see. A like scene
had been gone through at Bec when it was first sought
to raise Anselm to the abbacy.[3] The bishops fell at his
feet, and implored; Anselm fell at their feet, and implored
back again. There was nothing to be done save the last
shift of, so to speak, investing him with the bishopric
by physical force. A cry was raised for a pastoral staff; He is invested by main force.
the staff was brought, and was placed in the sick king's
hand.[4] The bishops seized the right arm of Anselm;
some pushed; some pulled; he was forced close up to

[1] "Regem turbas, turbatum penitus necas, quandoquidem illum jam
morientem obstinacia tua exacerbare non formidas."

[2] Of Baldwin we often hear again; he seems to have been Anselm's chief
helper at Bec in temporal matters.

[3] See above, p. 372.

[4] "Virgam huc pastoralem, virgam, clamitant, pastoralem. Et arrepto
brachio ejus dextro, alii renitentem trahere, alii impellere, lectoque jacentis
cœperunt applicare."

CHAP. IV.　the King's bed.　The King held out the staff; the Abbot, though his arm was stretched out against his will, held his hand firmly clenched.　The bishops strove to force open his fingers, till he shrieked with the pain.　After much striving, they managed to raise his forefinger, to place the staff between that one finger and his still closed hand, and to keep it there with their own hands.[1] This piece of sheer violence was held to be a lawful investiture.　The assembled crowd—we are still in the sick king's room—began to shout "Long live the Bishop." The bishops and clergy began to sing Te Deum with a

He is installed in the church.

loud voice.[2]　Then the bishops, abbots, and nobles, seized Anselm, and carried rather than led him into a neighbouring church—was it the great minster of Ealdred or its successor growing up under the hands of Serlo?[3]— while he still refused and struggled and protested that all that they did went for nothing.[4]　A looker-on, Anselm himself says, might have doubted whether a crowd in their right mind were dragging a single madman, or whether a crowd of madmen were dragging a single man who kept his right mind.[5]　Anyhow they reached the church and there went through the ceremonies which

[1] I am but translating Eadmer; "Indice levato, sed protinus ab eo reflexo, clausæ manui ejus baculus appositus est, et episcoporum manibus cum eadem manu compressus atque retentus."

[2] "Acclamante autem multitudine, 'Vivat episcopus, vivat;' episcopi cum clero sublimi voce hymnum Te Deum laudamus decantare cœpere."

[3] "Electum portaverunt pontificem potius quam duxerunt in vicinam ecclesiam."　On the works of Serlo, see N. C. vol. iv. p. 384.

[4] "Ipso modis, quibus poterat, resistente, atque dicente, nihil est quod facitis, nihil est quod facitis."

[5] This is Anselm's own comparison in his letter to the monks of Bec, Ep. iii. 1; "Quando me episcopi et abbates aliique primates ad ecclesiam trahentes reclamantem et contradicentem rapuerunt, ita ut dubium videri posset utrum sanum insani, an insanum traherent sani ; nisi quia illi canebant et ego magis mortuo quam viventi colore similis stupore et dolore pallebam." Presently he says ; "Huic autem de me electioni, imo violentiæ, hactenus quantum potui, servata veritate, reluctatus sum."　The last word may be taken in its original physical sense.

were usual on such occasions.[1] Anselm was now deemed CHAP. IV.
to have become, however much against his own will,
Archbishop-elect of Canterbury.

From the church Anselm went back to the King's Anselm's
chamber. He there renewed his protest against the ap- renewed
pointment, but he renewed it in the form of a prophecy. protest.
"My lord the King, I tell you that you will not die of this
sickness; I would therefore have you know how easily
you can undo what has been this day done with regard
to me, as I never agreed, nor do I agree, that it shall be
held valid."[2] He then left the sick room, and spoke to the
bishops and nobles in some other place, perhaps the hall
of the castle. Whether formally summoned as such or
not, they were practically a Gemót of the realm.[3] Anselm His parable
spoke to them in a parable, founded on the apostolic to the pre-
figure which speaks of the Church as God's husbandry.[4] nobles.
In England the plough of the Church ought to be drawn
by two chief oxen of equal strength, each pulling with
the same good will. These were the King and the Archbishop of Canterbury, one ruling by worldly justice and
dominion, the other by divine doctrine and teaching. So,
he implies, it had been in the days of William the Great
and of Lanfranc his yoke-fellow.[5] The figure is one
which will bear much study. It is perhaps in England

---

[1] Eadmer, Hist. Nov. 18. "Gestis vero quæ in tali causa geri in ecclesia
mos est, revertitur Anselmus ad regem."

[2] "Dico tibi, domine rex, quia ex hac tua infirmitate non morieris, ac
pro hoc volo noveris quam bene corrigere poteris quod de me nunc actum
est, quia nec concessi nec concedo ut ratum sit."

[3] The change of place is clearly marked in Eadmer. "Deducentibus
eum episcopis, cum tota regni nobilitate, cubiculo excessit, conversusque ad
eos, in hæc verba sciscitatus est." The parable which follows is placed
earlier by William of Malmesbury; but this is surely the right place.

[4] 1 Cor. iii. 9.

[5] Eadmer, Hist. Nov. 18. "Hoc aratrum in Anglia duo boves cæteris
precellentes regendo trahunt et trahendo regunt. Rex videlicet, et archiepiscopus Cantuariensis. Iste seculari justitia et imperio, ille divina
doctrina et magisterio." This must mean during the late reign.

alone that it could have been used. In the highest rank
of all, used to the loftier metaphors of the two great
lights of heaven and the two swords on earth, figures
drawn from ploughs and oxen might have seemed unworthy of the supreme majesty of the Roman Emperor
and the Roman Pontiff. In other lands the metaphor
would have failed from another side. The Primate of
Rheims or of Rouen could hardly be spoken of as in the
same sort the yoke-fellow of the French King or the
Norman Duke. In England the parable had more truth.
It set forth at once the supreme ecclesiastical authority
of the King, and the check which ancient custom put on
that authority in the shape of an archiepiscopal tribune
of the people. But the happy partnership of the two
powers had come to an end. The strong ox Lanfranc
was dead. His surviving yoke-fellow was a young and
untameable wild bull.[1] With him they wished to yoke
an old and feeble sheep, who might perhaps furnish them
with the wool and milk of the Lord's word, and with
lambs for His service,[2] but who was utterly unequal to
the task of pulling in fellowship with such a comrade.
His weakness and the King's fierceness could never work
together. If they would only think over the matter,
they would give up the attempt which they had begun.
The joy with which they had hailed his nomination
would be turned into sorrow. They talked of his raising
up the Church from widowhood; if they insisted on
forcing him into the see, the Church would be thrust

---

[1] "Horum boum unus, scilicet Lanfrancus archiepiscopus, mortuus est;
et alius ferocitatem indomabilis tauri obtinens jam juvenis aratro prælatus,
et vos loco mortui bovis, me vetulam ac debilem ovem cum indomito tauro
conjungere vultis."

[2] "Indomabilis utique feritas tauri sic ovem lanæ et lactis et agnorum
fertilem per spinas et tribulos hac et illac raptam, si jugo se non excusserit,
dilacerabit." So a little after; "Me, de quo lanam et lac verbi Dei, et
agnos in servitium ejus, nonnulli possent habere." The metaphor becomes
passing strange when it is thus worked out in detail.

down into a yet deeper widowhood, widowhood during CHAP. IV. the life of her pastor. He himself would be the first victim; none of them would dare to give him help, and then the King would trample them too under his feet at pleasure. He then burst into tears; he parted from the assembly, and went to his own quarters, whether in the city of Gloucester or at the unnamed place where he had before been staying.[1] The King, foreseeing no further difficulties, gave orders that steps should be taken for investing him without delay with the temporal possessions of the see.[2] But a whole train of unlooked-for hindrances appeared before Anselm could be put into possession of either the temporal or the spiritual powers of Lanfranc.

The King orders the restitution of the lands of the see.

At this first stage of the story, as at every other, as long as the scene is laid in England, we are struck in the strongest way by the fact that every one concerned takes the ancient customs of England for granted. If those customs have changed from what they may have been under Cnut or Eadward, they have at least not changed to the advantage of the Roman see, or indeed of the ecclesiastical power in any shape. Hildebrand has no followers either in England or in Normandy. No one has called in question the right either of the King of the English or of the Duke of the Normans to invest the prelates of his dominions with the pastoral staff. There is not one word in the whole story implying that any one had any scruple on the subject. Anselm clearly had none. He had received

The royal right of investiture not questioned.

No scruples on the part of Anselm.

[1] "Ad hospitium suum, dimissa curia, vadit."

[2] "Præcepit itaque rex, ut, sine dilatione ac diminutione, investiretur de omnibus ad archiepiscopatum pertinentibus intus et extra." Eadmer goes on to speak about the city of Canterbury, the abbey of Saint Alban's, and other things of which we shall have to speak again. But he can only mean that orders were given which were not immediately carried out; for the actual investiture was, as we shall see, delayed for some months.

the staff of Bec from the Duke; if he was not ready to receive the staff of Canterbury from the King, it was not because of any scruple as to the mode of appointment, but because he refused to accept the appointment itself, however made. Not a single English bishop has a word to say on the matter. We could not look for such scruples in Wulfstan who had received his staff from the holy Eadward; but neither do they trouble William of Saint-Calais, so lately the zealous champion of the rights of Rome. If anything, the bishops seem to attribute a kind of mystic and almost sacramental effi-

No ecclesiastical election. cacy to the investiture by the King's hand. Nor is there a word said as to the rights of any ecclesiastical electors, the monks of Christ Church or any other. It is taken for granted that the whole matter rests with the King. Anselm protests against the validity of the act, but not on any ground which assumed any other elector than the King. The nomination was invalid, because he did not consent to it himself, because the Duke of the Normans, the Archbishop of Rouen, and the monks of Bec, had not consented to it. Anselm is very careful as to the rights of all these three; he has not a word to say about the rights of the monks of Christ Church. Had he been a subject of the crown of England, a bishop or presbyter of the province of Canterbury, and himself willing to accept the archbishopric, there would clearly have been in his eyes nothing irregular in his accepting it in the form in which it was forced upon him, by the sole choice

Later change in Anselm's views. and sole investiture of the King. He afterwards learned to think otherwise; but it was neither at Canterbury nor at Bec nor at Aosta that he learned such scruples. He had to go beyond English, Norman, and Burgundian ground to look for them. At present he does at every stage, as an ordinary matter of

course, something which his later lights would have led
him to condemn. But it certainly does seem strange
when Bishop Gundulf of Rochester, in a letter to his
old companions the monks of Bec, tells them that the
King had given the government of the church of Canterbury to their abbot Anselm, by the advice and request
of his great men and by the petition and election of the
clergy and people.[1] We have often come across such
phrases;[2] and this case, where we know every detail,
may help us to estimate their meaning in some other
cases. That Anselm's appointment had been the general
wish of all classes before it was made, that it received
the general approval of all classes after it was made,
there is no manner of doubt. But there is no sign of
any formal advice, petition, or election, by any class of
men at any stage. It may be that the ceremony in the
church at Gloucester was held to pass for an election by
the clergy and people. But that was after the King had,
by the delivery of the staff, given to Anselm the government of the church of Canterbury. Even in Gundulf's
formula, the advice, petition, and election are mere helps
to guide the King's choice; it is the King who actually
bestows the see. And here again, of the rights of the
monks of the metropolitan church there is not a word.

Several months passed after this amazing scene at
Gloucester before Anselm was fully admitted to the full
possession of the archbishopric. He had not yet given
any consent himself, and the consents of the Norman

---

[1] Ep. iii. 3. "Ipsius namque inenarrabili potentia operante, dedit dominus noster rex Anglorum, consilio et rogatu principum suorum, cleri quoque
et populi petitione et electione, domino abbati Anselmo Cantuariensis
ecclesiæ gubernationem." So says Anselm himself in his letter to Archbishop Hugh of Lyons, Ep. iii. 24; "Subdidi me dolens præcepto archiepiscopi mei et electioni totius Angliæ."

[2] See N. C. vol. iv. pp. 591, 593.

CHAP. IV.

Anselm tarries with Gundulf.

Consent of the Duke, the Archbishop of Rouen, and the monks of Bec.

Duke, the Norman Archbishop, and the Norman monks, on all of which Anselm laid such stress, were still to be sought for. The King sent messengers to all of them, and meanwhile Anselm was, by the King's order, lodged on some of the archiepiscopal manors under the care of his old friend Bishop Gundulf.[1] One may suspect that it was the influence of this prelate, a good man plainly, but not very stout-hearted, and more ready than Anselm to adapt himself to the ruling powers, which brought Anselm to the belief that he ought to give way to what he himself calls the choice of all England, and which he now allows to be the will of God. At any rate Anselm brought himself to write letters to the monks of Bec, asking their consent to his resignation of the abbey and acceptance of the archbishopric.[2] For it was with the monks of Bec that the difficulty lay; Duke Robert and Archbishop William seem to have made no objection.[3] It was, after much hesitation, and by a narrow majority only that the convent agreed to part with the abbot who had brought such honour upon their house.[4] In the end all the needful consents were given. Anselm was free from all obligations beyond the sea. But he still had not given his own formal consent to the acceptance of the archbishopric. A long series of acts, temporal and spiritual, were needed to change the simple monk and presbyter, as he was now once more, into an Archbishop of Canterbury, clothed with the full powers and possessions of the Patriarch of all the nations beyond the sea. Those acts needed the consent, some of them needed the personal action, of the King. And

---

[1] Eadmer, Hist. Nov. 19.   [2] See Appendix Y.

[3] Ep. iii. 8. "Reverendo domino nostro principe Northmannorum Roberto concedente; et archiepiscopo nostro Guillelmo præcipiente, et vobis a Deo coactis, faventibus, a vestra cura sum absolutus, et majori involutus." Both Anselm and the King wrote letters; Eadmer, 19, 20.

[4] See the letter of the monks, Epp. iii. 6.

King William the Red was now again quite another CHAP. IV. man from what he had been when he lay on his sick bed at Gloucester.

The King's sickness is said to have lasted during the whole of Lent; but he seems to have been restored to health early enough to hold the Easter Gemót at Winchester.[1] Anselm was there, in company with his guardian Bishop Gundulf and his friend Baldwin the monk of Bec; but there is no mention of any business being done between him and the King. Doubtless the needful letters had not yet come from Normandy, even if Anselm had so soon brought himself to write those which were needful on his own part. By this time William was again in full health, and, with his former state of body, his former state of mind had also come back. He had repented of his repentance; he had fallen back into all his old evil courses with more eagerness than ever. All the wrong that he had done before he fell sick was deemed to be a small matter compared with the wrong which he did after he was restored to health.[2] It is to this stage of his life that one of the most hideous of his blasphemous sayings is assigned. Instead of thankfulness for his renewed health, he looked on his sickness as a wrong done to him by his Maker, for which he would in some way have his revenge. It was now that he told Bishop Gundulf, whom we can fancy faintly exhorting him to keep in the good frame of mind which he had put on while he lay on his sick bed—"God shall never see me a good man; I have suffered too much at his

The King's recovery.

The Easter Gemót. 1093.

William falls back into evil ways.

His renewed blasphemy.

---

[1] This seems implied in Anselm's presence at Winchester at Easter, which is recorded in the Life, ii. 1. 3. But his presence there is mentioned only to bring in a kind of miracle, in which Anselm, Gundulf, and the monk Baldwin all figure.

[2] Eadmer, Hist. Nov. i. 19. "Siquidem omne malum quod rex fecerat, priusquam fuerat infirmatus, bonum visu est, comparatione malorum quæ fecit ubi est sanitati redonatus."

CHAP. IV. hands."[1]   And his practice was such as became the fool
who said that there was no God, or rather the deeper
fool who said that there was a God, and yet defied him.

He recalls
his acts
of mercy.
He even went on to undo, as far as lay in his power, the
good works which he had done during his momentary
repentance. Some of the prisoners to whom he had
promised deliverance were already set free, and some of
those who were set free had taken themselves beyond his
reach. But those who were still in safe-keeping were
kept in yet harsher bondage than before; and of those
who had been set free as many as could be laid hold of
were sent back to their prisons. The pardons, the re-
missions of debts, which had been put forth were recalled.
Every man who had been held liable before the King's
sickness was held liable again. His gifts to monasteries
were also recalled.[2] But one thing which William had
promised to do he remained as fully minded to do as

He keeps
his pur-
pose as to
Anselm.
before. At no stage did he show the slightest purpose of
recalling his grant of the archbishopric to Anselm. This
distinction is quite in harmony with the general character
of William Rufus. The reforms which he had promised,
and which he had partly carried out, were part of the
ordinary duty of a man in that state of life to which
William had been called, the state of a king. As such,
they were reckoned by him among those promises which

[1] "Ipse prædicto Roffensi episcopo, cum illum, recuperata sanitate,
familiari affatu moneret ut se amplius circumspecte secundum Deum in
omnibus haberet respondit." (See above, p. 165.)

[2] The Chronicler says generally; "Ac þæt he syððan ætbræd, þa him
gebotad wæs, and ealle þa gode laga forlæt, þe he us ær behét." We get
the details from Eadmer; "Mox igitur cuncta quæ infirmus statuerat bona,
dissolvit et irrita esse præcepit. Captivi nempe, qui nondum fuerant
dimissi, jussit ut artius solito custodirentur, dimissi, si capi possent,
recluderentur; antiqua jamque donata debita in integrum exigerentur;
placita et offensiones in pristinum statum revocarentur, illorumque judicio,
qui justitiam subvertere magis quam tueri defendereve curabant, tracta-
rentur et examinarentur."

it was beyond his power to fulfil. But his engagement chap. iv.
to Anselm was of another kind. To say nothing of
Anselm being the old friend of his father, his engagement to him was strictly personal. If it was not exactly
done in the character of a good knight, it was done as
the act of a man to a man. It was like a safe-conduct;
it touched, not so much William's kingly duty as his
personal honour. William's honour did not keep him
back from annoying and insulting Anselm, or from
haggling with him about money in a manner worthy
of the chivalrous Richard himself. But it did keep him
back from any attempt to undo his own personal act
and promise. He had prayed Anselm to take the archbishopric; he had forced the staff, as far as might be,
into Anselm's unwilling hand. From that act he would
not draw back, though he was quite ready to get any
advantage for himself that might be had in the way of
carrying it out.

But we must not fancy that the affairs of Anselm and Events of March–December, 1093.
of the see to which he had been so strangely called
were the only matters which occupied the mind of
England during this memorable year. The months which
passed between the first nomination of Anselm and his
consecration to the archbishopric, that is, the months
from March to December, were a busy time in affairs of
quite another kind than the appointment of pastors of
the Church. The events of those months chiefly concerned the relations of England to the other parts of the
island, Welsh and Scottish, and I shall speak of them at
length in another chapter. Here it is enough to say Affairs of England and Wales.
that the very week of the Easter Gemót was marked
by striking events in Wales,[1] and that during the whole

[1] Florence notices the death of Rhys ap Twdwr in the Easter week, of
which I shall have much to say in the next chapter.

CHAP. IV.
Dealings
between
William
and Mal-
colm.
time from March to August, negotiations were going on
between William and Malcolm of Scotland. In August
Malcolm came personally to Gloucester, but William
refused to see him. Malcolm then went home in wrath,
and took his revenge in a fifth and last invasion of
England, in the course of which he was killed near
Alnwick in the month of November. By that time
Anselm was already enthroned, but not yet consecrated. The main telling of the two stories must be
kept apart; but it is well always to keep the joint
chronology of the two in mind. In reading the Lives
of Anselm, where secular affairs are mentioned only
casually, we might sometimes forget how stirring a time
the year of Anselm's appointment was in other ways;
while the general writers of the time, as I have already
noticed,[1] tell us less about Anselm than we should have
looked for. The affairs of Scotland and the affairs of
Anselm were going on at the same time; and along
with them a third chain of affairs must have begun

Designs of
Rufus on
Normandy.
of which we shall hear much in the next year. Rufus
was by this time already planning a second attack on
his brother in Normandy. Except during the short
season of his penitence, he was doubtless ready for such
an enterprise at any moment. And this same year,
seemingly in the course of its summer, a special tempter

Action of
William
of Eu.
came over from beyond sea. This was William of Eu, of
whom we have already heard as the King's enemy and
of whom we shall hear again in the same character, but
who just now appears as the King's counsellor. As the
owner of vast English estates, he had played a leading
part in the first rebellion against William, with the
object of uniting England and Normandy under a single
prince.[2] That object he still sought; but he now sought
to gain it by other means. He had learned which of

---

[1] See above, p. 370.　　　　　　[2] See above, p. 33.

the brothers was the more useful master to serve. He CHAP. IV.
was now, by the death of his father, Count of Eu, and His divided
allegiance.
Eu was among the parts of Normandy which Robert
had yielded to William.[1] For Eu then Count William
was the man of King William; but he was still the man
of Duke Robert for some other parts of his possessions.
He thought it his interest to serve one lord only; he He suggests
an attack
accordingly threw off his allegiance to Robert, and came on Nor-
over to England to stir up William to take possession mandy.
of the whole duchy.[2] And it must surely have been in
connexion with these affairs that, at some time between William
and Robert
March and September, William had an interview with Count of
Count Robert of Flanders at Dover. By this descrip- Flanders.
tion we are doubtless to understand the elder Count
Robert, the famous Frisian, of whom we have already
heard as an enemy to the elder William,[3] but who must
now have been at least on terms of peace with his son.
He was drawing near the end of his life, a memorable life, Death of
Count
nearly the last act of which had been honourable indeed. Robert.
October 4
He had, several years before the preaching of the cru- or 13, 1093.
sade, sent a body of the choicest warriors of Flanders to
defend Eastern Christendom against the Turk.[4] Robert
died in October of this year, and was succeeded by his

[1] See above, p. 276.

[2] This action of William of Eu is marked by Florence at the end of the
year, but without saying at what time of the year it happened; "Eodem
anno Willelmus comes de Owe, auri ingenti victus aviditate et pro-
missi honoris captus magnitudine, a naturali domino suo Rotberto Normannorum comite, cui fidelitatem juraverat, defecit et in Angliam ad
regem Willelmum veniens, illius se dominio, ut seductor maximus, subjugavit."

[3] See N. C. vol. iv. pp. 538, 684.

[4] Anna Comnena tells us this, vii. 6. Robert, on his return from
Jerusalem (ὁ Φλάνδρας κόμης ἐξ Ἱεροσολύμων ἐπανερχόμενος), does homage
to the Emperor (τὸν συνήθη τοῖς Λατίνοις ἀποδίδωσιν ὅρκον) and promises
five hundred knights (ἱππεῖς). In viii. 7 we find that he had fulfilled his
promise, and that they are ἱππεῖς ἔκκριτοι. In viii. 3 they figure as Κελτοί.
Cf. Will. Malms. iii. 257.

CHAP. IV.   son Robert of Jerusalem,[1] a name which the father had
Robert of   an equal right to bear. The younger Robert had been
Jerusalem.
associated by his father in the government of the county;
but one may suppose that, when our guide speaks of
Robert Count of Flanders, it is the elder Robert who is
meant. He was the enemy of the elder William rather
in his Norman than in his English character, and his
enmity may have passed to his successor in the duchy
Relation   and not to his successor in the kingdom. One can hardly
between
William   help thinking that this meeting of William of England
and the   and Robert of Flanders had some reference to joint
Flemish
Counts.   operations designed against Robert of Normandy. But,
if so, the alliance was put an end to by the death of
Robert the Frisian, and, when the time for his Norman
enterprise came, William had to carry it on without
Flemish help.

Interview   By this time Anselm had received the letters from
between
Anselm   Normandy which were to make him free to accept the
and the   archbishopric; but the letters to the King from the same
King at
Rochester. parties had not yet come. At this stage then Anselm
wished for an interview with the King, the first—unless
they met at Easter at Winchester—since they had parted
in the sick room at Gloucester. William was on his way
back from his meeting with the Count of Flanders at
Dover; he came to Rochester, where Anselm was then
staying with Bishop Gundulf. There Anselm took the
King aside, and laid the case before him as it then
stood.

Anselm's   Anselm was at this moment, in his own view, a pri-
position.   vate man. He was no longer Abbot of Bec. His monks
had released him from that office, and he had formally

---

[1] We have heard of him in N. C. vol. v. pp. 181, 850, and we shall come
across him again.

resigned it by sending back to them the pastoral staff.[1] CHAP. IV.
He was not yet Archbishop of Canterbury; he was not
yet, in his own view, even Archbishop-elect; all that had
been done at Gloucester he counted for null and void.
But he was now free to accept the archbishopric, and,
though he still did not wish for the post, he had got over
the scruples which had before led him to refuse it. In
such a case he deemed it his duty to be perfectly frank
with the King, and to tell him on what terms only he
would accept the primacy, if the King still persisted in
offering it to him.

The conditions which Anselm now laid before William His con-
Rufus were three. The first of them had to do with the ditions with the King.
temporal estates of the archbishopric. I have elsewhere
spoken of the light in which we ought to look at demands of this kind.[2] We may be sure that Anselm Restoration
would gladly have purchased the peace of the land, of the estates of
the friendship of the King, or anything that would profit the see.
the souls or bodies of other men, at the cost of any temporal possessions which were strictly his own to give up.
But, if he became Archbishop of Canterbury, he would
become a steward of the church of Canterbury, a trustee
for his successors, the guardian of gifts which had been
given to God, His saints, and His Church. In any of
these characters, it would be a sin against his own soul
and the souls of others, if he willingly allowed anything
which had ever been given to his church to be taken
from her or detained from her. If the King chose to
keep the see vacant and to turn its revenues to his own
use, that would be his sin and not Anselm's; but Anselm
would be a sharer in the sin, if he accepted the see with-

---

[1] Eadmer, Hist. Nov. 20. "Jam cum virga pastorali curam quam super
Beccum abbas susceperat, pro descripta superius absolutione, ipse Becco
restituerat."

[2] See N. C. vol. iv. pp. 327, 328.

CHAP. IV. out requiring full restitution of everything to which the see had a lawful claim. In the private conference at Rochester, he therefore demanded, as a condition of his accepting the see, that he should receive all that Lanfranc had held, without delay or dispute or process in any court. As for lands to which his church had an ancient claim, but which Lanfranc had been unable to win back, for those he demanded that the King should do him justice in his court.[1] The second demand touched the ancient relations between the crown and the archbishopric. The sheep, about to be yoked with the wild bull, sought to make terms with his fierce comrade.

He demands to be the King's spiritual guide.

Anselm demanded that, in all matters which touched God and Christianity, the King should take him as his counsellor before all other men; as he acknowledged in the King his earthly lord, so let the King acknowledge in him his ghostly father and the special guardian of his soul.[2]

Acknowledgement of Popes.

To these two requests Anselm added a third, one which touched a point on which the Red King seems to have been specially sensitive. It had been the rule of his father's reign that no Pope should be acknowledged in England without his consent.[3] William Rufus seems to have construed this rule in the same way in which he construed some others. From his right to nominate to

[1] This seems to be the distinction drawn by Anselm, Hist. Nov. 19, 20; "Volo ut omnes terras quas ecclesia Cantuariensis, ad quam regendam electus sum, tempore beatæ memoriæ Lanfranci archiepiscopi tenebat, sine omni placito et controversia ipsi ecclesiæ restituas, et de aliis terris quas eadem ecclesia ante suum tempus habebat, sed perditas nondum recuperavit, mihi rectitudinem judiciumque consentias." About anything which Lanfranc had actually held there could, it is assumed, be no question, either of law or of fact; about earlier claims there might easily be either.

[2] Ib. 20. "Sicut ego te volo terrenum habere dominum et defensorem, ita et tu me spiritualem habeas patrem et animæ tuæ provisorem." To this day it is held that, wherever the King may be, the Archbishop of Canterbury is his parish priest.

[3] See N. C. vol. iv. p. 436.

bishoprics and abbeys he had inferred a right not to CHAP. IV.
nominate to them; so, from his right to judge between
contending popes, he inferred the right to do without
acknowledging any pope at all. And, if the King acted
in this way for his own ends, the country at large seems
to have shown a remarkable indifference to the whole
controversy. To Englishmen and to men settled in England it was clearly a much greater grievance to be kept
without an Archbishop of Canterbury than it was to be
left uncertain who was the lawful pope. At this moment Schism in
the Western Church was divided between the claims of the papacy.
Victor the
Wibert or Clement, the Imperial anti-pope of the days of Third.
1086–1087.
Hildebrand, and those of Urban, formerly Odo of Ostia, Urban the
who, after the short reign of Victor, stepped into Hilde- Second.
1088–1099.
brand's place. In the eyes of strict churchmen Urban Urban and
was the true Vicar of Christ, and Wibert was a wicked Clement.
intruder and schismatic. Yet it will be remembered that
Lanfranc himself had, when the dispute lay between
Wibert and Hildebrand, spoken with singular calmness
and caution of a question which to more zealous minds
seemed a matter of spiritual life and death.[1] Our own English
Chronicler seems to have measured popes, as well as feeling on
the subject.
kings and bishops, by the standard of possession; he
found it hard to conceive a pope that "nothing had of
the settle at Rome."[2] Even Anselm's own biographer
speaks very quietly on the point. Two rival candidates
claimed the popedom; but which was the one rightly
chosen no one in England, we are told, knew—or seemingly cared.[3] Another of our guides describes Urban
and Clement as alike men of personal merit, and looks

---

[1] See N. C. vol. iv. p 435.   [2] Ib. p. 436, note.

[3] Ib. The language of Eadmer, Hist. Nov. 25, is nearly to the same effect;
"Erant quippe (illo tempore) duo, ut in Anglia ferebatur, qui dicebantur
Romani pontifices a se invicem discordantes, et ecclesiam Dei inter se
divisam post se trahentes."

CHAP. IV. on the controversy as one in which there was much to be said on both sides. The chief argument for Urban was that his supporters seemed to increase in number; otherwise no one really knew on which side the divine right was. In England opinion was divided; but fear of the King—so we are told—made it lean on the whole to Clement.[1] Earlier in the reign we have heard Bishop William of Durham talk a great deal about going to the Pope; but he had taken care not to say to which pope he meant to go, and in the end he had not gone to either.[2]

Anselm requires to be allowed to acknowledge Urban. With Anselm the matter was more serious. Urban was his pope. All the churches of Gaul had acknowledged him; Bec and the other churches of Normandy had acknowledged him along with the rest.[3] From the obedience which he had thus plighted he could not fall back. He told the King that, though he, King William, had not acknowledged Urban, yet he, Anselm, must continue to acknowledge him and to yield him such obedience as was his due.[4] To be allowed freely to do so must be one of the conditions of his accepting the archbishopric.

[1] There is a most important passage of William of Malmesbury in his first draught of the Gesta Pontificum (p. 86, note) which he afterwards, as in so many other cases, found it expedient to tone down. As he wrote it, it stood thus;

"Erant his diebus duo competitores Romani præsulatus, summi ambo et prestantes viri. Uterque causam verisimilibus rationibus fulciebat, Urbanus electione cardinalium, Guibertus electione imperatoris Theutonum, cujus esset Roma et Italia. Neuter ergo pro persona sua cedebat. Guiberto necessitatem subjectionis ministrabat terrarum tractus qui sub imperio illius jacet; Urbano favebat omnis Gallia et Normannia, et cetera usque ad oceanum Brittannicum. Incertum cui faveret Divinitas, nisi quod Urbani fama prosperius crementum sumebat. Consensu dubio fluctuabat Anglia, in Guibertum tamen inclinatior propter metum regis."

[2] See above, p. 117.

[3] Eadmer, Hist. Nov. 25. "Urbano jamdudum pro vicario beati Petri ab Italia Galliaque recepto; Anselmus etiam, utpote abbas de Normannia, eum pro papa receperat, et, sicut vir nominatissimus, necnon authoritate plenus ejus literas susceperat, eique velut summo sanctæ ecclesiæ pastori suas direxerat."

[4] Ib. 20. "De Romano quoque pontifice Urbano, quem pro apostolico

The King's answer was unsatisfactory, but not openly
hostile. He was however beginning to be on his guard; The King's
he called to his side the two subtlest advisers that the counsellors; Count
Church and realm of England could supply. The one was Robert and
Bishop
Count Robert of Meulan, at home alike in England, Nor- William.
mandy, and France. The other was William Bishop of
Durham, once the strong assertor of ecclesiastical claims,
who had appealed to the Pope against the judgement of
the King and his Witan. He had indeed both learned and
forgotten something in his exile. He had come back to The
be the special counsellor of Rufus, the special enemy of Bishop's
new policy.
Anselm, the special assertor of the doctrine that it was
for the King alone to judge as to the acknowledgement
of Popes. The King, having listened to Anselm, sent
for these two chosen advisers. He bade Anselm say over
again in their hearing what he had before said privately.
He then, by their advice, answered that he would restore The King's
to the see everything that had been held by Lanfranc; answer.
on other points he would not as yet make any positive
engagement.[1]

Up to this time the King had not yet received his The letters
expected letters from Normandy. They presently came, come
from Nor-
and Rufus evidently thought that some step on his part mandy.
ought to follow. He had asked the Duke, the Archbishop, and the monks of Bec, to set Anselm free to
accept the archbishopric. They had done so at his request. Unless then he wished to make fools of himself
and of everybody else, he could not help again offering
the see to the man whom he had himself chosen, and

hucusque non recepisti, et ego jam recepi atque recipio, eique debitam
obedientiam et subjectionem exhibere volo, cautum te facio ne quod scandalum inde oriatur in futuro."

[1] Eadmer, Hist. Nov. 25. "Terras de quibus ecclesia saisita quidem
fuerat sub Lanfranco omnes eo, quo tunc erant, tibi modo restituam, sed
de illis quas sub ipso non habebat, in præsenti nullam tecum conventionem
instituo. Veruntamen de his et aliis credam tibi sicut debebo."

CHAP. IV.

The King prays Anselm to take the archbishopric.

He asks for the confirmation of grants made by him during the vacancy.

Anselm refuses.

who was now free to take it. He sent for Anselm to Windsor, where he now was; he prayed him no longer to refuse the choice of the whole realm;[1] but in so doing, he fell back somewhat from the one distinct promise which he had made at Rochester. When the estates of the see came into his hands on the death of Lanfranc, he had granted out parts of them on tenure of knight-service. These grants he asked Anselm, as a matter of friendship to himself, to allow.[2] Was William merely seeking an excuse for backing altogether out of his offer of the archbishopric, or did he feel himself bound in honour to the men to whom he had made the grants? If so, his scruple of honour was met by Anselm's scruple of conscience. Anselm would not be a party to any alienation of the goods of the Church; above all, he would not make any agreement about such matters before he was invested with any part of them.[3] The point clearly is that so to do would be more than wasting the estates of the Church; it would be obtaining the archbishopric by a corrupt bargain. To agree to give up the estates of the see to the King's grantees would be the same thing as obtaining the see by a bribe to the King. Anselm therefore refused to consent to the grants which the King had made during the vacancy. The whole matter thus came to a standstill. Rufus refused the investiture unless his grants were to stand good. Anselm went away rejoicing.

The whole case was set forth at length by Anselm

[1] Eadmer, Nov. Hist. 25. "Quatenus et secundum totius regni de eo factam electionem pontifex fieri ultra non negaret." Here are the same kind of expressions with regard to Anselm's election of which we have already spoken in p. 405.

[2] Ib. "Et terras ecclesiæ quas ipse rex, defuncto Lanfranco, suis dederat pro statuto servitio, illis ipsis hæreditario jure tenendas, causa sui amoris, condonaret."

[3] Ib. "Nolens ecclesiam, quam necdum re aliqua investierat, exspoliare."

in a letter to his friend Hugh Archbishop of Lyons,
the head prelate of his native Burgundy.[1] The alienation to which Anselm was asked to consent was called
by the King a "voluntary justice," a phrase which has
a technical sound, but the meaning of which is not very
clear.[2] The King's argument was that, before the Normans invaded England, the lands in question had been
held of the archbishopric by English thegns, that those
thegns had died without heirs, and that it was open to
the King to give them what heirs he would.[3] It was
certainly strange, if, on the one hand, not one of these
thegns had been constrained to make way for a Norman
successor, and if, on the other hand, not one of them
had left a son to succeed him. But we must take
the fact as it is stated. Rufus seems to mean that,
during Lanfranc's incumbency, the lands which these
thegns had held of the see had fallen back to the lord
for lack of heirs, and had become demesne lands of the
archbishopric. The King asserts his right, during the
vacancy of the see, to grant out such lands by knight-
service, service to be paid of course to the King as long
as the vacancy lasted, but seemingly to the Archbishop,
as soon as there should be an archbishop in possession.
If this was the argument, an argument which savours of
the subtlety of Flambard, there is, from Flambard's point
of view, a good deal that is plausible about it. The
King, as temporary lord, claims to deal with the land as
any other lord might do, and, when his temporary lord-

---

[1] This letter (Ep. iii. 24) is a most important exposition of Anselm's own
views on the whole matter of the election and what followed it.

[2] Ep. iii. 24. "Sub occasione cujusdam *voluntariæ justitiæ*, secundum
quam de terris eisdem me vult placitare."

[3] Ib. "Hæc autem est illa quam dixi voluntaria justitia. Quoniam
terras easdem, antequam Northmanni Angliam invaderent, milites Angli
ab archiepiscopo Cantuariæ tenuisse dicuntur, et mortui sunt sine hære-
dibus, vult asserere se posse juste quos vult eorum hæredes constituere."

ship comes to an end, he calls on the incoming lord to respect his acts. The legal question would seem to be whether the new doctrine which gave the King the temporary profits of the archbishopric gave him any

Anselm's argument. right to turn its demesne lands into fiefs. Anselm's argument seems to be that anyhow the possessions of the archbishopric were practically lessened, as they undoubtedly were. Experience showed that such a lordship as the see would keep over the lands so granted out would be both hard to enforce and of little value if enforced.[1] Practically the grants were an alienation of the lands of the see. And to this Anselm could not consent. Open robbery from some quarter which owed no special duty to the archbishopric he might bear, and in such a case there would be more hope of gaining back what was lost by the help of the law.[2] But for the King, the advocate of the see, and for himself, its guardian, to come to an agreement whereby the see would be damaged, was a thing to which Anselm would

The King's advocatio of the arch- bishopric. never consent.[3] In this argument we hear the word *advocate*, the equivalent of the modern *patron*, in its elder sense. The *advocatio*, the *advowson*, of an ecclesiastical benefice carries with it, not only the right to name the incumbent of that benefice, but also the duty of acting as its protector.[4] For the King, the advocate of the see of Canterbury, to do anything against its rights was a

[1] See the instances collected in N. C. vol. v. Appendix G. The lands moreover would be yet harder to get back when they had been granted away on the new military tenures.

[2] Ep. iii. 24. "Si quis enim alius, ad quem ecclesiæ custodia non pertineret, hanc faceret ei violentiam, aut factam patienter sustineret, palam esset quia in futuro nihil dici posset cur res ecclesiæ ad eam redire non deberent."

[3] Ib. "Nunc autem cum et ipse rex advocatus ejus sit, et ego custos, quid dicetur in futuro nisi, quia rex fecit et archiepiscopus sustinendo confirmavit, ratum esse debet?"

[4] See N. C. vol. iii. p. 194; vol. v. p. 101.

greater crime than if another man did the same. For the CHAP. IV. Archbishop to betray the rights of his church and his successors was a greater crime still. And if King and Archbishop agreed to any such spoliation, all other men would naturally hold that the act could not be questioned. On these grounds Anselm refused to consent to the King's grants. He left the royal presence trusting that he was now free from the burthen of ecclesiastical rule in any shape. He had been set free from the abbatial rule of Bec; he had escaped being loaded with the primatial rule of Canterbury. He was, as he wished to be, a private man.[1]

But a private man Anselm was not to remain. After the scene in the sick room at Gloucester, neither William nor Anselm could act exactly as if that scene had never taken place. The momentary repentance of the King, and the acts done during the time of that repentance, had given a strength to public opinion which even William Rufus could not despise. The old abuses, the old oppressions, began again; but men were now less disposed to put up with them than they had been before. They would no longer go on without an archbishop, after an archbishop, and Anselm as that archbishop, had been more than promised, after he had been given to them. The general murmur became so loud that the King had to give way.[2] He could no longer help giving the archbishopric to Anselm, and that on Anselm's own terms. And what he did, he did in the most solemn and, as far as outward appearances went, the most thorough manner. An extraordinary Gemót of the kingdom—for the season was

Public feeling since the nomination at Gloucester.

Gemót at Winchester.

---

[1] Eadmer, Hist. Nov. 20. "Unde Anselmus oppido lætatus est, sperans se hac occasione, a prælationis onere, per Dei gratiam, exonerandum." And directly after; "Eo quod terras ecclesiæ injuria dare nolebat, episcopalis officii onus sese lætus evasisse videbat."

[2] Ib. "Cum decursu non exiguo tempore, clamorem omnium, de ecclesiarum destructione conquerentium."

CHAP. IV.

The King renews his promises.

neither Christmas, Easter, nor Pentecost — was summoned to Winchester. In the presence of the assembled Witan, William Rufus, in full health, renewed the promises which he had made in his sickness. The wrongs done in his kingdom, above all, the wrongs done to the Church, were a second time to come to an end.[1] Anselm was exhorted, and at last persuaded, to accept the archbishopric. He received it, seemingly without scruple, according to the ancient use of England; he became the man of the King.[2] Anselm kneeling before Rufus, with his pure hands between the polluted hands of the King, pledging himself as the King's man for all earthly worship, makes a scene which it is strange to think of.[3] The deed was now done, and it could not be recalled. Bishop in the spiritual sense Anselm was not as yet; but he was the legal possessor of all the temporal estates and temporal jurisdiction of the see of Canterbury.

Anselm receives the archbishopric, and does homage.

The King's writ.

The act which had just been done had now to be announced to the whole nation in the ancient form. The writ of King William went forth, announcing to all the King's faithful men, French and English, that he had granted to Anselm the archbishopric of Canterbury, with all the rights, powers, and possessions — rights, powers, and possessions, recited in the English tongue — which belonged to the see, with all liberties over all his men, within boroughs and without. And words were added which seemed meant expressly to enforce Anselm's

[1] Eadmer, Hist. Nov. 20. "Multis bonis et ecclesiæ Dei profuturis promissionibus illectus [Anselmus]."

[2] Ib. "More et exemplo prædecessoris sui inductus, *pro usu terræ,* homo regis factus est, et, sicut Lanfrancus suo tempore fuerat, de toto archiepiscopatu saisiri jussus est." Does not Eadmer, writing by later lights from Rome, feel scruples which Anselm did not feel at the time?

[3] When one thinks of this, one is less surprised at the astounding language of the Council in Eadmer, Hist. Nov. 53. Yet, after all, Henry the Fourth was not Rufus.

view of the point last in dispute. The new archbishop was CHAP. IV.
to have all these liberties over as many thegns as King The Arch-
bishop's
Eadward the King's kinsman had granted to the see of thegns.
Christ Church. This can hardly mean anything except the
annulling of the grants which the King had made during
the vacancy.[1] Anselm was to have all such temporal
rights as had been lawfully held by Lanfranc, as had
been before him unlawfully held by Stigand. The writ Clauses in
favour of
further contains provisions on behalf of the metro- the monks.
politan monastery. The estates of the convent were
distinct from those of the see; still, in such a time of
unlaw, it is likely that some excuse had been found to
do them some wrong also. To the monks of Christ
Church therefore the King confirms all their rights and
possessions, with all the tolls and dues from the haven
of Sandwich; no man, French or English, should meddle
with them or their servants.[2] Our Canterbury guide The city of
Canterbury
speaks also of a renewed grant, on more favourable terms and abbey
than before, of the city of Canterbury and of the abbey of Saint
Alban's.
of Saint Alban's.[3] These possessions were at least not
granted by the writ which announces the grant of the
archbishopric. Of one of them the local patriotism of Anselm
and Saint
Saint Alban's naturally knew nothing, though we hear Alban's.
of the friendship which Anselm showed to the house and

---

[1] We have the writ in the Fœdera, i. 5. It grants "omnes liber-
tates in terra et mari super suos homines, infra burgos et extra, et
super tot theines quot ecclesiæ Christi concessit Edwardus rex, cognatus
meus." This mention of the thegns, and the King's request about the
grants, and the words of Anselm to the Archbishop of Lyons, all hang
together.

[2] Ib. "Nolo pati ut aliquis hominum se intromittat de omnibus rebus
quæ ad eos pertinent, nisi ipsi et ministri eorum quibus ipsi committere
voluerint, nec Francus nec Anglus."

[3] Eadmer, Hist. Nov. 18 (see above, p. 403). "At civitas Cantuaria
quam Lanfrancus suo tempore in beneficio a rege tenebat, et abbatia sancti
Albani quam non solum Lanfrancus sed et antecessores ejus habuisse
noscuntur, in alodium ecclesiæ Christi Cantuariensis, pro redemptione
animæ suæ, perpetuo jure, transirent."

to its abbot Paul. This friendship could hardly have been shown in the character of archbishop, as Paul died during the year of Anselm's appointment.[1] And it is not wonderful that Anselm's friendship for the abbey did not avail to save it from the usual fate. For four years after the death of Paul, the church of Saint Alban remained without an abbot, while the King held the lands of the abbey, cut down its woods, and found many ingenious excuses, such as Flambard knew how to devise, for wringing money out of its tenants.[2]

It would seem that, of the three points which had been insisted on by Anselm at Rochester, two were left out of sight in the public assembly at Winchester no less than in the private conference at Windsor. The question about the grants of the archiepiscopal lands was settled, at least in name and for the time, in favour of Anselm; but nothing was said either about William's obligation to take Anselm as his spiritual guide or about the acknowledgement of Urban as Pope. The former of these two was in truth a matter for the King's private conscience; it was hardly a matter to be discussed and legislated about in an assembly of the kingdom. And even the matter of the Pope did not touch Anselm's conscience in exactly the same way as the question of the grants. If Anselm had allowed the grants, it would have been, in his view, an alienation of the rights of his see, and therefore a personal crime. But he might, without in any way giving up his position, receive the investiture

---

[1] They were old friends. The Gesta Abbatum (i. 61) go on to say; "Rex Willelmus secundus archiepiscopatum, quem diu in manu sua tenuit, immisericors depauperavit. Abbas autem Paulus Anselmum egentem juvit et consolabatur. Unde, inthronizatus, in multis beneficia potiora gratus abbati recompensavit, et quod imperfectum erat in ædificiis ecclesiæ sancti Albani juvit postea consummare."

[2] Ib. i. 65. "Nemora complanando, hominibus beati Albani pecuniam, causis cavillatoriis adinventis, extorquendo." Rufus is described as "nullius, præcipue mortui, verus amicus."

without saying anything about the papal question at
all. It was not yet held that the Bishop of Rome
was entitled to any voice as to the election, investiture,
or consecration, of any English bishop. In the case of
a diocesan bishop, there was no need for any reference
to the Pope at any stage; in the case of a metropolitan,
the pallium had to be asked for; but it was not asked
for till after consecration. Anselm had given fair warning
to the King that he meant to acknowledge Urban. But
at no stage of the business which had yet been reached
was there any need for any formal acknowledgement
of any Pope. Anselm might therefore fairly hold that
his first warning was enough, and that he was not called
upon to raise the question again, till the time came when
it would be his duty to seek for the pallium from one
Pope or the other. When that time came, he would be
ready to do or suffer as the circumstances of that yet
future day might dictate.

Before the time for any dealings with Rome should
come, there were still two more ceremonies to be done
in England. The process of making a bishop was, then
as now, a long one; but the order of the several stages
was different then from what it now is. Anselm had
done homage and had received restitution of the temporalities; but he was not yet enthroned, still less
consecrated. The order then was, homage, enthronement.
consecration. The present order is the exact opposite.
The bishop-elect is consecrated; then he takes corporal
possession of the see by enthronement; last of all, he
does homage to the King and receives restitution of the
temporalities. In the elder state of things the spiritual
office was bestowed on one who was already full bishop
for all temporal purposes. By the later rule the temporal
rights are bestowed on one who is already full bishop

for all spiritual purposes. The difference in order seems to arise from the different theory of the episcopate which has prevailed since the restoration of ecclesiastical elections was fully established by the Great Charter. In the irregular practice of the eleventh century, the notion of investiture of a benefice by the king had come to the front. The king had in his hands a great fief, which he granted to whom he would; that fief was chargeable with certain spiritual duties. It was therefore for the Church, by her spiritual rite of consecration, to make the king's nominee, already invested with his temporal rights, capable of discharging his spiritual duties. Such was clearly the established view of the days of Rufus, and the order of the process is in harmony with it. The office is treated as an appendage to the benefice. In the theory which is both earlier and later the benefice is treated as an appendage to the office. The order of the process is therefore reversed. The spiritual office is first filled by the three ecclesiastical processes of election, confirmation, consecration—the last of course being needless when the person chosen is already a bishop. The bishop then takes personal possession of his church by installation or enthronement. The spiritual functions over, the bishop, now in full possession of his office, lastly receives the attached benefice by homage to the king and restitution of the temporalities at his hands. That elections were hardly ever really free at any time, that the royal leave was needed for the election, that kings recommended, that popes "provided," that the later law requires the electors to choose only the king's nominee and requires the metropolitan to confirm the person so chosen, makes no difference to the theory. The royal power is kept in the background; it is the ecclesiastical power which formally acts. The king's hand pulls the wires of the ecclesiastical puppets; but the ecclesiastical puppets play their formal part. The whole is done according to a theory which naturally places the formal act of the temporal power last. In the days of Rufus the whole was done according to another theory which, as naturally, placed the formal act of the temporal power first of all.

The next stage then was for Anselm, still only a presbyter, but already invested with all the temporal powers and possessions of the archbishopric, to take personal possession of his see in the metropolitan church. It was the only time that such a rite was performed in the short eastern limb of the new church of Lanfranc. Anselm's own later days were to see the removal of the patriarchal throne of Britain to be the centre of the more stately apse of Conrad, as later days saw it again removed to be the centre of the yet more stately apse of the two Williams. On that throne, Anselm, chosen to be Pope of the island Empire, was placed on one of the later days of September in the presence of a rejoicing crowd of monks, clergy, and lay folk. Well might they rejoice; the Church had again a shepherd; the nation had again a defender. But even that day of joy did not pass without signs that the favour of the temporal lord of the island Empire was already turned away from its new pontiff. The King's sense of personal honour required him to carry out the promise made at Gloucester, to allow, even to compel, Anselm to become archbishop. But he had no sense of Christian or kingly duty to keep him from insulting and harassing the man whom he had promoted, or to constrain him to keep the promises contained in his own proclamation. Those things had not been done in the character of *probus miles*, of knight and gentleman. It was quite consistent with chivalrous honour to send Flambard to disturb the joyful day of enthronement

Enthronement of Anselm. September 25, 1093.

CHAP. IV. by the announcement of a hostile suit against the new

Flambard archbishop. We are not told what was its exact nature,
brings a
suit against only that it was something which, in the eyes of strict
Anselm on
the day of churchmen at least, wholly concerned the affairs of the
enthrone-
ment. Church, and with which the King's court had nothing to
do.[1] In the older days of England such a distinction
could hardly have been drawn; after the separation of the
jurisdictions under the Conqueror, it may have been fair
enough. Whatever the actual matter in dispute was, we
can understand the general indignation at the choice of
such a moment for the serving of the notice, at the malice
which would not let even the first day of the Primate's
new dignity pass unmolested. We can also easily picture
to ourselves the fierce swagger of Flambard, graphically
as it is set before us.[2] And we can listen also to the mild
grief of Anselm, inferring from such treatment on the
first day of his primacy what the troubles of his future
life were likely to be.[3]

Other   After the enthronement more than two months still
events of
the year. passed before the final rite of consecration admitted
Anselm to the fulness of his spiritual office. They were
months of no small moment in the history of Britain
They beheld the last invasion of Malcolm, his death,[4]
the death of his saintly wife, the uprising of Scottish

[1] Eadmer, Hist. Nov. 20. "Indignationi hoc quoque non parum doloris
adjiciebat, quod negotium unde agebatur ad jura ecclesiæ pertinebat, nec
in aliquo regalis judicii definitionem respiciebat."

[2] Ib. "A rege missus quidam nomine Ranulphus, regiæ voluntatis
maximus executor, qui, spreta consideratione pietatis ac modestiæ, placitum
contra eum ipsa die instituit, et ferus ac tumens, tantum ecclesiæ gaudium
conturbare non timuit." Directly after; "ut nec primum quidem suæ
dignitatis diem permitteretur in pace transigere."

[3] Ib. "Ex præsentibus futura conjecit, et quia multas in pontificatu
angustias foret passurus, intellexit atque prædixit."

[4] The consecration of Anselm and the death of Malcolm are oddly joined
together in the new Canterbury Chronicle published by Liebermann, (p. 4);
"1094. On ðison geare me bletsede Anselm to biscope ii. ñ. Decemb.; and
on ðison geare me scloch Malculm cing."

nationality against the foreign innovations or reforms chap. iv.
which Malcolm and Margaret represented in the eyes
of their native subjects. The affairs of Scotland, of
Wales, of Normandy, were all on the Red King's
mind at the same moment, as well as the affairs of
Anselm. But it is these last that we have to follow for
the present. Early in December, on the second Sunday Consecration of Anselm
in Advent, the more part of the bishops of England came at Canterbury.
together at Canterbury for the consecration of the new
metropolitan. At their head was the Archbishop of December 4, 1093.
York, Thomas of Bayeux. It was the privilege of his Thomas of York.
see—so the loyal historian of the church of York takes
care that we should know—when Canterbury was without an archbishop, to consecrate bishops and to put the
crown on the king's head within the vacant province.[1]
Whether the one available suffragan of the northern province came along with Thomas, in the form of William of
Durham, we are not distinctly told. But of the bishops Other bishops present.
of the province of Canterbury eight must have been there.
Robert Bloet was the elect of Lincoln; but he, like Anselm,
was himself awaiting consecration. Of the rest three
were absent, and among those three were the only two
who were English either by birth or by adoption, the two
whom we could have most wished to have a share in the
work. Herbert of Thetford must now have been on his Absence of Herbert,
penitential journey to Rome or on his way back.[2]
The holy Wulfstan, the one Englishman by descent
as well as by birth who was left among the bishops Wulfstan,
of England, the only one who had been a bishop in

[1] T. Stubbs, X Scriptt. 1707. He adds emphatically, "Hæc interim
fecit Thomas archiepiscopus, nec quisquam episcoporum erat qui hæc in
sua ipsius diœcesi præsente archiepiscopo præsumeret."

[2] Eadmer (Hist. Nov. 21) describes the consecrators as "Thomas archiepiscopus Eboracensis et omnes episcopi Angliæ," except the two who sent
excuses. But Dr. Stubbs does not seem to reckon the Bishop of Durham
among the number.

CHAP. IV.

and
Osbern.

the old days of King Eadward, was still in the land, but was kept away by age or sickness. So was Osbern of Exeter, the only one of the foreign stock who had thoroughly made himself an Englishman by adoption. These two sent letters of consent instead of their personal presence.[1] The others gathered round the high altar of Lanfranc's rearing at Christ Church. Most of them are men with whose names we are familiar; Maurice of London, Walkelin of Winchester, Gundulf of Rochester, Osmund of Salisbury, Robert of Hereford, John who had moved from Wells to Bath, Robert of Lichfield or of Chester, who had moved in a fiercer sort to Earl Leofric's Coventry. All of them, whatever they were in other ways, were mighty builders. If William of Durham, whose church had just begun to rise on the height above the Wear,[2] was really in their company, there was indeed the master-builder of all, whose heart might already swell to think how the work which he had begun would surpass the work of Lanfranc under whose roof they were met. These eight came together in the new metropolitan church to perform the rite which should make Anselm at once their brother and their father.

But, before the rite could be gone through, an old question was stirred again, by no means for the last time. The leader of the episcopal band was fully minded that the rank to which they were about to admit the prelate

Position
of Thomas.

elect should be clearly defined. Thomas of York had doubtless not forgotten the day when he had himself gone away unconsecrated from the spot where they were now met, because he could not bring himself to make such a submission to the higher dignity of Canterbury as Anselm's predecessor had required of him.[3] He now had his opportunity of raising his voice with greater

[1] See N. C. vol. iv. p. 417.

[2] The foundations had just been laid, as we shall see in the next chapter.

[3] See N. C. vol. iv. p. 340.

success on behalf of the dignity of his own church. Before CHAP. IV.
the consecrating prelates went on to the examination of the
bishop-elect, it was the business of the Bishop of London to
read the formal document declaring the cause why they had
come together.[1] Bishop Maurice handed over this duty to
the Bishop of Winchester. Walkelin began to read how
the church of Canterbury, the metropolitan church of all
Britain, was widowed of its pastor. The Archbishop of Thomas
York stopped him; "Metropolitan church of all Britain? objects to
the de-
Then the church of York, which all men know to be a scription
of Anselm
metropolitan church, is not metropolitan. We all know as "Metropolitan of
that the church of Canterbury is the primatial church of Britain."
all Britain; metropolitan church of all Britain it is not."[2]
This was not a distinction without a difference. To
allow the claim of Canterbury to be the metropolitan
church of all Britain would have been to admit that the
church of York was a mere suffragan see of Canterbury.
The other form simply asserted the precedency of Canterbury as the higher in rank of the two metropolitan
sees of Britain. So Anselm's correspondent at Lyons
was Primate of all the Gauls, without endangering the
metropolitan rank of Rheims and Rouen. But William
the Good Soul would have been stirred to wrath had it
been hinted that Lyons was the metropolitan church of
all Gaul, and Rouen simply its suffragan. A zealot for

[1] Eadmer, Hist. Nov. 21. "Cum ante ordinandi pontificis examinationem
Walchelinus Wentanus episcopus, rogatu Mauricii episcopi Lundoniensis
cujus hoc officium est, ecclesiastico more electionem scriptam legeret."
This is, I suppose, as Dean of the Province, an office still held by the
Bishops of London, and by virtue of which they do several of the things
which Thomas Stubbs claims for his own metropolitan.

[2] Eadmer, Hist. Nov. 21. Walkelin reads the writing till he comes to
the words which set forth how "hæc Dorobernensis ecclesia totius Britanniæ metropolitana suo sit viduata pastore." Then Thomas "subintulit, dicens
totius Britanniæ metropolitana? Si totius Britanniæ metropolitana, ecclesia
Eboracensis quæ metropolitana esse scitur, metropolitana non est. Et
quidem ecclesiam Cantuariensem primatem totius Britanniæ esse scimus,
non metropolitanam."

CHAP. IV.
His objection admitted.
Anselm's consecration.

the rights of Canterbury admits that the objection of Thomas was a good one.[1] The wording of the document was at once changed;[2] the rite went on, and Anselm was consecrated as Archbishop of Canterbury and Primate of all Britain. If the more northern suffragans of York had any objections to make, they were just then less likely than ever to be at Canterbury to make them.

Question of acknowledging the Pope.

The position of the newly-consecrated Primate within his own island was thus settled to the satisfaction of the man who thought that he had a special interest in the matter. It was perhaps more difficult to settle his relation to the ecclesiastical powers beyond his own island. Anselm had warned the King that, if he became archbishop, he must yield obedience to Urban. But, as the King had not acknowledged Urban, it would have been deemed unlawful to speak of Urban as Pope in any public act. The difficulty seems to have been got over by Anselm making a profession of obedience to the

[1] Eadmer, Hist. Nov. 21. "Quod auditum ratione submixum esse, quod dicebat intellectum est."

[2] Ib. "Tunc statim scriptura ipsa mutata est, et pro totius Britanniæ metropolitana, totius Britanniæ primas scriptum est, et omnis controversia conquievit. Itaque sacravit eum ut totius Britanniæ primatem."

The Yorkist version, as given by T. Stubbs (X Scriptt. 1707), is of course quite different. Thomas is there attended by several members of his church, Hugh the Dean and others. This might almost imply the absence of his one suffragan. The words objected to are in this version "Primas totius Britanniæ." As soon as they are heard, Thomas and his companions go out and take off their robes. Anselm and Walkelin follow them; they fall at the feet of Thomas, and ask for his forgiveness ("pedibus archiepiscopi affusi humiliter deprecati sunt, ne moleste acciperet"). Thomas stands firm. "Cum duo tantum, inquit, sint metropolitæ in Britannia, alter super alterum esse non potest." He might have erred in his youth by admitting the claims of Canterbury; he would at least not err in the like sort again. He would consecrate no man as primate. Anselm and Walkelin submit; the word "primate" is struck out, and Anselm is consecrated as "metropolitan." It will be seen that in this version the place of the two titles, "primate" and "metropolitan," is simply turned round. We can have no doubt as to preferring the contemporary account; but it is well to see how matters looked at York several centuries later.

Roman Church, without mentioning the name of any CHAP. IV.
particular pontiff.[1] Thus passed the day of the consecration; but, on the morrow, Thomas of York, successful Thomas
thus far, found yet another point to assert on behalf claims jurisdiction
of the alleged rights of his church. He had, it will be over
Lincoln.
remembered, striven to hinder Remigius from transferring the see of Dorchester to a spot which he deemed
to be in his own province and diocese.[2] Since that time,
notwithstanding his remonstrances, the minster of Lincoln had arisen; but it remained unconsecrated, and its
builder was dead. To the mind of Thomas these facts
perhaps seemed to be signs as clear in their meaning as
any which the Bishop of Hereford would find out from the
lore of the stars.[3] Thus emboldened, on the day after he
had consecrated Anselm to the see of Canterbury, Thomas
warned the new Primate against proceeding, as he had
purposed, to consecrate Robert Bloet to the see of Lincoln.
He might consecrate him, if he would, to the ancient see
of Dorchester; but not to Lincoln or to any other place in
that land of Lindesey which belonged to the jurisdiction
of York.[4] Anselm seems to have yielded; at least the Robert
Bloet's con-
matter remained unsettled, and the elect of Lincoln re- secration
mained unconsecrated for two months longer. delayed.

Anselm now, after so many difficulties, was at last
fully Archbishop. He remained in his metropolis for

[1] There is no mention of this in Eadmer's account of the consecration;
but such seems to be the meaning of Anselm himself in a letter to Walter,
Bishop of Albano, which I shall have to quote again (Epp. iii. 36). He
there says, "Sub professione obedientiæ Romani pontificis me consecrarunt." This is an answer to a charge of being schismatically consecrated
while the kingdom was not under the obedience of Urban.

[2] See above, p. 311.　　　　　　[3] See above, p. 312.

[4] T. Stubbs, X Scriptt. 1707. "Non prohibebat quin eum Dorkaces-
trensem ordinaret episcopum, sicut et antecessores sui fuerant; verum
Lyndecoldinum oppidum, et magnam partem provinciæ Lyndisiæ dicebat
fuisse, et jure esse debere, parochiam Eboracensis ecclesiæ, et injuria illi
erepta esse."

CHAP. IV. eight days only after his consecration. He then set forth
Christmas for the Christmas Assembly of the realm, to be held at
Gemót at
Gloucester. Gloucester.[1] The prayer which he had drawn up at the
1093-1094.
assembly held there twelve months before had indeed
been answered. The King's heart had been stirred; the
Archbishop had been appointed. Unhappily also the
King's heart had been stirred back again. William was
again the king who had mockingly bidden his bishops
to pray as they thought good, not the king who had
passionately called on Anselm to step in between him
and eternal death. The breach between King and Primate had begun before Anselm was fully Primate, when
Flambard had insolently summoned him in his own
church on the day of his enthronement. Whatever the
matter of the summons was, Anselm was now ready in
the King's court to answer it. But of that dispute we hear
Anselm re- no more. The Archbishop came to Gloucester, and was
ceived by
the King. courteously and cheerfully received, not only by the
assembled nobles, but by the King himself.[2] But the
Witan were not to depart from the place of meeting till
new grounds of quarrel had arisen between the two
unequal yokefellows who were at last fully coupled
together.

§ 3.   The Assembly at Hastings and the Second
Norman Campaign.   1094.

Events of   THE events of the year on which we have now en-
the year
1094. tered consist partly of warlike movements in Normandy
and Scotland, partly of matters directly touching ecclesiastical questions, above all touching Anselm. Of these,

---

[1] Eadmer does not mention the place; but it appears from the Chronicle
that it was at the usual place, namely Gloucester.

[2] Eadmer, Hist. Nov. 21. "Consummato ordinationis suæ die octavo,
Cantuariam egrediens, ad curiam regis pro imminente nativitate Domini
vadit. Quo perveniens, hilariter a rege totaque regni nobilitate suscipitur."

the affairs of Scotland and the affairs of Anselm have CHAP. IV.
hardly any bearing on one another. But the affairs of Affairs of
Normandy and the affairs of Anselm have a close con- their connexion. They were discussed in the same assemblies; and nexion with
one ground of quarrel between King and Primate arose Anselm.
directly out of the discussion of Norman affairs. Some
of the details of the two stories are so mixed up with
one another that it would be hard to keep them apart.
Again, the Scottish warfare of this year is part of a con-
tinuous series of Scottish events spread over several
years. But the Norman warfare is a kind of episode.
It is connected by the laws of cause and effect with
things which went before and with things which came
after; but, as a story, it stands by itself or is mixed up
with the story of Anselm. It cannot be dealt with, like
the King's first Norman war, as a distinct chapter of our
history. It will therefore be better, during the year
which follows the consecration of Anselm, to keep Scottish affairs apart from the history of the ecclesiastical
dispute, but to treat the Norman campaign as something
filling up part of the time between two great stages in
Anselm's history.

The chief business of the assembly which now met at Robert's
Gloucester was the reception of a hostile message from of William.
the Duke of the Normans. This fact makes us wish to 1093-1094.
know more in detail what Count William of Eu had
suggested, and what King William of England had done.
It is certain that King William needed no pressing to
make him inclined for another attempt on his brother's
dominions; but it is clear that the coming of Count
William had led to some special action which had given
Duke Robert special ground of complaint. The Norman
embassy came, and challenged one brother in the name
of the other, almost as an earlier Norman embassy had
challenged Harold in the name of the father of both of

them.[1] The diplomacy of those days was clear and outspoken. The *bodes* of Duke Robert seem to have spoken to King William in the midst of his Witan, much as the bodes of the Athenian commonwealth spoke, with a greater amount of personal deference, to King Philip on his throne. They told the King of the English that their master renounced all peace and treaty with him, unless he would do all that was set down in the treaty; they declared him forsworn and truthless, unless he would hold to the treaty, or would go and clear himself at the place where the treaty had been made and sworn to.[2] Such a message as this was hardly wise in Robert, whatever it might have been in a prince who had the resources of his dominions more thoroughly at his command. It was in some sort an appeal to arbitration; but it was put in a shape which was sure to bring on war. William had no doubt made up his mind for a Norman enterprise in any case; the message of Robert would really help him by turning a certain amount of public feeling to his side. An expedition was decreed; Normandy was to be a second time invaded by the Red King.

War decreed.

And now came the question how ways and means were to be found for the new war. That some of the ways and means which were employed were unworthy of all kingly dignity [3] is not wonderful in this reign. But the only one of which we distinctly hear seems in itself less un-

---

[1] See N. C. vol. iii. pp. 69, 260.

[2] Again it is from the Chronicler that we get the most formal statement of the words of the challenge. They would doubtless be uttered in French; but we may believe that we have an authorized English version; " Him þider fram his broðer Rodbearde of Normandig bodan coman, þa cyddon þæt his broðer griö and forewarde eall æftercwæð, butan se cyng gelæstan wolde eall þet hi on forewarde hæfdon ær gewroht, and uppon þæt hine forsworenne, and trywleasne clypode, buton he þa forewarda geheolde, oðöe þider ferde, and hine þær betealde þær seo forewarde ær wæs gewroht and eac gesworen."

[3] Eadmer, Hist. Nov. 21. "Adeo ut nonnullas etiam difficultates pateretur, quas regiam pati excellentiam indecens videbatur."

worthy than some others, though the particular form which
it took is eminently characteristic of Rufus. The great
men who had come together to the assembly made presents
to the King, forerunners of the benevolences of later times.
The great men of Normandy had, twenty-eight years before, made contributions of ships for the invasion of England.[1] Now the great men of England, some of them the
same persons, made contributions of money for the invasion of Normandy. This was at least less unworthy of
the kingly dignity than some of the tricks by which Flambard wrung money out of more helpless victims. But
the Red King's way of dealing with such gifts shows
the mixture of greed and pride which stands out in all
his doings. If the sum offered was less than he thought
it ought to be, he cast it aside with scorn; nor would
he ever again admit the offerer to his friendship, unless
he made amends by a second offer of such a sum as the
King might think becoming.[2] To this custom Anselm
now conformed, with the other nobles and prelates; but it
was with some pains that his friends persuaded him to
conform to it.[3] With his usual fear of being misconstrued,
he dreaded that if, so soon after his consecration, he gave
the King any sum which the King would think worth
taking, it might have the air of a simoniacal bargain.[4]
He might also hold that the goods of the Church ought
not to be applied to worldly, least of all to warlike,

[1] See N. C. vol. iii. p. 300.

[2] Eadmer, u. s. "Siquidem hunc ipse rex morem erga cunctos quibus
dominatur habebat, ut quum quis eorum aliquid ei pecuniarum, etiam
solius gratiæ obtentu, offerebat, oblatum, nisi quantitas rei voto illius con-
curreret, sperneret. Nec offerentem in suam ulterius amicitiam admittebat,
si ad determinationem suam oblatum munus non augeret."

[3] He does it only "suasus ab amicis suis."

[4] Anselm himself gives this motive in his letter to Archbishop Hugh (Ep.
iii. 24); "Gratias Deo, quo miserante simplicitatem cordis mei hoc factum
est, ne, si nihil aut parum promisissem, justam videretur habere causam
irascendi; aut si accepisset, verteretur mihi in gravamen, et in suspicionem
nefandæ emptionis."

uses; he might even feel some scruple in helping towards
a war against a prince who had so lately been his own
worldly lord. But he was won over by the argument that
a gift in season might win the King's favour for ever,
and that he might be allowed to give his mind with less
He gives disturbance to the spiritual duties of his office.[1] He
five
hundred brought himself therefore to offer the King five hundred
pounds. pounds of silver. William was satisfied with the amount,
and received the gift with courteous thanks.[2]

William   What followed showed that William Rufus had coun-
persuaded
to refuse sellors about him who were worse than himself, or
the money. who at any rate were not ashamed to play upon the
worst parts of his character to obtain their own ends.
In this case they are nameless. Are we to fill up the
blank with the names of the Bishop of Durham and the
Count of Meulan? Or is it safer to lay any evil deed
the doer of which is not recorded on the broad back of
Randolf Flambard? At any rate, some malignant persons, whoever they were, came about the King, and persuaded him that the gift of the Archbishop was a
contemptible sum which he ought to reject. One whom
he had exalted and enriched above the other great men
of England ought, in such need as that in which the King
found himself, to have given him two thousand pounds, or
one thousand at the very least. To offer so little as five
hundred was mere mockery. Let the King wait a little,
let him change his face towards the Archbishop, and
Anselm would presently come, delighted to win back the
King's favour with the gift of five hundred pounds more.[3]

---

[1] Eadmer (Hist. Nov. 21) gives these motives at length.

[2] Ib. Rex tali oblatione audita, bene rem quidem laudando respondit."

[3] These are the arguments which Eadmer puts into the mouths of the
King's advisers; "Quidam malignæ mentis homines regem, ut fieri solet,
ad hoc perduxerunt quatenus oblatam pecuniam spernendo recipere non
adquiesceret."

Thus the Primate's enemies, whoever they were, sought CHAP. IV. to frighten him, and to get more money out of him for the King's use. But their schemes were disappointed.[1] Anselm was presently surprised by a message to say that the King refused his gift—the gift which he had already cheerfully accepted.[2] He then sought an au- dience, and asked the King whether such a message was really of his sending. Some tyrants might have seen in this question an escape from a difficulty. It would have been easy for Rufus to have denied his own act; but his pride was up, and direct lying was never in his vein. He avowed his message. Then Anselm prayed him not to refuse his gift; it was the first that he had offered; it should not be the last. It would be better for the King to receive a smaller sum from him as a friend, than to wring a larger sum from him as a slave.[3] Of the alternative of increasing the amount of the gift he said not a word. One motive was that he could not raise a greater sum without doing wrong to his tenants—the wrong which he had declared Ælfheah to be a true martyr for refusing to do.[4] The King was now in the mood for short and wrathful speeches. "Keep your money and your jaw to yourself; I have enough of my own. Get you gone."[5] Anselm obeyed, remembering that at his enthronement the Gospel had been read which said that no man could serve two masters. He rejoiced that no one now could deem that he had been guilty of any corrupt bargain with

Anselm prays Rufus to take the money.

Rufus refuses it.

[1] Eadmer here quotes a psalm; "Mentita est iniquitas sibi." Ps. xxvii. 12.

[2] Ib. "Mandatur illi regem oblatam pecuniam refutare, et miratus est."

[3] Ib. 22. "Amica nempe libertate me et omnia mea ad utilitatem tuam habere poteris, servili autem conditione nec me nec mea habebis."

[4] See N. C. vol. iv. p. 441.

[5] Eadmer, u. s. "Iratus rex, Sint, inquit, cum jurgio tua tibi, sufficient mea mihi. Vade."

CHAP. IV. the King. Yet he tried once more through messengers to persuade the King to take his gift, but, as he steadily refused to double it, it was still thrust aside with scorn. The assembly broke up; the Archbishop, still in the King's disfavour, went away, and the money which the King had despised was given to the poor.

This business over, Anselm had now a few weeks, but a few weeks only, to give to his immediate pastoral work.

Dispute with the Bishop of London.

Even those weeks were disturbed by a dispute with one of his suffragans. The point at issue was the right of the Archbishop to consecrate churches and do other episcopal acts in such of his manors as were locally in other dioceses. This right was denied by Bishop Maurice of London, who sent two of his canons to forbid the Archbishop to consecrate the newly built church of Harrow.[1] The matter was settled by an appeal to one who knew the ancient laws of England better than either Maurice or Anselm.

Judgement of Wulfstan.

Wulfstan of Worcester, now "one and alone of the ancient fathers of the English," wrote back his judgement in favour of the Primate's right.[2] The question was thus

---

[1] The story is told by Eadmer, 22. The objection of Maurice takes this shape; "Dicebat ipsam ecclesiam in sua parochia esse, et ob hoc, licet in terra archiepiscopi fuerit, dedicationem illius ad se pertinere." The right of the Archbishop seems to have rested on good ancient precedent; but there is something odd in Eadmer's way of stating the controversy. The presumption was surely in favour of the diocesan bishop.

[2] The letter of Anselm to Wulfstan appears among the Epistles (iii. 19). Wulfstan's answer is given in the text of the Historia Novorum. Anselm speaks of the action of the earlier archbishops in this matter; "Quod etiam sanctus Dunstanus et alii prædecessores mei fecisse probantur, ipsis ecclesiis quas dedicaverunt adhuc stantibus." This is a little touch from a time when the churches of Dunstan's day were being largely rebuilt, that of Harrow most likely among them. Wulfstan is well described by Eadmer; "Super-erat adhuc beatæ memoriæ Wolstanus episcopus unus et solus de antiquis Anglorum patribus, vir in omni religione conspicuus, et antiquarum Angliæ consuetudinum scientia apprime eruditus." There is something very remarkable in the way in which Wulfstan speaks of the archbishop to whom he made his first profession (see N. C. vol. ii. pp. 473, 655); "Extant

decided; Maurice did not dare to set up his judgement
on such a matter against that of the venerable saint, the
relic of a state of things which had passed away.[1]

Those of the great men of England who had come to
the Gemót at Gloucester from the more distant parts of
the kingdom could hardly have reached their homes
when they were again summoned to give the King the
benefit of their counsels. William Rufus was so strong
upon his throne that in his days assemblies were sure to
be frequent. He was moreover planning a campaign
beyond the sea, so that it was very doubtful whether he
would be able this year to wear his crown in England at
the usual times of Easter and Pentecost. The Easter Assembly
at Hast-
Gemót was therefore in some sort forestalled. As the ings.
starting-point for his second invasion of Normandy the February 2,
1094.
King had chosen the spot which had been his father's
head-quarters in the great invasion of England. At
Pevensey he had once beaten back the invasion of his
Norman brother; at Hastings he now gathered the force
which was for the second time to avenge that wrong. The

quippe et in nostra diœcesi altaria, et quædam etiam ecclesiæ in hiis scilicet
villis quas Stigandus vestræ excellentiæ prædecessor, haut tamen jure eccle-
siasticæ hæreditatis sed ex dono possederat sæcularis potestatis, ab ipso de-
dicata." Wulfstan, speaking his own words in his own letter, speaks of
Stigand in quite another tone from that which he had used in the profession
which was put into his mouth by Lanfranc (see N. C. vol. ii. p. 655). The
places referred to are in Gloucestershire, and will be found in Domesday,
164 b. Most of the lands had passed to the Archbishop of York; some
of them first to William Fitz-Osbern, and then to the King. It would seem
then that, in whatever character Stigand held them, it was not as Archbishop of Canterbury. Wulfstan's witness therefore goes so far as to give
the archbishop the right to oust the diocesan bishop, not only on the lands
of the archbishopric, but on any lands which he may hold as a private man.

[1] There is something amusing in the tone of glee in which Eadmer records
his patron's triumph; "Secure deinceps suorum morem antecessorum emu-
labatur, non solum ecclesias, inconsultis episcopis, sacrans, sed et quæque
divina officia in cunctis terris suis per se suosve dispensans."

CHAP. IV. chief men of England were again brought together. We may perhaps see in this assembly a case of the military Gemót. Anselm and several other bishops were there; but it is said that their presence was required to give their blessing to the King and his army before they crossed

The fleet delayed by the wind. the sea.[1] But that final blessing could not be given till many weeks after the army or assembly first came together. When the younger William sought to invade Normandy, he was kept lingering at Hastings, as the elder William had been kept lingering at Saint Valery when he sought to invade England. For six weeks the north wind refused to blow. While thus kept back from warfare, the King seems to have amused himself with ecclesiastical business and ecclesiastical ceremonies, and he further brought on himself the sharpest of ecclesiastical rebukes.[2]

But one of the ceremonies which filled up the time of enforced leisure must have been something more than a matter of amusement to William the Red. Whatever traces of good feeling lingered in his heart gathered round the memory of his parents. And he was now called on to join in a rite which was the crowning homage to his father's name, the most speaking memorial of his father's victory and his father's bounty. Again was a William encamped at Hastings called on to make his way to the hill of Senlac. But this time he could make his way thither in peaceful guise. The

---

[1] Eadmer, 22. "Ex præcepto regis, omnes fere episcopi una cum principibus Angliæ ad Hastinges convenerunt, ipsum regem in Normanniam transfretaturum sua benedictione et concursu prosecuti."

[2] The Chronicler seems distinctly to mark the ecclesiastical business which we have now come to as casually filling up the time lost by the bad weather. The whole entry runs; "Ða ferde se cyng to Hæstingan to þam Candelmæssan, and onmang þam þe he þær wederes abad he let halgian· þæt mynster æt þære Bataille. And Herbearde Losange þam bishop of Theotfordan his stæf bename and þæræfter to midlengtene ofer sæ for into Normandige." We shall take these things in order.

place was no longer a wilderness or a camp, no longer CHAP. IV.
the hill of the hoar apple-tree, no longer bristling with The Abbey of Battle.
the thickset lines of battle, no longer heaped with the
corpses of the conquerors and the conquered. The height
which had once been fenced in by the palisade of the
English host was now fenced in by the precinct wall of a
vast monastery; its buildings, overhanging the hill side,
covered the spot where Gyrth had fallen by the hand of
William;[1] its church, fresh from the hands of the craftsman, covered the ground which had beheld the last act
of the day of slaughter; its high altar, blazing doubtless
with all the skill of Otto and Theodoric,[2] marked the
spot where Harold, struck by the bolt from heaven, had
fallen between the Dragon and the Standard. After so Completion of the building.
many years had passed since the Conqueror had bidden
that the memorial of the Conquest should rise on that
spot and on no other, the minster of Saint Martin of the
Place of Battle stood ready for consecration. Moved by
the prayer of Abbot Gausbert, prompted too by his own
reverence for the memory and the bidding of his father,
William the younger bade that his father's church should
at once be hallowed in his own presence.[3] On a Saturday Consecration of the church.
then in the month of February, in the twenty-eighth year February 11, 1094.
since the awful Saturday of Saint Calixtus, the two who
were so unequally yoked together to draw the plough of
the Church of England made their way to the place of
Battle. A crowd of nobles and commons came together to
the sight; and with them, besides the Primate, were seven

---

[1] See N. C. vol. iv. p. 404.   [2] Ib. 401.

[3] In the Battle Chronicle (40) the consecration is naturally an event
of great importance. But here too the presence of the King and so great
a company is accounted for by their presence in the neighbourhood on
other grounds; "Cumque jam operis fabricæ peroptata advenisset perfectio,
rege quibusdam causis obortis eandem provinciam cum multis optimatibus
forte adeunte, ex instinctu ejusdem abbatis, paterni memor edicti, eandem
dedicari basilicam decrevit."

CHAP. IV.

Bishops
present;
Ralph of
Coutances.

Death of
Geoffrey
Bishop of
Coutances.
February 3,
1093.

William
and Ans-
elm at
Battle.

bishops of three different provinces. There was Ralph of
Chichester, bishop of the diocese, whose jurisdiction
within the favoured abbey was so zealously denied by
every monk of Battle.[1] There were Walkelin of Winchester, Osmund of Salisbury, John of Bath, and Gundulf of Rochester. There was the Primate's great
northern enemy, William of Durham. And there too
was a suffragan of Rouen, the immediate successor of
one of the fierce prelates who had blessed the Conqueror's host on the morning of the great battle.[2]
Geoffrey of Mowbray, Bishop and once Earl, had died
a year before, and the episcopal chair of Coutances
was now filled by his successor Ralph.[3] How, it may be
asked, came a Norman bishop in the court, almost in
the army, of a king who was about to invade Normandy? The answer is easy. The Côtentin was now
again in the hands of Henry,[4] and the presence of its
bishop at the court of William was a sign of the
good understanding which now reigned between the
two younger sons of the Conqueror. But on such a day
as this all interest gathers round the two main figures
in the assembly, the two of highest rank in their several
orders. William the Red, strange assistant in any religious rite, seems less out of place than usual as assistant
in the rite which was to dedicate the work of his father.
And if prayers and offerings were to go up on that
spot for those who had fallen there on the defeated as
well as on the victorious side, there was no mouth
in which we should more gladly put them than in the
mouth of him who was the chief celebrant on that day.
Anselm, standing at the head of his foreign suffragans—

[1] See N. C. vol. iv. p. 405.   [2] See N. C. vol. iii. p. 453.
[3] He was consecrated the year before; the date of his death seems not
to be known. See Bessin, 531.
[4] See above, p. 321.

English Wulfstan stood not by him—before the altar of CHAP. IV.
Saint Martin of the Place of Battle, seemed like a representative of universal Christendom, of universal peace
and love. The holy man from Aosta sang his mass in
honour of the holy man of Tours. And he sang it on
the spot where Harold of England had stood by his
standard in the morning, where William of Normandy
had held the feast of victory in the evening, the morning
and evening of the most memorable day in the history
of our island since England became one kingdom.

From the hill of Battle William went back to the hill
of Hastings, now crowned by the castle into which the
hasty fortress of his father had grown.[1] Six years
earlier the Bishop of Durham, charged with treason,
had in answer, pleaded that he had kept Hastings and
its castle in the King's obedience.[2] Notwithstanding
that answer, he had been banished; he had been recalled, and he now stood, with all his former authority,
chief counsellor of the King, chief enemy of the Archbishop. On the morrow of the dedication of Saint
Martin's, William of Saint-Calais joined with Anselm in
the long-delayed consecration of the elect of Lincoln.
The rite was done in the church of Our Lady within the
castle of Hastings, by the hands of the same prelates
who had the day before dedicated the church of Battle.
It was to the see of Lincoln, not to the see of Dorchester,
that Robert Bloet was consecrated. Thomas of Bayeux
was not there to repeat his protest. He would have
been there in vain. The bishop-elect had, in the
course of his chancellorship, got together the means of
settling such questions. His bishopric, granted at the
time of the King's repentance, had cost him nothing.
It was now a matter of regret with Rufus that it had

Marginal notes: The King at Hastings. William of Saint-Calais. Consecration of Robert Bloet to Lincoln. February 12, 1094.

---

[1] See N. C. vol. iii. p. 411.   [2] See above, p. 29.

CHAP. IV. cost him nothing; Robert had therefore to pay all the more for the establishment of the rights of his see.

Robert's gift to the King. One who had the means of knowing says that he gave the King the great sum of five thousand pounds to decide the cause in favour of Lincoln.[1] This was done, the York writer complains, without the consent of the Archbishop of York and without the knowledge of his chapter.[2] The case must have been settled either at Gloucester or now at Hastings. It was most likely at Hastings, as we can hardly fancy Thomas keeping away from the great Christmas gathering. Our Canterbury guide tells us a not very intelligible story which may show us how the claim of Thomas was spoken of in the southern metropolis. The cause of York had found at least professing friends among the great men at Hastings, though it met with no favour from the King himself. Not knowing perhaps with what weighty arguments the elect of Lincoln had proved his case, certain unnamed bishops and lords deemed that they would please the King by anything which could annoy or discredit Anselm. They therefore insidiously tried to persuade the Archbishop to consecrate Robert without his making due profession to the church of Canterbury.[3] Anselm stood firm. The King, when he heard of the plot, took to his magnanimous vein. His personal quarrel with Anselm should

Plot against Anselm.

---

[1] See Appendix Z.

[2] So says T. Stubbs, X Scriptt. 1708. "Rex Willelmus quamdam concordiam, vel potius dispensationem, fecit inter illos, Thoma quidem archiepiscopo invito et renitente et coacto nec consentiente, sed inconsulto Eboracensi capitulo."

[3] Eadmer, 23. "Quidam de episcopis atque principibus conati sunt contra Anselmum scandalum movere, intendentes ad hoc ut eundem episcopum absolute absque debita professione consecraret. Quod nullo jure fulti, ea solummodo re sunt aggressi, quia putabant se animo regis aliquid ex conturbatione Anselmi, unde lætaretur inferre, scientes eum pro suprascripta caussa adversum ipsum non parum esse turbatum."

never lead him to do anything against the dignity CHAP. IV.
of the Church of Canterbury his mother.[1] The King
and Flambard perhaps enjoyed the joke together. But
Robert Bloet made the needful profession, and was consecrated as Bishop of Lincoln by Anselm and the assembled
prelates. The controversy with York was at last formally Compro-
settled, by a compromise which was announced in a York.
royal charter. By this the Archbishop of York accepted
the patronage of the new abbey of Selby in his own
diocese, and that of the church of Saint Oswald at Worcester—the city and diocese so long connected with
York—in exchange for his claims over Lindesey.[2] The
isle and city of Lindum has ever since remained an
undisputed member of the southern province.

The new Bishop of Lincoln, the first prelate conse- Character
crated to that see, has left a doubtful character behind Bloet.
him. He held his bishopric for thirty years, living on
far into the reign of Henry, and keeping the royal favour
till just before his death. Chancellor under both Wil- His offices.
liams, he, as usual, resigned that post on his consecration; but under Henry he ruled with great power in the
higher office of Justiciar.[3] Bountiful in his gifts to his
see and to his church, the number of whose prebends he
doubled, splendid and liberal in his manner of life, bountiful to the poor, winning the hearts of all around him,
not himself a scholar, but a promoter of scholars, skilful
in worldly business of every kind, he does not show us
the best, but neither does he show us the worst type of
the prelates of his day. He was charged with looseness
of life; but his chief accuser found it wise to strike out

---

[1] Eadmer, 23. "Asseruit se nullo pacto consensurum ut, pro inimicitia
quam contra archiepiscopum habebat, matri suæ ecclesiæ Cantuariensi de
sua dignitate quid quivis detraherat."

[2] See Appendix Z.

[3] On the history and character of Robert Bloet, see Appendix Z.

CHAP. IV. the charge, and his son Simon, Dean of his own church, was born while he was Chancellor to the Conqueror,

His death. 1123. quite possibly in lawful wedlock. His last days form a striking incident in the next reign; here he chiefly concerns us as being in some sort, however strangely, bracketted with Anselm, as the other bishop whom the Red King named during his short time of repentance.[1]

Local legends about him. Anyhow it was hard on him to tell in after days how his ghost hindered anybody from praying or giving alms near his tomb in the minster, and that only because he removed the monks of Stow to Eynsham, because he subjected his see to the gift of a precious mantle to the King, or because he agreed to the wise measure which lessened the extent of his vast diocese.

Return of Herbert of Thetford. Another bishop appeared at this gathering, whose coming was, for the time, less lucky for himself than that of Robert Bloet. Herbert of Thetford, struck with penitence for his simoniacal bargain, had, as it will be remembered, gone beyond sea on an errand which of all others was most offensive to the King. He had gone to receive again from the Pope—doubtless from Urban—the bishopric which he had

He is deprived by the King. already bought of the King.[2] For this offence William now took away his staff; that is, he deprived him of his bishopric. With whose advice or consent this was done, and what line Anselm took with regard to such a step, we are not told. At all events the King now deprived a bishop of his office on the ground of what he deemed to be treason done without the realm. This was the converse of the act by which, forty-two years before, the nation had deprived another bishop on the ground of what they deemed to be treason within the realm.[3] William however did not set up any doubtful

---

[1] See above, p. 395.   [2] See above, p. 355, and Appendix X.

[3] This deprivation of Herbert by the King—most likely with the consent of somebody, but we are not told—is quite as contrary to strict ecclesiastical

Stigand of his own in the church of Thetford. About a CHAP. IV.
year later Herbert was again in possession of his see.[1]
How he was restored to the King's favour we are not
told. He may have deemed it no sin to win it by means
which he had learned to look upon as sin when applied
to the obtaining of a spiritual office. Next year he removed the seat of the East-Anglian bishopric once more.
Herfast had moved it from Elmham to Thetford. With
the good will and help of Roger Bigod Herbert now
translated it to its final seat at Norwich. He there
began the foundation of that vast church and monastery, the creation of which caused his name to be ever
since held in at least local honour.

Meanwhile the north wind still refused to blow, and
the King with his prelates, lords, and courtiers, still
tarried at Hastings. Lent began before the fleet had Lent, 1094.
a chance of sailing. The penitential season began with
the usual ceremonies. The Archbishop said his mass and
preached his sermon in the ears of the multitude who
came together on the day of ashes, to receive, according to custom, the ashes of penitence from the hands
of the Primate. Among them came the minions and
young gallants of the court of Rufus, with their long
combed and twined hair, their mincing gait, defying
alike the commands of the Apostle and the dictates of
common decency and manliness. The voice of Anselm Anselm re-
rebuked them, as well he might, when the outward garb bukes the minions.
was but the sign of the deeper foulness within. Not a
few were moved to repentance; they submitted to the

notions as the deprivation of Stigand by the English people. The
Parliaments of Elizabeth, William and Mary, George the First, followed
that precedent. I will not speak of the reign of Edward the Sixth,
as that was a time of "unlaw" nearly equal to the days of Rufus
himself.

[1] See Appendix X.

CHAP. IV. loss of their flowing locks, and put on again the form of
men.[1]   Others were stubborn; they received neither
ashes nor absolution.   In this battle with a foolish
custom which was in truth far more than a foolish
custom, Anselm had not a few forerunners or followers.
Saint Wulfstan, Gundulf, Serlo of Seez, all preached and
acted vigorously against the long hair which was the
symbol of the crying vice of the time.[2]   Anselm deemed
that the evil called for something more than a single
act of discipline.   The man of God felt called on to
strike at the root of the mischief; he was moved to make
a warning appeal to the conscience, if any conscience was
left, of the chief sinner of them all, and he made it, after
his wont, at once gently and vigorously.

We may guess that the King had not been present at
the ceremonies of Ash-Wednesday; had he been there,
his presence would surely have been dwelled upon.   It
seems that Anselm, though openly out of the King's
Anselm's favour, still visited him from time to time.   One day
interview
with the therefore he went and sat down beside him, and spoke
King. what was in his heart.[3]   The King was setting forth to
His silence conquer Normandy.   It is to be noticed that Anselm
about the
war. does not say a word as to the right or wrong of the war.
Perhaps, after the challenge of Robert, the cause of
Rufus may have seemed, even to him, to be technically
just.   Perhaps he knew that anything that could be

---

[1] Here we come personally across the class of offenders of whom we
have before spoken generally (see above, p. 158, and Appendix G).   Eadmer
draws their picture; "Eo tempore curialis juventus ferme tota crines
suos juvencularum more nutriebat, et quotidie pexa, ac irreligiosis nutibus
circumspectans, delicatis vestigiis, tenero incessu, obambulare solita erat.
De quibus cum in capite jejunii sermonem in populo ad missam suam
et ad cineres confluente idem pater habuisset, copiosam turbam ex illis
in pœnitentiam egit, et attonsis crinibus, in virilem formam redegit."

[2] See Appendix G.

[3] This is pointed out by Eadmer.   "Die quadam ad eum ex more ivit, et
juxta illum sedens eum his verbis alloqui cœpit."   We shall come to other
instances of this custom of the Archbishop sitting down beside the King.

said on that subject would be fruitless. He may even CHAP. IV.
have deemed, a view which had much to be said for it,
that a conquest of Normandy by the Red King would
be a good exchange for the rule of its present sovereign.
And we must remember that wars of all kinds were in
those days so constantly going on that they would seem
like a necessary evil, a dark side of the economy of
things, but one which could not be hindered. Even
men like Anselm would come to look with less horror
than one might expect on wars which were waged only
by those whose whole business might seem to be warfare. Anyhow Anselm said nothing directly against the
war, even though it was to be waged against the prince
to whom he had lately owed allegiance and against the
land which had been to him a second birth-place. But He asks for help in his reforms.
he asked the King whether he had any right to look
for success in that or any other enterprise, unless he did
something to check the evils which had well nigh up-
rooted the religion of Christ in his realm. He called on
William to give him the help of the royal authority in
his own schemes of reform. The King asked what form
his help was to take,[1] and Anselm then put forth his
views at length.

First and foremost, the King was to help in the work He asks leave to hold a synod.
of reform by allowing Anselm to hold a synod of the
realm. It will be remembered that, by the laws of the
Conqueror, no synod could be held without the King's
licence, and the acts of the synod were of no force
without the King's confirmation.[2] But under the Conqueror Lanfranc had, on the conditions thus laid down,
held his synods without hindrance. That is to say,
the elder William, in all causes and over all persons

[1] "Obsecro primum, fer opem et consilium qualiter in hoc regno tuo Christianitas, quæ jam fere tota in multis periit, in statum suum redigi possit. Respondit, 'Quam opem, quod consilium?'"
[2] See N. C. vol. iv. p. 437.

CHAP. IV. within his dominions supreme, used that supremacy as the chief ruler of the Church from within, while the younger William turned that same supremacy into a weapon wherewith to assault the Church as an enemy from without. It is plain from the earnestness of Anselm one way—one might almost say, from the earnestness of Rufus the other way—that the synod was a real instru-

Advantages of the synod.

ment for the reformation of manners. It is plain that the assembled bishops, when they came together in a body, could do more both for ecclesiastical discipline and for moral improvement than they could do, each one in his own diocese. One cause may have been that, in a synod, the assembled prelates might seem to be really speaking as fathers in God, while the exercise of their local jurisdiction was too much mixed up with the petty and not always creditable details of their courts, with those tricks and extortions of archdeacons and other officials of which we have often heard. Anyhow, as the Roman Senate had good enough left in it to call forth the hatred of Nero, so an ecclesiastical synod had good enough left in it to call

No synod held under Rufus.

forth the hatred of William Rufus. Not one synod had he allowed to be held during the whole time of his reign, now in its seventh year.[1] Anselm earnestly prayed to be allowed to hold one for the restoration of discipline and the reformation of manners. The King answered; "I will see to this matter when I think good; I will act, not after your pleasure but after my own. And, pray," added he mockingly, "when you have got your

Anselm's appeal against the fashionable vices.

synod, what will you talk about in it?" The man of God did not shrink from going straight to the crying evil of the time. What weighed most on Anselm's mind

---

[1] Anselm is made to say; "Generale concilium episcoporum ex quo tu rex factus fuisti non fuit in Anglia celebratum, *nec retroactis pluribus annis.*" Yet Lanfranc had held many synods, and one notable one as late as 1085. See N. C. vol. iv. p. 687.

was not any mere breach of ecclesiastical rule—such
breaches he had to speak of, but he would not speak
of them first;[1] the burthen on his soul was the hideous
moral corruption, a new thing on English ground,
which had become rife throughout the land. Unless
King and Primate, each in his own sphere, each
with his own weapons, worked together to root out
this plague, the kingdom of England might share the
fate of the cities which it had come to resemble.
A strict law was needed, the very hearing of which
would make the guilty tremble.[2] The words of Anselm
were general; there was no personal charge against
William; the Archbishop simply appealed to him as
King to stop the sins of others. But all this makes
us feel more strongly the wonderful character of such
a scene, where two such men could be sitting side by
side and exchanging their thoughts freely. But the
heart of Rufus was hardened; he answered only by a
sneer. "And what may come of this matter for you?"
"For me nothing," said Anselm; "for you and for God
I hope much."[3]

[1] He passes by the smaller matters—"ut illicita consanguineorum connubia et alia multa rerum detestandarum facinorosa negotia taceam"—and goes straight to the sin of the reign, "noviter in hac terra divulgatum," which "jam plurimum pullulavit multosque sua immanitate fœdavit." See Appendix G.

[2] "Conemur una, quæso, tu regia potestate et ego pontificali auctoritate, quantus tale quid inde statuatur, quod cum per totum fuerit regnum divulgatum, solo etiam auditu quicunque illius fautor est paveat et deprimatur." What would have been the nature of the punishment? Something more, one would think, than an ecclesiastical censure, as it was to be a decree of the King. Anselm had no objection to very severe punishments on occasion (see N. C. vol. v. p. 159; cf. vol. iv. p. 621). But when he was able to legislate on this subject (see N. C. vol. v. p. 223), it was in an ecclesiastical synod, and the penalties are milder.

[3] "Non sederunt hæc animo principis, et paucis ita respondit, 'Et in hac re quid fieret pro te?' 'Si non,' inquit Anselmus, 'pro me, spero fieret pro Deo et te.'" I suppose the meaning is something like what I have given. Again one longs for the actual words in their own tongue.

CHAP. IV.

Ecclesiastical grievances.

There is so much of simple moral grandeur in this appeal of the righteous man against moral evil that we might almost have wished that Anselm's discourse had ended at this point, and that he had not gone on to speak of matters which to us seem to have less of a moral and more of a technical nature. Yet Anselm would doubtless have thought himself faithless to his duty, if he had left the King's presence without making a special appeal about the special grievances of ecclesiastical bodies. Moreover the wrongs of the bishoprics and abbeys were distinctly moral wrongs; the King's doings involved breach of law, breach of trust; they were grievances on which the head of the ecclesiastical order was, as such, specially bound to enlarge. But they were also grievances which did not touch the ecclesiastical order only; the wrongs done to the tenants of the vacant churches are constantly dwelled on as one of the worst features of the system brought in by Rufus and Flambard. Anselm therefore deemed it his duty, before he parted from the King, to say a word on this matter also, a matter in which there could be no doubt that the King himself was the chief sinner. No bishopric was now vacant; but several abbeys, Saint Alban's among them, were in the hands of Flambard. Such a state of things called for his own care as Primate; he appealed to William to give him his help as King. In the monasteries which were left without rulers discipline became lax; the monks fell into evil courses; they died without confession. He prayed the King to allow the appointment of abbots to the vacant churches, lest he should draw on himself the judgement which must follow on the evils to which their vacancies gave cause.[1] The King seems to have been less able to endure this rebuke

Wrongs of the church tenants.

He prays the King to fill the vacant abbeys.

---

[1] "Ne in destructione monasteriorum et perditione monachorum tibi, quod absit, damnationem adquiras."

than the other. The disorders of his courtiers and of CHAP. IV.
his own private life he could not defend on any showing;
but the demand that the abbeys should be filled touched
what he looked on as one of his royal rights. Rufus
burst forth in wrath. "Are not the abbeys mine? Tush, The abbeys in what
you do as you choose with your manors; shall not I sense the King's.
do as I choose with my abbeys?"[1] The answer of
Anselm drew a distinction which was a very practical
one in those days, and which affects our legal language
still. To this day the King, the Bishop, the Chapter,
all speak of any episcopal see as "our cathedral church,"
and all speak, from their several points of view, with
equal truth. Such a church is the king's church by
virtue of the fundatorial rights which he claims, in some
cases by real historic succession, in all cases by a legal
theory. By virtue of those fundatorial rights, he claims to
be informed of every vacancy, and to give his consent to
a new election. In this sense Anselm did not deny that
the abbeys were the King's abbeys; he did deny that they
were the King's in the further sense in which Rufus claimed
them. "The abbeys are yours," he said, "to defend and
guard as an advocate; they are not yours to spoil and lay
waste. They are God's; they are given that his servants
may live of them, not that you may make campaigns and
battles at their cost.[2] You have manors and revenues of
many kinds, out of which you may carry on all that
belongs to you. Leave, may it please you, the churches
to have their own." "Truly," says the King, "you know Hostile
that what you say is most unpleasing to me. Your pre- answer of Rufus.
decessor would never have dared to speak so to my
father. I will do nothing on your account." When

---

[1] "Quid ad te? Numquid sunt abbatiæ meæ? Hem, tu quod vis agis
de villis tuis, et ego non agam quod volo de abbatiis meis?"

[2] "Tuæ quidem sunt ut illas quasi advocatus defendas atque custodias,
non tuæ autem ut invadas aut devastes. Dei scimus eas esse, ut sui
ministri inde vivant, non quo expeditiones et bella tua inde fiant."

CHAP. IV. Anselm then saw that he was casting his words to the winds,[1] he rose and went his way.

Lanfranc and Anselm.

It may be that William Rufus spoke truly, and that Lanfranc would not, in any case, have dared to speak to the Conqueror as Anselm dared to speak to him. Lanfranc, with much that was great and good in him, was not a prophet of righteousness like Anselm. But it is far more certain that Lanfranc was never put to the test. The Conqueror never gave him any need to speak to him as Anselm had now need to speak to his son. What we blame in William the Great, what men like Wimund of Saint Leutfred dared to blame in him, Lanfranc could not blame. The position of Lanfranc in England involved the position of William. And, once granting that position, there was comparatively little to blame in the elder William. The beheading of Waltheof, the making of the New Forest, stand almost alone; and the beheading of Waltheof was at least no private murder; it was the judgement of what was in form a competent court. The harshness and greediness with which the Conqueror is justly charged was, after all, a small matter compared with the utter unlaw of his son's reign.

No need to rebuke the Conqueror on these points.

And on the two subjects of Anselm's present discourse, the elder William needed no rebuke at any time. His private life was at all times absolutely blameless, and, neither as Duke nor as King, did he ever turn his ecclesiastical supremacy into a source of gain. On both those points Lanfranc had as good a right to speak as Anselm; but on those points he was never called on to speak to his own master. Whether, in Anselm's place, he would have dared to speak as Anselm did, we cannot tell. But surely the holy boldness of Anselm cannot be looked on as in any way blameworthy, as either insolent or untimed. To him at least the time doubtless seemed most fitting.

Estimate of Anselm's conduct.

[1] "Intellexit ergo Anselmus se verba in ventum proferre, et surgens abiit."

He called on the King, before he exposed himself to the CHAP. IV.
dangers of a campaign beyond the sea, to do something
to win God's favour by correcting the two grossest of the
evils which were rife in his kingdom. The Assembly was
clearly not dissolved when Anselm spoke; William could
at once have filled the abbeys, he could at once have put
forth a law against the other class of offenders, in the most
regular form, by the advice of his Wise Men. Anselm
might even have held his synod while the wind was waiting. The synod in Lanfranc's day followed on the Gemót,
and it took up only three days.[1] Most of the bishops were
present at Hastings; those who were absent had doubtless been summoned and, by the rule of the Great Charter
and of common sense, they would be bound by the acts of
those who obeyed the summons. Moreover, according to The Arch-
the precedents of the late reign, Anselm would be the sole bishop's
claim to the
or chief representative of the King during his absence. regency.
He might fairly ask to be clothed with every power,
temporal and spiritual, which was needed for the fit
discharge of kingly as well as pastoral duties.

Anselm was deeply grieved at the ill success of his Anselm
personal appeal to the King. He was now wholly out attempts to
recover the
of the King's favour, and he felt that, without some King's
favour.
measure of support from the King, he could not carry
out the reforms, ecclesiastical and moral, for which he
longed.[2] He was ready to do anything that could be
done with a good conscience in order to win back the
King's good will. He sent the bishops to William, to
crave that he might, of the King's free grace, be again
admitted to his friendship. If the King would not grant
him his favour, let him at least say why he would not
grant it; if Anselm had wronged him in any way, he was

---

[1] See N. C. vol. iv. p. 687.
[2] "Considerans offenso principis animo nequaquam posse pacem rebus
dari."

CHAP. IV. ready to make the wrong good.[1] The bishops laid the
prayer of their metropolitan before the King. The answer
was characteristic. "I have no fault to find with the
Archbishop; yet I will not grant him my favour, because
I hear no reason given why I should."[2] What those
words meant in the mouth of Rufus the bishops knew very

Advice well. They went back to tell the Primate that the mys-
of the
bishops to tery was clear.[3] The King's favour was to be won only by
give more money, and by money in no small store. Their counsel
money.
was that Anselm should at once give the King the five
hundred pounds which he had before offered, and that he
should promise him another gift of the same amount as
soon as he could get it out of his men.[4] On those terms
they fully believed that the King would grant him his
peace and friendship. They saw no other way for him;
they were in the same strait themselves, and knew no
other way out of it.[5]

In the counsel thus given to Anselm by his suffragans
we hear the words, not of utterly worldly and unscrupulous men, but of the ordinary prelates of the time, good
men, many of them, in all that concerned their own personal lives and the ordinary administration of their
churches, but not men disposed to risk or dare much,
men disposed to go on as they best might in very bad
times, without doing anything which might make things

Anselm's still worse. In the eyes of Anselm, on the other hand,
grounds for things hardly could be made worse; if they could, it
refusing.
would be by consenting to them. By an unflinching

---

[1] "Deprecatus est ut in amicitiam sui sese *gratis* admitteret. Quod si,
ait, facere nonvult, cur nolit edicat, et si offendi, satisfacere paratus sum."

[2] "De nulla re illum inculpo, nec tamen ei gratiam meam, *quia non audio
quare*, indulgere volo." The words which I have put in Italics in the two
speeches must be taken together.

[3] "Mysterium hoc, inquiunt, planum est."

[4] "Tantundem pecuniæ quam ab hominibus tuis accipies illi promitte."

[5] "Aliam qua exeas viam non videmus, nec nos, pari angustia clausi,
aliam exeundi habemus."

assertion of principle things might be made better;
in the worst case the assertor of principle would have
delivered his own soul. In Anselm's eyes the course
which his suffragans suggested was sinful on every
ground; moreover—an argument which some of them
might better understand—it was utterly inexpedient.
He refused to make his way out of his difficulties by the
path which they proposed. The King allowed that he
had no ground of complaint; he was simply angry because he could not get five hundred pounds out of him
as the price of his favour. If now, while his appointment was still fresh, he should win the King's favour
at such a price, the King would get angry with him at
any other time that might suit him, in order to have his
wrath bought off in the same way. This last argument
seems to show that Anselm was after all not so lacking
in worldly wisdom as some have thought. But his main He will not
argument was that he would not commit the crime of oppress his
tenants.
wringing any more money out of his tenants. They
had been frightfully oppressed and robbed during the
vacancy; he had not as yet been able to do anything to
relieve them; he would not lay fresh burthens upon them;
he would not flay alive those who were already stripped
to their skins.[1] Again, he would not deal with his lord
the King as if his friendship was a thing to be bought
and sold. He owed the King faith and honour, and it
would be doing him dishonour to treat his favour like a
horse or an ass to be paid for in vile money. He utterly
refused to put such an insult upon his sovereign. He His answer
told his suffragans that they should rather do their best to the
bishops.
to persuade the King to deal of his free grace as it was
fit for him to deal with his archbishop and spiritual
father. Then he, on his part, would strive to do all that

---

[1] " Et ego cum hucusque nihil eis unde revestiri possint contulerim, jam
eos nudos spoliarem, immo spoliatos excoriarem."

CHAP. IV. he could and might do for his service and pleasure. This ideal view of the relation of King and Primate was doubtless above the heads of John of Bath, of Robert of Lincoln, of Robert of Chester, and of William of Durham in his present mood. It was surely one of them, rather than Osmund or Robert of Hereford, who answered; "But at least you will not refuse him the five hundred pounds which you once offered." Anselm answered that he could not give that either; when the King refused it, he had promised it to the poor, and the more part of it had been given to them already. The bishops went back to the

The King more hostile than ever. King on their unpromising errand. William bade them tell the Archbishop that he hated him much yesterday, that he hated him much to-day, and that he would hate him more and more to-morrow and every other day. He would never hold Anselm for father or archbishop; he cursed and eschewed his blessings and prayers. Let him go where he would; he need not stay any longer there at Hastings, if it was to bless him on his setting sail that he was waiting.[1]

Anselm leaves Hastings. The Red King had thus cast aside another offer of grace. Our guide tells us; "We departed from the court with speed, and left him to his will." The pronoun is emphatic. From that time, if not from an earlier time, English Eadmer was the inseparable companion of Anselm. Anselm and Eadmer then turned away, at what exact date we are not told. But the north wind seems not to have blown till more than half the month of March had passed. Then at last King William of England set sail from Hastings for the conquest of Normandy. He went without Anselm's blessing; yet some of the ceremonies which had been gone through during

---

[1] "Eat quo vult, nec me transfretaturum pro danda benedictione diutius exspectet."

his sojourn at Hastings" must surely have dwelled in his
mind. Fresh from the rite which in some sort marked
the completion of his father's work in England, the
younger William set out so far to undo his father's
work as to bring Normandy into political subjection to
England. At what Norman haven he landed we are William
not told; it was seemingly in some part of the lands of crosses to Normandy.
his earlier conquest, the lands on the right bank of the March 19, 1094.
Seine. Before swords were drawn, an attempt was Vain
made to settle the dispute between the brothers. King attempts to settle
and Duke met in person; what was their place of the dispute.
meeting we are not told; but no agreement could be
come to.[1] A second meeting took place, in which the
guarantors of the former treaty were appealed to, much
as Cnut had appealed to the witnesses of the treaty
between him and Eadmund.[2] The guarantors, the Verdict of the
twenty-four barons, twelve on each side, who had sworn guarantors against
to the treaty, agreed in a verdict which laid the whole William.
blame upon the King. The words of our account—it is
the English Chronicler who speaks—clearly imply that
the guarantors on William's side agreed in this verdict
no less than those who swore on behalf of Robert.[3]
And he adds from himself that Rufus would neither
allow that he was in fault nor abide by his former
engagement.[4] This meeting therefore was yet more

[1] Chron. Petrib. 1094. "Syððan he þider com, he and his broðer
Rodbeard se eorl gecwæðan, þæt hi mid griðe togædere cuman sceoldan,
and swa dydon, and gesemede beon ne mihtan." So Florence; "Rex . . .
ad fratris colloquium sub statuta pace venit, sed impacatus ab eo
recessit."

[2] See N. C. vol. i. p. 435.

[3] Chron. Petrib. 1094. "Syððan eft hi togædere coman mid þam ilcan
mannan þe ær þæt loc makedon, and eac þa aðas sworen, and ealne þone
bryce uppon þone cyng tealdon." The version preserved in one manuscript
of Florence says, "denuo in campo Martio convenere." Can this be the
"Champ de Mars" just outside Rouen? I had fancied that the name was
modern.

[4] Ib. "Ac he nolde þæs geþafa beon, ne eac þa forewarde healdan."

CHAP. IV. fruitless than the former; the brothers parted in greater anger than ever.[1] The Duke went back to Rouen; the King again took up his head-quarters at Eu.[2]

Again on Norman soil, William began to practise the arts which had stood him in such stead in his former enterprise on the duchy. He hired mercenaries; he gave or promised money or lands to such of the chief men of Normandy as were willing to forsake the allegiance of Robert; he quartered his knights both in the castles which he had hitherto held, and in those which he won to himself by these means.[3] Some of these last

Castles held by the King.

were very far from Eu. It shows how successful were the arts of Rufus, how wide was the disaffection against Robert, when we find castles, far away from one another, far away from the seat of William's power in eastern Normandy, but hemming in the lands in the Duke's obedience on two dangerous frontiers, garrisoned by the King's troops. We are reminded of the revival of Henry's power in the Côtentin when we read

La Houlme.

that the castle of La Houlme, at the junction of the two rivers Douve and Merderet, lying south-east from Valognes and nearly east from Saint Saviour, was

Argentan.

now held for William.[4] So was another stronghold in quite another quarter, not far from the Cenomannian border, the castle of Argentan on the upper course of the Orne, to the south of the great forest of Gouffers. Two

[1] Chron. Petrib. 1094. "And forþam hi þa mid mycelon unsehte tocyrdon."

[2] The mention of the places comes from Florence; "Comes quidem Rotomagum perrexit; rex ad Owe rediit et in illo resedit."

[3] Flor. Wig. 1094. "Solidarios undique conduxit, aurum, argentum, terras, quibusdam primatum Normanniæ dedit, quibusdam promisit, ut a germano suo Rotberto deficerent, et se cum castellis suæ ditioni subjicerent: quibus ad velle suum paratis, per castella, vel quæ prius habuerat vel quæ nunc conduxerat, suos milites distribuit."

[4] The "castel æt Hulme" of the Chronicler is the castle of Hulmus, Le Homme, or L'Isle Marie. See Stapleton, ii. xxv, xxviii. It must not be confounded with the "pagus Holmensis" or "Holmetia regio" in the Hiesmois. See Stapleton, ii. xc, xcv, and Ord. Vit. 691 C.

famous captains held these threatening posts. Argentan CHAP. IV.
was commanded by Earl Roger's son, Roger the Poitevin.[1]
La Houlme was held by William Peverel, the lord of Not-
tingham and the Peakland.[2] But the first military exploit Taking of
of the campaign was wrought in a land nearer to Eu. Bures.
Bures—whether still held or not by the faithful Helias
we are not told—was taken, and the garrison were made
prisoners; some of them were kept in Normandy, others
were sent by Rufus for better safe-keeping in his own
kingdom.[3]

Rufus thus pressed the war vigorously against his
brother, with the full purpose of wholly depriving him
of the duchy. Robert, in his distress, again called Robert
on his over-lord, and this time with more effect than King
before.[4] The French intervention was at least able to Philip.
turn the balance for a while against Rufus. No object
was more important for Robert than the recovery of
the two strongholds which threatened him, one in the
dangerous land on the upper Orne, the other in the
no less dangerous Constantine peninsula. A joint expe- Siege of
dition of the new allies was agreed on, and King and Argentan.
Duke appeared side by side before Argentan. The castle
stood on a height of no great elevation above the river,
with the town, as usual, spreading down to its banks.
The existing fragments show that the fortress and its
precinct covered a vast space, but no architectural feature
remains as a witness of the siege of Argentan by Philip

[1] See N. C. vol. iv. p. 488. See above, p. 57.

[2] Ib. vol. iv. pp. 200, 201.

[3] Chron. Petrib. 1094. "And se cyng syððan þone castel æt Bures
gewann; and þes eorles men þærinne genam; þa sume hyder to lande
sende." Florence adds, "partim in Normannia custodiæ mancipavit; et
fratrem suum multis modis vexans, exhæredare laboravit."

[4] The Chronicler casually mentions Philip's coming when speaking of the
siege of Argentan; Florence is more emphatic; "At ille, necessitate compulsus, dominum suum regem Francorum Philippum cum exercitu Normanniam adduxit."

CHAP. IV. and Robert. The town contains several attractive buildings of later date, ecclesiastical, civil, and military. There are churches, town-walls with their towers, the later *château* within the fortress ; but of the stronghold which Roger of Poitou had to guard against the powers of Rouen and Paris but little can be traced. There are some massive and irregular pieces of wall, and part of a polygonal donjon, the latter at least far later than Roger's day. But of the size and strength of the castle there can be no doubt. It is therefore with some little wonder that we read that the besiegers found its capture so easy a matter as they did, especially when its defender was one of the house of Montgomery and Bellême.

Surrender of Argentan. On the very first day of the siege the castle surrendered without bloodshed. Roger of Poitou, with seven hundred knights and as many esquires — a name which we are now beginning to come across—and his whole garrison were made prisoners and were kept in ward till they were ransomed.[1] Here we see the hand of Philip; we see, as in some other cases which we have come across already, Ransom of prisoners. the beginning of one of the institutions of chivalry. We shall presently see the custom of the ransom become a marked feature of the wars between France and England—so we shall soon find ourselves obliged to call them — in the eleventh century no less than in the fourteenth. But the bulky King of the French was for the present contented with this one exploit and with so valuable a stock of captives. Philip went back into France, and left his Norman vassal to go on with the campaign alone.[2] Robert now drew some spirit from

---

[1] The Chronicler (1094) says only, " Ðær togeanes se eorl mid þes cynges fultume of France gewann þone castel æt Argentses and þearinne Rogger Peiteuin genam, and seofen hundred þes cynges cnihta mid him." Florence adds, "ipso die obsessionis dcc. milites regis, cum his totidem scutariis et castellanis omnibus qui intus erant, sine sanguinis effusione cepit [rex], captosque in custodia tamdiu detineri mandavit, donec quisque se redimeret."

[2] So says Florence; "Post hæc in Franciam rediit." As however he

success. He marched westward, and attacked La Houlme. CHAP. IV.
The castle surrendered; the lord of the Peak, with eight Robert takes La Houlme.
hundred men, became the prize of the Duke's unusual
display of vigour.[1]

The war went on; each side burned the towns and
took the men of the other side.[2] But the tide had for
the moment decidedly turned against the Red King.
The loss of Argentan and La Houlme, with their com- Difficulties of Rufus.
manders and their large garrisons, was a serious military
blow. The payment of their ransoms might be a still
more serious financial blow. And the payment of a
ransom, by which he only got back again what he had
had before, would be less satisfactory to the mind of
Rufus than the payment of bribes and wages by which
he had a hope of gaining something fresh. The hoard
at Winchester seems at last to have been running low;
but when William Rufus was king and when he had
Randolf Flambard to his minister, there could be no
lack of ways and means to fill it again. Specially Further taxation.
heavy were the gelds laid on England both in this year
and in the following.[3] And money was gained by one
device which surely would have come into the head
of no king and no minister save those by whom it
actually was devised. A great levy was ordered; King Levy of English soldiers.
William sent over his bidding that twenty thousand
Englishmen should come over to help the King in Normandy.[4] Englishmen had by this time got used to service

says nothing of Philip's coming to Longueville, he may mean his return
after that.

[1] The Chronicler says only, after the taking of Argentan, "and syððan
þone [castel] æt Hulme." Florence makes it the special exploit of Robert;
"Comes vero Rotbertus castellum quod Holm nuncupatur obsedit, donec
Willelmus Peverel et dccc. homines, qui id defendebant, illi se dederent."

[2] Chron. Petrib. 1094. "And oftrædlice heora ægðer uppon oðerne tunas
bærnde, and eac men læhte."

[3] Flor. Wig, 1094. "Interea gravi et assiduo tributo hominumque mor-
talitate, præsenti et anno sequenti, tota vexabatur Anglia."

[4] Chron. Petrib. 1094. "Ða sende se cyng hider to lande, and hét

beyond sea. Nothing is said of any difficulty in getting this great force together. The troops were gathered at Hastings, ready to set sail. Each man had brought with him ten shillings, the contribution of his shire for his maintenance in the King's service. For the men who answered to Rufus' bidding were no mercenaries, not even housecarls; they were the *fyrd* of England, summoned, by a perhaps unjustifiable but not very wonderful stretch of authority, to serve their king beyond the sea. But, when they were ready to sail, Flambard came, and by the King's orders took away each man's money, and bade them all go home again.[1] One would like to know something of the feelings of the men who were thus strangely cheated; we should surely have heard if there had been any open resistance. Anyhow, by this amazing trick, the Red King had exchanged the arms of twenty thousand Englishmen for a sum of ten thousand pounds of English money. After all, the money might be of greater use than the men in a war with Philip of Paris.

If William thus reckoned, he was not deceived. He was still at Eu. Philip was again in arms; his forces joined those of Robert; again King and Duke marched side by side, this time with the purpose of besieging the King of the English in his Norman stronghold. The ten thousand pounds now served William's turn quite as well as the twenty thousand men could have served it. The combined French and Norman host had reached

Flambard takes away the soldiers' money.

Rufus buys off Philip.

abeodan út xx. þusenda Engliscra manna ['xx. millia pedonum' in Florence] him to fultume to Normandig."

[1] Chron. Petrib. 1094. "Ac þa hi to sæ coman, þa het hi man cyrran, and þæt feoh to þæs cynges behófe þe hi genumen hæfdon; þet wæs ælc man healf punda, and hi swa dydon." Florence tells us the place and the doer; "Quibus ut mare transirent Heastingæ congregatis, pecuniam quæ data fuerat eis ad victum Rannulphus Passeflambardus præcepto regis abstulit, scilicet unicuique decem solidos, et eos domum repedare mandavit, pecuniam vero regi transmisit."

Longueville on the Scie, with streams and forests between them and Eu.[1] Longueville was the last stage
of their march. Thither Rufus sent those who knew
how to bring his special arguments to bear on the mind
of Philip. The King again went back to France, and
the confederate army was broken up.[2]

There is something very singular in the way in which
this second Norman war of William Rufus is dealt with
by those who wrote at or near the time. Some make
no mention of it at all; others speak of it only casually;
our own Chronicler, who gives the fullest account of all,
does not carry it on to any intelligible issue of success
or of failure. In his pages, and in those of some others,
the war drops out of notice, without coming to any real
end of any kind.[3] The monk of Saint Evroul, so lavish
in local Norman details, seems to have had his head too
full of the local strifes among the Norman nobles to tell
us anything of a warfare which in our eyes comes so
much nearer to the likeness of a national struggle. It
must always be remembered that the local wars which
tore every district of Normandy in pieces did not stop
in the least because two hostile kings were encamped on
Norman soil. There cannot be a more speaking comment, at once on the difference between Robert and
either of his brothers and on the essential difference

Contemporary
notices
of the
campaign.

Difference
between
England
and Normandy.

[1] Chron. Petrib. 1094. "And se eorl innon Normandig æfter þison,
mid þam cynge of France and mid eallon þan þe hi gegaderian mihton,
ferdon towardes Ou þær se cyng W. inne wæs, and þohtan hine inne to
besittanne, and swa foran oð hi coman to Lungeuile."

[2] Ib. "Ðær wearð se cyng of France þurh gesmeah gecyrred, and swa
syððan eal seo fyrding tóhwearf."

[3] Florence, as we have seen, stops with the taking of La Houlme in 1094.
The Chronicler goes on to Henry's Lenten expedition in 1095. After that,
neither says anything about Norman affairs till the agreement of 1096,
though both of them imply (see below, p. 555) that the war lasted till that
time.

between the ordinary state of Normandy and of England. With us private war was never lawful; we needed not the preaching of the Truce of God.[1] William the Great, when his authority was fully established, kept England in peace; and in his later years the peace of Normandy itself, as distinguished from the border lands, was broken only by the rebellion of his own son. So in England there still were rebellions alike against Rufus and against Henry; but, when the rebellion was crushed, the land was at rest. In Normandy, as soon as the hand of the great ruler was taken away, things fell back into the state in which they had been during his own minority. And they remained in that state till William the Red in his later years again established order in the duchy. One can well understand that the endless ups and downs in the local struggles which went on close to every man's door really drew to themselves far more of men's thoughts than the strife of King William, King Philip, and Duke Robert himself. The two kings were but two more disputants added to the crowd, and they were disputants who really did much less harm to the land in general than was done by its own native chiefs. It is not very wonderful then that we hear so little of this war from the Norman side. It is not wonderful that, on the English side, when stirring events began again before long to happen in England, the Norman war dropped out of sight. And presently events in the world's history were to come which made even the warfare of England and France seem trifles amid the general stir of "the world's debate."

Private wars go on in Normandy.

For the last events of Rufus' second Norman war we have to go wholly to our one witness in our own tongue. It is plain that the King, even after his gold

Relations of Rufus and Henry.

---

[1] See N. C. vol. ii. p. 241.

had turned Philip back, did not feel at all at ease in
his Norman quarters. He seems to have distrusted two
important personages at the other end of the duchy, his
other brother and one of the mightiest of his own subjects. Henry, Ætheling and again Count, was safe in
his castle of Domfront, among the people who had chosen
him as their protector. At one period of this year, he
is described as at war with both his brothers at once.[1]
We find him taking the part of the lord of Saint Cenery,
Robert son of Geroy,[2] against the common enemy, Robert
of Bellême. His help however did not hinder the che- Saint
rished fortress from falling into the hands of the tyrant.[3] Cenery
 taken by
We hear of him before the end of the war in a way which Robert of
 Bellême.
implies at least some suspicious feeling between himself
and the King his brother. Besides Henry, Hugh of
Chester—rather Hugh of Avranches or Hugh of Saint-
James—was also in his own continental possessions. The Henry and
 Hugh
King summoned both of them to come to him at Eu, summoned
and, as the state of the duchy did not allow them to to Eu.
come across Normandy by land, he sent ships to bring
them.[4] But Henry and Hugh, from whatever causes,

[1] Ord. Vit. 706 C. See Appendix P.

[2] Ord. Vit. ib. See above, p. 217.

[3] This is one of Orderic's best stories (706 C, D). A false tale of its
lord's death is brought to Saint Cenery. His allies, Pagan of Montdoubleau (see above, p. 209) and Rotrou of Montfort, at once forsake the
castle which they had been defending. Robert's wife Radegund cannot
get them to wait till more certain news can be had. Robert of Bellême
comes just in time for dinner. "Ingressi castrum, lebetes super ignes fer-
ventes invenerunt carnibus plenas, et mensas mappulis coopertas et escas cum
pane super appositas." He spoils and burns the castle. Robert son of Geroy
is left homeless; his wife ("proba femina et honesta") dies; his little son
William, whom Robert of Bellême somehow has as a hostage, is poisoned;
he then defends his new castle of Montacute against Robert of Bellême.
Robert of Bellême brings Duke Robert to besiege him. Peace is made by
the mediation of Geoffrey of Mayenne; Montacute is destroyed, and Saint
Cenery is restored to Robert son of Geroy.

[4] Chron. Petrib. 1094. "Her onmang þison se cyng W. sende æfter his
broðer Hennrige se wæs on þam castele æt Damfront, ac forþi þe he mid

CHAP. IV.

They go to South-hampton. October 31, 1094.

They keep Christmas in London.

did not choose to meet the King face to face. Instead of sailing to Eu or its port, they made for Southampton, where they landed and seemingly stayed—with what objects we are not told—for some weeks.[1] Thence they went to London, and kept Christmas there. King William was not this year wearing his crown either at Westminster or at Gloucester. But it is clear that the movements of his youngest brother had an effect upon his own. For the first three days of the holy twelve he

The King comes to England. December 28, 1094.

stayed at Whitsand. On the fourth day, the feast of the Innocents, the anniversary of the dedication of the West Minster, he crossed the sea and landed at Dover.[2] Thence he seemingly came to London, where

William and Henry reconciled.

Henry was. Whatever quarrels or suspicions had sprung up between the King and the Ætheling were now made up. Henry was received into his brother's fullest confidence. He stayed in England till Lent began, when he went to spend the penitential season in Normandy.

Henry goes to Nor-mandy. c. Feb. 9, 1095.

But it was not to be an idle season; in the month between Epiphany and Lent, the Red King had made his preparations for a campaign in which Henry was to take his place. The Count of Coutances then went again beyond sea with great treasures to be used on the King's behalf against his brother—Earl Robert,

His war-fare with Robert.

as English lips called him. "And ofttimes upon the Earl he won, and to him mickle harm either on land and on men did."[3] Here ends our story. We get no further

friðe þurh Normandig faran ne mihte, he him sende scipon æfter, and Hugo eorl of Ceastre."

[1] Chron. Petrib. 1094. "Ac þa þa hi towardes Oú faran sceoldan þær se cyng wæs, hi foran to Englelande and úp coman æt Hamtune on ealra halgena mæsse æfne, and her syððon wunedon, and to Xp̄es mæssan wæron on Lunden.'

[2] Ib. 1095. "On þisum geare wæs se cyng Willelm to Xp̄es mæssan þa feower forewarde dagas on Hwitsand; and æfter þam feorðan dæge hider to lande fór, and úpp com æt Doferan."

[3] Ib. "And Heanrig þes cynges broðer her on lande oð Lengten wunode, and þa ofer sæ for to Normandig mid mycclon gersuman, on þæs cynges

details till William became master of all Normandy by
quite another process. But though we get no details of
the war from Norman sources, we do get a general
picture of its results. The no-rule of Robert is once
more set before us in speaking words. The soft Duke,
who feared his subjects more than they feared him, was
benumbed with softness and idleness.[1] He is contrasted
with both his brothers. Henry held his stronghold at
Domfront, together with a large but undefined part of
the duchy, including without doubt the more part of
his old peninsular county. Some places he had won by
arms; others, like Domfront itself, had sought his rule
of their own free will.[2] Within these bounds he yielded
to his brother the Duke just so much service as he
thought good,[3] which at this particular moment would be
little indeed. And the other brother who wore the diadem
of England held more than twenty castles on Norman
ground. He, unlike Robert, was a ruler whom men
feared; and his gifts, and the fear of him together, kept
many of the great men of the land, not only in his
allegiance, but in his zealous service.[4] If Normandy was
not conquered, it was at least effectually dismembered.

The list of the Norman nobles who joined the King
from beyond sea takes in most of the names with

heldan, uppon heora broðer Rodbeard eorl, and gelomlice uppon þone eorl
wann, and him mycelne hearm ægðer on lande and on mannan dyde."

[1] Ord. Vit. 722 D. "Rodbertus mollis dux a vigore priorum decidit, et
pigritia mollitieque torpuit, plus provinciales subditos timens quam ab illis
timebatur."

[2] Ib. "Henricus frater ducis Danfrontem fortissimum castrum possidebat,
et magnam partem Neustriæ sibi favore vel armis subegerat."

[3] Ib. "Fratri suo ad libitum suum, nec aliter, obsecundabat." I do not
see what is meant in Sigebert's Chronicle under 1095 (Pertz, vi. 367); "Rex
Anglorum a fratribus sollicitatur in Normania et Anglia."

[4] Ib. "Porro alius frater qui Angliæ diadema gerebat in Normannia, ut
reor, plusquam xx. castra tenebat, et proceres oppidanosque potentes muneribus sibi vel terroribus illexerat. . . . Perplures cum omnibus sibi subditis
munitionibus et oppidanis regi parebant, eique, *quia metuendus erat*, totis
nisibus adhærebant."

CHAP. IV. which we are most at home. There is Ralph of Conches, Gerard of Gournay, Richard of Courcy. We hear now too of Philip of Braose, a name to become famous in more than one part of our island. And we find the names of men yet higher in power, and nearer to the ducal house. There is the first author of the late troubles, Count William of Eu, for the present still an adherent of Rufus, before long to be heard of in quite another character. With him stands Count Stephen of Aumale, also before long to play a part in our story wholly different from that which we find him playing now. And it is needless to say that Count Robert of Meulan was the Red King's servant in his Norman, as well as in his English character.[1] Nor do we wonder to find in the same list—for he was Earl of Buckingham as well as lord of Longue-ville—the name of Walter Giffard, him who appeared as an aged man forty years before.[2] He still lived, while, during this very year, more than one of the elder generation of the famous men of Normandy passed away. The father of the Count of Meulan, the old Roger of Beaumont, renowned so many years before alike in arms and in council,[3] died on the Norman soil which he had guarded so well, and which he seems never to have left. He had for some years left the world, to become a monk in the monastery of Preaux of his father's rearing.[4] His estates had passed to his son at Meulan, the mighty vassal of three lords. His younger son Henry had his lot cast in England, where, perhaps before this time, the Red King bestowed on him the earldom of Warwick. And, in the same year as the lord of Beaumont, died, far away in England, another Roger,

William of Eu.

Stephen of Aumale.

Robert of Meulan.

Walter Giffard.

Death of Roger of Beaumont. 1094.

Henry Earl of Warwick.

---

[1] He appears in Orderic's list, 722 D.

[2] See N. C. vol. iii. p. 129.   [3] See N. C. vol. iii. p. 288.

[4] Ord. Vit. 708 C. He makes the remark just before, "In diebus illis antiqui optimates qui sub Roberto duce vel filio ejus Guillelmo rege mili-taverant humanæ conditionis more hominem exuerunt."

like him a monk, but four days before a mighty earl, CHAP. IV.
Roger of Montgomery, of Arundel, and of Shrewsbury, Death of
the youngest brother of the house beyond the Severn Mont-
bridge of which he at least claimed to be the founder.[1] gomery.
1094.

His vast possessions were divided at his death. Robert Robert of
of Bellême, already heir of his mother in the border-
land, now became heir of his father in Normandy. The
earldom of Shrewsbury and Roger's other English estates
passed to his second son Hugh, who bears the character
of being the only one of the sons of Mabel who was mild
and gentle[2]—mild and gentle, we must understand, to
Normans, perhaps even to Englishmen, but certainly not
to captive Britons. Of Hugh, as well as of Robert of
Bellême and Roger of Poitou, as well as of Arnulf of Montgomery, a fourth son of the same fierce stock, we shall hear
much as our tale goes on. In England too, perhaps within Death of
his sheriffdom of Leicester, died Hugh of Grantmesnil, of
whom we have lately heard in the civil wars both of
Normandy and of England, and whom his own shire
and his neighbours of Northamptonshire had no reason
to bless. His body, we need hardly say, found its way His burial
across the sea, to lie among his loyal bedesmen at Saint
Evroul.[3] These men all left the world in the year with
which we are now dealing, and left the hoary Earl of Death of
Buckingham to be for eight years longer the representative of an earlier day.[4] The hands which eight and
twenty years before had been too feeble to bear the banner
of the Apostle[5] were still, it would seem, ready to do
whatever was still found for them to do in the service of
the Red King. But the warfare of the King and his

Bellême
succeeds
his father
in Nor-
mandy,
and Hugh
in Eng-
land.

Hugh of
Grant-
mesnil.

at Saint
Evroul.

Walter
Giffard.
1102.

---

[1] Ord. Vit. 708 C. See N. C. vol. iv. p. 498.

[2] See above, p. 57. We shall come across his fuller picture in a later
chapter.

[3] Ord. Vit. 718 D. He adds the epitaph of his own making.

[4] He records his death and adds his epitaph, 809 C, D. William of
Breteuil and Ralph of Conches died the same year, 1102.

[5] See N. C. vol. iv. p. 465.

CHAP. IV.

Eadmer's judgement of the campaign.

partisans is set down simply as one among the many ways in which Normandy was torn in pieces by her own children.[1] An English writer meanwhile, on whose main subject the Norman campaigns of Rufus had but a very indirect bearing, speaks casually of this expedition as an undertaking on which a vast deal of money was spent, but by which very little was gained.[2]

Wretchedness of England.

Causes for the King's return.

It is indeed to be borne in mind, as supplying at least a partial explanation of the way in which the second Norman expedition comes to an end without any end, that things in England were, just as they had been three years and a half before, in a state which urgently called for the presence of the King within his kingdom. We know not whether it at all moved him that the heavy taxation which had been laid on his kingdom for the cost of his warfare had brought the land to the lowest pitch of wretchedness. Men, we are told, had ceased to till the ground; hunger followed; there were hardly left any who could tend the dying or bury the dead.[3] These things might not have greatly stirred the heart of the Red King; but he may, like other tyrants, have felt that there was a bound beyond which oppression could not be safely carried. And there were political and military reasons which called him back. He could not afford to jeopard his undisputed possession of England for the sake of a few more castles in Normandy. He

---

[1] Ord. Vit. 723 A. "Sic Normannia suis in se filiis furentibus miserabiliter turbata est, et plebs inermis sine patrono desolata est."

[2] Eadmer, Hist. Nov. 25. "Ipse quidem in Normanniam transiit, expensaque immensa pecunia eam sibi nullatenus subigere potuit. Infecto itaque negotio in Angliam reversus est."

[3] Will. Malms. iv. 327. "Septimo anno, propter tributa quæ rex in Normannia positus edixerat, agricultura defecit, qua fatiscente, fames e vestigio, ea quoque invalescente, mortalitas hominum subsecuta, adeo crebra ut deesset morituris cura, mortuis sepultura." This is copied by the Margam annalist.

could hardly afford to jeopard for their sake the imperial supremacy of his crown over the whole isle of
Britain, a supremacy which he was at that moment
specially called on to assert. The year of the second
Norman campaign was a year of special importance in
the history both of Scotland and of Wales. While the Affairs of
Scotland
Red King was warring and bribing in Normandy,
Scotland had, as in the days of Siward, received a
king from England, and, what had not happened in
the days of Siward, her people had slain the foreign
nominee, and had again chosen a king of their own.
The first reign of Donald, the momentary reign of
Duncan, the beginning of the second reign of Donald,
all of them events which were not mere changes of
sovereign, but real revolutions in the state of the
nation, had happened between the death of Malcolm and
the return of William from Normandy thirteen months
later. Wales too had risen in a movement which had and Wales.
more than was usual of the character of real national
insurrection, and the movement had called for all the
energies of the new Earl of Shrewsbury and of the King
himself on his return. And a plot yet nearer home, a Plots at
home.
plot to deprive the King of his crown and life, a plot
devised by men who had been just now the foremost in
supporting his cause, broke out soon after his return. It
broke out so soon after it that one is tempted to think
that it was already hatching, and that it was one of the
causes which brought him back. The seeming break-down
of the Red King's second Norman campaign thus becomes more intelligible than some of the other cases where
he began an undertaking and failed to finish it. William
had plenty to do in Britain, both in camp and in council.
As soon as he was assured of the adhesion of his brother
Henry, he could afford, indeed he was driven, to leave
him to do the work which had to be done in Normandy.

§ 4. *The Council of Rockingham.* *December,*
1094—*March,* 1095.

The year to which the last Christmas feast intro-
duces us brings strongly home to us the singular way in
which our general chroniclers follow one line of events,
while the special biographer of the Archbishop follows another. There is no contradiction; but the gaps
which have to be filled up in each narrative are remarkable. It is not perhaps wonderful that the biographer of Anselm should, even in a work which bears
a general title, pass by events which in no way affected
the history of Anselm. It is more remarkable that one
of the most striking scenes in Anselm's history should not
have been thought worthy of notice by the more general
annalists of our land. But so it is. The year 1095 is
a year of very stirring events, and it is preeminently a
year of councils. But, with a single exception, our two
authorities do not record the same events and the same
councils. Both tell us of the pallium being brought to
Anselm; but, while one tells us nothing of the most
striking of the assemblies in which Anselm bore a part,
the other tells us nothing of the conspiracy, the revolt,
the war, which specially mark this year in the general
story of England.

If our story is rightly told, the Christmas meeting of
William and Henry, followed before long by a Norman
campaign on the part of Henry, was followed yet more
immediately by a Welsh campaign on the part of William. The King took the affairs of his own island into
his own hands, and, for the present, he left those of
the mainland to the Count of Coutances. A winter campaign in Wales does not sound very promising, and we
are not surprised to hear that it did not add much to the

glory of the Red King's arms.[1] At all events it must have CHAP. IV.
been short, for, in the course of January and February
we find him at points at a considerable distance from the
Welsh border. In January he was at Cricklade in Wilt- Move-
shire; in February he was at Gillingham in Dorset, near William.
to Ælfred's monastery of Shaftesbury, and itself the scene January–
of the election of the Confessor.[2] In both cases we hear 1095.
of the King's movements through incidental notices in
our ecclesiastical story. The second is part of the story
of Anselm; the first does not concern Anselm himself;
it forms part of the tale of the holiest of his suffragans.

In this month of January the soul of the last surviving Death of
English bishop, the sainted Wulfstan of Worcester, passed Wulfstan.
away. In the eyes of one annalist his death was the
great event of the year, and was announced by signs
and wonders in the heavens. "There was a stir among

---

[1] Flor. Wig. 1094. "Post hæc rex Willelmus iv. kal. Januarii Angliam
rediit, et ut Walanos debellaret, mox exercitum in Waloniam duxit, ibique
homines et equos perdidit multos." I am not at all clear that this entry in
Florence is not a confusion. The Chronicle under the same year records the
return of the King, and directly after sums up the Welsh warfare of the year;
but it is not implied that the King took any part in it. He could not have
done so before his return from Normandy, and, to say nothing of the un-
likelihood of a winter campaign in itself, the incidental notices of the King's
movements hardly leave time for one.

[2] See N. C. vol. ii. p. 9. Eadmer writes the name *Illingham*, a change
which might easily have happened after the pattern of *Ilchester* (see above,
p. 63) and *Islip* (see N. C. vol. ii. p. 15), but the *g* remains in use to this
day. There is something very amusing in the note of Henschenius reprinted
in Migne's edition of Eadmer and Anselm, col. 394;
"Alia plura dominia, ut *Rochingeham, Ilingeham, Sæftesburia*, quæ jam
ante occurrerunt, et plura secutura, potuissent designato locorum situ ex-
plicari, si operæ pretium visum esset eorum causa totas Anglici regni
tabulas perlustrare, et esset qui exsoleta jam nomina, ubi requirenda sint,
indicaret. Poterit postea curiosior aliquis hunc defectum supplere."
Fancy a man reading his Eadmer, and not making the faintest effort to
find out where any place was. But perhaps this is better than M. Croset-
Mouchet, who always turns the Bishop of Exeter into a Bishop of *Oxford*
(cf. N. C. vol. iv. p. 779), and who has a place *Srewsbury*, which does duty
alike for the earldom of *Shrewsbury* and for the bishopric of *Salisbury*.

the stars, and Wulfstan Bishop of Worcester died."[1]

The health of the good old man had been for some time ailing; we have seen that he had latterly been unable to show himself in assemblies and ceremonies. At the

Easter of the year before his death, while the King was in Normandy, he told his steward that on the day of the feast he meant to dine in state with "good men."

The steward, mistaking the meaning of a phrase which is ambiguous in several languages and which was specially so in the English of his day,[2] got together many of the rich men of the neighbourhood—we are not told whether the Sheriff Urse was among them. The day came; the Bishop entered the hall with a large company of the poor, and ordered seats to be set for them among the other guests. The steward was displeased;[3] but Wulfstan explained that those whom he brought with him were the men who had the true riches; he had rather sit down with such a company than sit down, as he had often done, with the King of the English.[4] For Rufus, we are told, always received

---

[1] So say the Margam Annals, 1095; "Commotio fuit stellarum, et obiit Wlstanus Wigorniensis episcopus." But unluckily it appears from Florence that the stars did not shoot till April 4. Still it is edifying to mark the different results of the death of a saintly and of a worldly bishop. The next entry is, "Moritur Willelmus episcopus Dunelmensis, et hic commotio hominum." According to Hugh of Flavigny (Pertz, viii. 474) the stars paid regard to the death of an abbot who in no way concerns us; "Stellæ de cœlo cadere visæ sunt, et eadem nocte Gyraldus abbas Silvæ majoris [in the diocese of Bourdeaux] migravit ad Dominum." Sigebert's Chronicle (Pertz, vi. 367) has some curious physical details.

[2] See above, p. 297.

[3] The story is told by William of Malmesbury, Vit. Wlst. Angl. Sacr. ii. 266. "Præmonuerat ministros velle se ad illud pascha convivari accuratis epulis cum bonis hominibus." He then brings the poor people into the hall and "præcepit inter eos sedili locato epulas sibi apponi."

[4] The steward's doctrine is "competentius esse, ut episcopus convivaretur cum paucis divitibus quam cum multis pauperibus." The bishop makes his scriptural quotation, and adds, "illis debere serviri, qui non haberent unde redderent." He then winds up, "Lætius se videre istum consessum, quam si,

Wulfstan with honour; we may doubt whether either CHAP. IV.
knew enough of the other's language for rebukes to be General
respect for
met by repartees. The great men of the realm did the Wulfstan.
like. Foreign princes, prelates, and potentates honoured
him with gifts and asked for his prayers.[1] Among his His corre-
spondence.
correspondents were the Pope—doubtless Urban—Mal-
colm and Margaret of Scotland, and the kings of Ireland.
To this list are added the Archbishop of Bari and the His
Patriarch of Jerusalem, which last name suggests corre- increased
sickness.
spondence on the common needs of Christendom. At Whitsun-
tide, 1094.
Pentecost Wulfstan was very sick; he sent for his special
friend Bishop Robert of Hereford, him whose skill had
foretold that Remigius would never dedicate his min-
ster.[2] Robert came; the humble Wulfstan made his Wulfstan
and Robert
confession and submitted to the discipline.[3] But he of Here-
lived on during the rest of that year. Shortly after the ford.
beginning of the new year, he had another visit from
Bishop Robert and two abbots of his diocese, Serlo of
Gloucester and Gerald, abbot of the still unfinished
house which Robert Fitz-hamon was raising at Tewkes-
bury.[4] Wulfstan again confessed; he foretold his own

---

ut sæpe, consedisset regi Anglorum." One would like to have Wulfstan's
English. We must remember that Wulfstan was commonly surrounded at
dinner by a knightly following. Vit. Wlst. 259. "Excepto si quando
cum monachis reficeretur, semper in regia considentibus militibus palam
convivabatur."

[1] Vit. Wlst. 266. "Multo eum suspiciebat rex honore, multo proceres;
ut qui sæpe ipsum ascirent convivio, et assurgerent ejus consilio." Then
follows the list of his foreign admirers, but it is only of the Irish kings that
we read that "magnis eum venerabantur favoribus." Malcolm and Margaret
"ipsius se dedebant orationibus;" the foreign prelates "epistolis q3æ adhuc
supersunt ejus ambierunt apud Deum suffragia."

[2] See above, p. 312.

[3] Vit. Wlst. 267. "Humanorum excessum [had he given in a little too
much to foreign ways?] confessione facta, etiam disciplinam accepit. Ita
vocant monachi virgarum flagra, quæ tergo nudato cædentis infligit acri-
monia."

[4] Serlo we have heard of before; see N. C. vol. iv. p. 383. Of Tewkes-
bury I shall have to speak below, and see N. C. vol. v. pp. 628, 629.

CHAP. IV.

Death of
Wulfstan.
January
18, 1095.

His ap-
pearance
to Bishop
Robert.

His burial.
Jan. 22.

death; he comforted his friends; he gave himself to religious exercises, causing his seat in his chamber to be so
placed that he could see the altar in his chapel.[1] At last,
not many days after Robert's visit, the one remaining
bishop of the old stock passed away from his church and
from the world. Men believed that he appeared *in transitu*
to his friend Bishop Robert, who, as one who reconciled
his episcopal virtues with skill in the affairs of the world,
was now with the King at Cricklade.[2] The vision bade
Robert come to his friend's burial; he came, and the
ceremony took place four days after Wulfstan's death,
among a mighty gathering of those who had honoured
him in life. A generation later it was made a subject
of complaint, a subject of rebuke to an age which, we
are told, was loath to believe in signs and wonders, that
so holy a man was not formally enrolled on the list of
saints.[3] Aftertimes made up for this neglect. Wulfstan

---

[1] Vit. Wlst. 267. " Magis sedens quam jacens, aures psalmis, oculos altari
applicabat, sedili sic composito ut libere cerneret quicquid in capella fieret."
That is, there was a *squint* between his bed-room and the chapel, a not uncommon arrangement, one of the best instances of which is to be seen in
Beverstone Castle, in Wulfstan's diocese, though of a date long after Godwine's days and his. This use of the squint is only one of several ways
for enabling the inmates, whether of houses, hospitals, or monastic in-
firmaries, to hear mass without going out of doors.

[2] The vision is recorded by William of Malmesbury in the life of Wulfstan
(268), where he says that Bishop Robert was "in curia regis," and adds
that he was "homo sæculi quidem fretus prudentia, sed nulla solutus illecebra." Florence says that Robert was "in oppido quod Criccelad vocatur."
The inference is that the King was at Cricklade. Cricklade does not appear
among the King's lordships in Wiltshire; but both he (Domesday, 65) and
other lords had burgesses there, and there is an entry in 64 *b* about the third
penny, which brought in five pounds yearly.

In the Gesta Pontificum William of Malmesbury does not mention the
vision; but he brings Bishop Robert to Worcester to bury Wulfstan without
any such call. There is surely something a little heathenish in his description of the bishop's body lying in " Libitina ante altare."

[3] Gest. Pont. 289. " Profecto, si facilitas antiquorum hominum adjuvaret,
jamdudum elatus in altum sanctus predicaretur, sed nostrorum incredulitas,
quæ se cautelæ umbraculo exornat, non vult miraculis adhibere fidem etiamsi

became the chief object of local devotion, and no small chap. iv. object of devotion throughout the land. The saint whom Rufus had honoured in life became after death the special object of the devotion of King John, who hoped to be safer in the next world if his body lay in Wulfstan's church under the shadow of Wulfstan's shrine.

Another link with the past was thus snapped, and, what the King at least thought more of, another bishopric passed into the hands of Flambard. About a month after the shade of Wulfstan had appeared to Bishop Robert in the King's court at Cricklade, the living Anselm showed himself to the King in person in his court at Gillingham.[1] Notwithstanding the hatred which William had expressed towards him at Hastings, the Archbishop had reasons which urged him to seek another interview. The errand on which he came was Anselm and Urban. one at which he had hinted before he had been invested with the archbishopric. He had then fairly warned the King that, if he became archbishop, he must acknowledge Urban as Pope.[2] He had as yet done nothing towards acknowledging him; he had taken no step which involved the acknowledgement of Urban or of any other pope. With Anselm moral questions came first. The points on which he had first striven to awaken the conscience of the King had been the moral corruption of his court and kingdom, and the synod

conspicetur oculo, etiamsi palpat digito." Yet, though he says that prayers offered at Wulfstan's tomb were always answered, yet he says nothing about miracles being wrought there (unless we count the wonderful preservation of the tomb itself during a fire), and not much of miracles done during his lifetime. There is more in the Life.

[1] Eadmer, Hist. Nov. 25. "Quem consistentem in quadam villa quæ tribus miliariis a Sceftesberia distans Ilingeham vocatur Anselmus adiit." See above, p. 477. By what follows this must have been some time in February.

[2] See above, p. 414.

CHAP. IV. which, in Anselm's eyes at least, was the best means for
its reformation. But William had so utterly refused his
consent to the holding of a synod, he had so utterly
refused to give Anselm any help in his schemes of moral
reform, that Anselm perhaps thought it useless to press
those subjects again upon him. The point which he still
thought it his duty to press was one which to us seems
of infinitely less importance than either, but with regard
to which we must look at matters with the eyes of Anselm's day and not with the eyes of our own. Anselm
was full archbishop in all points spiritual and temporal,
as far as the spiritual and temporal powers of England

Need
of the
pallium.
could make him so. But he still lacked one badge of
metropolitan authority, without which his position
would certainly be deemed imperfect anywhere out of
England. He had not received the archiepiscopal *pallium* from Rome. He naturally wished for this final
stage of his promotion, this sign of recognition, as he
would deem it, on the part of the Universal Church and

Elder
usage as
to the
pallium.
her chief pastor. Now this supposed need of the pallium
was not, like some of the claims of the Roman see, anything new. English archbishops had gone to receive the
pallium at Rome, or they had had the pallium sent to
them from Rome, in the days of the elder William, in the
days of Eadward, in the days of kings long before then.[1]
Lanfranc had gone to Rome for his pallium with the full
good will of the Conqueror,[2] and one of the chief ecclesiastical difficulties of the time immediately before the
Conqueror's coming was the belief that Stigand had received his pallium in an irregular way.[3] The amount of
dependence on the Roman see which was implied in the
receipt of this badge of honour may perhaps be questioned.
It would be differently understood at Rome and at Can-

---

[1] See N. C. vol. ii. pp. 122, 462, and Hook, Archbishops, i. 27, 270.
[2] See N. C. vol. iv. p. 353.   [3] See N. C. vol. ii. p. 441.

terbury. It would be differently understood at Canterbury, CHAP. IV.
according to the temper of different archbishops, or
according to their English or foreign birth. But it is at The pal-
least plain that the possession of the pallium was not at needful
this time looked on as at all needful for the validity of for the
validity
any archiepiscopal act. Anselm, as yet unclothed with of archi-
it, had consecrated a bishop and had proposed to hold a acts.
synod. Still for the new archbishop to go to Rome to
receive that badge of his office which was still lacking
was a simple matter of course. Doubtless the journey
needed the formal leave of the king; but no king but
William Rufus would have thought of refusing his leave
for the purpose. William had indeed not acknowledged
Urban; but Anselm had warned William that, if he
became archbishop, he must continue to acknowledge
Urban, and William had allowed him to become archbishop on those terms. The earlier conduct of William
in such matters could not have led Anselm to think that
he attached much real importance to the matter. William
of Saint-Calais had put forth the loftiest views of papal
authority in the hearing of William and Lanfranc, and
they had been objected to on quite other grounds. King
and Primate had rightly objected when the Bishop of Durham appealed from the King and his Witan to the Pope
of Rome; they had not quarrelled with the Bishop of
Durham simply because he had implied that there was
a Pope of Rome. The refusal to allow Anselm to go for Character
the pallium could have come only from a king who was liam's
determined to raise every point which could annoy the refusal.
archbishop, above all to raise every point which could
by any chance drive him to a resignation of the archbishopric. Or better still than all in the Red King's
eyes would it be to find some point which could anyhow lead to Anselm's being deprived of the archbishopric. If such an end could be gained, it would

CHAP. IV. matter not by what power or by what process it was done; it would matter not if it involved the forsaking on William's own part of every position which he had taken up.

Anselm asks leave to go to Urban for the pallium. William will acknowledge no pope.

Anselm then came to Gillingham, and asked the King's leave to go to the Pope to ask for his pallium. William at once asked to which Pope he meant to go.[1] Anselm of course answered, To Urban. The King said that he had not yet acknowledged Urban as Pope, that it was neither his custom nor that of his father to allow any one in his kingdom so much as to call any one Pope without his leave. So precious was this right to him that to seek to take it from him was the same thing as

Anselm's argument.

to seek to take away his crown.[2] Anselm then set forth the case of the two contending Popes, and his own personal case in the matter. He reminded the King of what he had told him at Rochester before he took the archbishopric, that, as Abbot of Bec, he had acknowledged Urban, and that he could not withdraw from the

William's answer.

obedience which he had pledged to him. The King, in great wrath, said that Anselm could not at once keep his faith towards himself and the obedience which without his leave he had promised to Urban.[3] Now, when

Position of Anselm towards Urban.

Anselm pledged his obedience to Urban, he was not an English subject, and he needed no leave from the King of England for anything. He acknowledged Urban, as all the rest of Normandy acknowledged him. The obedience which he had thus pledged Anselm looked on as still personally binding on him, though his temporal

[1] Eadmer, Hist. Nov. 25. "Eique suam voluntatem in hoc esse innotuit, ut Romanum pontificem pro pallii sui petitione adiret. Ad quod rex, A quo inquit papa illud requirere cupis ?"

[2] Ib. "Quicunque sibi hujus dignitatis potestatem vellet præripere, unum foret ac si coronam suam sibi conaretur auferre."

[3] Ib. "Iræ stimulis exagitatus, protestatus est illum nequaquam fidem quam sibi debebat simul et apostolicæ sedis obedientiam, contra suam voluntatem, posse servare."

allegiance was transferred to a kingdom where Urban CHAP. IV.
was not acknowledged. William, not unnaturally, took
no heed of Anselm's personal obligations. Whatever the
Abbot of Bec might have done, neither the Archbishop
of Canterbury nor any other English subject could
acknowledge any Pope without the King's leave. After
all, Anselm's acknowledgement of Urban had not yet
gone further than speaking of him as Pope. He had had
no dealings with him of any kind. He indeed proposed
to do an act which would have been the fullest acknowledgement of Urban's claims. But he had proposed
to do it only with the King's leave. What he should do
in case the King refused to give him leave to go, he
had not said, very likely he had not settled in his own
mind. He would do nothing contrary to his obedience
to Urban; but as yet his obedience to Urban was wholly
in theory. The King's words now made it a practical
question; any kind of adhesion to Urban was declared
by the King's own mouth to be inconsistent with the
duties of one who was the man of the King of England.

Anselm, it is plain, was most anxious to do his duty Twofold
alike as churchman and as subject. He saw no kind of duty of
the Arch-
inconsistency between the two. No such questions had bishop.
been raised in the days of Lanfranc, and he had not
done, or proposed to do, anything but what Lanfranc
had done before him. Reasonably enough, he was not
prepared to admit the King's interpretation of the law
which declared that he could not be the friend at once
of Urban and of William. And, in a thoroughly consti- He asks
for an
tutional spirit, he demanded that the question should be assembly
referred to a lawful assembly of the kingdom. Let the to discuss
the ques-
bishops, abbots, and lay nobles come together, and let tion.
them decide whether the two duties were so inconsistent
with each other as the King said they were.[1] By their

[1] Eadmer, Hist. Nov. 26. "Petivit inducias ad istius rei examinationem

judgement on the point of law he would abide. If they ruled that it was as the King said, that obedience to Urban was inconsistent with allegiance to William, then he would shape his own course accordingly. If such should be their verdict, he could not abide in the land without either openly throwing off the obedience of Urban or else openly breaking his duty as subject and liegeman to William. He would do neither. In such a case he would leave the realm till such time as the King should acknowledge Urban.[1] By that means he would avoid all breach of either duty. The case might well have been argued on another ground, whether it was not being righteous overmuch to bring back again, for the sake of a technical scruple of any kind, all the evils which would at once follow if the land were again left without an archbishop. Anselm's answer would doubtless have been that he could not do evil that good might come. And it would be much clearer to the mind of Anselm than it would have been to the mind of any native Englishman that a withdrawal of obedience from Urban was the doing of evil. The feelings of Aosta, even the feelings of Bec, were not quite at home in the air of Gillingham. But the bringing in of foreign ideas, feelings, and scruples, was one of the necessary consequences of foreign conquest. Anselm obeyed his own conscience, and his conscience taught him as a

quatenus episcopis, abbatibus, cunctisque regni principibus, una coëuntibus communi assensu definiretur, utrum salva reverentia et obedientia sedis apostolicæ posset fidem terreno regi servare, annon." These words must be specially attended to, as they contain the whole root of the matter with regard to the council of Rockingham. The word "indutiæ" is rather hard to translate. It means an adjournment, but something more than an adjournment. The word "truce," commonly used to express it, is rather too strong; yet it is sometimes hard to avoid it.

[1] Eadmer, Hist. Nov. 26. "Quod si probatum, inquit, fuerit, utrumque fieri minime posse, fateor malo terram tuam, donec apostolicum suscipias, exeundo devitare, quam beati Petri ejusque vicarii obedientiam vel ad horam abnegare."

conscience schooled at Aosta and Bec could not fail to CHAP. IV.
teach him.

To Anselm's proposal for referring the matter to the Frequency
Witan of the kingdom William made no objection.   The of assemblies
Red King seems never to have had any objection to under
Rufus.
meeting either his great men or the general mass of his
subjects. He was in truth so strong that every gathering
of the kind became little more than a display of his
power. But it is not easy to see why the question could
not have been kept open till the ordinary Easter Gemót.
That Gemót was held this year at Winchester, and, as Easter
we shall see in another chapter, matters of no small Gemót.
March 25,
moment had to be treated in it. The King's authority 1095.
was beginning to be defied in northern England, and at
this Easter it had to be asserted. But, for whatever A special
reason, it was determined that a special assembly should meeting
summoned.
be summoned a fortnight before the regular meeting at
Winchester, for the discussion of the particular point
which had been raised between the King and the Archbishop. It illustrates the way in which the kings and
great men of that time were always moving from place
to place that a spot was chosen for the special meeting,
far away from the spot where William and Anselm then
were, far away from the place where the regular assembly was to be held so soon after. Gillingham and
Winchester were comparatively near to each other; but
the assembly which was to give a legal judgement as to Assembly
of Rock-
Anselm's conflicting duties was summoned to meet on ingham.
the second Sunday before Easter at the royal castle of March 11,
1095.
Rockingham on the borders of Northamptonshire and
Leicestershire, a place which had at least the merit of
being one of the most central in England.

In the question which was now to be argued, there
can be little doubt that the King was technically in the

The King technically right.

right, as the law was understood in his father's time. By the custom of the Conqueror's reign, no Pope could be acknowledged without the King's leave ; and, though Anselm had not taken any active or public step in acknowledgement of Urban, he had acknowledged him in words spoken to the King himself, and he had declared that he would not on any account withdraw his obedience from Urban. At the same time one can hardly conceive a more pettifogging way of interpreting the law, or a meaner way of abusing a legal power. There was no reasonable ground for refusing to acknowledge Urban, except on the theory that the deposition of Gregory and the election of Clement were valid. Urban represented the claims of Gregory; Clement still lived to assert his own claims. But though Lanfranc had used cautious language about the dispute,[1] England and her King had never thought of acknowledging Clement or of withdrawing their allegiance from Gregory. Gregory had been the Conqueror's Pope, as long as the two great ones both lived. And, if Clement's election was void from the beginning, Gregory's death could not make his right any better. Victor had succeeded Gregory, and Urban had succeeded Victor. There could be no excuse for objecting to Urban, except on a ground which William Rufus might have been glad to take up, but which he could not take up with any decency. He might, not unreasonably from his own point of view, have thrown himself into the Imperial cause, as the common cause of princes. But he could not do this without throwing blame on the conduct of his father. Or again, if he had tried, in any legal or regular way, either to limit the papal power like Henry the Second, or to cast it off altogether like Henry the Eighth, we at least, as we read the story, could not have blamed him.

Moral estimate of his conduct.

Position of the rival Popes.

[1] See N. C. vol. iv. p. 435.

But it was not in the nature of William Rufus to do
anything in a legal or regular way. It was not in him
to take up any really intelligible counter position, either
by getting rid of Popes altogether or by acknowledging
the Imperial Pope. It is true that he might have found
it hard to carry with him even his servile prelates, still
harder to carry his lay nobles, in either of those courses.
But then it was just as little in him honestly to take the
third course which was open to him, by frankly acknowledging Urban. It pleased him better to play tricks William's
with his claim to acknowledge popes, just as he played treatment of the
tricks with his claim to appoint bishops and abbots. question.
To keep the question open, to give no reason on either
side, but practically to hinder the acknowledgement
of any pope, was a more marked exercise of his own
arbitrary will than if he had ruled the disputed question
either way. But, just as he was ready to fill up a
bishopric as soon as he thought it worth his while in
point of money, so he was quite ready to acknowledge a
pope as soon as it seemed worth his while to do so, in
point either of policy or of spite. All this while he No real objection
had not the slightest real objection to acknowledge to Urban
Urban. Either now or very soon after, he was actually on his part.
intriguing with Urban, in hopes of carrying his point
against Anselm by his means.

And now the Assembly came together which was to
declare the law of England as to the point in dispute
between Anselm and the King. It was not gathered in Position
any of the great cities, or under the shadow of any of of Rock-ingham.
the great minsters, of the realm. Nor yet was it
gathered, as some councils were gathered before and
after, in one of those spots which were simply the seats
of the King's silvan pleasures. Rockingham, placed on
the edge of the forest which bears its name, the wooded

ground between the sluggish streams of Nen and Welland, was preeminently a hunting-seat; but it was not merely a hunting-seat; it was also a fortress. As in so many cases, the Norman, in this case the Conqueror himself, had seized and adapted to his own use the home and the works of the Englishman. On a height just within the borders of Northamptonshire, looking forth across the valley of the Welland over the Danish land to the north, the Englishman Bofig had in King Eadward's days held *sac* and *soc* in his lordship of Rockingham. His dwelling-place, like those of other English thegns, crowned a mound on a site strong by nature, and which the skill of Norman engineers was to change into a site strong by art. In the havoc which fell upon Northampton, borough and shire, when William went forth to subdue the Mercian land,[1] the home of Bofig had become waste; and on that waste spot the King ordered a castle to be built.[2] At Rockingham, as almost everywhere else, we find works earlier and later than the time of our story, but nothing that we can positively assign to the days of either William. There is no keep, as at Bridgenorth and at Oxford, which we can assign to any of the known actors in our tale. The mound of Bofig is yoked on to a series of buildings of various dates, from the thirteenth century to the sixteenth. But we can still trace the line of the walls and ditches which the Conqueror or his successors added as new defences to the primitive mound and its primitive ditch. Art and nature together have made the site almost peninsular; but a considerable space, occupied by the parish church

History of the place.

The castle.

---

[1] See N. C. vol. iv. p. 224.

[2] Domesday, 220. "Rex tenet Rochingeham .... Hanc terram tenuit Bovi cum saca et soca T. R. E. Wasta erat quando rex W. jussit ibi castellum fieri." On Rockingham Castle, see Mr. G. T. Clark, Archæological Journal, xxxv. 209.

and by the town which has sunk to a village, lies between CHAP. IV.
the castle and the stream that flows beneath the height.
The site is a lordly one, and is almost the more striking Descrip-
because it commands no other great object such as those the site.
which are commanded by those castles which were
raised to protect or to keep down a city. When the
forest was still a forest in every sense of the word, the
aspect of the castle of Rockingham, one of the wilder
retreats of English kingship, must have been at once
lonelier and busier than it is now.

At Rockingham then the Assembly met, a fortnight Meeting
before Easter. The immediate place of meeting was the Assembly.
church within the castle.[1] The church has perished, but March 11,
1095.
its probable site may be traced among the buildings to
the north of the mound. But it is hard to understand Place of
how the narrow space of a castle-chapel could hold the the castle-
great gathering which came together at Rockingham. chapel.
The King and his immediate counsellors sat apart in a The King's
separate chamber, while outside were a numerous body, council.
among whom we hear of the bishops and nobles, but
which is also spoken of as a vast crowd of monks,
clerks, and laymen.[2] It may be that, according to an
arrangement which is sometimes found elsewhere, but
of which there is no present trace at Rockingham, the
great hall opened into the chapel, so that, while the
church was formally the place of meeting, the greater
space of the hall would be open to receive the over-
flowing crowd.[3] The time of meeting was the early

---

[1] Eadmer, Hist. Nov. 26. "Fit conventus omnium dominico die, in
ecclesia quæ est in ipso castro sita, ab hora prima, rege et suis secretius
in Anselmum consilia sua studiose texentibus."

[2] "Anselmus autem, episcopis, abbatibus, et principibus, ad se a regio
secreto vocatis, eos et assistentem monachorum, clericorum, laicorum, nume-
rosam multitudinem hac voce alloquitur."

[3] See above, p. 480, for somewhat similar arrangements. But the present
hall of Rockingham, dating from the thirteenth century, is divided by the
width of the court from what seems to be the site of the chapel.

morning; a midnight sitting of the Wise Men was an unknown thing in those days. The King sat within in the outer space, whatever was its nature, Anselm addressed the assembly, calling forth the bishops and lords from the presence-chamber to hear him. We must remember that, in the absence of the King, he was the first man in the Assembly and its natural leader. He laid his case before his hearers. He had asked leave of the King to go to Pope Urban for his pallium. The King had told him that to acknowledge Urban or any one else as Pope without his leave was the same thing as trying to take his crown from him. The King had added that faith to him and obedience to Urban were two things which could not go together; Anselm could not practise both at once. It was this point which the Assembly had come together to decide; it was on this

point that their counsel was needed. He bade his hearers remember that he had not sought the arch-bishopric, that in truth he would gladly have been burned alive rather than take it.[1] They had themselves forced him into the office—the bishops certainly had in a literal and even physical sense. It was for them now to help him with their counsel, to lessen thereby the burthen which they themselves had laid on his shoulder.[2] He appealed to all, he specially appealed to his brother bishops, to weigh the matter carefully, and to decide. Could he at once keep his plighted faith

---

[1] Eadmer, Hist. Nov. 26. "Fateor verum dico, quia salva reverentia voluntatis Dei maluissem illa die, si optio mihi daretur, in ardentem rogum comburendus præcipitari, quam archiepiscopatus dignitate sub-limari."

[2] "Rapuistis me, et coegistis onus omnium suscipere, qui corporis imbecillitate defessus meipsum vix poteram ferre .... attamen videns importunam voluntatem vestram, credidi me vobis, et suscepi onus quod imposuistis, confisus spe auxilii vestri quod polliciti estis. Nunc ergo, ecce tempus adest quo sese causa obtulit, ut onus meum consilii vestri manu levetis."

to the King and his plighted obedience to the Pope? It CHAP. IV.
was a grave matter to sin against either duty. Could
not both duties be observed without any breach of
either?

This was indeed the question which the Assembly was The real
brought together to consider and to decide. The point avoided on
meeting had been called, at Anselm's own request, to the King's side.
inform him on the point of law, whether he could
acknowledge Urban without disloyalty to William. But
during a long debate of two days, that real issue is
never touched, till Anselm himself calls back men's
minds to the real object of their coming together. It Assumption of
is assumed throughout by the King and the King's the King's party
party that the point of law is already settled in the against Anselm.
sense unfavourable to Anselm, that Anselm has done
something contrary to his allegiance to the King, that He is
he is there as an accused man for trial, almost as a treated as an accused
convicted man for sentence. That he is a member of person.
the Assembly, the highest subject in the Assembly,
that the whole object of the meeting is to decide a
question in which the King and his highest subject
understand the law in different ways, seems not to
come into the head of any of the King's immediate
counsellors. Least of all does it come into the heads Conduct of the
of the bishops, the class of men who play the most bishops.
prominent and the least creditable part in the story.

To Anselm's question then the bishops were the first Answer of the
to make answer. They are spoken of throughout as bishops.
acting in a body; but they must have had some spokesman. That spokesman could not have been the Bishop
of Durham, who must surely have been sitting with the
King in his inner council. William of Saint-Calais comes
on the scene afterwards, but no bishop is mentioned by
name at this stage. The answer of the episcopal body
was not cheering. The Archbishop had no need of their

CHAP. IV. counsel. He was a man prudent in God and a lover of goodness, and could settle such points better than they could. If he would throw himself wholly on the King's will, then they would give him their advice;[1] or they would, if he wished, go in and report his words to the King.

The meeting adjourned till Monday. They did so; and Rufus, with a scruple which one would rather have looked for from Anselm, ordered that, as the day was Sunday, the discussion should be adjourned to the morrow. Anselm was to go to his own quarters, and to appear again in the morning. One might like to know where, not only the Archbishop, but the whole host of visitors at times like this, found quarters. Unless they were all the King's guests in the castle, and filled its nooks and corners how they might, it must have been much harder to find lodgings at Rockingham than it was at Gloucester. Monday morning came; Anselm, with his faithful reporter Eadmer, went to the place of meeting. Sitting in the midst of the whole Assembly,[2] he told the bishops, as it would seem, that he was ready to receive the advice which he had asked for yesterday.

Meeting of Monday, March 12.

Anselm and the bishops.

They counsel unreserved submission. They again answered that they had nothing to say but what they had said yesterday; they had no advice to give him, unless he was ready to throw himself wholly on the King's will. If he drew distinctions and reservations, if he pleaded any call on behalf of God to do anything against the King's will, they would give him no help.[3] So low had the prelacy of England fallen under

---

[1] Eadmer, Hist. Nov. 27. "Si, remota omni alia conditione, simpliciter ad voluntatem domini nostri regis consilii tui summam transferre velles, prompta tibi voluntate, ut nobis ipsis, consuleremus."

[2] "In medio procerum et conglobatæ multitudinis *sedens.*" Judges and bishops can still deliver charges sitting; but it would seem hard to carry on a debate in that posture.

[3] "Si pure ad voluntatem domini regis consilii tui summam transferre volueris, promptum, et quod in nobis ipsis utile didicimus, a nobis consilium certum habebis. Si autem secundum Deum, quod ullatenus voluntati regis

the administration of Rufus and Flambard. Neither as
priests of God, nor as Witan of the realm, nor simply as Position
freemen of the land, was there any strength or counsel of the
in them. Their answer seems almost to imply that they
cast aside the common decencies, not only of prelates
but of Christian men, that they fully accepted the ruling
of their sovereign, that the will of God was not to be
put into comparison with the will of the King. Anselm Anselm
is not doing like some before and after him, not even makes no
exclusive
like his chief enemy in the present gathering. He is claims.
not asserting any special privilege for his order; he is
not appealing from a court within the realm to any
foreign jurisdiction. He asks for counsel how he may
reconcile his duty to God with his duty to the King;
and the answer he gets is that he has nothing to do but
to submit to the King's will; the law of God, and
seemingly the law of England with it, are to go for
nothing. But there was at least some shame left in
them; when they had given their answer, they held
their peace and hung down their heads, as if waiting
for what Anselm might lay upon them.[1] Then the His second
Primate spoke, seemingly not rising from his seat, but speech.
with uplifted eyes, with solemn voice, with a face all
alive with feeling.[2] He looked at the chiefs of Church
and State, prelates and nobles, and told them that if
they, shepherds and princes,[3] could give no counsel save
according to the will of one man, he must betake him to
the Shepherd and Prince of all. That Shepherd and

obviare possit, consilium a nobis expectas, frustra niteris; quia in hujusmodi nunquam tibi nos adminiculari videbis."

[1] Eadmer, Hist. Nov. 27. "Quibus dictis conticuerunt, et capita sua
quasi ad ea quæ ipse illaturus erat demiserunt."

[2] "Tunc pater Anselmus, erectis in altum luminibus, vivido vultu, reverenda voce, ista locutus est."

[3] "Nos qui Christianæ plebis pastores, et vos qui populorum principes
vocamini."

Prince had given a charge and authority to Peter first, and after him to the other Apostles, to the Vicar of Peter first and after him to all other bishops, a charge and authority which He had not given to any temporal prince, Count, Duke, King, or Emperor.[1] He owed a duty to his temporal prince, for the Lord had bidden him to render to Cæsar the things that were Cæsar's. But he was bidden also to render to God the things that were God's. He would, to the best of his power, obey both commands. He must give obedience to the Vicar of Peter in the things of God; in those things which belonged to the earthly dignity of his lord the King, he would ever give his lord his faithful counsel and help, according to the measure of his power.

His two duties.

The words are calm and dignified, the words of a man who, forsaken by all, had no guide left but the light within him. There is indeed a ring about some of Anselm's sayings which is not pleasing in English ears; we may doubt whether Dunstan would have drawn the distinction which was drawn by Anselm. And yet that distinction comes to no more than the undoubted truth that we should obey God rather than man. The only question was whether obedience to Pope Urban was a necessary part of obedience to God. The foreign clergy doubtless held stronger views of papal authority than had been known of old in England; but we may be sure that every man, native or foreign, held that the Bishop of Rome had some claim on his reverence, if not on his obedience. The ancient custom that an English archbishop should go to him for the pallium shows it of itself. The craven bishops themselves would, if secretly pressed by their consciences or their confessors, have spoken in all things as Anselm spoke. And there was

Position of England towards the Popes.

---

[1] Eadmer, Hist. Nov. 27. "Non cuilibet imperatori, non alicui regi, non duci, non comiti." I have ventured to prefer the climax to the anti-climax.

one hard by, if not present in that company, yet within
the wall of the same castle, who had gone many steps
further Romeward than Anselm went. Closeted with the Anselm
King, caballing with him against the man of God, was William
Bishop William of Durham, the man who had openly of Saint-
appealed to the Pope from the sentence of an English Calais.
court, the man who had openly refused to Cæsar what
was most truly Cæsar's, who had denied the right of the
King and Witan of England to judge a bishop, even in
the most purely temporal causes.[1] Anselm had made
no such appeal; he had made no such exclusive claims;
it is needless to say that he did not, like William of
Saint-Calais, take to the policy of obstruction, that he did
not waste the time of the assembly by raising petty points
of law, or subtle questions as to the befitting dress of its
members.[2] Anselm was a poor Papist, one might almost
say a poor churchman, beside that still recent phase of
the bishop who had now fully learned that the will of
God was not to be thought of when it clashed with the
will of the King. It was not Anselm, but the man who Anselm
sought to supplant Anselm, who had taken the first and not the
greatest step towards the establishment of foreign and appeal to
usurped jurisdictions within the realm.   Rome.

The bishops heard the answer of their Primate. They Answer
rose troubled and angry; they talked confusedly to of the
one another; they seemed as if they were pronouncing bishops.
Anselm to be guilty of death.[3] They turned to him in
wrath; they told him that they would not carry to the
King such a message as that, and they went out to the
room where the King was. But it was right that the
King should know what Anselm's answer had been.

[1] See above, p. 104.   [2] See above, p. 95.
[3] Eadmer, Hist. Nov. 27. "Turbationem suam confusis vocibus expri-
mentes, ut eos illum esse reum mortis una clamare putares." The reference
seems to be to St. Matthew's Gospel, xxvi. 66.

CHAP. IV.

Anselm goes in to the King.

Anselm asleep.

The King's message.

Advice of the bishops.

Anselm had no one whom he could send on such an errand; it was not in his nature to thrust another into the mouth of the lion when he could brave the danger himself. He went into the presence-chamber; he repeated his own words to the King, and at once withdrew. The wrath of William was kindled; he took counsel with the bishops and the nobles of his party, to see what answer he could make; but they found none. As in the hall at Lillebonne, when the Conqueror put forth his plan for the invasion of England,[1] men were to be seen talking together by threes and fours, seeking for something to say which might at once soften the King's wrath and at the same time not directly deny the doctrine set forth by Anselm.[2] They were long over their discussion; the subject of their debates meanwhile sat leaning against the wall of the place of meeting, in a gentle sleep.[3] He was awakened by the entrance of the bishops, accompanied by some of the lay nobles, charged with a message from the King. His lord the King bade him at once, laying aside all other words—the words, one would think, of dreamland so cruelly broken in upon—to hear, and to give his answer with all speed.[4] They had not as yet to announce any solemn judgement of the King and his Witan; their words still took the form of advice; but it was advice which was meant to be final and decisive.[5] As for the matters which had

[1] See N. C. vol. iii. p. 295. Only the groups at Lillebonne seem to have been larger than those at Rockingham.

[2] Eadmer, Hist. Nov. 28. "Hic duo, ibi tres, illic quatuor, in unum consiliabantur, studiosissime disquirentes, si quo modo possent aliquod responsum contra hæc componere, quod et regiam animositatem deliniret et prælibatas sententias Dei adversa fronte non impugnaret."

[3] "Adversariis ejus conciliabula sua in longum protelantibus, ipse ad parietem se reclinans leni somno quiescebat."

[4] "Vult dominus noster rex, omissis aliis verbis, a te sub celeritate sententiam audire."

[5] "Hæc rogamus, hæc consulimus, hæc tibi tuisque necessaria esse dicimus et confirmamus."

been talked about between him and the King at Gillingham, the matter for whose decision he had sought the
present adjournment, the matter at issue was plain and
easy. The whole realm was complaining of the Archbishop, because he was striving to take away from the
common lord of all of them his crown, the glory of his
Empire. For he who seeks to take away the King's dig-
nities and customs seeks to take away his crown; the one
cannot be without the other.[1] They counselled Anselm
at once to throw aside all obedience and submission to
Urban, who could do him no good, and who, if he only
made his peace with the King, could do him no harm.
Let him be free, as an Archbishop of Canterbury should
be in all his doings; as free, let him wait for the will
and bidding of the King in all things.[2] Let him, like a
wise man, confess his fault and ask for pardon; then
should his enemies who now mocked at his misfortunes,
be put to shame as they saw him again lifted up in
honour.[3]

Such was the advice which the stranger bishops of
England, with such of the stranger nobles as acted with
them, gave to the stranger Primate. Such was their prayer,
such was their counsel; such was the course which they
insisted on as needful for Anselm and for all who held
with him. Among those was the true Englishman who
wrote down their words, and who must have smiled over
the definition of freedom which, even in their mouths,

[1] Eadmer, Hist. Nov. 28. "Noveris totum regnum conqueri adversum te
quod nostro communi domino conaris decus imperii sui, coronam, auferre.
Quicumque enim regiæ dignitatis ei consuetudines tollit, coronam simul et
regnum tollit."

[2] "Urbani illius, qui offenso domino rege nil tibi prodesse nec ipso pacato
tibi quicquam valet obesse, obedientiam abjice, subjectionis jugum excute,
et *liber*, ut archiepiscopum Cantuariensem decet, in cunctis actibus tuis voluntatem domini regis et jussionem expecta." What more could Henry the
Eighth have asked of Cranmer?

[3] "Quatenus inimici tui qui casibus tuis nunc insultant, visa dignitatis
tuæ sublevatione, erubescant."

has a sound of sarcasm. Anselm said that, to speak of
nothing else, he could not cast aside his obedience to the
Pope. But it was evening; let there be an adjournment
till the morrow; then he would speak as God should
bid him.[1] The bishops deemed either that he knew not
what more to say or else that he was beginning to yield
through fear.[2] They went back to the King, and urged
him that the adjournment should not be allowed, but
that, as the matter had been discussed enough, if Anselm
would not agree to their counsel, the formal judgement
of the Assembly should be at once pronounced against
him.[3]

And now for the first time we come across a distinct mention of an individual actor, standing out with
a marked personality from the general mass of the
assembled Witan. Foremost on the King's side, the
chosen spokesman of his master, was the very man who
had gone so far beyond Anselm, who had forestalled
Thomas himself, in asserting the jurisdiction of the
Bishop of Rome within this realm of England. William
of Saint-Calais, who, when it suited his purpose, had
appealed to the Pope, who had been so anxious to go
to the Pope, but who, when he had the means of going,
had never gone, stood now fully ready to carry out the
Imperial teaching that what seems good to the prince has
the force of law. This man, so ready of speech—that we
have seen long ago—but, in Eadmer's eyes at least, not
rich in any true wisdom, was all this time stirring the
King up to wrath against Anselm, and doing all that he

---

[1] Eadmer, Hist. Nov. 28. "Respondeam quod Deus inspirare dignabitur."

[2] "Suspicati illum aut quid diceret ultra nescire aut metu addictum statim
cœpto desistere."

[3] "Persuaserunt inducias nulla ratione dandas, sed causa recenti exami-
natione discussa, supremam, si suis adquiescere consiliis nollet, in eum judicii
sententiam invehi juberet."

could to widen the breach between them.[1] Men believed,
on Anselm's side at least, that his object was to bring
about the Archbishop's deprivation or resignation by any
means, in hopes that he might himself succeed him.[2] Was
this mere surmise, or had the Bishop of Durham any solid
ground for looking forward to a translation to Canterbury? Had he the needful means? William of Saint-
Calais was not a servant of the King's to make a fortune
in his service, like Randolf Flambard or Robert Bloet.
He had risen, like Anselm himself, through the ranks of
monk, prior, abbot, and bishop. But so too had Herbert
Losinga, who had managed to buy a bishopric for himself and an abbey for his father. William of Saint-
Calais had since his consecration spent three years in
banishment while his bishopric was in the King's hands.
Still he may, during his two terms of possession before
and after, have screwed enough out of the patrimony of
Saint Cuthberht to pay even the vast price at which
the archbishopric would doubtless be valued. Or he
may have fondly dreamed that, if Anselm could be got
rid of by his means, the service would be deemed so
great as to entitle him to Anselm's place as a free gift.
Anyhow he worked diligently on the King's behalf.
We are told—and the picture is not out of character—
that Rufus wished to get rid of Anselm as the representative within his realm of another power than his own.
He deemed himself to be no full king as long as there
was any one who put the will of God before the will of
the King, or who named the name of God as a power to

---

[1] Eadmer, Hist. Nov. 28. "Erat quasi primus et prolocutor regis in hoc
negotio Willelmus supra nominatus Dunelmensis episcopus, homo linguæ
volubilitate facetus quam pura sapientia præditus. Hujus quoque discidii
quod inter regem et Anselmum versabatur erat auctor gravis et incentor."

[2] "Omni ingenio satagebat, si quo modo Anselmum calumniosis objecti-
onibus fatigatum regno eliminaret, ratus, ut dicebatur, ipso discedente, se
archiepiscopatus solio sublimandum."

CHAP. IV. which even the King must yield.[1] In his hatred to
Anselm, he hoped to carry one of two points. Either the
Archbishop would abjure the Pope, and would abide in
the land a dishonoured man who had given up the cause
for which he strove. Or else, if he still clave to the
Pope, the King would then have a reasonable excuse for
driving him out of the kingdom.

To these intrigues of the blaspheming King the
Bishop of Durham was not ashamed to lend himself.
He recked nothing of the dishonour under which it
was thought that Anselm would hardly bear to live.

Bishop
William's
promises
to the
King.
He promised to the King that he would bring about
one of two things; either the Archbishop should
renounce the Pope, or else he should formally resign the archbishopric by restoring the ring and staff.[2]
Now seemingly was the time to press him, when he was
weary with the day's work and sought for a respite,
when his enemies were beginning to hope that, either
through fear or weariness, he would be driven to yield.
So the bishops again went back from the King to the
Archbishop, with him of Durham as their leader and
spokesman. The time-server made his speech to the

His
speech to
Anselm.
man of God. "Hear the King's complaint against you.
He says that, as far as lies in your power, you have
robbed him of his dignity by making Odo Bishop of
Ostia"—William of Saint-Calais had had other names
for him in an earlier assembly—"Pope in his England[3]
without his bidding. Having so robbed him, you ask

---

[1] Eadmer, Hist. Nov. 28. "Nec regia dignitate integre se potitum sus-
picabatur, quamdiu aliquis in tota terra, vel etiam secundum Deum, nisi
per eum quicquam habere (not dico) vel posse dicebatur."

[2] "Spoponderat se facturum ut Anselmus aut Romani pontificis funditus
obedientiam abnegaret, aut archiepiscopatui, reddito baculo et annulo, ab-
renunciaret."

[3] Ib. 29. "Dicit quod quantum tua interest eum sua dignitate spoliasti,
dum Odonem episcopum Ostiensem sine sui auctoritate praecepti papam in
sua Anglia facis."

for an adjournment that you may devise arguments to CHAP. IV. prove that that robbery is just. Rather, if you please, clothe him again with the dignity of his Empire,[1] and then talk about an adjournment. Otherwise know that he will invoke the wrath of Almighty God upon himself, and we his liegemen will have to make ourselves sharers in the curse, if he grants you an adjournment of an hour. Wherefore at once make answer to the words of our lord, or else expect presently a judgement which shall chastise your presumption. Do not think that all this is a mere joke; we are driven on by the pricks of a heavy grievance.[2] Nor is it wonderful. For that which your lord and ours claims as the chief thing in his whole dominion, that in which it is allowed that he surpasses all other kings,[3] that you unjustly take away from him as far as lies in your power, and by taking it away you throw scorn on the oath which you have sworn to him, and plunge all his friends into this distress."

Here are forms of words which may make us stop to study them. In this speech, and in the one which went before it, we see the ground on which William founded a claim to which he attached such special importance. It was not merely the King of the English, it was the *Basileus* of Britain, the Cæsar of the island world, whose dignity was deemed to be touched. To allow or to refuse the acknowledgement of Popes is here declared by William of Saint-Calais to be no part of the prerogative of a mere king; it is spoken of as the special attribute of Empire. He who, alone

William's Imperial claim.

---

[1] Eadmer, Hist. Nov. 29. " Revesti eum primo, si placet, *debita imperii sui dignitate*, et tunc demum de induciis age."

[2] " Nec jocum existimes esse quod agitur; immo in istis magni doloris stimulis urgemur."

[3] " Quod dominus tuus et noster in omni dominatione sua præcipuum habebat, et quo eum *cunctis regibus præstare* certum erat."

among Christian princes, knew no superior either in the elder or the younger Rome, was alone entitled to judge how far the claims of the Pontiff of one world should be acknowledged in another. This sole claim to Imperial power on behalf of the Monarch of all Britain[1] might have been disputed in the last age in Bulgaria and in the next age in Castile; at that moment William of England was without a rival. He might even, if he chose to take up Anselm's line of argument, bear himself as more truly Imperial than the German king whose Roman crown had been placed on his head by

William and the vassal kingdoms.

a schismatic pontiff. And yet at no moment since the day when Scot and Briton and Northman bowed to Eadward the Unconquered had the Emperor of the Isle of Albion been less of an Emperor than when Anselm met the Red King at Rockingham. The younger William had indeed fallen away from the dominion of the father who had received the homage at Abernethy and

His ill-success at this moment.

had made the pilgrimage to Saint David's. The Welsh were in open and triumphant revolt; the Scots had driven out the king that he had given them. The Welsh had broken down his castles; the Scots had declared their land to be barred against all William's subjects, French and English.[2] True he was girding himself up for great efforts against both enemies; but those efforts had not yet been made. William was just then as far away as a man could be from deserving his father's surnames of the Conqueror and the Great. At such a moment, we may really believe that he would feel special annoyance at anything which might be construed as casting doubt even in theory on claims which he found it so hard to assert in practice. In the moment of his first great success in England, there had been less to

---

[1] See Appendix F.

[2] We shall come to these matters in the next chapter.

bring the wider and loftier side of his dominion before CHAP. IV.
his mind. He had thought less of his right to allow or
to refuse the acknowledgement of Popes in the days
when the *regale* was asserted by Lanfranc and the *pon-*
tificale by William of Saint-Calais, than he thought now
that the *regale* was asserted by William of Saint-Calais
and the *pontificale* by Anselm.

The shamelessness of the words of William of Saint-
Calais in the mouth of William of Saint-Calais might
have stirred even the meek Anselm to wrath. But he
bore all with patience; he only seized, with all the skill
of his scholastic training, on the palpable fallacy of the
Bishop's argument. The Assembly had come together The real
to discuss and settle a point of law. Was the duty which question hitherto
Anselm professed towards the Pope inconsistent or not evaded.
with the duty which he no less fully acknowledged
towards the King? On that point not only had no judgement been given, but no arguments either way had been
heard. Messages had gone to and fro; Anselm had been
implored, advised, threatened; but prayers, advice, and
threats had all assumed that the point which they had
all come there to discuss had already been ruled in the
sense unfavourable to Anselm. William of Saint-Calais
could talk faster than Anselm; but, as he had not
Anselm's principle, so neither had he Anselm's logic.
Anselm saw both his intellectual and his moral advantage.
His answer to the Bishop of Durham took the shape of Anselm's
a challenge. "If there be any man who wishes to prove challenge.
that, because I will not give up my obedience towards
the venerable chief Pontiff of the holy Roman Church,
I thereby break the faith and oath which I owe to my
earthly King, let him stand forth, and, in the name of
the Lord, he will find me ready to answer him where
I ought and as I ought." The real issue was thus at He states
last stated; Anselm demanded that the thing should the real case.

at last be done which the Assembly had been called for the very purpose of doing. The bishops were puzzled, as they well might be; they looked at one another, but no one had anything to say; so they went back to their lord.[1] Our guide however puts thoughts into their hearts which Anselm had certainly not uttered, which his position in no way implied, and which one is tempted to think that both Anselm and Eadmer first heard of in later times when they came to talk with a pope face New posi- to face. The bishops, we are told, remembered, what tion of the bishops. they had not thought of before, that an Archbishop of Canterbury could not be judged on any charge by any judge except the Pope.[2] This may be so far true as that William of Saint-Calais may have remembered the day when he had urged those very claims on behalf, not only of an Archbishop of Canterbury, but of a Bishop of Durham. If the other bishops had any such sudden enlightenment, they did well to keep their new light to themselves. The doctrine that no one but a Pope could judge the Archbishop, combined with the doctrine that there could be no Pope in England without the King's leave, amounted, during the present state of things, to a full licence to the Archbishop to do anything that he might think good.

Meanwhile things were taking a new turn in the outer place of assembly. There a state of mind very unlike that of the King's inner council began to show itself. There were those, as there will always be in every gathering of men, whose instinct led them to insult and trample on one who seemed to be falling. By such men

---

[1] Eadmer, Hist. Nov. 29. "Aspicientes sese ad invicem, nec invenientes quid ad ista referrent, ad dominum suum reversi sunt."

[2] "Protinus intellexerunt quod prius non animadverterunt, nec ipsum advertere posse putaverunt, videlicet archiepiscopum Cantuariensem a nullo hominum, nisi a solo papa, judicari posse vel damnari, nec ab aliquo cogi pro quavis calumnia cuiquam, eo excepto, contra suum velle respondere."

threats, revilings, slanders of every kind, were hurled CHAP. IV. at the Archbishop, as he sat peacefully waking and Anselm insulted. sleeping, while William of Saint-Calais marched to and fro at the head of his episcopal troop. But threats and revilings were not the only voices that Anselm heard. The feeling of the great mass of the assembly was with Popular feeling on his side. him. Well might it be so. Englishmen still abiding on their own soil, Normans who on English soil were growing into Englishmen, men who had brought with them the spirit which had made the Conqueror himself pause on the day of Lillebonne, were not minded to see the assembly of the nation turned into a mere tool to carry out a despot's will. They were not minded that the man whose cause they had come together to judge according to law should be judged without law by a time-serving cabal of the King's creatures. English thegns, Norman knights, were wrought in another mould from the simoniacal bishops of William's court. A spirit began to stir among them like the spirit of the old times, the spirit of the day which called back Godwine to his earldom and drove Robert of Jumièges from his archbishopric. When Anselm spoke and William of Saint-Calais stood abashed and speechless, the general feeling of the assembly went with the man who was ready to trust his cause to the event of a fair debate, against the man who could do nothing but take for granted over and over again the very question which they had come there to argue. There went through the hall that deep, low murmur which shows that the heart of a great assembly is stirring and that it will before long find some means of clearer utterance. But for a while no man dared to speak openly for fear—it is Eadmer's word—of the tyrant.[1] At last a spokesman was found. A knight

---

[1] Eadmer, Hist. Nov. 29. "Ortum interea murmur est totius multitudinis pro injuria tanti viri summissa inter se voce querentis. Nemo quippe palam

CHAP. IV.　—we should gladly know his name and race and dwelling-

Anselm and the knight.

place—stepped forth from the crowd and knelt at the feet of Anselm,[1] with the words, "Father and lord, through me your suppliant children pray you not to let your heart be troubled at what you have heard; remember how the blessed Job vanquished the devil on his dunghill, and avenged Adam whom he had vanquished in paradise." Anselm received his words with a pleased and cheerful look; for he now knew

"Vox populi vox Dei."

that the heart of the people was with him. And his true companions rejoiced also, and grew calmer in their minds, knowing the scripture—so our guide tells us—

Perplexity of the King.

that the voice of the people is the voice of God.[2] While a native English heart was thus carried back to the feelings of bygone times, the voice of the stranger King, to whom God was as a personal enemy, was speaking in another tone. His hopes had utterly broken down; his loyal bishops had made promises to him which they had been unable to fulfil. When he heard how popular feeling was turning towards Anselm, he was angered beyond measure, to the very rending asunder of his

His speech to the bishops.

soul.[3] He turned to his bishops in wrath. "What is this? Did you not promise that you would deal with him altogether according to my will, that you would judge

William of Saint-Calais breaks down.

him, that you would condemn him?" The boasted wisdom, the very flow of speech, of their leader the Bishop of Durham now failed him; he spoke as one from whom

pro eo loqui audebat ob metum tyranni." We have had the word "tyrannis" already; see above, p. 397.

[1] Eadmer, Hist. Nov. 29. "Miles unus de multitudine prodiens viro adstitit flexis coram eo genibus."

[2] "Confidentes juxta scripturam, vocem populi vocem esse Dei." "Scriptura" must here be taken in some wide sense; Eadmer could hardly have thought that these words were to be found in any of the canonical books.

[3] "Ad divisionem spiritus sui exacerbatus."

all sense and reason had gone away.[1] All that he could CHAP. IV.
say who had so lately with curses and threats refused The
assembly
Anselm's plea for an adjournment was to propose an adjourned.
adjournment himself. It was night; let Anselm be bidden
to go to his own quarters; they, the bishops, would
spend the night in thinking over what Anselm had said,
and in devising an answer on the King's behalf.[2] The
assembly was accordingly prorogued till the next
morning, and Anselm went to his own quarters, uncondemned, with his cause as yet unheard and unanswered,
but comforted doubtless that he had put his enemies
to silence, and that he had learned that the hearts of the
people were with him.

Tuesday morning came, and Anselm and his compa- March 13,
nions took their seats in the accustomed place,[3] awaiting ¹⁰⁹⁵.
the King's bidding. That bidding was slow in coming.
The debates in the King's closet were perplexed. The
King and his inner counsellors were working hard to
find some excuse for the condemnation of Anselm. The Debates in
the inner
King asked the Bishop of Durham how he had passed council.
the night;[4] but the night thoughts of William of Saint-
Calais, sleeping or waking, did not bring much help to
the royal cause. He confessed that he could find no
way to answer Anselm's argument, all the more because
it rested on holy writ and the authority of Saint Peter.
We must always remember that the texts which
Anselm quoted, and the interpretation which he put
upon them, were in no way special to himself. Every

---

[1] Eadmer, Hist. Nov. 29. "Dunelmensis ita inprimis tepide et silenter per
singula loquebatur, ut omnis humanæ prudentiæ inscius et expers putaretur."

[2] "Cogitabimus pro te usque ad mane."

[3] "Mane reversi sedimus in solito loco exspectantes mandatum regis. At
ille cum suis omnimodo perquirebat quid in damnationem Anselmi componere posset, nec inveniebat."

[4] "Requisitus Willielmus Dunelmensis quid ipse, ex condicto, noctu egerit
apud se."

one acknowledged them; William of Saint-Calais had
appealed to them when it suited his purpose to do so.

William
of Saint-
Calais re-
commends
force.

But the bishop who had once laid the lands of northern
England waste could recommend force when reason
failed. He whose dealings towards the King in whose
cause he was now working had been likened to the deed
of Judas was now ready to play Judas over again
towards the Patriarch of all the nations beyond the
sea. " My counsel," he said in plain words, " is that he
be put down by force;[1] if he will not consent to the
King's will, let the ring and staff be taken from him,

The lay
nobles
refuse.

and let him be driven from the kingdom." This short
way of dealing with the Archbishop, proposed by the
man who had once argued that none but the Pope could
judge any bishop, suited the temper of the King; it did
not suit the temper of the lay nobles. Many of them
had great crimes of their own to repent of; but they
could see what was right when others were to practise it.
Besides Anselm was in one way their own chief; if they
were great feudatories of the kingdom, so was he, the
highest in rank among them. The doctrine that the
first vassal of the kingdom was to be stripped of his fief
at the King's pleasure might be dangerous to earls as
well as to bishops. The lay nobles refused their consent to the violent scheme of the Bishop of Durham.

Speech of
the King.

The King turned fiercely on them. " If this does not
please you, what does please you? While I live, I will
not put up with an equal in my kingdom." Speaking
confusedly, it would seem, to bishops and barons alike,
he asked, " If you knew that he had such strong grounds
for his cause, why did you let me begin the suit against
him? Go, consult, for, by God's face, if you do not con-

---

[1] Eadmer, Hist. Nov. 29. " Verum mihi violentia videtur opprimendus,
et, si regiæ voluntati non vult adquiescere, ablato baculo et annulo, de regno
pellendus. Non placuerunt hæc verba principibus."

demn him according to my will, I will condemn you."[1] CHAP. IV.
The common spokesman was found in him whose counsel
was held to be as the oracle of God.[2] Count Robert of Speech of
Meulan spoke, and his speech was certainly a contrast Meulan.
to that of Bishop William, though both alike, these two
special counsellors, confessed that Anselm had been too
much for them. "All day long were we putting together
counsels with all our might, and consulting how our
counsels might hang together, and meanwhile he, thinking
no evil back again, sleeps, and, when our devices are
brought out, with one touch of his lips he breaks them
like a spider's web."[3]

When the temporal lords, the subtlest of counsellors The King
among them, thus failed him, the King again turned to bishops.
his lords spiritual. "And you, my bishops, what do you
say?" They answered, but their spokesman this time is
not mentioned; Bishop William, it would seem, had tried
and had failed. They were grieved that they could not
satisfy the pleasure of their lord. Anselm was Primate,
not only of the kingdom of England, but of Scotland,
Ireland, and the neighbouring islands—lands to which
William's power most certainly did not reach at that
moment. They were his suffragans;[4] they could not

[1] Eadmer, Hist. Nov. 30. "Per vultum Dei si vos illum ad voluntatem
meam non damnaveritis, ego damnabo vos." The oath "per vultum Dei"
is the same as that "per vultum de Luca." See Appendix G.

[2] "Robertus quidam ipsi regi valde familiaris" would seem to be no other
than the Count of Meulan. We shall hear of him by name later in the
story. It might be Robert the *Dispenser* (see above, p. 331), but that seems
much less likely.

[3] "De consiliis nostris quid dicam, fateor nescio. Nam cum omni studio
per totum diem inter nos illa conferimus, et quatenus aliquo modo sibi co-
hereant conferendo conferimus, ipse, nihil mali e contra cogitans, dormit, et
prolata coram eo statim uno labiorum suorum pulsu quasi telas araneæ
rumpit."

[4] "Primas est, non modo istius regni, sed et Scotiæ et Hiberniæ, necne
adjacentium insularum, nosque suffraganei ejus." We have had one or two
other cases, in which, in Eadmer's language at least, the Archbishop of York
is spoken of as the suffragan of Canterbury.

CHAP. IV.   with any reason judge or condemn him, even if any crime
could be shown against him, and now no crime could
be shown.   "What then," asks William, "can be done?"

The king
bids the
bishops
withdraw
their obedi-
ence from
Anselm.

The question was answered by a suggestion of his own,
one which sounds as if it really were his own, and not
the device of Bishop William or Count Robert. If the
bishops could not judge him, could they not withdraw
from him all obedience and brotherly friendship? This,
they said, if he commanded it, they could do. It is not
clear by what right they could withdraw their obedience
from a superior whom they could not judge; but both
king and bishops were satisfied. The bishops were
to go and do the business at once; when Anselm
saw that he was left alone, he would be ashamed, and
would groan that he had ever forsaken his lord to follow
Urban.[1] And, that they might do this the more safely,
the King added that he now withdrew from Anselm all
protection throughout his Empire, that he would not
listen to or acknowledge him in any cause,[2] that he
would no longer hold him for his archbishop or ghostly
father. Though the King's commandment was urgent,
the bishops still stayed to devise other devices against
Anselm; yet found they none. At last the bishops,
now taking with them the abbots, a class of whom
we have not hitherto heard in the story, went out
and announced to Anselm at once their own withdrawal of obedience and friendship and the King's withdrawal of protection. The Archbishop's answer was
a mild one. They did wrong to withdraw their obedience and friendship where it was due, merely because

He with-
draws his
protection.

The
bishops
and abbots
carry the
message.

----

[1] Eadmer, Hist. Nov. 30. "Properate igitur, et quod dicitis citius facite,
ut cum viderit se a cunctis despectum et desolatum, verecundetur, et in-
gemiscat se Urbanum me domino suo contempto secutum."

[2] "Et quo ista securius faciatis, en ego primum in imperio meo penitus ei
omnem securitatem et fiduciam mei tollo, ac deinceps in illo vel de illo nulla
in causa confidere, vel eum pro archiepiscopo aut patre spirituali tenere volo."

he would not withdraw his where it was also due. But CHAP. IV.
he would not deal by them as they dealt by him. He Anselm's
answer.
would still show them the love of a brother and a
father; he would do what he could for them, as brethren
and sons of the church of Canterbury, to bring them
back from their error into the right way. And whereas
the King withdrew from him all protection and would
no longer acknowledge him as father and archbishop,
he would still discharge to the King every earthly duty
that lay upon him, and, so far as the King would let
him,[1] he would still do his duty for the care of the King's
soul. Only he would, for God's service, still keep the
name, power, and office, of Archbishop of Canterbury,
whatever might be the oppression in outward things
that it might bring upon him.

His words were reported to the King.[2] We are again The King
turns again
admitted to witness the scene in the presence-chamber. to the lay
The bishops had proved broken reeds; William would lords.
make one more appeal to the lay nobles. "Everything
that he says," began the King, "is against my pleasure, and
no one shall be my man who chooses to be his.[3] Wherefore, you who are the great men of my kingdom, do you,
as the bishops have done, withdraw from him all faith
and friendship, that he may know how little he gains by
the faith which he keeps to the Apostolic See in defiance of my will." But the lay lords were not like the
bishops; one would like to know by what mouth they
made their calm and logical answer. They drew a clear
distinction between spiritual and temporal allegiance.

---

[1] Eadmer, Hist. Nov. 30. "Paterno more diligentiam, animæ illius
curam, si ferre dignabitur, habebo."

[2] "Ad hæc ille respondit," says Eadmer; but it can only mean an answer
through messengers, as it is plain that the King and the Archbishop were still
in different rooms.

[3] "Omnino adversatur animo meo quod dicit, nec meus erit, quisquis
ipsius esse delegerit."

CHAP. IV.

The lay lords support Anselm.

The King had told them that no one could be his man and the Archbishop's at once, and he had bidden them to withdraw their faith—clearly using the word in the feudal sense—from the Archbishop. They answered that they were not the Archbishop's men, that they could not withdraw from him a fealty which they had never paid to him. This of course was true of the lay nobles as a body, whatever questions there might be about Tunbridge castle or any other particular fief. But they went on to say that, though Anselm was not their lord, yet he was their archbishop, that it was he who had to "govern Christianity" in the land; that, as Christian men, they could not, while in that land, decline his mastership, all the more as there was no spot of offence in him which should make the King treat him in any other way.[1]

The King's difficulties.

Such an answer naturally stirred up William's wrath; but the earls and great barons of his kingdom were a body with whom even he could not dare to trifle. He was stronger than any one among them; he might not be stronger than all of them together, backed as they now were, as the events of the day before had shown, by popular feeling. He had once beaten the Norman nobles at the head of the English people; he might not be able to beat the Norman nobles and the English people together. He therefore made an effort, and kept down any open outburst of the wrath that was in him.[2] But

[1] The answer of the lay lords must be taken as a formal setting forth of their position ; one would be glad to know whose are the actual sentiments and words. It runs thus (Eadmer, 30) ;

"Nos nunquam fuimus homines ejus, nec fidelitatem quam ei non fecimus abjurare valemus. Archiepiscopus noster est ; Christianitatem in hac terra gubernare habet, et ea re nos qui Christiani sumus ejus magisterium, dum hic vivimus, declinare non possumus, præsertim cum nullius offensæ macula illum respiciat, quæ vos secus de illo agere compellat."

[2] "Quod ipse repressa sustinuit ira, rationi eorum palam ne nimis offenderentur contraire præcavens." This is perhaps a solitary case of recorded self-restraint on the part of William Rufus, at all events since the death of

the bishops were covered with confusion; they felt that CHAP. IV.
all eyes were turned on them, and that their apostasy Shame of the bishops.
was loathed of all.[1] This and that bishop was greeted,
seemingly by this or that earl or baron, with the names
usual in such cases, Judas, Pilate, and Herod.[2] Then the The King further examines the bishops.
King put the trembling bishops through another examin-
ation. Had they abjured all obedience to Anselm, or
only such obedience as he claimed by the authority of
the Roman Pontiff?[3] The question was hard to answer.
Anselm does not seem to have claimed any obedience
by virtue of the authority of the Pope; he had simply
refused to withdraw his own obedience from the Pope.
Some therefore answered one way, some another. But
it was soon plain which way the King wished them to
answer. The real question in William's mind had nothing
to do with the Pope; any subtlety about acknowledging
this or that Pope was a mere excuse. It was Anselm
himself, as the servant of God, the man who spake of
righteousness and temperance and judgement to come,
that Rufus loathed and sought to crush. Those bishops
therefore who said that they had abjured Anselm's obedience utterly and without condition were at once

Lanfranc. It is significant that it should be in answer to the lay lords and
not to the bishops.

[1] Eadmer, Hist. Nov. 30. "Episcopi hæc videntes, confusione vultus
sui operti sunt, intelligentes omnium oculos in se converti, et apostasiam
suam non injuste a cunctis detestari." It must be remembered that
apostasia is a technical term, meaning, besides its usual sense, a forsaking
of his monastic vows and calling by a professed monk. Eadmer speaks of
the bishops as guilty of a like offence towards their metropolitan.

[2] The picture is very graphic; "Audires si adesses, nunc ab isto, nunc
ab illo istum vel illum episcopum aliquo cognomine cum interjectione indig-
nantis denotari, videlicet Judæ proditoris, Pilati, vel Herodis horumque
similium." One of the bishops had been likened to Judas some years before
on somewhat opposite grounds.

[3] "Requisiti a rege, utrum omnem subjectionem et obedientiam, nulla
conditione interposita, an illam solam subjectionem et obedientiam, quam
prætenderet ex autoritate Romani pontificis, Anselmo denegassent."

CHAP. IV.

His treatment of them.

bidden to sit down as his friends in seats of honour.[1] Those who said that they had abjured only such obedience as was claimed by the Pope's authority, were sent, like naughty children, into a corner of the room, to wait, as traitors and enemies, for their sentence of condemnation.[2] But they debated among themselves in their corner, and soon found the means of winning back the royal favour. A heavy bribe, paid at once or soon after, wiped out even the crime of drawing distinctions while withdrawing their obedience from a metropolitan whom the King hated.[3]

Anselm wishes to leave England.

While his suffragans were undergoing this singular experience of the strength of the secular arm, Anselm sent a message to the King. He now asked that, as all protection within the kingdom was withdrawn from him, the King would give him and his companions a safe-conduct to one of his havens, that he might go out of the realm till

[1] Eadmer, Hist. Nov. 31. "Hos quidem qui, nulla conditione interposita, funditus ei quicquid prælato suo debebant se abjurasse professi sunt, juxta se sicut fideles et amicos suos honorifice sedere præcepit."

[2] "Illos vero qui in hoc solo quod præciperet ex parte apostolici sese subjectionem et obedientiam illi abnegasse dicere ausi sunt, ut perfidos ac suæ voluntatis inimicos, procul in angulo domus sententiam suæ damnationis ira permotus jussit præstolari. Territi ergo et confusione super confusionem induti, in angulum domus secesserunt."

[3] "Reperto statim salubri et quo niti solebant domestico consilio, hoc est, data copiosa pecunia, in amicitiam regis recepti sunt."

All this suggests the question, what was the course taken by Gundulf of Rochester, Anselm's old friend, and the holder of a bishopric which stood in a specially close relation to the archbishop. In the Historia Novorum there is no mention of Gundulf; the bishops are spoken of as an united body, except so far as they were divided on this last question. But it seems implied that all disowned Anselm in one way or another. Yet in the Life (ii. 3. 24) the bishops disown him, "Rofensi solo excepto." How are these accounts to be reconciled? If Gundulf had stood out in any marked way from the rest, Eadmer would surely have mentioned him in the Historia Novorum. One might suppose that the Bishop of Rochester, as holding of the Archbishop, was not in the company of the King's bishops at all. But, if he had stayed outside with Anselm and Eadmer, one would have looked for that to be mentioned also. He can hardly lurk in the first person plural which Eadmer so often uses.

such a time as God might be pleased to put an end to CHAP. IV.
the present distress.[1] The King was much troubled and Perplexity
perplexed. He wished of all things for Anselm to leave of the King.
the kingdom; but he feared the greater scandal which
would arise if he left the kingdom while still in possession of the archbishopric, while he saw no way of
depriving him of it.[2] He again took counsel; but this
time he did not trouble the bishops for their advice. Of
them he had had enough; it was their counsel which had
brought him into his present strait.[3] He once more
turned to the lay lords. They advised yet another Another
adjournment. The Archbishop should go back to his adjourn-ment.
own quarters in the King's full peace,[4] and should come
again in the morning to hear the King's answer to his
petition. Many of the King's immediate courtiers were
troubled; they groaned at the thought of Anselm's
leaving the land.[5] But he himself went gladly and cheerfully to his lodgings, hoping to cross the sea and to cast
off all his troubles and all the burthens of the world.[6]

The fourth day of the meeting came, and the way Wednes-
in which its business opened marks how the tide was day, March 14, 1095.
turning in Anselm's favour. A body of the nobles came Anselm
straight from the King, asking the Primate to come summoned to the

---

[1] Eadmer, Hist. Nov. 31. "Donec Deus tantæ perturbationi modum
dignanter imponeret."

[2] "Licet discessum ejus summopere desideraret, nolebat tamen eum
pontificatus dignitate *saisitum* discedere, ne novissimum scandalum quod
inde poterat oriri pejus fieret priore. Ut vero pontificatu illum *dissaisiret*,
impossibile sibi videbatur." The feudal language creeps in at all
corners.

[3] "Episcoporum consilio per quod in has angustias se devolutum querebatur omisso, cum principibus consilium iniit."

[4] "Quatenus vir cum summa pace moneatur ad hospitium suum
redire."

[5] "Perturbatis etiam curialibus plurimis . . . rati sunt quippe hominem
a terra discedere, et ingemuerunt."

[6] "Lætus et alacer sperabat se perturbationes et onera sæculi, quod
semper optabat, transito mari, evadere."

to the royal presence.[1] Anselm was tossed to and fro
between the hope of leaving the kingdom and the fear
of staying in it. Eadmer was eager to know what
would be the end of the whole matter.[2] They set forth
and reached the castle. They were not however, at first
at least, admitted to the presence-chamber, but sat in
their wonted place. Before long the lay nobles, accompanied by some of the bishops, came to Anselm. They
were grieved, they said, as old friends of his, that there

had been any dispute between him and the King. Their
object was to heal the breach, and they held that the
best means towards that object was to agree to an
adjournment—a truce, a peace [3]—till a fixed day, during
which time both sides should agree to do nothing
which could be counted as a breach of the peace. Anselm
agreed, though he said that he knew what kind of peace
it would be.[4] But it should not be said of him that
he preferred his own judgement to that of others. To
all that his lord the King and they might appoint in
the name of God he would agree,[5] saving only his

obedience to Pope Urban. The lords approved; the
King agreed; he pledged his honour to the observance
of the peace till the appointed day, the octave of
Pentecost. The day seems to have been chosen in order
that the other business of the Whitsun Gemót might

---

[1] Eadmer, Hist. Nov. 31. "Ecce principes *a latere regis* mane directi"—
the style of Emperors and Popes.

[2] " Ascendimus, inimus, et supremam de negotio nostro sententiam avidi
audire, in quo soliti eramus loco consedimus." The word "ascendimus"
might show that Anselm's lodgings were at some point lower than the
castle.

[3] "Inducias utrimque de negotio dari quatenus hinc usque ad definitum
aliquod tempus inter vos pace statuta."

[4] "Pacem atque concordiam non abjicio; veruntamen videor mihi videre
quid ista quam offertis pax habeat in se."

[5] " Concedo suscipere quod domino regi et vobis placet pro pacis custodia
secundum Deum statuere"—Anselm's invariable reservation.

be got over before the particular case of Anselm came CHAP. IV.
on. If matters had not been brought to an agreement
before that time, the case was to begin again exactly
at the stage in which it had left off at Rockingham.[1]
It is not clear whether, even at this last moment, William
and Anselm again met face to face. But the Archbishop,
by the King's leave, went to Canterbury, knowing that
the truce was but an idle and momentary veiling of
hatred and of oppression that was to come.[2]

So it soon proved; yet the scene at Rockingham was Importance
a victory, not only for a moment but for ever. No slight of the meeting at
step had been taken in the great march of English freedom, Rocking-
when Anselm, whom the King had sought to condemn ham.
without trial or indictment, went back, with his own
immediate case indeed unsolved, but free, uncondemned,
untried, with the voice of the people loud in his favour,
while the barons of the realm declared him free from
every crime. It was no mean day in English history
when a king, a Norman king, the proudest and fiercest
of Norman kings, was taught that there were limits to
his will. It is like a foreshadowing of brighter days
to come when the Primate of all England, backed by
the barons and people of England—for on that day the
very strangers and conquerors deserved that name—
overcame the Red King and his time-serving bishops.
The day of Rockingham has the fullest right to be
marked with white in the kalendar in which we enter
the day of Runnymede and the day of Lewes.

The honour of the chivalrous King was pledged to
the peace with Anselm. But the honour of the chivalrous

---

[1] Eadmer, Hist. Nov. 31. "Dantur induciæ usque ad octavas Pentecostes, ac
regia fide sancitur, quatenus ex utraque parte interim omnia essent in pace."

[2] "Præsciens apud se pacem et inducias illas inane et momentaneum
velamen esse odii et oppressionis mox futuræ.

King was construed after a truly chivalrous fashion.

William doubtless thought that he was doing all that a true knight could be expected to do, if he kept himself from any personal injury to the man to whom he had personally pledged his faith. Anselm was unhurt; he was free; he went whither he would; he discharged the ordinary duties of his office undisturbed; it does not appear that he was in any way personally molested, or that any of the property of his see was taken into the King's hands. But William knew full well how to wreak his malice upon Anselm without breaking the letter of the faith which he had pledged. He knew how to grieve Anselm's loving heart far more deeply than it could be grieved by any wrong done to himself. The honour of the good knight was pledged to Anselm personally; it was not pledged to Anselm's friends and tenants. Towards them he might, without breach of honour, play the greedy and merciless king. A few days after Anselm had reached Canterbury, Rufus sent to drive out of England the Archbishop's cherished friend and counsellor the monk Baldwin of Tournay,[1] and two of his clerks. Their only crime was standing by their master in the trial which still stood adjourned.[2] The Archbishop's chamberlain was seized in his master's chamber before his master's eyes; false charges were brought against his tenants, unjust imposts were laid upon them, and other wrongs of many kinds done to them.[3] The church of Canterbury, it was said, began to doubt whether it had

---

[1] Eadmer, Hist. Nov. 31. "Baldwinum monachum, *in quo pars major* consiliorum Anselmi pendebat."

[2] "Præscripti discidii causa."

[3] "Quid referam camerarium ejus in sua camera ante suos oculos captum, alios homines ejus injusto judicio condemnatos, deprædatos, innumeris malis afflictos?" All this was "infra dies induciarum et præfixæ pacis." Eadmer reproaches the "regalis constantia fidei." Rufus would have said that his faith was plighted to Anselm, not to Baldwin.

not been better off during the vacancy than now that CHAP. IV.
the archbishopric was full.[1] And all this while, heavy
as William professed to deem the crime of so much
as giving Urban the title of Pope, William's own dealings
with Urban were neither slight nor unfriendly.

§ 5. *The Mission of Cardinal Walter.* 1095.

The months of truce between the King and the Arch- Events of
the months
bishop were, as our next chapter will show, busy months of truce,
in other ways. William Rufus was all this time engaged March–
May, 1095.
in another dispute with a subject of a rank but little
below that of the Primate, a dispute in which, at least
in its early stages, the King appears to much greater
advantage than he commonly does. A conspiracy against
William's throne and life was plotting; Robert of Mowbray
was making ready for revolt, and his refusal to appear,
when summoned, at the Easter and Whitsun assemblies
of this year was the first overt act of his rebellion. We Assemblies
of the year.
may conceive that Anselm did not attend either of those
gatherings; that of Whitsuntide we know that he did
not. It might be more consistent with the notion of
the truce that he should keep away from the King's
presence and court till the time which had been fixed for
the controversy formally to begin again. At Easter and
for some time after, Anselm seems to have stayed at
Canterbury, and, while he was there, the metropolitan
city received an unexpected visitor, who did not allow
himself to be treated as a guest.

The year which we have reached was one of the most Position of
Urban.
memorable in the history of the papacy. Urban, though
not in full possession of Rome, had kept his Christmas
there a year before, and his cause was decidedly in the

---

[1] Eadmer, Hist. Nov. 32. "Ut fere universi conclamarent melius sibi
absque pastore jam olim fuisse quam nunc sub hujusmodi pastore esse."

CHAP. IV. ascendant throughout the year of the Red King's second
Norman campaign.[1]   At the beginning of the next year,
after keeping Christmas in Tuscany, Urban went on
into Lombardy, where the Emperor still was, though
his rebel son Conrad, crowned and largely acknowledged
as King of Italy, was far more powerful than his father.[2]

Council of Piacenza. May 1-7. Almost on the same days as those which in England
were given to the council of Rockingham, Urban held
his great council of Piacenza, a council so great that no
building could hold its numbers; the business of the
assembly was therefore done, as we have seen it done in

Its decrees. our own land, in the open fields.[3]   There the Empress
Praxedes told her tale of sorrow and shame; there the
cry of Eastern Christendom, set forth in the letters of
the Emperor Alexios, was heard and heeded; there the
heresy of Berengar, already smitten by Lanfranc,[4] was
again condemned; there a new set of anathemas were
hurled at the married clergy,[5] and a more righteous curse
was denounced against the adulterous King of the

No mention of English affairs. French.   But no mention seems to have been made
of English affairs; one is a little surprized at the small
amount of heed which the dispute between the King
and the Archbishop seems to have drawn to itself in

---

[1] The movements of Urban at this time will be found in the Chronicle of
Bernold in the fifth volume of Pertz, p. 461. Cf. Milman, Latin Christianity, iii. 215.

[2] Bernold, ib. "Henricus autem rex dictus eo tempore in Longobardia
morabatur, pene omni regia dignitate privatus. Nam filius ejus Chon-
radus, jam dudum in regem coronatus, se ab illo penitus separavit, et
domnæ Mathildi reliquisque fidelibus sancti Petri firmiter conjunctus totum
robur paterni exercitus in Longobardia obtinuit."

[3] Ib. "Ad quam sinodum multitudo tam innumerabilis confluxit, ut
nequaquam in qualibet ecclesia illius loci posset comprehendi. Unde et
domnus papa extra urbem in campo illam celebrare compulsus est; nec hoc
tamen absque probabilis exempli auctoritate." He justifies the act by the
example of Moses; in England Godwine and William might have been
precedents enough.

[4] See N. C. vol. ii. p. 230.

[5] The matters discussed are reckoned up by Bernold, u. s.

foreign lands. Yet, next to the ups and downs of the Emperor himself, one would have thought that no change
could have so deeply affected the Roman see as the
change from William the Great to William the Red. It
is part of the same general difficulty which attaches to
the Red King's career, the strange fact that the worst of
all crowned sinners, the foulest in life, the most open
in blasphemy, the most utter scorner of the ecclesiastical
power, never felt the weight of any of those ecclesiastical
censures which so often lighted on offenders of a less
deep dye. But if Urban was not thinking about William,
William was certainly thinking about Urban. It was at
this stage that we light on the curious picture which we
have before seen, showing us England in a state of un-
certainty, and seemingly of indifference, between the rival
Pontiffs.[1] But just now it suited William to acknow- William's
ledge some Pope, because he thought that his only chance fresh
schemes to
of carrying out his purposes against Anselm was by the turn the
Pope
help of a Pope. He had found that no class of men in against
Anselm.
his kingdom, except perhaps some of the bishops, would
support him in any attempt to deprive the Primate
of his own arbitrary will. Mere violence of course
was open to him; but his Witan would not agree to any
step against Anselm which made any pretence to legal
form, and, with public feeling so strongly on Anselm's
side, with a dangerous rebellion brewing in the realm,
the King might well shrink from mere violence
towards the first of his subjects. His new device was
to acknowledge a Pope, and then to try, by his usual
arts, arts which Rome commonly appreciated, to get the
Pope whom he acknowledged to act against the Archbishop. To see Anselm deprived, or in any way humbled,
by an exercise of ecclesiastical power, would be to wound
Anselm in a much tenderer point, and would therefore be

[1] See above, p. 415.

CHAP. IV. a much keener satisfaction to his own spite, than anything that he could himself do with the high hand.

Mission of Gerard and William of Warelwast.

As soon therefore as William found, by the issue of the meeting at Rockingham, that Anselm could not be bent to his will, and that he could practically do nothing against Anselm, he sent two trusty clerks of his chapel and chancery on a secret and delicate errand. They were men of the usual stamp, both of whom afterwards rose to those high places of the Church which were just then commonly reserved for men of their stamp. They were Gerard, afterwards Bishop of Hereford and Archbishop of York, and William of Warelwast, afterwards

Their commission.

Bishop of Exeter. As we read our account of their commission, it would almost seem as if they were empowered to go to Rome, to examine into the state of things, and to acknowledge whichever seemed to be the true Pope, or rather whichever Pope was most likely

They are practically sent to acknowledge Urban.

to suit their master's purpose. But practically they had no choice but to acknowledge Urban. Local English feeling might indeed set little store by one who simply "hight Pope, though he nothing had of the settle at Rome;"[1] but Urban was plainly the stronger Pope, the Pope acknowledged by all who were not in the immediate interest of the Emperor. And, what was more, Urban was the only Pope who could carry out William's purpose. A censure from Urban would be a real blow to Anselm and to Anselm's partisans; a censure from Clement would in their eyes go for nothing, or rather it would be reckoned as another witness in their favour. Practically Gerard and William of Warelwast went to acknowledge Urban, and to see what they could make of him. They went secretly. Anselm knew nothing of their going. Most likely nothing was known

---

[1] So speaks our own Chronicler the next year. See above, p. 415.

of their errand by any man beyond the innermost cabal CHAP. IV.
of the King's special counsellors.[1]

Their mission is said to have been to Rome; but the
name Rome must be taken in a conventional sense for
any place where the Pope might be. It is not likely that
they really reached the Eternal City. In the former Urban at
Cremona.
part of April Urban was at Cremona, and was received April 10,
there with great state by the rebel King Conrad.[2] The 1095.
momentary effort of Henry which followed, his vain
attempt on Nogara, only raised the position of Urban
and the Great Countess yet higher.[3] It was most likely
at Cremona that the ministers from England met
Urban. They were to try, if possible, to win over the Dealings of
Gerard and
Pontiff, by gifts, by promises, by any means, to send a William
pallium to England for the King to bestow on the Arch- with
Urban.
bishop of Canterbury, without mentioning the name of
Anselm. They were, it seems, to try to obtain for the The Sicilian
King a legatine authority like that which, then or later, "Monarchy."
had been granted to the Norman princes of Sicily.[4]

---

[1] Eadmer, Hist. Nov. 32. "Siquidem ipse rex, ubi sensit Anselmum suæ
voluntatis in præscripto negotio nolle obtemperare, clam et Anselmo igno-
rante, eosdem clericos [Girardum et Willielmum] Romam miserat, Romanæ
statum ecclesiæ per eos volens certo dinoscere."

[2] Bernold (Pertz, v. 461) gives the details. The part which most concerns us is that the King and future Emperor is received only "salva
justitia illius [Romanæ] ecclesiæ, et statutis apostolicis, maxime de investi-
turis in spiritalibus officiis a laico non usurpandis."

[3] Bernold merely glances at this matter. It will be found described more
at length in the hexameters of Donizo, ii. 9, Muratori, v. 374; and in the
prose life of Matilda, 13, Muratori, v. 395.

[4] Eadmer, Hist. Nov. 32. "Scire veritatem hujus rei Romam missi sunt
hii duo clerici, eaque cognita, jussi sunt sacris promissionibus illectum ad
hoc si possent papam perducere, ut ipsi regi ad opus archiepiscopi Cantuariensis pallium, tacita persona Anselmi, destinaret, quod ipse rex, Anselmo
a pontificatu simul et regno dejecto, cui vellet cum pontificatu vice apostolici postmodum daret." The formal grant of the hereditary legation
to Count Roger comes somewhat later, being given by Urban himself
in 1099. (See William of Malaterra, iv. 29, Muratori, v. 602.) But the
language used seems to imply that some such power practically existed
already.

CHAP. IV. A Norman king of England was surely as worthy of such powers as a Norman Great Count of Sicily; and throughout these disputes we ever and anon see the vision of the "Sicilian Monarchy," as something at which kings of England were aiming, and which strict churchmen condemned, whether in Sicily or in England.[1] It is even possible that Gerard and William of Warelwast may have discussed the matter with some members of the Sicilian embassy which about this time brought the daughter of Count Roger to Pisa as the bride of King Conrad.[2] Close intercourse between the Norman princes of the great Oceanic and the great Mediterranean island is now beginning to be no small element in European politics. Some commission of this kind from the Pope was what William's heart was set upon; he thought he had good right to it; he thought that his hope of it could not be doomed to disappointment.[3] Did the proudest of men look forward, as an addition to royal and imperial power, to a day when he might fill a throne in the mother church of England, looking down on the patriarchal chair, as the empty thrones of later Williams still look down on the lowlier metropolitan seats of Palermo and Monreale?

Relations between England and Sicily.

Gerard and William come back,

The dates show that the journeys must have been hasty, and that the business was got through with all speed. The two clerks could not have left England before the middle of March, and May was not far

---

[1] Ep. S. Thom. ad Cardinales, Giles, S. T. C. iii. 93. "Eo jam perventum est ut sequatur rex noster etiam Siculos, immo certe præcedat." On the question of the legatine power supposed to have been granted, or designed to be granted, to Henry the Second, see J. C. Robertson, Becket, 106. For my purpose the general belief that something of the kind was done or designed is enough.

[2] Bernold, ap. Pertz, v. 461.

[3] Eadmer, Hist. Nov. 32. "Hoc quippe disposuerat apud se; hoc suspicatus est non injuria sibi concedi posse, hoc indubitato fieri promittebat opinioni suæ."

advanced before they were in England again, and a CHAP. IV.
papal Legate with them. This was the Cardinal Walter, and bring
Bishop of Albano, whose good life is witnessed by our Walter as
own Chronicler.[1] His Italian subtlety showed itself Legate.
quite equal to the work of outwitting the King and his
counsellors whenever he chose; but his Roman greediness could not always withstand their bribes. He He brings
came, bringing with him a pallium, but the whole affair a pallium.
was, by the King's orders, shrouded in the deepest
mystery. Not a word was said about the pallium;
indeed the Legate was not allowed to have any private
discourse with any man. His two keepers, Gerard and Secrecy of
William, watched him carefully; they passed in silence his errand.
through Canterbury, and took care not to meet the
Archbishop.[2] A few days before Whitsuntide, Cardinal His inter-
Walter had an interview with the King. He spoke so the King.
that William understood him to be willing to abet all
his purposes. Some special privilege was granted to
William, which amounted at the least to this, that no
legate should be sent into England but one of the King's
own choosing.[3] Not a word did Cardinal Walter say on

[1] Chron. Petrib. 1095. "Eac on þis ylcan geare togeanes Eastron com
þæs papan *sande* hider to lande, þæt wæs Waltear bisceop swiðe god lifes
man, of Albin þære ceastre." The date is strange, as he did not and could
not come till after Easter.

[2] Eadmer, Hist. Nov. 32. "Præfatus episcopus Angliam veniens, secum
archiepiscopatus stolam papa mittente clanculo detulit. Et silenter Cantuaria civitate pertransita, Anselmoque devitato, ad regem properabat,
nulli de pallio quod ferebat quicquam dicens, nullum in absentia ductorum
suorum familiariter alloquens. Rex denique præceperat ita fieri, nolens
mysterium consilii sui publicari."

[3] Ib. 33. "Sentiens rex episcopum ex parte Urbani cuncta suæ voluntati
coniventia nunciare, et ea, si ipsum Urbanum pro papa in suo regno susciperet, velle apostolica authoritate sibi dum viveret in privilegium promulgare, adquievit placito." This is put somewhat more distinctly in the
account by Hugh of Flavigny (Pertz, viii. 475, see Appendix AA); "Conventionem fecerat cum eo [Willelmo] Albanensis episcopus, quem primum
illo miserat papa, ne legatus Romanus ad Angliam mitteretur nisi quem rex
præciperet."

CHAP. IV. behalf of Anselm, not a word that could make peace
between him and the King, not a word that could give
Anselm any comfort among all the troubles that he was
enduring on behalf of the Christian religion and of the
authority of the Holy See.[1] Many who had looked for
great good from the Legate's coming began to murmur,
and to say, as Englishmen had learned to say already and
as they had often to say again, that at Rome gold went
for more than righteousness.[2] To King William everything seemed to be going as he wished it to go. Fully
satisfied, he put out a proclamation that throughout his
Empire—through the whole patriarchate of Anselm—Urban should be acknowledged as Pope and that obedience
should be yielded to him as the successor of Saint Peter.[3]
Walter had now gained his point; William fancied that
he had gained his. He at once asked that Anselm might
be deprived of his archbishopric by the authority of the
Pope whom he had just acknowledged. He offered a
vast yearly payment to the Roman See, if the Cardinal
would only serve his turn in this matter.[4] But Walter
stood firm; he had done the work for which he had
come; England was under the obedience of Urban.
And, much as gold might count for at Rome, neither the
Pope nor his Legate had sunk to the infamy of taking
money to oppress an innocent man and a faithful

William acknowledges Urban.

Walter refuses to depose Anselm.

---

[1] Eadmer, Hist. Nov. 32. "Nil penitus ipsi pro Anselmo locutus est,
quod pacem inter eos conciliaret, quod tribulationes in quibus pro fidelitate
sedis apostolice desudabat mitigaret, quod eum ad sublevandum in Anglia
Christianæ religionis cultum roboraret."

[2] Ib. "Papæ, quid dicemus? Si aurum et argentum Roma præponit
justitiæ," &c. It must be remembered that in this sentence "Papæ" has
nothing to do with "Papa." See above, p. 292.

[3] Ib. 33. "Præcipiens Urbanum *in omni imperio suo* pro apostolico
haberi, eique vice beati Petri in Christiana religione obediri."

[4] Ib. "Egit post hæc quibus modis poterat ipse rex cum episcopo, quatenus Romani pontificis autoritate Anselmum ab episcopatu, regali potentia
fultus, deponeret, spondens immensum pecuniæ pondus ei et ecclesiæ Romanæ
singulis annis daturum, si in hoc suo desiderio satisfaceret."

adherent. Anselm was indeed treated by them as Eng- CHAP. IV.
lishmen, whether by race, by birth, or by adoption, whether
Edmund, Thomas, or Anselm, commonly were treated
by Popes. He was made a tool of, and he got no
effectual support; but Urban was not prepared for such
active wickedness as the Red King asked of him.

William was now thoroughly beaten at his own William
weapons. The craft and subtlety of Randolf Flambard, and his
of William of Saint-Calais, of the Achitophel of Meulan outwitted
himself, had proved of no strength before the sharper Legate.
wit of Walter of Albano. The King complained with
good right that he had gained nothing by acknowledging
Urban.[1] In truth he had lost a great deal. He had
lost every decent excuse for any further attack upon
Anselm. . The whole complaint against Anselm was that
he had acknowledged Urban. But the King had now
himself acknowledged Urban, and he could not go on
persecuting Anselm for simply forestalling his own act.
In legal technicality doubtless, if it was a crime to
acknowledge Urban when the King had not yet acknowledged him, that crime was not purged by the King's
later acknowledgement of him. Rufus himself might
have been shameless enough to press so pettifogging
a point; but he had learned at Rockingham that no
man in the land, save perhaps a few servile bishops,
would support him in so doing. There was nothing He is
to be done but for William to make up his quarrel with driven to a
Anselm, to make it up, that is, as far as appearances tion with
went, to make it up till another opportunity for a Anselm.
quarrel could be found. But till such opportunity was
found, Anselm must be openly and formally received
into the King's favour.[2] The thing had to be done;

[1] Eadmer, Hist. Nov. 33. "Reputans apud se nihil in requisitione vel
susceptione Romani antistitis se profecisse."

[2] "Qualiter, servata singulari celsitudinis suæ dignitate, viro saltem specie

CHAP. IV. only if some money could be squeezed out of Anselm in the process of doing it, the chivalrous King would be the better pleased.

Whitsun Gemót at Windsor. May 13, 1095.

The feast of Pentecost came, and with it the second of the assemblies at which the rebellious Earl of Northumberland refused to show himself. The King and his Witan were at Windsor; the Archbishop was keeping the feast at his manor of Mortlake. On the octave he was himself, according to the truce made at Rockingham,

The King's message to Anselm.

to appear at Windsor. In the course of the Whitsun-week a message was brought to him from the King, bidding him go to Hayes, another of his manors nearer to Windsor, in order that messages might more easily go to and fro between him and the King.[1] He went, and Eadmer went with him. The next day nearly all the bishops came to him; some of them, it will be remembered, had kept the King's favour throughout, and the others who had lost it had bought it again. Their object was to try to persuade the Archbishop to give money to the King for the restoration of his favour. Anselm answered stoutly, as before, that he would not so dishonour his lord as to treat his friendship as something which could be bought and sold.[2] He would faithfully discharge every temporal duty to his lord, on the one condition of being allowed to keep his obedience to Pope Urban. If that was not allowed, he would again ask

The Legate's coming revealed to Anselm.

for a safe-conduct to leave the kingdom. They then told him—the secret must have been still kept, though Urban was acknowledged—that the Bishop of Albano had brought a pallium from the Pope; they did not

tenus amorem suum redderet, cui crudeliter iratus nihil poterat cupitæ damnationis pro voto inferre."

[1] Eadmer, Hist. Nov. 33. "Ad eum venire et verba regis illi et illius possent regi deferre."

[2] "Dixi vobis jam, quod nunquam domino meo hanc contumeliam faciam ut facto probem amicitiam ejus esse venalem."

scruple to add that he had, at the King's request, brought CHAP. IV.
it for Anselm.[1] Would not the Archbishop pay something
for so great a benefit?[2] Would he not at least, now that
the pallium had come to him instead of his going for the
pallium, pay the sum which the journey to Rome would
otherwise have cost him?[3] Anselm would pay nothing. Anselm
The King had thus to make the best of a bad bargain. will not
pay for the
As Anselm would not pay for either friendship or pal- pallium.
lium, there was nothing to be done but to let him have
both friendship and pallium without paying. The King Anselm and
once more consulted his lay nobles, and, by their advice,[4] William
reconciled.
he restored Anselm to his full favour, he cancelled all
former causes of quarrel, he received him as archbishop
and ghostly father, and gave him the fullest licence to
exercise his office throughout the realm. One condition
only seems to have been made; Anselm was to promise
that he would observe the laws and customs of the
realm and would defend them against all men.[5] The
promise was made, but with the express or implied
reservation of duty to God.[6] That was indeed the
reservation which William most hated; but in his present
frame of mind he may have brought himself to consent

[1] Eadmer, Hist. Nov. 33. "Dominus papa Urbanus, rogatu domini
nostri regis, stolam illi archiepiscopatus per episcopum qui de Roma venit
direxit." The pallium, they said, was sent to the King, but the words
which follow show that they wished it to be understood that it was meant
for Anselm.

[2] "Tuum igitur erit considerare quid tanto beneficio dignum regi
rependas."

[3] "Laudamus et consulimus ut saltem quod in via expenderes si pro hoc
Romam ires regi des, ne si nihil feceris injurius judiceris." They enlarge
also on the dangers of the way; these had certainly proved fatal to some of
Anselm's predecessors. [4] "Principum suorum consilio usus."

[5] This is not mentioned now, but it comes out afterwards; Hist.
Nov. 39. See below, p. 588.

[6] Ib. 39. "Scio quippe me [Anselmum] spopondisse consuetudines
tuas, ipsas videlicet quas per rectitudinem et secundum Deum in regno
tuo possides, me secundum Deum servaturum, et eas per justitiam contra
omnes homines pro meo posse defensurum."

Their
friendly
discourse.

to it. Anselm came to Windsor, and was admitted by
the King to his most familiar converse in the sight of
the lords and of the whole multitude that had come
together.[1] Cardinal Walter came in at the lucky
moment, and was edified by the sight. He quoted the
scripture, "Behold, how good and joyful it is brethren
to dwell together in unity." He sat down beside the
friendly pair; he quoted other scriptures, and expressed
his sorrow that he himself had not had any hand in
the good work of bringing them together.

The wild bull and the feeble sheep thus seemed for
a moment to pull together as friendly yokefellows. But
a Norman king did not, in his character of wild bull, any
more than in his character of lion, altogether cast aside
his other character of fox. He, or Count Robert for him,
had one shift left. Or it might almost seem that it was
not the King's own shift, but merely the device of
flatterers who wished to win the royal favour by pro-
posing it. Would not the Archbishop, for the honour
of the King's majesty, take the pallium from the King's
hand?[2] Anselm had made no objection to receiving
the staff from the King's hand, for such was the ancient
custom of England. But with the pallium the King
had nothing to do; it belonged wholly to the authority
of Saint Peter and his successor.[3] Anselm therefore
refused to take the pallium from the King. The refusal
was so clearly according to all precedent, the proposal
the other way was such a manifest novelty, that nothing
more was said about the matter. It was settled that, on a

Anselm
asked to
take the
pallium
from the
King.

He refuses.

[1] Eadmer, Hist. Nov. 33. "Cum curiæ illius apud Windlesorum se
præsentasset et familiari alloquio in conspectu procerum et coadunatæ multitudinis ipsum detinuisset."

[2] "Ut pro regiæ majestatis honorificentia, illud per manum regis
susciperet."

[3] "Rationabiliter ostendens hoc donum non ad regiam dignitatem, sed
ad singularem beati Petri pertinere auctoritatem."

fixed day, the pallium should be laid on the altar of Christ снар. iv.
in the metropolitan church, and that Anselm should
take it thence, as from the hand of Saint Peter himself.[1]
The expression used is remarkable, as showing that the
popular character of these assemblies had not utterly
died out. "The whole multitude agreed."[2] They agreed Assent
most likely by a shout of Yea, Yea, rather than by any Assembly.
more formal vote; but in any case it was that voice of
the people which Eadmer at least knew to be the voice
of God.

The Archbishop and his faithful comrade now set out Anselm
for Canterbury. But he was called on to do some two re-
archiepiscopal acts by the way. They had hardly left pentant
Windsor when two bishops came to express their repentance for the crime of denying their metropolitan
at Rockingham.[3] These were the ritualist Osmund of Robert and
Salisbury, and Robert of Hereford, the friend of Wulfstan. Osmund.
It was believed that, besides the visit at the moment
of his departure, the saint of Worcester had again
appeared to Bishop Robert. He had warned him of
divers faults in his life and in the administration of
his diocese, giving him however good hopes if he mended
his ways.[4] Notwithstanding this voice from the dead,
Robert had consented to the counsel and deed of them
at Rockingham; he now came with Osmund to ask

---

[1] Eadmer, Hist. Nov. 34. "Quasi de manu beati Petri, pro summi
quo fungebatur pontificatus honore, sumeretur."

[2] "Adquievit istis multitudo omnis."

[3] "Pœnitentiam apud illum agentes pro culpa suæ abnegationis, quam
cum aliis coepiscopis suis fecerant apud Rochingeham."

[4] William of Malmesbury (Gest. Pont. 302) has two appearances of Saint
Wulfstan to Robert; but both come before Wulfstan's burial. The one here
meant is recorded by Florence (1095). Robert was, according to the Worcester writer, "vir magnæ religionis," and we have a pleasing picture of
"ambo patres nimia caritate in Dei dilectione et ad se invicem conjuncti."
In the Life of Wulfstan (Ang. Sac. i. 268) the Bishop of Hereford is "homo
seculi quidem fretus prudentia, sed nulla solutus illecebra."

CHAP. IV. pardon. Anselm turned into a little church by the way-side, and gave them absolution. Then and there too he did another act of archiepiscopal clemency to a more distant suffragan. Wilfrith Bishop of Saint David's had been—we are not told when—suspended for some fault— we are not told what. Anselm now restored him to his episcopal office.[1]

Wilfrith of Saint David's restored.

Anselm receives the pallium at Canterbury. June 10, 1095.

The Archbishop went on to Canterbury, and there awaited the coming of the Roman Cardinal. On the appointed day, a Sunday in June, Bishop Walter came. He was met with all worship by the convents of the two monasteries, Christ Church and Saint Augustine's, by a great body of clergy, and by a vast crowd of layfolk of both sexes. The Bishop of Albano bore the precious gift in a silver casket. As they drew near to Christ Church, Anselm, with bare feet, but in the full dress of his office, supported on either side by the suffragans who had come to the ceremony, met the procession. The pallium was laid on the altar; it was taken thence by the hand of Anselm, and reverently kissed by those who were near him.[2] The Archbishop was then clothed with his new badge of honour; nothing was now wanting to his position. Already invested, consecrated, clothed with full temporal and spiritual powers within his own province by the King and the bishops of England, he now received the solemn recognition of the rest of the

---

[1] Eadmer, Hist. Nov. 34. "Ibi etiam Wilfrido episcopo sancti David de Gualis quæ vulgo Dewi vocatur, ipsa hora reddidit episcopale officium, a quo, exigente culpa ejus, jam antea ipsemet illum suspenderat." Was Wilfrith there in person ? We shall hear of him again.

[2] Flor. Wig. 1095. "Pallium . . . quod juxta condictum die dominica, quæ erat iv. idus Junii, ab eodem [Waltero] Cantuariam super altare Salvatoris delatum, ab Anselmo assumptum est, atque ab omnibus pro reverentia S. Petri suppliciter deosculatum." The details come from Eadmer; the Chronicler tells only how Walter "þam arcebisceop Anselme uppon Pentecosten, of þæs papan healfe Urbanus, his pallium geaf, and he hine underfeng æt his arcestole on Cantwarabyrig."

Western Church, in the person of its chief Pontiff.[1] CHAP. IV.
Anselm and England were again in full fellowship with
the lawful occupier of the apostolic throne. Nothing
now was wanting. The Archbishop, clad in his pallium,
sang the mass. But, as at his consecration, men found
an evil omen in part of the words of the service. The
gospel of the day told of the man who made a great
supper and bade many, but whose unthankful guests
began to make excuse.[2]

The reception of the pallium by Anselm was the last
great ceremony done in the metropolitan church during
this his first primacy; it was one of the very few great
ceremonies done in the unaltered church of Lanfranc.
And, if we are to understand that all the suffragans of
Canterbury were present, one of them was soon taken
away. Not many days after Anselm first put on the pal- Death of
lium, his late penitent, Bishop Robert of Hereford, left the Bishop Robert of
world, to join for ever, as the charity of Worcester believed, Hereford. June 26,
the saintly friend whom he had twice wonderfully seen.[3] 1095.
Cardinal Walter meanwhile stayed in England during the The Legate
greater part of that year, and according to some accounts stays in England.
for some months of the year which followed. Notwith-
standing the good life for which the Chronicler gives

[1] I hardly know what to make of the words of Hugh of Flavigny
(Pertz, viii. 475); "Adeo auctoritas Romana apud Anglos avaritia et
cupiditate legatorum viluerat, ut eodem Albanense præsente et consentiente nec contradicente, immo præcipiente, Cantuariensis archiepiscopus
fidelitatem beato Petro et papæ juraverat salva fidelitate domini sui regis."
One cannot conceive any time during the Cardinal's visit in which Anselm
could be called on to make any such oath either to Pope or King except
at the time of his receiving the pallium; there may be some confusion
with the promise mentioned in p. 531.

[2] This coincidence is noticed by Eadmer, Hist. Nov. 34.

[3] Such is the pious belief of Florence; "Credi fas est, ipsum qui prius de
hoc sæculo ad Deum migravit sollicitudinem egisse sui dilectissimi, quem
in hoc sæculo reliquit, et ut quam citius simul ante Deum gauderent operam
dedisse."

CHAP. IV. him credit, he seems, like other Romans, to have been open to the King's special means of influence, and a foreign writer who had good means of knowing seems to speak of his general conduct in England as having greatly tended to bring his office into discredit.[1] His commission from Pope Urban was a large one. Among other things, he had to look to the better payment of the Romescot,[2] which, it will be remembered, had not always flowed regularly into the papal coffers even in the days of the Conqueror,[3] and which of course did not flow at all in the days when no Pope was acknowledged in England. He had also to enquire generally into the state of things in England, and to consult with Anselm as to the means of reform. It is plain however from most independent testimonies that the Archbishop and the Cardinal were by no means suited to work together. Two letters from Anselm to Walter throw a singular light on some points in the story which are not recorded in any narrative. The personal intercourse of the two prelates was interfered with by a cause which we should hardly have looked for, namely, the occupation of Anselm in the duties of a military command. But it is plain that Anselm did not look for much good from any special intercourse between himself and the Cardinal. He writes that private conferences between the two were of no use; they could do nothing without the King's consent and help.[4] But

Objects of Walter's mission.

His dealings with Anselm.

---

[1] Hugh of Flavigny, directly after the passage just quoted (Pertz, viii. 475), goes on to say, " Quæ res in tantum adoleverat, ut nullus ex parte papæ veniens honore debito exciperetur, nullus esset in Anglia archiepiscopus, episcopus, abbas, nedum monachus aut clericus, qui litteras apostolicas suscipere auderet, nedum obedire, nisi rex juberet."

[2] This is noticed by the Chronicler; "And se bisceop Waltear has on lande þæs geares syððan lange wunode, and man syððan þæt Romgesceot be him sende, swa man manegan gearan æror ne dyde."

[3] See N. C. vol. iv. p. 430.

[4] Epp. iii. 35. " Vestra prudentia non ignorat quia nos duo nihil effice-

Anselm seems to have taken a more constitutional view CHAP. IV.
of the way by which the King's consent and help was
to be got than the Roman Legate was likely to take.
Anselm says that they would meet to no purpose, except
when the King, the bishops, and the nobles, were all
near to be referred to.[1] This reads very much as if
Anselm was aware of some underhand practices between
the King and the Legate, and had no mind to meet the
emissary of Rome except when he himself would have
the constitutional voice of the nation to back him. But
as things stood at the moment, circumstances seem to
have hindered the meeting for which Walter seems to
have wished and Anselm not to have wished.

We are now in the thick of the revolt of Earl Robert The King's northern march.
of Mowbray, the tale of which will be told in full in
the next chapter. The King was on his march northward to put down the revolt. King, Archbishop, and
Legate, had parted as if the Legate at least was not to
see either of the other two again in England.[2] At such
a time the desired conference could not be held; and
Anselm himself was bound for the time within a very
narrow local range. While the King marched on towards Anselm entrusted with the defence of Canterbury.
Northumberland, the Archbishop was entrusted with the
care of Canterbury, perhaps of Kent generally, against

remus, nisi regi suggestum esset, ut ejus assensu et auxilio ad effectum
perduceretur quod disponeremus." The military history which this letter
casually opens to us, and of which we have no mention elsewhere, will come
in the next chapter.

[1] "Expecto reditum domini mei regis, et episcoporum et principum qui
cum eo sunt, quatenus illi quæ agenda sunt, opportune et rationabiliter sug-
geramus." So in the next letter (Epp. iii. 36) he says more distinctly that
he would like to meet the Cardinal, "si congruo tempore factum esset, id est
quando dominus meus rex, et episcopi, et principes hujus regni vobis præsentes aut propinqui erant."

[2] Epp. iii. 36. "Vos ab illis et ego a vobis discessimus, veluti non nos
in hac terra amplius invicem visuri."

CHAP. IV. an expected Norman invasion.[1] If Anselm's conscience would have allowed him to take part in actual warfare, we can hardly fancy that he would have proved a captain to the liking of the Red King. Yet it does sometimes happen that a simple sense of duty will carry a man with credit through business the most opposite to his own temper and habits. It is more likely however that the duty really laid upon Anselm, as upon Wulfstan at Worcester, was rather to keep the minds of the King's forces up to the mark by stirring exhortations, while the task of personally fighting and personally commanding was given to others. Still he was, both by the King's word of mouth and by his writ and seal, entrusted with the care of the district,[2] and he deemed it his duty not to leave Canterbury, except to go to any point that might be immediately threatened.[3] Why Walter could not have come to Canterbury is not clear. Anyhow personal communication was hindered, and to that hindrance we owe a letter which gives us a further insight into the almost incredible shamelessness of the King's courtly bishops. Walter, it is plain, had been rebuking them for their conduct towards Anselm. They were open to ecclesiastical censure for denying their archbishop, and he blames Anselm himself for too great lenity towards them.[4] Anselm pleads that they had returned to him and had promised obedience for the future.[5] The others, it would seem, had followed the

Letters between Anselm and Walter.

Position of the bishops.

[1] Epp. iii. 35. See the next chapter.

[2] Ib. "Rex ore suo mihi præcepit ... et postquam Cantuarberiam reddi mihi mandavit per litteras proprio sigillo signatas."

[3] Ib. "Idcirco de Cantuaria exire non audeo, nisi in illam partem ex qua hostium expectamus adventum."

[4] Ib. 36. "Quod quæritis a me cur et qua justitia episcopi alii me abnegantes a me discesserunt, nec sunt reversi dignam agentes pœnitentiam, hoc potius ab illis quærendum erat quam a me."

[5] Ib. "Reversi hactenus sunt ut illam obedientiam quam Cantuariensi sedi promiserant se mihi servaturos faterentur."

example of the Bishops of Hereford and Salisbury. But CHAP. IV.
it comes out in the letter that some of these undutiful
suffragans had taken up the strangest and most self-
condemning line of defence. These men, cringing slaves
of the King, who had carried every mean and insulting
message from the King to the Primate, who had laid
down the rule that neither bishops nor other men had
anything to do but to follow the King's will in all things,
were not ashamed to plead that Anselm was no lawful The
archbishop, that he could claim no duty from them, object
simply because he had done what they had themselves to Anselm's
done in a far greater degree. These faithful servants position.
of King William were not ashamed to urge that their
master and his kingdom had been in a state of schism,
cut off from the Catholic Church and its lawful head, and
that Anselm had been a partaker in the schism. He had
received investiture from a schismatic King; he had done
homage to that schismatic King, and had received consecration from schismatic bishops. In other words, they
plead that Anselm is no lawful archbishop, because he
had been consecrated by themselves.

A more shameless plea than this could hardly be
thought of, but Anselm does not seem stirred by its
shamelessness. He simply answers the doubt which was His
cast on his own appointment and consecration as calmly answer.
as if it had been started by some impartial outsider.[1]
Those who consecrated him were not schismatics; no
judgement had cut them off from the communion of the
Church. They had not cast off their allegiance to the
Roman Pontiff; they all professed obedience to the Roman

[1] Epp. iii. 36. "Dicitis quosdam illorum vobis dixisse ideo non offendisse
in me, quia permisi me a catholica ecclesia transferri ad schismaticos et
ab illis consecrari, si fieri, sicut additis, potest; et a schismatico rege
investituram accepisse, et illi fidelitatem et hominium fecisse, quos omnes
sciebam esse schismaticos et divisos ab ecclesia Christi, et a capite meo Urbano pontifice, quem ipsi, me audiente, abnegabant."

CHAP. IV. See; they had not in any way denied that Urban was the lawful Pope; they had simply, in the midst of the controversy which was going on, doubted whether it was their clear duty to receive him as such.[1] That his own position was perfectly good was shown by the conduct of the Pope himself. Urban knew all that had happened between him and the King, together with all the circumstances of his consecration. So knowing, he had treated him as lawfully consecrated, and had sent him the pallium by Walter's own hands.[2] If such objections had any force, why had not Walter spoken of them before he, Anselm, had received

Question about the monks of Christ Church.

the pallium?[3] Another passage in this letter would seem to imply that some complaint had been made as to Anselm's dealings with the monks of his own church. The Cardinal asks Anselm to leave them in free possession of their goods.[4] Anselm answers that he earnestly desires the peace and advantage of his monks, and with God's help he will do all that lies in his power to settle everything for their advantage.[5] Anselm and his

---

[1] Epp. iii. 36. "Illi non abnegabant canonicum Romanum pontificem, quicunque esset, nec Urbanum negabant esse pontificem; sed dubitabant propter illam quæ modo nata est dissensionem, et propter dubitationem illum suscipere quasi certum differebant; nec ullum judicium illos ab ecclesia segregaverat, et omnino obedientiam Romanæ sedis tenere se fatebantur et sub professione obedientiæ Romani pontificis me consecrarunt."

[2] Ib. "Denique dominus papa sciebat me esse consecratum et a quibus, et cui regi feceram quod feci. Et tamen pallium quod archiepiscopus Cantuariæ solet habere, mihi per vestram caritatem, non ut schismatico, sed ut accepto, non ut reprobans, sed ut approbans misit, et sic quod de me factum erat confirmavit."

[3] Ib. "Si vobis hæc calumnia attendenda videtur, cur eam ante pallii concessionem mihi tacuistis? Si negligenda putatur, vos judicate quam diligenter sit a vobis inculcanda."

[4] Ib. "Rogatis me ut fratres nostros Cantuariensis ecclesiæ quiete ac pacifice possidere dimittam res suas."

[5] Ib. "Nullus magis desiderat quietem ac pacem illorum quam ego, nec magis sollicitus est pro utilitate ejusdem ecclesiæ; et idcirco voluntas mea est ut res ejus, Deo annuente, disponam ad utilitatem præsentem et futuram, prout melius sciam et potero."

monks seem to have been commonly on the best of
terms. Still we seem here to see the beginnings of those
disputes which grew into such terrible storms a hundred
years later. The lands of the monks had, as we have
seen,[2] not been spared during the vacancy of the archbishopric. And it may be that some wrong had been
again done to them when the King was molesting the
Archbishop's men during the time of truce. We heard
not long ago of great complaints going up during that
time; some of them may have taken the formal shape
of an appeal to the Cardinal. Anselm's reeves may have
been no more scrupulous than the reeves of other men.
Indeed we find a curious witness that it was so. The
question was raised why Anselm, a monk and a special
lover of monks, did not always live at Canterbury, among
his monks.[1] Several answers are given. The most Anselm
remarkable is that his presence in his manors was and his tenants.
needed to protect his poorer tenants from the oppression
of his reeves.[2] When such care was needed on behalf
of the tenants, it is quite possible that the reeves might
sometimes meddle wrongfully with the possessions of
the monks also.

A time of peace for Anselm followed, though hardly
a time of peace for England. Before the year was out
the King had put down the revolt in Northumberland;
Earl Robert of Mowbray was his prisoner. An expedition against the Welsh was less successful, and Scotland
still remained under the king of her own choice. The

---

[1] This question is argued by Eadmer in the Life, ii. 1. 9.

[2] Ib. "Si Cantuariam assidue incoleret, homines sui ex advectione vic-
tualium oppido gravarentur; et insuper a præpositis, ut sæpe contingebat,
multis ex causis oppressi, si quem interpellarent, nunquam præsentem haberent, magis ac magis oppressi in destructionem funditus irent." Of the
doings of reeves of all kinds we have often heard. See specially N. C.
vol. iv. p. 616.

CHAP. IV.

Gemót of Windsor and Salisbury. Christmas, 1095–1096.

Christmas Gemót, of which we shall have presently to speak at length, was a famous, and, what was not usual in our early assemblies, a bloody gathering. It was held at Windsor and was then adjourned to Salisbury; at the former place at least Anselm was present, and he had an opportunity of showing Christian charity to an

Anselm attends the Bishop of Durham on his death-bed. January, 1096.

enemy. At Windsor Bishop William of Durham sickened and died. His latter days are so closely connected with the fall of Earl Robert that they will be better spoken of elsewhere. It is enough to say here that his last hours were cheered by the ghostly help of the holy man against whom he had so deeply sinned. Meanwhile Anselm, comforted by the recall of his friend Baldwin,[1] was doing his duty in peace; ruling, writing, exhorting, showing love to every living creature,[2] ever and anon

Consecration of bishops.

called on to discharge the special duties of his office. In this interval he consecrated two bishops to sees within the realm. The churches of Worcester and Hereford were vacant by the deaths of the two friends Wulfstan and Robert. Both sees were filled in the year after they fell vacant. Were they filled after the usual fashion of the Red King's day, or was Anselm, now, outwardly at least, in William's full favour, able during this interval of peace to bring about some relaxation of the crying evil of this reign? There is no direct statement either way; we can judge only by what we know of the characters of the two men appointed. Neither of them, one would think,

Samson Bishop of Worcester.

was altogether to the mind of Anselm. In the place of the holy Wulfstan, the diocese of Worcester received as its bishop, and the monks of Worcester received as their abbot, a canon of Bayeux, Samson by name, a

---

[1] Eadmer, Hist. Nov. 34.

[2] This would seem to be the time when Anselm's practice of various virtues is so fully described by Eadmer in the first and second chapters of the second book of the Life.

brother of Archbishop Thomas of York. The influence CHAP. IV.
of the Northern Primate may perhaps be seen in the
appointment of his kinsman to a see so closely connected with his own. Samson was one of the school
of learned men with whom Odo—it was his one redeeming merit — had filled his church of Bayeux.[1]
He was as yet only in deacon's orders, and he was
possibly married, at least he is said to have been
the father of the second archbishop Thomas of York.[2]
He seems to have been one of those prelates, who,
without any claim to special saintship, went through
their course at least decently. He was bountiful to all;
to the monks of Worcester he did no harm—some harm
seems to have been looked for from a secular—beyond
suppressing their dependent monastery of Westbury.[3]
Of the new Bishop of Hereford we know more. He was Gerard
that Gerard who had helped to bring Cardinal Walter Bishop of
to England, one of the King's clerks, not even in deacon's Archbishop
orders, and a thorough time-server.[4] We cannot help 1100.

Gerard
Bishop of
Hereford,
Archbishop
of York
1100.

---

[1] See N. C. vol. iv. p. 340. He appears in the Gesta Pontificum, 289, as
"Samson, canonicus Baiocensis, non parvæ literaturæ vir nec contemnendæ
facundiæ. Antiquorum homo morum, ipse liberaliter vesci, et aliis dapsi-
liter largiri." But this last description is substituted for an amazing account
of his appetite, specially in the way of fowls and swine's flesh (cf. the account of King Æthelred in N. C. vol. i. p. 658), and how he died of fat.
He fed however three hundred poor men daily.

[2] His kindred to the elder and the younger Thomas appears in the sup-
pressed passage of William of Malmesbury. Eadmer (Hist. Nov. 35) says
of the two bishops-elect, " Qui cum in summum promovendi sacerdotium ad
Anselmum pro more venissent, necdum omnes inferiores ordines habuissent,
ordinavit eos pro instanti necessitate, ad diaconatum et presbyteratum unum,
et alium ad presbyteratum." The canon of Bayeux would be more likely
than the King's clerk to have the higher degree.

[3] Will. Malms. Gest. Pont. 290. But the first and second versions are
worth comparing. It has a curiously modern sound when we read, " Quotiens Lundonia rediret, aliquid pretiosum afferret, quod esset ornamento
ecclesiæ." But it is a witness to the growing importance of London.

[4] William of Malmesbury has a first and a second edition (Gest. Pont.
259) in the case of Gerard also. According to rumour, "multorum criminum
et maxime libidini obnoxius erat." He was suspected of magic, from his

CHAP. IV.

Consecration of Gerard and Samson. June 6, 1096.
suspecting that his bishopric was not granted for nothing, whatever may have been the case with Samson at Worcester. The bishops-elect came to Anselm for consecration. He was then with his friend Gundulf at Lambeth, then a manor of the see of Rochester. In the chapel of the manor Anselm ordained them priests.[1] The next day he consecrated them in the cathedral church of London, with the help of four of his suffragans, three of whom, Thomas of York, Maurice of London, and Gundulf of Rochester, had in different ways a special interest in the ceremony. The fourth was Herbert, described as of Thetford or Norwich. It was in the course of this year that he began his great work in his last-named see.[2]

Anselm consecrates Irish bishops.
This year too Anselm was able to show that his style of Patriarch of all the nations beyond the sea was not an empty title. It was now that he consecrated two bishops to sees in Ireland, Samuel of Dublin and Malchus of Waterford. They were both Irish by birth, but monks of English monasteries, Samuel of Saint Alban's, Malchus of Winchester. They came with letters from the clergy and people of their sees, and from King Murtagh or Murchard, of whom we shall hear again, and who takes to himself the sounding title of King of Ireland. Both were consecrated by Anselm, Samuel at Winchester, Malchus at Canterbury.[3] It was no new claim; two predecessors of Samuel had already been consecrated by Lanfranc.

constant study of Julius Firmicus. According to Hugh of Flavigny (Pertz, viii. 496), he sacrificed a pig to the devil, while of his brother more wonderful things still were told. See Pertz, viii. 496, and Appendix G.

[1] Eadmer, Hist. Nov. 35.   [2] See above, p. 448, and Appendix X.

[3] Eadmer gives the account of these Irish bishops (Hist. Nov. 34, 36). Samuel is described as being "a rege Hiberniæ Murierdach nomine, necne a clero et populo in episcopatum ipsius civitatis electus est, atque ad Anselmum, juxta morem antiquum, sacrandus cum communi decreto directus." Of King Muirchertach, whose name is written endless ways, and whom it is

§ 6. *The Crusade and the Mortgage of Normandy.*
November, 1095–*March,* 1097.

We must now for a while again turn our eyes to Normandy, but to Normandy mainly as affected by the most
stirring scenes in the history of the world. We have Council of seen Urban at Piacenza; we have heard him there make $\substack{\text{Piacenza.}\\ \text{March 7,}}$ his appeal to Western Christendom on behalf of the op- 1095. pressed churches and nations of the East. Their cry
came up then, as it has come up in our own ears; and it
was answered in those days as one only among Christian
nations has been found to answer it in ours. In those
days the bulwark and queen of the Eastern lands still
stood untouched. The New Rome had not then to be
won back for Christendom; it had simply to be pre-
served. By the prince who still kept on the unbroken Appeal succession of Constantine and Diocletian and Augustus $\substack{\text{of the}\\ \text{Emperor}}$ the appeal was made which stirred the hearts of nations Alexios. as the heart of one man. The letters of Alexios had
been read at Piacenza; the great call from the mouth of Council of the Western Pontiff was made in the ears of a vaster $\substack{\text{Clermont.}\\ \text{November}}$ multitude still in the memorable assembly of Clermont. 18, 1095. But the tale of the first Crusade needs not to be told The first here. The writers of the time were naturally called $^{\text{Crusade.}}$ away from what might seem the smaller affairs of their
own lands to tell of the great struggle of two worlds.
Some of the fullest accounts of the gathering and march

well perhaps to shorten into Murtagh, we shall hear again. He was King
of Leinster, and Bretwalda, so to speak, of all Ireland, though it seems that
he was not acknowledged always and everywhere. He signs the letter to
Anselm which appears in Eadmer (Hist. Nov. 36) on behalf of Malchus,
which professes to come from the "clerus et populus oppidi Wataferdiæ, cum
rege Murchertacho, et episcopo Dofnaldo." There are also two letters of
Anselm to him (Ep. iii. 142, 147), chiefly about ecclesiastical reforms in
Ireland. Anselm also speaks of a brother Cornelius, whom the Irish king
had asked for, but who could not go, because he was taking care of his aged
father. This is one of those little personal touches which make us wish to
know more.

of the crusaders are to be found in the writings to which we are in the habit of turning in every page for the history of England and Normandy.[1] Our native Chronicler can spare only a few words, but those are most pithy

Bearing of the crusade on our story. words, to set forth the great stirring of the nations.[2] And in our present tale the holy war directly comes home to us, chiefly because so many men whom we have already heard of took a part in it. Above all, it places two of our chief actors before us in parts eminently characteristic of the two. We see how Duke Robert of Normandy went forth to show himself among the foremost and the worthiest in the struggle, and how King William of England took occasion of his brother's zeal to gain his duchy by money wrung from English households and English churches. I have noticed elsewhere,[3] as has been often noticed before, that the work of the first crusade was strictly the work of the nations, and of princes of

No king engaged in the first crusade. the second rank. Dukes and counts there were many in the crusading army, but no king of the West joined in its march. The Western Emperor was at open war with the Pope who preached the crusade. The kings of Spain had their own crusade to wage. The kings of England and France were of all men in their kingdoms the least likely to join in the enterprise. The kingdoms of the North were as yet hardly stirred by the voice of

The crusades a Latin movement. Urban. It is indeed plain that the whole movement was primarily a Latin movement. It is with a true instinct that the people of the East have from those days onward

Name of Franks. given the name of *Franks* to all the Christians of the West. It is a curious speculation, and one at which I have already hinted elsewhere, what would have been the share of England in the crusades, if there had been

---

[1] Orderic and William of Malmesbury stand conspicuous.

[2] See the Chronicle, 1096. I quoted the passage in N. C. vol. iv. p. 93.

[3] Ib.

no Norman Conquest.[1] As it was, the part of the Teutonic nations in the crusades is undoubtedly secondary
to that of the Latin nations. Germany takes no leading
part till a later stage; Scandinavia takes no leading
part at all; England is brought into the scene as an
appendage to Normandy. The English crusaders served Share of
under the banner of the Norman Duke.[2] Among the Normandy
secondary powers Flanders indeed appears among the Flanders.
foremost; but Flanders, a fief of the crown of Paris, was,
as a power, though not as a people, more Latin than
Teutonic. The elder Count Robert had won the honour
of forestalling the crusade by sending help to the
Eastern Emperor on his own account.[3] It was fittingly Place
in a Latin city, in a Gaulish city, that Urban, himself chosen for
by birth a Frenchman in the stricter sense,[4] called the
nations of the West to arms. But it was equally fitting
that it should not be within the immediate dominion of
a king who had no heart for the enterprise, of a king
whose own moral offences it was one of the duties of
the Pontiff and his council to denounce. Not in the
dominions of any king, not in the dominions of any of
the great dukes and counts who were in power on a
level with kings, but in the land of the lowlier counts,
not as yet dauphins, of Auvergne, the assembly met
whose acts were to lead to the winning back of the Holy
City for Christendom, but with which we are more
directly concerned as causing William the Red to reign
at Rouen as well as at Winchester.

---

[1] See N. C. vol. v. p. 356.   [2] Ib. p. 93.

[3] See above, p. 411.

[4] Urban came from Rheims, but it is important to remember how little
entitled Auvergne was in that day to the French name. This comes out
oddly enough in an entry in the Chronicle, 1102, when thieves of all parts
seem to have conspired to rob the minster of Peterborough; "þa coman
þeofas sum of Aluearnie, sum of France, and sum of Flanders, and breokan
þæt mynstre of Burh."

CHAP. IV.

Decrees of the council.

The preaching of the crusade was not the only business of the great assembly at Clermont. A crowd of canons of the usual kind were passed against the usual abuses. Those abuses were not confined to England and Normandy. We are told that in all the lands on our side of the Alps—and we may venture to doubt whether things were likely to be much better on the other side— simony prevailed among all classes of the clergy, while the laity had taken to put away their wives and to take to themselves the wives of other men.[1] The great example of this last fault was certainly King Philip of France, whose marriage or pretended marriage with Bertrada of Montfort, the wife of Count Fulk of Anjou, was one of the subjects of discussion at the council. All abuses of all these kinds were again denounced,

Lay investiture forbidden.

as they had often been denounced before, and were often to be denounced again. But what concerns us more immediately is the decree that no bishop, abbot, or clerk of any rank, should receive any ecclesiastical benefice from the hand of any prince or other layman.[2]

[1] William of Malmesbury (iv. 344) draws a grievous picture of the state of things among the "Cisalpini," who "ad hæc calamitatis omnes devenerant, ut nullis vel minimis causis extantibus quisque alium caperet, nec nisi magno redemptum abire sineret." He then speaks at some length of simony, and adds; "Tunc legitimis uxoribus exclusis, multi contrahebant divortium, alienum expugnantes matrimonium; quare, quia in his et illis erat confusa criminum silva, ad pœnam quorundam potentiorum designata sunt nomina."

[2] The great provision of all is (Will. Malms. iv. 345), "Quod ecclesia catholica sit in fide, casta, libera ab omni servitute; ut episcopi, vel abbates, vel aliquis de clero, aliquam ecclesiasticam dignitatem de manu principum vel quorumlibet laicorum non accipiant." This decree does not appear among the acts of Piacenza in Bernold, 1095 (Pertz, v. 462).

Among so many more stirring affairs, one decree of this council, which has a good deal of interest, might easily be forgotten. This is one which was meant to reform the abuses of the privileges of sanctuary; "Qui ad ecclesiam vel ad crucem confugerint, data membrorum impunitate, justitiæ tradantur, vel innocentes liberentur." Are we to see here the first beginning of a feeling against mutilation, which came in bit by bit in the

This struck straight at the ancient use both of Eng- _{CHAP. IV.}
land and of Normandy. It forbad what Gregory the
Seventh had, if not allowed, at least winked at,
during his whole reign, in the case of the common
sovereign of those two lands.[1] This decree, we cannot
doubt, had an important bearing on the future position
of Anselm. Wibert, calling himself Clement, was of Sentences
course excommunicated afresh, along with the Emperor against Clement
as his supporter. So were the King of the French and and the Emperor;
his pretended queen, for their adulterous marriage. So against
were all who should call them King and Queen or Lord Philip and Bertrada.
and Lady, or should so much as speak to either of them
for any other purpose except to rebuke their offences.[2]
The thunders of the Church could have found only one
more fitting object than the reformation of this great
moral scandal. But we see to what a height ecclesiastical
claims had grown, when the council took on itself to declare the offenders deprived of their royal dignity and their
feudal rights. Then followed the great discourse which
called men to the Holy War. Urban told how, of the Urban
three parts of the world, the infidels had rent away two preaches the cru-
from Christendom; how Asia and Africa were theirs— sades;
a saying wholly true of Africa, and which, when the his geography.
Turk held Nikaia, seemed even more true of Asia than
it really was. Europe alone was left, our little portion.
Of that, Spain had been lost—the Almoravids had come

next century? The guilty man is to be punished, but in some other way
than by loss of limb.   [1] See N. C. vol. iv. p. 429.

[2] Philip had professed all intention of coming to Piacenza; he had even
set out; "Se ad illam itiner incepisse, sed legitimis soniis se impeditum
fuisse mandavit." (Bernold, u. s.) He was allowed, like Anselm, "indutiæ"
till Whitsuntide; but now the decree went forth (Will. Malms. iv. 345)
against Philip himself; "Et omnes qui eum vel regem vel dominum suum
vocaverint, et ei obedierint, et ei locuti fuerint nisi quod pertinet ad eum
corrigendum. Similiter et illam maledictam conjugem ejus, et omnes qui
eam reginam vel dominam nominaverint, quousque ad emendationem vene-
rint, ita ut alter ab altero discedat."

CHAP. IV. in since our last glimpse of Spanish matters[1]—while most of the northern parts of Europe itself were still shrouded in heathen darkness. It needs some little effort to remember how true to the letter Urban's religious geography was. The south-western peninsula was then, what the south-eastern is now, the land of Christian nations slowly winning back their own from infidel masters. And, before Swedish kings had crossed the Baltic, before Sword-brothers and Teutonic knights had arisen, before Russia had made her way northward, southward, and eastward, all north-eastern Europe was still heathen, while Scandinavia, Poland, and Hungary, were still recent conquests for the faith. Into the central strip of Christian land which lay between the heathen of the north and the Turks and Saracens of the south, east, and west, the enemy was now ready to cross. Urban called on his hearers to go forth and stop the way; and not a few of the men whose names have been famous, some whose names have been infamous, in our own story were among the foremost to go forth on the holy errand to which the voice of the Pontiff called them.

French and other crusaders.

Those among the recorded crusaders whose names come more immediately home to Englishmen did not join the holy war till a later time. But not a few names which have been long familiar to us are to be found in the list of those who joined in the first regular expedition which set forth in the course of the year which followed the assembly at Clermont. Beyond the bounds of England and Normandy we may mark the names of Hugh surnamed the Great, the brother of King Philip, Count of Vermandois, Count of Valois in succession to the holy Simon,[2] but who appears in our chief list of crusaders by the lowlier title of the Count of Crêpy. He went to the work, leaving his fiefs to

1096.

Hugh brother of King Philip.

---

[1] See N. C. vol. iv. p. 696.　　　　[2] Ib. vol. iv. p. 648.

his sons. His daughter Isabel or Elizabeth he gave in CHAP. IV.
marriage to Count Robert of Meulan, by this time no Robert of
Meulan
very youthful bridegroom.[1] Among princes of greater marries his
daughter.
power, but of less lofty birth, the foreign allies of the
Norman house were represented by the younger Count Robert of
Flanders
Robert of Flanders, nephew of the Conqueror's queen, and
and by Stephen Count of Chartres and Blois, husband of Stephen of
Chartres.
the Conqueror's noblest child, and father of a king of
England and of a bishop of an English see more personally
eminent than his royal brother. Rotrou of Mortagne and
Walter of Saint Valery went from the border lands so
closely connected with Norman history. In Everard of
Puiset we hear the name of a house which was in the
next century to become famous in England on the throne
of Saint Cuthberht, the throne at that moment empty and
widowed by the death of William of Saint-Calais. And The
brothers
from a house most hateful to England, but which had re-from
ceived no small share of the spoils of England, went forth Boulogne;
three brethren, one of whom was to show himself the worthiest, and to be placed the highest, in the crusading host.
Eustace of Boulogne, a prince beyond the sea but in Eustace,
England lord of lands scattered from Mendip to the
Kentish and East-Saxon shores,[2] marched with his two
brothers, both of whom were to reign as kings in the
Holy City. The part of Baldwin in the enterprise had Baldwin,
been already foreshadowed in visions told in the hall of
Conches.[3] Visions were hardly needed to foretell the

---

[1] The marriage is recorded by Orderic (vii. 23 D). There is a letter of
Bishop Ivo of Chartres addressed to the clergy of Meulan and to all persons within the archdeaconry of Poissy. He denounces the intended marriage
on the ground of kindred, and bids them send the letter to the Count of
Meulan. The kindred is said to be " nec ignota, nec remota ;" but it consisted
in this, that Robert and Isabel had a common forefather removed by four
degrees from Robert and five from Isabel. Robert was thus, as we should
have expected, a generation older than his wife.

[2] See N. C. vol. iv. pp. 130, 166, 744.

[3] See above, p. 269.

CHAP. IV.

Godfrey of Lorraine.

greatness of Godfrey of Lorraine, who had won his duchy as the prize of faithful service to the Emperor, but who was none the less ready to discharge the duties of a higher allegiance at the bidding of the Pontiff. From Normandy itself went, among a crowd of others, some of that younger generation which is beginning to supply

Norman crusaders.

the chief actors in our tale. Philip, the son of the lately deceased Roger of Montgomery, Ivo and Alberic the sons of the lately deceased Hugh of Grantmesnil,[1] all went forth; so did Gerard of Gournay and his wife Eadgyth, he to die, she to come back for another marriage.[2] And with them went another married pair whose names carry

Ralph of Wader.

us back to earlier times. The double traitor, Ralph of Wader, traitor to England, traitor to William, went forth with his valiant Emma, to do something to wipe out his old crimes by good service beneath the walls of Nikaia, and to leave his bones and hers in lands where his memory was not a memory of shame.[3]

Duke Robert.

We may be sure that among the crowd of men of every rank who were stirred by the voice of Urban none took up the cross with a more single mind than the Duke of the Normans. It was an appeal which spoke at once to the better side of him, an appeal which took him away from that land of his birth and dominion which was to him a land of such utter failure. As a son and a ruler, he had much to repent of; as a warrior, a worthy object of warfare was for the first time opened to him.

His need of money.

But how was he to go, at least how was he to go as became the prince of a duchy which under other princes had been so great? His hoard was empty; half his barons

[1] See above, p. 473.

[2] Her second marriage with Drogo of Moncey is recorded in Will. Gem. viii. 8. Drogo was a fellow crusader (Ord. Vit. 723 D).

[3] See Ord. Vit. 535 C, 724 C, 729 D, where we hear of him before Nikaia.

were in practical rebellion; his brothers held no small CHAP. IV.
part of his duchy. He had no resource but one, to seek He is
help, at whatever cost, from the brother who could com- driven to apply to
mand the wealth of England, even though the price should William.
be nothing short of yielding the whole of Normandy to
him who already held a part. It is needless to say
that King William of England had no thought of going
on the crusade himself. He was not indeed hindered, as Position of
the Emperor and the King of the French were hindered, William.
by actually lying under the censures of the Church.
But he was as little likely as either of them to gird on
his sword in the great quarrel. The voice which stirred
the heart of Robert to the quick found no kindred chord
to strike on in the mocking soul of Rufus. The enemy
of God felt no call to march in the cause of God. He
was not likely to spend his treasures or to display his
chivalry in warfare which could not bring him any direct
increase of wealth or power. It was rather for him to
stay at home, and to reap what he could in the way of
either wealth or power at the cost of those whose madness led them on errands which could bring in neither.
Palestine was far away and hard to win. Normandy,
so much as was left of Normandy, so much as was not
already his own, was near and was easy to win with his
own special arms. William Rufus was not at all likely
to turn aside from any offer of the kind which Robert
might make to him.

The brothers were however at war, and the services of Mission
a mediator were needed to open negotiations between of Abbot Jeronto.
them. The Pope becomingly undertook the office, and
sent a prelate from the more distant parts of Gaul,
Jeronto, Abbot of Saint Benignus at Dijon, to make
peace between the King and the Duke. We are told
that Walter of Albano's greediness and subserviency to

CHAP. IV.   the King had brought the name of Legate, and of Rome itself, into discredit. Jeronto was therefore trusted with a commission to make an appeal to William, such as Walter had clearly never made, about the evils which were allowed to go on under his government.[1]   Of the two branches of this commission one prospered better than the other.   At first, we are told, the Abbot's righteous boldness and plainness of speech seemed to have made an effect on the King, while it raised general hopes of reform among the nation.[2]   But the King or his counsellors knew how to deal, if not with Abbot Jeronto, at least with those in greater authority.   He had, so the story runs, sent a messenger of his own to the Pope— most likely during his sojourn in northern Gaul, of which we shall hear again—carrying with him the weighty argument of ten marks of the purest gold.[3]   Trusting to this means of gaining his end, the King kept the Abbot of Dijon with him, till the Easter of the next year.   By that time the King's messenger came back, bringing with him a commissioner from the Pope, a layman, the sister's son of Urban, by whose word of mouth it would seem the Abbot's commission was cancelled and all questions were adjourned till the next Christmas.[4]   When the next

Jeronto rebukes William.

The Pope sends his nephew. Easter, April 13, 1096.

---

[1] This comes from Hugh of Flavigny, Pertz, viii. 474; "Tunc temporis pro componenda inter fratres Willelmi regis filios concordia, Willelmum videlicet regem Anglorum et Robertum comitem Normannorum, abbas Divionensis ex præcepto papæ mare transierat, et ut præscriptum regem ammoneret de multis quæ illicite fiebant ab eo, de episcopatibus videlicet et abbatiis quas sibi retinebat, nec eis pastores providebat, et reditus proventusque omnium sibi assumebat, de symonia, de fornicatione clericorum."

[2] Ib. "Qui veniens tanta libertate usus est, ut rex, integritate ejus inspecta et inadulata mentis constantia, se consiliis et votis ejus adquieturum promitteret, ut omnes fideles gratularentur eum advenisse, ad cujus adventum quasi respiraret et resurgeret decus et vigor ecclesiæ Anglicæ et libertas Romanæ auctoritatis."

[3] Ib. "Sed quid imperturbatum relinquit inexplebilis gurges Romanæ avaritiæ? Rex suspectam habens viri auctoritatem, quem jam diu venturum audierat, legatum papæ præmiserat, et in manu ejus auri probati et purissimi 10 marchas."   [4] See Appendix AA.

Christmas came, the King was not in England, to attend CHAP. IV. to ecclesiastical reform or to anything else.

The other object for which Jeronto came to England Peace between Robert and William. was fully carried out, whether Jeronto himself had any real hand in bringing it about or not. Peace was made between the Duke of the Normans and the King of the English. In order that Robert might have money to go Normandy pledged to William. to the crusade, the duchy of Normandy was pledged to his brother for a sum of ten thousand marks. The trans- 1096. action was not a cession or a sale; it was a mere pledge. The duchy was to pass to William merely for a season, for three years, or for so long a time as Robert should be away. If the Duke should come back, and should find himself able to pay the money, the duchy was to be his again.[1] Still William's possession seemed likely to be a lasting one. There seemed but small chance of Robert's

---

[1] The accounts do not exactly agree; but every version makes the terms such that the duchy was not ceded for ever, but could under some circumstances be recovered. The Chronicler puts it pithily, but without details; "Đurh þas fare [that is the crusade] wearð se cyng and his broðor Rodbeard eorl sehte swa þæt se cyng ofer sæ fór, and eall Normandig æt him mid feo alisde, swa swa hi þa sehte wæron." Florence calls the transaction "vadimonium," and mentions the price, 10,000 marks, or 6,666*l.* With this William of Malmesbury agrees; Eadmer and Hugh of Flavigny make it a pledge for three years. Hugh's words (Pertz, viii. 475) are; "Pro componenda inter fratres pacis concordia in Normannia substitit donec, pace facta, decem milium marcarum pensione accepta, terram suam comes Normanniæ regi Anglorum usque ad trium annorum spacium custodiendam traderet." "Pensio" must here be taken in the sense of a single payment. Eadmer's words are; "Normanniam spatio trium annorum pecuniæ gratis in dominium tradidit." Orderic (723 A) makes the time five years; "Rex Anglorum .... Normanniam usque ad quinque annos servaturus recepit, fratrique suo ad viam Domini peragendam decem milia marcos argenti erogavit." Robert of Torigny (Will. Gem. viii. 7) mentions no number of years, but makes the bargain last as long as Robert shall be away; "Rex Willelmus in Normanniam transfretans, decies mille marcas argenti ea conditione Roberto duci commodavit, ut quamdiu idem Dux in prædicta peregrinatione moraretur, ipse ducatum Normanniæ pro eis vadem haberet, illum duci restituturus cum ipse sibi prætaxatam pecuniam rediens reconsignasset."

CHAP. IV. ever coming back, and smaller still of his coming back with ten thousand marks to spare out of the spoils of the infidels. If he ever did come so laden, William Rufus doubtless trusted that, by some means either of force or of fraud, his brother's restoration to his duchy might be either evaded or withstood.

The price not large. The price for which Normandy was thus handed over does not, when compared with other payments of the time, seem a large one. It was not very much higher than the sums which Herbert Losinga was said to have paid for a bishopric for himself and an abbey for his father.[1] The price to be paid for at least a three years' possession of all Normandy was not much more than three times the sum which courtiers at least had looked on as a reasonable contribution for an Archbishop of Canterbury to make towards a single Norman expe-

Heavy taxation to raise the money. dition.[2] Yet the sum which was now to be paid is spoken of as a drain upon the whole kingdom. Rufus had no thought of paying the money out of any rightful revenues of the crown or out of any stores which he had already wrung from his people. Something was to be wrung from them yet again for the special object of the moment. The time would seem to have been the summer of the year which followed the gathering at Clermont, the year which in England began with the death of Bishop William of Durham and the frightful punishment

Whitsun Assembly, 1096. of Count William of Eu. The matter may have been discussed at the Whitsun Assembly of that year, of which we have no record. At any rate a heavy tax was laid on the whole kingdom; we may be sure that the Red King took the occasion to wring more out of the land than the actual sum which he had to pay to his brother. Otherwise, except on the view that everything had been taken already, the payment of a sum less than

[1] See Appendix X.   [2] See above, p. 438.

seven thousand pounds could hardly have weighed on CHAP. IV.
the whole kingdom as this benevolence is said to have
weighed. For a benevolence it was, at least in form; Extortion
men were invited to give or to lend; but we gather that of the be-
nevolence.
some more stringent means was found for those who
failed to give or to lend willingly.[1] The English
Chronicler sends up his wail for the heavy time that it
was by reason of the manifold gelds, and he tells us
how, as so often happened, hunger followed in the wake
of the extortioner.[2] Other writers describe the King as
demanding loans and gifts from his prelates, earls, and
other great men. The great lay lords, we are told, raised Oppression
their share by the plunder of the knights who held fiefs of tenants.
of them and of the churls who tilled their demesne lands.[3]
It is the cry of these last that we hear through the voice
of the Chronicler. The bishops and abbots are said to Protest
have made a protest, a thing which almost passes belief of the
prelates.
on the part of the bishops of the Red King's day. When
called on for their shares, they are said to have answered,
in the spirit, or at least in the words, of Ælfheah, that
they could not raise the money by any means save the
oppression of the wretched tillers of the earth.[4] Judged
by the conduct of the two classes at Rockingham, the
prelates and the lay barons seem to have changed places.
It is the churchmen now who have the conscientious Compari-
scruple. Yet the difference is not wonderful. The barons son of the
prelates
were used to general havoc and violence of every kind; and the
lay lords.

[1] Eadmer, Hist. Nov. 35. "Quæ pecunia per Angliam, partim data,
partim exacta, totum regnum in immensum vastavit."

[2] Chron. Petrib. 1096. "Ðis wæs swiðe hefigtíme gear geond eall Angel-
cyn, ægðer ge þurh mænigfealde gylda and eac þurh swiðe hefigtymne
hunger, þe þisne eard þæs geares swiðe gedrehte."

[3] Flor. Wig. 1091. "Comites, barones, vicecomites, suos milites et
villanos spoliaverunt."

[4] Will. Malms. iv. 318. "Super violentia querimoniam facientes, non
se posse ad tantum vectigal sufficere, nisi si miseros agricolas omnino
effugarent."

CHAP. IV. what they scrupled at was the deliberate perversion of formal justice to crush a single man who claimed their reverence on every ground, official and personal. The prelates, on the other hand, might be ready for any amount of cringing and cowardice, and might yet shrink from being made the agents of direct oppression in their own persons. Anyhow another means of payment was suggested by the cunning agents of the impious King. It may have been the future Bishop of Durham who answered, "Have ye not chests full of the bones of dead men, but wrought about with gold and silver?"[1] In this strait the churchmen took the sacrilegious hint. The most sacred objects were not spared; books of the gospels, shrines, crucifixes, were spoiled of their precious ornaments, chalices were melted down, all the gifts of the bounty of the old time were seized on, not to relieve the poor, but to fill the coffers of the King with the money that was needed for his ambitious schemes.[2]

Plunder of the churches.

In all this we have learned to suspect some exaggeration; extreme measures taken at some particular places must have been spoken of as if they had been universal throughout the land. In one case, and that the case of the highest personal interest, we get the details, and they are a good deal less frightful than the general picture. Among the other great men of the land, the Archbishop of Canterbury was called on for his contribution. His friends advised compliance with the request, and he himself did not complain of it as

Contribution of Anselm.

---

[1] Will. Malms. iv. 318. "Quibus curiales, turbido, ut solebant, vultu, 'Non habetis,' inquiunt, 'scrinia auro et argento composita, ossibus mortuorum plena? nullo alio responso obsecrantes dignati.'"

[2] Ib. "Ita illi, intelligentes quo responsio tenderet, capsas sanctorum nudaverunt, crucifixos despoliaverunt, calices conflarunt, non in usum pauperum, sed in fiscum regium: quicquid enim pene sancta servavit avorum parcitas, illorum grassatorum absumsit aviditas." Cf. the account of the spoliation of Waltham in Appendix H.

unreasonable.[1] But Anselm had no great store of money
in hand. He consulted the Bishops of Winchester and
Rochester, Walkelin and Gundulf, and by their advice
he borrowed a sum of money from the hoard of his
monks, who seem to have been better provided than
himself. The convent, by a vote of the majority, agreed He mort-
to help the Archbishop with a present sum of two gages the
manor of
hundred pounds, in return for which Anselm made over Peckham
to them for seven years his manor of Peckham, which to his
monks.
brought in thirty pounds yearly. The money supplied
by the monks, together with what Anselm could raise
himself, made up a sum which seems to have satisfied
the King; at least no complaint or dispute is recorded.[2]

The ten thousand marks were raised and paid. We
may well believe that more than the ten thousand
marks were raised; but we may be sure that not a
penny more than his bargain entitled him to found its
way into the hands of Duke Robert. In September the
whole business was finished. King William crossed the Conference
sea, and met his brother in a conference held under the between
William
mediation of the King of the French, at some point of and Robert.
the border-land of the Vexin, at Pontoise or at Chaumont, places of which we shall have to speak again.[3]

[1] Eadmer, Hist. Nov. 35. "Conventus est et Anselmus per id temporis,
et ut ipse quoque manum auxilii sui in tam rationabili causa regi exten-
deret, a quibusdam suis est amicis admonitus."

[2] Eadmer describes this transaction at length; and adds that Anselm
gave the two hundred pounds to the King, "cum illis quæ de suis habere
poterat pro instanti necessitate, ut rebus consuleret."

[3] This fact comes from a letter of Bishop Ivo of Chartres (Du Chesne, iv.
219) addressed to King Philip; "Excellentiæ vestræ litteras nuper accepi,
quibus submonebar ut apud Pontesium vel Calvummontem cum manu
militum vobis die quam statueratis occurrerem, iturus vobiscum ad placitum quod futurum est inter regem Anglorum, et comitem Normannorum,
quod facere ad præsens magnæ et multæ causæ me prohibent." One of these
reasons is that he will not have anything to do with Bertrada, against
whom he again strongly exhorts the King. He himself will not be safe in

CHAP. IV.

Robert
sets forth
on the
Crusade.
September,
1096.

His com-
panions,
Robert,
Stephen,
and Odo.

The money was paid to the Duke; the duchy was handed over to the King, and Robert of Normandy set forth for the holy war. He went in company with his cousin the Count of Flanders and his brother-in-law the Count of Chartres. And with them went a kinsman of an elder generation, whose long history, though not specially long life, is now drawing to an end. Bishop Odo of Bayeux could not bear to stay in Normandy again to become a subject of the nephew to whom he had surrendered himself at Rochester.[1] He joined the forces of his elder nephew, and with him went the eloquent Bishop of Evreux, Gilbert, who had preached the

Conduct of
Robert.

funeral sermon of the Conqueror.[2] The Duke on his armed pilgrimage showed new powers. He could now, often but not always, overcome his love of idleness and pleasure, and whenever the moment of real danger came, he was ever foremost, not only in the mere daring of the soldier, but in the skill and counsel of the commander.[3] Another hand has traced his course with all

the King's court, because of her devices; such at least seems to be the meaning of the general remark, "Postremo novit vestra serenitas, quia non est mihi in curia vestra plena securitas, in qua ille sexus mihi est suspectus et infestus, qui etiam amicis aliquando non satis est fidus." Another reason is more curious, and seems to imply that some fighting was looked for; "Præterea casati ecclesiæ, et reliqui milites pene omnes vel absunt, vel pro pace violata excommunicati sunt: quos sine satisfactione reconciliare non valeo et excommunicatos in hostem mittere non debeo."

[1] Ord. Vit. 675 A. "Odo Baiocensis episcopus cum Rodberto duce, nepote suo, peregrinatus est. Tantus enim erat rancor inter ipsum et regem pro transactis simultatibus, ut nullatenus pacificari possent ab ullis caduceatoribus. Rex siquidem magnanimus et iracundus et tenacis erat memoriæ, nec injuriam sibimet irrogatam facile obliviscebatur sine ultione."

[2] See N. C. vol. iv. p. 714.

[3] We learn a great deal about Robert on the crusade from the Life of Lanfranc by Ralph of Caen, in the fifth volume of Muratori. One passage describing his character has been already quoted. We shall see some special cases as we go on. But it is worth while to compare the "regius sanguis Willelmides" of c. 22 with the picture in c. 58. In this last Robert makes up to the English at Laodikeia "spe dominationis." Were they to help him in any attempt on the English crown?

vividness, but with less sympathy than one could have CHAP. IV.
wished for the general objects of the holy war.[1] A few
points in Robert's eastern career are all that need now be
touched on. He and his companions passed by Lucca, and
there received the blessing of the orthodox Pope Urban.[2]
They went on to what should have been Urban's see, Robert at
and found how truly the English Chronicler spoke when Rome.
he said that Urban nothing had of the settle at Rome.
When they went to pay their devotions in the basilica of
Saint Peter, they met with much such entertainment
from the followers of the schismatic Clement as the
monks of Glastonbury had met with from their abbot
Thurstan.[3] They reached southern Italy, now a duchy His recep-
of the house of Hauteville, and the reigning Duke tion by
Roger of
Roger, son of the renowned Wiscard, is said to have Apulia.
welcomed his natural lord in the head of the ducal
house of his ancestral land.[4]

At the time of their coming, Duke Roger, his uncle
Count Roger of Sicily, who had won back a realm for
Christendom, and his brother Bohemond—Mark Bohe-

---

[1] I refer to Sir Francis Palgrave's chapter "Robert the Crusader," the
eleventh in the fourth volume of his "Normandy and England." He goes
further off from the scene of our common story than I can undertake to
follow him.

[2] Will. Malms. iv. 350. But our best account just at this moment is that
by Fulcher of Chartres in the "Gesta Dei per Francos," which Orderic
(718 B) witnesses to as a "certum et verax volumen." Here we read (385),
"Nos Franci occidentales, per Italiam excursa Gallia transeuntes cum
usque Lucam pervenissemus, invenimus prope urbem illam Urbanum apostolicum, cum quo locuti sunt comes Robertus Normannus, et comes Stephanus, nos quoque cæteri qui voluimus."

[3] Fulcher (u. s.) graphically describes this scene; "Cum in basilica
beati Petri introissemus, invenimus ante altare homines Guiberti, papæ
stolidi, qui oblationes altari superpositas, gladios suos in manibus tenentes,
inique arripiebant : alii vero super trabes ejusdem monasterii cursitabant ;
et inde deorsum ubi prostrati orabamus, lapides jaciebant."

[4] Ord. Vit. 724 D. "Rogerius dux, cognomento Bursa, ducem Normanniæ cum sociis suis, utpote naturalem dominum suum, honorifice
suscepit."

CHAP. IV.

Siege of
Amalfi.

Bohemond
takes the
cross.

The cru-
saders
winter in
Apulia.
1096-1097.

mond we find him accurately called[1]—were warring against the famous merchant town of Amalfi,[2] rebellious in their eyes against the Norman Duke, in its own eyes loyal to the Eastern Emperor. At the coming of the crusaders Bohemond took the cross, and rent up a goodly cloak into crosses for his followers.[3] Count Roger was left almost alone to besiege Amalfi, and he went back to his own island. Yet, after this outburst of pious zeal, those who were highest in rank among the warriors of the cross tarried to spend a merry winter in that pleasant land, while many of the lower sort, already weary of the work, turned aside and went back to their homes.[4] The Norman prelates, from whatever motives, crossed to the great island of the Mediterranean, a trophy of Norman victory only second to the yet greater island of the Ocean. There, under the rule of the Great Count of Sicily, the whilom Earl of Kent might see how conquerors of his own blood could deal

[1] He is "Marcus Buamundus" in Orderic, who afterwards (817 A) tells the story of his two names. When he went through Gaul, he stood godfather to many children, "quibus etiam cognomen suum imponebat. Marcus quippe in baptismate nominatus est ; sed a patre suo, audita in convivio joculari fabula de Buamundo gigante, puero jocunde impositum est. Quod nimirum postea per totum mundum personuit, et innumeris in tripertito climate orbis alacriter innotuit. Hoc exinde nomen celebre divulgatum est in Galliis, quod antea inusitatum erat pene omnibus occiduis." Orderic is always careful about names, specially double names. See another account in Will. Malms. iv. 387.

[2] Orderic (724 D) says merely "quoddam castrum," but it appears from Geoffrey Malaterra (iv. 24) and Lupus Protospata, 1096 (Muratori, v. 47), that the place besieged was Amalfi. Count Roger of Sicily brought with him ten thousand Saracens.

[3] Ord. Vit. u. s. "Sibi tandem optimum afferri pallium præcepit, quod per particulas concidit, et crucem unicuique suorum distribuit, suamque sibi retinuit."

[4] Fulcher, 585. "Tunc plurimi de pauperibus vel ignavis, inopiam futuram metuentes, arcubus suis venditis, et baculis peregrinationis resumptis, ad mansiones suas regressi sunt. Qua de re viles tam Deo quam hominibus facti sunt : et versum est eis in opprobrium." So William of Malmesbury, iv. 353, who adds that "pars pro intemperie soli morbo defecit."

with the men of conquered lands after another sort from CHAP. IV.
that in which he had dealt with the men of his English
earldom. There, in the happy city of the threefold
speech,[1] the Bishop of Bayeux might mark, in the
great temple of Palermo, once church, then mosque, and
now church once more, those forms of art of the Greek
and the Saracen, which had lost in grace, if they had
gained in strength, in taking the shapes which he had
himself followed in his great work in his own Saxon
city. There the Earl and Bishop at last ended a career of Odo dies
which Kent and Bayeux could tell so different a tale. at Palermo.
February,
Gilbert of Evreux discharged the last corporal work of 1097.
mercy for his fiercer brother; and the tomb of Odo of
Bayeux arose within the walls of the great church of
Palermo, soon to boast itself the head of the Sicilian
realm.[2] And, after all the changes of later days, amid
the small remains which the barbarians of the *Renais-*
sance have left us of the church of English Walter, we
may, even beside the tomb of the Wonder of the World,
stop for a moment to remember that the brother of our
Conqueror, the scourge of our land, found his last
resting-place so far away alike from Bayeux, from
Senlac, and from Rochester.

The Bishop went no further than Palermo; the Duke Duke
went on by the course which the warfare of the Apulian Robert
crosses to
Normans had lately made familiar. They entered the Dyrrha-
chion.
Eastern world at Dyrrhachion, where the valour of Normans and Englishmen had been lately proved.[3] They Use of the
passed, in the geography of our authors, through Bul- Bulgarian
name.
garia;[4] that is, they passed through those Illyrian and

---

[1] See Historical Essays, Third Series, 473, 474.

[2] Ord. Vit. 765 B, C. [3] See N. C. vol. iv. pp. 625, 626.

[4] Orderic (u. s.) says, "tranquillo remige in Bulgariæ partibus applicuit."
Fulcher is naturally more exact. They land at Dyrrhachion (386), and
then "Bulgarorum regiones, per montium prærupta et loca satis deserta,
transivimus." He gives several curious details of the voyage and march.

CHAP. IV.

Robert
does hom-
age to
Alexios.

Robert at
Laodikeia.

Macedonian lands where the rule of Byzantium had again displaced the rule of Ochrida, but to which the name of the people whom Samuel had made terrible still clave, as in the language of fact, though not of diplomacy, it cleaves still. They reached Thessalonica, they reached Constantinople, and wondered at the glories of the New Rome.[1] There, as in duty bound, they pledged their faith to the truest heir of the Roman majesty, whose lost lands they were to win back from the misbelievers. Before the throne of Alexios Robert the Norman knelt; he placed his hands between the Imperial hands, and arose the sworn liegeman of Augustus.[2] The homage of Harold to Robert's father was not more binding than the homage of Robert to Alexios; but an English earl and a Norman crusader were measured in those days by different standards. The host passed on; at Nikaia, at Antioch, at Jerusalem, Robert was ever foremost in fight and in council. Yet the old spirit was not wholly cast out. When the English Warangians at Laodikeia hailed their joint leaders in the son of their Conqueror and in the heir of their ancient kings,[3]

[1] Fulcher bursts into ecstasy at the sight of Constantinople, and William of Malmesbury takes the opportunity to tell its history. From iv. 356 and the note it appears that he knew his Emperors, and that his editor did not.

[2] See Fulcher, 386; Orderic, 728 A; Will. Malms. iv. 357. They all record the homage, except in the case of Count Raymond of Toulouse, who would only swear, but not do homage. The Count of Flanders seems a little doubtful; but the words of William of Malmesbury are explicit as to Robert; "Normannus itaque et Blesensis comites hominium suum Græco prostraverunt; nam jam Flandrita transierat, et id facere fastidierat, quod se meminisset natum et educatum libere." Orderic seems to take a real pleasure in speaking of Alexios as Augustus and Cæsar, the latter title being a little beneath him. His subjects however are not only "Græci," but "Pelasgi," "Achæi," anything that would do for the grand style. Presently Nikaia appears (728 B) as "totius Romaniæ caput." So William of Malmesbury speaks of "Minor Asia quam Romaniam dicunt." Here "Romania" means specially the Turkish kingdom of *Roum*; in more accurate geography it takes in the European provinces of the Empire.

[3] See above, p. 560, and Ord. Vit. 778 A, B, where he describes the coming of Eadgar, of which more in a later chapter, and his near friendship with Robert.

the pleasures of Asia, like the pleasures of Apulia, were CHAP. IV.
too much for the Duke, and it needed the anathemas of
the Church to call him back from his luxurious holiday to
the stern work that was before him.[1] Before the walls
of Jerusalem he found a strange ally. Hugh of Jaugy, Hugh of
one of the murderers of Mabel, after his long sojourn Jaugy
joins the
among the infidels, greeted his natural prince, returned crusades.
to his allegiance, and by his knowledge of the tongue
and ways of those whom he forsook, did useful, if not
honourable, service.[2] A worthier comrade was a noble
and valiant Turk, who of his own accord came to seek
for baptism and for admission to share the perils of the
pilgrims.[3] The Norman Duke ever appears as the fellow-
soldier of his kinsman and namesake of Flanders; the
two Roberts are always side by side. It is needless to The "rope-
dancers" at
say that neither of them shared in that shameful descent Antioch.
from the walls of Antioch which gained for some of the
heroes of Normandy the mocking surname of the *rope-
dancers*.[4] It is hard to find any absolutely contemporary

---

[1] The words of Ralph of Caen (c. 58) on this head are very emphatic;
"Normannus comes ingressus Laodiciam somno vacabat, et otio; nec in-
utilis tamen, dum opulentiam nactus aliis indigentibus large erogabat;
quoniam conserva Cyprus Baccho, Cerere, et multo pecore abundans, Laodiciam repleverat, quippe indigentem vicinam Christicolam, et quasi col-
lacteam; ipsa namque una in littore Syro et Christum colebat et Alexio
serviebat. Sed nec sic excussato otio, prædictus comes frustra semel atque
iterum ad castra revocatur. Tertio sub anathemate accitus, redit invitus;
difficilem enim habebat transitum commeatio, quæ comiti ministrare Lao-
dicia veniens debebat."

[2] Ord. Vit. 753 A. We have heard of Hugh before, N. C. vol. iv. p. 493.
We now read that "Susceptus a Normannico duce, multum suis profuit et
mores ethnicos ac tergiversationes subdolas et fraudes, quibus contra fideles
callent, enucleavit."

[3] Ib. "Cosan etiam, nobilis heros et potens de Turcorum prosapia,
Christianos ultro adiit, multisque modis ad capiendam urbem eos ad-
juvit. In Christum enim fideliter credebat, et sacro baptismate regenerari
peroptabat. Ideoque nostratibus, ut amicis et fratribus, ad obtinendum
decus Palæstinæ et metropoli Davitici regni summopere suffragari satagebat."

[4] "Furtivi funambuli" was the name given to Ivo and Alberic of Grant-

CHAP. IV. authority for the statement which was very soon afloat,
Robert said that the crown of Jerusalem was offered to Robert and
to have
refused the was refused by him.[1]　Robert could not have been as
crown of
Jerusalem. Godfrey; but we can believe that his career would have
been more honourable in a Syrian than in a Norman
dominion.　He was at least one of the first to stand on
the rescued walls of the Holy City;[2] and in the fight for
the newly-won realm against the Fatimite Caliph, it was
not merely by cutting down the Saracen standard-bearer
with his own hand, but by a display of really skilful tactics,
that Robert did much to win the day for Christendom.[3]

His return. He then turned his face towards Constantinople and
towards Apulia, and we shall meet him again in his own
land.

William　　As soon as Robert had set forth for Jerusalem, William
takes pos-
session of took possession of the duchy of Normandy—in modern
Normandy. phrase, he took upon him its administration—without
opposition from any side.　There was indeed no side,
except the side of mere anarchy, from which opposition
could come.　It was perhaps a little humiliating for a
great duchy to be handed over from one prince to another
by a personal bargain, like a house or a field.　But there

mesnil and certain others.　See Orderic, 738 D.　Stephen of Chartres too
decamped for a while in a manner which did not please his wife.

[1] The words of William of Malmesbury (iv. 389) are remarkable; " Robertus, Jerosolymam veniens, indelibili macula nobilitatem suam respersit,
quod regnum, consensu omnium sibi utpote regis filio delatum, recusaret,
non reverentiæ, ut fertur, contuitu, sed laborum inextricabilium metu."

[2] His exploits in the storm come out in all the accounts.　In William
of Malmesbury (iv. 369) he and his namesake of Flanders are as usual
grouped together; "Hæc quidem victoria in parte Godefridi et duorum
Robertorum evenit."

[3] Will. Malms. iv. 371.　"Duces, et maxime Robertus Normannus, qui
antesignanus erat, arte artem, vel potius virtute calliditatem eludentes,
sagittariis et peditibus deductis, medias gentilium perruperunt acies."
This seems to prove more than the story in iv. 389, where Robert, with
Philip of Montgomery and others, makes use of the worn-out stratagem of
the feigned flight.

was no practical ground for opposing William's entry. CHAP. IV.
All classes, save mere robbers, lordly or vulgar, must
have had enough of Robert. And now Robert was gone,
and in going, he had handed them over to the prince for
whom many of them had fought or intrigued, and who
already held some of the most important points of the
country. Whether it was good or bad for England and
Normandy to have the same ruler, it was clearly a gain
for all Normandy to have only one ruler. In one sense indeed this object was not even now attained. William's first
step was to dismember the duchy which he had bought.
Henry, it will be remembered, had been left in Normandy Grants to
a year and a half before, and had been, perhaps ever Henry.
since, acting in William's interests against Robert. He
now received the reward of his services in a noble fief
indeed. He became again acknowledged Count of the
whole Côtentin. And to his peninsular dominion he was
allowed to add the whole Bessin, except the city of
Bayeux and the castle and town of Caen.[1] The spot
which contained the foundations of his parents, the tombs
of his parents, William Rufus could not bring himself to
give up, even to reward the faithful service of a brother.

But for Henry, in full friendship with his brother, to
hold a corner of Normandy as a fief of his brother was a
partition of Normandy of quite another kind from such
a partition as had been when William, as Robert's
enemy, hemmed in Robert in his capital. There can be Rule of
no doubt that the exchange from Robert to William was William in
an unspeakable gain to the duchy. During the remainder Normandy.
of the life of Rufus Normandy had a stern master; but,
after the anarchy of Robert, what the land most needed

---

[1] Robert of Torigny, 1096. "Comes Henricus contulit se ad regem
Willermum, atque omnino cum eo remansit; cui idem rex comitatum Con-
stantiensem et Baiocensem, præter civitatem Baiocas et oppidum Cadomi,
ex integro concessit."

CHAP. IV.　was a master of almost any kind.　The kind of work

Synod of
Rouen.
1096.
which was needed is shown in the acts of a synod which had been gathered at Rouen by Archbishop William, while Robert still nominally ruled, almost immediately after the greater gathering at Clermont.　Three Norman bishops had been at Clermont in person, Odo of Bayeux, Gilbert of Evreux, and Serlo of Seez.　They brought back the decrees of the council to their brethren, who forthwith assembled to accept and enforce in their own province all that had been ordered at Clermont for the

Truce of
God con-
firmed.
Church and the world in general.　They confirmed the Truce of God[1] with all its enactments on behalf of the more useful and helpless members of society.　They drew up an oath to be taken under pain of anathema by all men, which bound them to observe the Truce in their own persons, and to give the help of the temporal arm to the efforts of the ecclesiastical powers against those who should break it.[2]　In those days at least peace could be had only through war, and the Truce of God itself became the occasion of more fighting against those who

Other
decrees.
scorned its wholesome checks.　Other anathemas were pronounced against robbers, false moneyers, and buyers of stolen goods, against those who gathered themselves together in castles for purposes of plunder, and against the lords who sheltered such men in their castles.　Such castles were put under an interdict; no Christian rite might be done in them.[3]　In going on to pronounce

---

[1] Ord. Vit. 721 B.　This decree heads the acts of the council; "Statuit synodus sancta, ut trevia Dei firmiter custodiatur," &c.

[2] Ib. C.　All persons from twelve years of age are to swear that they will keep the Truce, and will help their several bishops and archdeacons, "ita ut, si me monuerint ad eundum super eos, nec diffugiam nec dissimulabo, sed cum armis meis cum ipso proficiscar, et omnibus, quibus potero, juvabo adversus illos per fidem sine malo ingenio, secundum meam conscientiam."

[3] Ib. D.　"Hoc anathemate feriuntur falsarii et raptores et emptores prædarum, et qui in castris congregantur propter exercendas rapinas, et

further anathemas against the invaders of ecclesiastical CHAP. IV. rights, against the unlawful occupiers of Church lands, against laymen who claimed to have a right in tithes and other Church dues,[1] the synod uses a formula which shows how keenly Normandy felt the difference between the great William and his eldest son. What the days of The days the Confessor were in England, the days of the Conqueror ^{of King} William. were in his own duchy. The synod decreed that all churches should enjoy their goods and customs as they had been in the time of King William, and that no burthens should be laid upon them but such as King William had allowed.[2]

It would be too much to think that William the Red at once brought back the Norman duchy to the state in which it had been in those golden days of William the Great. And it is still less needful to stop to prove that even the days of William the Great would not have seemed golden days as compared with the state of any well-governed land in our own time. But there can be no doubt that the coming of the new ruler wrought a real reform. And a reform was grievously needed. We read Small re-that very little came of the well-intentioned decrees of the ^{sults of the} synod. synod. The bishops, Odo among them, did what they could—it is Odo's last recorded act in the lands with which we have to deal, and it is something that he leaves us in the shape of a reformer and not in that of an oppressor. But very little came of the efforts of the prelates. The Duke did nothing to help them—his mind was perhaps too full of the crusade—and things were at the moment of William's coming in almost greater confusion than

domini qui amodo eos retinuerint in castris suis. Et auctoritate apostolica et nostra prohibemus ut nulla Christianitas fiat in terris dominorum illorum."

[1] Ord. Vit. 721 D. "Et quod nullus laicus participationem habeat in tertia parte decimæ, vel in sepultura, vel in oblatione altaris."

[2] Ib. "Nec servitium, nec aliquam exactionem inde exigat, præter eam quæ tempore Guillelmi regis constituta fuit."

CHAP. IV. ever.[1] He at least gave the land the advantage of a
William's strong rule; he kept the luxury of oppression to himself.
rule in
Normandy. The lesser scourges of mankind were thoroughly put
down. We hear no more of that private warfare which
had torn the land in pieces in the days of Robert. William
recalled many of the lavish grants of Robert; what his
father had held, he would hold.[2] Even in ecclesiastical
matters Rufus is not painted in such dark colours in
His ap- Normandy as he is in England. He is not charged with
pointments
to prelacies. keeping ecclesiastical benefices vacant in order that he
might enjoy their revenues. He found two great abbeys
vacant, those of Jumièges and Saint Peter-on-Dives;
and he at once supplied them with abbots. They were
abbots of his own choosing, but it is not said that
Tancard they bought their places.[3] Tancard, the new abbot of
Abbot of
Jumièges. Jumièges, may lie under some suspicion, as a few years
1096–1101. after he was deposed on account of a shameful quarrel
with his monks.[4] Saint Peter's was vacant, not by the
death, but by the deposition and banishment—unjust we
Etard are told—of its abbot Fulk. William appointed a monk
Abbot of
Saint of Jumièges called Etard or Walter, who ruled well, we
Peter's.
1096–1107. are told, for eleven years, till Fulk came back with
letters from the Pope, on which his successor cheerfully
made way for him again.[5] No Norman bishopric was
vacant at the time of William's entry, nor did any become vacant for more than a year. Then in the midst
February, of events which are to be told hereafter, the news came
1098.

[1] Orderic draws a special picture (722 D, 723 C), winding up with "Sic
Normannia suis in se filiis furentibus miserabiliter turbata est, et plebs inermis sine patrono desolata est."

[2] Ord. Vit. 765 C. "Guillelmus itaque rex Normanniam possedit, et
dominia patris sui, quæ frater suus insipienter distraxerat, sibi mancipavit."

[3] Ib. "Ecclesias pastoribus viduatas electis *pro modulo suo* rectoribus
commisit." Or do these words imply simony ? They might merely imply
lay nomination and investiture.

[4] Ib.   [5] Ib.

that the throne of Bayeux was vacant by the death of CHAP. IV.
Odo far away at Palermo. William at once bestowed
the staff on Turold the brother of Hugh of Evermouth, Turold
seemingly the same Hugh who figures in the legend of Bishop of Bayeux.
Hereward as his son-in-law and successor.[1] This pre- 1098–1195.
late sat for seven years, and then, for reasons of his
own, gave up his see, and became a monk at Bec.[2]

§ 7. *The Last Dispute between William and Anselm.*
1097.

The year which followed William's acquisition of
Normandy was a busy year in many ways. The King Christmas,
passed the winter in the duchy; the greater part of the 1096–1097.
year he spent in England. He was largely occupied
with the affairs of Wales and Scotland, and in this year
came the last dispute between the King and the Archbishop, and the first departure of Anselm from England.
Since their reconciliation at Windsor two years before,
there had been no open breach between them. The State of
first difference arose out of the events of the Welsh war. the end of
At the end of the year which saw William master of 1096.
Normandy, he seemed to have wholly lost his hold on
Wales. Except Glamorgan and the one isolated castle
of Pembroke, the Britons seemed to have won back their
whole land.[3] The affairs of Wales brought the King Easter,
back from Normandy, and he designed to hold the April 5, 1097.
Easter Gemót in its usual place at Winchester. Stress of
weather however hindered him from reaching England William
in time for the festival. He landed at Arundel on Easter comes to England.

---

[1] Ord. Vit. 765 C. "Turoldo fratri Hugonis de Ebremou episcopatum
dedit." Hugh of Evermouth occurs in the false Ingulf, 77 (not so in Domesday), as lord of Bourne and Deeping.

[2] Ib. "Pro quibusdam arcanis ultro reliquit."

[3] I shall speak of these Welsh wars in full in the next chapter.

CHAP. IV.
Assembly
of Windsor.

Seeming
conquest of
Wales.

Good hopes
for the
future.

William
complains
of Anselm's
contingent
to the
Welsh war.

eve, and thence went to Windsor, where the Assembly was therefore held, somewhat later than the usual time.[1] The meeting was followed by a great expedition into Wales, and by a submission of the country which events a few months later proved to be very nominal indeed.[2] But there was at last an apparent success. William seemed to be greater than ever; he had, by whatever means, won Normandy and recovered Wales. And, more than this, the beginnings of his Norman government had been good; he had thus far shown himself a better nursing-father of the Church in his duchy than his brother Robert had done. A hope therefore arose in many minds that the days of victory and peace might be days of reformed government in England also, and that King and Primate might be able to join in some great measure for the improvement of discipline and manners.[3] In this hope they were disappointed, as they were likely to be, especially if they reckoned on any long time of peace with the Britons. But the first renewed breach between the King and the Archbishop arose from quite a new cause. When the King came back from the Welsh war, he sent a letter to Anselm, angrily complaining of the nature of the Archbishop's military contingent to his army. The knights whom Anselm had sent had been so badly equipped and so useless in war that he owed him no thanks for

---

[1] Chron. Petrib. 1097. "Se cyng Willelm .... togeanes Eastron hider to lande for, forðam he þohte his hired on Winceastre to healdenne; ac he wearð þurh weder gelét oððet Eastre æfen, þæt he up com ærost æt´Arundel, and forþi his hired æt Windlesoran heold."

[2] Eadmer (Hist. Nov. 37) makes a great deal more than enough of this submission, when he says; "Super Walenses qui contra eum surrexerant exercitum duxit, eosque post modicum in deditionem suscipit, et pace undique potitus est." But this would doubtless be the impression of the moment.

[3] Ib. "Cum jam multi sperarent, quod hæc pax servitio Dei deberet militare, et attenti exspectarent aliquid magni pro emendatione Christianitatis ex regis assensu archiepiscopum promulgare."

them but rather the contrary.[1] This story is commonly
told as if Anselm had been the colonel of a regiment whose
men were, through his fault, utterly unfit for service.
Anselm had indeed, as we have seen, once held somewhat Estimate
of a warlike command, but it had been of a passive kind; _{of the} complaint.
he was certainly not expected to go to the Welsh war
himself. In truth the complaint is against knights;
doubtless, if the knights were bad, their followers would
be worse; but it is of knights that the King speaks.
If I rightly understand the relation between the Arch- Position of
bishop and his military tenants, these knights were men _{the Arch-} bishop's
who held lands of the archbishopric by the tenure of knights.
discharging all the military service to which the whole
estates of the archbishopric were bound.[2] It was doubtless the business of their lord to see that the service was
paid, that the proper number of knights, each with his
proper number of followers, went to the royal standard.
But one can hardly think that it was part of the Archbishop's business to look into every military detail, as
if he had been their commanding officer. It was not
Anselm's business to find their arms and accoutrements;
they held their lands by the tenure of finding such
things for themselves. The King was dissatisfied with
the archiepiscopal contingent, and, from his point of view,
most likely not without reason. Anselm's troops might
be expected to be among the least serviceable parts of the
army. Gentlemen and yeomen of Kent—we may begin
to use those familiar names—could have had no great
experience of warfare; there were no private wars to keep
their hands in practice; they could not be so well fitted for

---

[1] Eadmer, Hist. Nov. 37. " Ecce spei hujus et exspectationis turbatorias
literas rex, a Gualis reversus, archiepiscopo destinat, mandans in illis se pro
militibus quos in expeditionem suam miserat nullas ei nisi malas gratias
habere, eo quod nec convenienter, sicut aiebat, instructi, nec ad bella
fuerant pro negotii qualitate idonei."

[2] See N. C. vol. v. p. 372.

CHAP. IV. war in general or specially for Welsh war, either as the picked mercenaries of the King or as the tried followers of the Earl of Chester and the Lord of Glamorgan. William, as a military commander, might naturally be annoyed at the poor figure cut by the Archbishop's knights; but there is every reason to think that, in point of law, his complaint against the Archbishop was unjust. It seems to be shown to be so by the fact that the charge which the King brought against Anselm on this account was one which in the end he found it better to drop. But he now bade Anselm to be ready to *do right* to him, according to the judgement of his court, whenever he should think fit to summon him for that end.[1]

Anselm summoned to the King's court.

Anselm's distress.

Anselm seems to have been thoroughly disheartened by this fresh blow. And yet it was no more than what he had been looking for. Over and over again he had said that between him and William there could be no lasting peace, that under such a king as William there could be no real reform.[2] And the new grievance was a personal one; whether the charge was right or wrong, it had nothing to do with the interests of the Church or with good morals; it simply touched his relations to the King as his temporal lord. Since the meeting at Windsor two years before, though William had given Anselm no kind of help in his plans, he does not seem to have openly thwarted them, except, as seems implied throughout, by still refusing his leave for the holding of a synod. At the same time there had been quite enough to make Anselm thoroughly weary of England and her King and of everything to do with her. And the visits of the Cardinal of Albano and the Abbot

His weariness of England.

[1] Eadmer, Hist. Nov. 37. "Præcepit ut paratus esset de his, juxta judicium curiæ suæ, sibimet rectitudinem facere, quandocumque sibi placeret inde eum appellare."

[2] Ib. "Licet jam olim sciverit se, eodem rege superstite, in Anglia Christo non adeo fructificaturum."

of Saint Benignus had done Anselm no good. From this CHAP. IV.
time we mark the beginning of a certain change in him Change in
Anselm's
which, without in any way morally blaming him, we feelings.
must call a change for the worse. Left to himself, he seems
not to have had the faintest scruple as to the customs
which were established alike in England and in Normandy. He was unwilling to accept the metropolitan
office at all; but he made no objection to the particular
way of receiving it which was the use of England and
of Normandy. He had, without scruple or protest,
received the staff of Canterbury from the son as he had
received the staff of Bec from the father. His wish to
go to Rome to receive the pallium was fully according
to precedent, and it was only the petty captiousness of
the King that turned it into a matter of offence. But His
yearnings
the mere talking about Rome and the Pope which the towards
discussion had led to was not wholesome; and every- Rome.
thing that had since happened had tended to put Rome
and the Pope more and more into Anselm's head. The
coming of the Legate, the rebukes of the Legate, even
the base insinuations of his undutiful suffragans against
the validity of his appointment, would all help to bring
about a certain morbid frame of mind, a craving after
Rome and its Bishop as the one centre of shelter and
comfort among his troubles. The very failure of Walter's
mission, the unworthy greediness and subserviency into
which the Legate had fallen, the utter break-down of the
later mission of Abbot Jeronto, would all tend the same
way. Anselm would hold, not that the Pope was corrupt,
but that none but the Pope in his own person could
be trusted. He would have nothing more to do with
his unfaithful agents; he would go himself to the
fountain-head which could not fail him. And he to
whom he would go was not simply the Pope, any Pope;
it was Urban the Second, the reformer, the preacher of

the crusade. Since Anselm's work had begun, the world had been filled with the personal fame of the Pontiff in whose cause he had striven. In the same council which had stirred the common heart of Christendom Urban had denounced those customs of England to which Anselm had conformed in his own appointment and which he had promised to defend against all men. The rules laid down at Clermont against the acceptance of ecclesi- astical benefices from lay hands not only condemned his own appointment, made before those decrees were issued; it condemned also the consecrations to the sees of Hereford and Worcester which he had himself performed since they had been issued. Amid the reign of unlaw, amid the constant breaches of discipline, the frightful sins against moral right, which he had daily to behold and which he was kept back from duly censuring, with none to support him outwardly, none but a few chosen ones to understand his inward thoughts, it is not wonderful if distant Rome seemed to him a blessed haven of rest from the troubles and sorrows of England. Let him flee thither at any cost, and have peace. Let him seek the counsel of the ghostly superior to whom he looked up in faith, and to whom he had been so faithful; to him he would open his soul; from him he would receive guidance, perhaps strength, in a course which was beset with so

many difficulties on all sides. Rome, seen far away, looked pure and holy; its Pontiff seemed the one embodiment of right and law, the one shadow of God left upon earth, in a world of force and falsehood and foulness of life, a world where the civil sword was left in the hands of kings like William and Philip, and where an Emperor like Henry still wielded it in defiance of anathemas. At such a distance he would not see that the policy of Popes had already learned to be even more worldly and crooked than that of kings and emperors. He had not learned, what Englishmen had already learned, that gold was as powerful in the counsels of the Holy See as ever it was in the closet of the Red King. The Pope's agents and messengers might take bribes; the Pope himself, the holy College around him, would never sink to such shame. The majestic and attractive side of the Roman system was all that would present itself to his eyes. He would flee to the blessed shelter and be at peace. He had had enough of the world of kings and courts, the world where men of God were called on to send men to fight the battles of this life, and were called in question if swords were not sharp enough or if horses were not duly trained and caparisoned. Weary and sick at heart, he would turn away from such a scene and from its thankless duties; he would, for a while at least, leave the potsherds of the earth to strive with the potsherds of the earth; he would go where he might perhaps win leave to throw aside his burthen, or where, failing that, he might receive renewed strength to bear it.

In all this we can thoroughly enter into Anselm's New position taken by Anselm. feelings, nor are we called upon to pronounce any censure upon either his feelings or his conduct. But it is plain that he was now taking up a wholly different position from that which he had taken at Rockingham, a position in which he could not expect to meet with, and in which he did not meet with, the same support which he had met with at Rockingham. At Gillingham and at Rockingham Anselm did nothing which could be fairly construed as a defiance of the law or an appeal to the Pope against any lawful authority of the King. All that he did was to ask the King's leave to go for the pallium, that is to do what all his predecessors had done, to obey what might be as fairly called a custom of the realm as any other. In the discussions which now began, his Aspect of his conduct. conduct would, to say the least, have, in the eyes of

CHAP. IV. any but the most friendly judges, another look. He was asking leave to go to Rome, not to discharge an established duty, but, as it might be not unfairly argued, simply to gratify a caprice of his own. He might rightly ask for such leave; but it rested with the King's discretion to grant or to refuse it, and no formal wrong would be done to him by refusing it. And to ask leave to go and consult the Pope, not because of any meddling with his spiritual office, not on account of any religious or ecclesiastical difficulty, but because the King had threatened him with a suit, just or unjust, in a purely temporal matter, had very much the air of appealing from the King's authority to the Pope. We must remember throughout that Anselm nowhere makes the claim which Odo and William of Saint-Calais made before him, which Thomas of London made after him, to be exempt from temporal jurisdiction on the ground of his order. As such claims had no foundation in English law, neither was it at all in the spirit of Anselm to press them. All that he wanted was to be allowed to seek help in his troubles in the only quarter where he believed that help might be found. But the petition for leave to seek it was put in a form and under circumstances which might well have awakened some distrust, some unwillingness, in minds far better disposed towards him than that of the Red King. We may not for a moment doubt the perfect singlemindedness of Anselm, his perfect righteousness from the point of view of his own conscience. But we cannot wonder that, in the new controversy, he failed to have the barons and people of England at his side, as he had had them on the day of trial at Rockingham and on the day of peace-making at Windsor.

Causes of his loss of general support.

The belief that the supposed season of peace might be a

season of reform had been shared by Anselm himself. CHAP. IV.
He had more than once urged the King on the subject; Anselm's
but William had always answered that he was too demands of
busy dealing with his many enemies to think about reform.
such matters.[1] Such an answer was a mere put-off;
yet a more discouraging one might have been given.
Anselm had therefore fully made up his mind to make
the most of this special opportunity, and to make yet
one more urgent appeal to the King to help him
in his work.[2] And now, at the meeting where he trusted
to make this attempt, he was summoned to appear as
defendant on a purely temporal charge. To that He deter-
charge he determined to make no answer. But surely to answer
the reason which is given is rather the reason of Eadmer the new
afterwards than of Anselm at the time. Anselm is Working of
made to say that in the King's court everything de- the King's
pended on the King's nod, and that his cause would be
examined in that court, without law, without equity,
without reason.[3] He had not found it so at Rockingham,

---

[1] Eadmer, Hist. Nov. 37. "Rogatus de subventione Christianitatis, non-numquam solebat respondere se propter hostes quos infestos circumquaque habebat eo intendere non valere."

[2] Ib. "Jam tunc illum pace potitum cogitaverat super hac re convenire, et saltem ad consensum alicujus boni fructus exsequendi quibus modis posset attrahendo delinire."

[3] Ib. "Quod ille dinoscens, et insuper cuncta regalis curiæ judicia pendere ad nutum regis, nilque in ipsis nisi solum velle illius considerari certissime sciens, indecens æstimavit pro verbi calumnia placitantium more contendere, et veritatis suæ causam curiali judicio, quod nulla lex, nulla æquitas, nulla ratio, muniebat, examinandam introducere." As I understand this, he does not decline the authority of the court; he simply determines to make no defence, and to leave things to take their course.

How far did the court deserve the character which Eadmer gives of it? At this stage of the constitution, we are met at every step by the difficulty of distinguishing between the greater *curia regis*, which was in truth the Witenagemót, and the smaller *curia regis* of the King's immediate officials and counsellors, the successor of the *Theningmannagemót* (see N. C. vol. v. pp. 423, 878). Eadmer's picture would, under Rufus, be true enough of the smaller body. The event at Rockingham had shown that it was not always true of the larger.

CHAP. IV. nor did he find it so now. But we can quite understand that, with his mind full of so much greater matters, he might think it better to let his judges settle matters as they might, for or against him, in questions as to horses and weapons and military training. The worst that could happen would be another payment of money.[1] Anselm believed that the charge was a mere pretence, devised simply to hinder him from making the appeal to the King which he designed.[2] He therefore made up his mind to make no answer to the summons, and to let the law, if there was any law in the matter, take its course.[3] When he looked around at the spoliation of the Church, at the evils of all kinds which had crept in through lack of discipline, he feared the judgement of God on himself, if he did not make one last effort.[4] His heart indeed sank when he saw that, of all the evil that was done, the King either was himself the doer or took pleasure in them that did it. But he would strive once more; if his last effort failed, he would appeal to a higher spiritual power than his own; he would see what the authority and judgement of the Apostolic See could do.[5]

He deter-
mines on a
last effort.

---

[1] We read directly after (Eadmer, Hist. Nov. 37) what was expected to happen;—"ut culpæ addictus, aut ingentem regi pecuniam penderet, aut ad implorandam misericordiam ejus, caput amplius non levaturus, se totum impenderet." Anselm was determined to avoid the latter alternative.

[2] "Causa discidii utique, non ex rei veritate producta, sed ad omnem pro Deo loquendi aditum Anselmo intercludendum malitiose composita."

[3] Ib. "Tacuit ergo, nec quicquam nuntio respondit, reputans hoc genus mandati ad ea perturbationum genera pertinere quæ jam olim sæpe sibi recordabatur illata, et ideo hoc solum ut Deus talia sedaret supplici corde precabatur."

[4] Ib. "Verebatur ne hæc Dei judicio sibi damno fierent, si quibus modis posset eis obviare non intenderet."

[5] Ib. "Sed obviare sibi impossibile videbat, quod totius regni principem aut ea facere aut eis favere perspicuum erat. Visum itaque sibi est aucto-ritatem et sententiam apostolicæ sedis super his oportere inquiri." Yet that he did design a last effort with the King, before he said anything about the Pope, is plain by his actually attempting it.

The Whitsun festival came, and Anselm went to the CHAP. IV.
Assembly. The place of meeting is not mentioned; Whitsun
Gemót.
according to usage it would be Westminster. Though May 24,
1097.
the suit was hanging over Anselm, he went, not as a defendant in a suit, but as a chief member of the Gemót.
He seems to have been graciously received by the King; Anselm
at least we hear of him at the royal table, and he had favourably
received;
opportunities of private access to the royal ear. Of these his last
appeal.
chances he did not fail to take advantage for his purpose;
but all was in vain; nothing at all tending to reform was
to be got out of William Rufus.[1] In this way the earlier
days of meeting, the days of the actual festival, were
spent. Then, as usual, the various matters of business
which had to be dealt with by the King and his Witan
were brought forward.[2] Among other questions men Surmises
as to the
were eagerly asking what would become of the charge charge
against the Archbishop as to the bad equipment of his against
Anselm.
knights in the late Welsh campaign. Would he have to
pay some huge sum of money, or would he have to pray
for mercy, and be thereby so humbled that he could
never lift up his head again?[3] Anselm's thoughts meanwhile were set upon quite other matters. He had made
his last attempt on the King's conscience, and he had
failed. There was nothing more to be done by his own
unaided powers. He must seek for the counsel and help He determines to
of one greater than himself. He called together a body ask leave

[1] Eadmer, Hist. Nov. 37. "Cum igitur in Pentecoste, festivitatis gratia,
regiæ curiæ se præsentasset, et modo inter prandendum, modo alias quemadmodum opportunitas se offerebat, statum animi regalis quis ergą colendam
æquitatem esset studiose perquisisset, eumque qui olim fuerat omnimodo
reperisset, nihil spei de futura ipsius emendatione in eo ultra remansit."

[2] Ib. "Peractis igitur festivioribus diebus, diversorum negotiorum causæ
in medium duci ex more cœperunt." This notice is important as showing
us the order in which business was done in these assemblies.

[3] Ib. "Ut culpæ addictus aut ingentem regi pecuniam penderet, aut ad
implorandam misericordiam, ejus caput amplius non levaturus, se totum
impenderet."

CHAP. IV.

to go to
Rome.

He declares
his purpose
to a chosen
body.
of nobles of his own choice, those doubtless in whom he
could put most trust, and he bade them carry a message
from him to the King, to say that he was driven by the
utmost need to ask his leave to go to Rome.[1] We ask
why he who had been on such intimate terms with the
King during the earlier days of the meeting, was now
forced to send a message instead of speaking to the King
face to face. We may suppose that the arrangement was
the same as at Rockingham, that there was an outer and
an inner chamber, and that, while the suit against the
Archbishop was pending, he was not allowed to take his
natural place among the King's counsellors. During the
days of festival, he had been a guest and a friend; now
that the days of business had come, he had changed into
a defendant. We are not told what the lords of his
choice said or thought of the message which he put into

their hands. Unless it was accompanied by a rather full
explanation, it must have been startling. With the help
of Eadmer we can follow the workings of Anselm's mind;
but to one who heard the request suddenly it must have
had a strange sound. Did the Archbishop wish to
complain to the Pope because the King was displeased
with the trim and conduct of his military contingent?
The King at least, when the message was taken to him,
was utterly amazed. But William was not in one of his
worst moods; he was sarcastic, but not wrathful. He

refused the licence. There could be no need for Anselm
to go to the Pope. He would never believe that Anselm
had committed any sin so black that none but the Pope
could absolve him. And as for counsel, Anselm was much
better fitted to give it to the Pope than the Pope was
to give it to Anselm. Anselm took the refusal meekly.

---

[1] Eadmer, Hist. Nov. 37. "Accersitis ad se quos volebat de principibus
regis, mandavit per eos regi se summa necessitate constrictum velle, per
licentiam ipsius, Romam ire."

"Power is in his hands; he says what pleases him. CHAP. IV.
What he refuses now he may perhaps grant another
day. I will multiply my prayers."[1] Anselm had therefore to stay in England. But the formal charge against The charge
him was withdrawn. Perhaps the King had merely made $_{\text{Anselm}}^{\text{against}}$
it in a fit of ill humour, and had long given up any withdrawn.
serious thought of pressing it. And, if he really wished
to annoy Anselm, he had now a way in which he might
annoy him far more thoroughly and with much greater
advantage than by any mere temporal suit.

This year was a year of gatherings, alike for counsel Affairs of
and for warfare. The seeming submission of Wales was $_{\text{June-}}^{\text{Wales.}}$
soon found to be utterly hollow. From Midsummer till $_{\text{1097.}}^{\text{August,}}$
August William was engaged in another British expe-
dition, one which brought nothing but immediate toil and
trouble, but of whose more distant results we shall have
again to speak. On his return he summoned, perhaps Another
not a general Gemót, but at any rate a council of pre- assembly.
lates and lords, to discuss grave matters touching the
state of the kingdom.[2] We would fain hear something of
their debates on other affairs than those of Anselm; but
that privilege is denied us. We only know that, when Anselm's
the council was about to break up, when all its members $_{\text{again}}^{\text{request}}$
were eager to get to their homes, Anselm earnestly craved refused.
that his request to go to Rome might be granted, and that
the King again refused.[3]

William Rufus seems never to have been happy save
when he was himself moving and keeping everybody else
in motion. It must have been in his days as in the days

[1] Eadmer, Hist. Nov. 38. "Potestas in manu sua est; dicit quod sibi
placet. At si modo non vult concedere, concedet forsitan alia vice. Ego
preces multiplicabo."

[2] Ib. "Insequenti mense Augusto cum de statu regni acturus rex
episcopos, abbates, et quosque regni proceres, in unum præcepti sui sanctione egisset."

[3] Anselm made his petition, "dispositis his quæ adunationis illorum
causæ fuerant, dum quisque in sua repedare sategisset."

CHAP. IV. of Constantius, when the means of getting from place to place broke down through the multitude of bishops who were going to and fro for the endless councils.[1] In the month of October the bishops and great lords at least, if no one else, were brought together for the fourth

Assembly at Winchester. October 14, 1097. time this year. This time the place of meeting was Winchester; the day was the day of Saint Calixtus, the thirty-first anniversary of the great battle. We hear nothing of any other business, but only of the renewed petition of Anselm. It is clear that the idea of going to the Pope had seized on Anselm's mind to an unhealthy degree. He could not help pressing it in season and out of season, clearly to the weakening both of his influence

Anselm renews his request. and of his position. He made his request to the King both with his own lips—this time he was no defendant—and by the lips of others. The King was now thoroughly tired of the subject; he was now not sarcastic, but thoroughly annoyed and angry. He was weary of Anselm's endlessly pressing a request which he must by this time know would not be granted. Anselm had wearied him too much; he now directly commanded that he should cease from his importunity, that he should submit to the judgement of the court and pay a fine for the annoyance which he had given to his sovereign.[2] The King had an undoubted right to refuse the licence; but it is hard to see why the Archbishop was to be fined for

Anselm again impleaded. asking for it. By this turn Anselm was again made a defendant. Anselm now offers to give good reasons, such as the King could not gainsay, for the course

Alternative given to Anselm. which he took. The King refuses to hear any reasons, and, with a mixture of licence, threat, and defiance, he

[1] Ammianus, xxi. 18.

[2] Eadmer, Hist. Nov. 38. "Conturbat me, et intelligentem non concedendum fore quod postulat, sua graviter importunitate fatigat; quapropter jubeo ut amplius ab hujusmodi precibus cesset, et qui me jam saepe vexavit, prout judicabitur mihi emendet."

gives the Archbishop a kind of alternative. Anselm
must understand that, if he goes, the King will seize the
archbishopric into his own hands, and will never again
receive him as archbishop.[1] There was some free expression of feeling in these assemblies; for this announcement of the King's will was met by a storm of shouts
on different sides, some cheering the King and some the
Archbishop.[2] Some at last, the moderate party perhaps, The meet-
proposed and carried an adjournment till the morrow, ing ad-
hoping meanwhile to settle matters in some other way.[3] journed.

The next morning came; as so often before, Anselm Thursday,
and his friends sat waiting the royal pleasure. Some October 15,
bishops and lords came out and asked Anselm what Anselm
his purpose now was about the affair of yesterday. and the
He had not, he answered, agreed to the adjournment bishops
because he had any doubt as to his own purpose, and lords.
but only lest he should seem to set no store by the
opinion of others. He was in the same mind in which he
had been yesterday; he would again crave the King's
leave to go. Go he must, for the sake of his own soul's
health, for the sake of the Christian religion, for the
King's own honour and profit, if he would only believe
it.[4] The bishops and lords asked if he had anything
else to say; as for leave to go to Rome, it was no use
talking; the King would not grant it. Anselm answers
that, if the King will not grant it, he must follow the
scripture and obey God rather than man. We here see
that Anselm had brooded over his griefs till he had

---

[1] Eadmer, Hist. Nov. 38. "Si iverit, pro certo noverit quod totum
archiepiscopatum in dominium meum redigam, nec illum pro archiepiscopo
ultra recipiam."

[2] Ib. "Orta est ex his quædam magna tempestas diversis diversæ parti
acclamantibus."

[3] Ib. "Quidam permoti suaserunt in crastinum rem differri, sperantes
eam alio modo sedari."

[4] Ib. "Indubitanter sciens quod causa meæ salutis, causa sanctæ Christianitatis, et vere causa sui honoris ac profectus, si credere velit, ire dispono."

CHAP. IV. reached the verge of fanaticism. Such language would
have been exaggerated, had it been used when he was
forbidden to go for the pallium according to ancient
custom; it was utterly out of place when no clear duty
of any kind, no law of eternal right, no positive law of
the Church, bade him to go to Rome in defiance of the
King's orders.

Speech of
Bishop
Walkelin.

At this stage we again meet a personal spokesman
on the other side; Bishop Walkelin of Winchester
speaks where doubtless William of Saint-Calais would
have spoken, had he still lived. Walkelin's argument
was one hardly suited to the mind of Anselm. The
King and his lords knew the Archbishop's ways; they
knew that he was a man not easily turned from his
purpose; but it was not easy to believe that he would
be firm in his purpose of casting aside the honour and
wealth of the great office which he held, merely for the
sake of going to Rome.[1] Anselm's face lighted up, and
he fixed his keen eyes on Walkelin, with the words,
"Truly I shall be firm." This answer was taken to
the King, and was debated for a long while in the inner
council. At last Anselm bethinks him that his suffragans
ought rather to be advising him than advising the King;
he sends and bids them to come to him. Three of them
come at the summons, Walkelin, the ritualist Osmund,
the cunning leech John of Bath. They sat down on
each side of their metropolitan. Anselm called on them,
as bishops and prelates in the Church of God. If they
were really willing to guard the right and the justice of
God as they were ready to guard the laws and usages
of a mortal man,[2] they will let him tell them in full his

Anselm
and the
bishops.

[1] Eadmer. Hist. Nov. 38. "In hoc scilicet, ut, spreto tanti pontificatus honore
simul et utilitate, Romam petas, non leve est credere quod stabilis maneas."

[2] Ib. "Si ita fideliter et districte vultis in mea parte considerare atque
tueri rectitudinem et justitiam Dei, sicut in parte alterius perpenditis
atque tuemini jura et usus mortalis hominis."

reason for the course which he is taking, and they will
then give him their counsel in God's name.[1] The three
bishops chose first to confer with their brethren; Walkelin
and Robert were then sent in to the King, and the whole
body of bishops came once more to Anselm. We now
see the portrait of the prelates of the Red King's day, as
it is drawn by their own spokesman. Anselm they knew
to be a devout and holy man who had his conversation
in heaven. But they were hindered by the kinsfolk
whom they sustained, by the manifold affairs of the
world which they loved; they could not rise to the
loftiness of Anselm's life or trample on this world as he
did.[2] But if he would come down to them, and would
walk in their way,[3] then they would consult for him as
they would consult for themselves, and would help him
in his affairs as if they were their own. If he would
persist in standing alone and referring everything to
God,[4] they would not go beyond the fealty which they
owed to the King. This was plain speaking enough;
the doctrine of interest against right has seldom, even
in these later times, been more openly set forth. One
would think that the bishops simply meant to strengthen
Anselm's fixed purpose; they could not hope to move
him with arguments which certainly did not do justice
to their own case. Anselm's scholastic training always
enabled him to seize an advantage in argument. "You
have spoken well," he answered; "go to your lord; I

---

[1] Eadmer, Hist. Nov. 38. "Audiam sequarque consilium quod mihi
inde vestra fida Deo industria dabit."

[2] Ib. 39. "Domine pater, scimus te virum religiosum esse ac sanctum,
et in cælis conversationem tuam. Nos autem, impediti consanguineis nostris
quos sustentamus et multiplicibus sæculi rebus quas amamus, fatemur, ad
sublimitatem vitæ tuæ surgere nequimus, nec huic mundo tecum illudere."

[3] Ib. "Si volueris ad nos usque descendere, et qua incedimus via
nobiscum pergere."

[4] Ib. "Si te ad Deum solummodo quemadmodum cœpisti tenere dele-
geris solus."

CHAP. IV. will cleave to God."[1] They did as he bade them; they went, and Anselm was left almost alone; the few friends who clave to him sat apart at his bidding, and prayed to God to bring the matter to a good ending.[2]

In all these debates it is the bishops who play the worst part. They seem to say in calm earnest the same kind of things which the King said in wrath or in jest. Part of the After a short delay, they come back, accompanied by lay lords. some lay barons, and the tone of their discourse is at once raised. Anselm has no longer the laity on his side, as he had at Rockingham; nor can we wonder at the change. The speech which is now made is harsh, perhaps captious; but at all events the stand is now taken on direct legal grounds, no longer on the base motives confessed to by the bishops. The King sent word that Anselm had troubled him, embittered him, tortured him, Anselm's by his complaints.[3] The Archbishop is reminded that, after promise to the suit at Rockingham and the reconciliation which fol-obey the customs. lowed at Windsor—a reconciliation which is now attri-buted to the earnest prayers of Anselm's friends[4]—he had sworn to obey the laws and customs of the realm, and to de-fend them against all men.[5] After this promise the King had believed that Anselm would give him no more trouble.[6]

[1] Eadmer, Hist. Nov. 38. "Bene dixistis, Ite ergo ad dominum vestrum, ergo me tenebo ad Deum."

[2] Ib. "Unoquoque nostrum qui admodum pauci cum eo remansimus ad imperium illius singulatim sedente, et Deum pro digestione ipsius negotii interpellante." There is something strange in this last word.

[3] We here get a climax; "Sæpe diversis eum querelis exagitasti, exa-cerbasti, cruciasti."

[4] The wording is remarkable and subtle; "Cum tandem post placitum quod totius regni adunatione contra te apud Rockingeham habitum est, eum tibi sicut dominum tuum reconciliari sapienter peteres; et, adjutus meritis et precibus plurimorum pro te studiose intervenientium, petitioni tuæ effectum obtineres."

[5] See above, p. 531.

[6] Hist. Nov. 39. "Quibus opem credulus factus sperabat se de cætero quietum fore."

But he had already broken his oath—the charge is CHAP. IV.
delicately worded—when he threatened to go to Rome He is charged
without the King's leave.[1] For any of the great men of with breach of promise.
the realm so to do was utterly unheard of; for him most
of all. Anselm's enemies had now the advantage of him;
he certainly had uttered words which might be not unfairly construed as an intended breach of the law. They
therefore called on him to make oath that he would
never appeal to the Holy See in any shape in any matter
which the King might lay upon him; otherwise he must Alterna-
leave the kingdom with all speed, on what conditions he tive given to him.
already knew. And if he chose to stay and take the oath,
he must submit to be fined at the judgement of the court
for having troubled the King so much about a matter in
which he had after all not stuck firm to his own purpose.[2] This last condition seems hard measure; there
was surely no treason in making a request to the King
which it rested with the King to grant or to refuse. With
regard to the alleged breach of promise they undoubtedly stood on firmer ground.

The King's messengers did not wait for an answer.
Anselm therefore rose; followed by his companions, he
went in to the King, and, according to custom, sat down
beside him.[3] He asked whether the message which he
had just heard had really come from the King, and he received for answer that it had. Anselm then said that he Anselm
had undoubtedly made the promise to observe the laws, and the King.
but that he made it only in God's name, and so far as
the laws were according to right, and could be obeyed in

---

[1] Eadmer, Hist. Nov. 39. "Hanc pollicitationem, hanc fidem, en tu patenter
egrederis, dum Romam, non expectata licentia ejus, te iturum minaris."

[2] Ib. "Tunc te ad judicium curiæ suæ præcepit sibi emendare, quod
de re in qua non eras certus te perseveraturum, ausus fuisti eum totiens
inquietare."

[3] Ib. "Dextram illius *ex more* assedit." Here is the distinct mention
of a custom which we have come across before.

CHAP. IV. God's name.[1] The King and his lords answered that in
Qualifica- the promise there had been no mention of God or of
tions and
distinc- right.[2] We should be well pleased to have the actual
tions.
words of the promise; but we need not suppose any direct
misstatement of fact on either side; the forms of oaths
and promises are commonly capable of more than one
interpretation. Words which one side looks on as sur-
plusage another side looks on as the root of the whole
matter. But the form of the answer gave Anselm, if
not a logical, at least a rhetorical, advantage. If there
was no mention of God or right, what was there mention
of? No Christian man could be bound to observe laws
which were contrary to God and right. We have here
reached the beginning of those distinctions and qualifi-
cations which play so great a part in the debates of the
next century; but with Anselm the appeal is simply to
God and right; there is not a word about the privileges
of his order. His hearers murmured and wagged their
Anselm's heads, but said nothing openly.[3] So the Primate went
discourse;
duty to on to lay down at some length the doctrine that every
God always promise of earthly duty involved in its own nature a
excepted.
saving of duty to God. Faith was pledged in earthly
matters according to the faith due to God; faith to God
was therefore excepted by the very terms of the promise.[4]
The argument is doubtless sound, as regards the individual conscience; it leaves out of sight, and any argument of that age would probably have left out of sight,

[1] Eadmer, Hist. Nov. 39. "Scio me spopondisse consuetudines tuas, ipsas
videlicet quas per rectitudinem et secundum Deum in regno tuo possides,
me secundum Deum servaturum."

[2] Ib. "Cum rex et principes sui cæca mente objicerent, ac jurisjurandi
interjectione firmarent, nec Dei nec rectitudinis in ipsa sponsione ullam
mentionem factam fuisse."

[3] Ib. 40. "Cum ad hæc illi summurmurantes contra virum capita mo-
verent, nec tamen quid certi viva voce proferrent."

[4] Ib. "Cum fides quæ fit homini per fidem Dei roboretur, liquet quod
eadem fides, si quando contraria fidei Dei admittit, enervatur."

the truth that men may differ as to what is duty CHAP. IV.
towards God, and that no lawgiver or administrator of
the law can possibly listen to every scruple which
may be urged on such grounds in favour of disobedi-
ence. To Anselm's mind the case was clear. A custom
which hindered him from going to consult the Vicar of
Saint Peter for his own soul's health and for the good
of the Church was a custom contrary to God and right,
a custom which ought to be cast aside and disobeyed.
No man who feared God would hinder him from going
to the head of Christendom on God's service. He ended
with a parable. The King would not think himself well
served if any powerful vassal of his should by terrors
and threatenings hinder any other of his subjects from
doing his duty and service to him.

It was perhaps not wholly in enmity that the Count Answer
of Count
Robert.
of Meulan, who at Rockingham had frankly professed
his admiration of Anselm, joined the King at this
stage in trying to turn off the matter with a jest.
The Primate, he said, was preaching them a sermon; but
prudent people could not admit his line of argument.[1]
And certainly Anselm's present line of argument, the
assertion of individual conscience against established
law, could not be admitted by any legislative or judi-
cial assembly. A disturbance followed; the barons who The barons
against
Anselm.
had stood by the Archbishop when he lay under a
manifestly unjust charge joined in the clamour against
him when he declared that the law of the land was
something to be despised and disobeyed. But Anselm's
conscience was not disturbed; he sat quiet and silent,
with his face towards the ground, till the clamour wore
itself out.[2] He then finished his sermon, as Count

---

[1] Hist. Nov. 40. "Tunc rex et comes de Mellento Robertus nomine, in-
terrumpentes verba ejus, 'O, O, dixerunt, prædicatio est quod dicit, prædicatio
est: non rei de qua agitur ulla quæ recipienda sit a prudentibus ratio.'"

[2] Ib. "Ipse inter ora perstrepentium, demisso vultu, mitis sedebat, et

Robert called it.　No Christian man ought to demand
of him that he would never appeal to the blessed Peter
or his Vicar.　So to swear would be to abjure Peter,
and to abjure Peter would be to abjure Christ who had
set Peter as the chief over his Church.　He then turned
to the King with a kind of gentle defiance; "When I
deny Christ, O King, for your sake, then will I not be
slow to pay a fine at the judgement of your court for
my sin in asking your leave."　Half in anger, half in
mockery, Count Robert said, "You will present yourself
to Peter and the Pope; but no Pope shall get the better
of us, to our knowledge."[1]　"God knows," answered
Anselm, "what may be in store for you; He will be
able, if He thinks good, to guide me to the threshold of
his apostles."　With these words the Archbishop rose,
and went again into the outer chamber.

The King and his counsellors seem to have been moved
by the calm resolution of Anselm, even when the letter of
the law was on their own side.　Either Rufus was not in
his most savage mood, or his wily Achitophel contrived
to keep him in some restraint.　Nothing could be gained
by keeping Anselm in the kingdom.　He had already

Anselm to
be allowed
to go, but
the arch-
bishopric
to be seized
if he went.
had the choice set before him.　He might go; but, if he
went, the archbishopric would be seized into the King's
hands.　He had made his choice, and he should be
allowed to carry it out without hindrance; only he knew
on what conditions.　The decision was on the whole not
altogether unfair; but the inherent pettiness of the magnanimous King could not help throwing in an insult or
two by the way.　If Anselm chose to go, all that he had,
in Rufus' version of the law, at once passed to the King.

clamores eorum quasi surda aure despiciebat. Fatigatis autem eis a proprio
strepitu, sedatoque tumultu, Anselmus ad verba sua remeat."

[1] Eadmer, Hist. Nov. 40. "His verbis præfatus comes indignando sub-
urgens, ait, Eia, eia, Petro et papæ te præsentabis, et nos equidem non trans-
ibit quod scimus." I can only guess at the meaning of these last words.

He was therefore told, in the message which was sent
out to him, that he might go, but that he might take
nothing with him which belonged to the King.[1] Anselm
did not, like William of Saint-Calais, bargain for the
means of crossing in state with dogs, hawks, and servants.[2] He seems tacitly to raise a point of law. The
lands of the archbishopric might pass to the King; but
that could not take from him his mere personal goods.
"I have," he said, "horses, clothes, furniture, which perhaps somebody may say are the King's. But I will go
naked and on foot, rather than give up my purpose."
When these words were reported to Rufus, for a moment
he felt a slight sense of shame.[3] He did not wish the
Archbishop to go naked and barefoot. But within eleven
days he must be ready at the haven to cross the sea, and
a messenger from the King would be there to tell him
what he and his companions would be allowed to take
with them. The King's bidding was announced to the
Archbishop, and Anselm's companions wished, now the
matter seemed to be settled, to go at once to their own
quarters. But Anselm would not leave the man who
was his earthly lord, who had once been, in form at
least, his friend, to whom he held himself to stand in
so close an official and personal relation, without one
word face to face. He entered the presence-chamber,
and once more the saint sat down side by side with
the foulest of sinners. "My lord," said Anselm, "I am
going. If I could have gone with your good will, it
would have better become you, and it would have been
more pleasing to every good man. But since things are

---

[1] Eadmer, Hist. Nov. 40. "Ecce ibis. Veruntamen scias dominum nostrum pati nolle te exeuntem quicquam de suis tecum ferre."

[2] See above, p. 93.

[3] Hist. Nov. 40. "In istis princeps pudore suffusus, dictum suum non
ita intellexisse se respondit."

CHAP. IV. turned another way, though it grieves me as regards you, as regards myself I will, according to my power, bear it with a calm mind. And not even for this will I, by the Lord's help, withdraw myself from the love of your soul's health. Now therefore, not knowing when I may again see you, I commend you to God, and, as a ghostly father speaking to a beloved son, as an Archbishop of Canterbury speaking to a King of England, I would, before I go, give you my blessing, if you do not refuse it." For a moment Rufus was touched; his good angel perhaps spoke to him then for the last time. "I refuse not your blessing," was his answer. The man of God arose; the King bowed his head, and Anselm made the sign of the cross over it. He then went forth, leaving the King and all that were with him wondering at the ready cheerfulness with which he spoke and went.[1]

He blesses Rufus.

Rufus and Anselm never met again. From Winchester the Archbishop went to his own home at Canterbury.[2] The day after he came there, he gathered together his monks, and addressed them in a farewell discourse.[3] Then, in the sight of a crowd of monks, clerks, and lay-folk, he took the staff and scrip of a pilgrim before the altar. He commended all present to Christ, and set forth amidst their tears and wailings. The same day he and his comrades reached Dover. There he found that the passing current of better feeling which had touched the King's heart as he bowed his head for Anselm's blessing had been but for a moment. Rufus had gone back to

Anselm at Canterbury.

He takes the pilgrim's staff.

---

[1] Eadmer, Hist. Nov. 41. "Mox ille surgens, levata dextra signum sanctæ crucis super regem ad hoc caput humiliantem edidit, et abscessit, viri alacritatem rege cum suis admirante."

[2] "Ubi sedes pontificalis, ubi totius regni caput est atque primatus," Eadmer takes care to add.

[3] For the discourse we have to go to the Life, ii. 3. 30. It contains the remarkable passage which I referred to in N. C. vol. iv. p. 52.

his old mind, to the spirit of petty insult and petty gain. CHAP. IV.
The King's obedient clerk, William of Warelwast, one William of
day to be the builder of the twin towers of Exeter, Warelwast at Dover.
was there already. For fifteen days Anselm and his
companions were kept at Dover, waiting for a favourable
wind. Meanwhile William of Warelwast went in and
out with Anselm; he ate at his table, and said not a
word of the purpose which had brought him.[1] On the
fifteenth day the wind changed, and the sailors urged the
Archbishop's party to cross at once. When they were
on the shore ready to start, William stopped the Archbishop as if he had been a runaway slave or a criminal
escaping from justice,[2] and in the King's name forbade
him to cross, till he had declared everything that he had
in his baggage. In hope of finding money, all Anselm's
bags and trunks were opened and ransacked, in the
sight of a vast crowd that stood by wondering at so
unheard of a deed, and cursing those who did it.[3] The
bags were opened and ransacked in vain. Nothing was
found that the King's faithful clerk thought worth his
master's taking. The Archbishop, with Baldwin and Anselm
Eadmer, was then allowed to set sail, and they landed crosses to Whitsand.
safely at Whitsand.

As soon as the King heard that Anselm was out of the The arch-
kingdom, he did as he had said that he would do; he bishopric seized by
again seized all the estates of the archbishopric into his the King.
own hands. This was only what was to be looked for;
it was fully in accordance with the doctrines of Flambard, and better kings than William Rufus would

[1] Eadmer, Hist. Nov. 41. "In qua mora idem Willielmus, cum patre
intrans et exiens et in mensa illius quotidie comedens, nihil de causa pro
qua missus fuerat agere volebat."

[2] Ib. "Patrem patriæ, primatem totius Britanniæ, Willielmus ille, quasi
fugitivum vel alicujus immanis sceleris reum, in littore detinuit."

[3] Ib. "Ingenti plebis multitudine circumstante ac nefarium opus, pro
sui novitate, admirando spectante et spectando exsecrante."

<small>CHAP. IV.</small> have done the like in the like case. But Rufus or his agents went much further. Our guide implies that he acted as if Anselm had been an intruder in the arch-

<small>Anselm's acts declared null.</small> bishopric. All the acts and orders of Anselm during his four years' primacy—that is, we must suppose, all leases, grants, and legal transactions of every kind— were declared null and void.[1] Much loss and wrong must have been thus caused to many persons. A man who had, in the old phrase, bought land of the archbishopric for a term or for lives[2] would lose his land, and, we may be sure, would not get back his money. A clerk collated by the Archbishop might be turned out of his living to make room for a nominee of the King. It is no wonder then that the wrongs which were done now were said to be greater than the wrongs which had been done when the archiepiscopal estates had before been seized after the death of Lanfranc.[3] For at any rate the acts of Lanfranc were not reversed. One feels a certain desire to know what became of the Archbishop's knights whose array had so displeased the King earlier in the year. But we hear nothing of them or of any particular class; all is quite general. In one case indeed it is quite certain that the rule that all Anselm's acts should be treated as in-

<small>The monks keep Peckham.</small> valid was not carried out. The monks of Christ Church clearly kept their temporary possession of the manor of Peckham. For they spent the whole income of it on great architectural works which Anselm himself had begun. The metropolitan church, so lately rebuilt by Lanfranc, had already become small in the eyes of a younger generation, as indeed it was smaller than many

---

[1] Eadmer, Hist. Nov. 41. "Irrita fieri omnia quæ per ipsum mutata vel statuta fuisse probari poterant, ex quo primo venerat in archiepiscopatum."

[2] See N. C. vol. v. p. 772.

[3] Hist. Nov. 41. "Ut tribulationes quæ factæ sunt in illo post mortem venerandæ memoriæ Lanfranci ante introitum patris Anselmi parvipensæ sunt comparatione tribulationum quæ factæ sunt his diebus."

minsters of the same date. The church of Lanfranc had CHAP. IV.
followed the usual Norman plan; the short eastern
limb, the monks' choir, was under the tower.[1] The Rebuilding
arrangements of the minster were now recast after a new of the choir
of Christ
pattern which did not commonly prevail till many years Church.
later. The eastern limb was rebuilt on a far greater
scale, itself forming as it were a cruciform church, with
its own transepts, its own towers, one of which in after
days received the name of Anselm. This work, begun Ernulf
Prior
by Anselm before his banishment, was carried on in his 1096 ?
absence by the prior of his appointment, Ernulf—Earn- Abbot of
Peter-
wulf—a monk of his old house of Bec, but perhaps of borough,
1107 ;
English birth, who rose afterwards to be Abbot of Peter- Bishop of
borough and Bishop of Rochester.[2] In marked contrast Rochester,
1115.
to the speed with which Lanfranc had carried through
his work, the choir begun by Ernulf and carried on by
his successor Prior Conrad was not consecrated till late
in the days of Henry.[3]

After reading the accounts of these two great debates Comparison of the
or trials, at Rockingham and at Winchester, it is im- trials of
possible to avoid looking both backwards and forwards. William of
Saint-
The story of these proceedings must be told, as I have Calais,
Anselm,
throughout tried to tell it, with an eye to the earlier and
proceedings against William of Saint-Calais, to the later Thomas.
proceedings against Thomas of London. The three stories

[1] See N. C. vol. iv. p. 359.

[2] Eadmer (Hist. Nov. 35) describes the new building as "novum opus
quod a majori turre in orientem tenditur, quodque ipse pater Anselmus
inchoasse dinoscitur." Its minute history must be studied in Gervase and
Willis.

[3] This was the time when Henry the First broke out into the fit of
devout swearing of which I spoke in N. C. vol. v. p. 844 ; Ann. Osney, 1130 ;
" Rex Henricus ecclesiam Christi Cantuariensis nobiliter dedicari fecit, adeo
ut, coruscante luminaribus ecclesia, et singulis altaribus singulis episcopis
deputatis, cum simul omnes inciperent canticum 'Terribilis est locus iste,'
et classicum mirabiliter intonaret, rex illustris, præ lætitia se non capiens,
juramento per mortem Domini regio affirmaret vere terribilem esse."

CHAP. IV. supply an instructive contrast. In each case a bishop is arraigned before a civil tribunal; in each case the bishop appeals to the Pope; but beyond that the three men have

Compari-
son of the
men.
little in common. William and Thomas were both of them, though in widely different senses, playing a part; it is Anselm alone who is throughout perfectly simple and unconscious. Through the whole of Anselm's life, we feel that he never could have acted otherwise than as he did act. He never stopped to think what was the right thing for a saintly archbishop to do; he simply did at all times

Position of
Thomas;
what his conscience told him that he ought to do. Thomas, perfectly sincere, thoroughly bent on doing his duty, was still following a conscious ideal of duty; he was always thinking what a saintly archbishop ought to do; above all things, we may be sure, he was thinking what Anselm, in the like case, would have done. Thus, while Anselm acts quite singly, Thomas is, consciously though

of William
of Saint-
Calais.
sincerely, playing a part. William of Saint-Calais is playing a part in a far baser sense; he appeals to the Pope, he appeals to ecclesiastical privileges in general, simply to serve his own personal ends. He appealed to those privileges more loudly than anybody else, when he thought that by that appeal he might himself escape condemnation. He trampled them under foot more scornfully than anybody else, when he thought that by so doing he might bring about the condemnation of Anselm and his own promotion. But it is curious to see how in some points the sincere acting of Thomas and the insincere acting of William agree as distinguished from the pure single-mindedness of Anselm. Both William and Thomas distinctly appeal to the Pope from the sentence of the

Anselm
does not
strictly
appeal to
the Pope.
highest court in their own land. We cannot say that Anselm did this; he does not refuse the sentence of the King's court; he does not ask the Pope to set aside the sentence of the King's court; the utmost that he does is

to say that it is his duty to obey God rather than man, CHAP. IV. and that his duty to God obliges him to go to the Pope. To the Pope therefore he will go, even though the King forbids him; but he is ready at the same time to bear patiently the spoiling of his goods as the penalty of going. This is assuredly not an appeal to the Pope in the same sense as the appeals made by William and Thomas.

Among the marks of difference in the cases is that both William and Thomas strongly assert the privileges of their order; none but the Pope may judge a bishop. Anselm never once, during his whole dispute with William Anselm Rufus, makes the slightest claim to any such privilege; does not assert he never breathes a word about the rights of the clerical clerical privileges. order. The doctrine that none but the Pope may judge the Archbishop of Canterbury—nothing is said about other priests or other bishops—is heard of only once during the whole story.[1] And then it is not put forth by Anselm; it is not openly put forth by anybody; it is merely mentioned by Eadmer as something which came into the minds of the undutiful bishops as a kind of after-thought. This most likely means that it was not really thought of at the time, either by the bishops or by anybody else, but that Eadmer, writing by fresh lights learned at Rome and at Bari, could no longer understand a state of things in which it was not thought of by somebody. The truth doubtless is that in Anselm's day the doctrine of clerical exemption from temporal jurisdiction was a novelty which was creeping in. It was well known enough for Odo and William of Saint-Calais to catch at it to serve their own ends; it was not so fully established that it was at all a matter of conscience with Anselm to assert it. By the time of Thomas every doctrine of the kind had so grown that its assertion had become a point of conscience

[1] See above, p. 516.

with every strict churchman. But there is another point in which the case of Anselm and the case of Thomas agree as distinguished from the case of William of Saint-Calais. In this last case nothing turned on any promise of the Bishop to obey the customs of the realm. Much in the case of Anselm, much more in the case of Thomas, turned on such a promise. In each case the Archbishop pleads a certain reservation expressed or understood; but there is a wide difference between the reservation made by Anselm and the reservation made by Thomas. The favourite formula with Thomas, the formula which he proposes, the formula which he is at Clarendon with difficulty persuaded to withdraw and on which he again falls back,[1] is "saving my order." Anselm has nothing to say about his order; he is not fighting for the privileges of any special body of men; he is simply a righteous man clothed with a certain office, the duties of which office he must discharge. It is not his order that he reserves; he reserves only the higher and more abiding names of God and right.

As for the cases themselves and the tribunals before which they were heard, we must always remember that our reports, though very full, are not official. Their authors therefore use technical or non-technical language at pleasure. They assume familiarity with the nature of the court and its mode of procedure; they do not stop to explain many things which we should be very glad if they had stopped to explain. But it is clear that the nature of the proceedings was not exactly the same in

the three cases. And it is singular that, in point of mere procedure, there seems more likeness between the case of Anselm and the case of Thomas than there is between either and the case of William of Saint-Calais. William

---

[1] "Salvo ordine meo." See Herbert of Bosham, iii. 24, vol. iii. p. 273, Robertson.

of Saint-Calais and Thomas were both of them, in the CHAP. IV.
strictest sense, summoned before a court to answer a William and Thomas
charge.   The charges were indeed of quite different Thomas
kinds in the two cases.   William of Saint-Calais was summoned to answer a
charged with high treason.   Thomas, besides a number charge.
of demands about money, was charged only with failing
to appear in the King's court in answer to an earlier
summons.   Anselm, on the other hand, cannot be said Anselm
to have been really charged with anything, though the seeks advice on
King and his party tried to treat him as though he had a point of law.
been.   The assembly at Rockingham was gathered at
Anselm's own request, to inform him on a point of law.
The King and his bishops tried to treat Anselm as a
criminal; but they found that the general feeling of the
assembly would not allow them to do so.   At Winchester
again, Anselm was not summoned to answer any charge,
for the charge about the troops in the Welsh war had
been dropped at Windsor.   The charges, such as they are,
which are brought against him turn up as it were casually
in the course of the proceedings.   Yet the order of things
seems much the same in the case of Anselm and in
the case of Thomas, while in the case of William of
Saint-Calais it seems to be different.   In the case of Proceed-
William of Saint-Calais everything is done in the ings in the case of
King's presence.   The Bishop himself has more than William of Saint-
once to leave the place of meeting, while particular Calais.
points are discussed; but there is not that endless going
to and fro which there is in the other two cases.   In the
case of Thomas, as in the case of Anselm, we see plainly
the inner room where the King sits with his immediate
counsellors, while the Archbishop waits in an outer place
with the general body of the assembly.   At Northamp- Architec-
ton we see the architectural arrangement more clearly tural arrange-
than either at Rockingham or at Winchester.   Thomas ments.
enters the great hall, and goes no further, while the

CHAP. IV.
Constitution of the several assemblies. King's inner council is held in the solar.[1] It is possible, as indeed I have already hinted,[2] that there was a difference in the nature of the assembly in the case of William of Saint-Calais and in the two cases of Anselm and Thomas. We must remember that in the reign of William Rufus the judicial and administrative system was still only forming itself, and that many things were then vague and irregular, both in fact and in name, which had taken a definite shape in the time of Henry the Second. Between the case of Anselm and the case of Thomas came the justiciarship of Roger of Salisbury and the chancellorship of Thomas himself. I am inclined to think that, at Rockingham, at Winchester, at Northampton, the assembly was strictly the great assembly of the nation, the ancient Witenagemót, with such changes in its working as had taken place between the days of the Confessor and the days of William Rufus, and again between the days of William Rufus and the days of Henry the Second. Each of these periods of change would of course do something towards taking away from the old popular character of the assembly. At Rockingham that popular character is by no means lost. We are not told where the line, if any, was drawn; but a multitude of monks, clerks, and laymen were there.[3] At Northampton we hear of no class below the lesser barons; and they, with the sheriffs, wait in the outer hall, till they are specially summoned

The Witenagemót;

its constitution becomes gradually less popular.

---

[1] The Archbishop enters the hall ("aula"), while the King is in "cœnaculo seorsum" (Herbert, iii. 37, vol. iii. p. 305). From pp. 307, 309 it appears that this *cœnaculum* was simply a solar or upper chamber; "Universis quotquot erant de cœnaculo ad domum inferiorem in qua nos eramus, descendentibus." William Fitz-Stephen (vol. iii. p. 57) seems to speak of the hall as "camera;" cf. p. 50.

[2] See above, p. 94.

[3] Will. Fitz-Steph. 58, vol. iii. p. 67. "A comitibus et baronibus suum exigit rex de archiepiscopo judicium. Evocantur quidam vicecomites et secundæ dignitatis barones, antiqui dierum, ut addantur eis et assint judicio."

to the King's presence. At Rockingham too and at CHAP. IV.
Winchester there seems much greater freedom of speech Lessened freedom of speech.
than there is at Northampton. The whole assembly
shouts and cheers as it pleases, and a simple knight
steps forth to speak and to speak boldly.[1] At Northampton, as at Rockingham and at Winchester, the Archbishop is allowed the company of his personal followers.
William Fitz-Stephen and Herbert of Bosham sit at the
feet of Thomas, as Eadmer and Baldwin sit at the feet
of Anselm. But at Northampton the disciples are
roughly checked in speaking to their master, in a way
of which there is no sign in the earlier assemblies. At
Rockingham and Winchester again, though the Archbishop stays for the most part outside in the hall, yet he
more than once goes unbidden into the presence-chamber,
and is even followed thither by his faithful monks. At
Northampton Thomas is never admitted to the King's
presence, and no one seems to go into the inner room who is
not specially summoned. This may be merely because, as
is likely enough, strictness of rule, form, and etiquette had
greatly advanced between William Rufus and Henry the
Second. Or it may have been because Thomas was
strictly summoned to answer a charge, while Anselm was
really under no charge at all, but came as a member of
the assembly.

Another point here arises. I cannot but think that in The inner and outer council;
these great assemblies, consisting of an inner and an outer
body, we must see the same kind of distinction which we
saw on the great day of Salisbury between the Witan
and the landsitting men. That is, I see in the inner and foreshadowing of lords and commons.
outer bodies the foreshadowing of Lords and Commons.
To this day there is one chamber in which the King's
throne is set; there is another chamber whose occupants
do not enter the presence of that throne, except by

[1] See above, p. 508.

CHAP. IV.

special summons. I am inclined therefore to see, both in the case of Anselm and in the case of Thomas, a true gathering of the Witan of the realm. Thomas comes, like Strafford or Hastings, to answer a charge before the Court of our Lord the King in Parliament,[1] that court, which from an assembly of the whole nation, gradually shrank up into an assembly of the present peerage. In the case of Anselm I see the same body acting, not strictly as a court, but rather as the great inquest of the nation, but at the same time fluctuating somewhat, as was but natural in that age, between its judicial and its legislative functions. But in the tribunal which sat on William of Saint-Calais I am, as I have already said, inclined to see, not the *Mickle Gemót* of the whole nation, but rather the King's court in a narrower sense, the representative of the ancient *Theningmannagemót*, the more strictly official body.[2] Here we have no division of chambers; the proceedings are strictly those of a court trying a charge, and the King, as chief judge, is present throughout.

Thomas tried before the Witan;

William before the Theningmannagemót.

---

[1] The distinction between the Court of our Lord the King in Parliament and the Court of the Lord High Steward is most clearly brought out in Jardine's Criminal Trials, i. 229. Lord Macaulay (iv. 153) is less accurate. He speaks of the Court of our Lord the King in Parliament as one form of the Court of the Lord High Steward. But in truth, the Court of our Lord the King in Parliament is simply the Witan sitting for a judicial purpose. The Lords alone sit, because the Commons have never attained to a share in the judicial functions of the Witan. The right to be tried before the Witan thus sitting judicially is naturally confined to those classes of persons who have kept or acquired the right to the personal summons, that is, to the peers.

If it should be objected that this privilege does not now extend to the spiritual peers, the reason is most likely to be found in the fact that for some ages a bishop would not be tried before any temporal court at all. When such trials began again in the sixteenth century, the later notion of peerage had grown up, and those peers whose holding was still strictly official was looked on as in some measure less fully peers than those whose peerage was "hereditary" in the modern sense.

[2] See N. C. vol. v. pp. 423, 878.

As for the matter of the three cases, the trial of CHAP. IV.
William of Saint-Calais was in itself the perfectly fair Estimate of the three
trial of a rebel who, in the end, after the custom of the cases.
age, came off very lightly for his rebellion. There really Behaviour of Rufus;
seems nothing to blame William Rufus for in that matter
—William Rufus, that is, still largely guided by Lanfranc
—except some characteristic pettinesses just towards the
end of the story.[1] Towards Anselm William appears—
save under one or two momentary touches of better
feeling—simply as the power of evil striving, by whatever means, to crush the power of good. He seems none
the less so, even when on particular points his own case
is technically right. Henry the Second, acting honestly of Henry the Second.
for the good of his kingdom, both technically and
morally right in his main quarrel, stoops to the base and
foolish course of trying to crush his adversary by a
crowd of charges in which the King seems to have been
both morally and technically wrong, and which certainly would never have been brought if the Archbishop
had not given offence on other grounds. William Rufus
again, and Henry the Second also, each forsook his own
position by calling in, when it suited their momentary
purposes, the very power which their main position bade
them to control and to keep out of their kingdom. Not Compari- son with Henry the First.
so the great king who came between them. The Lion of
Justice knew, and he alone in those days seems to have
known, how to carry on a controversy of principle,
without ever forsaking his own position, without ever
losing his temper or lowering his dignity, without any
breach of personal respect and friendship towards the
holy man whom his kingly office made it his duty to
withstand.

The three years of Anselm's first sojourn beyond sea

[1] See above, p. 115.

CHAP. IV.

Effect on
Anselm of
his foreign
sojourn.

concern us for the most part only indirectly. Of their most important aspect, as concerns us, I have spoken elsewhere,[1] and we shall again see their fruit before the present work is ended. In his journeyings to Lyons, to Rome, to Bari, Anselm learned a new doctrine which he had never found out either at Bec or at Canterbury. It was not for his good that he, who had, like the Primates who had gone before him, received his staff from the King's hands, and placed his own hands in homage between them, should hear the anathema pronounced against the prince who should bestow or the clerk who should receive any ecclesiastical benefice in such sort as no prince had scrupled to give them, as no clerk had scrupled to receive them, in the days of King Eadward and in the days of King William.[2] When Anselm came back to England, he came, as we shall see, the same Anselm as of old in every personal quality, in every personal virtue. But in all things which touched the relations of popes, kings, and bishops, he came back another man.

Change
in him.

His
journey.

But in the course of Anselm's adventures, in his foreign journeys, there are details here and there which no Englishman can read without interest. We come across constant signs of the place which England and her Primate held in the minds of men of other lands. We read how no less a prince than Odo Duke of Burgundy, already a crusader in Spain and afterwards a crusader in Palestine, was tempted by the report of the wealth of the great English see to sink into a common robber, and to set forth for the purpose of plundering the Primate as he passed through his land. We read how he was turned from his purpose, when he saw the white hair, the gentle and venerable look, of the Archbishop,

Alleged
scheme of
Odo Duke
of Bur-
gundy
[1078-
1102]
against
Anselm.

[1] See N. C. vol. v. p. 145.
[2] See the decree of the Council, Hist. Nov. 53.

the look which won all hearts. Instead of harming him, CHAP. IV.
Odo received his kiss and sought his blessing, and sent
him under a safe guard to the borders of his duchy.[1] We
read how the likeness of that venerable face had been
painted by cunning limners in the interest of Clement,
that the robbers who were sent to seize the faithful
follower of Urban might better know their intended
victim. We read with some national pride how, at his Anselm at
first interview with Urban, when Anselm bowed himself Rome.
at the Pontiff's feet, he was raised, received to his kiss,
and seated by him as one of equal rank, the Pope
and Patriarch of another world. We read how, in Council of
the great gathering in the head church of the city and Lateran.
of the world, when no man knew what was the fitting
place in a Roman council for a guest such as none
had ever seen before, the English Archbishop was placed
at the papal bidding in a seat of special honour.
Anselm took his seat in that apse which was spared
when papal barbarism defaced the long arcades of
Constantine, when the patriarchal throne of the world
was cast forth as an useless thing,[2] but which the more
relentless havoc of our own day, eager, it would seem,
to get rid of all that is older than the dogmas of
modern Rome, has ruthlessly swept away. We read how
visitors and pilgrims from England bowed to kiss the
feet of Anselm, as they would have kissed those of
Urban himself, and how the humble saint ever refused

---

[1] Eadmer, Hist. Nov. 42. We are told that the Duke, "succensus amore
pecuniæ quam copiosam illum ferre rumor disperserat, proponit animo eam
ipsi auferre." But there is really nothing in what Odo is said to have
done which implies any such bad purpose. Perhaps Eadmer judged him
uncharitably.

[2] See Historical Essays, Third Series, p. 20. On my last visit to Rome
(1881) I found the apse of Saint John Lateran destroyed, not by Huns or
Turks, but by its own chapter, with the approval, it is said, of its present
and late bishops. I believe there is some pretence of enlarging the church,
and of replacing the mosaics in a new apse.

CHAP. IV. such unbecoming worship.[1] And we are most touched of all to hear how, among all these honours, Anselm was commonly spoken of in Rome, not by his name, not by the titles of his office, but simply as "the holy man."[2] At Rome, that name might have a special meaning. It was well deserved by the one suitor at the Roman throne who abstained from the use of Rome's most convincing argument.

But in the record of Anselm's wanderings there is one tale which comes home more than any other to the hearts of Englishmen, a tale which carries us back, if not strictly to the days of English freedom, at least to the days when we had a conqueror whom we had made

Council
of Bari.

our own. The fathers are gathered at Bari, in the great minster of the Lykian Nicolas, where the arts of northern and southern Christendom, the massiveness of the Norman, the finer grace of the Greek, are so strangely blended in the pile which was then fresh from the craftsman's hand. There, in his humility, the pilgrim from Canterbury takes to himself a modest place amongst the other bishops, with the faithful Eadmer sitting at his feet.[3] The Pope calls on his father and master, Anselm Archbishop of the English, to arise and speak. There, in the city so lately torn away from Eastern Christendom, Anselm is bidden to justify the change which Latin theology had made in that

---

[1] Eadmer, Vit. Ans. ii. 5. 48. "Angli illis temporibus Romam venientes, pedes ejus ad instar pedum Romani pontificis sua oblatione honorare desiderabant. Quibus ille nequaquam acquiescens, in secretiorem domus partem fugiebat, et eos pro tali re nullo patiebatur ad se pacto accedere."

[2] Hist. Nov. 49. "Hinc etiam erat quod non facile a quoquam Romæ simpliciter homo vel archiepiscopus, sed quasi proprio nomine sanctus homo vocabatur."

[3] Eadmer brings this out with all vividness, Hist. Nov. 49; "Sedebat enim idem pater in ordine cæterorum inter primos concilii patres, et ego ad pedes ejus." Then the Pope calls him, "Pater et magister Anselme, Anglorum archiepiscope, ubi es?"

creed of the East which changeth not. The Pope CHAP. IV.
harangues on the sufferings of the Church in various
lands, and, above all, on the evil deeds of the tyrant
of England. The assembled fathers agree with one
voice that the sword of Peter must be drawn, and
that such a sinner must be smitten in the face of the
whole world. Then Anselm kneels at the feet of Urban, Anselm
and craves that no such blow may be dealt on the pleads for Rufus.
man who had so deeply wronged him.[1] But, while
these high debates were going on, the curious eye of
Eadmer had lighted on an object which spoke straight
to his heart as an Englishman and a monk of Christ
Church. Among the assembled prelates the Archbishop The cope
of Beneventum appeared clad in a cope of surpassing of Bene-ventum.
richness. Eadmer knew at once whence it came; he
knew that it had once been one of the glories of Canterbury, worn by Primates of England before England had
bowed either to the Norman or to the Dane. Eadmer,
brought up from his childhood in the cloister of Christ
Church, had been taught as a boy by aged monks who
could remember the days of Cnut and Emma. Those Dealings
elders of the house, Eadwig and Blæcman and Farman, between Canterbury
had told him how in those days there had been a mighty and Bene-
famine in the land of Apulia, how the then Archbishop ventum.
of Beneventum had travelled through foreign lands to
seek help for his starving flock, how he brought with
him a precious relic, the arm of the apostle Bartholomew, and how, having passed through Italy and Gaul,
he was led to cross the sea by the fame of the wealth of

---

[1] The whole story is charmingly told by Eadmer, Hist. Nov. 50. His
picture of himself and his curiosity in the new world which is opened to
him is delightful. So is his joy when he sees the cope of which he has so
often heard and shows it to Anselm; "Cum, ut dixi, concilio præsens antis-
titem Beneventanum, cappa reliquis præstante ornatum, viderem, et eam ex
his quæ olim audieram optime nossem, non modice lætatus et cappam et
verba mihi puero ex inde dicta patri Anselmo ostendi."

CHAP. IV. England and of the piety and bounty of Emma its Lady. She gave him plenteous gifts for his people, and he asked whether she would not give yet more as the price of the precious relic. The genuineness of the treasure was solemnly sworn to;[1] a great price was paid for it by the Lady, and, by the special order of King Cnut, it was added as a precious gift to the treasures of the metropolitan church. For in those days, says Eadmer, it was the manner of the English to set the patronage of the saints before all the wealth of this world. The Archbishop of Beneventum went back, loaded with the alms of England, and bearing with him, among other gifts from his brother Primate Æthelnoth, this very cope richly embroidered with gold with all the skill of English hands. Eadmer, taught by the tradition of his elders, knew the vestment as he saw it in that far land on the shoulders of the successor of the prelate who had come to our island for help in his day of need. He saw it with joy; he pointed it out to Father Anselm, and, feigning ignorance, he asked the Beneventan Archbishop the history of the splendid cope which he wore. He was pleased to find that the tradition of Beneventum was the same as the tradition of Canterbury.[2] Now that we have made our way into other times and other lands, it is pleasing to look back for a moment, with our faithful Eadmer, to days when England still was England, even though she had already learned to bow to a foreign King and a foreign Lady.

Emma buys the arm of Saint Bartholomew.

Æthelnoth's gift of the cope.

Eadmer recognises the cope.

More important in a general view than the details of

---

[1] Eadmer, Hist. Nov. 51. Some one, seemingly the Lady herself, requires that he shall swear "super corpus Dominicum et super sanctorum reliquias quas ei proponam jurejurando reliquias de quibus agitur veraciter esse de corpore beati apostoli Bartholomæi, et id remota omni æquivocatione atque sophismate." The Archbishop was quite ready to swear.

[2] Ib. "Inter alia mutuæ dilectionis colloquia cœpi de eadem cappa loqui, et unde illam haberet quasi nescius interrogavi."

Anselm's journey are the negotiations which went on CHAP. IV. during this time between William, Urban, and Anselm. The Red King's day of grace was now over. The last Position of Rufus. touch of feeling recorded of him is when he bowed his head to receive Anselm's blessing. Henceforth he stands out, in a more marked way than ever, in the character which distinguishes him from other kings and from other men. We have had evil kings before and after him; but we have had none other who openly chose evil to be his good, none other who declared himself in plain words to be the personal enemy of the Almighty. Yet, as we have already noticed, the bolts of the Church never lighted on the head of this worst of royal sinners. We have just seen how once at least he was spared by the merciful intercession of his own victim. We are tempted to stop Possible effect of excommuni- and think how a formal excommunication would have worked on such an one as William Rufus had now be- cation on him. come. We must remember that the weight of papal excom- Papal ex- munications of princes had not yet been lowered, as it came communi- cations to be lowered afterwards, either by their frequency or by not yet their manifest injustice. The cases which were then fresh despised. in men's minds were all striking and weighty. The ex- The Em- communication of the Emperor was, from the papal point peror Henry. of view, a natural stage of the great struggle which was still raging. Philip of France had been excommunicated Philip of France. for a moral offence which seemed the darker because it involved the mockery of an ecclesiastical sacrament. And no man could wonder or blame when, in the days Boleslaus of Hildebrand, Boleslaus of Poland was put out of the of Poland. 1079. communion of the faithful for slaying with his own hands before the altar the bishop who had rebuked him for his sins.[1] The case most akin to the wanton excommunications of later times had been when Alexander the

---

[1] The story is told in the Annales Capituli Cracoviensis (Pertz, xix. 588), 1079, and more briefly in other annals in the same volume.

CHAP. IV.
The case of
Harold.
Second in form, when Hildebrand in truth, had denounced Harold without a hearing for no crime but that
of accepting the crown which his people gave him. But
men are so apt to judge by results that the fall of
Harold and of England may by this time, even among
Englishmen, have begun to be looked on as a witness to
the power of the Church's thunders. In the days of
Rufus a papal excommunication was still a real and
fearful thing at which men stood aghast. It might not
have turned the heart of Rufus; it might even have
hardened his heart yet further. But among his people,
even among his own courtiers, the effect would doubtless have been such that he must in the end, like
Philip, have formally given way. As it was, the
bolt never fell; the hand of Anselm stopped it once;
other causes, as we shall soon see, stopped it afterwards. And, instead of the formal excommunication of
Rome, there came that more striking excommunication
by the voice of the English people, when, by a common
instinct, they declared William the Red to have no true
part in that communion of the faithful from which he
had never been formally cut off.

Probable
effect of an
excommu-
nication on
the people.

Anselm
writes to
the Pope
from
Lyons.

His new
tone.

The negotiations, if we may so call them, which followed the departure of Anselm may be looked on as
beginning with a letter written by Anselm to the Pope
from Lyons.[1] The Archbishop, once out of England,
seems to take up a new tone. His language with regard
to the King's doings is still singularly mild;[2] but he
now begins to speak, not only of God and right, but of
the canons of the Church and the authority of the Pope,

---

[1] Eadmer, Hist. Nov. 43.

[2] Ib. "Ipse rex faciebat quædam quæ facienda non videbantur de
ecclesiis, quas post obitum prælatorum aliter quam oporteret tracta-
bat."

as something to which the arbitrary customs of Eng- CHAP. IV.
land must give way.[1] To those customs he cannot agree
without perilling his own soul and the souls of his
successors. He comes to the Apostolic See for help and
counsel.[2] When he had reached Rome, he again set Anselm
forth his case more fully, as it had been set forth in the at Rome.
letter from Lyons. Letters both from Anselm and from Letters to
the Pope were sent to the King by the same messenger, the King.
letters which unluckily are not preserved. The summary
of the papal letter seems to point to a lofty tone on the
part of the Pontiff. He moves, he exhorts, he at last
commands, King William, to leave the goods of the Archbishop free, and to restore everything to him.[3] Anselm's
own letter was doubtless in a milder strain. The messenger came back, to find both Urban and Anselm again
at Rome after the synod at Bari. The letter from Urban His recep-
had been received, though ungraciously; the letter from tion of the
letters.
Anselm was sent back. As soon as the King knew that
the bearer was a man of the Archbishop's, he had sworn
by the face of Lucca that, unless the messenger speedily
got him away out of his lands, he would have his eyes
torn out without fail.[4]

The Pope however could hardly be left wholly with- Mission of
out some answer, however scornfully William might deal William of
Warelwast.

---

[1] Eadmer, Hist. Nov. 43. "Legem Dei et canonicas et apostolicas auctori-
tates voluntariis consuetudinibus obrui videbam. De his omnibus cum
loquebar, nihil efficiebam, et non tam simplex rectitudo quam voluntariæ
consuetudines obtendebantur."

[2] He gives among his reasons, "Nec de his placitare poteram; nullus
enim aut consilium aut auxilium mihi ad hæc audebat dare."

[3] Ib. 45. "Scribit literas Willielmo regi Angliæ, in quibus ut res Anselmi liberas in regno suo faceret, et de suis omnibus illum revestiret, movet,
hortatur, imperat."

[4] Ib. 51. "Susceptis quidem quoquo modo literis papæ, literas Anselmi
nullo voluisse pacto suscipere, imo, cognito illum [nuntium] esse hominem
ejus, jurasse per vultum Dei quia, si festine terram suam non exiret, sine
retractatione oculos ei erui faceret."

CHAP. IV. with the letter of his own subject. But the answer was not speedy in coming. Its bearer was the trusty clerk William of Warelwast, of whom we have already heard more than once. The King's business did not now call for the same haste as it had done when the same man was sent to find out who was the true Pope.[1] Much happened before he came. Amongst other things, not a few travellers came from England and Normandy, bringing with them fresh and fresh reports of the evil doings of the King, some of which we have already heard of. William was now in Normandy. He crossed at Martinmas,[2] and spent the whole of the next year in the wars of France and Maine. He did not come back to England till the Easter of the year following that.[3] It was now that he played at Rouen the part of a missionary of the creed of Moses.[4] But he kept his eye upon England also; for to this time is assigned the story of the fifty Englishmen who so enraged the blaspheming King by proving their innocence by the ordeal.[5] Nor was it merely rumours of William's doings at home which found their way into Italy from Normandy and England. While the King was devising his answer to the Pope, his emissaries were busy in other parts of the peninsula. The affairs of the Normans in their two great settlements are always joining in one stream. While Bohemund and Tancred were on their Eastern march, the reigning princes of their house, Roger of Apulia and Roger of Sicily, were carrying on their schemes of advancement west of Hadria. Their armies now lay before Capua. Meanwhile Anselm had with-

Margin notes:

William on the continent. November, 1097– April, 1099.

Affairs of Southern Italy.

Siege of Capua.

---

[1] See above, p. 526.

[2] Chron. Petrib. 1097. We shall come to his crossing and returning in another chapter.

[3] Ib. 1099.

[4] See above, p. 162.　　　　　　[5] See above, p. 155.

drawn with John Abbot of Telesia to seek quiet in a town CHAP. IV.
of the Abbot's on the upper Vulturnus, whose name of Anselm at Schiavia.
Schiavia may suggest some ethnological questions.[1] Our
guide specially marks that this journey was a journey
into Samnium; he may not have fully taken in how
truly Telesia was the heart of Samnium, alike in the
days of the Pontius of the Caudine Forks and in the
days of the Pontius of the Colline Gate.[2] Here, in his He writes
Samnite retreat, Anselm was moulding the theology of all "Cur Deus Homo."
later times by his treatise which told why God became
Man.[3] Meanwhile William of England, at war with righteousness in all its forms, held Helias in his prison at
Bayeux,[4] and plotted against Anselm in his hermitage at
Schiavia. When Duke Roger's army was so near, the
master of Normandy deemed that something might be
done for his purpose by Norman arms or Norman craft.
He sent letters—his letters could go speedily when speed
was needed—to stir up Duke Roger to do some mischief to the man whom he hated.[5] The plot was in
vain. Anselm was invited to the Duke's camp; he was Anselm and Urban before Capua.
received there with all honour during a sojourn of some
time, as he was at every other point of the Duke's
dominions to which he went.[6] The Pope and Anselm,

---

[1] Eadmer, Hist. Nov. 45. "Ducit eum [abbas] in villam suam *Sclaviam*
nomine, quæ in montis altitudine sita, sano jugiter aere conversantibus illic
habilis exstat."

[2] See Historical Essays, Second Series, p. 357, ed. 2; Arnold, Hist. Rome,
ii. 365.

[3] Vita Anselmi, ii. 4. 43.

[4] We shall come to this in another chapter.

[5] The reception of Anselm by Duke Roger is described by Eadmer in
both his works (Hist. Nov. 46, and in the Life, ii. 5. 45). The plots of
William Rufus come from William of Malmesbury (Gest. Pont. 98);
"Adeo ut Rogerus dux Apuliæ, apud quem rex Angliæ illum litteris in-
simulandum curaverat, spretis neniis, longe aliter sententiam suam in
viri honorem transferret."

[6] There is something rather singular in the picture of the Pope and
Anselm dwelling in the camp of the besiegers (Hist. Nov. 46); "Plures

CHAP. IV. patriarchs of two worlds, were Duke Roger's guests at the same time. But only the rich dared to present themselves in the presence of the Pope of the mainland, while the shepherd of the nations beyond the sea wel-

Anselm and the Saracens.

comed men of all kinds lovingly.[1] The very Saracens whom Count Roger had brought from Sicily to the help of his nephew pressed to visit the holy man of another faith, to be received and fed at his cost, to kiss his hands, and to cover him with prayers and blessings. Not a few of them were even ready to embrace Anselm's creed;[2] but proselytism among his soldiers formed no part of the policy of the conqueror of Sicily. Count Roger was ready enough to extend the territorial bounds of

exhinc dies in obsidione fecimus, remoti in tentoriis a frequentia et tumultu perstrepentis exercitus. . . . Sicque donec civitas in deditionem transiit, obsidio illius dominum papam et Anselmum vicinos habuit, ita ut familia illorum magis videretur una quam duæ." This is one of several passages in which Anselm and others seem to take a state of war for granted. There is no protest, no pleading of any kind, on behalf of the besieged city. There are some remarks of M. de Rémusat (Saint Anselme, p. 362) on this subject, with regard to the correspondence between Henry and Anselm after the battle of Tinchebrai. But in this last case the victory of Henry was surely a gain to humanity. In the Life Eadmer gives some curious details of their life in the camp, and of a remarkable escape of Anselm.

[1] Eadmer seems to take a certain pleasure in little hits against Urban, which his conduct presently made not wholly undeserved. Thus, in Hist. Nov. 46, he points out how the Pope came to the camp " ingenti sæcularis gloriæ pompa." So now in the Life (ii. 5. 46) he contrasts the demeanour of Urban with that of Anselm at some length, and ends, "Multi ergo, quos timor prohibebat ad papam accedere, festinabant ad Anselmum venire, amore ducti qui nescit timere. Majestas etenim papæ solos admittebat divites, humanitas Anselmi sine personarum acceptione suscipiebat omnes."

[1] Vita, ii. 5.46. "Et quos omnes ? Paganos etiam, ut de Christianis taceam." Eadmer then goes on to speak at some length of the Saracens brought over by Count Roger, whom he pointedly speaks of as the man of his nephew ; " Homo ducis Rogerus, comes de Sicilia." We read how Anselm received and entertained many of the Mussulmans, and how, when he passed through their camp, " ingens multitudo eorum elevatis ad cælum manibus ei prospera imprecarentur, et osculatis pro ritu suo manibus propriis necne coram eo genibus flexis, pro sua eum benigna largitate grates agendo venerarentur."

Christendom by his sword; but he found, as his great- CHAP. IV.
grandson found after him, that in war no followers were Count
to be trusted like the misbelievers. Once enlisted in his forbids con-
service, they had no motive to forsake him for any other versions.
Christian leader, while they had no hope of restoring
the supremacy of their own faith. With them too neither
Clement nor Urban, nor any votary of Clement or Urban,
had any weight. So useful a class of warriors was
not to be lessened in number. Whatever might be his
missionary zeal at Palermo or Syracuse, Count Roger
allowed no conversions in the camp before Capua. The
men who were ready to hearken to Anselm's teaching
had to turn away at the bidding of their temporal
lord, and the father of Christian theology was forbidden
the rare glory of winning willing proselytes to the
Christian faith among the votaries of Islam.[1]

Meanwhile the tales of William's misdoings in Nor- Anselm
mandy and England were brought in day by day. The wishes to resign
heart of Anselm was moved ever more and more; he the arch-
saw that, come what might, he and such a king could bishopric.
never agree; the only course for him was to cast aside
the grievous burthen and responsibility of his archbishopric. He earnestly craved the Pontiff's leave to
resign it into his hands.[2] Urban was far too wary
for this. He enjoined Anselm, by virtue of holy Urban for-
obedience, to do no such thing. The King, in his bids him.

---

[1] Vita, ii. 5. 46. " Quorum etiam plurimi, velut comperimus, se libenter ejus
doctrinæ instruendos submisissent, ac Christianæ fidei jugo sua per eum colla
injecissent, si credulitatem [crudelitatem?] comitis sui per hoc in se sævi-
turam non formidassent. Nam revera nullum eorum pati volebat Christianum impune fieri." He adds the comment; "Quod qua industria, ut
ita dicam, faciebat nihil mea interest; viderit Deus et ipse."

[2] Anselm's motives are set forth at length in Hist. Nov. 46. One reason
is that his teaching was so much more listened to on the continent than it
was in England. The stories of William's evil doings are brought in at
this point.

CHAP. IV. tyranny, might seize his temporalities and might keep him out of the land; but in the eye of the Church he remained none the less the Archbishop of the English kingdom, with his power of binding and loosing as strong as ever.[1] Anselm was not only not to give up his office; he was to make a point of always appearing with the full badges of his office.[2] Even now Anselm seems to have been in some difficulties how to reconcile his two duties to God and to Cæsar, difficulties which he would doubtless have got rid of altogether by resigning the archbishopric.[3] But he submits to the Pontiff's will, and he is bidden to meet him again at Bari, where judgement will be given in the matter of the King of the English and of all others who interfere with the liberties of the Church.[4]

Council of Bari. October 1, 1098.

Then came the meeting at Bari, the disputation against the Greeks, the excommunication of Rufus stopped by Anselm's intercession.[5] That Anselm was playing an arranged part we cannot believe for a moment; but we may believe, without breach of charity, that Urban threatened the excommunication of Rufus in the full belief that Anselm would intercede for him.

Anselm at Rome.

Urban and Anselm then went back to Rome; and thither presently came the messenger from Normandy, who had to tell of the King's frightful threats to-

[1] A debate on this head, in rather long speeches between Urban and Anselm, is given in Hist. Nov. 48. The main doctrine stands thus; "Si propter tyrannidem principis, qui nunc ibi dominatur, in terram illam redire non permitteris, jure tamen Christianitatis semper illius archiepiscopus esto, potestatem ligandi atque solvendi super eam dum vixeris obtinens."

[2] Ib. "Et insignibus pontificalibus more summi pontificis utens ubicunque fueris."

[3] He again describes his whole struggle between the two duties, how he believed that he could reconcile both, how others told him that he could not, and he asks, "Et ego, pater, inter tales quid facerem?"

[4] Ib. 49. "De ipso rege Anglico suisque et sui similibus qui contra libertatem ecclesiæ Dei se erexerunt."

[5] See above, p. 608.

wards himself. Soon after came William of Warel- CHAP. IV.
wast, with a message from the King to the Pope. William of Warelwast
The diplomacy of the future bishop of Exeter was at and Urban.
least straightforward. "My lord the King sends you
word that he wonders not a little how it can have
come into your mind to address him for the restitution of the goods of Anselm." He added, "If you
ask the reason, here it is. When Anselm wished to
depart from his land, the King openly threatened him
that, if he went, he should take the whole archbishopric
into his demesne. Since Anselm then would not, even
when thus threatened, give up his purpose of going,
the King deems that his own acts were right, and that
he is now wrongfully blamed." [1] The Pope asked
whether the King had any other charge against Anselm.
"None," answered the envoy. Urban had gained an
advantage. He poured forth his wonder at a thing so Urban's answer.
unheard of in all time as that a king should spoil the
primate of his kingdom of all his goods merely because
he would not refrain from visiting the Roman Church,
the mother of all churches.[2] William of Warelwast Excommu-
might go back to his master, and might tell him that nication threatened.
the Pope meant to hold a council at Rome in the
Easter-week next to come, and that, if by that time April 12,
Anselm was not restored to all that he had lost, the 1099. .
sentence of excommunication should go forth.[3]

[1] Hist. Nov. 51. "Si causam quæris, hæc est. Quando de terra sua
discedere voluit, aperte minatus est se illo discedente totum archiepiscopatum in dominium suum accepturum. Quoniam igitur, nec his minis constrictus, quin exiret omittere noluit, juste se putat fecisse quod fecit et
injuria reprehendi."

[2] Ib. 52. "Quis unquam audivit talia? pro hoc solo primatem regni suis
omnibus spoliavit, quia ne sanctam matrem ecclesiam omnium Romanam
visitaret omittere noluit? . . . . Et pro tali responso mirabilis homo huc
te fatigasti?"

[3] Ib. "Certissime noverit se in eodem concilio damnationis sententia
puniri quam promeruit."

CHAP. IV.
Brave words were these of Pope Urban, but William the Red knew how to deal with mere bravery of words, even in the Pope whom he had acknowledged. Walter of Albano had once outwitted William and his counsellors; but Walter of Albano had in the end yielded to

William of Warelwast's secret dealings with Urban.
William's most powerful argument. William of Warelwast was not the least likely to outwit Urban; but he had it in commission from his master to overcome the Pope by the same logic by which his Legate had been overcome. We may copy the words of our own Chronicler four-and-twenty years later; "That overcame Rome that overcometh all the world, that is gold and silver."[1] To Urban's well conceived speech the answer of William of Warelwast was pithy and practical; "Before I go away, I will have some dealings with you more in

The excommunication respited.

April–September, 1099.
private."[2] He went to work prudently, as the Red King's clerks knew how to do; he made friends here and there; the Pope's advisers were blinded; the Pope himself was blinded; a respite from Easter to Michaelmas was granted to King William of England.[3]

Position of Anselm.
This adjournment was a heavy blow for Anselm. He had in no way stirred up the Pope to any action against the prince whom he still acknowledged as his sovereign. At Bari, when no answer had as yet been received

[1] Chron. Petrib. 1123.

[2] Eadmer, Hist. Nov. 52. "Priusquam abeam, tecum secretius agam."

[3] Ib. "Prudenter operam dando hos et illos suæ causæ fautores efficere, ac, ut domini sui voluntati satisfaceret, munera quibus ea cordi esse animadvertebat dispertiendo et pollicendo parvi habere. Deductus ergo a sententia Romanus pontifex est." William of Malmesbury (Gest. Pont. 101) is still more distinct on this head; "Arte qua peritus erat negotium conficiens, singulos ambiendo, muneribus et pollicitationibus, regi terminum ad festum sancti Michahelis obtinuit. Cunctatus est multum ad id concedendum Urbanus, quod luctarentur in ejus animo Anselmi religio et munerum oblatio; sed prævaluit tandem pecunia. Itaque omnia superat, omnia deprimit nummus. Indignum factum ut pectori tanti viri, Urbani dico, vilesceret famæ cura, Dei respectus cederet, et pecunia justitiam præverteret."

from the King, Anselm had pleaded for him; it was CHAP. IV. indeed only common justice to give him that one more chance. But, when the answer had come, and had proved to be of such a kind as we have seen, Anselm most likely thought that the time for action had come. He might indeed fairly deem that the excommunication would in truth be an act of kindness towards William. All other means of reclaiming the sinner had failed; that final and most awful means might at last succeed. At all events, Anselm's soul was grieved to the quick at the thought that the Pope's sentence, whatever it might be, could be changed or delayed by the power of filthy lucre. He had borne Urban's every kind of grief, he had borne insults and banish- treatment of Anselm. ment and the spoiling of his goods, for the sake of Rome and the Pope, and he had now found out what Rome and the Pope were. He had found that the master was no better than his servants. He had found Rome to be what Rome was ever found to be by every English bishop, by every Englishman by birth or adoption, who ever trusted in her. Urban proved the same broken reed to Anselm which Alexander in after days proved to Thomas. Anselm had gone through much in order to have the counsel and help of the Pope. But no counsel or help had he found in him.[1] He craved leave to Anselm depart from Rome, and again to tarry at Lyons with a stay for the friend in whom he could better trust, the Primate of all Council of the Gauls.[2] The request was refused. Urban had still April 12, to make use of Anselm for his own purposes. He 1099. had to show his guest and the Church's confessor—

---

[1] Eadmer, Hist. Nov. 52. "Quod videntes vane nos ibi consilium, nihil auxilium operiri intelleximus."

[2] Will. Malms. Gest. Pont. 102. "Visum est ergo Anselmo circa tam venalem hominem expectationem non perdere, sed Lugdunum remeare. Sed enim licentiam impetrare non potuit, retinente papa, ut invidiam facti aliquo levaret solatio."

CHAP. IV. the guest and confessor whom he had sold for William's gold—to the whole world in his Lateran Council. The special honours which were there paid to Anselm must have been felt by him as little more than a mockery. It may have been a preconcerted scene, it may have been a burst of honest indignation, when Reingar, Bishop of Lucca, bore an emphatic witness on Anselm's side. Reingar, chosen on account of his lofty stature and sounding voice to announce the decrees of the Council, broke forth in words of his own declaring the holiness and the wrongs of the Archbishop of the English, and thrice smote his staff on the floor with quivering lips and teeth gnashed together.[1] The Pope checked him; Reingar protested, and renewed his protest. Anselm simply wondered; he had never said a word to the Bishop of Lucca on any such matter, nor did he believe that any of his faithful followers had done so either.[2]

Protest of Reingar of Lucca.

End of the Council.

The council broke up. The great general anathema was pronounced which would take in William along with the other princes of the earth;[3] but nothing was said or done directly for Anselm or his cause.[4] Anselm now at last left Rome for Lyons. He there heard of the deaths both of him who was to issue the excommunication and of him against whom it was to be issued. Urban did not live to hear how his preaching at Clermont was crowned by the deliverance of the Holy City. Yet the work was done while he still lived. Fourteen days after the storm of Jerusalem, seven days after the election

Anselm goes to Lyons.

Death of Urban. July 29, 1099.

[1] Hist. Nov. 53. "His dictis, virgam pastoralem quam manu tenebat tertio pavimento illisit, indignationem spiritus sui, compressis exploso murmure labiis et dentibus, palam cunctis ostendens."

[2] Ib. "Oppido miratus est, sciens se nec homini de re locutum fuisse, nec a se vel ullo suorum, ut talia diceret, processisse." A little characteristic touch follows; "Sedebat ergo uti solebat, silenter auscultans."

[3] See above, p. 606.

[4] Hist. Nov. 53. "Nil judicii vel subventionis, præterquam quod diximus, per Romanum præsulem nacti."

of King Godfrey, Pope Urban died. The news of his
death was brought to William while he was in the midst
of his last warfare for Le Mans. Let God's hate, he an- William's
swered, be upon him who cares whether he be dead or ^{words on his death.}
alive.[1] Fourteen days after Urban's death, the hosts of Battle of
Egypt were smitten at Ascalon; and the city which had _{Ascalon. August 12,}
just been won was again made safe. The next day a fresh 1099.
Pope was chosen, Paschal, who, in the course of a long Paschal
reign, had to strive alike with a Henry of Germany and _{the Second, Pope.}
with a Henry of England. The news of his election was August 13,
brought to William, and he asked what manner of man _{1099– January}
the new Pope might be. He was told that he was a man ^{21, 1118.}
in many things like Archbishop Anselm. "Then by God's William's
face," said the Red King, "if he be such an one, he is no _{words on Paschal's}
good." But William felt that his wished for time was now election.
come. Now at least there should be no trouble about
acknowledging Popes against his will. "Let the Pope be
what he will, he and his popedom shall not this time come
over me by little and little. I have got my freedom
again, and I will use it."[2] The time fixed for the excommunication passed unmarked over the head of the living
Rufus. But before a full year had passed from Paschal's
election, the dead Rufus was excommunicated by the
voice of his own kingdom.

We leave Anselm at Lyons; we shall meet him again
when he comes back in all honour to crown and to
marry a king and a queen who filled the English
throne by the free call of the English people. Meanwhile we must take up the thread of our story, and
see more fully what has been happening in the other
lands which come within the Red King's world,
while Anselm was so long and so wearily striving for

---

[1] Eadmer, Hist. Nov. 54. "Dei odium habeat qui inde curat."
[2] Ib. "Ego interim libertate potitus agam quod libet."

CHAP. IV. righteousness. The tale of Normandy, the tale of Jerusalem, so far as it concerned us to tell it, could hardly be kept apart from the tale of Anselm. But we have still to tell the tale of Scotland, of Northumberland, of Wales, of France, above all the tale of Maine and its noble Count, during the years through which we have tracked the history of Anselm. We have to go back to the beginning of the story through which we have just passed, and to begin afresh while Rufus in his short day of penitence lies on his sick-bed at Gloucester.

END OF THE FIRST VOLUME.